D0073611

Introduction to Forensic Psychology

Second Edition

Introduction to Forensic Psychology

Issues and Controversies in Crime and Justice

Second Edition

Bruce A. Arrigo
Department of Criminal Justice
University of North Carolina, Charlotte
Charlotte, North Carolina

Stacey L. Shipley
North Texas State Hospital
Vernon, Texas

ELSEVIER
ACADEMIC
PRESS

Amsterdam Boston Heidelberg London New York Oxford
Paris San Diego San Francisco Singapore Sydney Tokyo

The sponsoring editor for this book was Nikki Levy, the senior developmental editor was Barbara Makinster, and the senior project manager was Paul Gottehrer. The cover was designed by Eric DeCicco. Composition was done by Cepha Imaging PVT LTD, Bangalore, India and the book was printed and bound by Maple-Vail, Binghamton, NY.

Elsevier Academic Press
30 Corporate Drive, Suite 400, Burlington, MA 01803, USA
525 B Street, Suite 1900, San Diego, California 92101-4495, USA
84 Theobald's Road, London WC1X 8RR, UK

This book is printed on acid-free paper. ∞

Library of Congress Cataloging-in-Publication Data
Application submitted

British Library Cataloguing in Publication Data
A catalogue record for this book is available from the British Library

ISBN: 0-12-064351-0

For all information on all Elsevier Academic Press publications
visit our Web site at www.books.elsevier.com

Printed in the United States of America
05 06 07 08 09   9 8 7 6 5 4 3 2 1

Dedication

For Marc: Sometimes close, often deep, always my brother

B.A.A.

To Robert and Carol Shipley, Greg, and my family of friends
for your never ending support

S.L.S.

Contents

PART I

Courts and the Legal System: Criminal Forensics

1. Adult Forensics

PART II

Courts and the Legal System: Civil Forensics

PART III

Police and Law Enforcement

Corrections and Prison Practices

About the Authors

BRUCE A. ARRIGO, Ph.D., is Professor of Criminal Justice at the University of North Carolina, Charlotte, with additional faculty appointments in the Psychology Department, the Public Policy Program, and the Center for Applied and Professional Ethics. He served as Chair of the Department of Criminal Justice at the University of North Carolina, Charlotte (2001–2004) and as Director of the Institute of Psychology, Law, and Public Policy at the California School of

Professional Psychology, Fresno (1996–2001). Dr. Arrigo began his professional career as a community organizer and social activist for the homeless, the mentally ill, the working poor, the frail elderly, the decarcerated, and the chemically addicted. He received his Ph.D. from Pennsylvania State University in the Administration of Justice and holds a Master's degree in psychology and in sociology. He is an internationally recognized scholar, having authored more than one hundred and twenty-five (125) journal articles, chapters in books, and scholarly essays. In addition, he is the author, coauthor, or editor of sixteen (16) books. Recent volumes include *Psychological Jurisprudence: Critical Explorations in Law, Crime, and Society* (2005), *The French Connection in Criminology: Rediscovering Crime, Law, and Social Change* (with Dragan Milovanovic and Robert Schehr, 2005), *Police Corruption and Psychological Testing* (with Natalie Claussen, 2005), *Philosophical Foundations of Crime* (with Christopher R. Williams, 2006), and *Criminal Behavior: A Systems Approach* (2006). Dr. Arrigo was the Editor-in-Chief of *Humanity & Society* (1996–2000) and is founding and current Editor-in-Chief of the peer-reviewed quarterly, *Journal of Forensic Psychology Practice* (2001–Present). He is the Book Series Editor for *Criminal Justice and Psychology* (Carolina Academic Press) and *Critical Perspectives in Criminology* (University of Illinois Press). Professor Arrigo is a past recipient of the Critical Criminologist of the Year Award (2000), sponsored by the Division of Critical Criminology of the American Society of Criminology. He is also a Fellow of the American Psychological Association through the Law-Psychology Division (Div. 41) of the APA. He has been a (co)principal investigator for a number of public, private, and corporate grants and contracts totaling approximately $3,000,000. He lives in Concord, North Carolina with his wife and two children.

STACEY L. SHIPLEY, Psy.D., was awarded her doctoral degree in forensic psychology from the California School of Professional Psychology in Fresno, California and her Bachelor's degree from St. Edward's University in Austin, Texas, with a major in psychology and minor in criminal justice. Dr. Shipley is a forensically trained clinician, specializing in the provision of psychological services at the crossroads of psychology and the law or those that involve psycholegal issues. She completed her Predoctoral Internship at Milwaukee County Mental Health Division in Milwaukee, Wisconsin, where she worked with the County Forensic Unit conducting competency to stand trial evaluations. Additionally, Dr. Shipley provided clinical services for child, adolescent, and adult inpatient programs and a Mobile Urgent Treatment Team for children and adolescents that responded to mental health crises in the community. Dr. Shipley's clinical and forensic training focuses both on adults and adolescents in inpatient, outpatient, and forensic settings. She is licensed by the Texas Board of Psychology Examiners and is the Chief Psychologist on the Social Learning Rehabilitation Program at North Texas State Hospital—Vernon Campus. This facility is the only maximum-security forensic hospital in the state. Dr. Shipley specializes in forensic and clinical assessment, sex offender therapy, treatment for individuals adjudicated by the courts as not guilty by reason of insanity, incompetent to stand trial, or manifestly dangerous. In addition, she provides staff training on social learning principles and procedures, conducts risk assessments, creates dangerous management plans, and is a senior member of a multidisciplinary treatment team. In addition, Dr. Shipley is licensed by the Iowa Board of Psychology Examiners. In this capacity, she works as a consulting psychologist with the Clarinda Academy, a cognitive/behaviorally oriented program that promotes prosocial behavioral change and attitudes for at-risk and adjudicated adolescent girls and boys, and the Clarinda Youth Shelter for Boys and Girls providing psychological evaluations and dispositional recommendations. Dr. Shipley's related experience includes working in a maximum-security facility for women in California providing individual and group therapy, as well as psychological evaluations. Her research interests focus on psychopathy, women and crime, risk assessment, homicide, and serial offenders. Dr. Shipley has had extensive training on the assessment and conceptualization of the psychopathy construct. Her work in this area has resulted in two publications both appearing in the *International Journal of Offender Therapy and Comparative Criminology*. She was a senior writer and researcher for *Introduction to Forensic Psychology: Issues and Controversies in Crime and Justice* (2000), and was the lead author for the book, *The Female Homicide Offender: Serial Murder and the Case of Aileen Wuornos* (2004).

Preface for the First Edition

What *Is* Forensic Psychology?

Forensic psychology is a growing and popular field of inquiry. Its allure, in part fueled by sensationalized and glamorized media images, features psychologists tracking down serial killers, treating sexual psychopaths, and studying the criminal mind. Indeed, as a teacher, I see many of my students expressing considerable enthusiasm for careers as "profilers" engaged in the behavioral science pursuit of crime scene analyses. While there is certainly a need for trained specialists in this domain of forensics, the field itself is considerably more vast.

The expanse of the field is rooted in its sundry models of instruction and practice. Clinical practitioners emphasize the assessment, diagnosis, and treatment of different civil and criminal forensic populations. Law/psychology practitioners emphasize the development of the legally trained specialist whose overlapping skills in courtroom processes and human behavior make for a formidable expert in the treatment and policy arenas. Law–psychology–justice practitioners emphasize the development of a cross-trained specialist whose integrative knowledge base in psychology, criminology, organizational analysis, policy studies, and law readies the person for the increasing demands of a multifaceted profession. If appropriately prepared, this specialist moves skillfully among those in the psychotherapeutic, management, and advocacy communities.

Clearly, each of these models includes a unique set of strengths and limitations. What each of these approaches shares, however, is that its collective vision of forensic psychology is not so narrowly defined or so unidimensionally depicted as is the impression created for us by the popular media. Much of what forensic experts do is not stylish or seductive. Indeed, if anything, much of the work is often tedious and technical. This is not the same as suggesting that the contributions of forensic psychologists are insignificant or trivial to society. Nothing could be further from the truth.

Forensic psychologists are invested in crime and justice. They examine issues, controversies, social problems, psychological states, and other complex phenomena within the adult, juvenile, civil, and family domains of professional practice. They may not define the parameters of their work as such; however, they are unquestionably committed to this enterprise. What links various forensic specialists together, regardless of their particular academic orientation, is the problem of violence (e.g., physical, sexual, psychological, and symbolic) and its impact on different individuals or groups (e.g., offenders, victims, police officers, correctional guards), so that the experiences of intrapsychic pain, interpersonal conflict, and social unrest are identified, reduced, and, perhaps, altogether eliminated. Thus, it is not surprising that many people view the forensic arena as the study of psychology and law within the mental health and criminal/civil justice systems. In addition, though, forensic psychology is the study of both these disciplines and systems precisely where they intersect. Without question, at the crossroads of the field are a host of pressing general public concerns that warrant careful examination and close scrutiny by competently trained specialists.

Why Study Forensic Psychology?

The thoughtful study and effective practice of forensic psychology are compelling responses to the problems posed by crime, victimization, trauma, and other forms of violence. They are also laudable solutions to the demands placed upon us for restoring justice to society. These overlapping and interdependent aims are significant, and those interested in the field would do well to consider how these observations are integral to the successful administration of this specialty area.

Forensic psychology is not simply about reacting to crime. Yes, the discipline does address such disturbing and perplexing questions as: What do we do with kids who kill? What are the causes of prison riots? Are the mentally ill dangerous? Why do the police use (deadly) force? These matters, however, address only the violence variable. In addition, the field considers a number of related concerns that are equally critical and enduring: How do officers mediate conflict? Is the "least restrictive alternative" made available to the psychiatrically disordered? How do the legal and psychological communities promote the best interests of the child in forensic decision making? What treatment and care are available to mothers in prison? These subjects evaluate the justice variable. Forensic psychology, then, is as much about responding to crime and victimization as it is about preventing it or, better still, promoting peace and well-being whenever possible.

Organization of the Book

A textbook about the field of forensic psychology as defined above is therefore potentially quite useful, illuminating, and appealing. The organization of *Introduction to Forensic Psychology: Issues and Controversies in Crime and Justice* is distinct from that of other similar books on the market. This text is distinguishable from its competitors in four ways.

First, readers will note that the book is divided into three broad sections: (1) Police and Law Enforcement, (2) Court and the Legal System, and (3) Corrections and Prison Practices. For those more familiar with conventional psychology texts, this approach will be different and becoming acquainted with it may take some time. This strategy, however, is worthwhile. The three overarching components of the criminal justice system encompass the dimensions previously identified. Thus, as a starting point, working from within the police, court, and correctional orientations to forensic psychology makes perfect sense.

Second, each of the three broad sections to the text includes four subsections, creating a total of 12 chapters. These subsections include: (1) Adult Forensics, (2) Juvenile Forensics, (3) Civil Forensics, and (4) Family Forensics. For those comfortable with standard criminal justice textbooks, this approach will be unusual and familiarizing oneself with it may be awkward at first. Again, though, there is a justification for this strategy. The broad domains of (forensic) psychological practice emphasize these intervention areas. Thus, delineating the chapters accordingly is an appropriate and necessary way in which to define the contours of the police, court, and corrections sections.

Third, within each subsection of a given chapter, a number of selected issues or controversies are presented. Collectively, these topics do not exhaustively canvass the depth of a particular chapter's thematic possibilities. Rather, the carefully chosen entries reveal the diversity contained within the subspecialty area of forensic psychology under investigation. For example, Chapter 5 addresses several adult forensic topics in the court and legal system. The reader is introduced to where and how forensic professionals are called upon during the plea bargaining phase of a case, during the trial's unfolding, and following conviction. Traditional psychology and criminal justice textbooks tend not to adopt an issues/controversies perspective. I suggest that given the nature of the field, this approach is as logical to the introductory analysis of the forensic discipline as it is essential.

Relatedly, the core organizing theme for the selection of entries deliberately focused on capturing the breadth and variety of topics within a subspecialty domain of forensic psychology. This meant that some otherwise noteworthy issues had to be dismissed because they did not advance this goal. Moreover, the process of choosing topics was based on the promotion of introductory (rather than intermediate or advanced) knowledge and practical (rather than conceptual or technical) utility. Again, several worthwhile entries had to be omitted because they did not support this end.

Fourth, over 60 individual entries (i.e., topics) are found in *Introduction to Forensic Psychology: Issues and Controversies in Crime and Justice.* Most chapters examine between four and six topics. It is easy to imagine adding more entries within each chapter. Indeed, each chapter, if appropriately developed as such, could become the basis for its own, freestanding textbook. Standard introductory textbooks in psychology or criminal justice present students with a much more limited number of topics to investigate, but considerable depth is given to those matters that are reviewed. In *Introduction to Forensic Psychology*, greater care is given to the expanse of the field. Certainly, this sacrifices depth of critical analysis. But the aim of the book is to demonstrate something about the volume of compelling or "cutting edge" controversies influencing the development of the field. This is important to readers, particularly those who are cultivating interests in the field for future career possibilities.

Each section or entry of the textbook follows a structured format. The format includes a brief introduction, a case illustration, a review of the literature, an assessment of policy implications, and suggestions for future research. Most entries are between 4 and 6 pages long. Readers expecting to learn about the details of any one issue or controversy in a given chapter may be disappointed. Again, however, the book is designed to canvass an emerging field of inquiry that continues to grow considerably.

Additionally, because the organization of the project does not permit any more systematic assessment than what a provisional analysis would yield, the sections move very quickly and easily from one to the next. Readers could just as simply start in the middle of one chapter, explore a particular section, and then start at the beginning of the chapter and read to its completion. Either approach will not detract from the learning. To explain the broader context in which each individual chapter is organized, overviews introduce the material. The case illustrations (some factual and some fictitious) demonstrate the real-word impact or application of the issue investigated. The policy implications and future research sections are indicators of what needs to be done in a given subspecialty area. Policy implications address the current impact on the field given the state of knowledge regarding the individual entry. Future research considers where and how additional investigations could improve our understanding of the examined issue in relation to other facets of society. These include programmatic, scientific, political, economic, legal, and other notable remedies.

In many ways *Introduction to Forensic Psychology: Issues and Controversies in Crime and Justice* is a primer to the field. There are competitors; however, I believe that none attempts to so dramatically and comprehensively capture the breadth of the discipline. This project, then, arguably fills this gap in the literature. Mindful always that forensic practitioners operate within the justice and mental health systems, this book endeavors to reveal something about the complexities of where and how the forensic process succeeds and fails for those individuals and collectives who are most directly impacted by it. Clearly, a book of this sort can reveal but a tiny fraction of all that occurs in the functioning of a discipline. But it can offer us information that is useful, worthwhile, and insightful. I invite the readers, whether students or practitioners, to discover the possibilities contained in this book and to consider where and how such observations may serve them in their own educational pursuits or professional development.

Bruce A. Arrigo
Fresno, California
Spring 1999

Preface for the Second Edition

Five years have passed since the publication of the first edition of *Introduction to Forensic Psychology*. Our basic aim in preparing this new, second edition is to provide a text on the role of psychology in the criminal justice system, written so that it is accessible to undergraduates, sophisticated so that it appeals to educators and researchers, grounded so that it is of interest to practitioners, and cogent so that it is insightful for busy administrators. This is no small undertaking to be sure!

Although the book is designed as a lead text for forensic psychology courses, it also may be of use as a supplemental text in courses such as psychology and the legal system; criminal behavior; psychology public policy and the law; and topics in criminal justice and psychology. As these titles suggest, the field remains both interdisciplinary and integrative, thus ensuring that the interpretation of human behavior and the operation of the justice system is appropriately reviewed and synthesized, representing our secondary aim. Once again, we acknowledge the demanding nature of this project.

Four characteristics found in the previous edition—its readability, comprehension, scholarship, and practice orientation—have been retained and improved upon in this volume. Our position is that much of what is taken to epitomize the sub-field of forensic psychology is technical in nature. Demystifying this literature in thorough yet concise ways does much to facilitate student learning and general understanding. In addition, when guided by cutting-edge research that is tempered by a steadfast concern for the everyday world of the practicing forensic psychologist, a balance can be struck between the intellectual demands of the academic community and the professional needs of the forensic practitioner. Thus, we have endeavored to keep these worthwhile objectives in mind and to build upon them throughout this volume. If carefully developed and thoughtfully executed, the endproduct is a text that meaningfully satisfies the interests of all parties involved.

What's New in this Edition?

There are four features that distinguish this edition from its predecessor. Each of these additions stems from our commitment to making the world of forensic psychology relevant to a diverse (and growing) group of readers. Therefore, these new components represent our desire to link the burgeoning field of forensic psychology to those most noticeably impacted by it.

International Criminal Forensic Psychology

The development of the field extends well beyond the borders of the United States. Established and emerging periodicals such as *International Journal of Law and Psychiatry*, *International Journal of Offender Therapy and Comparative Criminology*, *International Journal of Forensic Psychology*, *Psychiatry, Psychology, and the Law*, and *International Journal of Forensic Mental Health* are publishing articles on a host of topics that canvass both civil and criminal aspects relevant to adult, juvenile, family, and community populations. *Introduction to Forensic Psychology, Second Edition* recognizes this growth and the need to comprehend it. Accordingly, we devote an entire chapter to the international and comparative landscape, exploring a number of contentious and enduring debates. In brief, these include the psychology of terrorism, the insanity defense and competency to stand trial, and violence risk assessment and mental disorders. The development and operation of these specific forensic psychological topics are reviewed in countries such as Japan, Australia, Brazil, the United Kingdom, and Canada.

Practice Updates

One of the more successful aspects of the first edition was the incorporation of factual and fictitious case scenarios that guided the subsequent commentary. Students, reviewers, practitioners, and educators all found this pedagogical tool useful and informative. Building upon this notion, the second edition includes a "Practice Update" at the conclusion of each chapter which identifies a key theme relevant to the chapter's overall thrust. The theme is grounded in the everyday difficulties or ongoing dilemmas confronted by the forensic psychological specialist. The purpose of these updates is to demonstrate for the reader the practical tensions at play when working in the forensic field. Thus, for example, psychopathy and antisocial personality disorder (ASPD) must be carefully assessed if the appropriate treatment regimen is to be recommended, knowing full well the success limits of various clinical interventions (Chapter 3). Submitting child custody evaluations to a legal tribunal necessitates that the psychological practitioner understand the assorted facets of the court process (e.g., discovery phase, subpoena process), as well as the specific matters to which the expert can accurately testify (Chapter 5). Psychologists assisting or otherwise treating offender populations entails a careful adherence to institutional regulations as well as to ethical standards of client intervention (Chapter 10). These and other identified "Practice Updates" situate the relevant literature in the complicated decision-making world of the forensic expert.

New Entries on Adult, Juvenile, Family, and Community Forensic Psychology

One way to stay abreast of the various changes impacting the forensic psychological field is to carefully evaluate the kind of issues in which academics and professionals invest their unique energies and particular resources. With this notion in mind, the second edition deliberately considers the development of new or emerging trends, as well as stagnant or faltering lines of inquiry. In both instances, we were cognizant of those contentious topics that could not be dismissed under any circumstances, given their enduring nature.

Fundamental to our efforts to review and discuss new and relevant entries in the second edition was a clear and unwavering commitment to incorporate topics germane to the areas of adult, juvenile, family, and community populations. Thus, throughout this volume, a number of themes not previously examined in the first edition now appear. Examples include malingering, mental illness, and issues of secondary gain; expert testimony; competency restoration and manifest dangerousness in maximum security facilities; termination of parental rights; evaluating psychiatric work-related disability; critical incidents debriefing; and crisis intervention in prisons. The inclusion of these entries, along with the elimination of others less central to the evolution of the field, helps to make the book more comprehensive in its coverage and more contemporary in its scope.

Race, Gender, and Class Dynamics

Consistent with our interest in international and comparative forensic psychology, this edition provides more cogent and concise information on how women, minorities, and the poor are affected by psycholegal policies and practices. Two principal areas where attention to this matter is most noticeable is found in the presentation of the literature—especially for a number of individual entries—and in the assessment of policy implications, especially given the state of the research on a specified issue or controversy. As our analysis repeatedly makes evident, more studies providing some explanatory and predictive insight regarding the impact of forensic psychological decision-making for diverse populations in a multicultural society are sorely needed.

Organization of the Book

There are a few changes to the organization of *Introduction to Forensic Psychology: Issues and Controversies in Law, Law Enforcement, and Corrections, Second Edition* that are worth noting. As the subtitle of this book suggests, our focus is on those psychological concerns found within the criminal justice setting affecting the lives of adults, juveniles, families, and communities. As such, three broad areas of psychological concern (i.e., law, law enforcement, and corrections) inform the way in which this edition is structured.

In addition, there are four parts to the text. Part I canvasses the legal system and criminal forensics. Part II examines the legal system and civil forensics. Part III investigates the relationship between policing practices and forensic psychology. Part IV explores the relationship between prison practices and forensic psychology. Each part of the text includes three chapters. Generally speaking, each of these chapters reviews the adult, juvenile, or family/community dimensions of the sub-discipline as linked to the specific section (Part I, II, III, or IV) under consideration. Overall, then, given the thrust of this edition and the manner in which it is organized, there are twelve separate chapters. A series of six to eight topics or entries are examined within each chapter. This means that this edition reviews approximately 75 individual entries. Much like its predecessor, the second edition emphasizes the expanse of the field (and, thus, its overall compelling nature), rather than the depth of a select number of topics. In this way, the reader is exposed to a range of issues influencing and shaping forensic psychology, its academic development, and its practical utility.

As an engaging and thought-provoking primer, *Introduction to Forensic Psychology: Issues and Controversies in Law, Law Enforcement, and Corrections, Second Edition*, continues where its highly acclaimed predecessor left off. Designed for students, researchers, practitioners, and administrators, the text demonstrates the breadth of the field through concise prose, cogent analysis, and a user-friendly format. Committed to accessibility and comprehensiveness, as well as to a scholarly approach and a practice orientation, this second edition incorporates a number of novel and stimulating features making it both intellectually rewarding and professionally appealing. Accordingly, we invite readers to explore the possibilities contained in this book. As the sub-discipline of forensic psychology evolves so, too, does our need to better comprehend the role of psychology and psychologists in the justice system. In the final analysis, *Introduction to Forensic Psychology, Second Edition* endeavors to facilitate and deepen this much-needed understanding.

Bruce Arrigo
Charlotte, North Carolina
Stacey L. Shipley
Vernon, Texas
Fall, 2004

PART I

Courts and the Legal System: Criminal Forensics

CHAPTER 1

Adult Forensics

OVERVIEW

The role of psychology in the legal system is both diverse and expansive. In addition, new and/or emerging application areas are discovered all the time. The adult forensic field is one domain where this particular focus is appreciable. The adult forensic arena encompasses all facets of criminal adjudication, from the pretrial stage to the postconviction phase, where the role of psychology in the court process is evident, necessary, and, ultimately, impactful.

In this chapter, seven controversies are explored. These topics include (1) competency to stand trial, (2) jury selection, (3) psychological tests and forensic evaluation instruments, (4) violence risk assessment, (5) forensic verdicts for mentally ill defendants (not guilty by reason of insanity, NGRI, and guilty, but mentally ill, GBMI), (6) expert testimony, and (7) maximum–security forensic hospitals. Individually, these controversies demonstrate the breadth of specialized roles that exist for forensic psychologists in the court system. Collectively, the issues explored in this chapter explain where and how the adult forensic field routinely relies upon the psychological sciences to inform effective legal practice and sound judicial decision making.

In order for a person to be prosecuted, the individual must be competent to stand trial. What is the legal standard for competency to stand trial? What role does psychology play in furthering our understanding of competency? How does the "psycholegal" standard relate to one's capacity to stand trial? How do symptoms of mental illness or other impairments impact relevant legal functional capacities? What role does psychiatric diagnosis play in a determination of competency to stand trial? Jurors are an indispensable component of most criminal (and civil) cases. The selection process can significantly affect the desired outcome of a case. How do the psychological sciences contribute to the scientific selection of a jury? Is it possible to assemble, through the selection process, an impartial jury panel? How does the pretrial publicity of a high-profile case impact the jury pool? Both prosecuting and defense attorneys increasingly rely upon forensic experts with psychological assessment skills who can testify in court. Do forensic tests provide accurate information about the personality, intelligence, ability, and psychopathology of an offender? Are such instruments and their findings legally admissible? What is the reliability and validity of testimony based on forensic assessments in the courtroom? One type of forensic evaluation is violence risk assessment. In short, the question posed is whether the defendant presents a risk for future violent behavior. How accurately do risk-assessment instruments predict future dangerousness? Do evaluations tend to be over- or underinclusive and what are the implications for defendants? What is the constitutionality of using risk evaluations in a criminal case? Mentally ill defendants can be found guilty or not guilty. In addition, however, they can be found not guilty by reason of insanity or guilty but mentally ill. How does the legal system understand insanity and mental illness? What are the various tests or standards the court uses for insanity? How do NGRI and GBMI verdicts differ?

Psycholegal questions in the criminal justice system necessitate that forensically trained mental health professionals educate or inform the court about relevant issues. It is critical for the forensic expert witness to not only understand both the underpinnings of human behavior and mental illness, but also the law applicable to the psycholegal question. Who is qualified to provide expert testimony? What types of issues warrant the evaluation and testimony of a forensic psychologist? What makes expert testimony more credible to jurors? Finally, what should the forensic mental health expert witness expect in the courtroom and what impact could his or her testimony have? What happens to a mentally ill defendant who has been adjudicated incompetent to stand trial or one who has been found NGRI? What type of setting accommodates the mentally ill defendant's unique treatment needs? How does a maximum-security forensic hospital differ from a general clinical facility? What is the role of the forensic psychologist working in this setting? What ethical dilemmas arise with the provision of psychological services and forensic evaluation services in a secure hospital setting?

The seven controversies examined in this chapter, though limited in scope, nonetheless explore several noteworthy subjects that dramatically reveal the interplay of law and psychology in the adult forensic arena.

Responses to the problem of crime entail sophisticated, scientific solutions. Whether the questions asked involve mentally disordered defendants at different stages of the adjudication process, the vagaries of selecting jurors, or the psycholegal consequences of functional impairments in competency to stand trial, one thing is clear: Psychology can and does impact what happens in the criminal courtroom and beyond. As the individual sections of this chapter explain, the policy implications for this continued trend necessitate that carefully trained specialists who understand the mechanics of law, the science of psychology, and the complexities of human behavior be called upon to assist the legal system. In part, as is suggested in the pages that follow, more and better research is therefore essential to accomplishing this end. Indeed, this level of training will ready the way for future generations of forensic specialists so that they can confront the challenges that await them in the adult forensic field.

COMPETENCY TO STAND TRIAL

Introduction

Some of the more frequently addressed issues concerning psychology and the legal system involve the concept of competency. *Black's Law Dictionary* (Garner, 1996) defines competency as "the mental ability to understand problems and to make decisions" (p. 117). The precise meaning of competency assumes different forms, however, depending on the context for which it is addressed. In general, there is long–standing agreement that an individual should not be subjected to the processes of the legal system if he or she is unable to understand the nature and purpose of those proceedings (L. Wrightsman, Nietzel, & Fortune, 1994). Further, it is important for defendants to be competent in order to ensure accurate results, maintain the dignity of the legal system, and justify the imposition of punishment (Weiss, 1997).

Questions of competency in the legal system can be raised at any point throughout the proceedings of the criminal process. Such questions may be raised by the prosecution, the defense, or the judge. The most frequent application of the competency rule concerns competency to stand trial. In addition, a number of other competency issues may be raised including competency to plead guilty, competency to confess, competency to refuse the insanity defense, competency to waive the right to an attorney, competency to testify, and competency to be sentenced and executed.

What exactly does the legal concept of competence refer to, and what implications ensue from its legal existence? This section explores these questions and looks more specifically at the issue of competence in the legal system. In addition, the issue of competency to stand trial is examined. For further analysis on competency to be sentenced and executed, refer to Chapter 10, page 369. The implications for forensic psychology, policy analysis, and practice that surface in light of the concept of competence are also briefly discussed.

Jenne Foster is a 28-year-old woman who was arrested for felony theft 3 months ago. Jenne has a history of moderate-to-severe psychological dysfunction. She has been hospitalized at various times since the age of 13 for mood-related issues, often accompanied by psychotic symptoms. Though her mental illness manifests only periodically, it is often compounded by her long history of substance abuse. In addition, Jenne has been diagnosed as mildly mentally retarded. Intelligence tests conducted by clinical and forensic psychologists consistently measure her within the 60–70 range.

    After initially interviewing Jenne in preparation for her trial, Jenne's defense attorney, John, questions her understanding of the upcoming proceedings and ability to assist him in the trial process. Having genuine concerns regarding these issues, John raises the question of Jenne's competency to stand trial. In other words: Is Jenne mentally capable of being a defendant in the criminal process? If so, what other competency issues might arise? If not, what will happen to Jenne?

Literature Review

The concept of competency to stand trial recognizes the potential implications of mental or emotional impairments on an individual's functional capacities as a criminal defendant. Stone (1975) referred to competency to stand trial (CST) as "the most significant mental health inquiry pursued in the system of criminal law" (p. 200). Perhaps one reason for the significance of competency applied in this context is the large number of persons found incompetent every year. Grisso (2003) reports that attorneys have doubts about their clients' competence in approximately 10–15% of their criminal cases but raise the issue in only half of them. A study conducted by H. Steadman, Monahan, Hartstone, Davis, and Robbins (1982) found that in the United States in 1978, approximately 25,000 CST evaluations resulted in over 6,000 individuals found incompetent to stand trial. Grisso (2003) indicated that there was no reason to believe that these numbers had decreased in recent years. Thus, the sheer number of individuals facing competency evaluations leaves competency to stand trial as one of the most significant issues confronted in the fields of law, psychology, and forensic psychology.

The legal definition of competency to stand trial was put forth by the Supreme Court in *Dusky v. United States* (1960). The *Dusky* standard requires the individual to have (1) "sufficient present ability to consult with a lawyer with a reasonable degree of rational understanding" and (2) "rational as well as factual understanding" of the general proceedings (*Dusky v. United States*, 1960, p. 402). Though competency standards vary somewhat from state to state, nearly every state has adopted some variation of *Dusky* (Grisso, 1996a). The purpose of raising this issue is to protect the due process rights of the defendant in question. He or she should be capable of being a rational, independent, decision maker and participant in the preparation and execution of his or her defense. Forensic experts are frequently called upon to assess for competency to stand trial and to address the standards set forth in *Dusky v. United States* (Rogers, Grandjean, Tillbrook, Vitacco, & Sewell, 2001). In *U.S. v. Timmins* (9th Circuit, 2002), the court ruled that when offering an opinion about a defendant's competence to stand trial, evaluators must be careful to closely scrutinize the independent decision-making abilities of the defendant (Osinowo & Pinals, 2003). This case demonstrated the necessity of utilizing a mental health expert to assist in a competency determination in part because "a lawyer is not a trained mental health professional capable of accurately assessing the effects of paranoid delusions on the client's mental process" (Osinowo & Pinals, 2003, p. 261).

Thus, the contemporary concept of CST concerns not only the presence of mental illness, but also centrally the individual's ability to function as a defendant in light of the effects of his or her mental illness. Slovenko (2002, p. 421) cautioned that psychiatric diagnosis may "play a role in the legal process but it is not always a *sine qua non* in the resolution of a legal matter." The primary concern, then, is whether mentally ill defendants are capable of fulfilling their role as defendants and to what extent their legal functional capacities are impaired. The knowledge and ability to do those things required by the court before and during the trial process are of primary importance (Grisso, 2003; L. Wrightsman et al., 1994).

Competency to stand trial must be differentiated from the standard of insanity. Competency refers only to a defendant's *present* ability to function. For example, an individual may have been legally insane at the time he or she committed a crime, but perfectly competent to stand trial and be sentenced. Likewise, an individual who was legally sane during the commission of a crime may not be competent several months later when he or she faces criminal trial. Thus, insanity and competence are entirely different legal constructs and, though often confused, must be considered as such. The inquiry into competence to stand trial involves a forensic evaluation by a mental health professional, with a finding of incompetence by the courts after the evaluation frequently leading to involuntary hospitalization for treatment with the primary goal to be restoration of trial competency (Grisso, 2003). Follow-up evaluations by mental health professionals at the admitting facility will be required periodically to ascertain whether or not the defendant has improved amply to merit a return to court. When the treating staff and evaluating clinician concur that the defendant is now clinically competent to stand trial, a written report which informs the referring court is sent recommending the issue is now appropriate for further adjudication (Poythress & Feld, 2002).

There is one important distinction between the treatment of those found insane or incompetent. Typically, the defendant found insane (i.e., NGRI or GBMI) faces a legal commitment or a sentence in a placement where psychiatric care is available. The NGRI individual may spend an indeterminate sentence in a psychiatric hospital. The incompetent-to-stand-trial individual, on the other hand, has not been tried, convicted, or sentenced for any wrongdoing and the court must determine the defendant's competence before proceeding with any elements of this process. He or she is simply treated in an effort to restore his or her ability (if possible) to understand the proceedings and assist his or her counsel in the trial. Grisso (2003, pp. 74–75) identified five main stages for determining and disposing of competence cases to include: (1) requesting a competence determination (often called "raising the question"); (2) the competence evaluation stage; (3) the judicial determination of competence or incompetence; in some cases, (4) disposition and provision of treatment; and (5) rehearings on competence. If it appears that the defendant's incompetence is amenable to treatment, admission to a forensic treatment facility for restoration of trial competency is the most common disposition (Grisso, 2003). For additional information on competency restoration refer to the section "The Maximum-Security Forensic Hospital."

How long can an incompetent individual be held in a psychiatric facility? The Supreme Court attempted to answer this very question in *Jackson v. Indiana* (1972). Prior to *Jackson*, it was not uncommon for incompetent defendants to be confined to psychiatric facilities for unlimited periods of time. At times, this period exceeded the sentence the individual would have faced if tried and convicted. Thus, it was not uncommon for the prosecution to raise questions concerning competency to essentially sentence an individual without the time and effort of a trial (L. Wrightsman et al., 1994).

The Court's decision in *Jackson* placed limits on the amount of time an individual who was found incompetent to stand trial (IST) could be confined. Thus, the time afforded to the state to treat defendants and restore their competence was subject to limitations. The proposed limits were defined as "... a reasonable period of time necessary to determine whether there is a substantial probability that [the defendant] will attain the capacity [competence] in the foreseeable future" (*Jackson v. Indiana*, 1972, pp. 737–738). The defendant found IST is not subjected to the trial process. He or she is generally placed in a psychiatric facility and treated until competency has been sufficiently restored. The *Jackson* decision, however, was the first Supreme Court case to place legal limits, though imprecise and not well defined, on the commitment of such individuals. According to the *Jackson* decision, forensic evaluators must address in their reports whether or not those individuals determined to be IST have a substantial probability of regaining competency through treatment in the foreseeable future (Hubbard, Zapf, & Ronan, 2003). Hubbard et al. (2003) warned that due to the infrequent occurrence of individuals who are unable to be restored to competency, forensic examiners are relatively poor at predicting which defendants will regain competency. In some cases, depending upon the severity of the charges, if a defendant is determined unlikely to regain competency in the foreseeable future, the charges may be dropped entirely. More often than not, this type of defendant will still spend some time in a forensic psychiatric facility before this occurs.

Forensic Psychology and Policy Implications

The implications of competency issues and developments for the forensic psychologist are profound. Research in this area has shown that the expert opinions of psychologists on the issue of competency are highly valued. It is uncommon for a judge to disagree with the recommendation of a mental health professional (Nicholson & Kugler, 1991). Often a full competency hearing is not necessary if all parties involved including the defense attorney, prosecuting attorney, and the judge stipulate that they are in agreement regarding the determination of the defendant's competence or incompetence, and if they agree after taking into consideration the forensic evaluation results (Grisso, 2003). Thus, the role of the practicing forensic psychologist is one that assists in defining the future of the defendant whose competency is in question. For Jenne in the above case study, the opinion of the psychologist conducting the competency evaluation may significantly influence the trier of fact in determining whether she must face the trial process in her present state or be committed for treatment to possibly restore her to a level of functioning that may enhance her ability to assist in her own defense.

For example, if it is determined that Jenne is competent to stand trial when she is in fact incompetent, the ensuing trial may not involve true due process and therefore be unjust. The reverse, however, is also true. If Jenne is judged to be incompetent when she is capable of standing trial, the public may regard her as "getting off easy" and not receiving due punishment if she were found guilty. Additionally, both defendants and society benefit from avoiding unnecessary delays in trial procedures or unnecessary hospitalization of defendants for evaluation or treatment as a result of a finding of incompetency (Grisso, 2003).

Perhaps even more significant, however, is the very issue of incompetence and the treatment of individuals such as Jenne. One who has been found incompetent to stand trial, for example, is deprived of liberty by being involuntarily confined without ever being found guilty of anything. The incompetent defendant not only faces the loss of liberty that may eventually follow a guilty verdict, but is also subjected to the loss of freedom, liberty, and sometimes the questionable conditions of the facility where he or she is confined (Bardwell & Arrigo, 2002). The very practice of confining the incompetent before they have been convicted raises important policy questions.

A more significant development concerning competency and policy is that of involuntary medication to restore competency. Often, an individual's competency may be restored following the administration of psychotropic medications. Questions then arise as to whether there is a justified basis for forcing medications on defendants in an effort to restore competency. Bullock (2002) explained that the defendant's interest in wanting to refuse medication is in conflict with the government's interest in obtaining an adjudication of the defendant's culpability in a criminal matter. The issue of the right to refuse treatment for both prisoners and civilly committed individuals is explored more fully in other sections of this book.

Suggestions for Future Research

What exactly constitutes a competent individual is perhaps the most controversial competency issue. Though cases such as *Dusky v. United States* (1960) shed light on the question, no distinct and specific conclusion has been reached by any court of law. This topic continues to receive substantial attention in both legal and social science literature. Given the inherent difference between individuals, forensic psychologists must consider whether it is even possible to adopt a specific standard of competency. Hubbard et al. (2003) expressed the need for continued research on characteristics of defendants not restorable to competency and those whose competency is restorable in order to improve the ability to accurately predict and classify them.

   Another area in need of future consideration concerns involuntary confinement of incompetent individuals. Many jurisdictions continue to allow for the automatic confinement of such persons (Melton, Petrila, Poythress, & Slobogin, 1987). Several proposals have been made to place limitations on the conditions under which this commitment should occur. Further, though the Court's decision in *Jackson v. Indiana* (1972) forbade unlimited confinement, it failed to define "reasonable period of time" and "substantial probability" (pp. 737–738). Thus, the Court has assumed some responsibility for the treatment of incompetent defendants. It has not, however, adequately resolved the issues with consideration of the best interest of the individual and the State (Bardwell & Arrigo, 2002).

JURY SELECTION

Introduction

The selection of jury members is one of the most important aspects of any given trial. The Sixth Amendment guarantees that "in all criminal prosecutions, the accused shall enjoy the right to a speedy and public trial, by an impartial jury." How then is an impartial jury selected? The last several decades have generated a substantial amount of criticism as to whether a jury can in fact be impartial, particularly with the rise in use of trial or jury consultants. Many factors, both sociological and psychological, can influence the means by which a juror reaches a decision about a defendant's guilt. The presumed impartiality of each juror is questionable, and several methods for assuring impartiality have been implemented.

Each of these factors and methods must be considered by both the defense and the prosecution in selecting a final jury. This section examines these as well as other important questions concerning jury selection.

Jen has been arrested and charged with felonious assault in a domestic dispute in which she was recently involved. Let us suppose that Jen has considered her plea bargaining options and decided against them, preferring instead to risk the trial process. She believes that she is completely innocent and that a jury of her peers will also see it that way. Thus, Jen has made the decision to place her future in the hands of the 12 jurors to be selected. Given this, it makes sense that Jen will want the jury to be composed of people most likely to find her innocent. The prosecution, on the other hand, will desire a jury composition that will be convinced of her guilt. Jen and her defense counsel must now be concerned with how the members of the jury are selected and what, if anything, they can do to impact Jen's chance of acquittal. To further complicate matters, Jen happens to be a well-known public figure, and anyone who watches television has heard about her case. What are the defense's chances of finding a juror who has not already developed an opinion about the case? The media has been quick to suggest Jen's guilt, and polls have shown that the majority of the public believes her to be guilty even before the trial has begun. These are important considerations which will undoubtedly affect the outcome of the trial.

Literature Review

The process of jury selection spans several stages, which involve both the prosecution and the defense. In many high-profile or high-stakes cases, this process begins with attorneys utilizing the services of trial consultants (Fischoff, 2003; Lord, 2001; Moran, 2001; Strier, 2001). After an initial jury pool is chosen, a panel is selected for a *voir dire* hearing. At this hearing, each prospective juror is questioned by the judge and often the defense and prosecution. The voir dire is intended to identify and dismiss those who would be unable to render an impartial verdict. An individual may be dismissed by the judge alone or *challenged for cause* by the prosecution or defense. Challenges for cause address specific issues, such as the prospective juror's relation to the defendant, exposure to media coverage of the case, or expressed personal biases about the defendant or case material. In addition, most jurisdictions allow the defense and prosecution a certain number of *peremptory challenges*. These challenges may be used to dismiss a juror without having to provide a specific reason (*Swain v. Alabama*, 1965). Peremptory challenges may not, however, be used to dismiss a prospective juror solely because of his or her race (*Baston v. Kentucky*, 1986).

This exception does not, as yet, extend to religion, gender, or national origin (Wrightsman et al., 1994).

The voir dire process has been the focus of much interest in the field of forensic psychology. Consider the issue of pretrial publicity. While many questions remain unanswered with regard to pretrial publicity, there is ample evidence that it can effect the juror's ability to be impartial (Dexter, Cutler, & Moran, 1992). The change of venue and much discussion about the Scott Peterson murder trial illustrate this complicated issue, particularly in light of the growing media saturation of high-profile cases. Several remedies for such effects have been investigated, yet their effectiveness has not been well established. One of these remedies is the voir dire, or jury examination, process. The use of the voir dire process as a remedy for pretrial publicity assumes that upon extensive questioning by the prosecution, defense, and/or judge, the impact of pretrial publicity on that juror can be assessed. Thus, each juror could be examined for potential biases resulting from media exposure to the case and discarded from the pool if it is suspected that they will be unable to remain impartial in rendering a verdict. In theory, using extended voir dire to assess for biases should work. However, research in this area has failed to reach a conclusive status. Dexter et al. (1992) found that subjects who were exposed to pretrial publicity perceived the defendant as more culpable (guilty) and that subjects who were exposed to extensive voir dire (as opposed to minimal voir dire) perceived the defendant as less culpable. It is safe to assume, then, that pretrial publicity has an impact on juror perceptions of culpability, and extended voir dire may be beneficial in these types of cases.

Pretrial juror bias, either pro-defense or pro-prosecution, has been shown to have a significant impact, particularly when more ambiguous evidence is presented (De La Fuente, De La Fuente, & Garcia, 2003). More recent research examined venire person's evaluations of aggravating and mitigating circumstances in capital trials by surveying 450 venire persons from the 11th Judicial Circuit Court in Miami, Florida. The results revealed that death-qualified venire persons, when compared to excluded persons, were more likely to endorse aggravating circumstances (Butler & Moran, 2002).

In the 1970s, the concept of scientific jury selection was introduced. This notion examined whether social scientists could be employed by the defense to select the most favorable jurors in an effort to increase chances of acquittal. Generally, a telephone survey was used to interview people who met the same eligibility standards of prospective jurors. Questions concerning biographical information and general beliefs and attitudes about the defendant, which may influence their verdict, were posed. The interviewees were also presented a brief description of the case and questioned as to how they would vote if they were part of the jury (Abadinsky & Winfree, 1992). Scientific jury selection generally relies on community surveys to "identify demographic, personality, or attitudinal correlates of potential jurors' inclinations to vote guilty or not guilty in a particular case" (Kovera, Dickinson, & Cutler, 2003, p. 161).

By measuring sociological variables, general beliefs, and attitudes of those who could potentially be jurors, it could be determined how certain types of jurors would vote before the jury selection process began. Thus, the defense would be able to predict how members of the jury pool might vote based on personal characteristics in an effort to increase the probability of acquittal. Lawyer-conducted voir dire could be used to determine whether the potential jurors "fit" their desired profile. Moran (2001) indicated that the two leading professions taking part in trial consultation were psychology and communications. He went on to warn that many such consultants have no pertinent professional training specifically in jury selection or simulation. Furthermore, Strier (2001) cautioned that the practice of trial consulting is virtually unregulated with no license required. There are also no explicit standards of education, training, or ethics for these consultants. Other research noted that jury selection experts are not utilizing solid psychological principles and therefore are not as effective as possible (Lord, 2001). The results of scientific jury selection have been noted to be modest at best, and it is generally believed that the success of such a process will continue to decrease in the future if better regulation of training and licensure is not created (Diamond, 1990; Lord, 2001; Moran, 2001).

Forensic Psychology and Policy Implications

When considering jury selection, a number of controversial issues arise. One of the most pervasive concerns in the modern system of justice is whether a truly representative jury is possible. The effects of pretrial publicity, particularly in highly publicized cases (e.g., Scott Peterson, Michael Jackson, O. J. Simpson, Timothy McVeigh), create a situation where trying to find jurors who are impartial about the case is extremely unlikely and perhaps even futile. Thus, in many cases, defendants (and their legal representatives) leave their freedom in the hands of jurors who most likely have preconceived ideas or opinions about the case. The legal system permits some exposure to cases through the media, yet it attempts to find those jurors who may be less biased than others in the pool. Consequently, the question of whether anyone can receive a truly *fair* trial by an *impartial* jury remains unanswered.

Steps to reduce jury bias, such as voir dire, may have some benefit. They allow for the exemption of jurors who are obviously biased or may show signs of being biased. One of the problems with the voir dire process is that both the defense and the prosecution are entitled to a certain number of dismissals. Consequently, any juror who is presumed to be a detriment to one side's case will be dismissed by the opposing counsel. A policy question arises when the voir dire process and the role of the defense and prosecution in that process is addressed. If each side is concerned with finding jurors who favor, or who they presume will favor, their view, then the final product (selection of jurors) is not truly representative. All individuals will have some biases but the nature, extent, and their willingness to keep an open mind to the presentation of evidence is particularly important.

Suggestions for Future Research

Additional research on the effects of pretrial publicity in influencing jury bias is needed. The available research has shown some influence, yet the extent of that influence remains somewhat speculative. When researchers in fields such as forensic psychology are able to determine the type and extent of bias from pretrial publicity, only then can steps be taken to ensure juror impartiality. Further, the voir dire process leaves many questions unanswered. Its effectiveness is questionable, particularly when addressing extended voir dire. Certainly research in the psychology of thought may provide some direction regarding this issue. Specifically, psychology has addressed how biases introduce themselves, why they exist, and why some individuals are able to look past bias-inducing experiences/thoughts while others are not. This information, applied specifically to the legal system, could provide direction for research and possibly a remedy for the issue at hand.

PSYCHOLOGICAL TESTS AND FORENSIC ASSESSMENT INSTRUMENTS IN THE COURTROOM

Introduction

Psychological tests are an objective and standardized measure of a sample of behavior (Anastasi & Urbina, 1997). Typically, psychological tests attempt to shed light on an individual's intelligence, personality, psychopathology,

<mark>or ability.</mark> Traditionally, these tests were formed on clinical or psychiatric populations and were used primarily for diagnosis and treatment. However, with the increasing presence of forensic psychologists in the court-room, these tests are used to help determine legal questions or legal constructs. As a result, there is a growing debate over the utility of these tests in the courtroom. A limited number of forensic assessment tools have been developed specifically for forensic evaluations such as competency to stand trial or criminal responsibility (insanity). Critics argue that the reliability and validity of these instruments have not been sufficiently tested, which indicates that future research is needed before these instruments can be used with confidence (Borum & Grisso, 1995; Weiner, 2003).

According to Wakefield and Underwager (1993), the consequences of a forensic evaluation regarding criminal issues, such as competency to execute, or civil issues, such as child custody, are potentially immediate and severe. Additionally, Weiner (2003) warned that psychological assessment data are much more dependable for describing an individual's current characteristics or functioning, rather than predicting how they might behave, or speculating on what they have done or been like in the past. These researchers argue that in a clinical setting if a test is misused or if an inaccurate interpretation of a test is made, the most likely result is a correctable misdiagnosis or an ineffective treatment plan. The controversy over the careful selection and interpretation of assessment tools, as well as their legal limits, is at the forefront of the debate over the role of forensic psychologists in the courtroom. The following case illustration demon-strates the impact of psychological tests and the responsibility held by forensic psychologists in their administration and interpretation.

A father in a divorce and custody dispute was accused of tying up his 3-year-old son with a bicycle chain and then sexually abusing him. Both parents were evaluated by a psychologist. The father was tested and interviewed by the psychologist who left the office, leaving him to finish his drawings. He took them home, finished them with the use of drafting instruments, and brought them to her office the next day.

The psychologist stated that the response style to the projective drawings suggested "obsessive-compulsive tendencies, high defensiveness, and an intense need to control ... [and] his rigidly defensive posture does not adequately bind the underlying anxiety and trepidation of doing poorly" (Wakefield & Underwager, 1993, p. 59). However, his Bender Visual Motor Gestalt Test results were completely normal. His House-Tree-Person (HTP) drawings were careful and detailed. He clearly attempted to do as good a job as possible. Given that his understanding was that these drawings would be interpreted to indicate whether he was an abuser, his choice to carefully complete them at home demonstrates an understandable effort to comply with the instructions and do the best job he could. None of this was noted in the report. There are no scientific data to support the interpretive comment quoted above. It is meaningless jargon with no connection to an empirical base.

Literature Review

Cases like the one presented by Wakefield and Underwager (1993) illustrate the potential for misuse or misinterpretation of psychological tests or other forensic assessment tools. This case illustration demonstrates the great care forensic psychologists must take in choosing, interpreting, and corroborating psychological tests with other relevant archival or third-party information. Forensic psychologists must address the issue of which assessment tools are appropriate in forensic settings. Conclusions reached by forensic psychologists can be challenged during cross-examination and are subject to close scrutiny in the legal arena (Knapp & VandeCreek, 2001; Wakefield & Underwager, 1993). Butcher (2002) explained that the quality of forensic evaluations, which include psychological tests, must meet the highest standard of practice and be able to withstand careful scrutiny in the adversarial system, particularly in the criminal courtroom. Therefore the primary focus of forensic assessment is on accuracy as opposed to a "therapeutic" focus in clinical settings (Acklin, 2002; Gacono, 2002; Heilbrun, 1992). Forensic assessments are significantly different from traditional clinical assessments in terms of the psycholegal question, the goals, scope, limits of confidentiality, the role of the examiner, and the nature of the relationship with the examinee (Melton, Petrila, Poythress, & Slobogin, 1997; Nicholson & Norwood, 2000).

Forensic assessments must also adhere to legal and ethical parameters of the referral question, and results and determinations must be communicated in a manner that is understandable to non–mental-health professionals. Traditional psychological tests have seen widespread use in forensic contexts; however, their utility is being challenged. Specialized forensic assessment instruments (FAIs) are being developed to address specific legal questions. The rigor by which these instruments have been validated has also come under fire. Forensic psychologists are questioning how to more effectively answer legal referral questions with the available assessment tools.

According to Heilbrun (1992), "the primary legal criterion for the admissibility of psychological testing is relevance to the immediate legal issue or to some underlying psychological construct" (p. 257). He stated that the courts typically will not limit the use of psychological tests or forensic instruments if their relevance to the legal standard is shown. Heilbrun explained that relevancy can be demonstrated either by directly measuring a legal construct included in the forensic referral question or by measuring a psychological construct that is considered to make up part of a legal standard. For example, intelligence testing could be used to measure an individual's ability to understand the charges against him or her. He concluded that this relationship could be demonstrated through a written report or testimony (Heilbrun, 1992).

The broad range of legal issues requiring the assessment of a forensic psychologist are subject to a standard that is determined from either statutes or case law. In the Federal Rules of Evidence, Rule 702 (Melton et al., 1997) considers the admissibility of expert opinions, stating that the primary criterion is whether the opinion will assist the factfinder (judge or jury). Rule 703 indicates that evidence presented by mental health professionals in the legal setting must be "reasonably relied upon" by professionals in the field (Melton et al., 1997, p. 59).

In the past, the majority of courts required that evidence follow the *Frye* test or that the evidence be based on procedures that have achieved "general acceptance" within that particular profession (*Frye v. United States*, 1923, p. 1013). Critics charge that under the *Frye* test evidence that is novel yet reliable is excluded while unreliable evidence that has gained general acceptance is allowed (Martin, Allan, & Allan, 2001; Melton et al., 1997). In 1993 the Supreme Court's decision in *Daubert v. Merrell* shifted the standard for the admissibility of evidence to focus on scientific validity, methodology, and the application of the expert opinion to the facts at issue. Martin et al. (2001, p. 77) summarized the *Daubert* test for the admissibility of evidence as follows:

- The theory it is based on is so precise and specific that it can be, or has been, tested
- The test has been subjected to peer review and publication
- It has a known or potential error rate
- It is generally accepted within the scientific community

Melton and his colleagues (1997) warned that if *Daubert v. Merrell* (1993) was strictly followed, a considerable amount of clinical testimony would not meet this threshold. They maintained that it would prevent the use of novel ways of thinking about human behavior that have relevance to the legal proceeding.

The Supreme Court has upheld rulings that a defendant can present "less reliable" evidence banned by a State statute (*Chambers v. Mississippi*, 1973; *Rock v. Arkansas*, 1987). The Court explained that a defendant's Fourteenth Amendment right to present evidence is paramount to the state's ability to ban such evidence. Heilbrun (1992) recognized the potential for "... a similar approach to the admissibility of expert mental health testimony based on psychological testing, even if they were inclined to exclude some tests on the grounds of limited psychometric rigor" (p. 261).

Holub (1992) found that in two-thirds of the cases in which clinicians used tests, the Minnesota Multiphasic Personality Inventory (MMPI), the Wechsler Adult Intelligence Scale-Revised (WAIS-R), the Rorschach Psychodiagnostic Inkblots (Rorschach), or the Bender Visual Motor Gestalt tests were used. In a study conducted by Borum and Grisso (1995), 68% of forensic psychologists rated psychological testing as essential or recommended in evaluations for criminal responsibility, with 32% rating it as optional. Of the 94% of forensic psychologists mentioning specific tests, 96% indicated that they used objective personality inventories (typically the MMPI or MMPI-2). Intelligence tests were utilized by 80% of the psychologists, followed by neuropsychological instruments at 50%, and finally projective tests at 42%. In CST evaluations, 51% of the forensic psychologists surveyed viewed psychological testing as essential or recommended and 49% considered it optional.

For criminal responsibility evaluations, 46% of the forensic psychologists in this sample reported they never used FAIs and another 20% reported rarely using them. Of the remaining 34%, the breakdown was as follows: 10% sometime users, 12% frequent users, and 12% almost always users. In CST evaluations, 36% of forensic psychologists reported that they almost always use FAIs and 36% reported that they never use them. Borum and Grisso (1995) reported that the Competency to Stand Trial Assessment Instrument and the Competency Screening Test were undoubtedly the most popular FAIs used. However, they indicated that their findings did not substantiate a standard requiring psychological testing in all criminal forensic assessments.

Skeem, Golding, Cohn, and Berge (1998) found that 70% of the relevant CST evaluations in their study did not articulate any relationship between assessment data and competency to stand trial. Moreover, the remaining 30% only provided ambiguous claims related to symptoms identified by testing and broad impairment in competency to stand trial. Out of the psychological tests used in this study, the results of intelligence tests were only sometimes correlated to functional capacities related to competency, and projective, objective, and neuropsychological test data were almost rarely or never associated with competency to stand trial (Skeem et al., 1998). Many forensic evaluators find that a thorough competency interview carefully structured around the psycholegal question and the defendant's relevant factual and rational understanding, as well as the necessary functional capacities, most closely approximates the attorney–client interaction. This interview designed to specifically address the functional capacities required by law for competence to stand trial can provide invaluable information about the defendant's ability to participate in a meaningful interchange with his or her attorney, which is essential for a determination of competency.

According to Podboy and Kastl (1993), frequent misuse of standard psychological tests included ignorance of the reliability and validity of a particular test, incomplete administration, over-reliance on a single test or scale, failure to correlate test results with other available data, and failure to address malingering. Researchers note that in many cases mental health professionals have the awkward task of trying to assess mental state at the time of the alleged offense with instruments that assess current mental functioning (Lanyon, 1986; Weiner, 2003). These types of evaluations are done retrospectively and require other sources of data including police reports, medical or mental health records, psychosocial history from friends and family, and the like (Heilbrun, 1992; Lanyon, 1986; Melton et al., 1997; Nicholson & Norwood, 2000; Weiner, 2003).

Melton et al. (1997) suggested there are limitations regarding traditional clinical methods in gaining accurate information from forensic populations. These researchers noted the potential for malingering, defensiveness, and even normal forgetfulness. Lanyon (1986) maintained that this population is greatly invested in a particular outcome and that attempts will be made to influence the conclusions of an evaluation in their favor.

Forensic assessment instruments have been under development for the past two decades. According to Melton et al. (1997), these instruments were more focused on specific legal criteria and had been tested on relevant legal populations. However, these researchers acknowledge that many of these instruments are conceptually flawed and lack empirical research. Forensic psychologists are left to determine the methodology of the various psychological tests and forensic assessment instruments available to them as well as their relevance to the legal question.

Forensic Psychology and Policy Implications

Research indicates that traditional psychological tests will continue to be used in forensic assessments. However, as more instruments are developed to address specific legal questions, their role will diminish. Lanyon (1986) pointed out that in the past traditional psychological instruments were considered adequate to answer all questions in the realm of neuropsychology, specifically, the presence or absence of organicity. He suggested that the area of forensic psychology will also develop its own psychometric instruments specific to legally relevant behaviors.

Some researchers are calling for ". . . the development of an independent set of standards for the selection, administration, and interpretation of psychological testing in forensic contexts" (Heilbrun, 1992, p. 269). The case illustration of the father who is assumed to have sexually abused his child due to his "response style to the projective drawings" demonstrates the need for more accuracy in test administration and interpretation as well as corroborating data if possible in forensic contexts (Wakefield & Underwager, 1993, p. 57). The consequences of a custody dispute as well as accusations of sexual abuse could result in the father losing his child and possible incarceration. Contemporary instruments designed specifically for use in custody determinations also require much more research, particularly on their validity (Otto, Edens, & Barcus, 2000).

Forensic psychologists are continually trying to improve their effectiveness in the legal arena. Unfortunately, many criticisms have been leveled regarding the role of psychologists in the courtroom by legal professionals. The subjective and unreliable nature of the instruments used for assessment is a primary criticism. Techniques by which forensic psychologists can be more effective, persuasive, and credible in legal proceedings are being developed and put into practice.

Suggestions for Future Research

Clearly, the development of methodologically sound forensic assessment instruments is needed. Those FAIs in current use are in need of additional research to determine their validity and reliability. Research is also necessary to determine if these instruments produce any positive trends when used in forensic evaluations. In general, more empirical data are called for on the uses of psychological tests in forensic evaluations: Which are more effective and with which type of evaluation? Additional research is needed to demonstrate if there is any substantial utility in using a measure of current functioning to speak to a mental state or behavior in the past or to predict characteristics or behavior in the future. The many differences between the fields of psychology and law should be continually explored to better prepare forensic psychologists for entry into legal settings.

RISK ASSESSMENT

Introduction

Mental health professionals who work in the arena of forensic psychology are often asked to conduct risk-assessment evaluations. This type of assessment involves making predictions about an individual's likelihood of engaging in future violence. In the criminal justice system, the sentencing hearing is a particularly common time for the court to ask a psychologist to generate an opinion as to an individual's risk for re-offending. In this regard, a psychologist serving as an expert for the court can have a significant influence on the sentence imposed. With a consistent movement toward a more stringent application of the retributive process in the criminal justice system, risk assessments have been utilized more and more frequently in the United States court systems.

Psychologists working in both correctional systems and in maximum-security hospitals are also conducting violence risk assessments to assist parole boards and dangerousness review boards. These boards consider insanity acquittees for release to less restrictive hospitals and make more informed decisions relating to violence risk. However, there are a number of very serious issues involved in risk assessment that need to be addressed. Of utmost concern is the lack of accuracy with which psychologists are able to predict future violent behavior. In many instances, a clinician's opinion regarding an individual's likelihood of committing future violence is no better than chance. Past research indicated that prediction by mental health professionals accurately predicted future violence only one third of the time (Monahan, 1981). Based on such knowledge, research in the area of risk assessment is currently focusing on how to improve the predictive models of violence, which are utilized by clinicians in making such predictions. More recent research has demonstrated that with the continued development and use of actuarial instruments, our ability to assess violence risk is improving (Moran, Sweda, Fragala, & Sasscer-Burgos, 2001). The constitutionality of risk assessment, as well as the crucial role that psychologists play in making such predictions, has been examined in such landmark cases as *Barefoot v. Estelle* (1983). The following case illustration summarizes this case as well as the findings by the court.

> Thomas Barefoot was convicted of first-degree murder and sentenced to death by a jury who based its opinion largely on the expert testimony of two psychiatrists. During Mr. Barefoot's sentencing hearing, the jury was instructed to consider whether "there is a probability that the defendant would commit criminal acts of violence that would constitute a continuing threat to society." If the jury found that such a probability existed, they were required to impose the death penalty on Mr. Barefoot. The jury listened to testimony by two psychiatrists, each of whom offered predictions as to Barefoot's likelihood for engaging in future violence. The conclusions by the two psychiatrists that Mr. Barefoot would continue to commit violent acts if he was not executed assisted the jury in delivering its decision that Mr. Barefoot did indeed deserve the death penalty. Mr. Barefoot challenged the constitutionality of risk assessment in an appeal to the United States Supreme Court. He argued that the expert testimonies of the psychiatrists were based on unreliable predictions. However, one of the psychiatrists who provided a risk assessment claimed that the accuracy of his prediction was "100% and absolute." Mr. Barefoot lost his appeal and the presiding Justice White stated that "the likelihood of a defendant committing further crimes is a constitutionally acceptable criterion for imposing the death penalty" (*Barefoot v. Estelle*, 1983, p. 880).

Literature Review

The case of *Barefoot v. Estelle* (1983) has repeatedly been used to illustrate the strength of the influence that psychological testimony has on jurors regarding an individual's perceived risk. While the controversy surrounding the accuracy of risk assessment remains unabated among psychologists and criminologists, certain issues are agreed upon by the vast majority of experts who research and conduct risk assessments. One such issue is that predictions of dangerousness are never 100% accurate. Thus, the psychiatrist who offered an expert opinion in *Barefoot v. Estelle* was misleading jurors at best and perhaps not only made an inaccurate statement, but also an unethical one. This has serious implications given that mental health professionals who provide expert testimony in court regarding a risk assessment carry a great deal of weight in terms of the eventual sentence delivered (Melton et al., 1997).

John Monahan, a leading expert on violence prediction, has examined the concept of risk assessment over the past 3 decades in order to offer some insight as to where this controversial issue is headed in the future (Monahan, 1996). He suggested that years ago the controversy was centered around the constitutionality of risk assessment. As illustrated by several cases, however, the courts have determined that regardless of the accuracy of the predictions, risk assessments will continue to be allowed in court (*Barefoot v. Estelle*, 1983; *Schall v. Martin*, 1984; *United States v. Salerno*, 1987). With this in mind, Monahan stated that rather than focusing on whether clinicians can make accurate predictions about violence, the focus has now shifted to researching ways in which the clinical models of prediction can be improved.

Research has suggested that one way in which the predictive models of future violence can be improved is to use actuarial data as the premise for the prediction as opposed to clinical opinion. M. Miller and Morris (1988) stated that clinical prediction is based on professional training and experience, whereas actuarial prediction is based on statistical models used to determine the commonalities between a particular individual and others with similar characteristics who have engaged in violent behavior. Research has consistently shown that actuarial methods are far more sophisticated in terms of predicting risk than clinical methods (Dernevik, Grann, & Johansson, 2002; G. Harris, Rice, & Cormier, 2002; McGrath, 1991; Milner & Campbell, 1995; Monahan, 2002; Moran et al., 2001). As noted by McGrath (1991), "it is imperative that decisions that can affect the liberty of offenders and the safety of the community are based not only on clinical experience but on empirical findings as well" (p. 331). However, limitations have also been noted with the use of actuarial data. For instance, the court system often has difficulty understanding information that utilizes statistical predictors (Melton et al., 1997). Milner and Campbell (1995) suggested that a combination of actuarial and clinical methods will provide the most accurate risk assessment. Although the literature remains controversial, there are certain factors that have consistently been shown to be significantly related to future violent behavior. Among such factors are the individual's score on the Hare Psychopathy Checklist (PCL), a history of criminal behavior, a history of substance abuse, and the age of the offender (G. Harris, Rice, & Quinsey, 1993; Meloy, 2000).

In the MacArthur Risk Assessment Study, Monahan et al. (2001) evaluated over 1,000 acute civilly committed patients at three mental health facilities in a variety of North American states and examined a wide variety of variables thought to be related to violent behavior. These researchers measured community violence by interviews with the patients, as well as by using collateral sources after their discharge in the community to include reviewing official records for the first 20 weeks after discharge and records after the first full year after discharge. Monahan (2002) described a number of specific risk factors that had a predictive relationship with violence. Despite much prior research that has found that men typically are more likely to be violent than women, results of this study suggested that the prevalence rates after one year were similar, but men were more likely to have been abusing substances and were less likely to have been adhering to prescribed psychotropic medications. The women who engaged in violent behaviors one year post discharge were more likely to have targeted family members and to have been violent in the home (Monahan, 2002). Prior violence and criminality were strong predictive factors as was prior physical abuse as a child. High-crime neighborhoods or the neighborhood context a patient was released into also had an effect. Diagnosis was also a significant factor, specifically a co-occurring diagnosis of substance abuse or dependence. A major mental disorder such as schizophrenia was less associated with violence than Axis II personality disorders or adjustment disorders.

The MacArthur Risk Assessment Study revealed that within the major mental disorders, a diagnosis of schizophrenia was associated with lower rates of violence than a diagnosis of depression or bipolar disorder, but associated with higher rates than a nondisordered comparison group from the community (Monahan, 2002). Psychopathy as determined by the Hare PCL:SV (screening version) added validity to a variety of other factors in predicting violence, which included history of recent violence, substance abuse, and the like. Most of its predictive power appeared to be a result of the behavioral factor (Factor II) versus the more narcissistic and detached personality structure measured in Factor I. Finally, command hallucinations with violent content, violent thoughts, and anger were significant factors in increasing violence risk (Monahan, 2002).

Other studies have attempted to develop predictive models for specific types of offenders. Blanchette (1996) stated that there are special considerations in conducting risk assessments for sexual offenders, such as assessing the individual's cognitive processes, and his or her general lifestyle and history of sexual deviance. Moreover, as noted by Quinsey, Lalumiere, Rice, and Harris (1995), risk assessments vary considerably depending on the specific type of sexual offender. G. Harris, Rice, Quinsey, Lalumiere, Boer, and Lang (2003) compared actuarial risk instruments for sex offenders for the prediction of violent and sexual re-offending using the Violence Risk Appraisal Guide (VRAG), Sex Offender Risk Appraisal Guide (SORAG), Rapid Risk Assessment for Sex Offender Recidivism

(RRASOR), and Static-99. All four instruments were found to predict violence, including sexual recidivism, with the VRAG and SORAG having some benefits. Overall, the predictive validity was higher for child molesters than for rapists, particularly for the Static-99 and the RRASOR. These researchers found that consistent with past research, those offenders with elevated scores in both psychopathy and sexual deviance were an exceptionally high-risk group (G. Harris et al., 2003).

As a result of greater risks associated with subtypes of offenders, mental health professionals who are not trained specifically in the assessment of sexual offenders are likely to draw erroneous conclusions regarding their risk. Another common population for whom mental health professionals tend to conduct inaccurate risk assessments is the mentally ill. It has been suggested that this may be due to the illusory correlation between mental illness and violence or the belief that an individual is more dangerous simply because he or she is mentally ill (Melton et al., 1997; Monahan, 2002). Therefore, it is crucial for mental health professionals to truly have expertise with the specific population on whom they purport the ability to conduct risk assessments.

Melton et al. (1997) provided guidelines for the most appropriate ways for mental health professionals to communicate the results of their risk assessments to the courts. These authors stressed the importance of refraining from using language that suggests that their opinion is absolute. They also suggested that experts present information to the court regarding the factors that have been empirically shown to enhance an individual's risk for violent behavior. Finally, these researchers encouraged mental health professionals to provide the court with a statement as to the poor validity of violence prediction. These suggestions are in stark contrast to the method employed by the psychiatrist who testified in the *Barefoot v. Estelle* (1983) case.

In California, even those mental health professionals who are not accustomed to their work entering the legal system have been faced with the issue of conducting risk assessments. In 1976, the landmark case of *Tarasoff v. Regents of the University of California* delivered a decision that requires therapists to take preventative measures if any reasonable therapist would believe that their client is likely to harm an identifiable victim in the near future. Most jurisdictions have a statute similar to that of *Tarasoff* (Melton et al., 1997). Thus, this statute brought the issue of risk assessment into the lives of all therapists. In so doing, controversy exists among mental health professionals concerning the damage that this form of risk assessment has on the therapeutic process and the ethical principle of confidentiality between a therapist and his or her client. This controversy is further examined in Chapter 4, page 137.

Forensic Psychology and Policy Implications

Experts have consistently agreed that predicting risk for future violent behavior is an extremely difficult task (G. C. N. Hall, 1990; McGrath, 1991; Monahan, 1981, 2002). However, it is likely that the courts will continue to turn to psychologists to provide risk assessments, despite the difficulties noted in providing accurate predictions. The courts have repeatedly ruled that expert testimony is permissible regarding the predictions of violent behavior (*Barefoot v. Estelle*, 1983; *Schall v. Martin*, 1984; *United States v. Salerno*, 1987). With this in mind, it is crucial for the mental health professionals who provide risk assessments to the courts to uphold their ethical duty and acknowledge the limitations of their expertise in making such predictions.

Tolman and Mullendore (2003) compared the practice patterns of generally licensed psychologists with those of specialist forensic diplomates in providing risk assessments for the courts. Their results suggested that risk evaluations are frequently conducted by general clinicians, but forensic diplomates are more likely to use more modern actuarial risk instruments, are more aware of the scientific literature, and provide the court with more information about the scientific basis of their testimony (Tolman & Mullendore, 2003). Considering the potential implications of probability statements about risk in the criminal courtroom, it appears that those who are forensically trained are better suited to conduct these evaluations. General clinicians who take on this type of work have an obligation to be familiar with relevant research and base their conclusions on solid empirical data relating to violence risk assessment.

As illustrated in the case of *Barefoot v. Estelle* (1983), there are decisions that juries make which require the risk assessment to be a primary consideration in their final decision. Suppose for a moment that the jury's decision to sentence Mr. Barefoot to death was primarily the result of the testimony by a psychiatrist who claimed to be able to predict with 100% accuracy that imposing the death penalty was the only way to keep Mr. Barefoot from committing another violent crime. There are currently no provisions against an expert witness providing such testimony in court. Given the weight that the judge and jurors give to expert testimony regarding violence risk assessments, the criminal justice and the mental health systems would do well to place parameters around the predictions that can be offered in court.

Suggestions for Future Research

To date, no predictive models exist that can predict future dangerousness with a high degree of certainty. Given that risk assessments from forensic psychologists continue to be commonly requested, it is imperative that research continues to explore factors which are associated with future dangerous behavior. The research on violence prediction has grown tremendously in the past 25 years and the accuracy of such predictions has improved. However, the predictive models that have been established thus far need to be tested in longitudinal studies across a diverse population of offenders.

An additional area of research that has not received as much attention concerns the jurors' decision-making process regarding expert testimony of risk assessments. This would shed light on the impact that mental health professionals have when providing risk assessments to the court. The decisions of jurors could then be compared to the decisions of judges in this regard in order to establish whether the judge is better able to consider the limitations of risk assessments when rendering his or her final decision.

FORENSIC VERDICTS OR PSYCHIATRIC JUSTICE: NOT GUILTY BY REASON OF INSANITY AND GUILTY BUT MENTALLY ILL

Introduction

The insanity defense has long been a debated issue within psychology, the legal system, and society in general. Melton et al. (1987) have referred to the defense of insanity as "probably the most controversial issue in all of criminal law" (p. 112). Although society and the law have historically been inclined to treat rather than punish mentally ill offenders, there are, nevertheless, a plethora of arguments that encourage an alteration in the legal system's present philosophy toward insanity and crime. Such strong opposition to the defense of insanity is founded upon several notable cases in which societal perception was that justice was not done. The current more stringent standard of legal insanity has recently left many mental health professionals feeling that justice was also not done when Andrea Yates was found guilty and sentenced to prison rather than found NGRI and placed in a maximum-security forensic hospital. In addition, there are several problems with the insanity defense as it stands. These problems encourage the perspective that such defenses should be at the very least modified, if not entirely eliminated, while other alternatives should be implemented.

One such alternative was established in the 1970s and is referred to as the guilty but mentally ill (GBMI) verdict. Thus, GBMI is not a defense per se, but a verdict that is reached wherein the defendant is found guilty, but his or her need for treatment is acknowledged. Melville and Naimark (2002) indicated that 14 states have attempted to reduce NGRI verdicts by presenting the alternative verdict of GBMI. The GBMI verdict, however, has also had its critics. Many are concerned that GBMI only serves to confuse jurors by appearing to offer an intermediate verdict that may result in more severe punishment than what would have resulted from a guilty verdict (Melville & Naimark, 2002). In addition to the proposal of a GBMI verdict and in response to the perceived inadequacy of the NGRI defense, several states have adopted other alternatives. Montana, for example, has completely eliminated the insanity defense. In this section, the purpose of the insanity defense and the different variations of "insanity," and tests for insanity, as well as several of the proposed alternatives, are explored.

On March 30, 1981, John Hinckley, Jr. attempted to assassinate President Ronald Reagan. Hinckley was apprehended and, a little over a year later, went to trial for his actions. One of the psychiatrists in the case offered the opinion that Hinckley was unable to control himself (i.e., that he did not know what he was doing). Hinckley's attorneys invoked the defense of insanity. It was argued that Hinckley was driven to action by the movie *Taxi Driver* in which the lead character stalks and attempts to assassinate the President of the United States in an effort to "win over" the 12-year-old prostitute played by Jodie Foster. Hinckley is said to have seen the movie numerous times and become infatuated with the "hero" of the movie to the degree that he was driven to reenact the events of the movie in real life.

The expert witnesses (mental health professionals) in the case were in general agreement that Hinckley suffered from schizophrenia. Hinckley's defense argued that if someone can be so influenced by a movie as to reenact those events in his real life, he must not be in a rational frame of mind and therefore should not be held responsible for his actions. His attorneys agreed with the prosecution in conceding that Hinckley had planned the attack

(continued)

(*Continued*)
(therefore establishing premeditation and a presumably "sound" mind), yet they claimed his entire "plan" was based on the movie and that he was acting upon forces that resulted from a diseased mind. Several months later, the jury returned the verdict of NGRI.

Literature Review

The Purpose of the Insanity Defense

It must first be noted that insanity does not refer to mental illness alone. It is a common misconception that "insane" equates to "mentally ill," "psychotic," or "crazy." It is often thought that "the insane" are those seeking (or not seeking) help from the mental health profession. In fact, insanity is specifically a legal term that is not used in the psychological literature, yet, its precise definition has serious implications for the determination of an individual's status in the legal system (Weinstein & Geiger, 2003). *Black's Law Dictionary* (Garner, 1996) defines insanity as "any mental disorder severe enough that it prevents one from having legal capacity and excuses one from criminal or civil responsibility" (p. 319). Thus, insanity is a legal standard that must be differentiated from the medical and psychological conceptions of mental illness, psychosis, and the like. Although the presence of a mental illness is often required for a finding of insanity, it alone is not sufficient. This distinction is later explored in this section.

The insanity defense is generally invoked by those considered to be of unsound mind at the time they committed their offense. Historically, society tends to hold criminals responsible for their actions. That is, we regard their crimes as having been committed by rational persons who have made a free choice concerning their actions. Naturally, society finds justice in punishing such offenders. In other cases, however, persons committing crimes are thought to be too irrational to have made a sound decision regarding criminal actions. In these cases, society has been reluctant to impose punishment on such individuals. In instances where persons have committed crimes without being aware of what they were doing, why they were doing it, or who may have been unable to control themselves, society often feels that these persons need not be held liable for their actions and, in some cases, are in need of compassion. Thus, the prevailing attitude has been that such persons are in need of treatment rather than punishment.

The American legal system is based upon the notions of morality and blameworthiness (Melancon, 1998; Morris, 2002). To be criminally responsible and therefore subjected to punishment for one's actions, one must be capable of making a moral decision regarding one's actions. Theories of punishment are founded upon the idea that humans are free to make rational decisions concerning the actions in which they engage. Therefore, such individuals are to be held accountable for their actions. Insanity (i.e., mental disease or defect) is thought to interfere with such free and rational decision making. Therefore, the presence of insanity does not allow for an individual to form "criminal intent." Such intent (i.e., *mens rea*) is necessary for a finding of blameworthiness under the American legal system. It is generally held, then, that the insane offender is better served by rehabilitation versus punishment. If one is unable to make a rational decision about one's actions, punishment is unlikely to persuade one (or others) not to engage in similar behavior. In light of the questionable value of punishing the mentally ill, rehabilitation through hospitalization and psychomedical treatment is generally considered to be in the best interest of the individual and society.

The Historical Basis of the Insanity Defense

The case of Daniel M'Naughten is generally regarded as the historical origin of the insanity defense. M'Naughten shot and killed the British Prime Minister's secretary in 1843. The jury found M'Naughten to be insane at the time he committed the offense and acquitted him of the charges. The verdict in the M'Naughten case was somewhat controversial at the time and consequently resulted in an official process of inquiry wherein English common law judges were given the task to determine the precise standards for competency. The first official test to determine a defendant's sanity developed out of these proceedings (Manchester, 2003; Moran, 1981).

The test that came to be known as the M'Naughten Test required clear proof that the individual was, at the time he or she committed the offense, under defect of reason resulting from a disease of the mind and that such a defect resulted in the individual's not being able to recognize the nature and quality of his or her actions (or not knowing that such actions were wrong). The idea behind such a rule concerns the presence of *mens rea*. It is often thought that insane persons do not possess sufficient *mens rea* (criminal intent) to be found guilty for the crimes they commit. As *mens rea* along with *actus reus* (wrongful act) are the necessary components for criminal liability, the absence of necessary intention on the part of the actor justifies not punishing the individual. The M'Naughten Test for insanity became the official determinant of sanity in Great Britain and its standard was adopted by the United States.

The M'Naughten Test eventually expanded to include an "irresistible impulse" component. In such cases, an insanity defense was raised on the grounds that the person knew the nature and quality of his or her actions and knew that it was wrong, but the person's mental disability resulted in an "overpowering compulsion" which did not enable the individual to resist the actions he or she undertook. The rationale for the irresistible impulse provision was that such a powerful compulsion was sufficiently strong enough so that the prospect of criminal punishment would not act as a deterrent and, thus, persons should not be held accountable for their actions. In 1954, Judge David Bazelon proposed an even broader test for insanity (*Durham v. United States*, 1954). Judge Bazelon opined that "an accused is not criminally responsible if his unlawful act was the product of mental disease or mental defect" (pp. 874–875). In reacting against the cognitive test of M'Naughten and in consideration of the available psychological literature at the time, the Durham Test held that "[o]ur collective conscience does not allow punishment where it cannot impose blame" (pp. 666–667). In other words, we punish those committing criminal acts of their own free will and criminal intent (i.e., *mens rea*). Those persons whose actions are the result of a mental disease are not to be held morally responsible for their actions and, consequently, should not be punished like other criminals.

Like the M'Naughten Test, the Durham Test also sustained its share of criticism. As a result, the American Law Institute (ALI) proposed its own test for insanity. This test would be known as the ALI Test. The ALI Test holds that "a person is not responsible for criminal conduct if at the time of such conduct as a result of mental disease or defect he lacks substantial capacity either to appreciate the [wrongfulness] of his conduct or to conform his conduct to the requirements of the law" (Model Penal Code, Section 4.01, as cited in Melancon, 1998, pp. 287–309). The ALI Test includes both a cognitive component (lack of appreciation for wrongfulness) and a volitional component (unable to control behavior) (Manchester, 2003). Thus, it is widely recognized as advantageous over either the M'Naughten or the Durham Tests. Further, the focus on "substantial incapacity" by the ALI test is thought more realistic than a necessary showing of total incapacity as is necessary with M'Naughten.

Forensic Psychology and Policy Implications

After the verdict was reached in the Hinckley case, the issue of insanity assumed one of the more controversial roles in American legal history.

The American public generally felt that justice had not been served in what they perceived as letting the man who attempted to assassinate President Reagan "go free" (Manchester, 2003; H. Steadman et al., 1993). In fact, Hinckley's acquittal, as with any successful insanity defense, is not grounds for immediate release back into society. Rather, the offender found NGRI is confined to a mental hospital for an indeterminate length of time. It is rare that such offenders are released from the hospital short of several years, and many remain there for most (if not all) of their lives. The criteria for release in these cases are far more restrictive than other cases of commitment (L. Wrightsman et al., 1994). In fact, it is not uncommon for an insanity acquittee to serve more time in a psychiatric hospital than he or she would have served in prison had the jury returned a guilty verdict.

Despite extensive criticisms of the narrowly defined M'Naughten Test and previous attempts at reform, most states returned to this standard for the insanity defense in the wake of Hinckley's NGRI verdict (Manchester, 2003). This standard focuses on whether or not the defendant knew the difference between right or wrong but not other relevant issues of mental illness that are equally pertinent. Manchester (2003, p. 739) stated: "The M'Naughten Test considers whether the individual was able to know that her actions were legally wrong and thus fails to account for irrational impulses and delusions that are common characteristics of many mental illnesses."

The primary beliefs of the public concerning the insanity defense are that criminals often employ the defense; many of these criminals are "set free" by naïve juries; those found NGRI are released back into society after the trial; and such persons present a threat to society, as they are dangerous and once again "on the streets" (Melton et al., 1987). Public outcry, however misinformed it may be, places a tremendous amount of pressure on the justice system to revise its handling of these cases. In fact, the reality of the insanity defense is much different than the public generally believes. The insanity defense is employed in only about 1 out of every 200 criminal cases. Of these, it is successful less than 1% of the time (L. Wrightsman et al., 1994). Kirschner and Galperin (2001) examined all defendants who were indicted for felonies and who raised any type of psychiatric defense in New York County from 1988 to 1997. Despite previous research that indicated that the general public believes that the NGRI defense is frequently used and is often successful, psychiatric defenses were only used in 16% of all indicted defendants during this time (Kirschner & Galperin, 2001).

The basis of the misconception that such acquittees go free is, perhaps, the use of the phrase "not guilty" with regard to the insanity defense.

In response to such public outcry, some states have implemented the GBMI verdict. The primary difference with regard to the GBMI verdict concerns the finding of guilty rather than not guilty and the defendant is still considered fully culpable for the crime. In states allowing for a finding of GBMI, the defendant generally pleads insanity, but the jury has the option of finding him or her GBMI rather than NGRI. In such cases the defendant is sentenced for the crime committed, but spends the sentence in a hospital until sanity is restored. If and when such a time arrives that the defendant is perceived to have regained his or her sanity, the person is transported to prison to serve the remainder of the sentence. Time in the hospital is not credited as good time spent toward earlier parole. Generally speaking, the public is often less likely to oppose a finding of GBMI. Presumably, this perception of justice being served relates, to some extent, to the fact that the offender has been found guilty of his or her crime in one way or another. Thus, had John Hinckley, Jr. been found GBMI rather than NGRI perhaps the public would have been more content. Yet, Manchester (2003) warned that this verdict reflects our ambivalence toward the mentally ill and numerous professional organizations such as the American Psychiatric Association (APA) and the American Bar Association have opposed the GBMI verdict.

There is sharp criticism of GBMI. Melville and Naimark (2002) contend that GBMI should be abolished on the grounds that it confuses and deceives jurors. They indicated that this verdict offers jurors a shortcut verdict, which enables them to avoid the difficult issues surrounding the insanity defense. Moreover, the majority of jurors do not adequately understand that the mental illness and treatment needs of a person found GBMI in no way guarantees that he or she will receive additional treatment in prison. These researchers point out that a GBMI verdict does not require mitigation of sentencing in any state and this verdict does not prevent the death penalty (Melville & Naimark, 2002). In addition, each state imposes extra requirements on those convicted GBMI, which are most typically mandated treatment as a condition of their parole. Finally, Melville and Naimark (2002) reported that the GBMI defendant is sentenced as fully responsible, sent to prison with the stigma of being mentally ill, and is often civilly committed at the end of his or her sentence. GBMI appears to represent the worst of both worlds and requires careful scrutiny by legislatures and policymakers in order to prevent a "double injustice" (Melville & Naimark, 2002, p. 554).

One of the more common criticisms of the insanity defense concerns its reliance on expert testimony. That is, the disposition of cases in which insanity is an issue is placed in the hands of psychologists and psychiatrists who ultimately may influence jurors' opinions as to the defendant's mental state at the time of the offense. This controversy raises important issues regarding the extent to which psychology is and should be involved in the legal process. Critics argue that psychologists are often unsuccessful in evaluations of insanity. This criticism often stems from the fact that psychologists are asked to provide opinions that are potentially extremely influential in court on matters in which they hold little understanding. In other words, psychologists are often untrained or undertrained in legal matters. This very point, perhaps, marks an intersection for the field of forensic psychology. Justice, it would appear, necessitates an understanding of both the legal and psychological disciplines when treating cases such as those employing the insanity defense. Until recently, this cross-disciplinary training has been essentially nonexistent. With the advent of programs stressing both psychology and law (i.e., forensic psychology), the system of justice may be turning in this direction.

Suggestions for Future Research

Given that criticism concerning the insanity defense often targets the role of psychology in the legal process, it seems necessary to ascertain the effectiveness of such involvement. In other words, are psychologists helping to inform justice? This raises important issues for future research in the field. In particular, it may be helpful to understand to what extent forensic psychologists can improve upon the previous wedding of psychology to the legal system. Does forensic psychology have something to offer that traditional psychology does not and what are the implications for education and training?

Additionally, the efficacy of insanity defense reform and proposals for reform must be examined in more depth. Does the current narrow standard for insanity address the complicated mental-health-related issues associated with women who experience postpartum psychosis and murder their children? More research and exploration into the nuances between legal and moral wrongfulness is needed, particularly with regard to delusions or hallucinations that clearly impact a person's perception of moral wrongfulness. As mentioned above, several states have adopted alternative policies including the GBMI verdict. Some states have taken it upon themselves to create their own standards for determining sanity. Are such alternatives more successful in the eyes of the law, the public, or justice?

This question does not resolve the issue and must be further examined in light of continuing developments. Longitudinal studies regarding the disposition of individuals found GBMI could help highlight the need for reform or the abolition of this verdict.

THE FORENSIC PSYCHOLOGIST AS EXPERT WITNESS

Introduction

The use of psychological and psychiatric expert witnesses flourished in the courtroom during the 1990s and shows no signs of diminishing (Coles & Veiel, 2001). Psychologists are called upon to provide expert testimony on specific psycholegal questions that have been put forth by the courts. This section will focus on the psychologist as an expert witness in the criminal court system, although the guidelines apply generally to civil contexts as well. Please refer to the section Child Custody Evaluations in Chapter 6 for issues specific to that context.

   Expert psychological testimony as evidence is allowed in the courtroom only when the issue at hand is deemed to go beyond the experience of jury members (McSherry, 2001). Major areas that frequently require expert testimony are competency to stand trial, mental state at the time of an offense, assessment of violence risk, diagnosis and syndromes, sentencing at capital and non-capital cases, and relevant psychometric testing, as these are considered areas that require special knowledge and experience that is outside the purview of the jury. A psychologist may become involved in a forensic evaluation as a result of court appointment or as an employee of an attorney (Knapp & VandeCreek, 2001). If a psychologist is hired by an attorney, his or her work may be considered under attorney–client privilege, and some courts have ruled that the hiring attorney, after reviewing the report or findings of the clinician, may choose not to reveal that information in court (Knapp & VandeCreek, 2001). No matter how they were initially retained, when the psychologist does appear in court he or she assumes the role of expert witness.

   A psychologist who is accustomed to the general clinical role as therapist is in for a rude awakening with regard to the adversarial process when providing expert testimony in the criminal court system. Every opinion must be carefully formulated and supported by reasonable decision making and accurate data, and will be subject to close scrutiny by opposing counsel.

Brodsky, Caputo, and Domino (2002) reported that in a forensic setting the expertise possessed by a doctoral-level psychologist is not automatically treated with respect and the expert has to be prepared for challenges aimed at his or her training, knowledge, methodology, results, and opinions. Qualification as an expert is up to the discretion of the presiding judge, based on the expert's education, training, and experience as well as its relevancy to the question before the court (Knapp & VandeCreek, 2001). In some instances, both attorneys will stipulate to an expert's qualifications, particularly to one who has testified on a particular issue many times before. Much debate has occurred within the professional community about whether or not psychologists should or should not testify on the ultimate issue. The ultimate issue is related to the legal question at hand, for example, whether or not a defendant's mental state at the time of the offense would reach the level of impairment necessary to qualify for a successful NGRI verdict or if a defendant should be adjudicated as incompetent to stand trial. This issue depends on the presiding judge and the laws of the jurisdiction. Many critics emphasize that testifying to this matter assumes the position of the jury and puts the mental health expert in the role of single-handedly determining what is in the interest of justice (Coles & Veiel, 2001; Tillbrook, Mumsley, Grisso, 2003). Consider the following case illustration (McSherry, 2001, pp. 13–14).

On November 12, 1990, in the Australian state of New South Wales, Andre Chayna, then aged 31, invited her sister-in-law, Cheryl Najim, to her house. While Najim was sitting at the kitchen table, reading a letter, Chayna made a frenzied attack upon her, first attempting to strangle Najim before cutting her throat and stabbing her until she was dead. Later that same day, Chayna went to the bedroom of her daughter, Sandy, and asked her to close her eyes while she read her a story. Chayna then stabbed her daughter in the throat, killing her. The bodies remained undiscovered until 3 days later when Chayna stabbed to death her second daughter, Suzanne, who had been away at camp when the first two killings occurred.

At her trial for murder, the prosecution argued that Chayna was motivated by jealousy and hostility to kill her sister-in-law and that she then killed her daughters to prevent her husband, with whom she had a problematic relationship, from having custody of them when she was in jail.

Seven psychiatrists were called to give evidence at the trial. All had examined Chayna and all agreed that she was in a floridly psychotic state when she arrived at the jail. She was given medication and responded to treatment.

(*continued*)

(*Continued*)
However, the psychiatric evidence as to her state of mind at the time of the killings differed markedly. Each witness was invited, without objection, to state an opinion not only as to Chayna's condition at the time of the killings but also as to the applicability of the defenses of insanity (New South Wales follows the M'Naughten Rules) and diminished responsibility (Section 23A of the Crimes Act 1900, NSW).

Literature Review

Chayna was convicted of murder but her verdict was appealed and the Appellate Court substituted a verdict of manslaughter. Chief Justice Gleeson delivered the judgment of the Court of Criminal Appeal of New South Wales and criticized the practice of trial judges allowing expert testimony regarding the ultimate legal issue. He stated (cited in McSherry, 2001, p. 14): "Psychiatrists not only express expert opinions, but go on to give their conclusions on the ultimate issues in the case, and those conclusions come to be regarded as the most important, and perhaps the only important, features of their evidence. This can be a misleading impression." Testifying on the ultimate issues and other pitfalls associated with providing expert testimony are equally relevant for psychologists. It is critical that psychologists who take on forensic evaluations are appropriately trained, qualify their opinions, and base their conclusions on accurate information.

Whether or not psychological expert testimony is admissible is subject to evidentiary rules and relevant case law. The Supreme Court case *Daubert v. Merrell* (1993) set forth that expert testimony must have demonstrable validity (Shuman & Sales, 2001; Slobogin, 2003). This ruling held that trial judges should only allow expert scientific testimony when "the reasoning or methodology underlying the testimony is scientifically valid, and . . . properly can be applied to the facts in issue" (as cited in Mossman, 2003, p. 229). Judge Alex Kozinski, in writing for the Court, stated that the role of the Court was "to analyze not what the experts say, but what basis they have for saying it" (*Daubert v. Merrell*, 1993). The 1997 decision in *General Electric Co. v. Joiner* resulted in providing wider discretion to the trial judge in the application of the *Daubert* standard (Reed, 1999). Presently all federal courts and 33 states have enacted some form of the *Daubert* standard. There is a split in the Circuit Courts of Appeals' interpretation on whether the *Daubert* standard should apply only to hard scientific expert testimony or should include all expert witness testimony such as psychological expert testimony (Reed, 1999). Psychologists in the courtroom who function in this capacity can review common factors compromising this standard.

Groscup, Penrod, Studebaker, Huss, and O'Neil (2002) indicated that although there is a greater reliance on *Daubert* criteria since the decision, only criteria related to the Federal Rules of Evidence are consistently related to the admissibility of expert testimony. "Rule 702 of the Federal Rules of Evidence states that 'if scientific, technical or other specialized knowledge will assist the trier of fact to understand the evidence or to determine a fact in issue, a witness qualified as an expert by knowledge, skill, experience, training or education may testify thereto in the form of an opinion or otherwise'" (as cited in Binder, 2002, p. 1819).

According to Snow and Weed (1998), general guidelines for expert witnesses include: (1) the expert testimony must provide information beyond the knowledge of the typical juror but in such a way that it is not beyond the juror's comprehension; (2) the testimony should be relevant and subject to the rules of evidence; (3) the testimony should be based on principles, methods, and techniques that have been proven to be reliable and valid; (4) the expert must be competent to do the evaluation and present relevant data; and finally, (5) the factual presentation to the jury must be clear, concise, and understandable.

There are many ethical considerations for psychologists undertaking forensic evaluations likely to result in expert testimony. Knapp and VandeCreek (2001) suggested that the evaluating psychologist be familiar with courtroom procedures and the role of expert witnesses. Additionally, in order to comply with the *Specialty Guidelines for Forensic Psychologists* (1991) and the APA's *Ethical Principles of Psychologists and Code of Conduct* (1992), the forensic psychologist should be mindful of competence or proficiency in the area of referral; informed consent as to the nature and purpose of the evaluation and limits of confidentiality; documentation for the basis of conclusions; qualification of the limits of testimony provided; exclusion of statements by the defendant that could be self-incriminating in reports and/or testimony; and avoiding multiple relationships, such as conducting a forensic evaluation on someone for whom the psychologist also assumes a treatment role (Knapp & VandeCreek, 2001). Finally, an expert witness should be objective, as there will be many external pressures to overlook evidence contrary to one's opinion or to manipulate the available evidence to fit a particular position (Chappelle & Rosengren, 2001; Goldstein, 1999). Clearly, being perceived as a "hired gun" will only hurt an expert's credibility (Chappelle & Rosengren, 2001).

Perhaps the most feared or anxiety-provoking aspect of providing psychological expert testimony is the cross-examination. Chappelle and Rosengren (2001) offered guidelines for the expert witness to maintain composure and credibility during cross-examination and these will be briefly summarized. The areas addressed included pretrial preparations and verbal (e.g., speech, word choice) and nonverbal behavior (e.g., demeanor, eye contact, dress/attire), as well as the content and style of the actual testimony. The expert must be viewed as knowledgeable and credible by the jury, but not condescending or difficult to follow and understand. Pretrial preparation should include being familiar with all updated, relevant research on the pertinent issue, keeping one's records in order, understanding court procedures, and meeting with the attorney who calls the expert to testify on direct examination. This meeting helps prepare the psychologist on the nature of the questions to be asked. During the actual testimony, direct or cross, the expert should be concise and organized, and only answer the question that is asked. During the cross-examination, no matter how sarcastic or disrespectful counsel might become, it is critical that the expert witness does not argue and remains unrattled (Chappelle & Rosengren, 2001). The expert should listen carefully to questions asked, pause, breathe, and not be afraid to say, "I don't know." The expert witness will likely lose more credibility by attempting to snowball the jury than by admitting to the limitations of their expertise. An expert witness should come across as confident, poised, honest, and well-mannered. Dressing in professional attire, making eye contact with the jury, and consistency in one's testimony are all frequently cited elements of a more effective expert witness. Please refer to Chappelle and Rosengren's (2001) article titled "Maintaining Composure and Credibility as an Expert Witness During Cross-Examination" for a more in-depth analysis of the nuts and bolts of providing expert testimony.

Redding, Floyd, and Hawk (2001) presented a hypothetical insanity defense case to 59 trial court judges, 46 prosecuting attorneys, and 26 defense attorneys throughout Virginia in order to assess their preferences for types of forensic mental health testimony and for types of mental health experts. There is considerable scholarly evidence to support the utility of actuarial instruments or empirical data in educating the courts about a psycholegal question and much criticism about clinically focused testimony (e.g., diagnosis, interview findings, and psychological testing). However, in the present study, the judges and attorneys found the clinically focused testimony more useful. In a national survey of trial judges, Redding and Reppucci (1999, p. 50) found that judges and attorneys often did not appreciate the value of research evidence. They believed instead that "nomothetic research had no bearing upon individual cases." In fact, in the study by Redding et al. (2001), the trial judges favored ultimate issue testimony and viewed research data, or statistically based data, as less helpful. This preference for ultimate issue testimony by mental health professionals occurred despite Virginia law and Federal Rule of Evidence 704, which specifically prohibited it. The study revealed, however, that more experienced attorneys gave much less credence to this type of expert testimony.

Redding et al. (2001) also found that judges, defense attorneys, and prosecuting attorneys had some differences in their preferences for types of expert testimony. Judges and prosecuting attorneys had the most similar preferences in types of testimony. Prosecutors were the least likely to favor theoretical or speculative information or testimony, most likely due to the potential mitigating effects. Defense attorneys were found to value clinical diagnostic testimony as well as theoretical explanations for a defendant's behavior and other speculative testimony related to exculpatory or mitigating circumstances (Redding et al., 2001). Defense attorneys were the least likely to favor ultimate expert testimony.

Participants in this study preferred the psychiatrist as an expert witness, but this was followed closely by doctoral-level psychologists, with other mental health professionals following far behind. Melton et al. (1997, p. 23) explained the preference for psychiatrists was a result of "internecine conflicts among the mental health guilds and the law's comfort with the medical model." The study by Redding et al. (2001) highlighted the importance of the legal community's responsibility to better understanding the utility of the social sciences and their place in the courtroom.

Forensic Psychology and Policy Implications

Redding et al. (2001) urged mental health professionals and social scientists to educate the courts and the bar about the dangers of ultimate issue testimony by mental health experts in criminal cases and the utility of actuarial and other research-based data in the courtroom. Additionally, psychological experts providing this type of testimony should take great care to explain its relevance to the court in terms that are meaningful and understandable for individuals who are not trained in scientific methodology. The best expert witnesses are excellent teachers who prepare their information or message and present it in a way that takes into consideration their audience.

Just as forensic psychology educational programs incorporate aspects of the legal system into their graduate instruction, more law school curricula should include training on social science evidence. Coles and Veiel (2001) also encouraged attorneys to be more familiar with these issues in order to identify when an expert witness is overstating his or her position. These authors stated: "There should be no poetic license in writing a professional report" (p. 623). The courts must be mindful of the potential for a criminal case to become a battle of the experts, particularly when the stakes are high. Martindale (2002) maintained that experts can frequently offer personal instead of expert opinions while on the witness stand.

Coles and Veiel (2001) warned that when expert testimony specifically addresses the ultimate issue, it has the potential to corrupt the whole trial process. Tillbrook et al. (2003) argued against testifying to the ultimate issue as there is "no basis in science or clinical knowledge for determining the degree of capacity that is required in order to reach the threshold of capacity associated with legal questions such as competency and criminal responsibility" (p. 77). These researchers fear that to do so threatens the integrity of both the mental health professional and the adversarial system in the courtroom. Yet some researchers (Rogers & Ewing, 2003) contend that categorically prohibiting ultimate issue testimony may have some untoward effect on juror's perceptions of the expert's credibility. Clearly, testifying about the ultimate issue is a topic that necessitates continued evaluation by both the mental health and legal communities.

Suggestions for Future Research

A great deal of scholarly literature has been written that focuses on the hired gun phenomenon. However, Miller (2003) indicated that little has been written about attorneys who use expert witnesses to present the testimony of their clients without ever having to undergo cross-examination. He maintains that even though this is much less common, when it is determined to be admissible, it can be very problematic. The courts that have not allowed this type of testimony have typically ruled that the intent of the testimony was not to clarify diagnosis or elucidate psycholegal questions, but rather to avoid cross-examination. Furthermore, Miller (2003) encouraged that this issue be more closely examined. For example, one question is whether or not this type of testimony should be allowed based on the medical records exception to the hearsay rules in the federal and state rules of evidence.

Future research needs to take a closer look at the impact of ultimate issue testimony by mental health expert witnesses on juror decision making. As more empirical and qualitative research explores the effect this type of testimony has on the judicial system, perhaps a more uniform approach could be agreed upon by both the mental health and legal systems. Additional investigations should also be conducted to further examine the effect of psychological expert testimony that does not directly speak to the ultimate issue. Also, this type of research, as well as the aforementioned inquiries, should be compared to illustrate their potential implications.

THE MAXIMUM-SECURITY FORENSIC HOSPITAL

Introduction

This section will address the dichotomous function of the maximum-security forensic hospital in providing both treatment and a secure environment for criminal defendants adjudicated incompetent to stand trial or NGRI for a felony offense. Psychologists who work in this setting have the delicate task of balancing their professional ethical obligations with the legal/forensic system. Individuals committed to this environment have a major mental illness, which requires treatment and they have typically been committed by a criminal court or have been determined by an Internal Review Board (IRB) at a less restrictive hospital to be manifestly dangerous and in need of a more secure locale. This finding usually occurs because the patient seriously assaulted other patients or staff. Psychologists working in this environment are charged with balancing the role of treatment provider for an offender population with that of a forensic evaluator for the institution.

Certainly, individuals who are court committed with felony charges including anything from drug possession, rape, child molestation, to multiple murder have unique security and management issues beyond those typically found with general psychiatric patients. The goal of this setting is to make available ethical mental health treatment, while also creating a secure environment for all patients. Maintaining a secure environment also serves to protect the community. The potential for ethical abuses is high and the clientele are often at high risk for future and institutional violence.

The psychologist working at a maximum–security forensic hospital specializes in the provision of treatment and general diagnostic assessments for a high-risk and seriously mentally ill offender population, leads multidisciplinary treatment teams, and conducts forensic evaluations such as competency to stand trial and violence risk assessments. Koetting, Grabarek, Van Hasselt, and Hazelwood (2003, pp. 114–116) provided the following case examples to depict the types of psychopathology and offenses that illustrate insanity acquittees and incompetent offenders who are committed to forensic inpatient hospitals. Consider the following case illustrations.

Case One

J. T., a 30-year-old Hispanic male diagnosed with chronic undifferentiated schizophrenia and polysubstance dependence, had ridden his bike over to a security guard at a local school and asked for directions. He was then asked by the security guard to leave because he appeared disheveled and suspicious. After returning to the school later, he dismounted his bike, unzipped his pants, and began masturbating. Several students and school personnel witnessed the incident before he fled on his bike. After the crime, he denied exposing himself to those present. J. T. never completed high school, although prior psychological testing revealed average intelligence. He was born the third of six children and had been married and divorced at least once. His psychiatric and criminal histories included one suicide attempt, five psychiatric hospitalizations, treatment for crack cocaine and/or marijuana abuse, and three prior arrests on felony charges. There is evidence that he was intoxicated on marijuana at the time of the aforementioned offense. J. T. received Social Security Disability Income and lived with his mother at that time as well.

Case Two

L. M. was a white male in his mid-30s who was diagnosed with paranoid schizophrenia when he shot and killed his brother, sister, and sister-in-law on one occasion in 1966. He believed that they were poisoning him and stealing his money. He reported later that he was the former heavyweight champion of the world. Having served in the Air Force for less than five years, he also identified himself as Catholic with no children. A history of medication noncompliance, in addition to at least six prior psychiatric hospitalizations and prior treatment for substance abuse, was recorded. While on conditional release in the 1990s, he committed battery on a law enforcement officer, but was found not guilty by reason of insanity.

Literature Review

A maximum-security inpatient forensic hospital is typically a licensed state hospital with special security measures (Weinstein, 2002). The security measures are often substantial as many of the individuals committed to the institution have violent felony offenses such as arson, assault, rape, child molestation, and murder. Although a mental illness significantly influenced the thinking of L. M. at the time of the offense, he still posed a significant risk to society and required maximum-security management in order to protect society. Security measures may include: tall, razor wire fences; electronic perimeter controls; a large security staff; metal detectors and personal searches; and strictly limited access to nonemployees, and no access to minors. Weinstein (2002) discussed the dual mission of the forensic hospital to include both caring versus management and treatment versus evaluation. To further complicate matters, the majority of individuals involuntarily hospitalized in forensic hospitals are those found incompetent to stand trial who have yet to be tried and convicted. Maximum-security forensic hospitals maintain a special relationship with the courts and legal system due to the fact that most persons admitted are committed there through the criminal courts by a finding of NGRI or incompetency.

Psychologists working in this setting also have a dual role; this requires them in some instances to be a treatment provider and in other instances to be a forensic evaluator. In order to comply with both ethical obligations as well as statutory requirements in some jurisdictions, psychologists must take care to only evaluate for competency those individuals who are not on their treatment team or for whom they do not provide other treatment services such as individual or group therapy. The spirit of this separation of duties is to preserve the objectivity that is required for the forensic evaluator, particularly in light of the potential for court testimony and the scrutiny of cross-examination. This can sometimes be a difficult task depending on the psychologist-to-patient ratio on a particular unit and it may in some instances result in a referral to another unit psychologist or outside consultation.

Line staff or "treatment assistants" as defined by the state of New York also have a complicated, multiple role that involves both treatment and management. Weinstein (2002) indicated that despite the title, these individuals' duties include security responsibilities that appear to outnumber their treatment-related interactions. He cited the security responsibilities listed in a position description for a Security Hospital Treatment Assistant as: "to provide 1:1 patient supervision, chart patient behavior, and to constantly monitor patients and provide safety through verbal and physical intervention, and, as a last resort, assist in the application of restraint" (Weinstein, 2002, p. 447). Employees of forensic psychiatric units are more likely to witness or experience threats or acts of serious physical violence by the patients with whom they work (Exworthy, Mohan, Hindley, & Basson, 2001; Morrison, Morman, Bonner, Taylor, Abraham, & Lathan, 2002). Overall, the use of seclusion and restraint is viewed as a necessary option for a severely disturbed patient, who, for example, is experiencing a psychotic agitation, will not respond to verbal intervention, and is either harming or attempting to seriously harm staff, another patient, or themselves (Exworthy et al., 2001). However, ethical dilemmas are inherent and the potential for misuse is present.

Forensic psychologists working in this setting also engage in interactions that take place for the benefit of the patient's treatment and those that occur to meet the needs of the criminal justice system. This is particularly the case with evaluations such as CST, insanity defense assessments, and risk assessments for the purpose of evaluation for transfer to less restrictive facilities by an IRB or Dangerousness Review Board (DRB). Moran et al. (2001) indicated that due to the violent felonies for which many patients are admitted as NGRI or IST, "virtually all patients are suited for risk assessment because all patients have a history of mental illness and a history of serious violence" (p. 425). The reader must be mindful that while most mentally ill individuals are not violent, those represented in a maximum-security forensic hospital are the minority and most have a history of violence. While in the hospital, the risk assessment and subsequent risk management plan will facilitate safety and inform treatment. "Because the clinical and forensic review board includes members from all disciplines, the risk assessment also provides a vehicle for vertical integration of services as the patient moves toward less restrictive environments" (Moran et al., 2001, p. 425).

In order to be discharged from an inpatient facility, the NGRI acquittee usually has the burden of proving in a court of law that he or she no longer requires hospitalization for their mental illness for public safety and that he or she may be released into the community under a set of conditions (i.e., conditional release) (Monson, Gunnin, Fogel, & Kyle, 2001). Mental health professionals are asked to provide expert opinions to the court about the probability of a patient's safe and successful reintegration into the community. This typically happens when a patient is potentially discharged from a less restrictive inpatient hospital. The IRB or DRB at a maximum-security forensic hospital, which is not affiliated with the court system, focuses on "manifest dangerousness" and determines whether or not the patient can be transferred to a less restrictive inpatient hospital. Once at a less restrictive inpatient hospital, the referring court must make the final decision about a patient's transition from a less restrictive hospital to the community.

Monson et al. (2001) examined the factors associated with NGRI acquittees and their maintenance of conditional release after discharge from the hospital. The medical and forensic records of 125 NGRI acquittees were reviewed. The results indicated that NGRI acquittees who were successfully released into the community tended to be white, with no previous criminal history, and were discharged to live alone or with their families. A statistical analysis indicated that minority status, substance abuse diagnosis, and a prior criminal history were the variables that significantly predicted conditional release revocation (Monson et al., 2001).

Criminal defendants are much more commonly committed to psychiatric hospitals after adjudication of incompetence to stand trial for the purpose of restoration of trial fitness (Noffsinger, 2001). The majority of these individuals are incompetent due to psychotic disorders and/or mental retardation and less frequently due to mood disorders. Noffsinger (2001) described the process of inpatient competency restoration to include treatment for the underlying mental illness while simultaneously receiving didactic instruction to teach the incompetent defendant legal concepts and court procedures. Clearly the barriers to learning suffered by those with mental retardation and the cognitive impairments experienced by those with schizophrenia can make this an arduous process. Competency to stand trial entails both factual and rational understanding. Therefore, a firm grasp of factual issues alone is insufficient if the defendant has paranoid delusions that directly impact the accused's rational understanding of the charges or renders the defendant unable to meaningfully participate in his or her defense. The potential for malingering incompetency is also quite common and will be discussed in more detail in the Practice Update section of this chapter. According to M. Davis (1995), "the clinical problem of incompetence to stand trial is the first priority of the hospitalization and is more important than other psychosocial problems defendants may be facing, such as lack of job skills, lack of education or housing, or residual psychosis" (as cited in Noffsinger, 2001, p. 358).

Although the majority of individuals in secure forensic hospitals have a diagnosis in the schizophrenic spectrum (Koetting et al., 2003), a substance abuse or dependence dual diagnosis is very common. J. T. in the above case illustration exemplifies the comorbidity of substance abuse and other symptoms of mental illness. Personality disorders are also frequently diagnosed. D'Silva and Ferriter (2003) examined the frequency and pattern of substance use by mentally disordered offenders committing serious offenses who were housed in three high-security hospitals at any point between 1972 and 1998. Their results indicated that, overall, 18.6% of patients had used substances at the time of the offense and 38.3% reported regular substance use in the 12 months preceding detention. However, when comparing the trends from the early 1970s until the late 1990s, the use of substances increased approximately threefold. The increasingly high prevalence of substance abuse in this population has important implications for the necessity of substance abuse (alcohol and drug) treatment programs in maximum-security forensic hospitals (D'Silva & Ferriter, 2003).

Forensic Psychology and Policy Implications

Ethical issues such as confidentiality and informed consent are different in a forensic setting than in community treatment. Upon admission, the limits of confidentiality are typically explained to patients, this discussion should occur again at the commencement of any type of forensic evaluation by informing the patient of the nature and purpose of the evaluation and by identifying who will have access to the information gathered. When evaluations are court ordered, the same degree of patient consent is not required; however, the clinician should take steps to obtain it nonetheless.

In 1999, a civil rights class action suit was filed by Sidney Hirschfeld, Director of the Mental Hygiene Legal Service of the Second Judicial Department of New York against the Commissioner of the New York State Office of Mental Health and several administrators and clinical staff of Mid-Hudson Forensic Psychiatric Center (Poythress & Feld, 2002). In summary, the complaint alleged that in notifying the court that the defendant had been restored to competency, the report style used by New York's largest forensic psychiatric hospital stated confidential medical and psychiatric information in violation of the patient's privacy and confidentiality rights established by the Fourteenth Amendment of the U.S. Constitution and state law. The defendants unsuccessfully argued that this release of information was in part justified based on the exception that "the interests of justice significantly outweigh the need for confidentiality" (as cited in Poythress & Feld, 2002, p. 53). The court's review of the fitness reports revealed that "all of [the] treating doctors issued fitness reports which revealed extensive confidential information related to patients' psychiatric and medical treatment, including medical information about HIV, tuberculosis, or hepatitis; sexual orientation and preference; and information regarding family histories of violence, mental illness, or substance abuse (p. 5)" (as cited in Poythress & Feld, 2002, p. 53).

The New York case of *Hirschfeld v. Stone* (2000) highlighted the difficulties encountered by the dual role inherent in the functioning of a forensic psychiatric hospital. Competency restoration, which is a legal mandate, had to be undertaken in a hospital that was also bound by laws that regulate medical and mental health records and was ultimately held liable for releasing too much information in its fitness reports to the referring courts (Poythress & Feld, 2002). Although the gathering of this information was necessary to provide adequate treatment, an individualized treatment plan, and risk assessment, it was not relevant to address competency restoration in a report to be seen by the court designed to inform on a narrow legal issue. Although the ruling of *Hirschfeld v. Stone* only applies to the forensic hospital named in the suit, mental health professionals working in these types of settings must be very aware of the fine line that exists at the crossroads of psychology and law. Poythress and Feld (2002) also asserted that the implications of this case were not relevant for the first line competency evaluators in the community who conduct the evaluation in the jail or in their offices. This is because the treatment role that can in some way be inferred in a psychiatric institution is not present for them. However, they maintain that the community evaluator should also target his or her assessment to the psycholegal question at hand.

The administrators of forensic hospitals must create their policies and procedures with both the ethics and laws related to mental health treatment and those specific to the criminal justice system. Generally, maximum-security forensic hospitals have a legal advisor on retainer to consult with regarding any ambiguous legal situations that might arise. Furthermore, the hospital usually has an ethics committee that is made up of a variety of professionals—both from within the organization and from the community—who can be consulted when ethical dilemmas arise regarding a particular case or patient. The conclusions of the ethics committee are typically advisory only.

Exworthy et al. (2001) urge that all forensic hospitals maintain rigorous monitoring of the use of seclusion and restraint by both internal and external bodies in order to ensure protection and reduce and ideally extinguish the punitive element of the seclusion process. Another important ethical requirement should be staff training on multicultural issues due to the overrepresentation of minority groups in forensic psychiatric hospitals.

This increased awareness could encourage a better understanding of how cultural diversity impacts the presentation of symptomatology and the delivery of mental health services (Weinstein, 2002).

Substance abuse is a very salient risk factor for future violence. The steady increase in the use of illicit substances both before and during the commission of violent crimes by mentally disordered offenders over the last 20 years highlights the absolute necessity of substance abuse treatment programs in maximum-security forensic hospitals. Additionally, defendants who are found NGRI for child molestation or rape are often sent to forensic hospitals that primarily treat their psychotic or affective disorders through prescribed psychotropic medications and psychosocial rehabilitation groups. The danger here is if the pedophilia, thinking errors, deviant arousal, deviant fantasies, and the like that lead to molestation or rape are not addressed, the individual will remain a significant threat to the community. Moreover, the danger is that the person might become a more organized sex offender upon release. More forensic hospitals should implement sex offender treatment programs for those sexual offenders who have stabilized enough to benefit from cognitive behavioral-type treatments. They should also have systems in place to provide a continuity of care with less restrictive hospitals and community providers for this disturbing and complex psycho-legal issue.

Suggestions for Future Research

Future research is needed to examine the adjustment of insanity acquittees who are conditionally released from forensic hospitals into the community and the utility of diagnostic (e.g., Hare Psychopathy Checklist Revised; PCL-R) and actual risk assessment tools (e.g., HCR-20, VRAG) in predicting success upon release or recidivism (Monson et al., 2001). Monson et al. (2001) also encouraged additional exploration into the constitutionality of removing insanity acquittees from the community in order to rehospitalize them for behavior that is not the result of Axis I psychopathology. Finally, they suggested further inquiries into the effectiveness of treatment programs that utilize long-term, cognitive-behavioral treatment strategies. This would include techniques to address criminal thinking errors, along with substance abuse treatment, and psychiatric intervention with the goal of reducing recidivism for insanity acquittees on conditional release. With respect to dually diagnosed individuals, additional research needs to be conducted regarding treatment strategies for the psychotic sexual offender. Research on treatment programs that use cognitive-behavioral strategies and also incorporate a symptom management component would be beneficial. This is a seriously neglected portion of the sex offender population that is cycled through the forensic hospital system. Koetting et al. (2003, p. 119) encouraged more "in-depth, descriptive analyses of small groups of individuals who have committed low base-rate, high-magnitude offenses" to give more insight into the motivations and behaviors of these individuals. Koetting et al. (2003) further suggested that future investigations on the intervening role of personality disorders were needed particularly, those characterized by anger in violence perpetrated by mentally disordered offenders. This research could help elucidate the relationship between major mental illness and the potential for violence.

Practice Update Section: Issues in Adult Forensics/Criminal Court

Forensic psychologists working with the criminal court system face several challenges in educating the courts about the many psycholegal questions referred to them. Unlike their counterparts working in general clinical practice, forensic psychologists must be proficient in the assessment of malingering and be mindful for the potential of its occurrence. The *DSM-IV* (APA, 1994) defines malingering as "the intentional production of false or grossly exaggerated physical or psychological symptoms motivated by external incentives such as avoiding military duty, avoiding work, obtaining financial compensation, evading criminal prosecution, or obtaining drugs" (p. 683). Criminal defendants may attempt to malinger mental illness in order to be found incompetent to stand trial and evade prosecution. Others will hope to give an exaggerated or falsified retrospective account of their mental illness at the time of the offense to support their insanity defense, and some individuals will malinger mental illness to receive psychotropic medications or to avoid work or other responsibilities. A common misperception is that someone who is malingering mental illness is not, in fact, mentally ill. The symptoms of a mental illness can be exaggerated in a person whose disorder is in remission, while some individuals claim to have deficits or symptoms beyond their actual degree of impairment.

Understanding the relevant literature on this topic is important. Familiarizing oneself with the typical presentations of symptoms such as auditory hallucinations or memory deficits associated with specific types of disorders is worth knowing. In addition, observing the defendant outside of the clinician's office in a forensic hospital setting will provide invaluable information. Far too often, the presentation of mentally disordered offenders is markedly different in front of mental health professionals than during their other day-to-day activities. A psychologist who will be conducting a CST evaluation has the ethical responsibility to inform the criminal defendant up front about the nature

(continued)

(*Continued*)

and purpose of the evaluation. The potential for secondary gain by presenting oneself in a less favorable light is immediately apparent for those motivated to malinger. If the defendant is evaluated in a jail setting, interviewing security staff about the defendant's presentation is also very useful.

In conjunction with an interview, direct observation, and collateral sources, psychological testing can often provide important evidence to help support or reject a hypothesis of malingering. According to Blau (1998), current literature suggests that diagnostic interviews alone are insufficient to reliably differenti- ate actual from malingered mental deficits, psychosis, or neurological impairment, particularly in a forensic criminal court context as compared to a medical one. The validity scales of objective instruments such as the MMPI-2 have long been used to serve as a red flag for possible malingering with dissimulation or invalidity determined by exaggerated profiles and sympto- matology (Blau, 1998). Other instruments are being developed to specifically address malingering; for example, the Structured Interview of Reported Symptoms (SIRS) was developed by Rogers, Bagby, and Dickens (1992) to differentiate honest response styles, irrelevant and inconsistent styles, defen- siveness, and malingering. The SIRS reliably demonstrates hit rates for Honest Responders and Probable Feigners in both civil and criminal litigation circumstances (Blau, 1998; Gothard, Viglone, Meloy, & Sherman, 1995). Lewis, Simcox, & Berry (2002) administered the SIRS and MMPI-2 to fifty-five men undergoing pretrial psychological evaluations for competency to stand trial or criminal responsibility in the federal system. Their findings indicated that both tests have potential utility as screens for malingering (Lewis et al., 2002). The Test of Memory Malingering (TOMM) was designed to specifically assess for malingered memory deficits and has also received good empirical support (Heinze & Purisch, 2001).

Many of the symptoms reported to clinicians are subjective experiences and, as a result, there are no absolutes in assessing malingering. However, mental health professionals should use multiple sources of data collection if possible and base their findings on research regarding the form and content of psychiatric symptoms in genuine patients. The consequences for a finding of malingering can be substantial for the criminal defendant or forensic psychiatric patient so the evaluating clinician should take care in building his or her case before making this determination.

CHAPTER 2

Juvenile/Family Forensics

OVERVIEW

The role of psychology in the juvenile justice system brings a different set of pressing and complicated issues from its adult counterpart to the forensic field. As various and recent media accounts depict, adolescent behavior can be no less gruesome and shocking than conduct committed by career criminals. While youth violent crime has typically been associated with minority gang members in urban areas, the Caucasian gunmen responsible for the small town school shootings in Columbine, Colorado; Jonesboro, Arkansas; and Santee, California; make it clear that youth rage and violence can cross both geographic and racial boundaries. The domain of juvenile forensic psychology examines the conduct of children and explains why they act deviantly and break the law. Although there are many more questions about adolescent (mis-)behavior than there are answers, the psychological sciences can help the court system make sense of what juveniles do and why.

Violence within the family also presents a multitude of difficult issues within the mental health and court systems. Other sections of this chapter explore how trauma and violence affect the behavior of family members and how the courts respond to such abuse. Domestic violence, particularly when physical, sexual, and emotional battering is involved, can be extremely painful for families. How does domestic violence impact couples, their children, and the family unit? Are there patterns to abuse in domestic violence cases? If so, can such patterns be traceable to one's family of origin? What is the role of the forensic psychologist in the area of domestic violence?

There are five controversies investigated in this chapter. These topics include (1) defining the age of criminal responsibility, (2) juveniles and the reliability of their courtroom testimony, (3) sentencing and the psychology of juvenile rehabilitation, (4) domestic violence, and (5) family violence and homicide. Certainly, many other contested subjects exist in the legal domain of juvenile and family forensics; however, these five issues represent key areas of considerable debate within the law and psychology communities. In addition, three issues explored in this chapter demonstrate where and how forensic psychological experts are called upon to assist the court system from the pretrial adjudication phase to the postconviction stage of a particular case. Additionally, the devastating effects of family violence and the difficulties faced by law enforcement and mental health professionals in this arena are explored.

Adolescents can behave recklessly and deviantly. They can also engage in illicit conduct. What decision-making capabilities do children exercise when breaking the law? How does psychology help us determine when youths are or are not responsible for their (criminal) actions? Is there a definable age of criminal responsibility?

Juveniles can provide testimonial evidence in a court of law. How does the child's age impact the admissibility and/or veracity of his or her testimony? Can youths tell the difference between right and wrong? Do adolescents understand the consequences of giving sworn testimony in a legal proceeding?

Youths who violate the law can be held accountable for their behavior. Are children who engage in illicit conduct troubled or dangerous? How do the psychological sciences assist the court system in treating at-risk youths? What prevention strategies, as developed in forensic psychology, exist to break the intergenerational cycle of abuse? People are at a greater risk to be victimized by a family member than by a stranger. Several manifestations of family violence include infanticide, parricide, and spousal abuse. What are the causal factors leading to these (and other) forms of family violence? How can law and psychology help us understand the phenomenon of family homicide? The field of mental health law affects the behavior and rights of individuals in families.

As the sections of this chapter demonstrate, there is an important role for forensic psychologists in the juvenile court and adult criminal court arenas. As a matter of policy, the entire juvenile adjudication process remains largely uncharted by mental health specialists. Notwithstanding, therapists, administrators, and advocates in the psychological community are routinely called upon to help address the problems of at-risk youths and to divert them, where possible, away from the formal justice system. Solutions to many of the remaining questions in the juvenile forensic arena require careful and thoughtful research strategies. As the sections of this chapter repeatedly make clear, this is one viable direction by which psychologists can assist those court practitioners who work in the field. The domain of forensic psychology also examines those situations where questions persist about the behavior, attitudes, and beliefs of parents and/or children in the family context. Some of these concerns are extremely serious in that immediate trauma, abuse, violence, and crime are at stake.

DEFINING THE AGE OF CRIMINAL RESPONSIBILITY

Introduction

> There is evidence ... that there may be grounds for concern that the child receives the worst of both worlds; that he (or she) gets neither the protections accorded to adults nor the solicitous care and regenerative treatment postulated for children (383 U.S., at 556, 1966).

The above statement was taken from the United States Supreme Court case of *Kent v. United States* (1966). In this case an intruder entered the apartment of a woman in the District of Columbia, raped her, and then took her wallet. The fingerprints at the apartment matched those of 16-year-old Morris Kent. He was soon taken into custody and interrogated from 3 to 10 p.m. the same evening. The next day Kent underwent further interrogation by the police. Kent's mother did not know that he was in custody until 2 p.m. on the second day. Kent's mother and her counsel visited Kent, at which time he was charged with housebreaking, robbery, and rape.

Consider another example as depicted by Gray (2001, p. 7).

Few people in her South Philadelphia neighborhood understood why 11-year-old Miriam White snapped that afternoon two summers ago. They learned later that she had been hysterical after an argument with a family member and, after seizing a kitchen knife and hiding it under her coat, had run out of the house and down the street. With the force of her frantic pre-adolescent body, Miriam, according to news reports, drove that knife blade deep into a stranger's chest. It cut through one of 55-year-old Rosemarie Knight's ribs and plunged six inches into her heart...Miriam later told the arresting officer, "I wanted to kill the lady. That's why I stabbed her in the heart."...According to court records, less than

(continued)

(Continued)

three weeks before she stabbed Rosemarie Knight, Miriam had been released from Horsham Clinic, an inpatient facility for children and adults with emotional and behavioral problems. She was back with her adoptive family, but receiving no community-based treatment services, she was having trouble adjusting. ... She told the psychiatrist that she left the house fully intending to stab somebody, but "a grown-up, not a teenager or a kid or a baby." ... "I stabbed that lady," she told the psychiatrist. "I didn't think she had any kids." The doctor asked Miriam why it was important for the adult she chose to not have children. "Kids need their mothers," responded Miriam, an ironic comment given her own circumstance: As a toddler she had been taken by child-welfare authorities from her own birth mother who, like Miriam, was mentally ill ... Today, in the Commonwealth of Pennsylvania, Miriam, now 14 years old, is the youngest person ever charged as an adult with murder and the youngest girl ever remanded to the Federal Detention Center in Philadelphia, an adult facility.

This section examines the issues stemming from these examples, especially the question of when juveniles are responsible for their actions and how juveniles should be treated in regard to these actions. This section examines the respective roles criminal justice and psychology assume in creating, sustaining, and responding to the issue of the age of criminal responsibility. Also examined is the age of criminal responsibility by looking at and providing examples of the juvenile and criminal court systems, relevant literature, case law, and current research.

At the turn of the century juvenile offenders were separated from adult offenders because they were seen as treatable. Today, however, there is a general trend in society to hold juvenile offenders accountable (Granello & Hanna, 2003; Umbreit, 1995). Society is moving away from rehabilitation and restorative justice and toward punishment and retributive justice. In the 1980s many state legislatures passed laws that enacted waivers which transferred juvenile offenders of serious and violent crimes from the juvenile justice system into the criminal justice system. These waivers lowered the age of criminal responsibility and held juveniles accountable, as adults, for their crimes. The Supreme Court said that with the lowering of the age of responsibility, due process should be present in the juvenile justice system (Fritsch & Hemmens, 1995).

The trend toward punishment creates a need for psychologists to determine when people are responsible for their actions and when they should be punished. When trying to determine the psychological age of responsibility, one cannot base the answer on a decision from a court, like the legal age of responsibility. This creates some tension between these two fields. Notwithstanding, the fields of psychology and law are continually merging closer together. To understand cases like *Kent v. United States* (1966) and the age of criminal responsibility, the relevant legal and psychological literature are examined.

Literature Review

According to Fritsch and Hemmens (1995), English common law held that children under the age of 7 were incapable of criminal responsibility. Children between the ages of 7 and 14 were still incapable, unless it could be established that they were able to understand the consequences of their actions. Juveniles over the age of 14 were considered fully responsible for their actions and would receive the same punishment as adult offenders. The *parens patriae* doctrine, which is derived from English common law, allows the state to intervene and act in the "best interests of the child" whenever it is deemed necessary (Reppucci & Crosby, 1993).

There is a general trend in society to lower the age of criminal responsibility and to punish rather than rehabilitate offenders. "This move away from rehabilitation has had a marked impact on every level of the criminal justice system, from the police to the courts to corrections" (Fritsch & Hemmens, 1995, p. 17). Legislatures responded to the public's desire to "get tough" on crime by passing laws that have toughened the adult criminal justice system. These laws included making prison sentences longer, eliminating "good time" credits used toward an earlier parole, and replacing indeterminate with determinate sentencing. The trend of holding the offender accountable carried over from the adult criminal system into the juvenile justice system due to the rise in adolescent crime. The juvenile courts then shifted away from rehabilitation and moved toward punishment. This shift caused a large increase in the use of waivers by judges (Fritsch & Hemmens, 1995). Judges use waivers to place juveniles into the adult justice system so that youth offenders can receive a more severe punishment. This procedure or waiver is also referred to as "certification," "transfer," "reference," "remand," or "declination" (Kinder, Veneziano, Fichter, & Azuma, 1995).

A February 2000 report from the Bureau of Justice Statistics found that every state had at least one provision for transferring juveniles to adult court (Federal Probation, 2000). "Twenty-eight states automatically exclude certain types of offenders from juvenile court jurisdiction, 15 permit prosecutors to file some cases directly to adult criminal courts, and 46 allow juvenile court judges discretion on whether to send cases to adult courts" (p. 79). A study done in April 2000 by the National Council on Crime and

Delinquency in Oakland, California, found that among juveniles with no prison record, African Americans were six times more likely than their Caucasian counterparts to be waived from juvenile to adult court for comparable crimes, and were punished more harshly when convicted (Gray, 2001). Boys make up approximately 95% of the juveniles transferred and remanded to adult facilities in the United States; however, over 400 girls, the majority who were disproportionately African American, were sent to adult women's prisons in 1994 and 1996 (Gaarder & Belknap, 2002; Puzzanchera, 2000). Allard and Young (2002, p. 65) stated, "Because there is considerable racial disparity in the assignment of children to adult prosecution, the harshness, ineffectiveness, and punishing aspects of transfer from juvenile to adult court are doubly visited on children of color."

According to the National Center for Juvenile Justice, 20% of arrests in 2000 involving youth who were eligible in their states for handling within the juvenile justice system were dealt with by law enforcement agencies; 71% were referred to the juvenile court; and 7% were referred directly to the criminal court (Cohn, 2003). Yet, others were referred to a welfare agency or to another police agency.

In the 1980s many state legislatures passed laws that enacted waivers. These certifications transferred juvenile offenders of serious and violent crimes from the juvenile justice system into the criminal justice system. The legislatures believed that the juveniles would then receive a harsher punishment for their offenses. In one research study this intention of greater punishment was found to only be true in a small number of cases (Kinder et al., 1995). In fact, the juvenile cases transferred to adult courts were far more likely to be pending or unresolved (see below for the results of a comparison study done by Kinder et al., 1995). Waivers are usually attached to the more serious and violent crimes like murder, rape, and aggravated assault because these offenses need more severe sanctions than the juvenile justice system can impose (Fritsch & Hemmens, 1995). During 2000, juveniles were involved in 9% of the murder arrests in the United States; 14% of the aggravated assault arrests; 33% of the arrests for burglary; 25% of robbery arrests; and 24% for weapons (Cohn, 2003).

There are several types of waivers to adult court, but the two most common are the judicial and the legislative (Fritsch & Hemmens, 1995). The judicial waiver is popular because it allows the juvenile court judges to use their discretionary power to waive jurisdiction and send the case to adult court. The juvenile court may decide on its own to use a waiver or base its decision on the prosecuting attorney's motion. The legislative waiver is sometimes called the automatic waiver, because this waiver can cause some juvenile offenders to completely bypass the juvenile justice system and go directly to the adult criminal justice system at the time of the arrest. For example, if a 14-year-old juvenile in Idaho is arrested for the possession of drugs and/or firearms near a school or at a school event, the youth is automatically sent to a criminal court (Fritsch & Hemmens, 1995). The judge in Idaho has no power of discretion in this case because the juvenile meets one of the requirements of the Idaho state government legislative waiver. In the example of *Kent v. United States* (1966), the juvenile court judge ordered a judicial waiver to place 16-year-old Kent into the criminal court system and he was tried as an adult. Kent's counsel filed a "question of waiver" motion. This motion was filed in the juvenile court asking for a hearing to present reasons why Kent should be tried as an adult but his motion was refused.

Juvenile offenders who appear before a judge in juvenile court are no longer seen or treated as immature children who deserve protection from the juvenile justice system. Instead juveniles accused of serious crimes are held accountable and punished (Fritsch & Hemmens, 1995; Granello & Hanna, 2003; Gray, 2001). This has led to treating juvenile offenders the same as adult offenders, especially those charged with violent crimes. This begs two questions: (1) If you are going to hold a juvenile accountable as an adult, then should the juvenile receive the same rights as an adult? and (2) What are the relationships that exist between children's responsibilities and children's rights? The Supreme Court said that with the lowering of the age of responsibility, due process should be present in the juvenile justice system (Fritsch & Hemmens, 1995).

A major reason for the courts granting juveniles more rights is the belief that because of their age and inexperience they lack the ability and/or capacity to protect their own best interests (Reppucci & Crosby, 1993). Nathaniel Abraham, a 13-year-old African American, was the youngest person in American history to be convicted of adult murder (Grisso, 2000). During his trial, mental health experts testified that he was emotionally and mentally impaired. While a 13 year old might have some of the basic cognitive skills to understand the nature and purpose of a trial, his rational and independent decision-making capacity might not be sufficiently developed to render him an effective participant in his legal defense (Grisso, 2000). Allard and Young (2002, p. 65) stated, "These transfers place children into a court setting in which they are at a disadvantage at every stage of the process." Theories regarding judgment in decision making postulate that throughout adolescence, judgment is impaired because the development of several psychosocial factors that are thought to impact decision making are less developed than the cognitive capacities that are required to make mature, rational decisions (Fried & Reppucci, 2001).

In *Kent v. United States* (1966), the Supreme Court outlined the procedures for using waivers and extended several due process rights to juveniles who are involved in the waiver process. The waiver hearing must be a full hearing in which the juvenile has the right to have counsel present (Fritsch & Hemmens, 1995).

When determining the psychological age of responsibility, one cannot base the answer on a decision from a court in regard to the legal age of responsibility. The age of responsibility differs from state to state, but federal law regards juveniles as adults at the age of 16. In *Thompson v. Oklahoma* (1988), the Supreme Court ruled that the Eighth Amendment to the U.S. Constitution prohibited the execution of a person who was under the age of 16 at the time of the offense. According to *Stanford v. Kentucky* (1989) and *Wilkins v. Missouri* (1989), executions are legal for crimes committed by juveniles ages 16 and 17 years. Sixteen is now the constitutional age of responsibility for capital punishment purposes. According to the Supreme Court, whatever type of environment a juvenile comes from, the legal age of responsibility is still 16 years (*Thompson v. Oklahoma*, 1988; L. Wrightsman, Nietzel, & Fortune 1994). Currently, only 22 states allow capital punishment for crimes committed before the age of 18 (Blum, 2002). Four states have death penalty eligibility for those 17 and above, 11 states for 16 and above, and 7 states have no minimum age specified (Weeks, 2003). Connecticut, New York, and North Carolina exclude all defendants aged 16 or older from their juvenile court systems. Ten other states automatically send juveniles age 17 and over to adult court, while the remaining 37 states and the District of Columbia put those 18 years and older in adult court (Federal Probation, 2000).

The law has long recognized that children are less mature and less capable than adults in many legal areas. The law, however, is not clear as to what degree certain capacities of responsibility vary with chronological age. For example, as we get older are we more responsible for our actions? The law is also unclear as to how levels of cognitive and socioemotional development affect levels of responsibility (Woolard, Reppucci, & Redding, 1996). When a juvenile court judge sends a youth to the criminal court, the youth is then supposed to meet the adult standard of responsibility, which includes the ability to make informed decisions.

Psychologists maintain that a person can learn from his or her mistakes and succeed in life if placed in the right environment. It would be ideal for the courts, when holding a juvenile offender accountable, to consider if the juvenile had both a cognitive meaning (understanding impact of his or her behavior on the victim) and a behavioral meaning (taking action to make things right) for his or her conduct (Umbreit, 1995). Umbreit also argued that the justice system should start practicing interventions or "restorative justice" in which the victim, the offender, and the community actively solve problems together. Psychologists would then be called in to assist the juvenile justice system with this proactive approach.

Forensic Psychology and Policy Implications

As more juveniles are waived to adult courts, forensic psychologists play an increasingly important role in educating the court about a juvenile's competency or capacity to function adequately in an adult system. It will be very important for the forensic psychologist to have a firm grasp on the differences between the juvenile court system and the adult criminal court system, which include the nuances of the psycholegal questions and capacities required to function adequately in each. Psychologists may be called to provide testimony about an adolescent's moral or cognitive development. A forensic evaluator could also be asked to speak to a juvenile's ability to plan and to make independent and rational decisions. It is important, however, for the courts to remember that juveniles are still growing and developing. "Our lack of scientific knowledge concerning child development and family functioning renders what is in the best interests of children largely indeterminate" (Reppucci & Crosby, 1993, p. 5). There is no way to guarantee that what psychologists and courts believe is actually in the best interest of an adolescent. If society is going to hold a juvenile accountable as an adult, then the juvenile should receive the same rights as an adult. Additionally, when the court treats a youthful offender like an adult, does the court protect the youth and society (now and in the future)? In the legal system many unlawful acts also constitute moral violations, consequently, how moral development affects the ability of a juvenile to understand why a particular action is "wrong" must be taken into account (Peterson-Badali & Abramovitch, 1993).

Suggestions for Future Research

In order to provide useful information for legal decision makers, future psychological research must be conducted with legal issues in mind. In this way, the findings will have a direct impact on the law (Reppucci & Crosby, 1993). We need to continue to examine legal cases like *Kent v. United States* (1966) and integrate psychological knowledge about children's best interests and capacities into the decision-making process of the juvenile justice system. If research is conducted carefully with the inclusion of legal issues, the relationship between psychology and law can be woven together and will enable judges to make decisions that are in the best interest of the juvenile. Legal standards and their assumptions about children's capacities must be investigated from both legal and psychological perspectives (Woolard et al., 1996). Studying children's capacities and performance in a legal context, however, is difficult because children can only be compared with adults or other "normal" children (Woolard et al., 1996).

Throughout this section, notions of whether to rehabilitate or to punish an individual have continually surfaced. It is important to conduct research on the effects of punishment versus treatment so that juveniles who need help can effectively obtain it. It is important as well to study age-appropriate legal decision making so that juveniles have the freedom to make legal decisions on their own while allowing them the opportunity to understand the law and their rights. It would also be beneficial to do research on the relationships that exist between children's responsibilities and children's rights. Research in this area is difficult because it is hard to determine at what age all juveniles can be allowed to make their own life decisions, considering how unique each juvenile is. Studying age-appropriate decision making raises other issues: Are we better decision makers as our age increases, and is age the most significant factor in determining responsibility? By studying the age of criminal responsibility, forensic psychologists can examine the effectiveness of the current juvenile justice system and make suggestions as to which changes are necessary in order to improve the treatment of juvenile offenders.

CHILDREN/JUVENILES AND THE RELIABILITY OF THEIR COURTROOM TESTIMONY

Introduction

More and more often, children are becoming involved in the legal system to provide courtroom testimony, especially in sexual abuse cases (Ceci & Bruck, 1993; Whitcomb, 2003;). It has been estimated that more than 200,000 children per year are in some way involved in the legal system

(Ceci & Bruck, 1995). Frequently, children provide key testimony because their word is the only evidence available in many abuse cases. The court must then determine whether the child is a reliable witness (J. E. B. Myers, 1993a). As discussed in this section, the court must examine various factors, such as the child's age, whether the child can tell the difference between the truth and a lie, and whether the child understands the consequences of the testimony he or she will provide.

> Martha is a 12-year-old girl who recently accused her old babysitter, a neighborhood friend named Mitch, of sexually abusing her when she was 8 years old. She never told anyone about this while it was occurring because she said he threatened to kill her favorite pet dog. However, recently she was behaving in an inappropriate sexual manner, so her parents questioned her about her behaviors until she finally admitted what had occurred several years ago. Her parents pressed charges against Mitch, and they are expecting the case to go to trial because Mitch denied his guilt. Martha is the only witness for the prosecution, and she has been questioned many times about the alleged abuse. Some of the details of her story have changed, and she has expressed great fear about having to be in the courtroom with Mitch. Because of the inaccuracies in her story, the prosecutor wants the judge to determine if she is a competent witness. He also requested the use of closed-circuit television so that Martha will not be in the room with Mitch when she testifies. The judge must determine whether Martha is a competent witness by deciding if she can distinguish the truth from a lie and understand the meaning of taking an oath. She also must decide whether allowing Martha to testify via closed-circuit television would be a violation of Mitch's constitutional rights.

Literature Review

As reflected in the case illustration above, having a child present testimony in court is not a simple, straightforward matter. There are many factors that need to be considered. Because prosecutors rely so much on children's testimony, especially in abuse cases, it is important to determine if children are competent to testify (Lyon, Saywitz, Kaplan, & Dorado, 2001; Saywitz, 1995; Trowbridge, 2003). It used to be common practice to have children below a certain age deemed automatically incompetent. Yet, a 1770 case, *Rex v. Brasier*, held that there should be nothing automatic in determining competency, no matter how young the child (J. E. B. Myers, 1993b). *Wheeler v. U.S.* (1895) stated that no age marker should determine competency to testify. However, there are a few states that still use this approach. The approach adopted in most states today is that everyone is competent, which comes from the Federal Rules of Evidence Rule 601. Some states also guarantee competency in sexual abuse cases (J. E. B. Myers, 1993b). Psychologists are frequently employed to evaluate child witnesses' competency. Trowbridge (2003) indicated that most tests of child witness competency stress three basic concepts: perception, memory, and ability to communicate. Evaluation for the ability to differentiate between the truth and a lie and one's ability to speak the truth, particularly when faced with the defendant, is another critical aspect of a child witness's competency (Trowbridge, 2003).

Whatever the state's approach, judges are ultimately responsible for determining children's competency, and they have broad discretionary powers. J. E. B. Myers (1993b) also describes three main requirements that judges use to determine competency. The first is whether children have certain capabilities. For example, they must be able to observe what occurs in the courtroom, yet not necessarily completely comprehend what happens. In addition, they must possess adequate memory. Firush and Shukat (1995) reported that even young children, ages 3 to 6, are capable of providing detailed descriptions of past events after long periods of time. J. E. B. Myers (1993b) described further capabilities that children must possess in order to be deemed competent to testify. Children must be able to communicate and be able to tell the truth from a lie and understand the importance of telling the truth. In other words, they must understand the consequences of lying. K. Bussey, Lee, and Grimbeck (1993) indicated that even 4 year olds have the capacity to distinguish a lie from the truth and that they are able to knowingly lie or tell the truth. The second requirement described by J. E. B. Myers (1993b) is whether children have personal knowledge about facts pertinent to their case. This comes from Rule 602 of the Federal Rules of Evidence. The final requirement is taking the oath. A. G. Walker (1993) stated that children can be found incompetent if they do not understand the meaning of the wording of the oath. However, some states allow children to forego this element and still testify (J. E. B. Myers, 1993b). In Martha's situation, described in the above case, the judge will have to determine if she possesses the afore-mentioned capabilities and whether she understands the meaning of an oath.

If the prosecutor wants to proceed with Martha's case and use her as the sole witness, the presecutor must decide whether her testimony is reliable so that the jury will believe her. According to Jaskiewicz-Obydzinska and Czerederecka (1995), evaluation of a child's reliability is imperative and is determined by the stability of his or her account after consecutive interrogations of the child. The authors conducted a study with juvenile witnesses/victims of sexual abuse, with the majority between the ages of 11 and 15. They found that in half of those examined, testimonial changes occurred. However, they found that the most common reason for these changes was the juvenile's low intellectual level. They concluded that in order to accept a child's testimony as reliable, psychological factors that include intellectual ability, significant fear of social evaluation, and increased self-criticism should be considered.

In addition to Martha's conflicting stories, her age also presents a problem with establishing reliability. Bottoms (1993) reported that younger children tend to be viewed as more reliable than older children and adolescents in testifying about sexual abuse. People believe that children are not cognitively efficient and therefore could not possibly invent such stories, whereas adolescents are believed to be more likely and/or able to have fabricated their story.

A "scientific case study" addressed the issue of reliability by using a detailed record of child sexual assault, documented by a "sex ring" leader. This was confiscated by police and compared to the child victims' reports (Bidrose & Goodman, 2000). Through police interviews and courtroom hearings, four girls, ranging from 8 to 15 years of age, testified about the sexual abuse they experienced at the hands of eight adult men (Bidrose & Goodman, 2000). The girls' allegations and reports were compared with evidence to include photographic and audiotaped records of the abuse. Overall, there was supportive evidence for approximately 80% of the allegations. The levels of proof for sexual act allegations were comparable for all four girls, regardless of age, but the youngest made more unsupported allegations of coercive behavior (Bidrose & Goodman, 2000).

Another factor affecting the reliability of children's testimony is the stress of the entire situation. Children must face an intimidating courtroom setting and discuss personal, traumatic events while confronting the alleged abuser (Batterman-Faunce & Goodman, 1993; Montoya, 1999). Having this feared person in the courtroom could reduce the likelihood of the child disclosing entire descriptions of the events. Therefore, allowing the child to testify in the absence of the accused may provide more reliable testimony (Montoya, 1999; Pipe & Goodman, 1991).

Westcott and Page (2002) examined portions of cross-examinations with child witnesses (ages 8, 10, 14, and 15 years) who were alleged victims of sexual abuse in order to identify ways the child's role of victim and witness were challenged. These researchers found that the child witness could be portrayed as "unchildlike," less than innocent, as instigators, or accused of being poor witnesses, as confused, untruthful, or having fallible memories.

Overall, they suggest that poorly conducted cross-examinations can further traumatize a child witness (Westcott & Page, 2002).

Tobey, Goodman, Batterman-Faunce, Orcutt, and Sachsenmaier (1995) suggested that if a child testifies in front of the defendant, then he or she might be psychologically traumatized because of facing the alleged abuser. They highlighted that this trauma could negatively affect the reliability and thoroughness of the testimony. The authors stated that the use of closed-circuit technology eliminates the need for children to testify in such a traumatic situation. They could provide their testimony from outside the courtroom via television monitors. The objection to this procedure is that it violates a defendant's Fourteenth Amendment right to due process because it interferes with the factfinder's capabilities of determining witness credibility. It also violates a defendant's Sixth Amendment right to confront witnesses directly (Goodman et al., 1998; Orcutt, Goodman, Tobey, Batterman-Faunce, & Thomas, 2001)

The Supreme Court has agreed with the opposition to testimony via television monitors to some extent. In *Coy v. Iowa* (1988), the Court ruled that the use of closed-circuit television (CCTV) did violate a defendant's Sixth and Fourteenth Amendment rights. However, 2 years later in *Maryland v. Craig* (1990), the Court decided in favor of allowing CCTV in child sexual abuse cases where the child would be so traumatized as to be unable to reasonably communicate. The Supreme Court does agree that such technology is a violation of a defendant's rights but that the psychological effects related to a child's testimony outweigh those rights. In Martha's case, the judge would need to determine if she would be so traumatized as to incapacitate her communication abilities, thereby necessitating the use of CCTV. Expert witnesses, frequently forensic psychologists, often evaluate a child and help to inform the court on this issue.

Goodman et al. (1998) conducted a study comparing children's testimony both in the courtroom and via CCTV. They found that CCTV reduced suggestibility for younger children and that these children made fewer errors related to misleading questions when compared to those testifying in the courtroom. Closed-circuit television overall fostered more reliable testimony in children. The authors also concluded that in the CCTV situation, the defendant had no greater chance of being convicted, and the trial was not identified as more unfair to the defendant. However, jurors in the study reported that children testifying by CCTV were considered less believable, even though they actually were more accurate, than children testifying in the courtroom. Orcutt et al. (2001) conducted a study to examine the influence of CCTV on jurors' abilities to detect deception in children's testimony and found that there was no support for the theory that jurors reach the truth better when children testify in open court versus testifying by CCTV.

There are many issues that can affect the reliability of children's testimony. It appears that the stress and trauma of testifying can reduce reliability. In the case illustration, Martha likely has legitimate fears about facing her alleged abuser, and these fears could decrease the reliability of her testimony.

Forensic Psychology and Policy Implications

The issue of whether children are competent witnesses seems to rest solely with judges. This allows judges a great deal of discretion in making decisions that may have psychological implications. The requisite abilities for a child to be deemed competent are psychological in nature, yet judges may or may not involve mental health professionals in their decision-making process (J. E. B. Myers, 1993b). Forensic psychologists should become involved in these types of cases, especially when a judge is uncertain. Increasingly, forensic psychologists are assisting the courts to identify whether or not a child witness is competent and whether or not a child witness will be able to testify in the presence of the defendant (Trowbridge, 2003). If forensic psychologists do not provide expert testimony on these matters, they can at least educate the court on psychological issues relevant to competency for child witnesses. In the case illustration, a forensic psychologist could offer the judge information as to whether Martha possesses the necessary abilities to testify.

Another important implication is to reduce the level of trauma and stress that children endure when they must testify, especially in abuse cases. Psychologists may provide a great deal of assistance in helping a child to testify (Small & Melton, 1994). One approach offered is to prepare children by providing a tour of the courtroom and teaching them information about the legal system. This would need to be conducted in age-appropriate language and may reduce their anxiety and thus increase the reliability of their testimony (Saywitz, 1995). Policies need to be developed to ensure that these children are not further traumatized, while keeping in mind the constitutional rights of the defendant. Although CCTV appears to be one possible solution, it is not currently a standard procedure due to constitutional dilemmas. However, more solutions like this must be implemented so that children can provide reliable testimony.

Suggestions for Future Research

Much of the research on children's testimony has focused on the suggestibility of child witnesses. Yet an important area related to reliability that should be examined is whether increased levels of suggestibility influence children's capability to offer reliable testimony (Ceci & Bruck, 1993). Because children are increasingly providing testimony, research must find the optimal techniques that limit the emotional stress that could compromise the reliability and credibility of their testimony (K. Bussey et al., 1993). Research on this topic should also examine which of these situations will provide a fair trial. It seems that CCTV is a step in that direction; however, there has not been enough empirical analysis to reach any definite conclusions (Batterman-Faunce & Goodman, 1993). Continued research needs to be done on CCTV as a possible solution to the problem of traumatizing children and whether it provides a fair trial. Another focus of research should examine how to prepare children to testify more competently and with minimal stress (J. E. B. Myers, 1993a). If it is found that CCTV is an unfair procedure, then children will have to continue to face their alleged abusers in court and do their best to provide reliable testimony.

SENTENCING: PSYCHOLOGY OF JUVENILE REHABILITATION

Introduction

The controversy surrounding the most appropriate way to deal with juvenile offenders remains unabated today. There are two opposing viewpoints that pervade the sentencing of youthful offenders. There are those who advocate a rehabilitative model when addressing juvenile crime, and those who advocate a retributive model. The rehabilitative model is based on the premise that youthful offenders are amenable to treatment and, if treated properly, will "age out" of criminal behavior. Those who promote the retributive model believe that juveniles who commit crimes are treated too leniently by the system and should receive more stringent punishment for their crimes. Rehabilitation used to be the primary goal of the juvenile justice system, but over the past decade there has been a shift to ensure retribution (Granello & Hanna, 2003; Gray, 2001; Melton, Petrila, Poythress, & Slobogin, 1997; Soler, 2002). The following case illustration depicts a notorious instance in which a juvenile committed a heinous crime that left many individuals throughout the nation wondering what to do with a boy like Kip. While some individuals perceive individuals such as Kip to be troubled teens in dire need of treatment, others think such youths deserve capital punishment.

On May 21, 1998, a 15-year-old freshman named Kipland Kinkel allegedly committed a series of heinous crimes. The young boy walked into his high school cafeteria and opened fire on a room full of students. He discharged a total of 52 rounds which some have described as sounding like fireworks. Kinkel's rampage left 2 people dead and another 22 injured. As if his killing spree at school was not tragic enough, Kinkel shot and killed both of his parents prior to arriving at school that day.

Reviewing the boy's history reveals that Kinkel announced to his literature class that he dreamed of becoming a killer and expressed his admiration for the Unabomber. Additionally, the day before the shootings, Kinkel was arrested for possession of a gun at school. Rather than being incarcerated or receiving any psychological counseling or treatment, Kinkel was released to the custody of his parents the same day.

Literature Review

As illustrated in the case above, juveniles commit crimes every bit as heinous as adults; however, determining what constitutes the most appropriate sentence for juvenile offenders is highly controversial. The execution of one's parents coupled with the mass murder in which Kinkel allegedly engaged, would make any adult eligible for the death penalty. However, imposing a sentence for a 15 year old oftentimes requires a great deal more consideration than imposing a sentence for an adult. The case of Kipland Kinkel highlights the kind of problems that ensue in the juvenile justice system. The overarching concern is whether juvenile offenders should be treated any differently than adult offenders.

When the juvenile court was initially established, one of the salient features of the system was its focus on rehabilitation. Inherent in the rehabilitative model was the notion that the disposition would be made based on its appropriateness for the offender, not the offense (Melton et al., 1997). Therefore, when the juvenile justice system was established as a separate entity from the adult system, it was presumed that the juvenile offender was indeed different from the adult offender. However, the differences recognized between adult and juvenile offenders had both positive and negative impacts on the juvenile justice system, and they led to a series of reform measures.

In landmark cases such as *Kent v. United States* (1966) and *In re Gault* (1967), juveniles were recognized as deserving many of the same constitutional rights that adult offenders were granted, and were therefore entitled to many of the same due process protections that adults received during criminal proceedings. On the one hand, these cases acknowledged the rights of juveniles. On the other hand, they highlighted the commonality between juveniles and adults, thereby making the position that the two should be treated fundamentally different in the legal system — something of a double standard. After the decision rendered in *In re Gault*, the juvenile court repeatedly encountered challenges to the due process clause as it pertains to juvenile offenders (*In re Winship*, 1970; *McKeiver v. Pennsylvania*, 1971). As a result, Grisso (1996b, 2000) noted that lawmakers became more and more supportive of retribution and less tolerant of any efforts to rehabilitate juvenile offenders.

Following the reforms aimed at protecting the due process rights of juvenile offenders were the initiatives geared toward promoting determinate sentencing (American Bar Association, 1980). Thus, this period of reform sought to reduce the arbitrariness inherent in the previous era of juvenile justice, which allowed for discretionary sentencing of youthful offenders. The move to determinate sentencing was temporarily supported by individuals with vastly different philosophies concerning the appropriate way to sentence youths. Grisso (1996b) stated that individuals who supported the retributive philosophy endorsed the determinate sentencing reform because, from their perspective, juvenile offenders received their just deserts. Likewise, individuals who advocated the rights of children supported this reform because it prevented the abuse of discretionary decision making by juvenile court judges. Grisso's final example acknowledges clinician support that recognized the therapeutic effect of teaching juveniles responsibility for their actions.

The current reform efforts are aimed at increasing the severity of the determinate sentencing for youths. As a result, the treatment of juvenile offenders is becoming a reflection of societal views. A national survey was conducted in 1991, which revealed that 99% of the public advocates punishment for violent offenders (Schwartz, 1992). The public's attitude is reflected in action taken by the legislature as new laws are created to implement stiffer punishment for juvenile offenders. The 1992 Attorney General for the United States, William Barr, clearly stated that serious juvenile offenders are beyond rehabilitation and laws must be enacted which provide the justice system with the flexibility needed to prosecute these youths as adults (Barr, 1992). Feld (1997) described how the same public outcry and political pressures to waive the most serious juvenile offenders to criminal court are increasingly influencing juvenile courts to more severely punish the remaining juvenile delinquents. In a more recent study conducted in Canada, Sprott and Doob (2000) found that the widespread support for dealing with very young violent children (10 or 11 years old) in the juvenile justice system diminished substantially when those polled were given the choice of mental health or child welfare systems instead.

As a result of these views, legal reforms in the juvenile justice system have primarily revolved around prosecuting juveniles in criminal court (Allard & Young, 2002; Granello & Hanna, 2003; Grisso, 1996b). By waiving the youth to the adult system, the juvenile essentially faces the same sentence as an adult charged with a similar crime. Moreover, the process by which a juvenile is waived to adult court has been reformed over the years. Initially, in the course of a waiver, the juvenile court took into account the juvenile's individual characteristics and the youth's potential for rehabilitation. However, currently there are laws in some states that require a juvenile to be waived to adult court based solely on the crime committed (Allard & Young, 2002; Grisso, 1996b). Thus, the flexibility and discretion that were once used in determining sentences for juvenile offenders are becoming increasingly less popular and, in some cases, nearly impossible. Allard and Young (2002, p. 65) stated: "The imposition of adult punishments, far from deterring crime, actually seems to produce an increase in criminal activity in comparison to the results obtained for children retained in the juvenile system. Reliance upon the criminal courts and punishment ignores evidence that more effective responses to the problems of crime and violence exist outside the criminal justice system in therapeutic programs."

Despite the movement toward retribution, a number of individuals remain in support of rehabilitation for youthful offenders. Weaver (1992) discussed a program in Florida designed to provide services to serious violent juvenile offenders. This program has successfully operated without incarcerating juveniles. The program is composed of three phases during which the juveniles engage in hard work, education, and obtaining job skills. The program has a behavioral component in which the youths receive "points" based on the degree to which they perform their daily tasks. The points can then be traded in for various privileges. The violent offenders in this program have more significant criminal histories, yet lower recidivism rates upon completion of the rehabilitative program as compared to juvenile offenders in Florida who did not participate in the program. This initiative is one of many in which rehabilitation demonstrates effectiveness in altering the criminal lifestyle of juvenile offenders.

In a similar fashion, policymakers in some states realize that community-based programs for juvenile offenders are more effective than facilities and institutions that are designed to incarcerate them (Allard & Young, 2002; Melton et al., 1997). This is perhaps due to the fact that juvenile detention facilities frequently do not offer services aimed at rehabilitating the offender. Moreover, from a fiscal perspective, community-based programs are much more cost-effective for juvenile offenders (Weaver, 1992). Furthermore, Straus (1994) presented a theoretical basis for diverting youths away from incarceration in the justice system. Straus reports that many individuals who advocate diversion programs believe that they will reduce the stigmatization associated with incarceration. Therefore, according to Straus, juvenile offenders can be better helped within their respective communities while being spared the detrimental effects of being labeled a delinquent.

There are numerous community programs designed to provide juvenile offenders with an alternative to incarceration in a juvenile institution. These programs are often structured to address problems within the families of juvenile offenders, as well as psychological issues affecting the youths. Straus acknowledged that there were a variety of programs available to meet the different needs of juveniles. Some of these programs include the following: peer support groups, work training programs, church-based programs, drop-in treatment centers, youth shelters, and inpatient treatment facilities. This list highlights the numerous opportunities for rehabilitative services that are available for youthful offenders. Thus, the dilemma concerning the most appropriate sentence to impose upon a particular juvenile remains at the discretion of the court judge. It is highly likely that the controversy surrounding rehabilitation versus retribution of youthful offenders will continue to spark debate among the legislature, the media, and individuals in the fields of mental health and criminal justice.

Forensic Psychology and Policy Implications

The issues involved in the sentencing of juvenile offenders raise numerous implications for the field of forensic psychology. Forensic psychologists are asked to complete evaluations of juvenile offenders to aid the courts with their decisions on dispositional placements (Hecker & Steinberg, 2003). The largest percentage of work that psychologists do for juvenile courts is the predisposition evaluation, which provides critical information about a juvenile to help inform the decisions of the court regarding postadjudication questions (Grisso, 1998; Hecker & Steinberg, 2003). See the Practice Update at the end of this chapter for additional information regarding these evaluations.

With the gravity of offenses committed by young persons, such as Kipland Kinkel, the public is intent on "solving" the problem of juvenile crime. Forensic psychologists are needed on both sides of the sentencing debate. On the one hand, those who promote the rehabilitation of juvenile offenders must be able to account for the recidivism rate among those who do receive such services. Perhaps the rehabilitative services that are currently available do not meet the comprehensive guidelines as suggested by Straus (1994), which would target social and structural changes in the families as well as in the juvenile. Without data unambiguously documenting how rehabilitative programs serve to protect the community from future acts of violence, it is unlikely that the communities and the legislature will refrain from imposing more stringent retributive sentences on juveniles.

On the other hand, those who support the retributive model in sentencing juvenile offenders must be able to offer explanations as to why especially young boys such as Kip Kinkel continue to commit heinous crimes, in an era of severe determinate sentencing. From 1992 to 1998, there were 16 publicized cases of juveniles shooting people on school grounds in the United States, and this number has continued to climb in more recent years (National Broadcasting Corporation Research, 1998). These cases do not provide evidence that determinate sentencing is reducing the severity or frequency with which juveniles commit crimes. Moreover, those who support the retributive model need to provide evidence that determinate sentencing does in fact curb recidivism among juvenile offenders. However, some current literature refutes this position by showing that youths who receive alternative dispositions versus incarceration have lower rates of recidivism (Weaver, 1992).

Suggestions for Future Research

The existing research does not include longitudinal studies comparing the rehabilitative approach of juvenile sentencing to the retributive approach. These studies are difficult to conduct due to the legalities involved in obtaining juvenile records; however, these inquiries are imperative for drawing conclusions regarding the effectiveness of either approach.

Moreover, there are few inquiries that attempt to detect the basis for the discretionary decisions made by juvenile court judges. It is crucial to understand why judges are sentencing some juveniles to life in prison, while others are sentencing juveniles, with comparable crimes, to juvenile detention facilities or treatment programs.

Additionally, research needs to be designed to examine the existing rehabilitative programs. These analyses would include program evaluations, the examination of the scope of treatment services offered, the provision of specialized treatment programs, and the nature and quality of treatment juvenile offenders receive in such programs.

DOMESTIC VIOLENCE

Introduction

Domestic violence is a pervasive social problem that plagues couples and families nationwide. A disproportionate amount of heterosexual domestic violence is male-to-female and generally affects anywhere from 2 to 28 million women. This variability may be attributed to the ambiguity regarding what constitutes spousal abuse or battery. Hence, definitions of domestic violence are likely to vary among existing counties, states, and nations.

It is readily apparent that women are at an appreciably higher risk in their homes due to the potential volatility that exists in their relationships with their intimate partners. The preponderance of research literature attempts to identify distinct characteristics of the abusers. However, perpetrators cannot be succinctly classified into one global category because they are essentially a heterogeneous group. There is an increased likelihood for partner-assaultive men to report childhood histories of physical abuse. Furthermore, the laws and policies pertinent to domestic violence offenders are continually evolving and are subject to change with new legislation. Currently, limited efforts exists that address issues such as prevention, intervention, and the implementation of new laws and policies. The following case studies were selected to illustrate the seriousness of this issue.

A jury of eight women and four men rejected Ms. Malott's claim of self-defense based on battered woman syndrome and convicted her of second-degree and attempted murder. She was sentenced to life in prison with no possibility of parole for at least 10 years (S. Bindman, 1991).

On December 26, 1993, Marsha Brewer Stewart was found with a knife in her chest. Police say she was murdered by her husband, Gregory. Just 7 months earlier, Marsha defended her husband in a suburban Chicago courtroom by testifying that he did not attempt to murder her. She dismissed the episode as a drunken fit of rage. Police and prosecutors begged her not to post his bond or move back in with him. Like many other women, she forgave him. On December 26, Marsha called the police in a desperate plea for help. By the time a squad car arrived, Marsha was dead. Hours later, her husband was charged with murder (Shalala, 1994).

Literature Review

Cases such as those illustrated above exemplify that domestic violence, all too often, leads to disastrous consequences. Early intervention can be facilitated by neighbors, community members, and a legal system that implements stringent arrest policies for the accused perpetrators. However, how can victims, police officers, and the courts identify such abusers? As alluded to earlier, a plethora of research has been geared toward identifying characteristics of male spousal abusers. Thus far, researchers have been unable to consistently identify a profile which is inclusive of most abusers, in terms of personality, psychopathology, and demographics. In this section, the predominant patterns of abusers and their families of origin are discussed. Furthermore, issues pertinent to court mediation and legal interventions regarding the deterrence of abusers are explored. The primary objective is to provide clarification on the preceding issues.

The increasing prevalence of cases such as those shown above has resulted in considerable research linked to the incidence of such harm and the characteristics of abusive individuals. In the United States alone, 4 million women of all races and classes are battered by a spouse or intimate partner (L. Mills, 1996). Battery by a spouse or intimate partner is the single most common reason for women entering emergency rooms, exceeding the rate of childbirth, automobile accidents, muggings, and all other medical emergencies (L. Mills, 1996). Cross-cultural research indicates that American women are not alone in this regard. A cross-cultural study of family violence found that domestic abuse occurs in over 84% of the 90 societies examined (D. Levinson, 1988). In countries such as Canada, Guatemala, Chile, Columbia, Belgium, and parts of Europe, domestic violence figures range from 4 to 60%. These alarming statistics have mobilized a number of battered women and feminists nationwide to address the issue of domestic violence.

In an effort to reveal theoretical and treatment implications, research has focused on describing the characteristics of abusers. Hastings and Hamberger (1988) suggested that the preponderance of identified male batterers showed evidence of a personality disorder. These researchers found that in comparison to age-matched, nonviolent males, batterers showed higher levels of dysphoria, anxiety, and somatic complaints. The batterers in their sample presented as more alienated, moody, labile, and passive-aggressive. Alcoholic batterers showed the highest levels of pathology, followed by nonalcoholic abusive batterers. Both batterer subgroups showed a greater disadvantage in terms of higher unemployment rates; lower education; and higher rates of reported, experienced, and witnessed victimization in the family of origin. In general, their findings provide support for the notion that batterers are a heterogeneous group that cannot be adequately explained by a unified "batterer profile."

Another study that examined the instances of partner violence in young men with early onset alcoholism who had committed suicide found that half of the men had histories of domestic violence (Conner, Duberstein, & Conwell, 2000). Those who were violent in their intimate relationship were found to have an earlier age of onset of alcoholism.

Research literature on psychopathology and anger suggests that both significantly contribute to interpersonal violence. Greene, Coles, and Johnson (1994) conducted a cluster analysis with data gathered from 40 court-referred abusers. The Minnesota Multiphasic Personality Inventory-2 (MMPI-2) and the State-Trait Anger Expression Inventory (STAXI) were utilized as measures of personality functioning and the expression of anger among abusers in the sample. The MMPI-2 scores demonstrated that domestic violence offenders indicated some degree of depression, antisocial attitudes, distrust, anxiety, and other psychopathologies. Results confirmed four clusters of violent offenders, with the most pathological cluster angrier than their nonpathological counterparts. Furthermore, these results were also consistent with the literature in that there was not a single, homogeneous "abuser" profile (Hastings & Hamberger, 1988).

Researchers have also emphasized the importance of traumatic child-hood experiences, such as severe physical abuse, in an effort to classify abusers. C. M. Murphy, Meyer, and O'Leary (1993) examined associations between family of origin violence, levels of current abusive behavior, and self-reports of psychopathology in a clinical sample of male abusers. Compared to nonviolent men in discordant and well-adjusted relationships, partner-assaultive men were significantly more likely to report childhood histories of physical abuse as well as physical abuse of the mother in the family of origin. When compared to batterers without such histories, those who were severely abused in childhood displayed more evidence of psychopathology on the Millon Clinical Multiaxial Inventory-II (MCMI-II), and expressed higher levels of aggression directed toward their current partner. These results suggest that violence in the family of origin, and in particular a history of severe childhood physical abuse, can differentiate partner-assaultive men (C. M. Murphy et al., 1993).

Whitfield, Anda, Dube, and Felitti (2003) studied the relationship of childhood physical abuse, sexual abuse, or growing up with a battered mother to the risk of being a victim of intimate partner violence for women or a perpetrator for men. The Adverse Childhood Experiences Study had 8,629 participants and was conducted in a large health maintenance organization (HMO). Results indicated that each of the three violent childhood experiences increased the risk of either victimization or perpetration of intimate partner violence about twofold. For those persons who had all three forms of violent experiences, the risk increased 3.5-fold for women and 3.8-fold for men.

Literature on the legal attempts to punish perpetrators of domestic violence has become more prevalent during the past 2 decades. Some of the legal responses include an increased reliance on civil protection orders and numerous options for prosecuting batterers, including, most notably, mandatory arrest. Police officers are more likely to arrest the perpetrator when the victim is visibly injured or when there is probable cause to believe a crime has been committed (L. Mills, 1996). Although mandatory arrest tends to reduce domestic violence, high recidivism rates for the abusers continue to adversely affect the lives of many women. The new law, Uniform Interstate Enforcement of Domestic-Violence Protection Orders Act, makes it easier and safer for domestic violence victims to travel from state to state (Saunders, 2003). This law mandates that a court must enforce all terms of a protection order from another state, even if the terms are typically prohibited in their jurisdiction. This law was first enacted in California, Delaware, Idaho, Indiana, Montana, and Texas, and 20 other states implemented it in 2003 (Sauders, 2003).

Civil protection orders, which enjoin a batterer from further violence, may curtail domestic violence. In most states, civil protection orders can be used either in conjunction with criminal proceedings or in civil court (Keilitz, 1994). However, L. Mills (1996) contends that the problem with civil protection orders, prosecution, and arrest policies is that they require women to terminate their abusive relationships and subject them to even more serious attacks by their batterers. Many studies show that battered women who attempt to leave their abusers may be at a higher risk for being harmed or killed (Campbell et al., 2003). Ironically, criminal strategies which aim to curb abuse and violent relationships through legal interventions may instead place victims in more dangerous predicaments. A descriptive study that retrospectively examined 485 victim surveys gathered in a domestic violence advocacy center over 12 months sought to explore the reasons why a victim of domestic violence would return to the abusive relationship (Anderson, Gillig, Sitaker, & McCloskey, 2003). The reasons for returning included lack of money (45.9%), the lack of a place to go (28.5%), and the absence of police assistance (13.5%). These obstacles were considered to directly impact the safety of the victim (Gillig et al., 2003).

Forensic Psychology and Policy Implications

Domestic violence is a widespread problem that affects families from every socioeconomic level in our society. Psychologists, judges, and lawmakers have struggled with devising an efficient means of preventing, assessing, and deterring perpetrators of such violence. Whereas studies have undoubtedly placed an emphasis on identifying the primary characteristics of abusers, the research suggests that batterers are a relatively heterogeneous group. The heterogeneous composition of the batterers unequivocally hinders efforts geared toward prevention and rehabilitation.

Research literature also clearly indicates the increased likelihood of abusers to endorse psychopathological symptoms and express bouts of anger and hostility. Hence, it is readily apparent that domestic violence offenders are likely to need extensive counseling for varying degrees of psycho-pathology as well as anger management interventions to modulate their intense feelings of anger. Also, victims are at an increased risk to develop psychopathological symptoms, including mood disorders and posttraumatic stress. Accordingly, group or individual counseling is likely to be a necessary component when working with victims of domestic violence. However, attrition continues to be a major problem for domestic violence rehabilitation programs (Gerlock, 2001). A study on domestic violence rehabilitation attrition with 62 male batterers (aged 20–62 years) and 31 female victims found that those who completed the program were more likely to be young and court-monitored. In addition, they had lower levels of stress and posttraumatic stress and higher levels of mutuality in their relationships (Gerlock, 2001).

Mandatory arrest laws and civil protection orders are currently utilized by many states to reduce domestic violence. There is, however, an implicit precursor within these statutes that requires women to end their relationships with their abusers, which subsequently places them at a great risk for being attacked. These women should be encouraged not to not directly confront their abusers about their intentions to leave, as this action is related to increased violence or even femicide (Campbell et al., 2003). Clearly, battered women need ample information about arrest policies and protection orders. If battered women decide to take steps to ameliorate their difficulties with violent partners, it is imperative that they receive adequate protection. Once these matters are thoroughly considered and implemented, then dilemmas like the case studies above might be avoided. Conversely, if domestic violence continues to be underprioritized, the issue is likely to go unabated and remain an intractable problem.

Suggestions for Future Research

Over the past 2 decades, research on domestic violence offenders has expanded. However, relatively scant research exists that assesses the legal and psychological impact of the victims in question. Additional inquiry is needed to learn what legal and psychological interventions can be implemented that will better serve those who are victimized by such abuse. Future studies will need to ascertain the efficiency and effectiveness of such interventions and analyze the feasibility of devising remedial methods that also can be implemented.

As research on the profiles of abusers gains more validity, treatment studies can be included to determine what type of treatment works best with what type of abuser. It would be beneficial to study whether varying treatment modalities differ in terms of effectiveness and, if so, more efficient interventions may evolve. In addition, researchers need to more closely examine the options available for handling domestic violence situations including mandatory arrest, protection orders, and options for prosecuting batterers. For example, states that utilize mandatory arrest laws, or any other laws pertinent to domestic violence, can be compared to those that do not. Studies such as these are likely to enhance the opportunities and resources available to victims of domestic violence.

FAMILY VIOLENCE: HOMICIDE

Introduction

When most people think of violence, they think of an innocent victim attacked by a total stranger. The media exacerbate these fears by depicting the perpetrator as an unknown, unidentifiable psychopath that sneaks around hunting for prey. An obvious means of avoiding contact with such a person is to stay away from the "bad" neighborhoods where such crimes are more likely to occur. The safest place appears to be the confines of your own home, behind locked doors and set alarms. The reality, though, is that the risk of dying at the hands of an acquaintance or family member far exceeds the threat of being killed by a complete stranger.

Familial violence, more specifically familial homicide, is much more common than most people would like to believe. This section explores the various forms of familial homicide such as battered women, infanticide, Munchausen syndrome by proxy, parricide, familicide, and the causal factors that lead to such incidents.

According to the 1994 Bureau of Justice Statistics report, focusing on murders within families, 16% of all murders committed in 1988 were committed against family members. The breakdown of these findings indicated that 6.5% of the victims were murdered by their spouses, 3.5% by parents, 1.9% were killed by their children, 1.5% were victims of sibling violence, and another 2.6% were victimized by other family members (Dawson & Langan, 1994). Between 1976 and 2000, about 11% of murder victims were determined to have been killed by an intimate. During this same time period, spouses and family members comprised approximately 15% of all murder victims (U.S. Department of Justice, Bureau of Justice Statistics, 2002). The following case study is an illustration of family violence.

After an exhausting day of caring for the children, cleaning the house, and working at her part-time job, Carla was laying down for a quick nap. Sleeping a bit longer than expected, Carla was late preparing dinner. When her husband Charlie came home, he was infuriated by her tardiness, laziness, and insensitivity to his needs. He had just lost a big contract at work and did not appreciate her lack of consideration. Believing it was his obligation to set her straight, which he had continually done in the past, Charlie picked up a pot of boiling water from the stove and threw it in Carla's face. Screaming for help, Carla charged toward the door where Charlie proceeded to hit her over the head with the pot. Carla died 3 days later from a subdural hematoma.

Literature Review

Domestic homicides are one of the most common forms of familial violence. According to the Presidential Task Force on Violence in the Family, in 1996 as many as 1,300 battered women were killed by their abusers (Ewing, 1997). Forty percent of all homicides in the United States are the result of domestic violence (K. Browne & Herbert, 1997). The U.S. Department of Justice, Bureau of Justice Statistics (2002) indicated that the number of women killed by intimates was stable for 2 decades, declined from 1993 to 1995, then remained stable through 2000. "Femicide, or the homicide of women, is the leading cause of death in the United States among young African American women aged 15–45 years, and the seventh leading cause of premature death among women overall" (Campbell et al., 2003, p. 1089). Intimate partner homicides are responsible for approximately 40% of femicides in the United States but only for a small percentage of male homicides (5.9%). Finally, the majority (67–80%) of intimate partner homicides includes the physical abuse of the female by the male prior to the murder, no matter if it is the male or the female partner who is killed (Campbell et al., 2003). Campbell et al. (2003) stressed the importance of identifying and intervening with at-risk battered women as a critical way to decrease intimate partner homicide.

Domestic violence is nothing new to society but has gained public attention given the shift in opinions regarding domestic relations. In an historical context, women were seen as the property of their husbands and, therefore, occasional beatings for their disobedience were expected. Rarely, if ever, were men charged with a crime for beating or killing their wives.

Even with the increased awareness of domestic violence, many women are left legally powerless and vulnerable to the abuse. Research has demonstrated that women are abused by intimate male partners more frequently than any other type of family violence, and that this abuse crosses all racial, ethnic, religious, and age groups (Leonard, 2000). Women who sought the protection of law enforcement found themselves beating against closed doors or, if they were helped, it was only with the granting of a restraining order. In reality, though, a piece of paper will not be effective when an angered spouse is on a mission (C. R. Snow, 1997). In all fairness, the elevated number of domestic violence cases is not entirely due to shortcomings within a faulty system. At times, battered women refuse to press charges against their abusive spouses, given the ramifications they face once the assailant is released. Because of the way our legal system is structured, a person is rarely detained for attempted murder if he simply makes threats. If the victim presses charges, the perpetrator will experience at most a night or two in jail, which will more than likely enrage him even more.

Research has consistently found that there is an elevated risk of intimate partner homicide for women who have separated or left the relationship versus those who remain (H. Johnson & Hotton, 2003). An 11-city study that examined the risk factors for femicide in abusive relationships found that preincident risk factors associated with increased risk of intimate partner femicide included the perpetrator's access to a gun and previous threat with a weapon, perpetrator's stepchild in the home, and estrangement, particularly from a controlling partner (Campbell et al., 2003). Farr (2002) found that women who had survived an attempted domestic homicide shared patterns in their experiences. For example, the year prior to the attack was typically fraught with a buildup in tension from ongoing contact with an angry, domineering batterer. Generally, the batterer was an alcoholic or drug addict, a gun owner, and was actively engaging in stalking the victim if the couple was estranged (Farr, 2002). The vast majority of the women had either left or announced to their perpetrators that they were leaving them. Most of the women felt afraid of their assailants, but prior to the incident they did not believe that their victimizers were capable of killing them. These women were often left feeling isolated and alone after the attacks and in need of mental health services (Farr, 2002).

In recent times, shelters and special interest groups have been organized to help women in battering relationships. Unfortunately, as the number of shelters has increased, so too have the number of domestic homicides. Once the perpetrator targets his victim, there is little that law enforcement is able to do to prevent the crime from eventually occurring (C. R. Snow, 1997).

Considering the lack of effective support available for victims of domestic abuse, those individuals harmed have begun to take matters into their own hands. Although husbands are more likely to be the perpetrators in domestic homicides, wives commit a portion of these murders. From 1976 to 2000, about one third of female murder victims were killed by an intimate, while only about 4% of male murder victims were killed by an intimate (U.S. Department of Justice, Bureau of Justice Statistics, 2002). According to the U.S. Department of Justice, Bureau of Justice Statistics (2002), from 1976 to 2000 the number of men murdered by intimates dropped by 68%. Although much less frequent, women are sometimes the perpetrators of domestic violence. In a study examining the treatment needs of females arrested for domestic violence, female offenders were noted to be demographically similar and few differences were noted in their childhood experiences (Henning, Jones, & Holdford, 2003). However, women were more likely to have previously attempted suicide; whereas a greater proportion of the men had conduct problems as children and substance abuse problems as adults (Henning et al., 2003).

The fate of women who kill their abusive husbands has become the topic of many debates in recent years. Some would consider these women to be acting in self-defense, while others would argue that there are other avenues that battered women should take. In terms of Carla, the women in the case illustration presented above, if she had grabbed a knife to protect herself prior to Charlie's reaching for the pot of water and Charlie had died as a result of his wounds, should she be charged with and convicted of murder?

In situations such as this, women have tried a variety of strategies for defending their fate during trial. Some have pled insanity, self-defense, guilt, and more recently, battered woman's syndrome. It has been hypothesized that women who are the constant recipients of physical and verbal abuse by their spouses suffer from a mental disorder known as battered woman's syndrome. Several expert psychologists and psychiatrists have defended this theory. Their testimony enables jurors to "understand why the women endured such allegedly serious abuse for so long, why they did not leave their abuser, and why they felt it was necessary to use deadly force at a time when she was not being battered" (Ewing, 1997, p. 34). Of course, those women who kill their abusers at the time of their victimization are more likely to find success in a self-defense plea as opposed to women who kill while not in immediate danger. Although battered woman's syndrome is becoming increasingly popular in the mental health arena, it has yet to receive substantial support in the courtroom.

In the case of *People v. Aris* (1989), Dr. Lenore Walker, a clinical and forensic psychologist, testified in Ms. Aris' defense on the premise of the battered woman's syndrome. The jury found Ms. Aris guilty because her husband was sleeping at the time of the offense and therefore her actions could not be considered self-defense (*People v. Aris*, 1989). There is no consistency in the sentencing of these women and verdicts depend largely on the jury of each particular case and the differences from crime to crime. Currently, few women are acquitted based upon battered woman's syndrome.

Another form of homicidal violence that occurs within the family is the killing of children by their parents. Fifty-seven percent of the murders of children under the age of 12 have been committed by the victims' parents (Dawson & Langan, 1994). According to the U.S. Department of Justice,

Bureau of Justice Statistics (2002), out of all the children under age 5 who were murdered between 1976 and 2000, 31% were killed by fathers; 30% were killed by mothers; 23% were killed by male acquaintances; 7% were killed by other relatives; and 3% were killed by strangers.

In October 1994, Susan Smith and her husband stood in front of media cameras and pled for the return of their two sons who had reportedly been kidnapped by a black man with a gun. For 9 days the country prayed for the safe return of the Smiths' children. It was later discovered that it was the tearful mother the public had seen on the news who was the actual killer. It was hard to imagine that a mother could drive her car into a lake with her two young boys strapped into their seats. Philip Resnick, a forensic psychiatrist, was the first to categorize infanticides based on the age of the child when they were killed (Manchester, 2003). He categorized neonaticide as the killing of a child directly after birth or shortly thereafter, infanticide as the killing of a child up to one year, and filicide as the killing of a child older than one year (Manchester, 2003). As appalling as it may seem, infanticide and neonaticide are common causes of childhood deaths (Dawson & Langan, 1994).

Pitt and Bale (1995) highlighted the characteristic differences between parents who commit infanticide as opposed to neonaticide. The results indicated that mothers in the neonaticide group were significantly younger than the mothers in the infanticide group. The mothers in the infanticide group were more likely to suffer from depression or psychoses and have histories of attempted suicide. "Eighty-eight percent of the infanticide mothers were married, while 81% of the neonaticide mothers were unwed" (Pitt & Bale, 1995, p. 378). "Studies have documented that neonaticide offenders are often single, young women who deny the pregnancy and kill their newborn infants in an effort to avoid the social and parental pressure against an illegitimate child" (Manchester, 2003, p. 724).

There are a variety of reasons why parents kill their children. Explanations range from postpartum depression, particularly postpartum psychosis, and schizophrenia. Postpartum depression is a mental disorder that occurs with some new mothers shortly after they give birth. According to the American Psychiatric Association's *Diagnostic and Statistical Manual of Mental Disorders, Fourth Edition (DSM-IV)* (1994), the most severe form of postpartum depression, postpartum psychosis, often presents episodes of delusions in which the mother feels that the infant is possessed, or it presents hallucinations that tell her to kill the child. Not all incidents of postpartum depression present delusions or hallucinations, but often there are suicidal ideations, obsessional thoughts of violence toward the child, and psychomotor agitation. Whereas the postpartum blues are very common, only about 0.2% of childbearing women will experience postpartum psychosis, which typically emerges within 2 weeks after childbirth and frequently requires hospitalization (Dobson & Sales, 2000; Manchester, 2003).

Postpartum depression is widely acknowledged by many in the mental health field, but little is known about its causes. Some have hypothesized that environmental stressors associated with becoming a parent, along with the immediate demands required of the parent, can overwhelm and cause this disorder in even the most psychologically sound mother (Ewing, 1997). Hormonal changes have also been reported to be a factor in explaining the incidence of severe depression and unusual actions by some mothers after the birth of a child (Ewing, 1997). Postpartum depression is more likely to occur in women who have experienced it with previous children.

On June 20, 2001, in Clearwater, Texas, Andrea Yates drowned all five of her children in the family bathtub after her husband, Rusty, left for work. Mrs. Yates had a long-standing history of mental illness, which included four hospitalizations since 1999, as well as two attempted suicides. She also had an outpatient prescription for Haldol, an antipsychotic medication used to help control hallucinations and other symptoms of psychosis (Gesalman, 2002; Manchester, 2003). She was suffering from a severe postpartum psychosis and had numerous delusions and hallucinations. The Texas jury rejected her insanity defense despite the overwhelming psychiatric evidence. Manchester (2003, p. 715) writes:

> In the United States, courts continue to evaluate postpartum depression defenses and other mental illnesses under the existing insanity defense [M'Naughten test]. The prevailing insanity defense test applied across United States jurisdictions is extremely narrow and makes proving legal insanity exceptionally difficult for even the most severely postpartum psychotic women. Therefore, the Yates case is most significant because it demonstrates the pressing need for insanity defense reform to address the realities of postpartum psychosis and other mental illnesses.

Schizophrenics have been found guilty of infanticide as well. Depending on the defense team's strategy, many of these women will plead insanity due to their disorder. Most likely, these women are not considered victims of postpartum depression considering their past and/or current history of schizophrenia, although the symptoms are similar.

Another explanation for why a mother would kill her child is Munchausen syndrome by proxy (MSBP). Munchausen syndrome is a disorder found in the *DSM-IV* as an appendix to factitious disorder. It differs from factitious disorder in that a person with Munchausen syndrome has a psychological need to feign certain illnesses but for no external purpose, as is found with factitious disorder. Patients with Munchausen syndrome have been known to inject themselves with poisons, urine, and feces so that they will become ill and be admitted to a hospital, or otherwise receive medical attention. Munchausen by proxy occurs when parents cause illness in their children through these means, which causes the child to require constant medical attention. Although the incidences of MSBP are rare, there have been enough cases to support its existence (O'Shea, 2003). In most of the known cases, death is the ultimate fate of the children because the parent will stop at nothing to fulfill his or her own need (Pitt & Bale, 1995). Sheridan (2003) found that mothers were the perpetrators in 76.5% of 451 cases reviewed. Lasher (2003) stated that there is an underidentification of MSBP due to a lack of public awareness and professional expertise, and that overall awareness must increase in order to protect victims.

Just as it is odd to conceive of a mother killing the child to which she has given birth, it is difficult to fathom a child killing the parent(s) who gave him or her life. Nevertheless, parricide, the killing of one's parent(s), is more common than expected. Parricide was highly publicized by the Menendez trial in Southern California where Eric and Lyle Menendez were charged with killing their wealthy parents for the purpose of receiving their inheritances. The defense team claimed that the boys killed their parents in an act of self-defense because of the continual abuse they received from their father. Nevertheless, after much debate, the boys were charged with the murders, but spared from the death penalty.

Similar to battered women, some children kill their parent(s) because of a history of abuse suffered by them, or witnessed toward the other parent. Further, some youths kill in self-defense during an episode of their abuse; others kill on random occasions as a result of their continual abuse. In terms of Carla, the scenario may have had a different conclusion had her son entered the kitchen and witnessed his father beating his mother as described. Out of fear and anger, the son could have run into his parents' room, grabbed the loaded gun from his father's nightstand, and returned to the kitchen to shoot and kill his father. Heide (1992, p. 3) claims that "these children, typically adolescents, were psychologically abused by one or both parents and often witnessed or suffered physical, sexual, and verbal abuse as well."

Baxter, Duggan, Larkin, and Page (2001) compared those individuals committed to high-security care who committed parricide and those who killed strangers. These researchers found that those who committed parricides were more likely to suffer from schizophrenia but less likely to have had a disrupted childhood and criminal history than those individuals who committed stranger homicide. The individuals in the parricide group had made a previous attack on their victim in 40% of cases (Baxter et al., 2001).

Other factors associated with parricide are mental illness, antisocial personalities, and greed. These can be sole factors but are most likely exhibited as combinations. Greed is rarely found to be a full explanation for why children commit parricide, although some cases have been reported. Children whose immediate motivation for killing their parents is greed will most likely have evidence of antisocial characteristics, abusive pasts, or mental illness. In these instances, the child is usually convicted on terms associated with insanity. In those cases where greed was found to be the sole determinant for the murder, other factors such as antisocial personality were most likely not effectively explored or not accepted by the jury (Ewing, 1997). This does not mean, however, that the children were not suffering from some sort of disorder in addition to greed.

Forensic Psychology and Policy Implications

A consistent theme throughout most of the above forms of familial homicide is the issue of abuse. For some, the killing of their victimizer becomes the only means of protection from experiencing further harm. The legal system has provided little help for victims of abuse. Even if the victims are fortunate enough to receive legal intervention through documentation or incarceration of the abuser, the reality is that the system provides little to no protection once the offender is released.

It is quite difficult to intervene or prevent obsessed abuser from continuing to harm or from eventually killing their victim. Campbell et al. (2003) suggested more proactive measures. For example, increasing employment opportunities, preventing substance abuse, and restricting abusers' access to guns as methods to reduce the rate of intimate partner femicide, as well as the overall homicide rate. Law enforcement should also treat abuse as a priority. The fact that domestic violence calls are common and dangerous for police officers should not be a justification for not responding to them. Instead, the increased number of domestic violence calls should indicate that a special domestic violence unit is needed to deal with this escalating problem. With the push of special interest groups advocating for victims' rights, many law enforcement agencies have organized units to specifically combat this epidemic. In addition to a law enforcement response, the Austin Police Department dispatches a crisis unit comprised of mental health professionals that aids in interviewing and supporting family violence victims.

Child abuse has received a great deal of public attention because society feels a responsibility to care for those who cannot care for themselves. Policies have been established so that fewer children will have to experience abuse from their parents. Programs exist, but they are so crowded and understaffed that too many children are "falling through the cracks." This partially explains why many homicides committed in this country are parricides. Psychopathic personalities and greed are also likely to blame, especially in some of the most notorious (e.g., the Menendez brothers).

Being abused should not be a justification for killing someone. Much of the debate surrounding sentencing for these perpetrators has centered on this issue. There are mixed feelings about how to punish someone who takes another's life for the purpose of saving one's own life. If there were effective programs, community outlets, and judicial supports for victims of abuse, then murder would be a less likely end result. The mental health field provides support for the plea of self-defense in relation to abuse cases, but it has not been accepted by the judicial system. It appears that insanity defense reform is needed to address those women who commit infanticide as a result of severe postpartum psychosis. Mental health professionals and the general public need to become much more knowledgeable about postpartum depression and psychosis in order to help prevent this tragedy for both the victim and the perpetrator of infanticide. There are several recent cases and articles that address this phenomenon; more research on policy implications needs to be undertaken and developed.

Suggestions for Future Research

Research needs to be conducted so that more effective programs can be established in order to decrease the occurrence of abuse and possible murder. As it stands, programs are not necessarily the problem; however, the lack of funding and inadequate staffing causes these programs to be less effective. Frequently, money is hard to raise when benefits are not immediate or apparent. Abuse intervention at crucial moments will help to decrease the number of familial homicides by eliminating murders by abusers as well as retaliation by the abused.

Many victims who kill their victimizers are sentenced to prison terms similar to those of other violent offenders. They are placed in the same units as the other predatorial offenders simply because their crime was murder. This can create many problems for the individual, as well as environmental problems within the prison. The individual sentenced to prison for self-defense tends not to have the same predatorial personality as other violent criminals, and, such as, may encounter unnecessary problems while incarcerated. With the increase of mental health care for inmates in California, for example, special groups have been developed specifically for incarcerated subjects whose crimes involve issues of abuse (*Coleman v. Wilson*, 1995). More programs such as these need to be instituted on a national level, and further research needs to be conducted regarding the effects of criminal confinement on these individuals.

An additional area that needs continued research is postpartum depression and psychosis, as well as, MSBP. Without the proper understanding of these forms of familial homicide, and how they originate, the risk of continued unnecessary deaths is inevitable.

Practice Update Section: Issues in Juvenile and Family Forensics

This section will first discuss some of the important issues concerning evaluations conducted by psychologists for the juvenile court system, specifically evaluations prior to placement. The next section will focus more on how family violence issues effect the criminal courts, in particular, some important concerns for clinicians working with domestic violence victims and those at risk for intimate homicide.

"Providing evaluative services within the framework of the juvenile court requires specialized knowledge and skill not typically received in most generalist clinical training programs" (Hecker & Steinberg, 2002, p. 304). Predisposition evaluations provide essential information to aid juvenile courts to make decisions about a juvenile's amenability to treatment and appropriate placement/treatment options. A clinician's specialized training in the psycho-legal questions that arise in juvenile and criminal court contexts will be critical in appropriately addressing the referral question. Melton et al. (1997) indicated that the only time juveniles are referred for evaluation for competency to stand trial, or a mental state at the time of the offense (insanity defense) evaluation, is when the juvenile may be transferred to adult court. Depending on the jurisdiction, requests for predisposition evaluations are left to the discretion of the judge, probation officers, and attorneys (Hecker & Steinberg, 2002).

General guidelines that have been suggested for predisposition evaluations typically indicate that the evaluator should begin with a thorough review of the juvenile's file. A detailed interview with the juvenile should be conducted including information on the juvenile's functioning over a number of situations

(continued)

(*Continued*)

relevant to the referral question. Topics correlated with recidivism and violence should be specifically queried, for example, substance abuse, history of violence, and mental heath history. Collateral contacts are also recommended to gather pertinent information, particularly if the juvenile is uncooperative and/ or has a vested interest in being presented in a more or less favorable light.

In addition to a thorough file review and clinical interview, the juvenile's intellectual, academic, and vocational abilities should be evaluated. This is to help make informed opinions about the juvenile's appropriateness for certain placements, and to ensure that any special educational needs are met as required by federal law (Hecker & Steinberg, 2002; Melton et al., 1997). A personality measure may be warranted if relevant to the referral question; for example, whether or not the juvenile has a major mental illness that necessitates inpatient or another type of treatment setting, rather than a more peer-run, behavioral modification type of program. Psychologists should only use psychological tests or instruments to inform judgments, diagnoses, or recommendations about issues for which they have been validated (Hecker & Steinberg, 2002; Heilbrun, 1992, 2001).

The mental health and cognitive needs of the juvenile should be addressed and reflected in appropriate treatment options provided in the recommendations section of the disposition evaluation. Careful consideration of the juvenile's family context is important in helping to determine the causes of the juvenile's delinquent behavior, or, perhaps, the level of support or detrimental effects provided by the family in the juvenile's rehabilitative goals (Hecker & Steinberg, 2002). Thoughtful attention regarding the resources available in the community is significant when making realistic recommendations. Unfortunately, these resources are frequently limited. Reports to be used by court participants should be free of psychological jargon and should only provide information that is relevant to the psycholegal question. These reports are often quite different from general psychological evaluations completed in a nonforensic environment.

Some psychologists provide treatment to domestic violence victims and/or their batterers. Psychologists who provide treatment for women at high risk of intimate partner femicide should consider the following suggestions. Campbell et al. (2003) suggested that if a woman tells her therapist she is planning to leave her abuser, she should be warned not to confront the abuser, but should instead leave when he is not present. She should be encouraged to leave a note or contact him by phone at a later time. The mental health professional should query her about the risk factors previously identified that put her at risk for intimate partner homicide. "Under these conditions of extreme danger, it is incumbent on health professionals to be extremely assertive with abused women about their risk of homicide and their need for shelter" (Campbell et al., 2003, p. 1093). Whether working with juveniles or domestic violence victims, forensic psychologists are required to have specialty training with very complex and challenging issues. Careful attention to research and an understanding of the psycholegal issues are required because there is so much at stake for those evaluated or treated.

CHAPTER 3

International Criminal Forensics

OVERVIEW

This chapter examines selected topics and practice issues in international criminal forensic psychology. Although the field of forensic psychology has grown rapidly during the past decade, most research and professional organizations focus on the national concerns relevant to specific jurisdictions (Eaves, 2002). This chapter gives an overview of the state of international forensic mental health as a whole and then proceeds to present three topics that illustrate the complexity and importance of examining forensic issues across nations. In some cases, there is significant overlap, while in others, unique cultures and laws dictate distinctive procedures and standards of practice. Increased awareness of international aspects of forensic practice will encourage an attitude of globalization versus isolationism. Conducting research between nations without consideration of borders on topics such as terrorism and risk assessment will facilitate a more thorough and sophisticated understanding of issues germane to forensic psychology. Overall, this comparative approach will help facilitate and contribute to a safer society. In total, three subjects are examined. These topics include (1) the psychology of terrorism, including motivations, implications, and healing; (2) the insanity defense and competency to stand trial; and (3) violence risk assessment and mentally disordered offenders. Although the scope of this chapter does not allow for a thorough assessment of all of the topics relevant to international criminal forensics, the issues presented will provide the reader with an awareness of the importance of international and comparative collaboration in forensic psychology, as well as a better understanding of the similarities and differences in our respective criminal justice systems.

As technology grows, so do the boundaries that used to restrict our global community's exchange of ideas and competencies. Terrorist acts in recent years have also increased our international awareness of the plight and progress of other nations. An exchange of expertise and data will be critical in improving our ability to identify, prevent, and protect ourselves from terrorists. The international community can also take lessons from one another about the process of healing and the provision of mental health services to those affected directly and indirectly by terrorism. What is the psychology of terrorism? How can a sense of safety, security, and dignity be restored to those who have experienced a mass terror attack? What is the role of psychology in the provision of emergency mental health services and aftercare for those affected by the trauma? Do residents of different countries or regions react differently to attacks by militant extremists and are they affected by media coverage of terrorism internationally?

Criminal courts around the world are confronted with mentally disordered offenders. What are the international protections for a fair trial? How are the rights of mentally disordered offenders protected? How do mental health criminal justice systems interface internationally? Is the insanity defense similar to or different from the standards commonly applied in the United States? Mentally disordered offenders are increasingly committed to forensic secure hospitals in a variety of countries. Are risk assessment instruments or actuarial measures developed in one country useful in helping to determine risk for violence in another country? Are the risk factors in these nations the same? What are the standards of practice for assessment of violence risk and release to a less restrictive setting? What treatment modalities are available for mentally disordered offenders in other countries? Clearly, then, the topics examined in this chapter internationally and comparatively explore issues at the crossroads of criminal law, the criminal justice system, and psychology.

The State of the Field: An Overview

There are many organizations with a focus on forensic mental health; however, most have a national focus and only include a specific profession (Eaves, 2002). The American Psychological Association (APA) has a division titled the American Psychology-Law Society/Division 41 (APLS), which emphasizes research and the clinical roles of forensic psychologists. The APLS has an annual conference where the newest research on a wide variety of forensic psychology topics is presented. During the March 2004 conference, research on topics such as competency to stand trial, the insanity defense, juror selection, sex offender research, psychopathy assessment, mitigation testimony, psychologists' contributions to terrorism, juvenile adjudication, malingering, and stalking were discussed. The APLS sponsors a journal titled *Law and Human Behavior*. In the UK, the journal *British Journal of Forensic Practice* is available. There are other forensic mental health organizations in the United States such as the American Academy of Forensic Examiners and the American College of Forensic Psychology. The Australian Psychological Society's College of Forensic Psychologists follows the standards of practice for Australian forensic psychologists, and this organization takes proactive measures, when necessary, to improve or remedy the provision of services (Martin, Allan, & Allan, 2001). Professionally sanctioned and proposed guidelines for forensic practice are now available to increase the quality of psychological services provided in legal arenas across the world (Nicholson & Norwood, 2000).

In the United States, national board certification in forensic psychology has been available since 1978, after the American Board of Forensic Psychology (ABFP) and the American Academy of Forensic Psychology (AAFP) were created (Nicholson & Norwood, 2000). According to Otto, Heilbrun, and Grisso (1990), a diploma awarded by the ABFP or becoming a diplomate of forensic psychology is reflective of the highest level of credentialing in forensic psychology. "The diploma recognizes the diplomate's forensic experience (minimum of 1,000 hours within 5 years, 4 of which must be postdoctoral), training (minimum of 200 hours of supervision), and proficiency (based on submitted professional work samples and an oral examination)" (Nicholson & Norwood, 2000, p. 13).

The number of forensic psychology programs is increasing in the United States and abroad. Programs at universities such as John Jay College of Criminal Justice in New York City offer a master's degree and a doctoral degree in forensic psychology. In addition, the California School of Professional Psychology — now known as Alliant International University — offers doctoral programs in forensic psychology. Similar programs such as these are found at Simon Fraser University (Canada), the University of Arizona, and Florida International University. Still other universities such as the University of Nebraska, Lincoln, offer combined PhD and JD (Psychology and Law) programs to better prepare practitioners who wish to be legally trained psychologists. Australia, New Zealand, and the UK also have a number of graduate training programs in forensic psychology.

More recently, the need for international organizations, journals, and research has become apparent. The International Association of Forensic Mental Health Services was founded in 2001 at a conference in Vancouver, British Columbia. According to Eaves (2002, p. 3), its defined goals are

- To enhance the standards of forensic mental health services in the international community
- To promote an international dialogue about forensic mental health, in all its aspects, including violence and family violence
- To promote education, training, and research in forensic mental health
- To inform professional communities and the public about current issues in forensic mental health
- To promote and utilize advanced technologies in the pursuit of the above goals
- To form informal and formal liaisons with organizations having a similar purpose

Hodgins (2002, p. 7) defines forensic mental health as "the study, treatment, and management of persons with mental disorders who engage in illegal or violent behaviors. It is a larger and more encompassing field than either forensic psychiatry or psychology. ... Along with many others — nursing, social work, education, occupational therapy, pharmacology, toxicology, sociology, criminology, neurobiology — it cares for persons with mental disorders who have committed crimes and conducts research that advances knowledge about this population, about effective treatments, and about factors relating to offending." Recently, the International Association of Forensic Mental Health Services sponsored the journal, *International Journal of Forensic Mental Health*. Additional journals whose scope is deliberately international in the realm of forensic psychology or psychiatry include such periodicals as the *International Journal of Law & Psychiatry*; *Psychology, Psychiatry, and Law*; *International Journal of Offender Therapy and Comparative Criminology*; and *Criminal Behavior and Mental Health*.

Ogloff, Roesch, and Eaves (2000) maintained that it is becoming less common and suitable for national forensic systems to run without an understanding of international practices. These researchers stress the importance of seizing the opportunities that technology has provided to expand the scope of research and practice. Studies comparing different criminal justice systems — forensic hospitals, mental health courts, and correction agencies — would be of considerable benefit, especially because they would broaden competencies and improve programs and policies affecting mentally disordered offenders all over the world. Eaves (2002, p. 5) suggests that the International Association of Forensic Mental Health could be a vehicle for "international focus groups in different areas to communicate more effectively, to plan collaborative studies, and discuss findings with program planners and policymakers."

Forensic Psychology/Mental Health Law in Australia, Japan, and the UK: An Overview

Mullen, Briggs, Dalton, and Burt (2000) indicated that during the last decade in Australia, the role of forensic psychologists included much more emphasis on therapy, particularly with government funding for the counseling of crime victims and with the creation of management strategies for sex offenders. These researchers describe progress and some transformation in forensic psychology in Australia to include not only the provision of assessment and treatment services for mentally disordered offenders, but also research regarding the impact of various crimes on crime victims and on developing services for those individuals.

In Australia, sex offender treatment is being explored to address the potential management, ethical, and political issues that arise (Birgden & Vincent, 2000). The state of Victoria with the CORE Sex Offender Programs has designed a statewide approach in the public correctional system to evaluate, manage, and treat male sexual offenders. Birgden and Vincent (2000) described the issue of motivation, denial, and willingness to participate in sex offender treatment as a significant hurtle that was overcome by the involvement of the Victorian Adult Parole Board, which mandates treatment for an offender before he can be considered for parole.

Easteal (2001) identified the difficulties faced by women in Australian prisons. As she describes it, the majority of incarcerated Australian women are drug addicts who have experienced violence as children or adults. The small number of women, as compared to men, has led to many inappropriate placements of females in maximum-security facilities. This practice has resulted in the limited availability of vocational and educational programs for these offenders, as well as a reduction of programs addressing issues linked to substance abuse and violence (Easteal, 2001). Howells, Hall, and Day (1999) explained the serious problems of suicide and self-harm in Australian prisons and the need for forensic psychologists in assessment, intervention, and prevention linked to these behaviors. The role of forensic psychologists in Australia is diverse and a considerable amount of research contributing to the ongoing improvement of useful and effective standards of practice is conducted in this country.

According to Sakuta (2003), the constitutional and organizational components of forensic psychology and psychiatry have only recently emerged in developed countries. However, Sakuta indicated that Japan handles mentally disordered offenders only by the use of mental health and welfare law monitored by the Ministry of Health, Welfare, and Labor.

These patient/offenders are admitted to psychiatric hospitals by way of involuntary admission by the Prefectural Governor and their discharge is solely in the hands of a designated physician. Sakuta (2003) reported that no probation exists to mandate outpatient aftercare and this perpetuates the cycle of recidivism and rehospitalization. He indicated that a bill addressing the psychiatric treatment and probation for individuals who commit serious crimes resulting in serious injury or death to others "under conditions of insanity" is being discussed by the Japanese parliament.

According to Towl (1999, p. 9), "The prison service is the largest single employer of forensic psychologists in the UK (England and Wales)." When broadening the definition of forensic psychology to include corrections, penal institutions provide more job opportunities for forensic psychologist in developed countries worldwide. Similar to Australia, health policy in the English National Health Service (NHS) is undergoing a period of rapid change, which serves as a catalyst for growth in the provision of specialist mental health services, including forensics (J. Bindman, 2002). As he indicated, national quality standards have been set and there is mounting political pressure for forensic mental health services to be accountable for assessing and managing violence risk, both to patients and to society.

The scope of this chapter does not allow for a thorough assessment of forensic psychological practice and mental health law in individual countries, nor does it allow for a review of all the controversial topics impacting the work of forensic psychologists internationally. However, the issues presented below highlight the relevance of information sharing and better inform the reader about international and comparative research approaches to critical aspects of forensic psychological practice. For the purposes of this chapter, these include the psychology of terrorism, competency to stand trial, insanity defenses, violence risk assessment, and treatment for mentally disordered offenders.

THE PSYCHOLOGY OF TERRORISM: MOTIVATIONS, IMPLICATIONS, AND HEALING

Introduction

Countries around the world such as Ireland, South Africa, Israel, Spain, Japan, and Lebanon have been the target of terrorist threats and attacks for years. Yet, the horrific terrorist attack on the United States on September 11, 2001, had a profound impact on the worldview of terrorism. The sheer magnitude of casualties and destruction forced many countries, especially the United States, to realize the international community's vulnerability to terrorism. In the wake of the devastation, American citizens have been forced to shift from an isolationist perspective to a global point of view. The March, 11, 2004, terrorist bombings on commuter trains in Madrid, Spain, further heightened awareness that the need exists to unite as a global community, in order to better comprehend and prevent terrorism, as well as to heal from its debilitating effects.

Acts of terrorism are psychological by nature. They typically intend to disrupt ways of life and effect political change by sending ripples of fear throughout a society, which far outreaches the relatively small numbers of physical victims killed or injured in the actual bombings, shootings, or other displays of violence. Often, those killed or injured are random targets selected to create a media fervor and to send shock waves of panic and distress into the political, economic, and social sectors of a country targeted (i.e., United States, Israel). This section will provide a broad, sweeping overview of the definition of terrorism, its emotional impact on people and society, its psychological consequences, and the need and role of psychological first-aid responders during and after these tragic and horrific events. Additionally, a brief description of the impact of the attacks on the World Trade Center and the Pentagon on September 11, 2001, as well as the ongoing Israeli and Palestinian conflict, will be used to illustrate the impact of terrorism on mental health symptoms, quality of life, and emergency mental health systems in the United States and abroad. The importance of assistance for caregivers also is stressed. Stout (2002) warned that terrorism is a very complicated and complex issue that is not easily comprehended or reduced to clear, understandable components. As such, this section will be broad and brief. It will review only some of the controversial issues relevant to forensic psychologists and will highlight topics addressing a response to and/or the prevention of terrorism, as well as treatment of trauma survivors.

Although countries such as the United States and New Zealand are new to developing mental health response programs and protocols to terrorist attacks, mental health professionals in Israel have been working with those who have either directly or indirectly suffered from terrorism for years. Consider the following case examples.

Judy is a mental health professional who was traveling on a bus shot at by Palestinian terrorists. Although the bus was bulletproof and no one was injured, Judy developed heavy somatic pains and depression, which prevented her from working for more than half a year. Judy was diagnosed as suffering from depression and posttraumatic stress disorder (PTSD). She entered psychotherapy, which allowed her gradually to get back to work. In conversations with her supervisors, she expressed the effects of the trauma that continued to influence her. About a year after the incident, she attended a staff meeting in which the discourse "hardship as an opportunity for personal growth" was presented. This alternative discourse resonated with Judy. She told us it was a new revelation for her. This discourse informed her of the possibility of being in control of the meaning of the incident and not falling victim to it. This revelation enabled her to take a ride back home at dusk in a private car for the first time since the shooting incident (Shalif & Leibler, 2002, p. 63).

In the case of a suicide bomb attack in a shopping mall, Joy saw many injured people in terrible states, as well as body parts scattered around. When talking to me (Y. S.) after the event, she was very upset and told me that she "almost went crazy." I asked her what kept her from running away or "going crazy." She then remembered that a woman who had been trying on some clothing had handed over her baby at the very moment that the bomb exploded. She realized that her responsibility to the baby helped her to stay "together" and not to run away or "fall to pieces." When asked why this experience had had that effect on her, she mentioned the issue of responsibility. The conversation that ensued turned toward the topic of how a sense of responsibility toward others who are vulnerable can help us deal with even the most terrible situations (pp. 68–69).

Literature Review

The U.S. State Department (2000) defines terrorism as "premeditated, politically motivated violence perpetrated against noncombatant targets by subnational groups or clandestine agents, usually intended to influence an audience." The FBI defines it as "the unlawful use or threat of violence against persons or property to intimidate the government, the civilian population, or any segment thereof, in furtherance of political or social objectives" (U.S. Department of Justice, Federal Bureau of Investigation, 1999a). After the events of September 11, 2001, there is growing concern and question about how terrorism is defined and who is at risk. Shamir and Shikaki (2002, p. 537) suggested that there is no universally accepted description of terrorism and that the majority of definitions offered by the international community are colored by "self-serving motivations."

Terrorism also has been characterized as psychological warfare whereby the "explicit goal of the terrorist act is to create a condition of fear, uncertainty, demoralization, and helplessness as a coercive and/or punitive force" (Everly, 2003, p. 57). The actual physical targets of a terrorist attack are meant to break the will and spirit of the perceived enemy and to irrevocably alter their lifestyle. These casualties are typically only symbolic targets and the message of fear is perpetuated through round-the-clock media coverage (Shamir & Shikaki, 2002).

Conventional wisdom maintains that terrorists are not able to combat or overcome their enemy by way of military force. Consequently, their only recourse is millitant extremism and psychological warfare. Yet, some scholars warn that most Western countries attempt to separate the means from the intended goals and define terrorism based on the targeting of civilians. This notion causes many third world and Muslim countries to fear that the complete separation of goals from methods will result in all national liberation, resistance, and guerilla movements to be defined as terrorist organizations (Shamir & Shikaki, 2002). Many terrorist groups justify their activities as retaliation when they see no other alternative. Although society collectively conjures up the image of Osama Bin Laden upon the mention of terrorism, care in who and what we define as extremist aggression is exemplified through the words of Nelson Mandela, South Africa's first democratically elected president. As he explained, . . . I argued that the state had given us no alternative to violence. . . . Violence would begin whether we initiated it or not. Would it not be better to guide this violence ourselves, according to the principles where we saved lives by attacking symbols of oppression, and not people? (Mandela, 1994, p. 322). The word terrorism has strong negative connotations and implications and must be used carefully. Clearly, the leadership efforts of Nelson Mandela cannot be classified with those of Osama Bin Laden.

Shamir and Shikaki (2002, p. 553) described the old adage that "one man's 'terrorist' is another man's 'freedom fighter' " as demonstrated by the Israeli-Palestinian debate on the matter. Connolly (2003) took a psychoanalytic approach and used the psychological mechanisms of dehumanization and splitting to explain the terrorist's justifications for his or her actions. In many cases, the other or the target is seen as oppressive, evil, or less than human. Therefore, the means (i.e., acts of violence) clearly justify the ends (i.e., the end of oppression). Frequently, terrorist acts are fueled by religious fanaticism with the belief that they are on a crusade. According to Reich (1998), feelings of hatred, revulsion, and revenge motivate many terrorists. The recent attacks by al-Qaeda were justified by

Islamic fundamentalism and religious fanaticism with Western culture, and any who consorted with Westerners are demonized. Terrorists typically are acting as groups or cells or in units that share common goals or beliefs (Lawal, 2002). Lawal (2002) maintained that terrorists will act as individuals (i.e., suicide bomber) when they are extremely inspired by their group and that, as such, these violent displays still can be classified as collective acts.

Researchers indicate that the true impact of terrorism cannot be measured by casualties, but rather by the impact of fear on the individual's thoughts, feelings, behavior, and personal freedom (J. M. Davis, 2002). There are many other consequences of terrorism. Economic costs were evidenced after the September 11th attacks by a decline in the stock market, as well as appreciable financial problems with the airline and travel industries. In essence, our way of life changed. The bombings on the commuter trains in Madrid, Spain, just days before their national elections, may have significantly contributed to the defeat of the incumbent party, which was known to be a firm ally with the United States during the war with Iraq. This is one example of how acts of terrorism can weaken political unity. Everly (2003, p. 58) described four salient terrorist threats to the United States at this time: (1) threats of physical destruction and death; (2) perceived threat of injury/death to individuals, families, and communities; (3) threat of sociological turmoil; and (4) the threat of economic recession, with the potential for particular industrial sectors to collapse. By undermining the most basic human needs of safety and security, terrorists can infiltrate many aspects of society and can obliterate day-to-day living in the targeted country.

The etiology of terrorism is unclear and although theories abound, there is no agreed upon understanding of this phenomenon. Crenshaw (1998) maintains that terrorists' actions are based on logical thinking and strategic choices with the intent of accomplishing a reality-based goal. Bandura (1998) suggests that terrorists have become morally detached and are driven more by psychological forces. Arena and Arrigo (2005) argue that terrorism is linked to group identity and the need to take on roles, advance symbols, and locate personal meaning consistent with this identity. Yet, other researchers suggest that the factors contributing to aggressive actions taken by terrorists are a complex combination of biological processes in combination with cultural/environmental situations and psychological correlates. For example, J. M. Davis (2002) described the interaction of frustration, intense negative emotions, poor impulse control, and social and group norms that support and validate violence as contributing to the phenomenon of terrorism. He further described the research from social psychology that suggests attack and threat or even a perceived threat is the most reliable predictor of or catalyst for aggression. When an individual or group responds with preemptive aggression toward a perceived threat, the person does not identify the behavior as aggressive but, rather, as legitimized conduct (J. M. Davis, 2002).

Terrorists typically perceive a hostile world that is not responsive to their needs, religions, ideologies, or miseries (Shamir & Shikaki, 2002). To illustrate, the ideologies of many current terrorist movements of Middle Eastern origin advance the belief that the government of Saudi Arabia is corrupt and only remains in power because of its support from Western governments. Additionally, they maintain that Israel unfairly occupies land and oppresses the Palestinians precisely because of Western (especially U.S.) assistance (J. M. Davis, 2002). With these observations on the phenomenon of terrorism in mind, one thing is certain: There is no silver bullet or singular psychology to account for this behavior; rather, there is a complex picture entangled with culture, politics, real and perceived social injustices, social and environmental factors, and, in some cases, psychopathology (Stout, 2002).

Spencer (2002) noted that suicide bombers were not typically suffering from a diagnosable mental illness but instead were engaging in "altruistic suicide." Spencer described altruistic suicide as "self-inflicted death owing to powerful beliefs, resulting in individuals losing their sense of autonomy" (2002, p. 436). Moreover, as he described it, "When a central belief that life is but a temporary prelude to everlasting utopian existence is one of these regulatory norms, the definition of suicide itself becomes ambiguous, and the role of psychiatry as a valid therapeutic intervention is also questionable" (p. 436).

Israel was established in 1948 and since that time, its residents or civilian population have experienced many periods of terrorist attacks (Shalif & Leibler, 2002). Bleich, Gelkopf, and Solomon (2003) reported that by April 30, 2002, 472 individuals, including 318 civilians, had been killed by terrorist attacks and 3,846 had been injured, including 2,708 civilians in Israel. According to Shalif and Leibler (2002), from 1987 to 1993 and the signing of the Oslo Accord between the government of Israel and the Palestinian Liberation Organization (PLO), the first Intifada or uprising occurred. During this time, there was an increase in the terrorist attacks on Jewish residents of Judea, Samaria, and the Gaza coastal region, and there were terrorist bombings in populated areas such as shopping malls, city buses, and markets. The second Intifada began in October 2000 and created increasing levels of terrorism which included repeated suicide bombings (Shalif & Leibler, 2002). The previous case examples of Judy and Joy represent the trauma experienced by many individuals who live in this region.

This Middle Eastern region has been plagued by violence for many years and has experience with psychological first-aid responders. Shalif and Leibler (2002, p. 61) wrote: "Every municipality in Israel employs school psychologists who specialize in counseling, testing, group interventions, and crisis intervention. News broadcasts that inform the population about a mass civilian disaster are most often accompanied by the announcement of available services provided by school psychologists in the area." Shalif and Leibler (2002) stressed the importance of involving community support to those affected by terrorism as a foundation of crisis intervention in Israel. Debriefing groups are very common and mental health professionals act as consultants to the community. As these investigators explain, the communities themselves are the primary source of empowerment for their members. Researchers find that those who experience or are affected by acts of terrorism engage in "meaning-making" as a strategy for coping (Shalif & Leibler, 2002). Davis and McKearney (2003) found that individuals who are faced with loss and trauma are motivated to perceive their lives as highly meaningful and interpret their purpose in life as a sign of well-being, based on a self-protective process. This ability to face trauma with a positive outlook is an important key to adaptive coping. Culture and religion are important components of this process of making sense out of tragedy. Those who experience the trauma associated with terrorism can have a wide variety of reactions. Notwithstanding the reaction (e.g., fear, anxiety), it should be normalized in an effort to avoid marginalizing individuals, given their unique responses to the trauma (Shalif & Leibler, 2002).

Strous, Stryjer, Keret, Bergin, and Kotler (2003) explored the effects of terrorism in Israel on the subjective mood and behavior of medical and psychiatric inpatients there. To accomplish this, they surveyed 42 medical and 36 psychiatric inpatients with 54 staff members at the two hospitals serving as the control population. The results indicated that the level of worry in response to security instability in the region was the highest in clinical staff, was midrange in medical patients, and was lowest in psychiatric inpatients with schizophrenia. Those who did report that their mood was affected were of similar severity. Strous et al. (2003) suggested that the lower level of anxiety or worry in psychiatric patients might have been linked to their inability to make sense out of the situation. This study highlighted the need to assist mental health caregivers in order to facilitate the provision of optimal psychiatric care of others under conditions that affect the emotional (and traumatic) needs of clinical personnel.

Bleich et al. (2003) conducted a nationally representative telephone-based survey of Israeli residents undertaken from April through May 2002 in order to ascertain the prevalence of PTSD symptoms and the methods of coping used to deal with exposure to terrorism and its ongoing threat. There were 512 participants: 250 men (48.9%), 262 women (51.1%), and 444 Jews (86.6%) and 68 Arabs (13.2%). The interviews were conducted by telephone using a structured questionnaire. Overall, the results indicated that 84 (16.4%) Israeli adults surveyed had been personally involved in an attack in the year and a half prior to the survey, 113 (22.1%) of the respondents indicated that a friend or family member was wounded or killed in an attack, and 78 (15.3%) reported that they knew someone who survived an attack uninjured (Bleich et al., 2003). Moreover, the results indicated that nearly two thirds of the sample (60%) feared for their lives and more than two thirds (67.9%) stated that they feared for the lives of their friends and family.

Respondents also reported trauma- and stress-related mental health symptoms. Greater than one third (37.4%) reported having at least one trauma-related symptom for at least one month, with an average of four symptoms reported per person. The most commonly reported symptoms were avoidance/numbing (55.5%), followed by hyperarousal symptoms (49.4%), and re-experiencing trauma-related scenes (37.1%). Additionally, 26.9% of the respondents reported at least one dissociative symptom, 46.3% reported being distressed by symptoms, and 22.7% reported that their work or social functioning was impaired. Greater than half (58.6%) reported feeling depressed or gloomy and 28% reported feeling "very" depressed. Overall, 9% of the participants met the *DSM-IV* criteria for PTSD. Bleich et al. (2003) reported that the number and severity of trauma-related symptoms reported in their sample were comparable to those found among a national sample of American residents after the September 11th terrorist attack on the World Trade Center, as well as comparable to a sample of New York residents overall. However, the prevalence of trauma-related symptoms reported for persons in the immediate vicinity of the World Trade Center one to two months after the attack was greater (20%) (Galea et al., 2002).

The terrorist attacks that took place on September 11, 2001, in both New York City and Washington, D.C., left approximately 3,000 people dead and several thousands of people in grief, anger, and shock (Taylor, 2002). Numerous official and unofficial agencies were involved in the counseling response to this enormous tragedy. During the first eight weeks after the attacks across the United States, the American Red Cross alone had 135,800 mental health and grief contacts (Taylor, 2002). Schuster et al. (2001) indicated that the World Trade Center terrorist attacks on the United States affected Americans far beyond New York City with substantial symptoms of stress. Clearly, the saturation of these events, particularly through sustained media coverage, had a significant impact on the emotions and feelings of security throughout the United States. Indeed, in response to the first anniversary of September 11th, one New Yorker observed the following (cited in Jordan, 2003, p. 110):

> We remembered the many lives we lost on the 11th, last year. The children that lost one parent, or worse, were orphaned that day. But you know, today we once more all became one country. There's no race, no ethnicity, and no poor or rich, we are all Americans. And we grew united out of the dust of the 11th.

Jordan (2003) discussed not only the tremendous impact of the actual events of September 11, 2001, but also the intense emotional reactions to the first-year anniversary. She described the need to deal with anniversaries of trauma proactively to help minimize the potential escalation of stress responses or other emotional reactions and to help the individual move toward closure and to move forward in the grieving process. The first anniversary was described as the most difficult for individuals who had (1) a group affiliation with a victim; (2) shared characteristics, interests, or attributes with a victim; (3) previously demonstrated poor coping skills; (4) exhibited extreme or atypical reactions; and (5) a personal history of trauma ... and concurrent adverse reactions (e.g., family problems, health problems, psychiatric history) (Roberts, 2000, cited in Jordan, 2003, p. 111). Mental health professionals should reassure those clients affected by an anniversary of a trauma that the intensity and duration of the experience varies from person to person and that their reactions are normal insofar as they are not: "(a) contemplating harming themselves or others, (b) resorting to using alcohol and other substances to numb the pain, and (c) abusing or being abused (Jordan, 2003, p. 112)."

Mental health professionals are not immune to the psychological trauma associated with terrorism and fear. Although mental health professionals are aware of the long-term potential of burnout, particularly forensic psychologists who typically come into contact with the darker side of human nature, psychologists responding to the emergency work at the World Trade Center and the Pentagon could not have been prepared for the physical and emotional effects of their task (Taylor, 2002). Those involved in emergency work are vulnerable to compassion fatigue, secondary traumatic stress, or "vicarious traumatization" (Taylor, 2002, p. 105). The APA advised responding psychologists to attend to self-care strategies and to seek professional support. Crime scene photos and police records detailing gruesome crimes would have insufficiently desensitized forensic psychologists to the death, destruction, and gruesome sights and smells that they experienced from the mass casualties at the World Trade Center in New York.

According to the National Center for PTSD in the United States (2001), the prevalence rates for PTSD are 4–5% from natural disasters, 28% from mass shooting, 29% from a plane crash into a hotel, and 34% from a bombing. Galea et al. (2002) found that after the September 11, 2001, terrorist attack on the United States, there was a rise in PTSD symptomatology in the United States. The Longitudinal Aging Study in Amsterdam demonstrated the long-range effects of the September 11th attacks (Van Zelst, De Beurs, & Smit, 2003). These militant extremist attacks caused a rise in the PTSD symptomatology on the elderly Dutch population. Victims of the September 11th attacks experienced anxiety about the future, engaged in avoidance and fear of public transportation, and were fearful of being random targets in crowded areas such as sports events (American Red Cross, 2001; Pawlukewicz, 2003).

Everly (2003, p. 57) indicated that the fight against terrorism must occur on three levels: "(1) prevention of the terrorist attacks themselves; (2) mitigating the adverse impact of the persistent threats of terrorist acts, as well as terrorist attacks when they do occur; and (3) psychological treatment of the lingering adverse effects of threatened or actualized terrorist attacks." He referred to the third level as "psychological counterterrorism" (p. 57). Everly stressed the importance of the psychology of terrorism as paramount in its understanding and as foundational for rebuilding a community devastated by its effects, not only structurally but psychologically as well. This approach is essential to restoring a sense of humanity. Therefore, the role of psychologists in assisting law enforcement personnel with profiling guidance or otherwise apprehending terrorists, with providing crisis counseling to trauma survivors, and with conducting research relating to counterterrorism are all of critical importance.

Forensic Psychology and Policy Implications

Everly (2003) described psychological efforts to prevent terrorism as falling into four domains (p. 58). These included (1) efforts to remove terrorism as a tactical option by encouraging the global community to view it with extreme legal, moral, and political disdain so as not to render it viable; (2) efforts to remove it as a strategic option by not negotiating with terrorists under any circumstances; (3) responding to terrorism with immediate and overwhelming force, wherein the costs outweigh the gains; and (4) establishing a global climate where "justice" is perceived to be accessible to all. Everly (2003, p. 58) also described psychological efforts to mitigate the negative impact of terrorism. These include: (1) the provision of pre-incident training and education; (2) the provision of "acute psychological first aid"; (3) the provision of community "town meetings" as a means to provide important updates, stress management information, and to build personal and community empowerment; and (4) the implementation of a multifaceted system of crisis intervention and emergency mental health services. Finally, Everly (2003) outlined psychological efforts to treat and rehabilitate those affected by way of using individual and group psychotherapy (with psychotropic medications where indicated), and even acute inpatient hospitalization in the most severe cases, especially where less restrictive means were ineffective or contraindicated.

The United States has several agencies that aid trauma victims and survivors. Examples include the American Red Cross (ARC), the Critical Incident Stress Management group (CISM), and the Green Cross. The Green Cross was established in 1995 after the Oklahoma City bombing and focuses on post-disaster work. This organization responds mostly in connection with employee assistance programs, and provides a comprehensive three-tiered training service for its staff with ascending degrees of certification based on progressive coursework and supervision (Taylor, 2002). The ARC, CISM, and the Green Cross all address the following: (1) clinical signs and symptoms of acute and chronic trauma, (2) differentiation between reactions attributable more to recent trauma rather than an unresolved psychiatric disorder or normal grief, (3) identification of the kinds of support victims may require at various stages of disaster recovery and designations as to where this support should be provided, (4) consideration of the spiritual impact of behavior, (5) description of procedures that encourage survivors to adaptively manage their trauma into manageable memories, and (6) the requirement that potential volunteers be adequately self-disciplined and responsive to organizational demands in order to fulfill their duties while minimizing embarrassment, stress, and fatigue (Taylor, 2002, pp. 105–106).

The enormity of the terrorist attacks on the United States forced many other nations to consider their vulnerability to terrorism and their response preparedness with emergency mental health care. With respect to the New Zealand mental health system, Taylor (2002) noted that this country is overburdened, sparsely located, and virtually unfamiliar with components of immediate disaster trauma. Moreover, Taylor (2002, p. 106) indicated that the immediate goal of crisis responders is to help victims return to their "psychological status quo." In his assessment of critical aspects to consider when developing a crisis plan in New Zealand, Taylor (2002, p. 106) observed the following: "As members of a multicultural society in which for many citizens English is a second language, and in a country that increasingly is becoming a popular tourist destination, they will need either to be multilingual or have access to interpreters to facilitate contact with casualties." Multicultural issues were also very significant in the United States, particularly in New York City, as some residents of Middle Eastern descent experienced further revictimization when they were looked upon with suspicion and anger by their fellow residents.

Some educational institutions in the United States and Great Britain are beginning to address issues specific to terrorism and trauma psychology, and they are lobbying for support to form a Division of Trauma Psychology within the APA to advance their professional and research concerns (Taylor, 2002). While forensic psychologists are expanding their role in consulting with law enforcement agencies to profile potential terrorists, some psychologists specialize in crisis counseling with trauma victims only. The Australasian Society for Traumatic Stress Studies and the Australasian Critical Incident Stress Association aid their members in sharing personal experiences, professional expertise, and research ideas (Taylor, 2002).

Psychologists responding to scenes of disaster should be aware of safety concerns for survivors and try to connect individuals with their family and support groups within their cultural and religious networks (Taylor, 2002). Pamphlets with appropriate contact information, as well as education relating to possible reactions that may arise, should be made available. Taylor (2002) stresses the importance of psychologists working with trauma survivors to take time and to not press for the removal of psychological defenses such as avoidance and hyperarousal too soon. Furthermore, the clinician is encouraged to refer victims to general practitioners for medication or for more intensive professional care services if no significant improvement is made. The attacks on September 11th resulted in work groups, group debriefings/process groups, and spiritual gatherings offered at hospitals, schools, mental health clinics, job sites, community centers, and the like (Pawlukewicz, 2003). Research suggests that giving individuals an opportunity to discuss their experiences shortly after the trauma may reduce symptoms of PTSD (Pawlukewicz, 2003).

Finally, there are several policy implications regarding research on terrorism. As J. M. Davis (2002, p. 47) stated: "Language differences are the greatest barrier to worldwide sharing of information." He indicated that few psychological databases regarding terrorism are available in English, which is the language spoken by the majority of psychologists worldwide. He encourages policymakers to have these databases translated into other languages for wider accessibility. Psychologists who are researching terrorism should familiarize themselves with cultural meanings and contexts of the groups under scrutiny in order to better understand them and to contribute to the field (Arena & Arrigo, in press). In addition, psychologists can help to educate the public with accurate and reliable information about terrorism in order to help increase vigilance and empowerment. As J. M. Davis (2002, p. 49) explained: "With increased alertness, initiative, and vigilance, ordinary people can find ways to maintain privacy and other norms of an open society while still countering the dangers of terrorism."

Suggestions for Future Research

Future research should compare the efficacy of terrorist profiles developed by forensic psychologists based on psychological and criminological research to that of the FBI and other intelligence agencies. Terrorists are part of groups that are shrouded in secrecy. Future research should continue to focus on exploring the individual psychological correlates leading to terrorism, as well as the interfacing social, political, economic, religious, and other ideological influences that contribute to developing the blueprint for a terrorist individual or the motivation for a terrorist act. Social science research should be conducted and used to help aid policymakers with regard to foreign affairs and to better inform our intelligence-gathering agencies. Additionally, continued research comparing the demographics and prevalence (or lack thereof) of mental illness in those who act as suicide bombers is needed. Additional studies evaluating the impact of more recent trends regarding extreme violence on attitudes of isolationism versus globalization among Western, European, and other countries must be undertaken.

It is also important to assess and interpret the process of effective coping and meaning-making for individuals who have faced significant trauma. More long-term or longitudinal studies with regard to the impact of security threats on a person's mental health, specifically symptoms related to anxiety, depression, and PTSD of vulnerable populations (e.g., the mentally ill, children, or the elderly), should be conducted in relation to the prevalence of these psychiatric/psychological problems as found in the general population.

THE INSANITY DEFENSE AND COMPETENCY TO STAND TRIAL

Introduction

The common law system of criminal law is built on the foundation that individuals should not be convicted of an offense unless they volitionally chose to commit the crime and had the presence of mind to make a rational choice at the time of the crime (Nemitz & Bean, 2001). Moreover, in order to be tried, the defendant must be able to understand the charges filed against the accused, comprehend the nature of the offense and the possible consequences if found guilty, understand the roles of the various court personnel and the operation of court procedure, and assist the attorney in the preparation of a defense (Bardwell & Arrigo, 2002). The accused has a right to be both physically and mentally present. A fundamental aspect of criminal law is that an individual should be given the opportunity to respond to those charges that are brought against a person (Veiel & Coles, 1999). Most countries have special provisions for mentally disordered offenders. Three areas that address special provisions for the mentally disordered offender include (1) competency to stand trial, (2) responsibility for conduct whereby a mental disorder was present at the time of the alleged offense and so impacted the crime such that the defendant could not be adjudicated as a criminal, and (3) sentencing of mentally disordered offenders.

Competency to stand trial evaluations are by far the most common and convictions can be overturned in cases in which a defendant was potentially incompetent and was not evaluated (Viljoen, Roesch, & Zapf, 2002). When mental illness and the criminal justice system interface, there is an inherent clash between individual autonomy, state authority, and public safety (Nemitz & Bean, 2001). Although provisions in the law for competency to stand trial and the insanity defense are designed to protect the rights of the mentally ill, the disposition of these individuals with affirmative findings has been the source of many debates regarding one's civil liberties. Consider the following case illustration:

In the case of *Regina v. Swain*, Mr. Swain was found "not guilty by reason of insanity," having been charged with an assault causing bodily harm involving his wife and children. His behavior during the offense was both violent and bizarre. He swung his children over his head, scored a cross on his wife's chest, spoken about spirits, and fought with the air. At his arrest, he conversed excitedly in religious themes. He later testified that he believed his family was being attacked by devils, and he was attempting to protect them. Mr. Swain has since been successfully treated with antipsychotic drugs, and at the time of his trial, he was living in the community without incident for well over a year.

The insanity defense was proffered by the Crown over the objections of Mr. Swain. Despite Mr. Swain's recovery and successful community reintegration, the only provision following a successful finding of insanity was indeterminate detention. Therefore, Mr. Swain was reincarcerated and held at the pleasure of the Lieutenant Governor for some 3 months before being granted an absolute discharge. The law did not provide a mechanism for taking into consideration his mental condition at the time of trial (as opposed to at the time of the offense), and there was no provision for judicial discretion with respect to sentencing. The Supreme Court of Canada found the section of the Criminal Code relating to mentally ill offenders to be unconstitutional under the new Charter by its clear deprivation of liberty, lack of procedural safeguards, and infringement of the right of psychiatrically disordered persons not to be arbitrarily detained (Stuart, Arboleda-Florez, & Crisanti, 2001, p. 528).

Literature Review

Criminal Responsibility

Canada has made revisions to their criminal code on matters pertinent to criminal responsibility and the requirements for fitness to stand trial evaluations and dispositions (Stuart et al., 2001). Mentally ill individuals who face criminal charges may need psychiatric treatment and a close examination of the effects of their disorder on their criminal responsibility or their mental state at the time of the offense (S. Brown, 1999). Mentally disordered offenders represent a tension of sorts for legislators, policy-makers, and administrators in which management and treatment needs must be delicately balanced. These issues have been varyingly addressed at different times and by different jurisdictions, states, provinces, or countries. For example, during the 1970s and 1980s the mandatory indeterminate confinement of defendants found not guilty by reason of insanity (NGRI) or unfit to proceed to trial increasingly came under fire and eventually was abolished when the Parliament ratified extensive changes to the mental health sections of the Criminal Code in 1992 (Menzies, 2002). Although specific "caps" that the new legislation put on the duration of psycholegal detention have not been set forth, a review board examines every forensic case in the province periodically (p. 400). Similar to other provinces and nations, the inpatient population in British Columbia, Canada, reached its peak in the mid-1950s and has since declined steadily. The Forensic Psychiatric Services Commission Act created one centralized organization to regulate all psycholegal policies and practices in the province (Menzies, 2002).

According to Hopper and McSherry (2001), there was growing concern in England and Wales that the traditional insanity defense based on the M'Naughten Rules was in violation of international human rights requirements set forth by the European Convention for the Protection of Human Rights (ECHR). The ECHR was activated on September 3, 1953. In 1999, all forty members of the Council of Europe unanimously supported the Human Rights Act 1998 (UK) that incorporated the convention into domestic law (Hopper & McSherry, 2001).

There also was growing concern that if an individual met the psycholegal criteria of insanity this did not necessarily mean the person met the psychiatric or medical definition of mental illness requiring involuntary confinement. In *Winterwerp v. The Netherlands* (1979) 2 ECHR 387, the European Court of Human Rights found that the involuntary commitment and treatment of the applicant into a psychiatric hospital in accordance with Dutch emergency procedure violated Article 5(1) (e) of the ECHR. This article holds that "no one shall be deprived of his or her liberty save in the case of the lawful detention of persons of 'unsound mind'" (Hopper & McSherry, 2001, p. 161). The Court held that the phrase "persons of unsound mind" could not be operationalized or given a clear interpretation (p. 162). The Court's ruling established that an individual could not be confined without medical evidence stipulated a current mental state that would justify involuntary confinement. This ruling had implications for the psycholegal interpretation of "insanity" and the disposition of those with a successful verdict of insanity (Hopper & McSherry, 2001). Ashworth (1999, p. 216) described the three requirements created by the ruling in *Winterwerp* as follows:

1. There must be a close correspondence between expert medical opinion and the definition of the mental state required to satisfy the defense.

2. The court's determination of mental impairment must be based upon objective medical expertise.
3. The court must have discretion to determine whether or not the mental state is "of a kind or degree warranting compulsory confinement."

The M'Naughten Rule is the basis for the traditional insanity defense in the UK. This defense stipulates that the defendant suffered from a "defect of reason, from disease of the mind, as not to know the nature and quality of the act ... or that he [or she] did not know what he [or she] was doing was wrong" (cited in Hopper & McSherry, 2001, p. 162). Ashworth (1999) indicated that the M'Naughten Concept, "disease of the mind," does not meet the *Winterwerp* criteria because it is so broad that many qualifying disorders would not meet the standard of compulsory confinement (e.g., epilepsy) (McSherry, 1993).

Criticisms of the insanity defense in England and Wales center around the disposition of mandatory indeterminate sentencing for those found NGRI (Hopper & McSherry, 2001). The Criminal Procedure (Insanity and Unfitness to Plead) Act of 1991 allowed the court the ability to decide between commitment to a hospital, a guardian or supervision and treatment order, or a complete discharge upon a finding of insanity for a less serious offense. However, involuntary confinement to a hospital remains mandatory when the psychiatric verdict is for an offense for which the sentence is mandated by law, and this applies predominantly to murder (Hopper & McSherry, 2001). This confinement can occur even if the mental illness is not found to be of the type or seriousness to warrant a current mandatory commitment.

Australia and New Zealand are not under the jurisdiction of the ECHR, but they are subject to the International Covenant of Civil and Political Rights (ICCPR). The ICCPR was enacted in 1980 for Australia and in 1978 for New Zealand. It is similar to the ECHR in that it states, in essence, that no one should be deprived of their liberty, except where allowed by the law. However, the mental health law in Australia and New Zealand indicates that there must be a system of mandatory and periodic review of the psychiatric/medical grounds for continuing the involuntary confinement (Hopper & McSherry, 2001).

All nine Australian criminal law jurisdictions and New Zealand have an insanity defense standard mostly based on the M'Naughten Rules. The Northern Territory, Queensland, South Australia, Tasmania, and Western Australia currently include an additional "volitional" prong in regard to whether or not the defendant lacked the capacity to control his or her conduct (Bronitt & McSherry, 2001, p. 210). Consistent with criticism leveled against the UK, critics of the traditional insanity defense in Australia and New Zealand contend that given a lack of congruency between the psychiatric and legal definitions of insanity, any mandatory confinement based on the legal definition violates the requirement set forth in the ICCPR. The convenant stipulates that everyone has the right to liberty (Hopper & McSherry, 2001). Different regions or jurisdictions use assorted phrases to help describe the psycholegal references to insanity. Some of these include the following: disease of the mind, mental impairment, and abnormality of mind. These descriptions are all subject to various interpretations and remain ambiguous and vague; thus, they are not equivalent to psychiatric or psychological definitions of mental illnesses.

Unlike other jurisdictions such as New South Wales, the Northern Territory, and Queensland where no discretion is available with respect to the disposition of insanity acquittees, New Zealand, South Australia, Tasmania, Victoria, Western Australia, and the Australian federal level allow courts the discretion to either commit an insanity acquittee or release the person conditionally or unconditionally (Hopper & McSherry, 2001). This available range of options ensures that these jurisdictions are in compliance with international human rights obligations.

Mental health legislation in Australia is a state responsibility and, as a result, each state and territory has a unique legislation (Jager, 2001). Queensland, Tasmania, and Western Australia have criminal codes; however, in the rest of the states, criminal law exists by statute. Tasmanian law is unique in that the insanity defenses allowed under M'Naughten criteria, as well as irresistible impulse and intoxication, are all available to defendants (Jager, 2001). In most jurisdictions, including the United States, involuntary intoxication does not qualify for an insanity defense.

In the Australian state of Queensland, the duty to determine criminal responsibility lies with the Queensland mental health tribunal (MHT), in a special sitting of the Supreme Court (S. Brown, 1999). The MHT is made up of a senior judge and two psychiatrists who take an inquisitorial approach to examining psychiatric evidence. An order for involuntary commitment to a psychiatric hospital is typically given for those with a successful special verdict and a serious crime, whereas community treatment can be ordered for those with less serious crimes. This system is very popular with the mental health community but criticized by the press and politicians who complain that it allows criminals to avoid responsibility for their behavior (S. Brown, 1999). The MHT was established in 1984 with the goal of extricating the mentally ill and the intellectually disabled from the criminal justice system and placing them in the mental health system. The MHT examines competency to stand trial hearings, cases where the defendant claims to have been mentally ill at the time of the offense, and examines cases when the diminished responsibility defense is raised in murder cases (S. Brown, 1999). The defense of diminished responsibility found in England, New South Wales, the Australian Capital Territory, the Northern Territory, and Queensland traditionally considers whether an "abnormality of mind" substantially impacts the defendant's "mental responsibility" in relation to his or her actions (McSherry, 2001, p. 15).

An application to the MHT can be raised at any point during a legal proceeding by the accused, a family member, a court officer, and the like. The court can reject a guilty plea and refer the defendant to the MHT over the objections of the accused (S. Brown, 1999). A defendant is assumed to be of sound mind unless there is any evidence to dispute this assumption. The judge alone makes the decision about whether or not the defendant was or was not of sound mind. The judge can use the testimony of advising psychiatrists to clarify the clinical and assessment evidence.

There are many similarities in the treatment of mentally disordered offenders in Canada, the UK, Australia, New Zealand, and the United States. Although several similarities exist within Central and South American countries as well, there are certainly more appreciable differences. For example, Brazil has no provisions in their criminal justice system for competency to stand trial; however, NGRI pleas are much more common there than in North America (Taborda, 2001). Typically, there are three phases to the Brazilian criminal justice process. These include the inquest, the judicial proceedings, and the judgment execution. The judicial proceedings phase represents the adversarial process, and this is when the Penal Imputability Exam (PIE) is conducted. In the United States, this is equivalent to assessing the mental state at the time of the offense for an insanity plea (Taborda, 2001). Conviction can only occur if the accused is fully imputable at the time of the crime, or, at least, "semi-imputable" (p. 372). Conviction with substitution of the punishment by criminal commitment involves "coercive application of psychiatric treatment, generally of a hospital nature" and this occurs when the accused is found semi-imputable at the time of the crime (p. 372). This verdict is similar to the guilty but mentally ill verdict in the common-law system. Finally, acquittal based on the "inimputability of the defendant" occurs when the defendant is judged as having been inimputable or not responsible at the time of the offense (p. 372). In this instance, the defendant also would typically undergo treatment by way of involuntary confinement in a psychiatric hospital. This verdict corresponds to the NGRI outcome found within common law. Acquittal occurs regardless of the accused's imputability if innocence is demonstrated (Taborda, 2001). Even if mentally ill, the defendant in this situation will not be committed as there is no concept of competency to stand trial in the Brazilian criminal justice system.

According to Taborda (2001, p. 384), the Brazilian rule for responsibility or imputability "is a kind of blend of the concept of *irresistible impulse*, formulated in Ohio in 1834, and the M'Naughten rule [developed] in 1843." The difference, however, is that the Brazilian system requires that the criminal not be completely cognizant of the wrongfulness of his or her actions, whereas in the U.S. system it is necessary to understand that the act was wrong in order to be considered criminally responsible for one's behavior. North American standards for insanity do not allow antisocial personality disorder or any other related personality pathology to be used as a basis for an insanity defense. Moreover, since the acquittal of John Hinckley, Jr., in 1984, the burden of proof with respect to insanity shifts to the party who raises it (i.e., the defense). Clearly, then, the North American standards are far more narrow and limiting than those set forth in Brazilian law. Brazilian law allows those with personality disorders only to be considered semi-imputable. Unlike countries of Anglo-Saxon tradition where the insanity defense is extremely rare, it is commonly invoked and is much more likely to be successful in Brazil (Taborda, 2001).

Competency to Stand Trial

Some unique aspects of the Brazilian criminal justice system help to explain why there is no concept of competency to stand trial in their criminal court system. Taborda (2001, p. 385) described some peculiarities of the Brazilian system as follows: (1) no one is given the right to defend oneself, unless the party in question is an attorney legally qualified to practice law; (2) any transactions between defense attorneys and prosecutors are forbidden and, as such, this forestalls any hope that a less severe sentence might be "negotiated" in a case where the accused previously admits his or her guilt; (3) the defendant holds a thoroughly passive attitude — that is, the accused is *defended* by an attorney — and the fact that the defendant is, or is not, in condition to actively cooperate with the defense is irrelevant; and (4) the defendant can be indicted and tried in default, that is, the accused may be a fugitive or may be absent from the courthouse. These provisions in Brazilian law make it less essential that the mentally ill defendant be an active participant in his or her defense or even understand court procedure. In this system, the lack of the accused's autonomy in preparing a defense makes the presence of rational, independent decision making, as well as other relevant legal functional capacities, moot.

In Tasmania, Australia, the Criminal Justice (Mental Impairment) Act 1999 defines the criteria for an individual to be found unfit to stand trial (UST) (Jager, 1999). The criteria for UST occurs when a person is unable to understand the charges, unable to plead to the charge or exercise the right of challenge, unable to understand court procedure, or unable to assist the attorney in preparation of a defense. Under Australian law, memory loss is specifically excluded as a factor for unfitness to stand trial (Jager, 1999). A defendant is presumed fit and unfitness is determined based on probabilities (Jager, 1999). Unfitness must be decided by a jury and if a defendant is determined to be unfit, the jury must then decide if he or she will be fit within 12 months and, if so, the hearing is adjourned; otherwise, another special hearing is initiated (Jager, 1999). In Queensland, a defendant who is found to be unfit for trial is referred to a psychiatric hospital and his or her fitness is then evaluated every three months by the patient review tribunal until he or she becomes fit to proceed (S. Brown, 1999). If there is no improvement or the mentally disordered offender has not been restored to fitness after three years, the Attorney General will drop the criminal charges but continue the restriction or hospitalization order.

The specific criteria for unfitness to proceed in England developed through case law during the 19th century (Mullen, 2002). The case of *R. v. Frith* (1790) created a general standard of procedural fairness in the courtroom insofar as the accused must be able to understand and participate in the criminal trial put forth against the defendant. This standard was further clarified in *R. v. Pritchard, Carrington and Payne* (1836). *Pritchard* is still the foundation for common law criteria with respect to fitness; however, specific procedures relating to determinations of trial competency are now set forth by legislation (Mullen, 2002). The *Dusky v. U.S.* (1960) decision and its progeny also had a significant impact on the fitness criteria and procedures. In Australia, the common law of England and Wales was changed slightly as a result of local decisions, the most important of which was *R. v. Presser* (1958) (Mullen, 2002). In more recent years, several Australian states have initiated legislation to regulate the criteria and procedures for determining trial fitness. The specific criteria and case law relevant for the United States was outlined previously in Chapter 1.

According to Mullen (2002), the criteria for competency to stand trial in the United States is far broader with respect to functional capacities as compared with England and the commonwealth countries. Mullen (2002, p. 486) described how the state of Victoria's legislation outlines the specific standards for fitness to plead, including the following criteria: (1) understand the nature of the charge, (2) ability to enter a plea, (3) ability to understand the nature of the trial and follow its course, (4) ability to understand the substantial effect of any evidence, (5) ability to challenge jurors or the jury, and (6) ability to give instructions to one's legal practitioner. The understanding required in competency cases in the UK is quite basic as compared with what is expected in the United States. Mullen (2002) reported that prior to 1992, defense counsels and most courts in British or Australian jurisdictions would go to great lengths to avoid a determination of unfitness due to the possibility of indeterminate sentencing or confinement in a prison or hospital. In general, these countries regard the "unfit to proceed" notion with some caution given the absence of any secondary gain for the defendant when it is invoked. As such, it is sparingly used. This interpretation stands in stark contrast to the possible advantages that befall an accused found incompetent to stand trial in the United States.

A fundamental principle of Canadian law is that criminal defendants must be competent or fit to stand trial (Stuart et al., 2001). The Canadian laws regulating the treatment of mentally disordered defendants in the criminal justice system were reformed in 1992. This reform was the first in approximately one hundred years. The Supreme Court of Canada found a section of the Criminal Code regarding mentally disordered offenders to be unconstitutional based on its apparent "deprivation of liberty, lack of procedural safeguards, and infringement of the right of the mentally disordered persons not to be arbitrarily detained" (Stuart et al., p. 528). The new legislation was termed Bill C-30. It was enacted on February 4, 1992, and addressed issues related to criminal responsibility and fitness to stand trial assessments and dispositions (Stuart et al., 2001). The primary goal of the new fitness provisions was to substantially decrease the amount of time the accused spent confined or in custody. The legal standard was reduced from an initial 30-day inpatient evaluation period to 5 days, in an attempt to more quickly answer the fitness question in the least restrictive environment. Moreover, the new legislation clearly separated assessment from treatment by mandating that fitness assessments were *not* for the purpose of treatment and that the defendant, therefore, could not be treated against his or her will (Stuart et al., 2001). The length of the assessment could be extended to 30 days with compelling evidence. This shift in attraction from a longer treatment-focused remand to a shorter assessment-focused remand was contentious. Directors and staff of various forensic facilities in Canada indicated that the 5-day period would not allow for a comprehensive assessment, nor would it allow them to meet other therapeutic goals that would have a direct impact on fitness.

Stuart et al. (2001) examined descriptive data collected over a 6-year period: three calendar years prior to the enactment of Bill C-30 (1989–1991); and three years after its enactment (1992–1994). The findings indicated that judicial and clinical practice changed very little after the enactment of the legislative reforms. Generally, the average length of fitness evaluation periods remained three to four times higher than the new legal standard. The occurrence of shorter periods of pretrial assessment increased to approximately 10%. This failed to become the standard of forensic practice, but remained the exception rather than the rule (Stuart et al., 2001). These researchers suggested that one possible explanation for this was related to court and correctional system resistance to give up the therapeutic role of fitness to stand trial determinations or competency commitments. Another explanation was their ability to mandate treatment under these particular conditions. Indeed, as Stuart et al. (2001, p. 536) stated: "For many correctional systems fitness remands provide a backdoor way of obtaining treatment for their mentally disordered offender populations, or [they are] a means of diverting mentally disordered offenders out of criminal justice to mental health systems."

Based on Canadian law (Viljoen et al., 2001), fitness assessments evaluate the following: (1) the defendant's mental state to determine if he or she has a mental disorder and (2) the presence of impairment in one or more functional capacities relating to legal abilities necessary to stand trial. If the assessment determines that the defendant currently has impaired psycho-legal abilities, a mental disorder, and the impaired abilities are a result of the mental disorder, the accused can be found unfit to stand trial. Fitness evaluations should focus on the relevant legal capacities and descriptions of mental illness should be related to these capacities. A psychotic disorder alone would be insufficient for a finding of unfitness if it did not substantially impair the person's abilities as a defendant.

A 5-year review of fitness to stand trial remands in Quebec, Canada, was undertaken to the study examined and compared the characteristics and processing of female and male fitness to stand trial (FST) remandees, identified factors associated with FST evaluations, and explored gender differences and similarities in the factors related to those found fit and unfit (Crocker, Favreau, & Caulet, 2002). The results indicated that in the sample examined, women were twice as likely as men to be recommended as unfit to stand trial (UST) even when age, offense severity, symptoms of psychosis, and a history of criminal convictions were controlled. The only factor significantly associated with a UST recommendation for women was the presence of psychotic symptoms. For men, both signs of psychosis and being charged with a violent offense were predictors of UST recommendations. Therefore, being charged with a nonviolent offense would decrease the probability of a UST recommendation for men but not for women. In Canada, more women (12.1%) than men (3.3%) charged with a nonviolent offense are found UST. This finding has implications for women involuntarily confined for nonviolent offenses, particularly when they are psychiatrically confined for periods that are longer than if the person had been criminally convicted and sent to prison. Crocker et al. (2002) maintained that what, on the surface, may appear to be a chivalrous action designed to protect a mentally disordered woman from a harsh trial process, may, in actuality, turn out to be paternalistic and punitive.

Forensic Psychology and Policy Implications

Hopper and McSherry (2001) stress the importance of a critical and systematic review of the current versions of the insanity defense in the UK, Australia, and New Zealand so that these countries can comply with international human rights law. In addition, they suggested that it might be better to list in the Criminal Code specific disorders that, if present, would make individuals who use a particular plea and receive a special verdict eligible for involuntary confinement under the appropriate conditions. Forensic psychologists have a clear obligation to be familiar with the relevant legislation and psycholegal definitions in the jurisdictions in which they practice. Moreover, it is essential that psychologists conducting fitness/competency or responsibility evaluations relate descriptions of symptoms or diagnoses of mental illness to the legal functional capacities outlined in the relevant law.

Care must be taken in the MHT system not to subject mentally ill defendants charged with relatively minor offenses to prolonged detention, especially while they wait for psychiatric reports to be completed. Along these lines a report created by the Commonwealth Government advocated mental health legislation that would empower the police to use their discretion to waive minor charges against mentally disordered offenders. The report intimated that such determinations (followed by judicial review) represented the less restrictive option (S. Brown, 1999). Moreover, the report emphasized the notion that a finding of insanity would result in a longer detention period than if convicted and sentenced, and would result in the unnecessary criminalization of the mentally ill for a minor offense that could be a direct result of their psychiatric disorder. However, a flaw exists in this proposal. In short, it would require untrained mental health professionals such as the police and court officials to recognize mental illness. Even with the existing MHT system, some training for non-mental-health personnel with regard to symptoms of psychiatric disorder could help prevent the dramatic under-referral of mentally ill offenders to the MHT.

In regard to FST determinations, forensic psychologists conducting these evaluations in England, Australia, and the like must be mindful that instruments such as the MacArthur Competency Assessment Tool are based on functional legal capacities that are more broadly defined in the laws of the United States. As such, this instrument and these capacities were normed on specific populations with different criteria. While there may be some overlap, results may not be valid. Forensic psychologists who test for competency to stand trial must remember that a determination of fitness is relative to the demands of a given case. For example, the standard would be higher for more complex legal charges, particularly with the potential of a lengthier trial. Finally, Canadian legislation requires that fitness evaluations can only be performed by *psychiatrists* (Viljoen et al., 2002). Canadian legislatures and policymakers would do well to consider the relative prevalence and identified success of *forensic psychologists* conducting competency to stand trial evaluations in other countries.

Suggestions for Future Research

S. Brown (1999) suggested that future research should examine whether or not the MHT improves the assessment and treatment of mentally disordered offenders, reduces these numbers in prisons, or improves the safety of the community. Also, empirical evidence could help determine if judges on the MHT are more or less likely to be influenced by psychiatric expert testimony. In addition, studies exploring long-term success outcomes (and recidivism) of mentally disordered offenders who have gone through this system should be conducted.

Continued research is needed in England, Canada, Australia, and other countries regarding the development of forensic assessment instruments that address the FST issue, normed on their own relevant populations and based on the criteria for competency as set forth in their laws. In addition, studies that compare the differences in the treatment for women versus men in the criminal justice system of different countries, particularly the criteria for determining insanity and competency, are needed. These data could help improve the accuracy of unfitness prediction, encourage cross-jurisdictional comparisons, and ultimately eliminate apparent gender biases in psycholegal evaluations (Crocker et al., 2002).

VIOLENCE RISK ASSESSMENT AND MENTALLY DISORDERED OFFENDERS

Introduction

Violence risk assessment has been a contentious issue for the past three decades (Woods, Reed, & Collins, 2003). Rather than considering clinical assessments of dangerousness as dangerousness prediction, these evaluations should be regarded as assessments of risk (Molbert & Beck, 2003). This debate has received international attention. In both North American and European countries the public's outcry for accountability with mental health services has only increased during the past decade, especially because violence risk assessment and management of mentally disordered offenders have only increased. Although the link between psychiatric illness and violence is not as strong as is perceived by the general public, there is significant political pressure to accurately predict future acts of violence and to employ effective management strategies to prevent future acts of harm. The media tend to sensationalize any instances of violence perpetrated by the mentally ill. In fact, as discussed in Chapter 1, the majority of mentally ill individuals are not violent. Risk factors are both static (historical or unchanging) or dynamic (fluid or changeable, typically present factors). Some typical risk factors that have been correlated to future acts of violence include: history of violence, negative social history, an antisocial value system, psychopathy, age, socioeconomic status, gender, the nature of the current offense and relating circumstances, history of substance abuse, history of mental illness, paranoia, fear, noncompliance with prescribed treatment, lack of insight, history of head injury, and subaverage intelligence. Other factors that impact risk include: current attitudes, motivation for treatment, current mental health status, and socially acceptable goals and values (Woods et al., 2003). Violence on psychiatric wards, especially in forensic hospitals is common (Bhui et al., 2001). This should not be shocking as violent behavior is frequently part of the admission criterion. Bhui et al. (2001) indicated that the risk of violence in inpatient psychiatric settings is high for a variety of reasons: the combination of mental disorders such as psychosis and personality disorders; the increasing prevalence of substance misuse among psychiatric admissions; the impoverished ward milieu, and the social deprivation and past experiences of traumatic violence in the development histories of those admitted. Consider the following case illustration.

Henry is a 30-year-old man who has spent most of the past 12 years in psychiatric hospitals or halfway houses. He also has spent some time in local jails and in the forensic psychiatric hospitals after committing various minor crimes. Henry has been diagnosed with paranoid schizophrenia, antisocial personality traits, and intermittent alcohol abuse. His most recent stay in the halfway house was, for the most part uneventful. Henry took his antipsychotic medication, attended the group meetings, and appeared to be doing satisfactorily. One evening he went to the local tavern and consumed enough alcohol to appear visibly inebriated and was asked to leave after getting into a loud argument with the bartender. Upon his return to the halfway house, he proceeded to beat his roommate, accusing him of controlling his thoughts. He was subsequently readmitted to the local community hospital where the emergency room staff appeared to be most familiar with him, telling the on-call psychiatrist that Henry had been admitted many times under similar circumstances (Citrome & Volavka, 2001, pp. 164–165).

Literature Review

During the last two decades in Germany, the number of admissions to forensic psychiatric hospitals has increased from 2,500 to approximately 3,800 (Seifert, Jahn, Bolten, & Wirtz, 2002). Currently, there are about 60,000 convicts imprisoned in Germany (Seifert et al., 2002). Although the occurrence of homicide or sex crimes committed by released forensic patients is rare, the emphasis on much of the current forensic research in Germany remains focused on the issue of risk of violence or the potential for recidivism for these groups. In practice, release from a forensic institution is almost exclusively based on a patient's behavior and development during his or her admission. Following the relevant law, patients are likely to be released if they have made the sort of progress that shows "it is not expected that the person will commit any further illegal acts after release" (Seifert et al., 2002, p. 62). However, basing release on institutional behavior has little empirical support. Moreover, there are many complaints about the reduction in criteria used for risk assessment in forensic practice as adaptive behavior in an institution does not necessarily translate into social competence and low risk for future violence (Seifert, 2002).

The number of individuals released from German forensic hospitals has been reduced dramatically. According to Seifert et al. (2002), this more cautious release standard was due in large part to patients with a personality disorder diagnosis and/or those convicted of a sexual offense. These researchers suggested that German forensic psychology and psychiatry have become a matter of extreme politics in the last decade with a tendency toward overpredicting the risk of violence posed by the mentally ill, resulting in overinclusive standards for psychiatric hospitalization.

Seifert et al. (2002) conducted a prospective study whereby 188 participants filled out a prognostic questionnaire immediately before release. They were monitored for 5 years after their release from forensic hospitals in order to test the prognostic validity of the questionnaire. The questionnaire consisted of sociostatistical and historical items, psychological testing and biological items (e.g., intelligence tests, CCT, and EEG), and clinical items. The clinical questionnaire was designed based on predictive factors in the literature and the prediction index items used in almost all German correctional institutions (Seifert et al., 2002).

The distribution of diagnoses differed from previous German release or cross-sectional studies in that the percentage of schizophrenic patients was disproportionately high (45.2%), whereas patients with personality disorders (31.9%) were clearly underrepresented (Seifert et al., 2002). An increase in substance misuse problems was noted since the 1980s, with a substance use disorder listed as the first or second diagnosis for 37.2% of the subjects. The percentage of sexual offenses was 13.3% and more than two thirds (70%) of the patients with schizophrenic psychosis had committed crimes against persons (homicide and physical injury). Two patients had committed sexual homicides and 70% of the patients had previous convictions.

The results of this study indicated that if a patient's treatment team in the forensic hospital assessed the patient's behavior and social skills as generally positive, the person was most likely given a favorable legal prognosis. However, if the patient's interactions with the treatment team were tense, strained, and required great caution, a high risk of recidivism was assumed (Seifert et al., 2002). A treatment team's assessment of a patient is established by long-term observations and daily interactions with the patient, as well as the personality profile that emerged during the admission. An aggressive demeanor and/or a schizoid presentation typically were evidence for a negative legal prognosis. The results further indicated that the legal prognosis of patients with a personality disorder was significantly worse than that of other diagnostic groups. The presence of a marked violent attitude and conspicuous social behavior were decisive criteria that significantly distinguished between personality disordered and schizophrenic patients. Patients with schizophrenia were classified as less prominent on both factors in contrast to those with personality disorders (Seifert et al., 2002). This study suggested that psychologists in forensic hospitals do consult clinical criteria to assess their patient's legal prognosis or risk for recidivism. The importance of using clinical and case history aspects was highlighted.

In addition, there is considerable political pressure in England for mental health providers to be accountable for assessing and managing risk among mentally disordered offenders (J. Bindman, 2002). During the past decade in the UK, the government has become more concerned with the risk of violence that psychiatric patients may pose to the public. J. Bindman (2002) described the sensationalized media coverage of homicides committed by individuals who come into contact with the mental health system as evidence of this preoccupation. In 1994, mental health services were mandated to identify and create registers of patients at risk for violence or self-harm, and to give them priority in access to appropriate care (Bindman, 2002). Although many mental health service providers in the UK established registers, the lack of agreement about defining risk and risk management resulted in variable implementation and doubtful benefit. Moreover, some treatment providers abandoned the registers altogether (J. Bindman, 2002). Notwithstanding these problems, policy documents continue to set forth the duty of mental health agencies to assess and manage the risks of violence to others. For example, in a 1998 policy document titled "Modernizing Mental Health Services: Safe, Sound and Supportive" (Department of Health, 1998), the link between violence and mental illness was highlighted. As the document stipulated: "There is a relationship between active mental illness and violence. The risk is significantly greater if the individual loses contact with services or receives inadequate care. The public is understandably concerned about the risks of violence ... services should be safe to protect the public" (cited in J. Bindman, 2002, p. 8).

Despite the growing public attention about risk assessment for the mentally ill in the UK, the rate of violent crime associated with mental illness is not rising and violent crime overall is falling (J. Bindman, 2002).

However, there remains a sharp increase in government pressure on mental health services to manage risk as a consequence of a political culture in which public services and forensic specialists are held responsible for the behavior of individuals (J. Bindman, 2002). With this pressure in mind, another highly controversial proposal for legal change has been suggested. In short, the government has established a new classification of mentally disordered offenders to include "dangerous severe personality disorder" (DSPD). This is a "diagnosis without a well-defined or understood medical or legal definition" (J. Bindman, 2002, p. 9). Individuals with DSPD may or may not have a treatable mental disorder or a conviction for a violent crime, and they could be involuntarily committed indefinitely in a secure hospital for possible future risk of violence. Overall, these British proposals have been strongly criticized on both ethical and theoretical grounds much like the sexually violent predatory laws and subsequent civil commitment statutes found in the United States (Bindman, 2002). In the UK, these laws have been deferred as a result of strong opposition; however, experimental treatment programs for individuals thus classified have been funded.

Watts, Leese, Thomas, Atakan, & Wykes (2003) conducted a prospective longitudinal study to address the prediction of violence in acute psychiatric units. The predictors of violence during the first two weeks of admission to two psychiatric units in London for 100 consecutive admissions were collected. Two definitions of violence were utilized which included actual assault on another person and aggressive behavior such as an attempted assault, violence to property, and specific threats. The results indicated that 32 patients completed actual assaults, 41 behaved aggressively, and 27 did not engage in any acts of violence. Furthermore, although preadmission violence had some predictive power, clinical variables, such as current mental status and response to treatment, were most predictive (Watts et al., 2003).

Actuarial methods or tools of violence prediction have been empirically proven to be superior to clinical judgment alone (M. Doyle, Dolan, & McGovern, 2002). These instruments are designed to complement and structure clinical decisions about violence risk, not take their place (Hart, 1998). Many risk-assessment tools are normed on populations in one region but used by clinicians in other regions. M. Doyle et al. (2002) carried out a study to examine the validity of North American (e.g., Canadian) actuarial violence risk-assessment tools employed in Britain. Specifically, these researchers explored the validity of the Psychopathy Checklist: Screening Version (PCL:SV), Violence Risk Appraisal Guide (VRAG), and the historical part (H-10) of the Historical/Clinical (HCR-20) scheme in predicting inpatient violence in 87 mentally disordered offenders in a medium-secure unit in the Northwest region of England.

Studies in North America have found the Hare Psychopathy Checklist-Revised (PCL-R), PCL:SV, VRAG, and HCR-20 to be valid predictors of inpatient violence (Heilbrun et al., 1998). The PCL:SV (Hart, Cox, & Hare, 1995) is a 12-item instrument that is quicker and easier to administer than the PCL-R, is empirically related to the PCL-R, and is psychometrically sound (Doyle et al., 2002). Both instruments were designed by Canadian researchers (e.g., Robert Hare). These instruments test for the construct of psychopathy. They were not expressly designed as risk-assessment tools. The concept of psychopathy in some form has been around since medieval times and the modern construct was pioneered by Cleckley's seminal work titled *The Mask of Sanity* (1941) (Arrigo & Shipley, 2001; Shipley & Arrigo, 2004). Hare (1991, 1993) created the most empirically validated method of assessing for psychopathy with primarily correctional inmates in Canada. The PCL-R is made up of 20 items that address both interpersonal items (grandiose sense of self-worth, superficial charm, lack of empathy) and behavioral aspects or criminality (criminal versatility, early behavioral problems, and juvenile delinquency) (Arrigo & Shipley, 2001; Rice, 1997; Shipley & Arrigo, 2004). The scores on the PCL-R range from 0 to 40 with 30 to 32 being the most commonly used criterion for a score reflecting psychopathy (Rice, 1997). Despite the fact that the PCL-R and the PSL:SV were not developed specifically as risk-assessment instruments, research has demonstrated that the PCL:SV is effective in predicting aggression and treatment noncompliance in forensic inpatients (Doyle et al., 2002; Hill, Rogers, & Bickford, 1996). Additionally, the MacArthur Foundation Violence Risk Assessment Study found that scores >12 on the PCL:SV were significantly related to violent behavior in the community in released psychiatric patients (Monahan et al., 2000).

The VRAG (G. Harris, Rice, & Quinsey, 1993) was developed in a sample of 618 male mentally disordered offenders evaluated in maximum-security hospitals in Canada and discharged into the community. It consists of 12 variables: a PCL-R score (which can be omitted if not available), behavioral problems in elementary school, age (negatively associated with violence), personality disorder diagnosis, separation from parents before the age of 16, revocation of previous conditional release, history of nonviolent offenses, never married, diagnosis of schizophrenia (negatively associated with violence), severity of injury to the victim with respect to the index offense (negatively associated with violence), history of alcohol abuse, and male victim of the index offense (Doyle et al., 2002, p. 144). The 12 items are weighted from -5 to $+12$ with the highest weighting given to the PCL-R score. Past research indicates that the VRAG predicts violent recidivism moderately well (Doyle et al., 2002; Harris et al., 2002). Rice (1997) reported that the research on the VRAG and that of others on the prediction of violence have shown that long-term criminal violence can be predicted with a fair degree of accuracy among men previously arrested for a violent criminal offense.

The HCR-20 (Webster, Douglas, Eaves, & Hart, 1997) is a 20-item scale that is rated as 0, 1, or 2 in a similar fashion to the PCL:SV. The historical (H) variables represent background static risk factors associated with violence and the clinical (C) variables represent risk related to the individual's current presentation or dynamic factors such as the nature of their psychiatric symptoms, insight, and attitudes (Doyle et al., 2002). Finally the risk management (R) variables represent a structured assessment of future risk, such as the feasibility of future plans, social supports, and other contextual factors. The HCR-20 has been proven to be a reliable predictor of violent recidivism in the community and in inpatient settings (Doyle et al., 2002).

The sample by Doyle et al. (2002) primarily included male Caucasians who were detained under the legal classification of mental illness with a diagnosis of schizophrenia or an affective disorder with only 4% carrying a diagnosis of personality disorder. This sample had a relatively high base rate of violence with 52% having at least one aggressive incident in the first 12 weeks. The factors found to be associated with subsequent violence were source of referral, with prison and district hospital transfers more likely to be violent than special hospital transfers. This is not surprising, especially since special hospital transfers generally include those persons transitioned to the community, unlike those transferred from prison or district services that tend to be acutely ill and manifesting behavioral disturbances. Individuals having a prior history of a violent index offense were not found to be more violent as inpatients. For example, Doyle et al. (2002) found that having an index offense of homicide was more likely to be related to classification in the nonviolent group.

The primary factors associated with being violent were elevated scores on the three risk-assessment tools (PCL:SV, VRAG, HCR-20). However, Doyle et al. (2002) found that only the PCL:SV contributed significantly to the prediction of violence in their inpatient sample in Britain. All three tools correlated significantly with the frequency of institutional violence, but the PCL:SV demonstrated the most robust association (Doyle et al., 2002).

Dernevik, Grann, & Johansson (2002) suggested that clinicians were more interested in preventing violence than predicting it. According to Hart (1998, p. 123), "Clinicians are bound — morally, ethically and legally — to prove themselves wrong when they 'predict' violence: They must take every reasonable action to ensure that those at high risk for violence do not act violently." Therein lies the inherent problem of distinguishing between a successful prediction and a false positive prediction error (Dernevik et al., 2002). When examining inpatient violent behavior, there is great disparity in the reported occurrence of inpatient violence (Dernevik et al., 2002), which ranges from 2.7% for hospitalized patients (Spissel, Krischker, & Cording, 1998), 45% for outpatients (Lidz, Mulvey, & Gardner, 1993), to 61% for admitted patients (Zeiss, Tanke, Fenn, & Yesavage, 1996). The occurrence or base rates of violence will also fluctuate during any given hospital admission with some studies indicating that the majority of violent incidents occur shortly after admission (Dernevik et al., 2002). Additionally, these researchers concluded that inpatient violence is also impacted by staff to patient ratio, the physical environment and atmosphere of the unit or ward, and the administration style and notable alliances. Inpatient violence can lead to staff injuries, patient restraint, a reduction in staff morale, and it can increase the cost and effectiveness of treatment (Dernevik et al., 2002).

Dernevik et al. (2002) conducted a study to demonstrate that risk assessment was of little value on its own and needed to be used to create effective risk-management strategies. The goal of the study was to estimate the types of inpatient violence (along with their frequency) in a Swedish psychiatric facility and examine their relationship within the context of care episodes (high, medium, or low security). Another goal was to assess the predictive ability of the HCR-20, including the PCL:SV, on a Swedish population, under a variety of risk-management conditions. The study had a prospective design with 54 mentally disordered offenders assessed with the HCR-20 upon admission to the Swedish forensic hospital. Each of the participants had a violent index offense (assault 16, murder 10, grevious bodily harm (GBH) 4, robbery 3, sex crimes 6, arson 10, and other 5) and was classified as suffering from a severe mental disorder. They were then monitored for violent incidents during their admission to the forensic hospital (mean = 60 weeks) and a follow-up of the patients, who were either transferred to other facilities or conditionally released, was initiated for up to 52 weeks (Dernevik et al., 2002).

The subjects included 6 women and 48 men. Twenty-nine percent of the subjects had an Axis I diagnosis only (60% schizophrenia), 14% had an

Axis II (personality disorder) diagnosis only, 27% had both an Axis I and an Axis II diagnosis (36% schizophrenia), 9% had an Axis I diagnosis and learning difficulties and/or neuropsychological impairment, 7% had a personality disorder and learning difficulties and/or neuropsychological impairment, and 14% had all three diagnoses as stated above (Dernevik et al., 2002). Overall, 69% of the participants had an Axis I disorder with 36% having a schizophrenic disorder. The violent behavior was classified into five categories: (1) verbal aggression, (2) physical aggression to others, (3) self-harm, (4) violence to objects, and (5) other behaviors (e.g., telephone terror, stalking behavior, etc.). Three levels of risk management were coded and included: level one (high security), level two (medium security), and level three (low security).

The results of the study indicated that the base rate of inpatient violence was high considering the broader characterization of violent behavior as defined above. More than half of the subjects engaged in violent behavior on one or more occasions during their admission. There was also a drop in frequency of violence from high to low risk management with the patients who reacted violently in the high-security condition not likely to have advanced to the low-security condition. A third of the incidents in the high-security condition were categorized as the self-harming type. Physical violence to others was low in the high- and medium-risk management conditions, whereas it constituted 40% of the occurrences in the low condition. This was the most common factor for patients to be reintegrated into the high-security condition.

With respect to the risk-assessment instruments in the present study, the HCR subscales and the PCL:SV were not significantly related with inpatient violence in the high-security conditions but made a more accurate assessment in the medium- and low-security conditions. Dernevik et al. (2002) indicated that a tentative conclusion is that the risk factors in the HCR are accurate in predicting risk but that the intensive risk-management conditions in high security can reduce the risk. They pointed out that the PCL was not developed as a risk prediction instrument and the PCL:SV was not found to be related to violence in any of the inpatient settings. However, it was associated with violent recidivism in the follow-up condition. Psychopathy is a risk factor for future violence and tends to remain relatively constant throughout a patient's life span (Arrigo & Shipley, 2001; Shipley & Arrigo, 2004). Dernevik et al. (2002) suggested that psychopathy is a fundamental issue in risk management and, hence, subject to intervention and prevention measures. These researchers also noted the severity of the violent incident (e.g., a patient who is verbally threatening on one occasion and who commits repeated physical attacks on staff) had significant qualitative differences in consequences warranting fuller consideration with risk management.

Forensic Psychology and Policy Implications

In order for risk assessments to be more effective, it is important that they are systematic and that the assessment procedures or instruments are based on the population being examined. Moreover, the targeted risk factors should be broken down into more manageable components, they should be addressed and further evaluated through treatment planning, and the outcomes should be carefully evaluated (Woods et al., 2003). Watts et al. (2003) stressed the importance of considering the prevalence or base rates of violence in the population under scrutiny when interpreting the predictive accuracy of a risk assessment. Forensic psychologists must take into consideration both clinical dynamic criteria as well as historical static factors. Seifert et al. (2002) suggested that an individual prognosis is required with risk assessments, wherein particular items play a more central role than others. This model takes into consideration the existence and causal relationships of specific risk factors and the potential for negative outcomes for the individual in question. Risk assessment tools help to structure clinical judgments regarding potential violence. "Incorporating tools such as the HCR-20, which includes an assessment of psychopathy, into clinical assessments is likely to enhance the assessment process by structuring clinical judgments, informing risk management and treatment strategies, justifying and rationalizing clinical decisions, and by making the decision-making process more transparent" (Doyle et al., 2002, p. 152).

Research suggests that violent recidivism would be more effectively reduced and public safety enhanced if release decisions were based on risk of future violence alone, instead of recovery from a mental disorder (Rice, 1997). Rice (1997) suggested that when making policies regarding sentencing, decision brokers should consider that violent recidivism could be reduced without overall greater rates of incarceration if sentencing tribunals weighed the research-based likelihood of future violent offending. Moreover, she intimated that violence by psychopaths could be decreased through careful monitoring and supervision that reduced for the individual the personal gain to engage in the violent behavior, as a result of the increased likelihood of detection. Additionally, she reported that the close monitoring of, supervision pertaining to, and consequences for aggression and related antisocial behaviors by primary caretakers early on in one's life might help prevent the development of psychopathy in those persons with this genetic predisposition (Rice, 1997). Thus, as Rice (1997, p. 421) concluded: "There is every reason to believe that applying the results of violence research to make policy changes in the criminal justice system would make society safer."

Suggestions for Future Research

Future research should focus on risk assessments structured to assess for acute inpatient violence. Many of the most secure forensic hospitals have to make an assessment of "manifest dangerousness" to determine if a patient can be managed in a less restrictive hospital setting. This concept is ill defined and risk assessments and factors are based on empirical research for more long-term risk of violence and recidivism in the community. Additional prospective studies in British and other samples are needed to assess the predictive validity of risk-assessment tools (e.g., VRAG, HCR-20) for violent recidivism and other more long-term outcome measures (Doyle et al., 2002). Doyle et al. (2002, p. 152) also suggested that future research could enhance risk-assessment tools by adding other critical variables such as "symptom severity, interpersonal style, underlying beliefs, anger, and impulsivity" into violence risk assessment. Finally, future research should continue to explore the effects of risk management (Dernevik et al., 2002). Risk assessment should not be an isolated endeavor, especially because the point of risk assessment is to facilitate effective risk management. As Dernevik et al. (2002, p. 108) stated: "It is perhaps time to put more attention to this process of guidance, both in terms of communicating risk and designing effective interventions and management strategies to lower the risk of violent behavior." Rice (1997) indicated that while current strategies for offender therapy are not effective for psychopaths, clinicians should concentrate future efforts on developing more effective techniques that are more congruent with current theories of psychopathy.

Practice Update Section: Issues in International Criminal Forensic Psychology–Psychopathy

The empirical research on the construct of psychopathy has been largely undertaken by Canadian forensic psychologists. However, the implications of

(continued)

(Continued)

psychopathy assessment and its relevance for potential violent criminal offending or re-offending are witnessed internationally. Additionally, a clear understanding of the nature and consequences of psychopathy has critical implications for forensic psychology practice worldwide. Research has consistently demonstrated that psychopathic individuals are disproportionately more likely to commit violent crime when compared with the general population (e.g., Hare & Hart, 1993; Monahan, 1998). Clearly, psychopathy has a significant impact on risk for future violence, including the likelihood that an individual will engage in institutional violence. Hare (1993) described psycho-paths as "human predators who coldly, callously, and ruthlessly use charm, deceit, manipulation, threats, intimidation, and violence to dominate and control others and to satisfy their own selfish needs and desires" (p. 3). Therefore, it is critical that psychopaths are correctly identified for their own good and for the protection of those with whom the psychopath interacts (Shipley & Arrigo, 2001).

Typically, diagnosis represents a clinical shorthand that enables assessors to quickly identify a constellation of symptoms and to appropriately target certain areas for treatment. However, clinicians often do not speak a shared language when discussing psychopathy (Shipley & Arrigo, 2001). There is considerable diagnostic confusion between antisocial personality disorder (ASPD) and psychopathy. Shipley and Arrigo (2001) questioned how the most recent conceptualization of ASPD could take the place of psychopathy when it virtually ignores most of the prominent personality or interpersonal characteristics (e.g., malignant narcissism) found in Factor 1 that significantly defines it. The diagnostic criteria for ASPD emphasize criminal acts that only approximate Factor 2 of the psychopathy construct. Psychopathy refers to a more lifelong pattern of both certain personality traits and socially deviant behaviors.

Many researchers criticize the current diagnosis of ASPD as confounding it with criminality in general (Hart & Hare, 1997). According to Hare (2000), the vast majority (almost 90%) of criminals classified by the PCL-R as psychopathic are diagnosed with ASPD, but only 30% of those with the diagnosis of ASPD can qualify as psychopathic. A classification of psychopathy is much more serious within the context of risk assessment, and individuals do not age out of their criminal lifestyles in the same way that persons who are only diagnosed with ASPD would. Furthermore, in the offender population, the base rate for ASPD ranges from 50 to 80%, whereas, the base rate for psychopathy is 15 to 25% (Hare, 2000). The two classifications clearly overlap on behavioral criteria or on Factor 2, but otherwise, a determination of psychopathy is much more discriminative (Hare, 2000; Shipley & Arrigo, 2001).

The psychopathic designation typically is equated with being untreatable. Therefore, the consequences of misidentification are "severe, substantial, and enduring" (Shipley & Arrigo, 2001, p. 410). Clinicians have a responsibility to be well educated in diagnostic criteria, current research, and assessment instruments used to classify psychopathy. Therefore, forensic psychologists must be clear if they are diagnosing or classifying solely on the basis of antisocial behavior or psychopathic traits (Shipley & Arrigo, 2001).

As psychopathy gains momentum in the world of forensic mental health and as it has implications for sentencing, parole, sexually violent predator commitments, conditional release, amenability for treatment, and risk assessment in general, forensic mental health specialists should be trained to assess for it. When assessing for psychopathy, it is critical to use collateral data and to look for consistencies or inconsistencies across data sets. It is unacceptable to accept what an offender says at face value (Shipley & Arrigo, 2001). Psychopaths are very skillful at providing assessors information that is expected, particularly if these proclamations will advance the psychopath's self-interests. It is imperative that psychopathy be evaluated with care and professionalism (Shipley & Arrigo, 2001).

If a well-trained clinician is appropriately using the PCL-R, a classification of psychopathy should be based on well-validated personality and behavioral traits. Each of the 20 items should be rated on the definition carefully explained in the PCL-R manual and not on the clinician's perception of what the item (e.g., remorse) is (Hare, 1991). Furthermore, a determination of 0, 1, or 2 is based on the existence and pervasiveness of the trait or behaviors throughout the individual's life span as evidenced through interviews and historical information, not based on one incident alone (Hare, 1991; Shipley & Arrigo, 2001).

Finally, the psychopathic label carries significant consequences; therefore, mental health professionals have a significant responsibility when reaching this determination. Following a risk assessment, psychopaths are likely to be considered a high risk to the community (Rice, 1997). Whereas other psychiatric disorders can facilitate an insanity defense, diminish responsibility, or mitigate the consequences of a crime, psychopathy functions as an aggravating factor at the sentencing phase (Zinger & Forth, 1998). As such, "a determination of psychopathy at any stage of the criminal justice system can have severe and long-lasting consequences for persons so identified" (Shipley & Arrigo, 2001, p. 414).

PART II

Courts and the Legal System: Civil Forensics

CHAPTER 4

Civil Forensics

OVERVIEW

The legal system assumes an important role in the adjudication of noncriminal matters impacting the lives of persons with mental illness. In addition, nonadjudicatory remedies affecting parties injured by offenders, or those emotionally suffering because of the pain they may have caused the public, represent alternative societal responses to the problem of crime and violence. Broadly defined, these are efforts designed to produce civil justice. Psychologists assist the court system or other administrative boards in determining how best to realize specific outcomes in this forensic area.

There are six civil justice issues examined in this chapter. These particular topics demonstrate the variety of avenues wherein forensic psychologists, invested in the effective operation of the formal civil and informal civil court system, influence overall decision making. Subjects investigated include (1) defining mental illness, (2) the right to refuse (medical) treatment, (3) the "least restrictive alternative" doctrine, (4) evaluating psychiatric work–related disability, (5) duty to inform versus client confidentiality, and (6) victim–offender mediation. Similar to other chapters in this textbook, emphasis is placed on presenting a breadth of topics to canvass. This allows one to consider the broader justice implications for the field (i.e., civil forensics) in relationship to the various roles of the psychologist or expert practitioner.

Persons with mental illness can be, under specified conditions, hospitalized against their will. What is the meaning of mental illness for lawyers and psychologists? How is the mental illness construct employed for purposes of involuntary commitment? Persons identified as psychiatrically disordered can, under the law, exercise their right to refuse (medical) treatment. To what extent can the mentally ill invoke this right in the context of antipsychotic medication? What role does one's informed consent play in the decision to refuse treatment? How do the legal and psychological communities endorse the individual autonomy of a mentally disordered citizen in the wake of one invoking a treatment refusal right? The law requires that the psychiatric care persons receive must occur in the most nonrestrictive environment possible so that the individual's liberty (e.g., freedom of movement) is protected. How does the psycholegal establishment operationalize this standard? In addition to the locus of care, the least restrictive alternative doctrine refers to the type and quality of medical intervention and whether it is the least invasive form of psychiatric care. How, if at all, does the least restrictive alternative doctrine protect a person's freedom from unnecessary, unwanted, and harmful treatment? Mentally ill individuals may be eligible for social security benefits. What is the difference between the clinical and legal definition of disability? Who is eligible for benefits and what role do psychologists play in this process?

In addition to formal courtroom outlets and legal mechanisms for advancing the aims of civil forensics, psychologists are called upon to promote the interests of justice in the informal legal system as well. Mental health clinicians are, on occasion, presented with clients who may act violently toward others. Psychologists are also entrusted with safeguarding the confidentiality of what their clients describe to them. What are the legal and ethical obligations and limits of mental health professionals when a client poses a threat to a third party? Are there circumstances in which client confidentiality can (and must) be breached? Increasingly, jurisdictions around the country are adopting the philosophy of restorative justice at the postconviction phase of a case. A key dimension to restorative justice is reconciliation through victim–offender mediation (VOM). How does VOM work? How can forensic psychologists assist in the restorative justice process? How does VOM promote the interests of reconciliation for offenders, victims, and the community of which both are a part?

The legal system has a vested interest in the resolution of noncriminal disputes that affect citizens who are users of mental health services or are victims of crime. When the tools of the psychological sciences are relied upon to address these matters, forensic experts are responding to issues of civil justice. The six controversies presented in this chapter reveal the degree to which psychologists influence outcomes in both the formal and informal court system. Clearly, this chapter demonstrates that citizens are impacted by the legal system in a number of noncriminal contexts and that trained forensic specialists assume vital roles in the process of determining how best to address these concerns. As a matter of policy, then, the civil forensic field, in relation to the legal system, presents the skilled practitioner with a different set of issues to understand and/or interpret versus its adult and juvenile counterparts.

DEFINING MENTAL ILLNESS

Introduction

What exactly *is* mental illness and what is the significance of the concept for issues in law and psychology? Although the mental health community has generally used the term "mental illness" somewhat haphazardly for purposes of diagnosis and treatment (B. Winick, 1995), it assumes greater significance when its legal relevance appears in a wide variety of contexts. Most important, it is a prerequisite for civil commitment (as in the case of Gina illustrated below), and if a mental illness impacts critical functional capacities designated in the law, it has implications for the insanity defense and trial competency as well. Mental illness can also have a dramatic impact on determining competencies, such as competency to stand trial, to execute a will, or to manage property (B. Winick, 1995). However, a diagnosis of a mental illness alone is insufficient to determine if someone is incompetent to perform a function as described in the law (e.g., competence to stand trial). The forensic evaluator must explain the functional deficits present for the specific competency in question, as a result of mental illness or some other condition (e.g., mental retardation or medical condition). For example, the plea of insanity was rejected by a jury in the case of Andrew Goldstein, a man with a history of schizophrenia, who pushed a woman to her death in front of a subway train in New York City (Barnes, 2000).

Further, the definition of mental illness becomes an issue *after* an individual is found incompetent or legally insane. The sustained confinement of those found not guilty by reason of insanity (NGRI) is only permissible by law if a continued manifestation of mental illness exists. Individuals committed to a psychiatric hospital as incompetent to stand trial must still demonstrate substantial functional deficits relating to their factual and/or rational understanding of court-related issues or in their ability to participate in their defense as a result of a mental illness.

Given the importance of the mental illness concept in issues such as those described above, its legal definition and operationalization have significant consequences for psychology and the criminal justice system.

The concern, however, is that the very definition of mental illness is rarely (or perhaps never) made precise by legislators, and often results in broad, general descriptions. Despite the continuing controversy over the meaning of mental illness as a legal concern, legislators and courts have done very little to clarify the issue. The legal definition of "insanity" is different from the definitions of mental disorders/diagnoses commonly understood in the mental health arena. Slovenko (2002, p. 421) examined the question of whether or not psychiatric diagnosis should play a role in the legal process and concluded that it should, but it is "not always a *sine qua non*" in the disposition of a legal issue. It is now necessary to turn to the concept of mental illness in more detail, specifically within the context of civil commitment and insanity defenses.

> Gina Hampton is a 27-year-old musician in a large metropolitan area. Gina has a history of mental instability with diagnoses of narcissistic and antisocial personality disorders, as well as severe depression and occasional suicidal ideation. Recently, she was exposed to several stressful events, which included the death of a close friend and the breakup of a 5-year relationship. Her friends and family have noticed her mental state worsening over the past few weeks and fear that she may present a danger to herself or those around her. Some suggest that she be placed in a psychiatric hospital for further observation. Gina, however, insists that she is "fine" and resists any attempt at psychological intervention. Unconvinced, her friends and family wonder under which conditions Gina may be hospitalized against her will, as they feel it would be in her best interest at this time. The involuntary hospitalization of Gina, however, requires a finding that she is "mentally ill" and presents an imminent danger to self or others. Given that she has recently engaged in several dangerous behaviors, jeopardizing her own safety as well as that of others, the primary question is whether she is mentally ill in the eyes of the law.

Literature Review

Civil Commitment

The first substantive criterion for civil commitment is the presence of a mental impairment. Most jurisdictions define this as the existence of a mental illness or a demonstration that the individual is suffering from a "mental disorder" (Reisner & Slobogin, 1990). Consistent with basic due process, the Court has held that an individual who is not mentally ill cannot be involuntarily committed for civil purposes (see *Foucha v. Louisiana*, 1992). Because the existence of mental illness is a necessary prerequisite for civil commitment, the primary interest is then in the constitution of mental illness. What exactly must be found if an individual is to be hospitalized against his or her will?

Poletiek (2002) explored how psychiatrists and judges assess the dangerousness of mentally ill individuals evaluated for civil commitment. Results indicated that judges more often define "dangerousness" as harming others, as compared to psychiatrists who typically include harm to self in the definition. Werth (2001, p. 348) examined the civil commitment statues of all 50 states and the District of Columbia to determine "(1) what is required for a person who is believed to be at serious and imminent risk of self-harm to be eligible for involuntary hospitalization and (2) whether an attempt to involuntarily hospitalize was required or was merely an option when the requirements in number 1 were met." The results indicated that 85% of the jurisdictions mandated that dangerousness to self be the result of a mental illness, and just two jurisdictions required attempts at involuntary hospitalization if a person was found to be an imminent risk of harm to self.

A Canadian study found that individuals detained under civil commitment statutes were more likely to be male, diagnosed with schizophrenia, and already known to the criminal justice system, whereas those voluntarily committed were not (Crisanti & Love, 2001). Additionally, these researchers found that once hospitalized, involuntary patients stayed considerably longer than voluntarily admitted patients. In a study that examined the relationship between involuntary commitment and arrest ($N = 1,064$ involuntary subjects; $N = 1,078$ voluntary subjects), results indicated that subsequent criminal behavior was higher among those admitted under civil commitment legislation (Crisanti & Love, 2002).

Despite the involuntary commitment reform movements of the 1970s contesting that mental illness is a "bankrupt term easily manipulated" (Melton, Petrila, Poythress, & Slobogin, 1987, p. 217), many legislative attempts to define and operationalize the term create only vague and circular meanings (see Levy & Rubenstein, 1996; Melton et al., 1987). The law has imposed only minimal limitations on the term, often using broad and general definitions (B. Winick, 1995). Melton et al. (1987) cited one of the most specific legislative attempts to define mental illness as:

> ... a substantial disorder of thought, mood, perception, orientation or memory, any of which grossly impairs judgment, behavior, capacity to recognize reality, or ability to meet the ordinary demands of life, but shall not include mental retardation. (p. 221)

Such a proposal is far more precise than another statute, which reads, "a mentally ill person means a person whose mental health is substantially impaired" (Melton et al., 1987, p. 221). The legislative effort is, however, still controversial as it relies on equally vague terms such as "substantial," "grossly impaired," and "ordinary demands of life." Many statutes have, however, attained some degree of success by excluding conditions such as mental retardation, substance abuse, and epilepsy (Levy & Rubenstein, 1996; Melton et al., 1987). Additionally, alcohol and substance abuse problems are generally not considered a mental illness for legal purposes. Thus, by excluding some mental impairments, the law has limited the scope of psychiatric disorder to some degree. Nonetheless, the meaning of mental illness remains open to individual interpretation. Who, then, interprets?

The consistent imprecision with and neglect for operationalization by the legislature has left the courts to "fashion a definition for the words 'mentally ill' . . . thereby fill[ing] the void in the statutory hospital law" (*Dodd v. Hughes*, 1965, p. 542). With the responsibility of defining and assessing potential mental illness as it stands before them, the courts have further deferred to the profession of mental health (i.e., expert testimony by psychiatrists and psychologists) (Arrigo, 1993; Melton et al., 1987; Reisner & Slobogin, 1990; Slovenko, 2002). This power given to, or, more appropriately, *dependent on*, the medical and mental health communities in the decision-making process persists, even though substantial research has documented a lack of consensus among professionals in matters of diagnosis (Arrigo, 1993; 2002). Research has shown that psychologists and psychiatrists are not necessarily any more in agreement about what mental illness is than anyone else. There is a general consensus regarding criteria for a diagnosis in the mental health community but there is often debate regarding whether or not a particular individual meets the criteria for a disorder. Thus, the failure to legally define mental illness may be, in part, a function of psychology and medicine's lack of precision in defining and describing it, particularly in the concrete fashion often necessitated in the law.

For example, the M'Naughten standard for the insanity defense used by many jurisdictions often does not clarify if the reference to the defendant's understanding or appreciation of the wrongfulness of his or her actions refers to legal or moral wrongfulness. The case of Andrea Yates highlights this issue. She may have understood the legal wrongfulness of her actions, but her delusions rendered her unable to appreciate the moral wrongfulness of her actions. The severity of her postpartum depression coupled with psychosis led to delusions that she was saving her children from eternal damnation; yet, in her case, the insanity defense was not successful.

Insanity Defense

The various insanity defenses (tests) can only be used by individuals suffering from a mental disease or defect. In order to be "excused" from criminal behavior, the individual must not only be mentally ill, but the mental illness must directly cause a dysfunction that is relevant when the offense was committed (Melton et al., 1987). When it is a psycholegal question, a specific diagnosis is not the central issue. However, its impact on functional capacities or one's ability to know the difference between right and wrong and to conform one's behavior to the law is paramount. Thus, the functional impact of mental illness becomes the key issue. Melton et al. noted that with mental illness imprecisely defined, it would seem that "any mental disability that causes significant cognitive or volitional impairment will meet the threshold [of mental illness needed for insanity defenses]" (p. 199). The legal emphasis of "insanity" is on the cognitive and/or volitional impact of the disorder on the defendant's thinking, feeling, and behavior at the time of the alleged offense. Historically, however, the successful insanity defenses have generally arisen from individuals who were suffering from a psychosis or mental retardation. Studies suggest that 60–90% of defendants acquitted for reasons of insanity have been psychotic (Melton et al., 1987).

Very few case opinions attempt to define mental disease or defect. The few cases that have, however, define the concept narrowly. In other words, the courts generally have disapproved of many insanity conceptions including mildly psychotic individuals, dissociative disorders, and drug- and alcohol-induced insanity (Melton et al., 1987). Further, the American Psychiatric Association (APA) has defined "mental disease or defect" in a narrow sense, suggesting it should only include "severely abnormal mental conditions that grossly . . . impair a person's perception or understanding of reality" (APA, 1983). Thus, the definition of mental disease or defect for purposes of insanity defenses varies from state to state and is probably more broadly defined than some have suggested (Arrigo, 2002).

Foucha v. Louisiana

The Supreme Court shed some light on the meaning of mental illness in the case *Foucha v. Louisiana* (1992). Although the case considered the extent to which an individual could be confined *after* being found NGRI, it has some important implications for the meaning of mental illness in civil commitment and insanity defense matters. The Court held that it would be unconstitutional to detain an individual who was diagnosed only with antisocial personality disorder. The primary issue was whether it was constitutional to continue to detain an individual who had been acquitted but had recovered from his or her illness. The short answer from the Court was "no." The more relevant issue, however, was the meaning of mental illness. For purposes of involuntary commitment an individual must be shown to be mentally ill and dangerous, but the *Foucha v. Louisiana* case found that dangerousness and antisocial personality disorder were not sufficient. Thus, the implication was that personality disorders, at least antisocial personality disorder, did not constitute mental illness for purposes of involuntary confinement. The Court did not justify this finding, which left the issue unresolved. Thus, the impact of the Court's decision in *Foucha* may be more apparent in future decisions.

Forensic Psychology and Policy Implications

The long-standing failure of the legislature and the courts to adequately define mental illness leaves a number of issues for forensic psychological analysts and practitioners. Most important, it leaves the decision as to what constitutes mental illness and who is mentally ill to the attending forensic examiner. Regardless of the specific (or general) reasons arguing for or against psychology's involvement in the courtroom, its "expertise" is judged central to civil commitment and mental illness affairs. Thus, the *legal* meaning of mental illness has been "passed on" by the courts, only to be adopted by the "expert(s)" attending to the particular circumstances of individual cases (i.e., the treatment team) (Arrigo, 1993). In all likelihood this will continue. Thus, above all else, the meaning of mental illness becomes a significant issue for forensic psychologists.

Despite the disagreement among mental health professionals defining what mental illness is, the legal system finds it appropriate to leave the decision in the hands of a select few individuals in the mental health and/or medical field. Persons included in this definition would then differ depending on the case in question. Thus, two individuals with identical psychiatric conditions might be found "mentally ill" and "not mentally ill" depending on the definer. Unfortunately, because the courts rely almost entirely on disagreeing professionals to define this construct, someone like Gina (as seen in the case study above) may be involuntarily hospitalized in one city (or by one treatment team) and not in another city (or by another team). In general, however, the medical community has shown a preference for presuming mental illness. Given the medical community's *presumption* of illness when confronting uncertainty (Arrigo, 1993), it is not unreasonable to assume that borderline cases are frequently labeled mentally ill for legal (i.e., involuntary commitment) purposes. Thus, it would seem that forensic psychological practitioners are overinclusive in these matters. In other words, more non-mentally-ill individuals are involuntarily hospitalized than is warranted (Arrigo, 2002).

The forensic psychology implications are profound for individuals like Gina who face (potentially) legal intervention. While individual freedom, liberty, and self-determination must be recognized, forensic psychologists also must be concerned with more general matters of public safety and health. The line between the two is not clear, as evidenced in the law's failure to define mental illness. Thus, forensic psychology practitioners and policy analysts are left to determine where this line should be drawn. At this point, there is no correct answer. There is no determined future for Gina or others like her. If we know, however, that the legislature and the courts cannot define mental illness, psychology should at the very least assume the task of creating a *consistent* definition, one in which we could know what mental illness stands for in the legal context.

Suggestions for Future Research

To a large degree, the future of mental illness in the legal system depends on establishing an adequate psycholegal definition of mental illness. Consequently, it is imperative that research be targeted in this direction. Many attempts have been made by legislatures, courts, and even the APA to define mental illness, but none seem to have proposed any conclusive interpretations. Thus, the varying definitions of mental illness found in psychology, psychiatry, federal and state, statutes, court decisions, and the like necessitate comparative analyses. Research focused on establishing commonalities between proposed definitions in an attempt to establish a single, definitive concept of mental illness would be useful. More importantly, the effects of cases such as *Foucha* need to be analyzed in order to assess their future impact on other court and legislative decisions regarding mental illness and the law. Defining mental illness, is a very contentious and problematic area of study. It is an area where a significant amount of inquiry has already been conducted; however, these investigations have been of limited practicality. Thus, future case decisions and their implications must be systematically evaluated.

RIGHT TO REFUSE TREATMENT

Introduction

The concept of personal liberty is, perhaps, the most treasured of all human rights in contemporary American society. The long-standing contention that lies at the historical core of American legal and social thought holds that the individual should have the right to decide what does or does not happen to his or her body and mind. If one becomes physically ill, for example, one can often choose not to receive medical treatment. The same should arguably apply to mental illness. The legal reality is, however, that this freedom from unwanted intrusion is not always enjoyed by the mentally disordered citizen. In fact, in some situations, individuals are subjected to psychological treatment against their will. This is the controversy surrounding the "right to refuse treatment."

In the case of *In Re Commitment of Dennis H.* (2002), (cited in Vitacco & Packer, 2003), the Wisconsin Supreme Court upheld Wisconsin's Fifth Standard for civil commitment based on the inability to make informed choices regarding medication or treatment. The Wisconsin Supreme Court contended that it endeavored to balance the state's interest in protecting citizens unable to make informed decisions based on mental illness against their civil liberties. In this case, the constitutionality was upheld and the laws allowing for commitment of the mentally ill found incompetent to make treatment decisions were expanded (Vitacco & Packer, 2003).

Although questions of treatment refusal are relevant when considering the legal ramifications of *any* form of treatment, such questions are generally raised regarding psychotropic medications. The question of the right to refuse antipsychotic medication has been called "the most important and volatile aspect of the legal regulation of mental health practice" (Perlin, Gould, & Dorfman, 1995, p. 111). Issues including personal autonomy of the mentally ill to refuse medication, subjection to drugs which occasionally cause irreversible neurological side effects, and questions of "informed consent" and "competency," as well as the least restrictive alternative, all potentially become significant when confronting the right to refuse treatment. This section explores these concerns in the context of the right to refuse treatment.

Alyssa is a 34-year-old woman diagnosed by her psychiatrist as suffering from a thought disorder. Her symptoms, including delusions and occasional auditory hallucinations, have become progressively worse over the past year and a half.

Although there is no dispute as to whether Alyssa is mentally ill, she shows no signs of dangerousness to herself or others. Alyssa has been able to maintain a reasonably "safe" lifestyle and, although she is in a state of obvious mental discomfort, she is not a candidate for involuntary commitment at this time.

Following her diagnosis, her attending psychiatrist recommends that she be placed on Thorazine, an antipsychotic drug that may help to alleviate her symptoms. Following extensive consideration by Alyssa, she asks that the recommended treatment *not* be implemented. In other words, she asks not to be placed on Thorazine. Alyssa reached her decision after learning about the drug. She found that it often causes severe side effects, which may be permanent. Alyssa decides that the risk is too high and she wishes to seek alternative treatment(s).

Upon learning of Alyssa's request, however, her psychiatrist questions her competence to make such a decision. He questions whether a reasonable person in need of psychiatric treatment could reach such a decision, as it would clearly not be in her best interest at this time. In light of her wishes and his concern, does Alyssa have a right to refuse medication? Does her psychiatrist have a right to involuntarily treat her as he sees fit? How exactly does the issue of competence come into play?

Literature Review

The right to refuse treatment is considered the "most controversial issue in forensic psychiatry today" (Perlin et al., 1995, p. 111; Winick, 1997). To fully understand its impact, one must consider the issue in light of a number of other important legal concerns; namely, the least restrictive alternative (LRA) doctrine, competency issues, and the doctrine of informed consent. Each of these matters as they relate to the right to refuse treatment are briefly discussed in this section.

Least Restrictive Alternative Doctrine and Right to Refuse Treatment

For individuals in need of psychiatric attention, the right to refuse treatment becomes relevant within the context of the LRA doctrine. The LRA doctrine holds that individuals be placed in the least restrictive setting when their condition necessitates state intervention. This doctrine also implies that the least restrictive *method* of treatment be employed. Thus, the goal is to treat the individual in a manner that is least intrusive upon his or her personal liberty (Atkinson & Garner, 2002; Lin, 2003). Some researchers suggest that the least restrictive alternative should also be interpreted to take into consideration the patient's views, as well as clinicians and legislatures (Atkinson & Garner, 2002; Say & Thomson, 2003). Say and Thomson (2003, p. 542) stated: "Health professionals are increasingly encouraged to involve patients in treatment decisions, recognizing patients as experts with a unique knowledge of their own health and their preferences for treatments, health states, and outcomes." However, these researchers point out that some doctors may wish to maintain the imbalance of power between themselves and their patients, and patients may be hesitant to share their preferences.

Without question, the administration of any treatment could be regarded as an intrusion on personal liberty if the citizen did not wish to receive the treatment (Winick, 1997). For example, the administration of psychotropic medication(s) to alleviate symptoms may be regarded as necessary, but may also significantly effect the individual's mental functioning. In this instance, one may not wish to be subjected to certain primary effects and side effects of medication. Thus, if a less restrictive alternative is available, it must be considered.

Doctrine of Informed Consent

The doctrine of informed consent requires that persons be supplied adequate information concerning treatment prior to consenting. In this way, the individual is able to make a well-informed decision regarding the suggested treatment they might receive. Generally, adequate information consists of the risks and benefits of treatment, the potential side effects, the chance of improvement both with and without the treatment, and any other treatments that may be available. The doctrine applies in a number of situations, which include administration of medication, tests, and surgical procedures (Levy & Rubenstein, 1996).

While the doctrine of informed consent applies to the general adult public, it also applies to the mentally ill to the extent that they are competent to make such decisions. Thus, the existence of a mental disability alone does not take the right to make treatment decisions away from an individual. In order for such a right to be lost, the individual must be found incompetent by a court of law. While this seems simple enough, some controversial issues arise concerning the incompetent or civilly committed mentally ill and their right to refuse treatment.

Competency

A competent consent to treatment requires that the individual make a reasoned decision to accept or refuse a proposed procedure. As noted, this generally means that the individual understands the treatment, its risks and benefits, and the potential alternatives. Thus, weight is not placed on the final decision itself, but rather on the manner in which the person came to such a conclusion.

An individual is not regarded as incompetent simply because his or her decision is not consistent with the majority of patients, is irrational, is not in the person's best medical interest, or is not consistent with the psychiatrist's recommendation (Winick, 1997). In the above case of Alyssa, her refusal of antipsychotic medication, given the potential side effects, is not an incompetent decision for the reasons mentioned above. Her choice must be assessed in light of what she considers a better quality of life (Levy & Rubenstein, 1996; Say & Thomson, 2003).

Thus, the standards for competency concerning the right to refuse treatment are similar to other competencies. Although there is currently no standard test to determine competency, it generally follows that the individual must understand the implications of the treatment and be able to make a rational choice based on this understanding. If the individual is not competent to make such a decision, another important controversy arises. That is, who makes the decision in his or her place? Generally, this decision is made by a panel of psychiatrists who must decide if, in fact, the individual is not capable of making such a decision and whether the proposed treatment is in the individual's best interest. Treatment-related decisional capacity is a frequently debated issue that invokes the question of guardianship (Chopra, Weiss, Stinnett, & Oslin, 2003; Palmer, Nayak, Dunn, Appelbaum, & Jeste, 2002; Teaster & Roberto, 2002). Teaster and Roberto (2002, p. 176), identified "third-party behavior, mental illness or personal behavior, and cognitive impairments or limitations" as the events most likely to precipitate guardianship.

Following the Court's decision in *Washington v. Harper* (1990), however, no finding of incompetency is necessary if the individual is judged to be mentally ill and either "gravely disabled" or poses a "likelihood of serious harm" to self or others (Slobogin, 1994, p. 687). Thus, similar to civil commitment law, individuals may not have a right to refuse treatment if it is in the state's best interest to protect the community. For further information, The section in Chapter 10, An Offender's Right to Refuse Treatment.

Forensic Psychology and Policy Implications

One of the prevailing controversies regarding the right to refuse treatment it is theoretical application versus practical application. In theory, the right was intended to place final decisions regarding the type and extent of treatment in the hands of the citizen rather than the medical or mental health professional (Arrigo, 1996). In practice, however, the patient merely has the right to object to treatment decisions made by the attending clinician. In such cases, the decision may be reviewed by a team of clinicians to determine the appropriateness of the chosen treatment. Thus, in practice, the final decision concerning treatment of the mentally ill and its consequent effect on the individual's personal liberty ultimately remain in the hands of the clinician or forensic expert. Although the intention of the doctrine was to consider individual interests in the name of unwanted intrusions on personal liberty, the practice of mental health treatment essentially disregards this perspective and reinforces the power that the medical community holds over those judged to be mentally ill.

Yet, in many cases the mental health professional is concerned about the best interest of the patient, who if decompensated may be incapable of rational decision making for his or her own welfare. For example, a patient who was released from an inpatient psychiatric hospital into the community during the Texas summer heat died shortly thereafter from heat stroke on the streets. His inability to make rational decisions regarding his own personal welfare and lack of resources contributed to his death. It is very common to observe schizophrenic patients in inappropriate dress, sometimes wearing several layers of clothing, when it is hot outside. Ideally, our communities would abound with resources for the mentally ill. However, in reality, community resources are woefully inadequate and the welfare of those who are unable to adequately care for themselves must be considered (Arrigo, 2002). In many cases, mental health professionals are not the oppressors, instead they are attempting to improve the quality of life, and in some instances sustain the physical life, of the mentally ill patient. Clinicians are in the precarious position of balancing patient care with civil liberties (Failer, 2002).

Similarly, questions of competency are often raised only when acceptance or refusal of treatment differs from the opinion of the medical community. Decisions that are consistent with the psychiatrist, for example, are rarely questioned. In the above case of Alyssa, the psychiatrist recommended Thorazine to treat her thought disorder. Had Alyssa concurred with the psychiatrist's recommendation, there would have been no issue regarding competency. Psychiatrists often accept a patient's consent without further consideration if it is consistent with the physician's opinion. When a patient challenges the treatment recommendation, however, questions of competency are likely to be raised, particularly if they could compromise the health and safety of the patient and others. Often, it is thought that the individual lacks insight into his or her own condition and, thus, is not capable of making rational treatment decisions. In this instance, the individual may be subjected to a competency hearing to determine his or her capacity to make such a decision (Levy & Rubenstein, 1996). Thus, the right to refuse treatment is often not a right at all, but rather a right to object and be subjected to a hearing (Winick, 1997).

Considerable literature and public attention surround the "antitherapeutic" aspect of the right to refuse treatment, but the "therapeutic" aspect also must be considered. Examples of the beneficial nature of the right to refuse treatment include judicial or administrative hearings (following the citizen's refusal of recommended treatment) to ensure that the mentally ill individual has the opportunity to fully present his or her case in a formal legal setting; the consequent procedures that help to prevent the inappropriate use of medications (e.g., for punishment or convenience); and the hearings that ensure that psychiatrists are not prescribing the wrong medication, wrong dosages, or ignoring concerns of the patient regarding side-effects (Perlin et al., 1995). Thus, in addition to the negative or antitherapeutic aspects of the right to refuse treatment, forensic psychology must also consider the beneficial or therapeutic aspects of such a right (Winick, 1997).

Suggestions for Future Research

Some research has been conducted exploring treatment outcomes of refusers and differences between clinical and judicial reviews of petitions for involuntary medication (Perlin et al., 1995). Overall, however, there is a lack of quality research concerning the various therapeutic and antitherapeutic effects of the right to refuse treatment (Arrigo & Tasca, 1999). Thus, research on quality of life, impacted after a decision to accept or refuse treatment, may be beneficial. As noted above, there is no standard test for competency. Although competency to accept or refuse treatment stands as a major legal issue, it seems that a more direct confrontation of this issue is needed.

LEAST RESTRICTIVE ALTERNATIVE DOCTRINE

Introduction

One of the most significant developments in mental health law and policy over the past 20 years concerns what may be regarded as the third substantive criterion for commitment. The LRA doctrine requires that individuals be placed in the least restrictive setting when their condition necessitates state intervention. In situations involving persons who are considered dangerous to self or others, and are, thus, candidates for involuntary commitment, the restrictiveness of the setting must be a consideration. In addition to setting, however, the doctrine also requires the least restrictive method of treatment. The ultimate goal, then, is to protect the individual's freedom from "unnecessary and harmful treatment" (Arrigo, 1993, p. 152) while serving the individual's interest in receiving effective treatment and services.

Given that the restrictiveness of a setting and the type of treatment administered become a concern of the state, several issues arise. First, the concept of restrictiveness (like the concepts of mental illness and dangerousness) must be adequately defined and operationalized. In other words, what settings and treatment plans constitute less restrictive ones versus others? The traditional assumption has been that hospitalization is the most restrictive setting and that other settings such as community-based programs become progressively less restrictive. This assumption, however, has been the subject of much debate. In particular, this debate hinges on the issue of what is truly in the best interest of the individual. Like many forensic controversies, this matter becomes a common point of disagreement between psychology and the law. This section explores some of the key issues with regard to the LRA doctrine.

> John is a 42-year-old librarian with a history of mental illness. Though prone to bouts of mental deterioration, his functioning has historically returned to "normal" within a few weeks. John is currently single with no children and no living family members. During this particular week, John's functioning has been markedly poor. He is unable to perform his work-related duties and is clearly unable to care for himself. While he represents no danger to himself or others, he is unquestionably in need of psychiatric care. John's coworkers were concerned for his well-being, and this

prompted him to seek help. After examination by several mental health professionals, it was decided that John be required to participate in some treatment program. Thus, John is a candidate for commitment. The question for John is such: What is the best placement and treatment for him given that he represents no danger to himself or others? Is involuntary hospitalization really the best alternative given John's individual needs?

Literature Review

The legal basis for the LRA doctrine is rooted in First Amendment rights. The First Amendment states that the state may only impose on individual liberty to the extent that it is necessary to ensure state interests (Melton et al., 1987). Because civilly committing individuals is a significant imposition on individual liberty, the argument posed by the LRA doctrine is that the state may only commit persons to the extent that it is absolutely necessary to protect the individual, the community, and provide treatment (Melton et al., 1987; Perlin, 1999). Therefore, if release to the care of family or friends, community outpatient services, or a stay in a supervised community facility are all that is necessary to effectively treat an individual and protect state interests, this form of release becomes a less restrictive alternative than hospitalization. Moreover, it is in the best interest of individual liberty. In such cases, commitment to a state hospital would arguably be unconstitutional (Perlin, 1999).

The first case to apply the LRA concept to mental health (the commitment process) was *Lake v. Cameron* (1966). In this case an elderly, demented woman opposed her commitment to a hospital. Though disoriented and prone to wandering, her danger was not significant enough to demand confinement in a locked psychiatric facility. Although supervision may have been necessary for Ms. Lake, involuntary confinement in a hospital was clearly unnecessary (Munetz & Geller, 1993). Judge Bazelon wrote that "deprivations of liberty solely because of dangers to the ill persons themselves should not go beyond what is necessary for their protection" and that ". . . an earnest effort should be made to review and exhaust available resources of the community in order to provide care reasonably suited to [Ms. Lake's] needs" (*Lake v. Cameron*, 1966, p. 657). Such efforts are the duty of the court when deprivation of liberty is at stake. The court implied this by stating that it had an "affirmative duty to explore alternatives to hospitalization before committing Lake to an institution"

(Melton et al., 1987, p. 224). Thus, the concept of least restrictive alternative should be employed in situations involving commitment for mental health reasons. The goal is to meet the patient's needs in the least restrictive setting (Durbin, Cochrane, Goering, & Macfarlane, 2001). Durbin et al. (2001) applied a level-of-care model to 307 inpatients and 284 outpatients in Ontario, Canada, and found that only 10% of current inpatients needed to remain in the hospital, and greater than 60% could live independently in the community with adequate supports.

After the *Lake v. Cameron* decision, a number of states began to implement the concept of LRA into their commitment laws. By 1977, two-thirds of the states incorporated it, in some way, into their laws (Hoffman & Faust, 1977). Shortly after the Hoffman and Faust study, the President's Commission on Mental Health (1978) stated that the concept of LRA concerns the "objective of maintaining the greatest degree of freedom, self-determination, autonomy, dignity, and integrity of body, mind, and spirit for the individual while he or she participates in treatment or receives services" (Munetz & Geller, 1993, p. 967). Thus, by the late 1970s the LRA concept was a significant national concern. By the early 1990s, the mental health laws and policies of nearly every state included the concept (Munetz & Geller, 1993).

Perhaps the most fundamental and disputed matter with regard to LRA centers upon the question: "What is restrictive?" According to Bachrach (1980), several assumptions are employed when considering "restrictive" in individual cases. First, that certain environments (e.g., hospital, halfway house, etc.) are inherently good or bad regardless of the individual in question. Second, there is a correlation between the quality of restrictiveness and the class of the facility in question. The last assumption identified by Bachrach, and, perhaps more of a summary of the first two, is that a continuum exists in which a hospital is the most restrictive environment and living in the home is the least restrictive. This final assumption places importance on the type of facility in question rather than those facilities within a specific category. For example, there is an assumption that all hospitals are more restrictive than all halfway houses. According to Bachrach, this is a false assumption. In reality, it is entirely possible that what is commonly regarded as a more restrictive type of residential facility may in fact be less restrictive than a poorer quality facility that is of a lesser presumed restrictiveness. Thus, the type of facility appears to be of less significance than the individual's needs and the quality of the particular facility.

Several proposals have been made with regard to what determines the restrictiveness of a given residential facility. Perhaps the most informative is that of Carpenter (1978), who noted that, in addition to the type of facility, we should consider the

> ... location, staffing, specific programs, treatment provided, patient mix, emphasis on rehabilitation, degree of expectations of patients' performance, degree of autonomy granted to patients, extraresidential programs for patients, limitations on length of stay, and the facility's track record of success and its specified and unspecified goals (Munetz & Geller, 1993, p. 969).

With each of these variables, as well as others, equally contributing to the level of restrictiveness, it is easy to understand how a given type of institution may be only one consideration. Thus, a more restrictive type of facility (e.g., state hospital) that ranks high on several of these variables, may in fact be less restrictive than a facility that is presumed to be less restrictive (e.g., halfway house) and that ranks low on many of the aforementioned variables.

As previously reviewed, one of the commonly used alternatives to hospitalization is commitment to outpatient treatment. A considerable amount of clinical research has addressed the issue of outpatient commitment since the late 1980s and several attempts to establish clinical guidelines have followed (R. Miller, 1992). The problem, however, is that no standard definition or consensus among states exist, which outline what practices are consistent with involuntary outpatient commitment (Arrigo, 1993). J. D. Brown (2003) contends that involuntary outpatient commitment statutes were developed in response to disorganized community mental health service delivery and patient treatment noncompliance. He indicated that significant problems have been evident in the implementation, enforcement, and successful measurement of involuntary outpatient commitment. Cornwell and Deeney (2003), however, supported the use of preventative outpatient commitment as a useful adjunct to conditional release or to a least restrictive placement alternative.

Proponents of involuntary outpatient commitment argue that mentally ill persons benefit from such practices as their freedom and autonomy increase. For a majority of the time, they are not subject to the impositions that may be present in hospitals. At the same time, some structure remains. The mentally ill enjoy the benefits of hospitalization (i.e., treatment, rehabilitation) while their lives are not governed to the extent that they would be in an inpatient facility.

Though initially recommended by legal scholars as an alternative to involuntary hospitalization, there has been an increasing focus of late by the legal field concerning the efficacy of such an option (Perlin, 1999). Two common concerns voiced by legal scholars are that involuntary outpatient commitment will (1) lead to broader social control over persons who are not subject to hospitalization and (2) contribute toward the depletion of already scarce community resources (R. Miller, 1990). Availability of community resources continues to be the primary obstacle to the effective employment of outpatient commitment.

Forensic Psychology and Policy Implications

The LRA doctrine, as with most mental health law and policy, is not without significant controversy. One of the major concerns with the LRA doctrine is similar to those identified with the criteria for civil commitment. First, the statutes are imprecise. As Munetz and Geller (1993) noted: "Physicians and other mental health professionals are mandated to choose the least restrictive treatment alternative for psychiatric patients without necessarily understanding what the mandate means or how to carry it out" (p. 967).

Second, and related to the first concern, statutes often specify only treatment in the least restrictive environment. The doctrine's intention was to ensure that hospitalization occurs only as a last resort and when absolutely necessary (Melton et al., 1987). The legal concept, however, has essentially been understood as treatment "anywhere but in the state hospital" (Munetz & Geller, 1993, p. 968). Thus, the treatment setting has often been the only basis for measurement. In light of this, there is a presumption that hospitalization is the most restrictive alternative (setting) with progressively less restrictive settings available (e.g., community). As Melton et al. (1987) noted, however, such a presumption fails to consider that treatment modalities also are restrictive. Thus, certain types of treatment in the community may be more restrictive than the physical constraints of a hospital under different treatment modes (Failer, 2002).

For example, is community-based treatment accompanied by long–term psychoactive medication less restrictive than hospitalization not requiring the use of heavy medications? This question alone has been the topic of considerable debate. In fact, in *Guardianship of Richard Roe III* (1981) the court noted that it was unable to answer such a question. Thus, when the issue of least restrictive environment includes a decision assessing whether forced medication is more of an intrusion on personal liberty than hospitalization, even the court has not been able to reach a suitable conclusion. In this sense, treatment modalities are important when considering the extent of state intervention, the least restrictive of which is the ideal.

Another important consideration regarding the LRA doctrine was raised by Arrigo (1993). He noted that decisions regarding the individual's best interest are often left to state mental hospitals. Thus, mental health professionals are the primary figures in LRA decisions. It is, however, unlikely that such professionals would opt against drug treatment or confinement in psychiatric hospitals when questions arise concerning treatment. Doing so would essentially require mental health professionals to admit that their current methods of treatment are, perhaps, ineffective or only marginally effective. Thus, it seems unlikely that recommendations by the very people in charge of the decisions would include options other than the conventional restrictive settings and treatment methods.

In general, then, much of the disagreement concerning the LRA doctrine can be regarded as a fundamental difference in perspective. The legal goal is to minimize intrusions of liberty, while the clinical goal is to determine the most effective treatment available for the mentally ill individual and, subsequently, to implement that treatment plan (Munetz & Geller, 1993). Thus, the goals of the legal system and the mental health system may often conflict. The concept of LRA requires involvement by the mental health field, which ascertains what the least invasive and most effective psychiatric intervention is as well as deciding what the least restrictive environment is, for that treatment. Thus, effective policy analysis and implementation of new initiatives require the insight of psychological, medical, and legal scholars. Forensic psychology, perhaps, provides this insight by addressing both mental health and legal issues from within one framework.

Suggestions for Future Research

Based on the literature concerning the LRA doctrine, several important considerations are apparent when questioning its future status. First, it is necessary to determine exactly what "restrictive" implies. As discussed earlier, there has been considerable debate exploring what settings and treatments (and combinations thereof) are, in fact, less restrictive. The answer depends on the needs of the individual in question. Thus, methods of relating "least restrictive" to the specific necessities of the individual become crucial in the future employment of the LRA doctrine. In this sense, psychology and law must realize that the resolution of the issue requires joint cooperation. Future research must explore the differences inherent in each of these disciplines and calculate ways to reach mutual agreement on what the LRA doctrine implies for given individuals.

Second, and related to the first issue, is the need for more empirical studies concerning individuals affected by the doctrine. In other words, what are the experiences of persons subjected to commitment (both hospitalization and outpatient) compared to those in community facilities? Are there fundamental differences in individual well-being, treatment effectiveness, and feelings of self-determination? While legal and mental health scholars continue to debate the issue, the input of the very persons affected by the doctrine have been somewhat neglected (Arrigo, 2002). Additional research in these two areas may help resolve some of the controversy surrounding the LRA doctrine and its implications for individuals and for forensic psychological practice.

EVALUATING PSYCHIATRIC WORK-RELATED DISABILITY

Introduction

Many mentally ill individuals are unable to maintain gainful employment due to the debilitating effects of their psychiatric symptoms (e.g., paranoia, severe depression, and panic attacks). The onset of mental illness prevents some individuals from learning vocational skills and chronic symptoms negatively impact their social and cognitive abilities, emotions, and behavior in such a way that they are unable to support themselves through employment. Forensic psychologists working in the civil forensics arena are increasingly asked to conduct disability evaluations based on mental illness. Persistent, severe mental illness is one of the most common reasons for disability claims. Psychologists and psychiatrists often are asked to evaluate whether or not psychiatric symptoms prevent an individual from functioning in a work setting (Enelow & Leo, 2002). Title I of the Americans with Disabilities Act (ADA) regulates employment discrimination against "qualified individuals with a physical or mental disability that substantially limits a major life activity" (cited in Gioia & Brekke, 2003,

p. 302). A study examined the work experiences of 20 young adults with recent-onset schizophrenia referred to the California Department of Vocational Rehabilitation (DVR) for vocational assessments. Some of the individuals in the study were able to maintain employment and some were not. Consider the following case illustration (Gioia & Brekke, 2003, p. 303):

> Mr. E, a 24-year-old white man, was the only one of the four participants in group 3 to resume his job bagging groceries after his diagnosis of schizophrenia. He was also the only one to earn more than minimum wage. His symptoms were initially job related. He believed he was receiving messages from the products he was bagging and that he had to perform actions by rhyming key words from the message. He stated that things got worse, "every decision was based on a sign."
>
> When these incidents began, Mr. E did not know what was happening to him. However, after his hospitalization he became aware of how severe his problems had become and how difficult it might be for him to return to work. He took a break from work and school to recuperate. However, his paranoid thoughts continued to be a daily presence. After two months Mr. E received a call from the store manager asking him to come back to work because the store was short staffed. ... Mr. E did return to work with a reduced hourly schedule, and along with his father he worked out an accommodation plan with the store manager.

Vocational rehabilitation programs and employers who are willing to accommodate the mentally ill are rare. Furthermore, the refractory symptoms of some mentally ill people prevent them from working altogether. The stigma of mental illness and the fears and misconceptions regarding psychiatric disorder often preclude many employers from accommodating the mentally ill as they would the physically handicapped. The following section explores the role of mental health professionals in evaluating for disability based on mental illness and the issues and potential pitfalls of disability benefits.

Literature Review

The national unemployment rate for persons with mental illness is approximately 80–90% (Finch & Wheaton, 1999). Several empirically supported reasons for the high unemployment rate for this group include stigma and the belief that the mentally ill are always violent, unreliable, unpredictable, and irrational (Hong, 2002; Marini, 2003). Employers are more skeptical about hiring the mentally ill than other disability groups (Black, 1988; Marini, 2003). Since 1935, the Social Security Administration (SSA) by way of the Social Security Act, provides income to retired workers, disabled individuals, and families of deceased workers (R. J. Leo, 2002). The SSA defines "disability" as:

> ...the inability to engage in any substantial gainful activity by reason of any medically determinable physical or mental impairment which can be expected to result in death or which has lasted or can be expected to last for a continuous period of no less than 12 months. (Social Security Act, Section 223 (d), cited in MacDonald-Wilson, Rogers, & Anthony, 2001, p. 218).

The SSA disability programs are made up of the Social Security Disability Insurance (SSDI) and Supplemental Security Income (SSI) programs (R. J. Leo, 2002). SSDI benefits are derived from a person's prior work (FICA payments), as compared to SSI benefits paid out from revenue funds of the U.S. Treasury. Individuals who receive SSI typically have very little or no previous work history. SSI provides a form of financial support for the marginalized and often indigent mentally ill. According to the Social Security Advisory Board (2001), psychiatric problems resulted in 22% or the largest single factor in disability awards during the 1999 fiscal year. R. J. Leo (2002) reported that over half of disability claimants have a mental disorder and many are diagnosed with mental retardation. Out of the remaining mental impairments, schizophrenia accounts for one-third.

According to the SSA, disability prevents an individual from engaging in simple, repetitive work (Enelow & Leo, 2002). Characteristics essential to work such as attention and concentration, ability to relate to others, ability to adapt to change, and to effectively maintain activities of daily living are seriously impaired. Factors affecting work performance such as attention and concentration can be assessed by observing the patient's ability to attend appropriately to an interview and to the surroundings, and more formally, through psychological testing. Data sources involve interviewing claimants as to their typical daily activities to ascertain their skill level, as well as any available third party or corroborating records or sources. The SSA may require formal psychological testing, for example, the Wechsler Adult Intelligence Test, Third Edition (WAIS-III), to evaluate the degree of cognitive impairment or the like, related to mental retardation, dementia, or head injury (Enelow & Leo, 2002). These researchers stated that, if required for the disability claim, the SSA will often request and pay for the formal psychological testing.

The evaluator must consider whether or not this individual has the capacity to participate in simple, repetitive tasks or adapt to concrete routines. For example, psychomotor retardation or slowing in depression could interfere with an individual's ability to keep up with the required pace at work (Enelow & Leo, 2002). Enelow and Leo (2002, p. 294) identified several essential work tasks for individuals to function in the competitive work force that are organized as either cognitive/intellectual functions or social functions. The six cognitive/intellectual functions include the ability to: (1) comprehend and follow instructions; (2) perform simple, repetitive tasks; (3) maintain a work pace appropriate to a given work load; (4) perform complex or varied tasks; (5) make generalizations, evaluations, and decisions without immediate supervision; and (6) accept and execute responsibility for direction, control, and planning. The two main social functions include the ability to relate to other people beyond giving and receiving instructions and the ability to influence others.

These authors also claimed that it is important to assess whether or not a patient can follow through with tasks in a timely fashion, maintain attendance, and be punctual. Certainly, if Mr. E in the case illustration above had been observed responding to internal stimuli or talking to the groceries he was bagging, customers might have been frightened. Regarding social factors, the capacity to interact with others appropriately is critical. Communicating appropriately with coworkers, supervisors, consumers, and not exhibiting behavioral extremes are all important component of maintaining gainful employment. Enelow and Leo (2002) further described the necessity of social skills such as maintaining appropriate interpersonal space; using clear, goal-directed speech with rational and organized thoughts; dressing appropriately; maintaining personal hygiene; and above all else, not engaging in hostile or aggressive behaviors.

The evaluator or treating sources must be able to provide clinical information to the SSA in such a way that it can be applied meaningfully to essential work-related abilities (Enelow & Leo, 2002). They pointed out that the evaluator must consider that even if the individual is unable to perform prior work (e.g., accounting), it does not necessarily preclude their ability to perform in other areas. If they can still work in some lesser skilled or different area, despite their mental illness, their claim will be rejected. SSI or SSDI does not indicate that you must be able to work at your prior level unless you are over the age of 55, which is considered "advanced age." In that instance, the SSA presumes that you would be less adaptable to new job-related skills and you are not expected to take on a new line of work.

Criterion to be applied to the review of case material includes a determination of whether or not the claimant's earnings are substantial. If so, the disability claim is rejected. Beginning on January 1, 2001, wages are considered substantial if one's monthly earnings exceed $740 (R. J. Leo, 2002). Severity of psychiatric impairment is another criterion that is based on the chronicity or expected course and the effect on four areas of functioning to include: "activities of daily living, social functioning, concentration and adaptation, and frequency and duration of episodes or symptom exacerbation" (R. J. Leo, 2002, p. 286). Serious impairment of any two of these areas, or severe impairment in any one, will also qualify for substantial psychiatric impairment. The SSA provides listings of psychiatric impairments in terms of symptoms and behaviors based on *DSM-IV* criteria that presume disability. If the history, course, symptoms, and severity of the mental disorder, described by the treating clinician, are compatible with those provided in the listings, the claimant is awarded disability benefits. If the symptom or disorder is not found in the listings, they are then evaluated to determine whether or not the impairments would prevent the claimant from returning to prior work, or if under the age of 55, performing any other work available (Enelow & Leo, 2002; R. J. Leo, 2002).

The chronicity or continuation of residual symptoms of some mental disorders such as schizophrenia and affective and anxiety disorders for a minimum of two years, despite treatment, may still support the finding of a disability claim. A claim that is rewarded is contingent upon compliance with treatment (e.g., attending psychotherapy and medication compliance) and little evidence for continued improvement (R. J. Leo, 2002). If awarded, disability benefits eligibility is typically reevaluated every three years.

A treating clinician may be asked to provide relevant clinical data on psychological impairments that affect vocational abilities when a patient has filed a disability claim (R. J. Leo, 2002). According to the SSA (2001, p. 64–039), the treating mental health professional is "neither asked nor expected to make a decision as to whether the patient is disabled." After all, this is the ultimate issue to be decided by the SSA. Just as a diagnosis of schizophrenia does not necessarily result in a finding of incompetency to stand trial, a clinically disabling condition does not necessarily result in the legal definition of disability (Druss et al., 2001; R. J. Leo, 2002). After a disability claim has been filed with the SSA, the file is evaluated by a psychologist or psychiatrist hired by the SSA who acts as a disability reviewer (R. J. Leo, 2002). These evaluators apply the legal standard to their paper review to determine eligibility. They do not reevaluate the patient. The ability to adjudicate the case is contingent upon the usefulness of the clinical information provided by mental health professionals and information provided by the claimant, particularly the report of the treating clinician (R. J. Leo, 2002).

Forensic Psychology and Policy Implications

There are many inconsistencies from region to region and state to state in awarding benefits. According to Marini (2003), there is typically a 5- to 12-month waiting period for those applying for SSI/SSDI. Thirty-three percent of applicants are successful on their first attempt. Approximately 50% of those denied will appeal the decision, and after more records are collected, the SSA will conduct a second review with 15% on average approved. Out of the 85% denied a second time, approximately 68% will appeal for a third time. At this point, an administrative law judge reviews the case and often a vocational expert is retained to assist the court in the evaluation. Approximately 58% of these appears successful (Marini, 2003). During the 2000 fiscal year, out of 584 claims, 540 claims were appealed, 16% were reconsidered by the SSA, and 59% of those reconsidered were awarded benefits after being heard by the administrative law judge (R. J. Leo, 2002). Five appeals are allowed with the final appeal heard by the U.S. District Court. However, success rates drop off dramatically for the fourth appeal to approximately 4% (Marini, 2003). There are no firm guidelines on determining the degree to which mental impairments will affect vocational impairments and most decisions are very subjective.

Additionally, some of the guidelines for benefits to be awarded may penalize those mentally ill individuals who are managing to avoid hospitalization by adhering to their treatment. However, they may require a level of structure or supervision in a work environment that is not readily available, yet, still fail to clearly meet the severity and/or chronicity with marginal treatment outcomes criteria needed for initial eligibility or renewal. Furthermore, those individuals with improved functioning could be denied; however, the stress of a work environment could likely lead to decompensation, increased impairment, or the inability to maintain employment. It is important for treating or evaluating clinicians to clearly document those limitations or those accommodations that are necessary. When these risk factors potentially preclude successful employment, the treating clinician should carefully document the implications for vocational impairment.

More programs and policies focusing on the provision of job coaches and community case managers, as well as more intensive supervision in the work environment could help many mentally ill individuals from falling through the cracks (R. J. Leo, 2002). Moreover, the structure of this type of employment could help a mentally ill individual maintain their autonomy and dignity. Marini (2003) reported that much research indicated the following strategies for placing and maintaining mentally ill individuals successfully in work environments:

> ... training available support systems to be aware of signs where medication noncompliance is occurring and to catch it early on; supported employment where follow-along contact is ongoing and natural coworker support at the work-site is strong; negotiating strong supervisor and coworker support as well as educating them about the disability; appropriate job matching; flex time work schedules where feasible; and positive feedback in addition to constructive feedback regarding work performance.

Dewa and Lin (2000) also suggested early treatment through employee assistance programs, if available, to provide confidential on- and off-site mental health counseling, when the more subtle signs of mental illness begin. Additionally, individuals lose their disability benefits when they are incarcerated or placed in a forensic hospital as incompetent to stand trial or NGRI for committing a felony offense. Often, when the individual is released it takes some follow-up time for their benefits to be reinstated. This period before reinstatement could increase the likelihood of failure with treatment follow up, the need for emergency services, or re-offense, resulting in new charges (R. J. Leo, 2002).

Suggestions for Future Research

MacDonald–Wilson et al. (2001) discussed the need for mental health professionals to have reliable and valid measures for work functioning. They expressed the need for future research to psychometrically test old and new instruments when assessing work capacity. This could enable a more standardized approach to a very imperfect and subjective system. Additionally, they suggested longitudinal studies of current disability claimants be undertaken for those both awarded and denied benefits. Continued investigations of this sort could help alleviate the tremendous disagreement between evaluators regarding the essential domains of functioning, particularly with respect to clinical impairments (e.g., symptoms, diagnosis) versus functional impairments (e.g., social functioning, cognitive functioning) (MacDonald-Wilson et al., 2001). Finally, future research should further explore the efficacy of varied strategies to successfully employ the mentally ill and to keep them engaged in their communities.

DUTY TO INFORM VERSUS CLIENT CONFIDENTIALITY

Introduction

Duty to inform versus client confidentiality stands as one of the more nebulous areas of forensic psychology. The controversy generally involves a mental health professional's ethical and legal obligation to protect client confidentiality and his or her duty to warn third parties to whom the client may pose a threat. Although the concept of confidentiality stands historically as one of the primary underpinnings of psychology, the legal ramifications of the duty to warn have caused substantial debate, especially with respect to the limits of confidentiality. In short, the question is: "When must and when should confidentiality be breached?"

The legal limits imposed on confidentiality are the result of the California Supreme Court's 1976 decision in *Tarasoff v. Regents of the University of California*. Generally, *Tarasoff* imposed an additional obligation on mental health professionals to consider the potential consequences of *not* releasing confidential information under certain circumstances. Thus, the ethically bound psychologist not only has the responsibility to uphold the value of confidentiality in his or her client relationships, but also must consider the interests of *other* individuals, organizations, and society in general in the process. Lee and Gillam (2000, p. 123) indicated that when considering the *Tarasoff* decision, psychologists must take into consideration the following relevant issues: "confidentiality, informed consent, ethical codes, identifiability of victims, level of dangerousness, and communicated threat."

In this section the concepts of confidentiality, the duty to warn or protect, and other relevant issues are more fully explored. The decision rendered in *Tarasoff* and its implications for psychological and forensic psychological practice are considered in detail. Further, a more recent controversy with regard to duty to warn is addressed: the implications of duty to warn for psychologists treating clients infected by the HIV virus or diagnosed with AIDS.

Peter is a 32-year-old man who recently began a therapeutic relationship with Dr. John to address issues of reported depression. Peter's depression appeared to Dr. John to revolve around several interpersonal concerns common to all of Peter's relationships. After approximately 2 months of therapy, Peter told Dr. John that he was beginning to feel very secure in their therapeutic relationship and that there was something he needed to address. Peter then confessed that he was bisexual which, because he had not told anyone, caused him a great deal of stress. Peter further reported that his first homosexual encounter was about a year ago and he had since engaged in several short-term relationships with other men. While Peter enjoyed the company of men, he stated that he had every intention of continuing to date women. In particular, Peter noted an 8-month relationship with a woman named Michelle.

Dr. John and Peter continued to address this issue over the course of the next several months. One day, seeming particularly tense, Peter confessed to Dr. John that he had been diagnosed as HIV positive. He maintained that he had been tested "just to be safe" about a month ago and had been informed of the results about 2 weeks ago. Peter told Dr. John that he was concerned, but "it hadn't quite sunk in yet." Further, Peter stated that he was continuing to have unprotected sex with several of his companions because it was unlikely that he could infect others in such a short time. In particular, Peter said he did not want to inform Michelle. He had come to the conclusion that Michelle would end the relationship upon hearing the news, and Peter did not want this to happen.

Literature Review

The ethical principles of the APA (1992) emphasize the psychologist's obligation to respect the privacy interests of the client. Maintaining confidentiality (assuring that a client's privacy will be protected) over the course of a relationship ensures that clients will feel free to engage more fully (i.e., fully disclose) with the psychologist (Kagle & Kopels, 1994). Further, the establishment of confidentiality standards serves to protect the client from the negative effects of stigmatization (Stanard & Hazler, 1995). Thus, confidentiality, from its original intent to foster therapeutic relationships to its expanded consideration as an ethical responsibility, assumes a significant and necessary role in the effective psychologist–client relationship.

Confidentiality includes most information obtained over the course of a psychologist's contact with a client. Revealing confidential information is ethically acceptable only upon consent of the client or upon consent from the client's legal representative. Because it undermines the trust that is often difficult to build in the first place, violating standards of confidentiality may result in termination of the relationship, poor outcome, and/or malpractice suits against the psychologist (Kagle & Kopels, 1994).

Recently, however, confidentiality has become more difficult to maintain. The ability of the psychologist to protect privacy through confidentiality has been curtailed by a number of issues. Namely, these issues revolve around the court's expanding interest and involvement in professional decisions (Kagle & Kopels, 1994). Clients must be made aware of the limits of confidentiality at the outset of the relationship and, additionally, must be made aware of the process of breaching confidentiality. Thus, psychologists are often forced into onerous decisions which necessitate the weighing of confidentiality against third-party interests in obtaining that information. This issue is, perhaps, most profound when violent or potentially violent clients are involved.

The "duty to warn," which has more recently invoked limits on client privacy and confidentiality rights, stems from the 1976 California Supreme Court case *Tarasoff v. Regents of the University of California*. In *Tarasoff*, client Poddar informed psychologist Dr. Moore over the course of their therapy that he intended to kill a woman when she returned from vacation. Taking the threats seriously, Dr. Moore consulted with his supervisors and campus police. Poddar did not meet the California standards for involuntary civil commitment and, thus, was not hospitalized. Further, the campus police detained Poddar briefly, yet released him after deciding that he presented no imminent and immediate harm. Two months later, after Tatiana Tarasoff returned from vacation, Poddar killed her. Tarasoff's parents initiated lawsuits for wrongful death against Dr. Moore, his supervisors, campus police, and the Board of Regents, claiming that their daughter should have been made aware of the danger that Poddar posed. The defendants claimed that Tarasoff was not their patient and that warning her would have breached confidentiality. The California Supreme Court, in response to their defense, would forever change the way psychology and related fields view confidentiality. The court held that:

> ... when a therapist determines, or pursuant to the standards of his profession should determine, that his patient presents a serious danger of violence to another, he incurs an obligation to use reasonable care to protect the intended victim against such danger (*Tarasoff v. Regents of the University of California*, 1976, p. 34).

The Court added that this duty entailed warning the intended victim or others who may alert the victim to the potential danger, notifying the police, and/or taking any other steps that may be necessary under the circumstances to protect the victim.

Following *Tarasoff*, a number of similar cases began to emerge in other parts of the country. In general, *Tarasoff* was used as the precedent case in the courts' rulings that therapists had a duty to warn third parties under certain circumstances (Felthous & Kachigian, 2001; Kagle & Kopels, 1994; Walcott, Cerundolo, & Beck, 2001). Thus, the dilemma posed by confidentiality versus duty to warn has profound nationwide implications at this time. Some states had statutes that provide for the protection of confidentiality. However, *Tarasoff* caused many of these statutes to be amended by allowing for exceptions in cases where a danger to a third party was a factor. Thus, it generally stands that confidentiality should, or must be, breached when a therapist believes that disclosing information is necessary to protect others from a "clear, imminent risk of serious physical or mental injury, disease, or death" (Kagle & Kopels, 1994, p. 219). Since the *Tarasoff* decision, the courts have expanded the scope and role of a clinician's duty to protect, with warnings only as one option for fulfilling this obligation (Felthous & Kachigian, 2001; Walcott et al., 2001). The precise implications of the duty to warn or protect, as are presented in the following section, remain somewhat vague.

Forensic Psychology and Policy Implications

Before discussing the implications of Peter's case, let us examine several of the issues more broadly related to the duty to warn. First, while courts have generally ruled that therapists have a duty to warn, the specifics of this duty have not been clearly elaborated. Court decisions have inconsistently determined whether the duty is limited to specific victims or more globally to all third parties. In other words, exactly which third parties the therapist is responsible for protecting varies widely among jurisdictions (Kagle & Kopels, 1994). Herbert (2002, p. 417) reported that 27 states mandate an actual duty to warn, but there is great disparity in the approaches leaving a "substantial burden of guesswork on clinicians." Several states and federal jurisdictions have even extended *Tarasoff* to include violence against property, and have extended therapist responsibility to include violent acts where the therapist "should have" known that a danger existed. Further, courts have mostly not specified what this protection entails. What exactly a therapist must do to protect third parties remains extremely vague (Oppenheimer & Swanson, 1990).

Moreover, questions remain about dangerousness and its prediction. One of the greatest difficulties pertaining to this is determining when a client is truly dangerous to a third party and when he or she is merely fantasizing (Oppenheimer & Swanson, 1990). Is it asking too much of psychologists to be able to identify when a client may "really do" what he or she has brought to the therapist's attention? If the therapist remains "on the safe side," he or she may be unnecessarily violating another's confidentiality rights. If that person does the opposite, he or she risks being held legally responsible for harm that may be inflicted upon another individual.

Additionally, how can we hold therapists responsible for the violent behavior of their clients when predicting whether a client will engage in a violent act is beyond the current ability of psychology (*Barefoot v. Estelle*, 1983; Monahan, 1981)? Studies have shown that psychology's success rate in predicting dangerous behavior is a mere 33–40%. Thus, we must ask ourselves if holding the therapist legally responsible is justifiable when the toss of a coin could better predict such outcomes. Borum and Reddy (2001) suggested that evaluation of risk in these cases should be primarily fact-based and deductive, as compared to the more inductive risk assessment approach used for general violence recidivism. Tolman (2001, p. 387) argued that improving the training of professional psychology students to include more risk assessment education, relevant legal information, and conceptual models of potential patient violence will "improve clinical practice, reduce legal liability, and improve public safety."

Let us now return to the above mentioned case of Peter. One of the most controversial aspects of the duty to warn involves the potentially violent sexual behavior of those infected with HIV. There are varying professional opinions regarding the implications for psychologists of duty to warn with HIV-infected clients. Some authors have pointed out that the sexual activity, not the person, is responsible for the risk (Kain, 1988; D. Martin, 1989). Thus, because different types of sexual activity create different risks, the level of danger must be addressed with specific regard to the activity. For example, the therapist must consider whether the activity involves the exchange of bodily fluids and whether preventive measures (e.g., protected sex) are being taken (Stanard & Hazler, 1995).

Others have suggested that the fatal nature of the disease creates a duty to warn which surpasses any ethical obligation to confidentiality. These commentators recommend directly informing the client's sexual partners if the client refuses to do so, and, where unidentified partners are at risk, informing the appropriate authorities (Gray & Harding, 1988). Regardless of the varying opinions, the majority of professionals seem to agree that HIV-positive clients engaging in high-risk behavior with uninformed partners are subject to *Tarasoff* (Stanard & Hazler, 1995). In other words, they are dangerous and steps must be taken to assure that, if a substantial threat exists, third parties are warned. Kain (1988) however, stated that with regard to unidentified third parties, the "identifiable victim" criterion of *Tarasoff* is absent. Given this, he believed that breaching confidentiality in such situations is "highly questionable" (p. 224). In a more recent study, Huprich, Fuller, and Schneider (2003) concluded that there is still no clear professional standard for whether or not a clinician has a duty to warn the unknowing partner of an HIV-positive client.

Thus, with regard to HIV and duty to warn for psychologists, several important issues must be addressed. First, the nature of the threat must be evaluated: whether specific, identifiable third parties are present; the exact nature of the sexual behavior; whether there is an imminent danger to others; and which third parties or authorities to notify. Next, given our undeveloped knowledge about HIV and AIDS, defining which behaviors put an individual at risk is difficult. Further, identifying victims is often difficult because the virus can lay dormant for many years (Stanard & Hazler, 1995). As Lamb, Clark, Drumheller, Frizzell, and Surrey (1989) noted:

> Given the incomplete knowledge about the diagnosis and transmission of AIDS, there is little agreement as to who is likely to contract the disease from infected persons. Such a lack of certainty about the conditions under which the disease can be contracted make it even more difficult to identify a potential victim (p. 40).

While cases such as Peter's may seem reasonably clear, others are far more controversial. As with the transmission of most illnesses, it is nearly impossible to identify potential victims and make an unconstestable risk assessment. Thus, HIV poses yet another difficult ethical and legal concern for psychologists to confront.

Suggestions for Future Research

Many fertile areas for future research have been addressed thus far. Generally, psychology is not efficient in assessing dangerousness or determining under which conditions dangerous behavior is likely to occur. Like other areas of civil forensics, methods for more accurately predicting dangerousness are necessary if psychology is going to remain in the position of interfering with individual civil rights. Further, we must better understand which third parties are best to contact if such a decision is reached. Clearly, as in the *Tarasoff* case, contacting certain third parties is often not enough to ensure that an individual will be protected from potentially violent acts. With regard to HIV, as our knowledge of the disease continues to grow, we must continue to adapt our strategies for dealing with it in clinical and/or forensic situations. As previously noted, to identify potential victims and potentially violent behavior, we must know which individuals are at risk and under what conditions.

VICTIM–OFFENDER MEDIATION

Introduction

Victim–offender mediation programs were created and are utilized in nearly 100 jurisdictions throughout the United States (Umbreit, 1993). Growing for three decades, victim–offender mediation (VOM) programs have spread throughout the United States and Europe, with initiatives in more than 1,200 communities (Umbreit, Coates, & Roberts, 2000). Mediation programs for victims and offenders offer the victim an opportunity to play a role in determining the offender's punishment, to explain to the offender the impact the crime had upon the party harmed, and give the victim closure after being violated. VOM gives offenders an opportunity to voice their personal problems and explain their crime, to avoid a possible harsher punishment such as imprisonment, and allows them to personalize their crime; that is, see first-hand the impact it had upon another human being. Ultimately, this personalization can help reduce recidivism (K. L. Joseph, 1996; Nugent, Umbreit, Wiinamaki, & Paddock, 2001; Reske, 1995; Umbreit & Bradshaw, 1997). The goal of mediation programs is to provide a conflict resolution that is fair for both parties involved and to develop an acceptable restitution plan (Umbreit, 1993; Umbreit et al., 2000).

Despite a variety of victim–offender mediation programs, most initiatives aim to achieve the same goals and have principles based on the concept of restorative justice (Severson & Bankston, 1995; Sullivan & Tifft, 2001; Umbreit, Coates, & Vos, 2001; Umbreit et al., 2000). Restorative justice is an age-old concept emphasizing that crime should be perceived as an act against individuals within the community, not only as an act against the state (Roach, 2000; Umbreit & Bradshaw, 1997). Most mediation programs are based on the same principles and follow the same process for mediation (Sullivan & Tifft, 2001). First, either a victim or offender is referred to a mediation program. Second, each party is seen individually by an unbiased mediator who informs them about the process and the possible benefits of participating in such a program. Third, after each party agrees, the mediator schedules a joint meeting between the two parties. During this phase, both the victim and the offender are given the opportunity to talk to each other without interruption. Finally, some programs may have a follow-up phase in which the referral agency approves the restitution agreement and closes the case; approving the agreement may include making sure payments or services that were agreed upon are fulfilled (K. L. Joseph, 1996; Umbreit, 1993). The types of offender mediation programs and how they differ are discussed later in this section.

The following case illustration is a real situation in which victim–offender mediation was successfully utilized. This section uses this case to describe the types of VOM initiatives and how they differ; to discuss the effectiveness of victim–offender mediation programs; and to address arguments against the appropriateness of such programs, including examples of how the following scenario could have been unsuccessful had circumstances been different.

Geiger was working as an auditor on the 11 a.m. to 7 p.m. shift that summer night when five men ages 18 to 21 entered the motel and demanded money. Geiger was punched and kicked, followed quickly by a pistol-whipping that knocked him to the ground. He jumped to his feet when he thought the crooks had left. Then he heard an explosion. The bullet tore into his chest, penetrating his right lung, breaking two ribs, and lodging in his stomach muscles. At the time of the robbery Geiger was a nationally ranked sprinter. Before the shooting he could do 100 meters in under 11 seconds; afterward, he could barely walk the distance. Facing unwanted publicity, motel management fired him.

At the trials of the black defendants, Geiger, who is white, was accused of racism and drinking and was made to feel guilty. He felt left out and angry at a system that had victimized him a second time. He was depressed and he needed answers. He wanted to confront his shooter and tell him about the damage that had done, and he wanted an apology.

Geiger found answers to many of his questions in mediation. He found that the offender was a substance abuser, out of work, and on parole. He had planned a simple robbery. He had not intended to shoot Geiger but instead wanted to fire a warning shot. At the end of his session, Geiger shook hands with the man who shot him. "I saw the burden of guilt lifted from him and the anguish from me." Geiger testified on behalf of the man last February at his parole hearing. He was granted parole after serving 12 years of a 12- to 25-year term for first-degree robbery (Reske, 1995, pp. 1–3).

Literature Review

Types of Victim–Offender Mediation Programs

In the Middle Ages, a criminal act was punished by the criminal making reparations directly to the victim; this is the basis upon which victim–offender mediation programs are utilized today (Severson & Bankston, 1995). There are various types of mediation programs that differ in several ways. Some programs offer mediation after conviction of a crime but prior to sentencing, whereas others offer mediation upon parole and make restitution a condition of parole. In some programs the victim and offender meet face-to-face whereas in other programs they do not (K. L. Joseph, 1996; Roy, 1993). In addition, programs may differ on the cases they accept; some programs may only accept juvenile cases while others accept adults (Kilchling & Loeschnig-Gspandl, 2000). Some programs only accept cases of violent crimes, while others accept nonviolent criminal cases (Severson & Bankston, 1995). Finally, programs differ in who they use to mediate, in the model they utilize to run the initiative, and in their administration. Most VOM programs use trained volunteers as mediators; however, other initiatives may use social work professionals. Although many mediation initiatives are supported by religious agencies, some are run and financed by probation departments and private foundations (K. L. Joseph, 1996; Severson & Bankston, 1995).

The most popular model used to run victim–offender mediation programs is the Victim/Offender Reconciliation Program (VORP) model (Sullivan & Tifft, 2001). The VORP model was developed in 1974 by the Mennonite Central Committee in Kitchener, Ontario, Canada (Roy, 1993; Umbreit & Bradshaw, 1997). In 1978, the first victim–offender program in the United States was put together in Elkhart, Indiana (Reske, 1995). The Elkhart program, like most victim reconciliation programs nationwide, is based on the VORP model. Programs based on the VORP model provide face-to-face meetings between the victim and offender (Roy, 1993). In addition, the VORP is usually a postadjudication program in which the offenders and their victims explore reconciliation and build a plan together for reparation (Roy, 1993; Severson & Blackston, 1995). Most likely, in the case illustrated above, the program Geiger went through utilized the VORP model because he had a face-to-face meeting with his offender and because the mediation took place after the offender had served time in prison (postadjudication).

According to an article by Severson and Blackston (1995), 30 states have reconciliation programs and most of them utilize the VORP model. In addition, more recent research suggests that the number of programs utilizing the VORP model is increasing (Umbreit & Bradshaw, 1997). Despite the majority of reconciliation programs that employ the VORP model, there are successful initiatives that do not. A restitution program in Kalamazoo County, Michigan, is operated by the Juvenile Probate Court, is a preadjudication program, and does not provide face-to-face meetings between the victim and offender; however, it does offer restitution to the victim similar to the VORP model (Roy, 1993). Despite the differences between the Kalamazoo program and the VORP model programs, Roy found that the Kalamazoo program was just as effective as the Elkhart, Missouri VORP program.

Umbreit and Vos (2000, p. 65) presented two case studies that examined capital murder cases involving victim–offender mediation/dialogue sessions between surviving family members and two offenders about to be executed. These researchers concluded that this intervention brought some measure of relief and healing to those involved. Additionally, they suggested that more opportunities for these types of encounters should be made available if "initiated and requested by victims and surviving family members of severely violent crime." However, opponents argue that this type of mediation does not fit the model of restorative justice in at least three critical ways (Radelet & Borg, 2000, p. 88).

1. There should be a "willingness and ability to change attitudes and understandings as a result of their communication."
2. "Restorative justice emphasizes recompense by the offender, actively taking steps to atone for the harm and injury he or she has caused."
3. "Restorative justice seeks to reduce the state's role in the justice process and to revitalize the ancient model in which victims, offenders, and communities all were actively involved in responding to crime and restoring peaceful relationships."

There are clearly many different types of victim reconciliation programs. A discussion of every type of program is beyond the scope of this section;

however, it is important to understand how such programs differ, and how these differences can have an impact on the effectiveness of the program. Because there are so many victim reconciliation initiatives and because many of these programs differ, it is difficult to assess their effectiveness as a whole. However, research on the effectiveness of individual programs, as well as on the effectiveness of initiatives utilizing the VORP model, have been conducted.

Effectiveness of Programs

Effectiveness of restitution programs is generally measured by program completion rates, the impact of restitution on lowering recidivism rates, and by victim satisfaction with the program (Nugent et al., 2001; Roy, 1993; Umbreit & Bradshaw, 1997). For example, in the Geiger case, the mediation was considered successful because the offender and Geiger came to an agreement, the offender showed compassion, and Geiger felt satisfied by the meeting. However, program completion percentages vary from program to program.

Roy (1993) conducted a study in which two programs were compared on recidivism rates and program completion. One of the programs was the Elkhart VORP initiative and the other was the Kalamazoo probate program described above. In his study, Roy found 59% of the offenders in the Elkhart program and 62% of those in the Kalamazoo program failed because of financial hardship. In addition, he found that 41% of the offenders in the Elkhart program and 38% in the Kalamazoo program re-offended. Despite the high rate of program failure in Roy's research, other studies have found successful completion rates as high as 98% (Fishbein, Davis, & Hamparin, 1984).

In an evaluation of a restorative justice program implemented by the Vermont Department of Corrections for nonviolent offenders, data suggested that the program worked. According to one researcher, the program was no less effective than the traditional retribution model of corrections and freed up space and resources to deal with more violent criminals (Hansen, 1997). Nugent et al. (2001) combined the data from four studies and ran a statistical analysis of the combination samples of 1,298 juveniles, which indicated that the recidivism rate of victim–offender mediation participants was 32% lower than nonparticipants. These researchers concluded that victim–offender mediation participation was related to significant decreases in delinquent behavior.

Research focused on victim satisfaction with the process has found high rates of victim satisfaction with reconciliation programs (Umbreit & Bradshaw, 1997; Umbreit et al., 2000). When Geiger met his offender, it provided him closure to an occurrence which had a negative impact on his life. When an offender shows compassion, as in Geiger's case, many victims are satisfied with the program. In a 1994 study, Umbreit found 90% of victims were satisfied with the mediation outcome; however, no research was found on the satisfaction rate among offenders. Arguments against victim–offender mediation suggest that offenders are often less than satisfied (J. G. Brown, 1994); however, other researchers posit that when a victim's needs are met, the offender's needs will be met as well (Evers, 1998).

Advocates for restorative justice believe that there is a reason why people commit crime again and again. One of these reasons is a lack of empathy for victims. With restorative justice, offenders are held accountable for their crimes, while the needs of the victim are met (Evers, 1998; Sullivan & Tifft, 2001). Geiger needed an apology, and he received that and much more (Reske, 1995). In addition, his offender showed empathy and regret for what he did. Ultimately, this could have reduced the potential that he would commit another crime of this nature in the future. According to advocates for mediation programs, one of its benefits is that it allows offenders to become aware of the impact of their crimes and to see their victims as people rather than as objects (Reske, 1995). When offenders are able to see their victims as people and possibly have empathy for them, the likelihood of recidivism is reduced (Umbreit & Bradshaw, 1997). As a result, fewer offenders circulate through the prison system, which helps to alleviate overcrowding. In addition, mediation initiatives such as the one implemented in Vermont help curb overcrowding simply by providing an alternative response to jail or prison.

Proponents for VOM suggest that prisons have become nothing more than "colleges for crime," which return to the public "meaner" and "craftier" criminals (Evers, 1998; Severson & Bankston, 1995; Snyder, 2001). These advocates suggest that the United States spends more on punishment and less on programs to prevent crime, and indicate that restorative justice is a response designed for prevention (Evers, 1998; Snyder, 2001). Restorative justice programs not only benefit victims, they benefit offenders as well. Proponents note that offenders need to be punished; however, also need help. Restorative justice can do both for some offenders (Evers, 1998; Sullivan & Tifft, 2001). However, other investigators are not so optimistic about restorative justice programs. They suggest that offenders often feel pressured to achieve an agreement during mediation and indicate that such programs often do not benefit the offender (Arrigo & Williams, 2003; J. G. Brown, 1994; K. L. Joseph, 1996). Additionally, some offenders have little capacity for victim empathy and would only utilize such an opportunity to further victimize a surviving victim or family members.

Arguments Against Victim–Offender Mediation

Although most research is supportive of victim–offender mediation, some researchers note problems with the programs, which results in debate about whether such initiatives should be utilized at all (Arrigo & Williams, 2003). The primary argument against mediation is whether true voluntariness exists for the offenders involved in the program (J. G. Brown, 1994; K. L. Joseph, 1996). Since many offenders are referred to mediation programs from the court, they participate because they feel it is required (K. L. Joseph, 1996). In addition, offenders may come to an agreement that they cannot afford or cannot complete because they fear if they do not reach consensus in mediation they will be punished for noncompliance (J. G. Brown, 1994). In response, researchers who support VOM suggest that giving the offender the opportunity to have a say in his or her punishment will more likely result in a sanction the offender complies with and accepts (Reske, 1995).

There are also arguments against restitution programs. J. G. Brown (1994) contends that such initatives represent a disservice to both victims and offenders. Victims may experience an injustice because reconciliation programs stress reconciliation before the victims "have the vindication of a public finding that the offender is guilty" (J. G. Brown, 1994, p. 3). However, this is not true for all programs; in Geiger's case, the offender was not only found guilty, he served 12 years in prison. Victim–offender mediation programs may pressure the victim into suppressing his or her anger and sense of loss through the assumption that these feelings can be expressed to the offender in merely a period of hours. In addition, these initiatives underserve the offender in several ways. First, the selection criteria are not related to the goals of the program. Second, such programs eliminate procedural protections, including the right to counsel. Third, programs attempt to gain advantages for the victims by using the threat of a pending criminal trial.

Some researchers argue against the use of victim–offender mediation programs for certain criminals such as sex offenders and wife batterers. Women's rights advocates believe restorative justice may reduce any progress battered women have made. However, the appropriateness of victim–offender mediation programs for certain populations does not appear to be much of a debate. Even Mark Umbreit, the director of the Center of Restorative Justice and Mediation, does not recommend mediation for some sexual assault cases and for all domestic violence disputes (Evers, 1998). Proponents argue that in some cases mediation can be beneficial for sexual assault incidents, and many initiatives require that sexual assault cases be victim initiated. Certainly, VOM programs for primary psychopaths would be inappropriate due to the high risk of manipulation and further victimization of survivors and family members (Shipley & Arrigo, 2001).

Despite evidence, which supports victim–offender mediation programs, questions remain regarding the efficacy of these initiatives. There are few examples of cases that went wrong; however, they are sure to exist. For instance, imagine if Geiger met the man who shot him and the man showed no remorse, guilt, refused to apologize, and did nothing but make excuses for his behavior. It is questionable whether Geiger would have experienced the closure he desired. In fact, such a meeting could have forced Geiger to relive some of the pain he dealt with during the past 11 years. Clearly, problems persist with mediation programs, and there will always be instances where the intervention is unsuccessful. The issue is whether the problems warrant giving up completely on such initiatives or whether they warrant changing existing programs to be more effective. Because restitution programs threaten to alter the way in which some criminals are punished, there are several some policy implications stemming from their continued existence.

Forensic Psychology and Policy Implications

A problem with victim–offender mediation programs is that they are run by many agencies. As a result, there are no set criteria about who can mediate, how offenders will be selected, and how the process of mediation should take place (Severson & Bankston, 1995). Most mediation initiatives rely on trained volunteers who know little or nothing about psychology or sociology. Several researchers suggest using trained professionals as mediators for these programs and that laws are needed to require mediators to have advanced training (Severson & Bankston, 1995). In addition, there is a need for policies based on research to be adopted for VOM practices. Although some researchers have suggested reforms that should be adopted, there is a need for enquiries that determine what guidelines create the most effective programs. One policy that most researchers do agree upon is a provision against mediation for domestic violence cases (Evers, 1998). It is essential that studies on mediation programs and procedural guidelines be adopted immediately; the concept is becoming more popular and lawmakers are passing legislation to create restorative justice programs in states such as Vermont and Maine (Sullivan & Tifft, 2001). The programs, however, are diverse and there are few provisions that indicate how the initiatives could be successfully run. As demonstrated by the opponents of restorative justice programs, the negative effects of unsuccessful initiatives can be huge. Without guidelines based on research, it will be difficult to minimize the negative effects.

With prison overcrowding, it is more likely that many states will look for alternatives to traditional sentencing. States may begin to implement legislation for the development of restitution programs. They may be met, however, with opposition from the general public, whose current attitude is that punishment equals imprisonment (Severson & Bankston, 1995). The public must be educated about the deficiencies of prisons and how these institutions financially impact them. Before legislation can be changed, society must become informed about alternatives to incarceration. As long as society equates imprisonment with punishment, politicians will continue to build prisons instead of invest in prevention programs. Perhaps the beginning of public education could occur through research results on the effectiveness of restorative justice programs. Because of the diversity of such initiatives, it is difficult to determine which aspects of various programs do or do not work.

Suggestions for Future Research

Further research on the effectiveness of victim–offender mediation programs is needed (Severson & Bankston, 1995; Umbreit et al., 2001). Although some studies have reported recidivism rates and program completion rates on individual programs, there is a need for research which examines the benefits and consequences of all restorative justice initiatives in order for recommendations to be made for program guidelines (Roy, 1993; Severson & Bankston, 1995). Also, there has been scant investigation of long-term recidivism rates for those who participated in a mediation program (Roy, 1993). These data are essential when states are enacting legislation to develop VOM initiatives. If program developers do not have findings indicating which initiatives have successful long-term effects and therefore would serve as models to pursue, then the implementation of these mediation programs will be no more successful at reducing recidivism than our overcrowded prisons.

The case of Geiger is a clear illustration of how VOM programs can benefit the victim and offender; however, the outcome of this case is not known. Quite possibly, the offender recidivated after his parole, perhaps this time shooting and killing an individual. There is no way to absolutely know this information for the majority of cases that have completed mediation programs, simply because long-term research on effectiveness is limited. Various studies indicate that victim–offender mediation programs do work. Studies demonstrate a high victim satisfaction rate and a recidivism rate no worse than those criminals who went through the traditional sentencing model. With prison overcrowding and the United States spending less on prevention and more on imprisonment, mediation programs appear to be promising.

Practice Update Section: Issues in the Court and Legal System/Civil Forensics

The *Tarasoff* duty to warn or protect has been at the center of many debates and requires well-informed decision making. In many cases, the *Tarasoff* warnings exemplify the gray area that lurks between the concrete black and white world of perfect answers and textbook solutions. Ethics courses around the nation attempt to broach the conflict between legal and ethical duties and balancing the best interests of the client (e.g., confidentiality, etc.) as well as the safety of a foreseeable victim. In some states, for example, Texas, there is no legal duty to warn. However, a clinician must take into consideration the more stringent ethical guidelines and do one's best to adhere to them within the boundaries of the law. If a forensic psychologist is in a situation where, based on a careful risk assessment, clear and imminent danger exists to an identifiable victim, taking reasonable steps to protect the welfare of a potential victim appears justified, even when not mandated by law.

The *Tarasoff* case created a new legal duty to protect third parties from a mentally ill patient's "foreseeable violence" (Walcott et al., 2001, p. 325). The courts initially expanded the scope of a clinician's duty to protect; however, subsequent cases began to substantially limit cases where *Tarasoff* warnings would apply. Some more recent cases have rejected a clinician's duty to warn. Furthermore, the creation of state statutes that codify the applicability and discharge of a *Tarasoff* duty to warn also have added a limit to the duty to protect. Finally, Walcott et al. (2001) have advocated for a "thorough, well-documented assessment of risk of violence as the best means for addressing concern about potential legal liability." Individualized responses will be needed for the risk posed by patients.

What happens after a clinician contacts the police as a means of fulfilling their *Tarasoff* duty? Are law enforcement officers aware of a mental health professional's duty to warn or protect potential victims of a psychiatric patient or client? In two states police officers were surveyed about their experience with *Tarasoff* warnings. The survey revealed that many police officers have very limited experience with *Tarasoff* warnings (Huber et al., 2000). Out of 48 Michigan and 52 South Carolina police stations surveyed, respondents at 45 stations reported receiving warnings from mental health professionals, with an average of 3.7 warnings a year. Only three respondents were familiar with the *Tarasoff* rulings. Out of the stations surveyed, only 24 had a specific policy on *Tarasoff* warnings and 27 stations noted that they would not warn a potential victim (Huber et al., 2000).

The duty to warn or protect has many potential moral, ethical, and legal implications for forensic psychologists. The preceding research highlights the boundaries of a mental health professional's ability to prevent potential violence. Psychologists are not law enforcement and cannot act in that capacity. If they assess clear and imminent danger and contact law enforcement, as well as appropriately document their actions, they may still be unsuccessful in preventing harm to the intended victim. However, if the responsible authorities fail to respond, then the moral and legal liability will likely shift to law enforcement. Psychologists are experts in risk assessment not at enforcing laws and foiling crimes.

Weiner (2003) discusses two cases where the patients were criminally prosecuted as a result of *Tarasoff* warnings. In both cases, each individual was arrested while undergoing evaluation as a patient in a locked psychiatric emergency service in a California hospital. Each individual was charged with "criminal threats," as defined by 422 of the California Penal Code. In both cases, the charge was a result of the *Tarasoff* warnings made by mental health professionals, and the *Tarasoff* warning itself was the means by which the threat was carried to the intended victim (Weiner, 2003). Although this is undoubtedly a more stringent application of law enforcement's response to *Tarasoff* warnings, the consequences in these instances weigh heavily with the patient. The failure to warn may have serious or even fatal fall-out for a potential victim and legal ramifications for the clinician, whereas *Tarasoff* warnings may have serious legal implications for the patient with a minimum of a loss regarding the therapeutic alliance. Expertise in violence risk assessment, the ethics code, and laws in one's state of practice, as well as good clinical judgment, should guide a psychologist's course of action.

CHAPTER 5

Juvenile/Family Forensics

OVERVIEW

This chapter examines selected topics and practice issues in forensic psychology impacting juveniles and families, specifically related to child custody. Divorce in the United States has become an epidemic and psychologists are called on in growing numbers to play a critical role in family court custody determinations. Central to this professional involvements, both legally and morally, is the best interests of the child. As such, three topical areas are addressed that identify all participants in the often contentious child custody arena.

Research has consistently demonstrated that divorce and battles for custody are damaging to children. Even though the setting for this controversy is family court, some argue that the stakes and emotions run as high if not higher than those typically seen in criminal courts. The work of forensic psychologists conducting custody evaluations is subject to intense scrutiny by parents and their legal advocates. The legal system relies heavily on mental health professionals to help define the very ambiguous Best Interest of the Child Standard. Any psychologist who participates in this process should be very aware of the legal guidelines, have training in relevant areas, and most importantly, have the positive adjustment and best interest of the child in mind when making recommendations.

This chapter provides an overview of the legal issues and professional guidelines involved in custody evaluations and determinations, and discusses the impact of family law and custody concerns on children and adolescents. In total, three subjects are examined. These topics include (1) family law and the "emotional rights" of children, (2) best interest of the child, and (3) the psychologist's role in child custody evaluations. Although the topics reviewed in this chapter do not exhaustively examine the issue of child custody determinations in juvenile/family court, they do represent an important foundation for understanding the vital role of well-trained, competent, mental health professionals working in this noncriminal subspecialty area of forensic psychology. Indeed, the stakes can be very high for the professional, the parents, and certainly the children involved.

The legal system is frequently asked about the issue of child custody when divorcing parents cannot agree on a coparenting plan or when one partner feels the other lacks adequate parenting skills or may pose a physical threat to the child. Judges, attorneys, and families often turn to mental health professionals to help educate the court and to provide recommendations about custody determinations. They also inform all parties in the dispute about what is in the best interest of the child in question. The experience of divorce and adoption can be traumatic for families, especially when children are involved. How are children impacted by these events? What is the emotional impact of the custody dispute for children? How does family law, if at all, protect the emotional rights of children in custody disputes when divorce and/or adoption are at issue?

Child custody cases involve a decision about the placement of a youth with a particular parent or parental surrogate. Typically, judges rely upon the "best interest of the child" doctrine. What is this standard and how do psychologists interpret it? How, if at all, does the juvenile court system promote it? To what degree does the Best Interest of the Child Standard aid judges in child custody determinations? How do custody evaluators formulate their recommendations and how do they ensure that they are in the best interests of the child? Are there structured guidelines that most custody evaluators follow and are they consistent with the American Psychological Association's (APA, 1994) best practices in child custody evaluations? What assessment techniques are currently used and how much influence do forensic psychologists have on family court decisions? Finally, how common are ethical complaints and litigation against psychologists who conduct custody evaluations and what strategies can ensure that ethical and legal standards are being applied? The subjects examined in this chapter explore the way in which the legal system, with the aid of psychologists, makes decisions about what is in the best interest of the child, how they formulate recommendations, and what potential impact these decisions have on parents and their children.

FAMILY LAW AND EMOTIONAL RIGHTS

Introduction

Children are involved in custodial disputes every day. In 1991, it was estimated that approximately 1 million children experience parental divorce every year in the United States (M. Bussey, 1996; Short, 1998). Other children are involved in disputes between their biological and potentially adoptive, or psychological, parents (Bracco, 1997; Levin & Mills, 2003; Oppenheim & Bussiere, 1996; Wynne, 1997). Both divorce and adoption are events that are lifelong processes affecting the mental well-being of children (Amato & Sobolewski, 2001; M. Lee, 1997; Leon, 2003; Oppenheim & Bussiere, 1996; Sun & Yuanzhang, 2002; Wertlieb, 1997; Weyer & Sandler, 1998; Wynne, 1997). Children of divorced parents are more likely to have lower levels of social competency, poor academic performance, conduct difficulties, and lower self-esteem than children from intact homes (Crockenberg & Forgays, 1996; Katz & Gottman, 1997; M. Lee, 1997; Short, 1998, 2002; Wertleib, 1997). Laws have begun to recognize the emotional impact custody disputes can have on children, especially for custodial decisions for divorce (Bauserman, 2002; Gunroe & Braver, 2001; Lowenstein, 2002a). However, children's emotional rights are not always considered in legal decisions, especially for custody disputes in which spousal abuse occurred in the home, or in those cases where adoption went wrong (W. G. Austin, 2001; Logan, Walker, Horvath, & Leukefeld, 2003; Zuberbuhler, 2001). Laws vary from state to state and while some apply the Best Interest of the Child Standard for custody issues, others do not. Even when such standards are applied, some researchers indicate they may not, in reality, protect the child's emotional rights (Kurtz, 1997).

In most states, the Best Interest of the Child Standard is applied for child custody cases (Azar & Cote, 2002; Kaltenborn, 2001; Kurtz, 1997). In fact, states are mandated to consider the best interest of the child in making custody decisions for divorce cases (Bracco, 1997; Oppenheim & Bussiere, 1996). Rather than allowing divorcing parents to make whatever decisions they want regarding the custody of their children, judges are now required to consider what portions of the divorce will affect the children and make certain their needs are met (Bracco, 1997). However, despite the best interest of the child mandate for divorce custody decisions, a child's right to a loving family and emotional support is not always considered. For other custody decisions, courts may use the parents' rights standard

(Wynne, 1997). This standard does not even acknowledge the emotional rights of the child. The following case illustration gives an example of such a ruling.

Jessica Deboer was 2 when she was taken away from the only parents she had ever known. Baby Jessica's biological mother, Cara Clausen, signed away her parental rights to the Deboers only 40 hours after the birth of her daughter, despite the Iowa law that prohibits signing a release before at least 72 hours expired after the birth of a child. When the Deboer's attorney called and asked Cara who the father of the child was, she lied and named Seefeldt, an ex-boyfriend, who signed away what he thought were his parental rights.

Two days after the Deboers received custody of baby Jessica, Cara told Dan Schmidt that he was really the father of the baby. When Jessica was 3 weeks old, Cara sued to have her parental rights restored, and Dan made a legal claim later the same month. The Deboers refused to give Jessica back without a fight, and when Iowa courts continued to rule against them, they took the case to Michigan, hoping to win on the question of the child's best interest. The Deboers won the case in Michigan, but the ruling was appealed when Iowa argued that Michigan did not have jurisdiction. The Iowa court did not consider the child's best interest, arguing that it was not required under Iowa law. By the time the court had determined a ruling, Jessica was 2 years old and did not know her biological parents.

Psychologists argue that nothing is more devastating than losing both parents as a toddler. Nevertheless, baby Jessica was returned to her biological parents. In August, 1993, the Deboers packed baby Jessica's things and tried to explain to her why she had to leave. When the van arrived to pick Jessica up, she began crying and screaming and continued to do so as the van drove away. Follow-up reports indicate baby Jessica, now named Anna, has adjusted well and is happy; however, there is no way to determine the long-term effects this court decision may have on her psychological well-being (Cowley, Springen, Miller, Lewis, & Titunik, 1993; Hansen, 1994b; Ingrassia & Springen, 1993, 1994).

Literature Review

In some states, family law clearly does not focus on the child's best interest when it comes to custody disputes between the biological family and the custodial, psychological parent. Wynne (1997) indicated that the case of Baby Jessica illustrates "that as a nation, Americans do not think enough of their children to consider their rights or interests, or to discuss even if they have rights or interests" (p. 187). In fact, most states make a primary effort to give biological parents custody of the child as long as there is no evidence of parental unfitness (Oppenheim & Bussiere, 1996). Even in states where the Child's Best Interest Standard is applied, there are different statutory orders of preference for the placement of the child. These preferences do not always take into consideration the child's emotional rights. For example, in California, the child is placed with a relative unless the court determines that such placement is not in the child's best interest. However, the law does not necessarily specify what the best interests are. Although some states do provide factors which should be considered in the best interest determination, much discretion is left to the judge (Oppenheim & Bussiere, 1996). As a result, the child's emotional well-being is not necessarily considered.

Riggs (2003) noted that more recent trends increasingly focused on psychological research and testimony when determining custody and visitation privileges. However, she explains that the U.S. Supreme Court's majority decision in *Troxel v. Granville* prefers the right's of biological parents over the best interests or psychological interests of children. In many instances, the unilateral decision about what is in a child's best welfare is determined solely by adults. However, A. B. Smith and Gollop (2001) recommended that separating parents should keep their children informed, listen to them, elicit and respect their views, and consider their point of view while making decisions about their care and living arrangements.

Bracco's (1997) examination of Canada's Best Interest Test illustrated the court's difficulty in determining the best interest of the child. Bracco explained that the test is a change in mentality from "every parent has the right to a child" to "every child has the right to a family." However, Bracco recounted the difficulty with assessing the best interest; she posed the question of whether it is truly in the best interest of the child to keep adoptions secret. In Canada, there is to be no contact between the adopted child and his or her biological parents.

The issue of children's emotional rights and family law is complex because laws differ from state to state (Oppenheim & Bussiere, 1996). However, most researchers agree that family law does not adequately acknowledge children's emotional rights (Bracco, 1997; Oppenheim & Bussiere, 1996; Shapiro, 1993; Wynne, 1997). There tends to be a bias toward biological parents in determining custody between biological parents and a third party (Riggs, 2003; Shapiro, 1993; Wynne, 1997). This bias was evident in the Baby Jessica case. Wynne (1997) argued that the courts need to recognize and support a child's need for a "stable relationship with his or her psychological parent" (p. 189). In addition, Wynne asserted that in order for family reunification attempts to work, the courts need to reassert what they consider real family relationships. According to Wynne, the family reunification policy using a biological definition of family had resulted in abuse, neglect, and even the deaths of many children. Perhaps Wynne's argument can be best illustrated by the statement of Kimberly Mays, a 14-year-old girl who was switched at birth and whose biological parents sought custody. At a news conference, she stated "Biology doesn't make a family" (Shapiro, 1993, p. 13). Mays clearly identified her "psychological" father as her family and wanted to divorce her biological parents.

Fortunately, shortcomings of family law have not been ignored when addressing the emotional well-being of children. The National Task Force for Children's Constitutional Rights has begun to write a children's amendment to the constitution which affords children certain rights (Wynne, 1997). The amendment grants children several protections, including the right to a safe home and "the right to the care of a loving family or a substitute which approximates such a family as closely as possible" (Wynne, 1997, p. 187). This amendment affects every state, and it could potentially help protect children's emotional rights by forcing every state to consider the child as a person, rather than the property of his or her biological parents, as Wynne suggests. However, the amendment does little for Baby Jessica and cases like hers when both families appear to be loving. Although the changes in family law are under way for third-party custody disputes, laws already exist for custody disputes between biological parents. These laws, and the degree to which they consider the emotional well-being of children, are discussed next.

Some specifications have been outlined for custody decisions in divorce cases. The Uniform Marriage and Divorce Act of 1970 provides a list of factors judges should consider in child custody cases (Crosby-Currie, 1996). Because laws in every state differ, the factors vary from state to state. One factor that is considered in custody decisions in every state is the child's wishes. Utilizing this standard in a custody determination was designed to protect the child's emotional best interests, some research indicates that asking a child about his or her wishes has a negative impact on the child's well-being (Crosby-Currie, 1996). In fact, some investigators note that regardless of whether the child is asked about his or her wishes, custody disputes are detrimental to children (M. Bussey, 1996). A longitudinal study that evaluated a child's relationships and residence preferences as custody criterion found that (1) a living arrangement that is commensurate with a child's wishes and relationships contributes to the child's welfare and represents a positive living arrangement in the family and social environment; (2) the child's personal relationships change and a timely transition of residence that occurs with the changed emotional preferences of the child is beneficial; (3) a living arrangement that contradicts the child's attachments and preferences can lead to either adjustment, a course of suffering, or attempts to change the living situation (Kaltenborn, 2001).

Amato and Sobolewski (2001) used 17-year longitudinal data from two generations and examined the effects of divorce and marital discord on adult children's psychological well-being. Results indicated that divorce and marital discord were predictive of children's subsequent lower levels of psychological well-being. Marital discord had a negative impact on children's emotional bonds with their mother, whereas both marital discord and divorce lessened or weakened children's emotional bonds with their father. Short (2002) compared 87 college students who experienced parental divorce between the ages of 8 and 18 with 67 students who experienced parental death during the same ages and 87 students whose parents remained married. Adult children of divorced parents reported significantly more present life stress, family conflict, and less family cohesion and friend support than the comparison groups. Additionally, children of divorced parents reported greater levels of current antisocial behavior, anxiety, and depression than their peers, related to the aforementioned factors. Research also has demonstrated that children with recent bouts of parental divorce are at a relatively high risk for behavioral and emotional problems (Harland, Reijneveld, Brugman, Verloove-Vanhorick, & Verhulst, 2002).

M. Bussey (1996) used a systems perspective to examine the detrimental effects of divorce on children. Some of the systemwide interventions for children of divorce have included legal reform. Because of the abundance of psychological literature that indicates divorce has long-term detrimental effects on most children (M. Bussey, 1996; Crockenberg & Forgays, 1996; M. Lee, 1997; Short, 1998, 2002), some states have begun to change the legal process for divorce (M. Bussey, 1996). For example, parent-targeted interventions are often mandatory instead of voluntary, and some states such as California have court-mandated mediation for all disputed cases. Family law has begun to work with psychologists in an effort to reduce the negative impact divorce has on children's emotional well-being. In 1992, a program to help children cope with divorce was established, and referrals were primarily from a family court judge, who posed the question of whether such programs should be mandated on a state- or nationwide basis (M. Bussey, 1996).

Zuberbuhler (2001) described the Early Intervention Mediation research project which lasted for 15 months at the Court of Domestic Relations of Hamilton County, Ohio. The goal of this initiative was to measure the efficacy of early introduction of mediation into divorce proceeding to resolve custody issues. The research project entailed half of all divorcing parents who could not agree on custody arrangements for their children to attend mediation within 6 weeks of filing for divorce. The other half of divorcing parents, operating under similar circumstances, acted as the control group and followed existing court procedures. The results indicated that in 61% of divorce cases ordered to participate in mediation, the parenting or custody issues were fully resolved. Zuberbuhler (2001) suggested that emotionally and financially damaging litigation was avoided in these cases and that the court reduced judicial hours.

Kelley (2003) described focused mediation interventions with parents in ongoing custody disputes. She discussed a design that emphasized areas of parental behavior that negatively affected children's adjustment, specifically, parent's conflict patterns, postseparation and postdivorce parenting relationships, appropriate communication patterns, and competent and desirable postdivorce parenting. Regarding the value of mediation in child custody disputes, Lowenstein (2002b, p. 739) stated: "The mediator's role is to help parents to value the contributions made by the other parent, to encourage parents always to put the children first, and to avoid allowing one parent's hostility and mistrust toward the other parent to undermine promoting the physical and psychological health of their children."

Although studies indicate that law and psychology do intersect when it comes to custody disputes between biological parents, there are criticisms regarding the adequacy of the law for such disputes. As discussed previously, states use the Best Interest of the Child Standard when determining custody cases between biological parents. Kurtz (1997) argued that the best interest standard may be detrimental to both the child and the parents in cases of spousal abuse. Judges are not required to take spousal abuse into consideration when determining the custody of the child. When the laws changed to the Best Interest of the Child Standard, courts were no longer required to assess parental behaviors. As a result, the courts are less concerned with the parental relationship as long as the relationship does not appear to have a physical impact on the child. In fact, because statutes do not require a judge to take parental abuse into account when determining custody, an abuser may be granted custody. Oftentimes, the abuser is the financial supporter for the family, and the judge may believe such assistance is in the best interest of the child and that placement with this parent is therefore warranted. Kurtz (1997) argued that legislation "must create a statutory presumption against awarding a spousal abuser custody of a child.

Only then will the best interests of the child truly be met" (p. 2). Consider the following case illustration.

> When his infant son was 6 months old, this father pushed his wife off an overlook. She plunged into a ravine and survived, thanks to some bushes that cushioned the impact. Her husband evaded indictment. For the 8 years this case was pending, the courts showed not a particle of compassion or concern for the mother. The first inexplicable affront to justice was awarding the father custody of the infant at the moment the mother was being discharged from the hospital to recover from her injuries. After finally winning her struggle for custody, the mother dared not attempt to curtail the father's visitation lest she involve her son in a new custody suit. Still suffering flashbacks from the assault, the mother stoically sent her son on alternate weekends to spend two nights with his father. The child invariably returned in an agitated, out-of-control state that subsided only in time for the next visitation. Why would the court not use its broad discretion to give this mother authority to raise her son free from the influence of a father known to be capable of murder and diagnosed by its own forensic specialist as a "sociopath?" (Sachs, 2000, pp. 212–213).

Sachs (2000) also described the very detrimental effect that visitation with known spousal abusers can have on children. She indicated that protective parents are justified in their attempts to insulate their children from the destructive influence of an antisocial role model or coparent. Requests to reduce or cut off visitation with a parent known to be violent or criminal should be afforded respect by judges. Sachs (2000, p. 224) illustrated her point with the following cases of fatalities linked to visitation.

> National Public Radio carried the story the morning of December 23, 1998, of the tragic death of a mother and child murdered by the father in an encounter after a supervised visitation outside a community center near Seattle. According to the reporter, the mother had obtained a protective order prohibiting her estranged husband from contact on the grounds that "he choked her, beat her, and threatened to kill her. She found his gun and turned it in to the police. Still he retained the right to see his daughter." (In newspaper accounts following the murder, the father was quoted expressing regret that the bullets intended for his wife had also struck his child.)
>
> In August 1998, a Brooklyn man was convicted of murdering his former wife, a policewoman, while she sat in his car holding their baby after a visitation she
>
> *(continued)*

(Continued)
had agreed to arrange to appease his demand for time during the supervisor's vacation. After the verdict, members of the jury commented to spectators from the National Organization for Women that they had heard sufficient testimony about the father's harassing phone calls, constant stalking, and maneuvers to obtain an illegal gun that they felt he should have been forbidden to have contact with the baby. Several noted that he had been grinning inappropriately throughout the trial.

Family law is beginning to take into consideration children's emotional well-being and their rights of emotional stability. However, the law has been criticized for not protecting these interests in all situations. Based on the literature, it is apparent that the law has progressed further toward protecting children's emotional rights when it comes to custody disputes between biological parents than it has in those disputes involving third parties. Possibly, the changes in law for custody disputes between biological parents are more advanced because they have a longer history and the detrimental effects on children have therefore been more publicized. Prior to the 1960s adoptions were closed. As a result, no disputes between biological parents and potentially adoptive parents existed. These cases are now more common, and activists have proposed legislation that they believe would protect the child's emotional interests.

Forensic Psychology and Policy Implications

Activist groups for children's rights have begun to recommend amendments that could potentially help protect their rights (Wynne, 1997). The National Task Force for Children's Constitutional Rights began writing an amendment to the United States Constitution that would grant children protections such as the right to a safe home, the right to adequate health care, the right to an adequate education, and the right to the care of a loving family or a substitute as close to a loving family as possible. In addition, the amendment would provide children with the right to an attorney in any legal matter affecting their interests (Wynne, 1997). The amendment is clearly a starting point toward protecting children's rights; however, the wording in the amendment is ambiguous. What one may consider adequate health care or a loving family may be quite different from another's point of view. Children's emotional rights cannot be protected unless legislation specifically consider psychological research on children's emotional needs. Had psychologists' opinions been considered in the Baby Jessica case, it is doubtful that she would have been taken from the only parents she knew.

Other researchers suggest defining the child's best interest standard more clearly and consistently (Oppenheim & Bussiere, 1996). The ambiguity of the best interest practice allows the court to be flexible and meet the needs of each individual child; however, it does not protect children against the biases and prejudices of judges (Sachs, 2000). To reduce the ambiguity, Oppenheim and Bussiere (1996) suggested that the effect of blood relationships on children's well-being be assessed, and that coherent laws based on the findings be enacted. In order to establish coherent laws, several questions, such as "How much weight should be given to blood relationships in determining custody?" and "Under what circumstances should relatives be able to maintain a relationship with their kin following an adoption by a nonrelative?" (pp. 480–481), need to be considered.

Not only do Oppenheim and Bussiere address specific questions that must be answered prior to policy change, they provide guidelines to accomplish this. They argue that the child's best interests should be considered more important than the interests of the adult parties, that the court should protect the continuity of personal relationships, and that the court should respect the importance of the child's relationships with the extended biological family because this family will encourage connections to one's history and culture. If Oppenheim and Bussiere's policy recommendations had been accepted prior to the Baby Jessica case, the judge might have ruled that she remain in the Deboer's home and receive regular visits from her biological parents. It is difficult to determine the effects that such a ruling would have had on the child.

Family law experts are proposing measures which could help protect children from the negative emotional impact that results from unsatisfactory court decisions (Braver, Fabricus, & Ellman, 2003; Cowley et al., 1993; Lowenstein, 2002; Sachs, 2000). In an effort to prevent adoption custody disputes, some activists have proposed making adoptions closed, despite research indicating that positive ties to biological family can be beneficial for adoptees (Bracco, 1997; Brooks, 2002; Oppenheim & Bussiere, 1996). An open adoption could have prevented the Baby Jessica custody dispute completely. Perhaps if the biological mother was granted regular visits with her daughter, she might not have felt like she was missing out on her daughter's life.

Neil, Beek, and Schofield (2003) discussed postplacement contact with biological family members. These researchers stated: "Children permanently separated from their birth families have to manage life-long issues of attachment, identity, and loss" (Neil et al., 2003, p. 401). Bracco (1997) suggested that the law redefine what is considered family. She argued that adoption law is based on patriarchal child development theories and the current perception of the nuclear family may be too rigid. Bracco further argued that policy changes in Canada should be made in which an adopted child's biological parents had a role in raising the child. Although Bracco's arguments are primarily for adoption considerations and not necessarily custody disputes, her efforts to redefine familial considerations relate to policy suggestions made by other investigators. Brooks (2002) discussed the tremendous potential of utilizing extended biological family members as a resource for at-risk children in a more creative and inclusive approach to adoption. Wynne (1997) suggested that courts work to redefine what are considered "real" family relationships. He argued that children's emotional needs will not be met until courts define family according to a psychological definition. This definition would place more emphasis on psychological ties with parents rather than on blood ties.

The analysis of policies concerning custodial disputes between biological parents and third parties is difficult because custody matters are confounded with adoption regulations. One cannot examine policy concerning custodial disputes without examining adoption law. A thorough examination of adoption law is beyond the scope of this section; however, the issue is important for the protection of children's emotional well-being and merits further examination.

Family law appears to be more adequate for custodial disputes involving biological parents. Psychological research indicates that conflict in divorce situations is what is most detrimental to children (Amato & Sobolewski, 2001; M. Bussey, 1996; Katz & Gottman, 1997; M. Lee, 1997). States have changed statutes regarding custody to protect children emotionally. Although there is still room for family law to change in order to protect children to an even greater extent, the fact that courts and psychologists are working together to help determine the best interests of the child is promising. Only when special circumstances such as spousal abuse are considered do investigators make bold suggestions for policy change.

Kurtz (1997) argued that statutes need to be created that prevent abusive fathers from receiving custody of their children. She argued that even joint custody should not be allowed because this forces the abused parent to maintain contact with his or her abuser. Kurtz alleged that the Best Interest Standard is inadequate when it comes to spousal abuse cases and that policies must be more specific to prevent further abuse of the spouse and the emotional trauma of the child. Spousal abuse is only one circumstance that may require a change in certain statutes regarding child custody. There are certainly many other circumstances in which current custody laws are insufficient; however, an examination of each circumstance is beyond the scope of this section. Spousal abuse provides one example of how policies might not protect children's emotional well-being in every given situation.

Suggestions for Future Research

The ambiguity of the law suggests a lack of consensus among experts on the importance of blood ties versus psychological ties (Neil et al., 2003; Oppenheim & Bussiere, 1996). Research is not consistent regarding what the best interests of the child are. While some studies indicates that blood relationships are more important, other inquiries recommend that psychological relationships take precedence. Further research needs to be conducted to determine the psychological impact of not knowing one's biological parents, of being raised by adoptive parents but maintaining a relationship with biological parents, and of being removed from one's psychological parents as a toddler and placed with biological parents. Psychologists have speculated about each of the above, but longitudinal research to determine the impact of each has not been undertaken. Studies of this sort will provide social scientists with individual characteristics of children who are more or less emotionally stable after living through a custodial dispute and possibly, when taken from one's psycho-logical parents. For example, research on divorce has shown that gender, degree of conflict in parental relationship, and the child's IQ all have an effect on the extent to which the divorce negatively impacts the child; however, research on adoption custody disputes of this nature has not been conducted.

There is ample research on the impact of divorce on children. This research has contributed to changes in family law regarding custody disputes. In fact, programs have been implemented such as the Children Cope With Divorce Program (M. Bussey, 1996). Although studies have been conducted with 2-year follow-ups for children who have passed this program, longitudinal research to determine the long-term effects of program attendance would be useful for future policy implementation.

BEST INTERESTS OF THE CHILD DOCTRINE

Introduction

The Best Interests of the Child Doctrine was established in the legal system to determine the components of child custody that ensures the best environment for a child's adjustment and development (Kelley, 1997; Smith & Gollop, 2001). According to Mason (as cited in Skolnick, 1998), approximately 50% of children born in 1990 will become involved in a child custody case. The Best Interests of the Child Doctrine is typically invoked during an adversarial divorce, which is the reason for most custody disputes (Kelley, 1997; Logan, Walker, Jordan, & Horvath, 2002; Riggs, 2003; Skolnick, 1998). Divorce can have significant consequences for the child, and the purpose behind the best interests doctrine is to determine which adult provides the most positive relationship with and the best environment for one's offspring (Bauserman, 2002; G. Miller, 1993; Pedro-Carroll, Nakhnikian, & Montes, 2001; Riggs, 2003). Although positive aspects of the doctrine have been noted, including the idea that every decision can focus on an individual child's need and that it permits society to address shifting morals, values, and situations (Kelley, 1997), much of the literature highlights the standard's limitations.

> Joe and Sarah have three children, ages 6, 10, and 13. The two youngest are girls, and the oldest is a boy. The parents have abused both drugs and alcohol. In addition, Joe went to prison several years ago for committing a sexual offense against a 12-year-old girl. Sarah remained married to Joe during this time but began having an affair with a coworker by whom she became pregnant. While Joe was in prison, their children were temporarily removed from Sarah's custody because of her drug use. However, she was able to straighten herself out and they were returned to her. When Joe was released from prison, he and Sarah did not initiate divorce proceedings; they shared joint custody of the two girls while the boy lived solely with his father. Joe does not have steady employment. He works odd jobs as a mechanic and lives with his girlfriend in a trailer in his

parents' backyard. Sarah does not work at all and lives with her new fiancée in a one-bedroom apartment. They both claim to be drug free. Recently, Joe and Sarah became angry with one another, and Sarah filed for a divorce. In an effort to hurt Joe, she has sued for sole custody of the two girls, stating that Joe is a threat to them because of his prior sex offense. The question before the court is which parent will provide the best environment for the children.

Literature Review

When deciding between Joe and Sarah as sole custodians of their children, many people might feel that neither should be awarded custody. However, the question before the court is to choose between these two individuals, and the judge must make the decision. In times past, a judge might have based his or her decision on very different criteria. For example, prior to the mid-19th century, children were perceived as property, and therefore fathers were entitled to such property. Courts then turned to the idea that children of young ages should be allowed to stay with their mothers until they were weaned. This was commonly referred to as The Tender Years presumption (A. S. Hall, Pulver, & Cooley, 1996). It was not until 1925 that the Best Interests of the Child Standard was initially proposed. This occurred in the case of *Finlay v. Finlay* (1925). A father was suing for custody of his child, and the court ruled that the concern should be for the child's welfare, not for the argument between the parents. However, the Tender Years presumption continued to prevail until 1970, when it was officially supplanted by the Best Interests of the Child Standard (A. S. Hall et al., 1996).

A major complaint lodged against this relatively new standard is that it is very vague. It allows for judicial bias that leads to different results in similar cases (Skolnick, 1998). Dolgin (1996), for example, reported that many criticize the standard because it does not provide enough substantial guidance for courts to follow regarding child custody decisions. The author also suggested that using the Best Interests Standard could lead to opposing decisions in child custody cases, depending on the presiding judge. Part of the problem is that there appears to be no widely recognized operational definition for the standard (Banach, 1998). Indeed, one study found that the codes and statutes in all of the states had very little in common when it came to standardized guidelines (A.S. Hall et al., 1996).

The criticisms about vagueness extend beyond the problem of judicial bias. There also appears to be a lack of agreement among mental health and legal professionals about the necessary requirements for the best interests of a child. This leads professionals to arrive at conflicting decisions in particular cases (Horvath, Logan, & Walker, 2002; Kelley, 1997). Horvath et al. (2002) examined 60% of custody evaluations in one circuit court over a 2-year period and found much variation in techniques used and a lack of consistency between guidelines and clinical practice. On an even broader level, the standard has been criticized because societal consensus about what is in the best interests of children does not exist (J. Goldstein, Solnit, S. Goldstein, & Freud, 1996; Skolnick, 1998). Azar and Cote (2002) contended that during the 20th century both the rights of women and children evolved, as well as the needs of children beyond just physical ones. These researchers maintained that the expansion of child protection laws, the increased willingness and speed in terminating parental rights, and the increase in rights for other interested parties (e.g., grandparents) prove that the pendulum is swinging away from parental rights to a greater emphasis on children's rights.

However, other investigators (Dolgin, 1996; Sachs, 2000) assert that the lack of guidance may lead judges to focus on the interests of the parents rather than on the interests of the child. A judge may do this by basing his or her decision on protecting the constitutional rights of the parents. G. Miller (1993) stated that courts often examine other factors in addition to the best interests of the child. These factors include the constitutional rights of those involved. G. Miller indicated that Supreme Court decisions reflect the idea that constitutional rights precede the best interests standard. This has lead other courts to examine the interests of the adults over the children (Sachs, 2000). In the case of Joe and Sarah, a judge might have to consider Joe's constitutional rights of losing his children because of a crime he may never commit, even if this supersedes the best interests of the children.

Kandel (1994) suggested that the best interests standard "does not rise to constitutional dimensions; it implicates neither substantive nor procedural due process rights. Further, it is subject to limitation in the interests of the state, the interests of the parents, and the interests of children themselves" (p. 349). He also pointed out that the standard is more of an infringement on the rights of children than parents, because a judge substitutes his or her opinion for the choice of the children. Sachs (2000) adamantly opposed judicial decisions that force joint custody or visitation with parents who have a violent or criminal background against the best interests of the child. As she stated: "Judges do not seem to see the contradiction of upholding the law by forcing children to spend time with criminals. The callous disregard for children's feelings shown by some decision makers is troubling to witness" (pp. 223–224).

In forming such an opinion, the judge does not have to consider psychological suggestions. In fact, G. Miller (1993) indicated that the best interests standard is defined differently both legally and psychologically, which leads to further complications. For mental health workers, the best interests of the child are the conclusive factor in recommending an appropriate placement, while for the courts, it is not; constitutional and legal factors rank higher than the best interests standard. Sachs (2000) noted: "Child advocates with no background in forensics are incredulous to learn that many judges, lawyers, and psychologists do not deem it necessary to weigh domestic violence as a factor in custody unless so instructed by state law" (p. 216). According to Kandel (1994), when the court does request psychological assistance, it does so to justify its decision. It appears that by creating "scientific validity" (p. 348) this is the best choice; however, often the court asks mental health professionals the wrong question. Sachs (2000) warned that some protective parents and judges are "cowed by the supposed unanimity among 'experts' that children should maintain relationships with both parents" (p. 222).

Another factor that appears to bias judges' decisions is that since the early 20th century mothers have been given preference with regard to custody of their children, even though this has never been statutorily recognized (Kandel, 1994). Skolnick (1998) suggested that though the best interests standard prevails, most custody decisions still are made in favor of the mother. There are four explanations provided by Warshak (1996) for this phenomenon: (1) women by nature make better parents and are more essential to children; (2) most mothers are better parents, not because they possess innate superiority, but because they have more experience than fathers in raising children; (3) custody should be a reward for the types of contributions a mother has made to her children; and (4) mothers suffer more emotionally than fathers from the loss of custody. Warshak (1996) also indicated that only 1 in 10 children resides with their fathers, and this has been a steady proportion for decades. Despite evidence showing that divorced fathers can provide nurturance for their children and can handle the responsibilities of child rearing, those who desire custody "must still prove mothers grossly negligent or abusive" (p. 399).

Stamps (2002) reported that presently all states have gender-neutral child custody laws, which supercede statutes and precedents that favor mothers in custody disputes. However, he argued that the legal literature suggests that a maternal preference still exists. To further examine this issue, Stamps (2002) surveyed state judges in Alabama, Louisiana, Mississippi, and Tennessee ($N = 149$) by mail in order to ascertain their beliefs related to maternal preferences in custody decisions. Results of the study indicated that the judges surveyed demonstrated continuing maternal preference with regard to quality of parenting, children's adjustment following divorce, and the preferred custodian following divorce. If a judge believes that mothers are better caregivers for children, then it can be fairly simple to favor a particular parent by highlighting the negative behaviors of the other caregiver (Dolgin, 1996). In the case of Joe and Sarah, if the judge preferred that mothers retain custody, then the judge could focus on Joe's prior sexual offense as evidence that he would be an unfit caregiver.

Forensic Psychology and Policy Implications

Based on the arguments against the Best Interests of the Child Standard, there should be some type of uniformity in the guidelines (A. S. Hall et al., 1996; Horvath et al., 2002). Kelley (1997) suggested that a consensus be created detailing what critical guidelines should be included. Banach (1998) noted that creating more specificity for all professionals involved might decrease the bias associated with decision making. She also suggested that an operational definition be included in state statutes to create some uniformity. In addition, professionals should not rely solely on their own judgment but evaluate their decisions with other professionals to avoid biases.

Skolnick (1998) provided some recommendations to create more uniform criteria. She stated that a child's psychological well-being should be one consideration. This would include examining emotional ties the child has with the parents and the child's need for stability. Also, rules should be developed that prevent a judge from considering lifestyle choices or parental conduct that does not directly damage the relationship with the child. In Joe and Sarah's situation, this could be a difficult task to accomplish because they both engaged in behaviors that were potentially harmful to their children.

J. Goldstein et al. (1996) suggested changing the Best Interests of the Child term to the Least Detrimental Alternative because it is more realistic and less subject to a magical idea of finding the best interest. They also suggested that child placement decisions remain as free as possible from state intervention and be as permanent as possible because continuity is critical for children. The state should interfere only if it can provide the least detrimental alternative. Krauss and Sales (2000, p. 843) critically examined the roles of forensic evaluators and psychological researchers when determining the Best Interest of the Child Standard in custody battles. These researchers maintained that current data did not support most "expert testimony" offered by mental health professionals in court. Instead, they argued that the Best Interest of the Child Standard does not represent the needs of the legal system or the expertise of psychology. Moreover, they asserted that the Least Detrimental Alternative to the Child Standard more precisely met the needs of both the legal and psychological arenas (Krauss & Sales, 2000).

Creating new guidelines for this standard should include cooperation between legal and mental health professionals. Wall and Amadio (1994) indicated that child custody decisions must consider the entire family and the needs of each member when endeavoring to provide the most beneficial and continuous relationships between parents and children. They stated that if legal and mental health professionals could cooperate, this task would be easier to accomplish and the best interests of the family would be realized.

Suggestions for Future Research

Research needs to focus on exactly which factors to consider when making custody decisions based on the best interests of the child. Before specific guidelines can be proposed, however, they first have to be discovered. Conducting research on those areas of development and functioning most appropriate for children, at various ages, should be pursued by mental health professionals, specifically child development specialists. Leon (2003, p. 258) suggested that the following questions be addressed in future research: "How does parental divorce affect developmental outcomes? What risk and protective factors influence adaptation? How does early parental divorce affect later adjustment?"

Studying various decisions made by judges and determining which constitutional factors are important in these situations are also warranted, especially because courts are not going to let psychological issues prevail over constitutional ones. Moreover, there needs to be some clarification regarding those factors regularly considered and how different conditions change the factors that are deemed important (Banach, 1998). Once these are learned, they can be incorporated into guidelines for those making child custody decisions.

In the area of gender bias decision making, further research should be conducted on fathers who are awarded sole custody of their children in order to verify that they can be appropriate caregivers. Although findings exist in this area, additional studies are needed because courts continue to favor mothers in custody cases. This bias can adversely impact someone like Joe, who might have made a horrible mistake but could still be a good caregiver.

THE ROLE OF PSYCHOLOGISTS IN CUSTODY EVALUATIONS

Introduction

Approximately one-half of all marriages end in divorce in the United States, impacting greater than one million children a year (Bernet, 2002). Children are involved in 40% of divorce cases (Horvath et al., 2002). Approximately 10% of divorce cases involve litigation over custody or visitation, resulting in about 100,000 children a year at the center of a custody battle (Bernet, 2002). Contested custody disputes are purported to have the most detrimental psychological impact on the children involved and even the process of divorce can have a long-term, negative psychological affect on children (Krauss & Sales, 2000).

When divorcing couples cannot agree on custody arrangements, custody disputes are often brought to family court, and mental health professionals are typically retained to conduct custody evaluations. According to the American Psychological Association (APA, 1994, p. 677), custody evaluations are assessments by professionals that examine "individual and family factors that affect the best psychological interests of the child." Although custody evaluations can be conducted by a variety of mental health professionals, doctoral-level psychologists with appropriate training are typically found to be among the most credible and thorough as reported by attorneys and judges (Gourley & Stolberg, 2000).

The APA published recommended ethical guidelines for custody evaluations performed by psychologists and are considered the professional standard of competent practice (Horvath et al., 2002). However, there is much concern that structured guidelines for performing child custody evaluations are lacking and that operationalizing and measuring what is in the best interest of the child remains ambiguous. The vast majority of parents who divorce do not require a custody evaluation by mental health professionals; however, a formal psychological custody evaluation may be particularly beneficial to the parents and the legal system in the following circumstances (Bernet, 2002, p. 784):

- One or both of the parents have a mental disorder that may affect the person's parenting skills

- The child may have specific mental health needs that should be considered in developing the custody arrangements or parenting plan
- The divorce has been unusually hostile and the custody evaluation is seen as a less adversarial approach to making decisions involving the children
- The child's relative attachment to the parents seems like an important issue
- It is suspected that one of the parents has tried to indoctrinate the child and alienate him or her from the other parent
- One parent has accused the other of physical or sexual abuse

Depending on the age and maturity of the child, the child's wishes about who they would like to live with can also be a significant factor, particularly if custody of a teenager is in question. However, the evaluator must be aware of the many elements that could influence a child's proclamation of where he or she wants to live. Additionally, Sachs (2000) warned that seeking custody should not always be confused with being a fit parent. She indicated that some parents seek custody of their children for the wrong reasons which are certainly not in the best interest of the children, for example (p. 217):

- To evade responsibility for paying child support
- As a strategy to force the opposing parent into a reduced financial settlement
- As a strategy, sometimes on advice of counsel, to add to the opponent's burden by expanding the scope and increasing the cost of litigation
- To hold on to children with the intention of exploiting them sexually, physically, or emotionally
- For self-gratification
- To compensate for inner feelings of emptiness and isolation
- For the satisfaction of defeating or tormenting the opposing parent

Consider the following case example about Janina; as documented by Kaltenborn.

Ten-year old Janina lived in her father's household at the time of the evaluation. She maintained good relationships with both parents, but showed preference for her mother and wished to live with her. Although the

(continued)

(Continued)
expert recommended that she should live with her mother, the court did not agree. In the first follow-up study about ten years after the child psychiatric evaluation, the father refused to be interviewed. I was, however, able to conduct a lengthy interview with Janina, now almost 20 years old, and her mother on the occasion of a visit by Janina to her mother. Both regarded the custody decision in favor of Janina's father negatively. To the question as to why her father sought custody, the young woman replied that he wanted to use the custody dispute as revenge against his wife for leaving him; as a result of the divorce he had regarded Janina as his property...In the second interview, about 6 years after the first survey, ... Janina felt that the fact that both of her parents had partners was particularly difficult for her. She told us that custody in favor of the mother would have resulted in the advantage of actually being cared for by her mother, but, as it was, during the time with her father, she was 'cared for by a strange woman.' In both interviews, she emphasized her good relationship with her mother, and how difficult it was only seeing her during the agreed visiting times. She also had painful memories of leaving her mother at the end of visits (Kaltenborn, 2001, pp. 99–100).

Literature Review

All 50 states mandate that the child's best interests be the main determinant in custody decisions (Horvath, et al., 2002; Keilin & Bloom, 1986). Over the last 2 decades, research has been undertaken to determine whether or not there is consistency in standards of practice among mental health professionals conducting child custody evaluations. Gourley and Stolberg (2000) state that the adversarial nature of the courtroom and ambiguous guidelines make the task of conveying research, and evaluating results regarding child custody, an arduous task.

In an effort to help create a standard of practice, and in response to the numerous ethical complaints brought against psychologists, the APA created practice guidelines for psychologists who perform custody evaluations (APA, 1994; Krauss & Sales, 2002). The guidelines offer 16 principles for psychologists to follow while conducting custody evaluations for the court. These principles emphasize the importance of using multiple sources of data collection, explaining the limits of confidentiality and obtaining written informed consent; warn against overinterpreting or inappropriately using or interpreting assessment or psychological testing data for a custody evaluation; and highlight the significance of parenting capacity, the psychological and developmental needs of the child, and the subsequent relevance to what would be in the best interest of the child involved (Quinnell & Bow, 2001). However, the guidelines are considered aspirational goals, not mandatory behavior on the part of psychologists participating in these evaluations. In other words, the guidelines do not require certain assessments and techniques or mandate certain expert opinions as ethical (Krauss & Sales, 2000). For example, these researchers noted that constructs such as "parenting ability," as set forth in the guidelines remain somewhat illusive and poorly defined.

Empirical psychological research exploring child custody decision making has increased tremendously over the last ten years (Krauss & Sales, 2000). In an empirical study by Keilin and Bloom (1986), 82 mental health professionals who conducted child custody evaluations were surveyed. The participants included 78.1% doctoral-level psychologists, 18.3% psychiatrists, 2.4% masters-level psychologists, and 1.2% other specialists. The results indicated that interviews were the primary means of data collection. However, the majority did use psychological testing. The Minnesota Multiphasic Personality Inventory (MMPI), Rorschach, and Thematic Apperception Test (TAT) were the assessment instruments most commonly used with adults and intellectual achievement, whereas projective testing was most commonly used with children (Keilin & Bloom, 1986). Overall, the psychological tests commonly used have changed over the years and will be briefly discussed later in this analysis.

In a replication study, Ackerman and Ackerman (1996, 1997) surveyed 201 psychologists and found that their standard of practice was congruent with the APA's 1994 guidelines. Bow and Quinnell (2001) surveyed 198 psychologists and found that evaluators used almost all of the recommended APA guidelines. Quinnell and Bow (2001) found that the majority of participants in the study viewed psychological testing as one source among many and did not overinterpret their significance. Results also indicated that the national survey of psychologists revealed that they were discriminative in their choice of testing instruments with a greater focus on objective assessment, particularly with the use of parent inventories and rating scales. Horvarth et al. (2002) suggested that this close adherence to APA guidelines was likely attributed to the fact that the studies utilized a self-report format, which allowed those surveyed to err on the side of presenting their more ideal standards of practice. Additionally, these researchers pointed out that the majority of persons surveyed in the aforementioned studies were doctoral-level psychologists in private practice, and that these individuals were not the only mental health professionals conducting these evaluations.

In order to more accurately reflect the standard of practice of custody evaluators generally, Horvath et al. (2002) examined 60% of custody evaluations in one circuit court over a 2-year period. These investigators found that in 63.6% of the cases, the final custody decisions were consistent with the recommendations of the custody evaluator. Overall, significant variability in the content and procedures of the child custody evaluations in the sample were found. In general, evaluators failed to conduct assessments of important factors such as domestic violence and child abuse, adequate evaluation of parenting skills, evaluation of parent's health status, and formal psychological testing. Horvath et al. (2002) found that approximately 40% of the evaluators sampled used only two methods of assessment to decide on a custody arrangement. In order to comply with APA guidelines and respect the significance of the impact of the evaluation on the parents and children, a variety of assessment techniques, including collateral sources (e.g., teachers, pediatricians, school records, etc.) should be utilized. Among private evaluators, doctoral-level psychologists typically adhered most closely to the APA guidelines. Horvath et al. (2002) concluded that evaluators should use multiple sources of information to include family interviews, psychological testing, observations of each parent and child, a review of available records, interviews with other relevant collateral sources, and home visits in some instances if indicated.

Gourley and Stolberg (2000, p. 1) conducted a study to define the current standard of practice for those psychologists who were viewed as "credible" by family law attorneys. These researchers surveyed 20% of the licensed psychologists in the state of Virginia regarding their participation in custody evaluations and surveyed family law attorneys to obtain nominations regarding those psychologists regarded as credible. Finally, the "credible" psychologists were surveyed to determine their training as well as their standards of practice.

The majority of psychologists in the broader sample, as well as those nominated as credible custody evaluators, identified self-teaching through workshops, conferences, and professional reading materials as the primary method of training.

Formal training and supervision in custody evaluations are rare and no licensing or accrediting bodies for this specialty area of forensic work exist. Psychologists can more generally be certified through boards such as the American Board of Professional Psychology (ABPP), although many well-regarded custody evaluators do not have this board certification and it does not signify any specialty training in this area. Forensic programs that provide specialized training in psycholegal issues are very new and many individuals currently practicing as custody evaluators learned by self-teaching.

Gourley and Stolberg (2000) found that one-third of the "credible" sample had some graduate training in custody evaluations, while the broader sample did not. These authors indicated that this finding was troublesome considering the lack of other areas in psychology where one could be considered an expert without formal training, including many hours of supervision by a more experienced professional. They also maintain that the lack of set guidelines to define who is considered an "expert," typically left this decision to the discretion of the judge; a person not likely trained in behavioral science, child development, research design, or psychological testing or assessment. As Gourley and Stolberg (2000, p. 22), however, "There are no guidelines, requirements, or licensing procedures established by most states or by the profession to help guide judges or the general public."

Overall, the surveyed psychologists in this study were in agreement about the relevant factors to be evaluated as set forth by research relating to child adjustment after divorce (Gourley & Stolberg, 2000). The results indicated that most psychologists give the most weight to the clinical interview or adapt instruments that measure psychopathology to inform on issues such as parenting and family functioning. A minority utilized home observations or surprise visits to obtain data on family functioning. The results of the study also reported that while the majority of custody evaluators were in agreement about the critical components to be assessed and the relative weight to assign to each, there was much less agreement on the techniques used to assess these factors (Gourley & Stolberg, 2000). The paucity of well-researched, standardized assessment instruments specifically designed to measure parenting skills, or other factors related to the determination of child custody, also was noted.

Quinnell and Bow (2001) found that, overall, psychologists are becoming more selective and discriminative in their administration of psychological tests in child custody evaluations. Presently, reliance on IQ testing or a single battery of tests, despite the type of forensic referral question, is antiquated. Rather, there has been an increase in the use of parent rating scales and parenting inventories, which indicates greater efforts to measure parenting capacity. Furthermore, objective testing is used more frequently with adults. Projective testing is also being used but is largely discouraged in the forensic arena, given its lack of psychometric or empirical support (Quinnell & Bow, 2001). As Horvath et al. (2002) cautioned psychologists who routinely base custody recommendations on clinical interviews alone without including psychological testing or behavioral assessment instruments for hypothesis development. As Horvath et al. (2002, p. 563) stated, "There is a substantial risk to the intended objectivity of child custody recommendations when there are no independent anchors for opinions such as those that can be obtained through the use of validated instruments."

Based on their national survey of 198 psychologists, Bow and Quinnell (2001) found that the main referral sources for child custody evaluations were attorneys (41%) and judges (41%) with only a very small percentage directly from parents (4%). Eighty-four percent of the child custody evaluations were court ordered. The majority of psychologists surveyed (65%) indicated that they charged an hourly fee for child custody evaluations with the average hourly rate reported as $144, with a range of $75–400 per hour. The majority of the remaining psychologists (33%) charged on a case-by-case basis. The most commonly reported costs for the evaluation by all survey psychologists were $2,500 and $4,000. On average, 24% of the child custody cases required expert testimony and 12% required depositions. The fee for expert testimony ranged from $0 to 400 per hour, with a mean of $177 per hour (Bow & Quinnell, 2001). When respondents were queried about the age at which they seriously considered a child's expressed preference for custody decision, the average age reported was 11.6 years, with 12 years as the most common response. When asked if they made specific recommendations about the ultimate issue or about custody/visitation, 94% responded affirmatively and 3% responded no, leaving the remainder to indicate "sometimes" (Bow & Quinnell, 2001, p. 265). Psychologists surveyed reported that they recommended joint custody 73% of the time and sole legal custody in 27% of the cases evaluated. The three most important reasons provided for recommending sole custody included (1) inability to coparent (e.g., lack of cooperation), (2) severe mental illness of a parent, and (3) abuse/neglect.

Results also significantly supported the notion that child custody evaluation participation is a high-risk specialty area for psychologists (Bow & Quinnell, 2001). Ten percent of the psychologists indicated they were involved in malpractice suits and 3% had been sued twice. Two of the participants had been sued three and five times. Thirty-five percent of those surveyed had received board complaints on at least one occasion based on child custody work. Ten percent reported 2 or more complaints and 2 psychologists had received 14 and 15 complaints based on child custody work. Many of the respondents added in their self-reports that the suits had been dismissed (Bow & Quinnell, 2001).

Psychologists are required to consider many ethical factors while conducting child custody evaluations. If a psychologist is prevented from completing a comprehensive evaluation due to circumstances out of his or her control, (for example, if one parent refuses to participate), it is critical that the psychologist make limited recommendations and acknowledge the limited scope of the evaluation. Additionally, if the evaluator has only assessed the father and the child, he or she can only comment on the psychological status of the father and child, their attachment to one another, and the father's parenting skills, but not the status of the mother (Bernet, 2002). Typically, in this instance the evaluator could not make specific recommendations regarding custody, as a comparison between the father and mother could not be accurately made. Finally, if the child custody evaluator has been asked to participate in a one-sided evaluation, it is imperative to ascertain whether or not the parent who requests the evaluation and brings in the child actually has the legal standing to authorize the evaluation (Bernet, 2002). Without permission from the custodial parent, such an evaluation would be unethical.

Forensic Psychology and Policy Implications

Bow and Quinnell (2001, p. 261) noted that "child custody evaluations are among the most difficult in the forensic field" due in large part to hostility between the parents, extreme emotions for even minor issues, vague standards, and balancing ethical obligations to all. Some critics argue that the lack of a clear, workable definition regarding what constitutes the Best Interest of the Child Standard allows far too much judicial discretion and permits judicial biases to influence custody decisions (Coons, Mnookin, & Sugarman, 1993; Krauss & Sales, 2000). These researchers also suggested that the lack of guidance provided by the standard has led to a significant deference toward mental health professionals when it comes to child custody evaluations and what is in the child's best interest. According to Davis and Dudley (1985, as cited in Krauss & Sales, 2002, p. 862), "It is hoped that mental health professionals will have what judges lack. The means to determine objectively what is the best interest of the child." The focus on the best interest of the child requires a thorough assessment of each parent's capacity to care for the child as the central feature of the evaluation (Horvath et al., 2002).

In order to better achieve this goal and to adhere to a higher standard of practice, Gourley and Stolberg (2000) suggested that formal training and licensing procedures be created to help regulate custody evaluations. Training which includes coursework on theory and research relating to "child development, postdivorce adjustment of children, adult and child psychopathology, family systems, and psychological assessment," as well as a procedure for postdoctoral supervision in custody evaluation by more seasoned, practicing custody evaluators, all should be required (Gourley & Stolberg, 2000, p. 26). Individuals who conduct competency to stand trial (CST) evaluations or other criminal court-related evaluations are more commonly held to this standard. More standardized procedures for conducting child custody evaluations should be established based on continuing research regarding critical, empirically supported variables (e.g., child adjustment, attachment issues, family functioning, etc.). Horvath et al. (2002) noted that there is a collective effort from mental health experts, judges, and attorneys to develop these guidelines and standards. In addition, they highlighted the importance of ongoing training and education of custody evaluators regarding critical areas that could significantly impact custody determinations such as domestic violence, substance abuse, and mental illness.

Parents who suffer from severe mental illness may have significant hurtles in caring adequately for their children, requiring extra support, and/ or treatment to facilitate their ability to parent (Krauss & Sales, 2000). Children with mental illness will also require specialized care, resources and a level of parenting ability different from a child with no evidence of mental illness. Krauss and Sales (2000) identified psychologists as the most able health professionals to assess for signs of psychiatric illness and to draw conclusions about how these factors likely affect parenting ability, a child's postdivorce adjustment, or the needs of the child.

In many custody cases, there are two parents who may appear equally capable of caring for the child in question. Yet, in others there may be only one capable parent, or two parents with significant barriers to healthy parenting or to providing an appropriate home environment. Horvath et al. (2002) suggested that more custody evaluators should be encouraged to recommend that special advocates be assigned when there are serious concerns about a child's physical and emotional needs. The special advocate can assist in the ongoing monitoring of the child's welfare and report back to the court far beyond the participation of the custody evaluator.

Forensic psychologists need to conduct highly competent work in order to formulate what is in the best interest of the child in question, while also reducing their chances of ethical complaints and possible litigation. In order to reduce the risk of being the litigant in a malpractice suit or an ethical or board complaint, Bow and Quinnell (2001) suggested the following:

Such strategies include familiarity with the APA Guidelines (APA, 1994) and APA Ethical Principles (APA, 1992), obtaining court appointment, securing informed consent and waiver of confidentiality, maintaining impartiality, avoiding one-party evaluations and dual relationships, providing complete disclosure, preserving a well-documented file, and avoiding ex parte communication. In some states, court-ordered custody work falls under the immunity of the court (Stahl, 1994); therefore, obtaining a court order may reduce the risk of a malpractice action in some states (as cited in Bow and Quinnell, 2001, p. 267).

The stakes for a custody determination are high and the implications are far reaching. Forensic psychologists need to set a very high standard of training and expertise before taking on the enormous responsibility of custody evaluations.

Suggestions for Future Research

Krauss and Sales (2000) strongly suggested that the Best Interest of the Child Standard be reevaluated and modified. These researchers indicated that the social sciences have been unable to demonstrate empirical foundations or support for current and past conceptualizations of the standard. Other investigators highlighted the lack of standardized and objective measures available to assess parenting capacity and other constructs specifically related to child custody, rather than objective measures of psychopathology (e.g., MMPI-2, Millon Clinical Multiaxial Inventory III, MCMI-III) that *could* have implications for parenting. Gourley and Stolberg (2000, p. 27) stated, "Psychologists should be encouraged to develop research protocols that would allow families to be assessed in a clinic in a way that could provide data for criterion and construct validity of custody evaluation procedures, aid in the development of more objective measures of parenting and family functioning as they relate to custody evaluation, and provide training for psychologists and others performing custody evaluations."

Bow and Quinnell (2001) recommended research to explore the specific issues that are usually cited as the underlying causes for malpractice suits or ethical or board complaints. Having a better understanding of these issues could better prepare psychologists to reduce their risk of litigation.

Quinnell and Bow (2001) also suggested further research regarding the situations in which specific assessment measures are used in order to better understand the role of psychological tests in custody evaluations.

Finally, other investigators call for additional research to explore the assessment of a child's level of sophistication and decision–making abilities in order to assist judges and evaluators in deciding on how much weight to give a child's expressed wishes regarding custodial preference (Krauss & Sales, 2000). Psychologists should also continue to explore the issue of the most appropriate way to ascertain a child's preferences without further damaging a parent–child relationship while minimizing the emotional impact on the child (Grisso, 1986; Krauss & Sales, 2000; Melton, Petrila, Poythress, & Slobogin, 1987).

Practice Update Section: Child Custody Evaluations and Juvenile/Family Court

The work of forensic psychologists who interact with courts is subject to a high degree of scrutiny, perhaps none more than the child custody evaluator. This Practice Update section will summarize the article by Martindale (2001) titled "Cross-Examining Mental Health Experts in Child Custody Litigation." The title alone is enough to raise anxiety levels but the points made serve to not only better prepare the attorney but also the mental health professional for cross-examination.

The intense emotions and hostility that are often a part of heated custody battles serve to critically impair the objectivity of the parents involved. The "nonfavored" litigant will not uncommonly register complaints with his or her attorney that the child custody evaluator did not consider all information that was presented; complains of irregular methods of evaluation; and insists that the evaluator was not impartial (Martindale, 2001, p. 484). Although some parents seek custody for their own agendas far from the best interest of the child, the vast majority view themselves as the more capable parent and are profoundly disappointed, confused, and quite angry when the child custody evaluator recommends otherwise. Martindale (2001) maintained that the nonfavored parent will often search for causes outside of his or her own potential parenting deficiencies or strengths of the other parent for the recommendation made by the evaluator. Some consider errors made by the evaluator as the likely culprit. Although this is a claim far too frequently made, in some instances, the nonfavored parent may have been placed at a disadvantage by a biased evaluator or one who was insufficiently trained to consider all relevant factors.

Cross-examination by the nonfavored litigant's attorney is one opportunity to expose such biases or substandard practices. The forensic psychologist who conducts custody evaluations must be very mindful of the potential implications of one's procedures and preconceptions about "family" prior to engaging in this work. It is critical that the evaluator not let personal biases prevent an adequate assesment of all factors and a thorough review of all hypotheses based on the data collected from each evaluation on a case-by-case basis. It is the job of the mental health expert to assist the trier of fact in making a custody determination. While it is the judge who makes the ultimate decision, research has demonstrated that the opinions offered by the evaluator often heavily influence the final outcome.

During the discovery phase of the court process, the attorneys should have familiarized themselves with the evaluator's *curriculum vitae* and the agreement the evaluator made with the parties involved (Martindale, 2001). Martindale (2001) encouraged attorneys to look for any training in the forensic specialty area of child custody, including conferences, workshops, and coursework. He stated: "It is inappropriate for a mental health professional whose background is treatment oriented to accept forensic assignments without first having secured education and training aimed specifically at preparing one for forensic work" (p. 485). As forensic psychology programs are relatively new, it is rare for a mental health professional to have originally received their education and training in a forensic specialty. If an evaluator lacks sufficient training on relevant issues by any of the previously mentioned methods, his or her credibility could be challenged at trial. The evaluator should also be very careful about listing "vanity boards" that do not conduct a thorough assessment of a candidate's expertise (e.g., work samples, oral and written examinations) on their *curriculum vitae* (p. 486). Attorneys are encouraged to follow up on claims of board certifications in order to gather information about the credentials-granting process.

The forensic mental health expert should also be very familiar with the subpoena process and the potential for their complete file, including evaluation notes, to be requested and the possibility of being part of the discovery process at trial. Martindale (2001) further suggested that attorneys attempt to obtain a reasonable number of the expert's previous custody evaluation reports and to scan them for identical passages, as well as for inconsistencies in rationales for recommendations. If the descriptors used to outline the interaction of one litigant and their child are repeatedly used to portray other litigants, it is important to challenge the evaluator on "corner cutting" and whether or not the evaluator explored all relevant individual differences (p. 490).

Forensic psychologists are also cautioned to assess any other individuals who are presently playing a parent role or will likely in the future (e.g., a fiancee of one of the litigants). Martindale (2001) indicated that to do otherwise would be offering an opinion on insufficient information. One critical difference between the forensic evaluator and the more typical treatment provider is the necessity to investigate all self-reported information by the litigants through follow-up with collateral information (e.g., records, uninvested collateral

(continued)

(*Continued*)

sources, etc.). Particularly in custody evaluations, the litigants are quite motivated to present themselves in the most favorable light. Forensic evaluators are obligated to list in their reports all collateral sources used and the information gleaned from each within the body of the report.

The suggestions for the mental health expert to avoid impeachment at trial provided in this Practice Update section are far from exhaustive but highlight the degree of inquiry to be expected for the child custody evaluator. Refer to Chapter 1 for more information on expert testimony. Ultimately it is the child who may suffer the greatest consequences based on the opinions offered and decisions made on their behalf. "The best interests of the children are ill served when flawed reports go unchallenged and become the basis upon which the trier of fact rests her judicial decision" (Martindale, 2001, p. 504).

CHAPTER 6

Family Forensics

OVERVIEW

This chapter examines selected controversies and issues in forensic psychology impacting families. For purposes of this chapter, the use of the term "family" is broadly defined. When the legal and psychological communities promote policies and/or therapeutic interventions that affect how parents and their children are to interact, then the structure and process of what it means to be in a family are called into question. In some instances, the law dictates which individuals are allowed to become a family, while in others the law allows individuals to retain their parental rights.

This chapter addresses the legal rights of families and the implications of neglectful and abusive care on children. Some sections consider how trauma and violence affect the behavior of family members and how the courts respond to such abuse. In total, four subjects are examined. These topics include (1) the role of paternalism and *parens patriae* in mental health law on the family, (2) family trauma and the cycle of crime, (3) the termination of parental rights, and (4) gay/lesbian rights and definitions of the family. While the issues reviewed in this chapter do not exhaustively canvass the family forensic field, the topics chosen are, nonetheless, controversial, significant, and demonstrate the pressing need for skilled practitioners in this subspecialty area of law and psychology.

The doctrines of paternalism and *parens patriae* are two legal principles demonstrating the power that the state possesses and exercises in the lives of persons suffering from psychiatric illness. How do paternalism and *parens patriae* work? What influence do these doctrines exert on families? How are these legal principles used in relation to civil commitment? Repeated exposure in childhood to family trauma and abuse can be devastating for young boys and girls. How does exposure to such violence affect a person in adulthood? What are the behavioral and situational risk factors involved in cycles of crime? What is our response to these children and the pathogenic care they are receiving? At what point is the termination of parental rights in the best interest of these children? What are the implications for the parents and children involved in termination of parental rights hearings? What role do forensic psychologists play in this process? In today's society, gay and lesbian citizens have redefined the meaning of family life and the family unit. Are children of nonheterosexual couples at any greater psychological risk when growing up in homosexual families? How does law and psychology assist us in our understanding of gay and lesbian family rights?

The legal system has a vested interest in protecting the rights and ensuring the responsibilities of families and their respective members. Often, the issue is about understanding how the law, with the assistance of psychology, can better address the changing and emerging needs of different families. The forensic specialist assumes a pivotal role in the intervention and policy process. As the individual sections of this chapter make clear, the field of family forensics requires additional research into the nature of family life in general, as well as the social, psychological, and legal factors that limit parents and their children from experiencing the joys of such a healthy existence in particular.

IMPACT OF MENTAL HEALTH LAW DOCTRINES ON FAMILIES: PATERNALISM AND *PARENS PATRIAE*

Introduction

At 6 years of age, a child was admitted indefinitely to a state hospital. The child's parents sought treatment for their son because of his aggressive and uncontrollable behavior. His diagnosis was "hyperkinetic reaction of childhood." Four years later, the parents relinquished their parental control to the county, whereupon the boy was placed in a mental hospital. Not long after, the youth filed a lawsuit requesting that the court "place him in a less drastic environment suitable to his needs" (*Parham v. J. R.*, 1978).

This example demonstrates the ramifications of what may occur when a person is deemed incapable of making his or her own decisions and placed under the guardianship of the state. The majority of these individuals are juveniles, elders, and persons who are found to be "out of sound" mind or mentally ill. This is the basic premise at work in the doctrines of *paternalism* and *parens patriae*; namely, that the intervention of the state in the life of an individual determined to be a serious threat to him- or herself and/or others is warranted and necessary. The historical context of the *parens patriae* doctrine comes from the authority of English kings to act or take responsibility for the presumed best interest of a disabled or impaired subject (Quinn, 2002). Today, it is often the police who manage the mentally ill when they are in crisis. According to Lamb, Weinberger, and DeCuir and Walter (2002, p. 1266), there are two principles that provide the justification for the police to take responsibility for the mentally ill which include: "their power and authority to protect the safety and welfare of the community and their *parens patriae* obligations to protect individuals with disabilities." What matters when the family of the mentally ill individual seeks out treatment over the objections of their psychiatrically disordered loved one? This section explores the development of *parens patriae* and paternalism in the realm of civil commitment and how, specifically, it has influenced the role of the family in such instances.

> In the 1860s, E. P. W. Packard was committed to a mental institution by her husband. Mrs. Packard, who was not in need of such care, was nevertheless institutionalized due to an 1851 Illinois statute that stated: Married women and infants who, in the judgment of the medical superintendents of the state asylum...may be entered or detained in the hospital at the request of the husband of the woman or guardian of the infant, without the evidence of insanity required... (J. E. Myers, 1983–1984, p. 376).
>
> Upon her release, Mrs. Packard began a nationwide campaign to adjust this law and others like it. Through her efforts, several bills were eventually passed that restricted the institutionalization of any person not found to be "insane or distracted by a verdict of a jury..." (J. E. Myers, 1983–1984, p. 376).

Literature Review

Much of Western civilization perceives the family as a unit in which its members have a duty to protect those who cannot care for themselves. This perception rests upon the assumption that adults, due to maturity and experience, are more knowledgeable than children and are better equipped to make decisions for their offspring. This concept was fundamental in establishing the historical notions of *parens patriae* and paternalism, whereby the state, similar to knowing family adults, is entrusted with the responsibility of caring for those persons in need of mental health care. Slobogin and Fondacaro (2000) proposed three separate models to rationalize the deprivation of personal freedoms by governmental institutions which include (1) the punishment model that deprives liberty as a sanction for blameworthy behavior; (2) the prevention model to curtail harm by way of deterrence or restraint; and, finally, (3) the protection model, which deprives civil liberty in order to ensure independent decision making.

Analysis of parental obligation to care for family members depicts a different picture. In reality, as the increasing number of child and elder abuse cases indicates, this familial belief system is not always practiced. "Some parents may at times be acting against the interests of their children" (*Bartley v. Kremens*, 1975, p. 1041). Specifically, in terms of commitment, some parents, or other family members, may not have the desire or energy to care for their unruly children or senile parent. In addition, there are instances in which family members are motivated by financial gain, such as inheritance or property control, culminating in the institutionalization of another relative. Hence, they request that the individual child or elder be admitted into a mental hospital despite the consequences that may transpire. Essentially, commitment may not be the most appropriate treatment for a given individual.

To demonstrate the susceptibility of civil commitment, one can analyze the above mentioned case of J. R. As unmanageable as J. R. might have been, placing him in an institution was not appropriate for his needs, according to the court's opinion (*Parham v. J. R.*, 1978). However, as a juvenile, J. R. was not able to overcome the request of his parents and psychologists when the initial decision to commit him was made. Prior to the *Parham* decision, there was virtually no judicial input that existed to ensure that the liberties and rights of the mentally ill were considered when a relative requested the hospitalization of a child family member.

Before the 1970s, civil commitment was an informal arena that was perceived as medical, not legal (Reisner & Slobogin, 1990). Hearings questioning whether a person should have been committed rarely occurred, if at all, until after the person had been confined. Because the mentally ill were considered incapable of knowing what was best for them, their opinions did not weigh heavily in court. In other words, if a family member requested a relative's commitment and there was a doctor's consent, then regardless of the wishes of the individual, he or she would most likely be committed. Once committed, the person was labeled mentally ill and it became difficult to cast off the stigma. Consequently, the probability of wrongfully or erroneously committing an individual to a mental institution was highly likely, given the nature of mental health policies defining commitment.

A recent study surveyed state statutes, which restricted the civil rights of the mentally ill or those found mentally incompetent (Hemmens, Miller, Burton, & Milner, 2002). The study examined the restriction of civil rights in five areas: jury service, voting, holding public office, marriage, and parenting. The results of a 1999 study were compared to those of a 1989 study in order to examine trends in the restriction of civil rights for the mentally ill. The study revealed that the restriction of the mentally ill's civil rights continues with an increase in the restriction of familial rights; specifically, marriage and parenting (Hemmens et al., 2002).

Provisions in the mental health field regarding the issue of commitment have only been developed within the past few decades. Previously, questions were not raised regarding the intentions of the family members who suggested it. Now that the courts are more actively involved in the process, there is a more watchful eye over family members, hospital administrators, and their respective motivations for civil confinement. Public defenders and specialists are assigned by the court to defend those individuals who are evaluated for commitment. This procedure is essential in those instances when family members do not look out for the best interest of a specific relative (e.g., as we have seen in cases such as *Parham v. J. R.*, 1978).

A judicial-type hearing is held prior to confinement during which time decisions surrounding commitment and the best medical care are addressed. These judicial guidelines are necessary, considering the unjust institutionalization some individuals faced as a result of past unethical standards for commitment. Yet, some major problems have developed with these new restrictions in relation to *parens patriae* and paternalism.

One difficulty with this transition can be observed when families that act in the best interest of a given member are penalized due to the actions of other members who harmfully suggest the commitment of a certain relative. New policies can marginalize the voices of good-intentioned families when deciding what is best for their relatives. Psychologists and judges make judgments with respect to the rights of individuals who are committed. However, these individuals place a professional standard on civil commitment determinations. Ultimately, these decisions lack a more personal understanding from those family members who represent the true needs of the committed patient. To illustrate, Shaw, Hotopf, and Davies (2003) found that discharges from psychiatric hospitals by the nearest relative against psychiatric advice were not related to poor clinical outcomes.

There are aspects of familial relations that are beneficial for determining what is best for an individual. For example, family members may possess a better awareness about the types of programs and activities to which an individual could respond. This is because family members have a personal connection with the individual. Court-appointed servants, however, lack this subjective knowledge about the committee. Thus, their decisions often do not embody all of a given situation's dynamics, and solely reflect documented information.

Despite the obvious advantages, good-intentioned family members, representing the interests of another individual, have often found it virtually impossible to get the care they feel would be most effective for their relative. As a result, the voices of invested family members frequently have been silenced. For these family members, in order to obtain the care they deem proper, several legal barriers must be hurdled. Then, too, there is the risk that the courts will not respect the wishes of family members for a variety of political and economic reasons (e.g., the case of Mrs. Packard).

Many debates exist which argue over whether the current implementation of *parens patriae* and paternalism in the civil commitment arena is any better than it was decades ago, especially considering the effect it has had on the family. In the process of protecting the mentally ill from family members who did not represent the best interests of the patient, relatives who are genuinely concerned now have to prove their well-meaning intentions to commit a relation, in order for that person to receive proper care. This practice is far removed from the historical assumption that family members will look out for the best interest of their relatives.

Forensic Psychology and Policy Implications

It is difficult to balance the views of the individual, family, and the state when dealing with the issue of mental hospital commitment. First and foremost, the individual should always have his or her liberties protected, yet, in most instances, the individual is incapable or too young to fight for such rights. This is why the doctrines of *parens patriae* and paternalism were established. However, when the state is given the power to act as a parent for an individual, the decisions made are going to reflect the politics and economics of that time. There needs to be some consistency in how these doctrines are implemented and what foci should be taken. As it stands, we have come to a point where the interests of the mentally ill are determined by public defenders and specialists. These specialists need to be appointed by the courts and not by advocates on either side of the debate. The experts, whether psychologists or doctors, need to be impartial to the situation at hand. Furthermore, the family needs to be recognized when decisions are made regarding an individual. In providing more protection for the mentally ill, the impact of the family has become less of a force in the entire process. It seems that while trying to protect the individual from family members with ill intentions, others are categorized as guilty of exploiting the mentally ill when they are not.

Suggestions for Future Research

When the doctrines of *parens patriae* and paternalism were first introduced, our society was very different. Since then, we have been trying to fit these antiquated notions into our modern values and beliefs. It seems as though we have done a successful job, considering the slim probability of pleasing everyone. Yet, it appears as if we have gone too far in making generalizations about the role of the family in this process. Some would argue that it is better to be pessimistic than optimistic in regard to predicting the motivations for people's actions. We have become so paranoid with this new system that we have drifted from making decisions based on human factors and are more concerned with making choices based on the judicial system.

Further research is needed to determine if current legal proceedings regard the patient as the most important figure. Along with that, since the family has become less of a voice in this process, it may be beneficial to investigate the ramifications of losing such a personal figure in the decision-making process.

FAMILY TRAUMA AND THE CYCLE OF CRIME

Introduction

An increasing number of children are living in chaotic familial and communal environments. Conservative estimates indicate that over 1 million children are abused and neglected each year in the United States alone (National Center on Child Abuse and Neglect, 1994). The United States is one of the most violent countries in the world and the lifetime exposure rates of young adults for victimization ranges from 76 to 82% and 93 to 96% for witnessing violence (Scarpa, 2003). According to Guadalupe and Bein (2001, p. 157), "A long history of violence and social and institutional oppression in U.S. society has reinforced violent behavior among children and youth." These children are often exposed to exorbitant levels of trauma characterized by parental neglect, physical abuse, sexual abuse, domestic violence, and inconsistent discipline from parental figures. The biological, psychological, and social repercussions of children growing up with such trauma are numerous.

According to Scarpa (2003), young adults with high levels of violence exposure by way of either victimization or witnessing report more psychological difficulties to include depressed mood, aggressive behavior, posttraumatic stress disorder symptoms, and interpersonal problems. Of particular interest, however, is the significance of family trauma and its relation to intergenerational cycles of antisocial and criminal behavior. The relationship between one's traumatic upbringing and the perpetuation of criminal behavior in adolescence and adulthood has been clearly noted in the literature. Empirical evidence does suggest that the growing numbers of adolescent and adult criminal offenders come from backgrounds plagued with varying levels of trauma. However, currently there are no concentrated efforts to address this issue in terms of prevention and effective intervention measures. The following case illustrates how a young male, who lived in a chaotic familial environment, resorted to violence.

Fifteen-year-old Arnold was arrested and incarcerated after he fatally stabbed his mother's boyfriend of 2 months. As a young child, Arnold had been exposed to numerous distressing events. On many occasions he observed his biological father physically assaulting his mother. Arnold's father physically abused him and often used objects such as belts, electric cords, and wooden planks. As a young child, Arnold was left alone in the house for days at a time without any guidance or supervision. Subsequently, Arnold began having numerous difficulties both at home and at school. His teachers reported that during class, he seemed distracted and irritable and he would often engage in physical altercations with other classmates. He began to exhibit increasingly dangerous and reckless behaviors; spoke perseveratively about weapons, stabbings, and the physical abuse he had witnessed; and expressed vague fears that he himself would come to harm others. The night of the stabbing, Arnold witnessed his mother and her boyfriend arguing in the living room. Arnold was unable to tolerate the argumentative behavior of his mother's boyfriend and, hence, Arnold impulsively reached for a kitchen knife and proceeded to stab him. Arnold was charged with assault with a deadly weapon and is currently awaiting sentencing.

Literature Review

As a result of Arnold's case, and those that are similar, it is apparent that the perpetuation of violence within families needs to be thoroughly examined and, ultimately, prevented. The results of exposure to severe familial violence is not randomly distributed within the population. Some children are substantially more likely to have such experiences associated with where they reside and with whom they live. Inner-city youth are exposed to especially chaotic environments, often marked by poverty and violence (Sklarew, Krupnick, Ward-Wimmer, & Napoli, 2002). Children who have risk factors in their lives such as domestic violence, parental substance abuse, and living in poverty are certainly at an increased risk for exposure to trauma and violence. Many children are unable to adapt or cope with intense feelings of helplessness, hopelessness, grief, and violent fantasies. In addition these children typically manifest an underlying depression, often expressed through aggression and self-destructive behaviors (Sklarew et al., 2002). Children can experience such violence within a number of different contexts; however, it is likely that the family, and especially a child's relationship with caregivers, is one of the most important of these contexts. The following literature review explores the risk factors involved in the cycle of crime. Preventative measures geared toward breaking the intergenerational cycle of crime are also discussed.

A common setting for violence is the home. Problems of parental abuse, neglect, and spousal abuse account for a major component of the physical and emotional trauma suffered by children. It is therefore not only important, but also necessary to examine the effects of familial violence, abuse, and neglect on the development of children who live within these contexts. In Helfer and Kempe's (1986) study, 82% of a group of adolescent offenders were found to have a history of abuse and neglect, and 43% recalled being knocked unconscious by one of their parents. Their sample of violent adolescents were victims of, as well as witnesses to, severe physical abuse. The sample provided a clear indication of how extreme physical disciplinary practices in the home correlated with aggressive and destructive delinquency. More recently, study that examined abuse perpetrated by siblings, as compared to parental abusers, found that abuse by siblings, like abuse by parents, may be associated with a cycle of violence in the life of the victim (Simonelli, Mullis, Elliott, & Pierce, 2002).

A study by McCord (1991) came from a larger longitudinal investigation of males who had been in a program designed to prevent delinquency. McCord (1991) examined families in which fathers were criminals and those in which fathers were not criminals, and found significant differences that helped explain the cycle of violence among sons of criminals. Results indicated that sons of criminals were more, rather than less, likely to become offenders. The data suggested that aggressive parental models increased the likelihood that their sons would be involved in criminal activities. Furthermore, maternal affection, self-confidence, and consistent nonpunitive discipline or supervision helped protect their sons from engaging in criminal behavior. This discovery led to the tentative conclusion that intervention techniques designed to develop competence among parents might be particularly effective when the targets are children at high risk (McCord, 1991).

Who are the children at high risk and how do these risk factors perpetuate a cycle of violence? Blumenthal (2000) described a pattern where a child's early context of how to function in relationships with others was damaged. The child learned to identify with the aggressor and repeats early childhood traumas in adulthood. Attachment theory provides some explanation of how a child in this environment develops a pattern of preemptive aggression. In other words, the child learns that the world is a hostile place made up of victims and victimizers where the youth must strike first to protect themselves in future relationships or interactions with others (Shipley & Arrigo, 2004).

One longitudinal study, completed by Widom (1992), looked specifically at the cycle of violence. Widom (1992) tracked 1575 cases from childhood through young adulthood and compared the arrest records of the two groups. One group contained 908 subjects who experienced some form of substantiated childhood abuse or neglect and a comparison group of 667 children who were not officially recorded as abused or neglected. Both groups were matched for age, race, sex, and socioeconomic status. Clear and succinct operational definitions of abuse and neglect allowed for a separate examination of physical abuse, sexual abuse, and neglect.

Results indicated that children who had been abused or neglected were 58% more likely to be arrested as juveniles, 38% more likely to be arrested as adults, 38% more likely to be arrested for a violent crime, and 77% more likely to be arrested if they were females. Abuse and neglect cases on average were nearly 1 year younger at first arrest, committed twice as many crimes, and were arrested 89% more frequently than the control group. A noteworthy conclusion was that a child who was neglected was just as likely as a child who was abused to be arrested for a violent crime. The aforementioned study further exemplified how childhood abuse and neglect can precipitate violent behavior in adolescence and adulthood. In order to test the hypothesis that victimized children grow up to victimize other children, a nationally representative data set made up of 6,002 participants was examined (Heyman & Slep, 2002). Results found that exposure to both physical violence and a witnessing of domestic violence between parents significantly increased the risk of adulthood family violence for women.

Researchers have also explored the familial and communal backgrounds of criminal offenders. Briscoe (1997) examined the familial histories of youths who were committed to the Texas Youth Commission (TYC). The TYC is a state agency that is responsible for the most seriously delinquent and disturbed youths. The findings indicated that the vast majority of the youths in TYC had histories of abuse and neglect. A majority of youth offenders had family members with histories of violence, substance abuse, criminal behavior, and mental impairments. Approximately 71% of these delinquent youths came from chaotic environments and 80% of the subject's parental figures lacked adequate disciplinary skills. This youth offender study further highlighted the relationship between traumatic childhood experiences and the increased likelihood of engaging in delinquent behavior.

A similar study (A. Levinson & Fonagy, 1999) examined 22 male patients in a prison sample and matched them with a group of psychiatric controls. Their crimes included attempted burglary, theft, property damage, car theft, gross indecency, importation of drugs, armed robbery, kidnapping, rape, and murder. They were interviewed with a structured clinical interview for *Diagnostic and Statistical Manual of Mental Disorders* (1983), *Third Edition, Revised (DSM-III-R)* disorders. They all had at least one clinical disorder and 91% had at least one personality disorder; 50% had a DSM–III–R diagnosis of borderline personality disorder. The average Global Assessment of Functioning (GAF) score for the group was 47. The GAF was generally indicative of serious symptoms or serious impairments in social and occupational functioning. A number of striking findings indicated that among this group of 22 criminals, extreme deprivations in childhood, severe physical abuse, and neglect were commonly and convincingly reported. Although this was only a pilot investigation, the results were promising to the extent that they linked histories of abuse with the perpetuation of criminal behavior and psychopathology.

Forensic Psychology and Policy Implications

The crisis of family trauma and the perpetuation of violence affects tens of thousands of families nationwide. Increasingly, children are not only witnessing, but experiencing, varying degrees of violence in their homes and communities. This exposure to violence changes the way children view the world and may change the value they place on life itself (Groves, Zuckerman, Marans, & Cohen, 1993). It can certainly affect their ability to learn, to establish and sustain relationships with others, and to cope with life's stressors. Yet there is a general lack of knowledge and understanding in terms of how growing up in such chaotic environments affects young children's social, emotional, and cognitive development. Factors such as the public's lack of understanding about the effects of family trauma only serve to hinder efficient and effective intervention methods.

The literature clearly points to a link between family trauma and an intergenerational cycle of violence and crime. Children who grow up in unstructured, chaotic, and abusive homes are at an increased risk of engaging in violent or antisocial behavior. Thus, it is imperative that policymakers endorse services for children and families which interface with police, schools, courts, community programs, and health care settings. Solutions must encompass preventing trauma, early intervention, and swift and clear repercussions for chronic or violent behavior. It is crucial to reach children who experience such trauma long before they arrive at an age where they act out their experiences in a violent manner.

Another inherent component to helping traumatized children is to provide information and counseling to the caregivers in the children's lives. Psychologists should play a vital role in treatment and evaluation of these issues. Children who have witnessed and/or experienced violence should be provided with therapy to not only address grief and anger-related issues, but also to help them build adaptive coping strategies to prevent the perpetuation of the cycle of violence. These children are more likely to come in contact with the family court system and/or mental health system. Violence risk assessments are a likely referral, as well as dispositional evaluations. Mental health professionals should play an active role in prevention or intervention programs that focus on problem solving, communication skills, conflict resolution skills, and anger management skills (DuRant, Barkin, & Krowchuk, 2001).

Suggestions for Future Research

Research has suggested that while the majority of those who perpetrate violence have a history of abuse or trauma as a child, most childhood victims of abuse do not perpetrate violence or abuse in adulthood. Investigators needs to continue to examine what mitigating factors prevent the majority of abuse survivors from perpetuating the cycle. What are the intermediating variables that lead from abuse to violence in adulthood for those who do become perpetrators (Fagan, 2001)? Future investigations of family trauma must investigate how familial trauma affects children, and how it impacts communities and society in general. Existing findings provide some important insights into these issues; however, a great deal of research still needs to be conducted. If family trauma perpetuates itself by producing a vicious cycle of violence, then it is imperative to explore what interventions can break this cycle. Studies are needed which elucidate more fully the range and effects of familial trauma and, more so, assess the effects of early treatment measures. We therefore need a closer look at the extent to which some interventions may be more effective than others in terms of differences between parental education, counseling for families in crisis, or stricter accountability measures for perpetrators of such violence. In addition, a gamut of preventative measures needs to be explored and utilized in order to thwart the cyclical nature of family trauma and violence. Finally, future research could help to elucidate the harmful effects of extreme stress in childhood on brain development (Koenen, Moffitt, Caspi, Taylor, & Purcell, 2003).

TERMINATION OF PARENTAL RIGHTS

Introduction

In cases where the abuse and neglect of children are evident, the state may find it necessary to petition for the termination of parental rights in order to act in the best interests of the child. Some view this as an extreme measure by the state to forever sever the legal bonds between the biological parent(s) and child (Wattenberg, Kelley, & Kim, 2001). Serious risk factors are evident in both the decision to reunite a child with an abusive or neglectful parent or to terminate their parental rights. Forensic psychologists are called upon for parental rights termination consultation. Psychologists are frequently utilized to conduct assessments and to provide testimony in these hearings. Experts are often presented by all parties involved.

In 1980, Congress passed the Adoption Assistance and Child Welfare Act (AACWA), in which the goal was to preserve families that had engaged in child abuse and neglect (Erickson, 2000). During the last decade, there has been a shift from an emphasis on rehabilitation and reunification to a focus on the safety of the child being paramount with provisions for expedited termination of parental rights and speedier adoptions. This paradigm shift occurred in part as a result of the wave of serious child abuse and death cases in the 1980s and 1990s. The attempts at rehabilitation were marginal at best and many children languished in the foster care system. When President Clinton signed the 1997 Adoption and Safe Families Act (ASFA), the focus shifted to permanency planning within an expedited time frame (Wattenberg et al., 2001).

Much debate still exists as to what is in the best interests of the child in question and at what point the legal ties to the biological parent must be dissolved. Some argue that while the intent of the shift is understandable, it may just encourage an already overburdened family court system, in some instances, to terminate parental rights without close enough scrutiny or just cause. When one considers the extreme cases of child abuse or neglect that end in the death of the child, it is not difficult to imagine the Court erring on the side of caution and the termination of parental rights with potentially irreversible consequences. Media accounts during the 1980s and 1990s described stories of children who had been reunited with their families, only to be later killed by the abusive parent (Erickson, 2000). Consider the following case illustration.

The cover story "A Shameful Death" in *Time* magazine on December 11, 1995, documented the case of Elisa Izquierdo, a 6-year-old child who had been returned to an abusive mother by social services only to be brutally tortured and murdered. Elisa's mother, a crack addict, came to believe that her father had put Elisa under a spell that had to be beaten out of the child. Elisa was also repeatedly sexually assaulted with a toothbrush and a hairbrush. Elisa's mother confessed to killing her by throwing her against a concrete wall. 'She confessed that she made Elisa eat her own feces and that she mopped the floor with her head. The police told reporters that there was no part of the 6-year-old's body that was not cut or bruised" (Van Biema, 1995, p. 36; cited in Erickson, 2000, p. 84).

Those involved in research and policy called for reform of the child welfare system. Gelles, in *The Book of David* (1996), eloquently argued that AACWA was not protecting vulnerable children. Like Elisa, 15-month-old David was killed by his mother, and also like Elisa, it was a death that should not have occurred given the known history of child abuse in the family. Gelles described how the model of family preservation that was based on rehabilitation of parents was failing to protect children. He questioned the assumption that all parents were motivated to change their behavior, arguing that many parents simply agreed to participate in rehabilitative programs in order to avoid further court action. Gelles stated the need to "abandon the fantasy that child welfare agencies can balance the goals of protecting children and preserving families,

(continued)

(*Continued*)
adopting instead a child-centered policy of family services" (1996, p. 148; cited in Erickson, 2000, p. 84).

Literature Review

Elisa's case demonstrates the extreme example of what can go horribly wrong with reuniting a child with an abusive family. Parental rights termination is a permanent severing of ties between a parent and child that results in a loss of custody and any legal authority over the child's welfare in the future, as well as making the child eligible for adoption (M. B. Johnson, Baker, & Maceira, 2001). M. B. Johnson et al. (2001) indicated that the state's responsibility to petition for parental rights termination and the court's ability to grant the order draws from the *parens patriae* doctrine, which places the state in a position to maintain societal interests.

During the past 3 decades, there has been a shifting focus on the federal government's position on what action should be taken to protect children who experience abuse or severe neglect while in the care of their families (Erickson, 2000). Prior to the mid 1970s, the federal government had little involvement in child welfare policy. By the mid 1970s, child welfare policies in the United States focussed more and more on removing children from unsafe homes and placing them in the foster care system.

In 1980, with the passage of the AACWA, the government acknowledged the obligation the states owed to parents whose children were in foster care to provide rehabilitative and prevention services and a time line to help with the process of reunification as the primary goal (Erickson, 2000). The services included group and individual counseling, substance abuse treatment, parenting classes, and regular visitation of the parent with the abused or neglected child in the home of the foster parent. This legislation was aimed at targeting the growing drift in foster care, specifically, those children caught in limbo.

Initially, it appeared that this strategy was successful with a decline in the foster care population from 1980 until 1986. However, from 1986 until 1993, the foster care population grew from 280,000 to 445,000 (House Ways & Means Committee, 1998). In addition to the overall criticisms of the ineffectiveness of this approach, researchers argued that there was little empirical evidence to support that these rehabilitative interventions were effective under these circumstances (Erickson, 2000). Costin, Karger, & Stoesz (1996) explained that the belief was that once the parents of these children understood the causes of their behavior, they would then change it. However, critics alleged that this model ignored the myriad of more complex environmental factors that contributed to the cycle of violence for many of the families involved (Costin et al., 1996; Erickson, 2000).

In 1993, Congress allowed 930 million dollars to be used over five years for family preservation by way of the Family Preservation and Support Program, which was designed to prevent out-of-home placements for children who were abused or neglected (Erickson, 2000). "Permanency planning" has been a consistent concept throughout the past 3 decades, but the means by which policy, the government, and the courts believe this should happen has shifted. Both the 1980 and 1993 legislation addressed this issue by way of reasonable efforts at family reunification or preservation. Once again, critics of the 1993 legislation compared it to the 1994 Violence Against Women Act and noted that the legislation for children only received half of the money, and that the legislation did not include a pro-arrest strategy for parents who physically abused their children (Costin et al., 1996; Erickson, 2000). The child abuse and neglect policy mandated home-based services, which included psychological treatment for parents who abused their children, while the Violence Against Women Act mandated arrest for husbands who were physically abusive toward their wives. Researchers thus asked the question: "Why does violence against women result in arrest, whereas violence against children lead to treatment" (Erickson, 2000, p. 85)?

Ultimately, the critics of the AACWA were instrumental in shaping the 1997 Adoption and Safe Families Act (ASFA) (M. B. Johnson et al., 2001). ASFA strives to improve on the deficits of the previous legislation by expediting parental rights termination or reunification if possible, providing financial incentives to the states for adoption placements, and by making the safety and welfare of the child the paramount issue rather than family preservation. All 50 states passed legislation that enacted ASFA by the end of 1999 (Erickson, 2000). This legislation attempts to reunify families using reasonable efforts; however, the time line is well defined and much shorter. ASFA also promotes concurrent planning or that states may pursue alternative placements, while attempting reunification, in order to speed up placement if parental conduct changes or is deemed unfit. ASFA mandates a state to file a termination of parental rights petition if a child has been placed in foster care for at least 15 of the last 22 months (Erickson, 2000).

There are three exceptions in place that do not require the petition to be filed: (1) a relative is caring for the child, (2) the agency documents a compelling reason why termination is not in the best interests of the child, or (3) if the state failed to provide reasonable efforts or services to safely reunite the child with their family within that time frame (Erickson, 2000). However, "reasonable efforts" are not operationally defined and the standard is not clearly set out. Three exceptions also exist wherein reasonable efforts for family preservation are not required: (1) the parent has forced the child to experience an aggravating circumstance to include torture, abandonment, or sexual abuse; (2) a person has killed another one of his or her children or has in some way conspired or aided another person in doing so; and, finally, (3) reasonable efforts are not mandated when the parental rights have been terminated for a sibling of the child in question (Erickson, 2000). Clear and convincing evidence is the burden of proof required to demonstrate that a child cannot safely remain with his or her parents and that a safer option, which is in the best interest of the child, exists (Wattenberg et al., 2001).

Some criticize ASFA for failing to take into consideration the ability of children to form multiple attachments and that severing parental ties quickly can have enduring negative effects (Erickson, 2000; Garrison, 1996). As long as the child is in foster care, visitation by parents is possible. Another criticism is the assumption that expediting termination of parental rights will lead to adoption. Some researchers have found that the number of adoptions cannot keep up with the larger number of children whose parental rights have been terminated, and many of these children just age out of the system (Erickson, 2000).

Another difficulty regarding parental rights termination hearings is that many of the parents involved are indigent and have marginal representation from attorneys who may have little experience dealing with these issues (M. B. Johnson et al., 2001). Additionally, the child welfare agency that attempts to provide services to them also collects evidence at the same time that might be used against the parents at trial. Furthermore, as M. B. Johnson et al. (2001) stated: "If a judge errs in terminating the parental rights, the consequences are minimal in that the aggrieved, typically indigent, parent and child can only suffer quietly. While if the judge errs in the direction of returning a child to a parent who later harms the child, the response from the press and the public will be substantial" (p. 17).

Research has demonstrated that parents who are involved with termination of parental rights typically have a long history of multiple problems including mental illness, substance abuse, lower intellectual functioning, involvement with the criminal justice system, limited formal education, poverty, and their own childhood history of out-of-home placement, as well as abuse and neglect (Wattenberg et al., 2001). The characteristics of parents who are facing a termination of parental rights petition is an example of the previously discussed cycle of violence.

The children involved were generally very young, typically lived in poverty-stricken, chaotic homes, and spent an extended amount of time in the system, when placed out of the home (Wattenberg et al., 2001). Past research has noted that a number of children from these home environments manifest a variety of disorders, including gross behavioral problems and below average IQs (Borgman, 1981). Critics of parental rights termination also point out that this strategy does little to benefit the older child with strong attachments to their parents as well as scant desire and probability to be adopted (M. B. Johnson et al., 2001). Children often remain fiercely loyal and attached to their parents, even when they have experienced serious abuse or neglect (Borgman, 1981; Garrison, 1996; M. B. Johnson 1996, 1999; M. B. Johnson et al., 2001). M. B. Johnson et al. (2001, p. 16) stated: "For instance, an early adolescent female responded to the state's petition to terminate her parental ties to her birth-mother by running away from her foster home of 7 years and returning to the home of her psychiatrically impaired mother." The termination of parental rights not only has implications for the child's abusive or neglectful parent(s), but for the child's relationship with siblings and extended family as well (M. B. Johnson et al., 2001).

Janko (1994) highlighted the role of environmental or sociocultural factors which contribute to the problem of abuse and neglect. These are factors that need to be addressed in order to reduce this problem overall and to more successfully reunify families with some expectation of success. In brief, the question is whether certain environmental circumstances, such as having "adequate money, food, housing, health care, and available adults to share care-giving responsibilities" will add stress or relief to parents (Janko, 1994, p. 3).

A recent study examined the records of 97 children ages 6 and under whose parental rights were terminated in Minnesota between 1991 and 1997 (Wattenberg et al., 2001). The study was initiated to identify risk factors or a "risk pool" of families who were likely to have a high probability of parental rights termination. The racial makeup of the sample data was approximately 48% Caucasian and 34% African American, as the two largest groups. About 64% of the mothers were Caucasian, 21% were African American, and 9.3% were American Indian, with the remaining 5.7% multiracial. More than half of the mothers had their first child before the age of 18 with approximately 12% having their first child when they were age 15 or younger. The median age of the mothers at termination was age 26. More than 80% of the mothers in the sample had multiple disorders, which included substance abuse currently or in the past (57.7%); disorders such as major mental illness (i.e., depression, bipolar disorder, schizophrenia, or personality disorders) (47.5%); developmental disabilities (12%); and almost one-third had a childhood history of abuse or out of home placement. Greater than one-quarter were involved with the correctional system and more than one-fifth had experienced one or more relationships with a history of domestic violence (Wattenberg et al., 2001). Substance abuse was identified as the problem that led to a termination of parental rights judgment in the majority of cases. Overall, 80% of cases documented varied, overlapping conditions resulting in a chaotic and unsafe living environment (Wattenberg et al., 2001).

Forty-one of the 97 cases did not have any information regarding the father of the child. Out of the 56 remaining case files, greater than 60% of the fathers also had multiple problems (Wattenberg et al., 2001). Greater than one-third had a current or past substance abuse problem, 25% had a criminal record, approximately 20% engaged in domestic violence with their partner, 15% had a history of childhood abuse and/or placement, and 14% were incarcerated at the time of the termination hearing.

Children of color were overrepresented in the sample taking into consideration the demographics of Minnesota with 57.7% Caucasian, 25.8% African American, and 13.4% American Indian. The Latino/Chicano children and Asian American children were more evenly represented in the sample at 2.1% and 3.3%, respectively. Approximately 20% of the sample were biracial. Almost two-thirds or 63.7%, of the children were the age of three or younger at the termination of parental rights. Greater than 75% of the children in the sample had siblings also in the process with more than one-third having had three or more siblings. Approximately 80% of the children had most recently lived with nonfamilial or nonrelative foster homes. Almost 60% of the children were identified as having disabilities including: emotional disturbance (26.8%), physical disability (9.3%), developmental disability (7.2%), learning disability (5.2%), and other conditions (11.4%). Evidence of sexual abuse was present in 18.5% of the cases. More than one-quarter of the children had been born either drug- or alcohol-exposed (Wattenberg et al., 2001).

Finally, the "reasonable efforts" at family preservation included counseling (52.6%), substance abuse treatment (48.5%), and parenting classes (47.4%). Mental health assessments occurred in 36.1% of the families and chemical dependency assessments in 29.9% of the cases. Parenting assessments occurred in 21.6% of the cases, home-based services (18.6%), and domestic violence treatment (14.4%). Direct services to children included special education (20.6%), therapy (15.5%), and developmental and psychological assessment (13.4%). However, the vast majority of children had no documented services (Wattenberg et al., 2001). The role that psychologists can play in this process is substantial. Certainly, additional services for these at-risk children are desperately needed.

Forensic Psychology and Policy Implications

Child welfare policy and practice in the United States continues to be criticized. The resources available to this system are overwhelmed by the number of children and families who experience abuse and neglect. Wattenberg et al. (2001) described the need for courts, child welfare workers, and mental health professionals to identify early on those families who are unlikely to be reunited with children, so that resources can be effectively used to investigate other permanency options. There are risks inherent in both the foster care system and in the abusive or neglectful parental home.

Regarding the Canadian system, Burford, Pennell, MacLeod, Campbell, and Lyall (1996) noted that, "Disclosures of widespread abuse in foster care and in children's institutions during the past decade have laid bare as false belief that placing a child into protective custody or substitute care is a guarantee of safety or long-range well-being for that child" (cited in M. B. Johnson et al., 2001, p. 26). What is also striking is the lack of therapeutic resources currently provided to these very high-risk children. Not only have they experienced abuse and/or neglect, but their parental bonds are severed and no matter how toxic the relationship, it is often quite traumatic for the children involved. Although the cycle of violence is present in the national consciousness, our society puts little resources toward prevention and intervention programs for these children. Our nearsightedness prevents us from contemplating the far more expensive human and financial costs our lack of action will create in the future. Wattenberg et al. (2001) cautioned that the "reasonable efforts" phrasing in the AACWA legislation from the 1980s did not provide a workable guideline for how much intervention or services was adequate in the attempt for reunification. For those children who cannot or should not be reunited with their biological families, expediting the adoption process by shortening stays in foster care would reduce costs and would bring the security of a permanent home to numerous children each year (Festinger & Pratt, 2002).

Erickson (2000) suggested that interventions should increase social supports for high-risk families, rather than just focusing on the psychological problems of the parent accused of abuse or neglect. As a whole, our society must recognize the impact of prolonged margin-alization, poverty, and inequality. These broad societal changes, however, will not come quickly enough to aid the parent facing parental rights termination in a little over a year or the children whose lives are in danger in an abusive home. Some critics also question the policy soundness of not criminally prosecuting more parents who fail to feed or who physically beat their children. Erickson (2000) speculated that perhaps our society values our indigent children less or wishes to limit governmental control over the institution of the family. Child welfare policies could be focused toward strengthening families and their connections to the larger community (Costin et al., 1996).

Mental health professionals, particularly psychologists who will testify as experts, should have extensive training in assessing the parent–child relationship. The evaluating psychologist will likely also be asked to opine about whether or not the parent's behavior or condition will change in the foreseeable future. Training in assessing the nuances of whether or not the parent(s) are likely to comply with reunification requirements is also recommended (Wattenberg et al., 2001). The forensic expert will frequently testify regarding the potential risks and benefits of either termination or reunification. Some mental health professionals should also have a more prominent role in providing developmental and mental health assessments for these children, while other scientists should take on the treatment role of providing individual or group therapy for the myriad of problems and stressors the family faces.

Suggestions for Future Research

Future research should develop a better understanding of the interaction of high-risk factors such as substance abuse, mental illness, poverty, intellectual disabilities, domestic violence, and a history of childhood abuse in a family's involvement in the child welfare system and in the criminal and family courts (Wattenberg et al., 2001). Comprehending these factors could aid in the development of more appropriate programming and therapeutic interventions for the families. Wattenberg et al. (2001) also recommended further examination of multicultural issues in the service delivery to at-risk families. Research should be explored to determine the effectiveness of concurrent planning in expediting permanent placements for children whose parental rights are terminated. Studies should also be conducted to help refine our risk assessments of children in both reunification and termination situations, in order to more fully appreciate the detrimental effects either of these scenarios might have on a particular child. A better understanding of a child's attachment to an abusive parent and their ability to form multiple attachments can aid in the development of permanency planning that is truly in the best interest of the child.

GAY/LESBIAN RIGHTS AND DEFINITIONS OF THE FAMILY

Introduction

The dynamics of contemporary families have shifted away from the "ideal" context of the nuclear family. Single-parent households are becoming increasingly commonplace and, more importantly, there has been an increase in the formation of gay and lesbian families. Recently, the state of Massachusetts legalized gay marriages, allowing homosexual couples to receive the legal benefits and protections that heterosexual couples have always been afforded. Along these lines, Dillen (2003) described the oppression of gay and lesbian individuals by the heterosexual, white, and middle class. Massachusetts also prohibits discrimination against individuals who apply to become adoptive parents, and enables adults to adopt a partner's child through second-parent adoption (Shelley-Sireci & Ciano-Boyce, 2002).

However, overall, little attention is paid to how parental rights have often been denied to lesbian or gay individuals. Common misconceptions about gay and lesbian families only serve to hinder the development of laws and policies, which favor artificial insemination, adoption, and foster care. For example, many people believe that children of homosexuals are apt to acquire parental sexual proclivities as well as to be subjected to additional sexual harm. Concerns also arise as far as children in nonconventional families experiencing difficulties with gender identity, gender roles, and having an increased likelihood of moving toward a homosexual orientation. A second category of concerns is that children living with homosexual parents may be stigmatized, teased, or otherwise traumatized by peers. Some courts have expressed fears that children in the custody of gay or lesbian parents will be more vulnerable to psychological maladjustment or will exhibit interpersonal difficulties and subsequent behavior problems. These are just some of the pertinent issues that are discussed within the context of gay and lesbian families. The following case illustrates the family dynamics of a young girl raised by lesbian parents.

Sarah is a 10-year-old in the fourth grade. She is healthy, bright, curious, and determined. She was born to Marsha into a white family consisting of two parents, Marsha and Jane. The donor of the sperm, Bill, is a heterosexual man who is a friend of Marsha and Jane and liked the idea of physically participating in helping his friends create a family. Marsha and Jane have all along chosen to counter external threats to their family by being out as lesbians. They live in a large city in a part of town friendly to lesbian-headed families. Marsha is active at Sarah's school, where she works to educate the teachers about lesbian and gay parents and the needs of the children. They belong to a local lesbian-and-gay parents group and attend gatherings as a family. In addition, they have consciously tried to give Sarah tools for interacting with the larger world. They talk to her about homophobia, helping her recognize it so she can learn to separate someone else's prejudice from a statement about her personally. However, to her parents' dismay, Sarah is signaling a need to know about her biological roots. Her parents have feelings in common with many parents whose families are created through adoption or donor insemination. They want Sarah to be only their child. Sarah's parents want to protect her from the pain and confusion that may be generated by needing to integrate the complex roots of her identity. On the other hand, her parents want Sarah to feel whole and integrated. They want to do all they can to prepare Sarah by giving her the support and the skills to maneuver through a complex process (Barrett, 1997).

Literature Review

Sarah's case elucidates some of the dynamics which may arise in gay and lesbian families. For example, gay and lesbian families have to continually struggle with prejudicial notions such as homophobia and gross stereotyping. On the basis of their sexual orientation, homosexual parents are continually labeled as unfit parents who are incapable of rearing well-adjusted children. Yet there is an absence of literature indicating any significant difficulties experienced by children brought up in households of lesbian or gay parents relative to those experienced by children growing up in comparable heterosexual households (Franklin, 2003; Tye, 2003). The existing body of research suggests that gay and lesbian parents are as likely as heterosexual parents to provide home environments that are conducive to positive developmental outcomes among children growing up within them. The following literature review further exemplifies the preceding premise and counters many commonly held misconceptions of gay and lesbian families.

There are between 1.2 and 3 million individuals who are in homosexual-partnered household relationships in the United States (Tye, 2003). The American Civil Liberties Union Lesbian and Gay Rights Project (2002) indicated that estimates of the prevalence of children raised by gay parents varies significantly with the high end being as many as 9 million. In the United States, the number of lesbian mothers is estimated to range from about 1 to 5 million, and gay fathers ranging from 1 to 3 million (Gottman, 1990). A more recent national study found that out of a random sample, 8% of lesbians and gay men were parents or a legal guardian of a child under the age of 18, and 49% of participants indicated that although they were not currently parents they would like to be (Henry J. Kaiser Family Foundation, 2001). Many lesbians and gay men who became parents within heterosexual marriages before adopting homosexual identities are also becoming parents after coming out. Therefore, it is likely that the preceding estimates minimize the actual number of homosexual parents.

Franklin (2003) described the growing trend of the planned gay and lesbian family. She described the impact of such public figures as Melissa Etheridge and Rosie O'Donnell, as well as the crisis in the U.S. child welfare system with greater than a half a million children in long-term foster care, as contributing to the growing awareness and increasing acceptance of the homosexual family through adoption or assisted fertilization. Additionally, the diversity of their family systems is described to include donor insemination, frequently used by lesbian couples, whereby one woman carries the child and the other obtains legal parental rights through a second-parent adoption process. Some lesbian couples adopt through the public adoption system, which is the most likely means used by gay men to parent (Franklin, 2003).

Heterosexual individuals are typically expected to become parents and many do so without planning, which is very different from the way many homosexual couples become parents (Franklin, 2003). She discussed how the minority of lesbian and gay men who become parents are a "self-selected, highly motivated" group who often endured a great deal of thought and planning, as well as financial expense prior to becoming parents. These individuals are also highly sensitive to outside criticism and negative expectations, so they may strive to be "super parents" (Franklin, 2003, p. 51). Thus, it is imperative for social scientists and the general public to take a closer look at the dynamics of gay and lesbian families.

Tasker and Golombok's (1995) longitudinal study of 25 young adults from lesbian families and 21 young adults raised by heterosexual single mothers revealed that those raised by lesbian mothers functioned well in adulthood in terms of psychological well-being, family identity, and relationships. The commonly held assumption that lesbian mothers will have lesbian daughters and gay sons was not supported by the findings. Furthermore, young adults from lesbian family backgrounds were no more likely to remember general teasing or bullying by their peers than were those from heterosexual single-parent homes. With respect to teasing about their sexuality, young adults from lesbian families were more likely to recall having been teased about being gay or lesbian themselves. No significant differences were found between young adults from lesbian and hetero-sexual single-mother households in the proportion who had experienced sexual attraction to someone of the same gender. Moreover, the majority of young adults from lesbian backgrounds identified themselves as hetero-sexual. No significant difference between young adults from lesbian and heterosexual single-parent homes was found for anxiety level as assessed by the Trait Anxiety Inventory. The groups did not differ with respect to depression level as assessed by the Beck Depression Inventory.

The study clearly indicated that this sample of young adults who were raised in lesbian households did not experience any detrimental effects as a result of their familial upbringing.

Overall, current research not only fails to substantiate assumptions of significant detrimental effects to children of homosexual parents, but also identifies specific strengths, such as more egalitarian and authoritative parenting styles, and children who are more emotionally attuned (Franklin, 2003; S. Johnson & O'Connor, 2001; C. J. Patterson & Chan, 1999).

A recent study examined the experience of lesbian adoptive parents as compared to heterosexual adoptive parents (Shelley-Sireci & Ciano-Boyce, 2002). Eighteen lesbian adoptive parents, 44 heterosexual adoptive parents, and 49 lesbian parents who utilized donor fertilization were surveyed to assess the similarities in the adoption process. Results indicated that the adoption process was similar for parents of both sexual orientations, but lesbian parents perceived more discrimination and were more likely to be guarded with information during the home study (Shelley-Sireci & Ciano-Boyce, 2002). On the basis of a literature review on the children of lesbian and gay parents, C. Patterson (1994) concluded that the development of these children was well within normal limits. Patterson studied 37 four- to nine-year-olds and found only two differ-ences between children of lesbian and heterosexual parents: (1) children of lesbian parents reported more symptoms of stress, but also (2) a stronger sense of well-being. Lesbian mothers who did not conceal their sexual orientation and who maintained supportive relationships with extended family members and adults in the community were better able to protect their children from prejudicial experiences. The author concluded that the common misconception that children of gay men and lesbians were more likely to adopt a homosexual orientation was completely unfounded.

Flaks, Ficher, Masterpasqua, and Joseph (1995) compared 3- to 10-year-old children born to 15 lesbian families through donor insemination with those of 15 matched heterosexual families. The families were white, well educated, and drawn from a fairly affluent population. As demonstrated by their performance on a broad range of parent and child outcome measures, couples of both sexual orientations were assessed in terms of parental awareness skills and child-care problems and solutions. Compared with fathers but not with mothers in heterosexual couples, lesbian couples exhibited more parental awareness skills and identified more child-care problems and solutions. The results of this study should generalize well to young children of affluent, stable, and committed lesbian couples who have used anonymous donor insemination. The traditional hypothesis that the healthy development of children requires two heterosexual parents is certainly called into question. The results within this sample show few differences among children of lesbian and heterosexual couples in terms of their psychological and social adjustment.

How important are family structural variables, such as the number of parents in the home and the sexual orientation of parents, as predictors of children's development? Chan, Raboy, and Patterson (1998) conducted a study of 80 families, all of whom had conceived children using the resources of a single sperm bank, including 55 families headed by lesbians and 25 families headed by heterosexual parents. Children averaged 7 years of age and biological mothers averaged 42 years of age. Results showed that children were developing in a normal fashion and that their adjustment was unrelated to structural variables such as parental sexual orientation or the number of parents in the household. Variables associated with family interactions and processes were, however, significantly related to children's adjustment. Not surprisingly, parents who were experiencing higher levels of stress, higher levels of interparental conflict, and lower levels of love for each other had children who exhibited more behavioral problems. The results are consistent with the general hypothesis that children's well-being is more a function of parenting and relationship processes within the family than the function of household composition.

Forensic Psychology and Policy Implications

To many individuals, getting married and raising children are central aspirations; however, these basic rights have been denied to lesbian and gay citizens in many states across America. Common misconceptions allude to the notion that lesbians and gay men are unfit parents or that children suffer irreparable harm if brought up in the households of lesbian or gay parents. Evidence from recent research indicates otherwise and suggests that children raised within lesbian- or gay-headed households are generally well adjusted. In Sarah's case illustrated above, her parents countered external threats to their family by educating Sarah and providing her with the support and encouragement that she needed.

A question then arises as to why half of the states in America consider parental sexual orientation relevant to child custody, visitation rights, foster care, and adoption rights. State laws on child custody, visitation, and adoption are based on what is in the "best interest of the child." Unfortunately, this particular clause opens the door to a consideration of the parent's sexual orientation and may introduce a certain level of subjectivity as far as court decisions about child custody, visitation rights, and adoption cases. Most states, however, utilize the Best Interests Standard and consider the parent's homosexual conduct, only as far as it can be shown that this has some adverse effect on the child. Indeed, the evidence to date suggests that home environments provided by gay and lesbian parents are as likely as those provided by heterosexual parents to support and to enable children's psychosocial growth (C. J. Patterson & Redding, 1996). Accordingly, social scientists can work to expand the body of research on lesbian and gay families and can make efforts to ensure that the results become available to the public and policymakers through appropriate publications. Not only can scientific evidence help alleviate misconceptions about lesbian- or gay-headed households, it can also facilitate changes in judicial or legislative decision-making processes. Thus, as certain elements change within the legal system, securing child custody cases and gaining adoption rights may eventually be a less arduous process for gay or lesbian families.

Suggestions for Future Research

Goldfried (2001) stressed the importance of future research on many gay, lesbian, and bisexual issues such as life span development, teenage suicide, substance abuse, victimization and abuse, and family and couple relationships. Research on lesbian and gay families is still relatively new, and additional work is needed if we are to expand our understanding of the lives of homosexual parents and their children. Future research that explores the predominant child-rearing styles of such families and their effects on children's adjustment in comparison to heterosexual families is certainly needed. James (2002, p. 475) stated, "The changing face of gay and lesbian parenting demands that researchers, educators, clinicians, and policymakers explore the issues of gay and lesbian adoptive parents and their children in their own right, not assuming that they are necessarily the same as those faced by other lesbian and gay families." Less research is conducted on children of gay fathers than on children with lesbian mothers. There is a lack of research assessing the development of children of gay or lesbian parents during adolescence and adulthood. Longitudinal studies which follow gay or lesbian families over a certain time period are also needed. However, the costly and time-intensive nature of such studies have, to date, hindered such efforts. Nonetheless, longitudinal studies with representative samples of homosexual and heterosexual families, including observational as well as questionnaire and interview assessments, would be better able to enhance our understanding of parents and children within these contexts. Research in this area would help expand our understanding of Sarah's family and those that are similar as well as many others headed by gay fathers and would elucidate more fully the dynamics of such families.

Practice Update Section: Family Issues in Court and Civil Forensics

Forensic psychologists can become involved in parental rights termination litigation in a variety of ways. Anytime psychologists address an issue as contentious as parental rights, they must be very well trained and expect their work to be carefully scrutinized. A psychological examiner in this situation should be very familiar with pertinent research and the forensic standard of practice in assessing the issue at hand. Even more important, the forensic evaluator should have a firm grasp and understanding of the relevant laws in his or her jurisdiction. M. B. Johnson et al. (2001) described the engagement of psychologists in termination of parental rights proceedings as occuring as early as the initial stages of removing a child from the home and foster care placement. Psychologists may be asked to educate the family court regarding the risk of future harm to the child, the parent's probability of complying with reunification requirements, clinical issues relating to the negative impact of the abuse/neglect on the child, or the potential impact of a parent's myriad of problems on the person's ability to care for the child. Psychologists are also asked to provide intervention services to parents and children in some cases, albeit, far too few in light of current research. In order to provide relevant and beneficial services, the mental health professional should have a good understanding of the needs and risk factors of the parties involved.

M. B. Johnson et al. (2001, p. 22) also described the critical role forensic psychologists often assume when providing evidence and testimony that are crucial to the state's "persuasive proof" case that the parent is unfit, that reasonable efforts for rehabilitation were made, and/or that the termination of parental rights is in the best interests of the child. Then the battle of the experts is likely to ensue. The parent's representing counsel retains a psychologist to conduct assessments to contradict the important facts regarding the state's case.

The child often has an appointed legal guardian that can be used as his or her own psychological expert witness. Alternatively, the judge can appoint an expert, or a specialist can be retained by foster parents. In the latter instance, this is particularly the case when foster parents are attempting to adopt the child in question (M. B. Johnson et al., 2001). It is crucial for psychologists participating in this process to be informed about the legal criteria in their jurisdiction, as well as the relevant case law. Parental rights termination proceedings typically involve two parts: the initial phase that focuses on why the parent is unfit, and the applicable legal grounds for termination. These stages are then followed by discussion of dispositional issues and the potential impact of the varying options on the child's well-being. M. B. Johnson et al. (2001) warns that far too often there is an assumption that parental rights termination is warranted without a careful look at the potential risks involved. As they note (2001, p. 23): "These risks are not only the loss of the relationship with the parent but also the loss of ties to siblings and extended family, risk of languishing indefinitely as a ward of the state, risks of maltreatment and abuse in foster care or institutional setting, and risks of adoption disruption.

If the interests of children are to be pursued vigorously, it is imperative that psychological examiners are made aware of and conduct inquiries that inform the courts of these various risks, as well as risks associated with maintaining parental ties. Forensic psychologists acting in this capacity have a tremendous burden to adhere to ethical, legal, and overall, high professional standards. With so much at stake, accepting consultation for parental rights termination cases should not be taken lightly.

PART III

Police and Law Enforcement

CHAPTER 7

Adult Issues in Policing

OVERVIEW

Traditionally, the fields of law enforcement and psychology have made for strained, if not strange, bedfellows. Policing by its very nature requires that officers responsibly exercise restraint and caution, be alert and suspicious, and exert power and force where appropriate. Psychology, by contrast, encourages considerable openness, reflection, and introspection. In short, the "protect and serve" function of policing does not seem easily assimilable with the "touchy-feely" sentiment of psychology. This notwithstanding, there are certainly a number of instances where the tools of psychology help officers interface with the public (for example, see the sections on Police and the Mentally Ill, and Police as Mediators in Domestic Disputes, Chapter 9, pp. 323, and Policing Minority Populations below.).

In this chapter, five issues and/or controversies are examined, which explore different facets of this relationship. These include (1) adult criminal profiling, (2) the use of force, (3) coerced confessions, (4) the police personality and pre-employment screenings, and (5) policing minority populations. Clearly, there are a number of other domains where the psychological sciences impact the practice of policing; however, the selected topics were carefully chosen because they collectively suggest considerable breadth in forensic application. In other words, the adult issues in this section canvas a wide array of law enforcement psychology topics, which reflect the expanse of the field.

State and federal law enforcement personnel investigate crimes that are committed by very troubled individuals. This has led to the criminal profiling of offenders. What are the personality and behavioral characteristics that officers consider when evaluating the profile for a serial homicide killer, a mass murderer, a sex offender, or other seriously disturbed persons? How do these processes contribute to the apprehension of offenders?

Police officers, on occasion, use force. What are the psychological variables that impact the use of it, and what "dangerous" circumstances inform an officer's decision to use excessive and even deadly force? Police officers are responsible for eliciting information from suspects that may result in a confession. What psychological and sociological techniques, manipulative or otherwise, do law enforcement personnel employ to arrive at (in)voluntary confessions? How, if at all, do officers balance the suspect's right against self-incrimination with the precinct's and/or the public's demand for apprehension of (factually) guilty criminals during the interviewing phase?

Patrol officers can, on occasion, confront dangerous citizens, aggressive suspects, and agitated groups. How, if at all, do exchanges such as these relate to the development of a police personality? Are officers susceptible to psychopathology? Can pre-employment (mental health) screening of officers assess for such characterological traits? Does cynicism and violence, as dimensions of law enforcement, draw certain individuals to this line of work?

Officers exercise a wide range of discretion in different contexts. This discretion is operative when making decisions about racial and ethnic minorities. What attitudes do police officers engender toward such constituencies? Where do these sentiments come from, and are they institutionalized within the organization of policing?

These and other questions are examined in the various sections below. This chapter, therefore, demonstrates that psychology is very much a part of what happens in ongoing police practices. Interestingly, however, very little is known about the extent of its role in routine law enforcement. What is known suggests that the implications for officers, for police departments, for suspects/offenders, for the public at large, and for communities in general need to be considered. More research on the identified controversies is needed, and better evaluations of how the adult issues in policing and psychology interface is essential. These conditions are necessary if we are to address the problem of crime and the search for justice at the crossroads of psychology and law enforcement.

ADULT CRIMINAL PROFILING

Introduction

The area of forensic psychology dealing with criminal profiling is an increasingly popular one. A greater number of movies and prime-time television shows attempt to portray the glamorous and interesting process of profiling criminals (most often serial murderers). Although much profiling is accomplished through intuitive processes possessed by law enforcement agents or their consultants, a scientific grounding does exist for profiling and is discussed in this chapter. The following case provides an example of a "typical" serial murder scenario and gives a hypothesis or "profile" used to apprehend the murderer (Turco, 1990).

> The homicide scene revealed a 21-year-old woman shot on each side of the head with a small-caliber weapon. She was found nude, lying face up on the stairway of her home and had been found sexually molested. Crime scene evidence led this author to the belief that she had been murdered while walking down the stairs. The investigation led to the comparisons of similar homicides in the area and "a profile" of the perpetrator was developed. We believed he was a young, athletic male with a casual acquaintance with his victims. We believed he was nonpsychotic and "organized" in his behavior. The detective team hypothesized that he was a "smooth-talker" and capable of easily winning a woman's confidence. This led to the "hunch" that he likely had good relationships with women, at least on a superficial basis. The possibility of "splitting" was entertained as a hypothesis in which we believed the perpetrator "divided" women into good (his friends) and bad (his victims). Investigators looked for physical patterns consistent with this hypothesis. This led to an examination of telephone records of public and private phones in the geographic vicinity of sequential homicides. This revealed a pattern of telephone calls to the same phone in another city. Interviews with the suspect and his girlfriend were arranged at the time of his arrest. Police learned that following each murder he telephoned his live-in girlfriend "just to talk." Examination of his telephone bills revealed collect calls made from the vicinity of previous homicides. He was an intelligent, good-looking psychopath who was later convicted of murder. (p. 152)

Literature Review

This case illustration demonstrates how a series of facts regarding a particular case can be used to develop profiles of criminals based on their behaviors. According to Woodworth and Porter (2000, p. 241), "A criminal profiler is a psychological consultant or investigator who examines evidence from the crime scene, victims, and witnesses in an attempt to construct an accurate psychological (usually concerning psychopathology, personality, and behavior) and demographic description of the individual who committed the crime." Despite the scientific grounding of criminal profiling and its increasing use in criminal investigations, many researchers contend that there is a paucity of empirical research to support its validity (Alison, Bennell, Mokros, & Ormerod, 2002; D. Davis & Follette, 2002; Kocsis, 2003a, 2003b; Kocsis, Cooksey, & Irwin, 2002).

According to the Federal Bureau of Investigation (FBI), profiling is defined as a technique which serves to identify the major personality and behavioral characteristics of an offender based on an analysis of the crime the offender committed. This process generally involves seven steps: (1) evaluation of the criminal act itself, (2) comprehensive evaluation of the specifics of the crime scene(s), (3) comprehensive analysis of the victim, (4) evaluation of preliminary reports, (5) evaluation of the medical examiner's autopsy protocol, (6) development of a profile with critical offender characteristics, and (7) investigative suggestions predicated upon construction of the profile (Douglas & Burgess, 1986). The authors in the same article equated the profiling process with that of making a psychiatric diagnosis. In this respect, data are obtained through assessment; situations are reconstructed; hypotheses are developed, formulated, and tested; and these results are reported back to the interested party. Palermo (2002) warned that although profiling can be a helpful tool in apprehending offenders, it should only be considered a working hypothesis due to the unique personality and behavioral characteristics of each offender. Additionally, he indicated that a profiler should have sound psychological and psychiatric knowledge, as well as crime scene expertise.

The goal of any law enforcement agency is not only to enforce laws, but also to apprehend those who have broken the law; however, the latter part of this process is often difficult. Investigators must struggle with a multitude of evidence, reports, and inferences regarding each particular crime. Criminals are not often immediately apprehended, leaving the law enforcement agency to deal with a criminal at large. When the crime is serious enough, as in arson, rape, or murder, a psychological or criminological profile of the subject is obtained in order to facilitate apprehension.

Criminal profiling has conceivably existed since the inception of crime itself. Documented attempts of profiling such heinous killers as Jack the Ripper date back to the 1800s. The majority of modern literature focusing on profiling examines crimes such as murder, sexual offences, and rape. These typologies are further broken down into subcategories. For example, murder is often subdivided into categories such as serial murder, sexual murder, and mass murder. Both professionals and nonprofessionals have made attempts to establish profiles of those who have broken the law — each utilizing their own preferred school of thought. For example,

West (1988) described the extensive use of the Minnesota Multiphasic Personality Inventory (MMPI) to predict future offenders based on a series of commonly found personality characteristics. The author also discussed the use of such devices as projective measures (Rorschach, Thematic Apperception Test, etc.) and the effects of neurological insult on future aberrant behaviors.

West (1988) also stated that biological theories underlying criminal or even homicidal tendencies are becoming increasingly popular. He claimed that research on genes and their correlation to aggressive criminal behaviors exists and should be further examined. The XYY sex chromosome irregularity was implicated in some studies in criminal behavioral effects through aggressive and disinhibition syndromes. Also, electroencephalograph studies examining the electrical activity of brain regions also implicated biological anomalies as a possible cause of criminal behavior. The reader must be cautioned, however, that attributing an offender's behavior to a biological or brain disturbance may lead to a belief that such behavior cannot be helped due to its uncontrollable biological nature. In addition, sentencing implications may be present due to a diagnosed brain abnormality.

Turco (1990) emphasized a psychoanalytic orientation in the production of psychological/criminological profiles of offenders. He stated that a crime scene is like a projective device such as a Rorschach ink blot. There are a number of personality characteristics derived from evidence and manipulation of the crime scene which can be interpreted much like a subject's response to an inkblot. Turco's psychoanalytic background stresses the importance of early childhood experiences and relationships, as well as unresolved conflicts and their relation to current behavior. Further, this information can be used to predict future behaviors based on these same variables.

The FBI has done a great deal of research in the area of criminal profiling. Special agents in the FBI have developed, through archival and current case information, typical characteristics likely to be found in particular types of offenders. Woodworth and Porter (2000) found that the two approaches to crime scene and offender profiling which are the most promising include the holistic approach developed by the FBI. This approach integrates aspects of the rational/deductive method and the empirical/ inductive method, developed mostly by investigative psychologists.

In a study examining expertise in psychological profiling, Kocsis, Irwin, Hayes, and Nunn (2000) compared the accuracy of psychological profiles for a closed murder case created by individuals with varying degrees and types of expertise. The study compared the profiles generated by 5 professional profilers, 35 police officers, 30 psychologists, 31 university students, and 20 self-declared psychics. The results indicated that the professional profilers had a superior set of profiling skills as compared to all other groups. Furthermore, the psychologists performed better in some areas than the police officers and the psychics, which suggested that knowledge and insight into human behavior is possibly relevant to psychological profiling. Finally, the authors suggested that the psychic group did little more than rely on the social stereotype of a murderer in their profiles (Kocsis et al., 2000).

In an article that examined the conclusions of empirically derived studies on profiling expertise, Kocsis (2003b) found that professional profilers create a more accurate prediction of an unknown offender than other groups. More specifically, Kocsis (2003a) found that professional profilers tended to write more detailed profiles which had more information about nonphysical attributes of the offender, and more information about the crime scene or the offender's behavior, at every stage of the crime. Hazelwood (1983) described how a profile of a rapist could be obtained primarily through competent and informed interviewing of rape victims. He noted that in profiling the rapist, three basic steps are critical: (1) careful interview of the victim regarding the rapist's behavior, (2) analysis of that behavior in an attempt to ascertain the motivation underlying the assault, and (3) a profile compilation of the individual likely to have committed the crime in the manner reported with the assumed motivation. A more recent study examining the homology of offender characteristics in rapists and their crime scene behavior found that rapists who offend in a similar way are not more similar with regard to age, sociodemographic features, or their criminal records (Mokros & Alison, 2002).

In establishing a profile of a rapist, Hazelwood described how the rapist behaves within his environment relative to his personality structure. Behaviors are broken down into a number of categories and the victim is asked for detailed information regarding the behavior in an attempt to classify the rapist. Three basic forms of behavior are exhibited by the rapist: physical (force), verbal, and sexual. For example, the rapist who dominates his victim primarily through the use of verbal degradation and threats may be portraying a personality characteristic consistent with an intense desire to emotionally harm his victim. This may be indicative of a recent break-up between the rapist and his girlfriend. The rape therefore serves as revenge on the girlfriend through the victim in order to satisfy a psychological need. Based on this information, profilers can then begin to formulate the type of offender personality that might use rape as a means of rectification and revenge.

Profiling victims can also give increased insight into a particular type of offender. Graney and Arrigo (2002) consolidated the criminological research on rape and the victimological research on victims to develop an increased understanding about the offender, his or her victims, and sexual crimes in general. Understanding a sexual offender's victim selection process can help prevent future victims, as well as provide increased knowledge about the offender, potentially aiding in his or her apprehension.

Other, more common techniques of profiling offenders come from aquiring detailed information from a criminal population convicted of committing the same or similar crimes. These data are used to establish patterns or norms based on that particular type of offender. According to the FBI (1985b), individual development of offenders is based on two primary factors: the dominance of a fantasy life and a history of personal abuse. These factors are used to develop a working profile of a murderer. In-depth interviews of 36 sexual murderers revealed a number of characteristics typical of this type of offender. For example, the sexual murderer tends to be intelligent, good-looking, of average socioeconomic status (SES), and an oldest son or first/second born. However, they also tend to have an attitude of devaluation toward people (having failed to form significant attachments), view the world as unjust, have an unstable or inconsistent view of authority and justice, and tend to have an obsession with dominance through aggression. These sexual murderers also tend to have few attachments outside their immediate families, tend to live in a created fantasy world in which they feel comfortable, and have a history of deviant behaviors. Based on these sets of characteristics, a profile can be developed (see Table I).

Some researchers (Reming, 1988) noted that the habitual criminal shares many personality characteristics with the supercop (a police officer who consistently performs within the top 90th percentile). Supercops score essentially the same on a test measuring perceived descriptive characteristics of habitual criminals. Further, there were similarities found between habitual criminals and supercops on such dimensions as control, aggressiveness, vigilance, rebelliousness, energy level, frankness in expression, intensity of personal relationships, self-esteem, feelings of uniqueness, extroversion, sociability, jealousy, possessiveness of a sexual partner, a tendency not to change opinions easily, philandering, and a tendency to avoid blame. Remming (1988) has also observed that many of the positive traits of good police officers were beneficial in examining the characteristics of the habitual criminal. Thus a complete understanding of officers' strengths and weaknesses might help in profiling criminals.

TABLE I   General Characteristics, Resultant Attitudes and Beliefs, and Deviant Behaviors of 36 Sexual Murderers[a]

Background characteristics		
Family background	Individual development	Performance
Detachment	Dominance of fantasy	School failure
Criminality	History of personal abuse	Sporadic work record
Substance abuse		Unskilled
Psychiatric problems		Poor military records
Sexual problems		Solo sex
Resultant attitudes and beliefs		Deviant behaviors
Devaluation of victim society		Rape
World viewed as unjust		Mutilation
Authority/life viewed as inconsistent		Torture
Autoerotic preferences		
Obsession with dominance through aggression		
Fantasy as reality		

[a]FBI (1985a, p. 6).

As previously stated, certain criminals tend to receive the spotlight in regard to psychological/criminological profiling. Not surprisingly, these crimes are often the most serious, such as homicide. It is therefore not surprising that the majority of research focuses on these criminals, since conceivably they are the most dangerous. Profiling sexual murderers seems to dominate the literature due to the nature of the crime itself. The sexual murderer often appears to be unmotivated and engages in a series of bizarre behaviors inconsistent with any other type of criminal typology (Arrigo & Purcell, 2002).

In examining a sample of sexual murderers, the FBI (1985b) has developed a series of profile characteristics based on both demographic and crime scene traits. These traits have broken down homicide into an organized and disorganized type. Each typology allows the law enforcement agent to create a profile of the murderer, thus expediting the arrest of the suspect (Tables II and III).

Dividing sexual murderers into organized and disorganized types allows for more accurate profiling based on information obtained through arrests. The crime scene characteristics described in Table III enable the investigator to develop a profile based solely on behaviors exhibited at the scene of the homicide, thus allowing for a psychological profile and description based on these data.

TABLE II   Profile Characteristics of Organized and Disorganized Murderers[a]

Organized	Disorganized
Average to above average intelligence	Below average intelligence
Socially competent	Socially inadequate
Skilled work preferred	Unskilled work
Sexually competent	Sexually incompetent
High birth order status	Low birth order status
Father's work stable	Father's work unstable
Inconsistent childhood discipline	Harsh discipline as child
Controlled mood during crime	Anxious mood during crime
Use of alcohol with crime	Minimal use of alcohol
Precipitating situational stress	Minimal situational stress
Living with partner	Living alone
Mobility with car in good condition	Lives/works near crime scene
Follows crime in news media	Minimal interest in news media
May change job or leave town	Significant behavioral change (drug/alcohol abuse, religiosity, etc.)

[a]FBI (1985b, p. 19).

TABLE III   Crime Scene Differences between Organized and Disorganized Murderers[a]

Organized	Disorganized
Planned offense	Spontaneous offense
Victim a targeted stranger	Victim/location unknown
Personalized victim	Depersonalized victim
Controlled conversation	Minimal conversation
Crime scene reflects overall control	Crime scene random and sloppy
Demands submissive victim	Sudden violence to victim
Restraints used	Minimal use of restraints
Aggressive acts prior to death	Sexual acts after death
Body hidden	Body left in view
Weapon/evidence absent	Evidence/weapon often present
Transports victim or body	Body left at death scene

[a]FBI (1985b, p. 19).

Forensic Psychology and Policy Implications

A number of U.S. Supreme Court cases have dealt with the use of opinions from psychologists and other mental health professionals regarding the "goodness-of-fit" of a criminal into a particular profile based on their assessment of the criminal. Much of this research stems from results obtained from the MMPI and mental status exams.

Peters and Murphy (1992) described a variety of issues related to the admissibility and inadmissibility of mental health professionals' expert opinions of profile fitting. According to their research, every appellate court in the United States, with the exception of California, has ruled on the admissibility of expert testimony regarding the psychological profiles of child molesters. These appellate courts have consistently rejected the psychological profile concept as evidence either defending or attempting to help convict the child molester.

The psychological profile as court testimony has been used in child sexual abuse cases for three primary reasons: (1) to prove the defendant committed the crime, (2) to prove the defendant did not commit the crime, and (3) to solidify the credibility of the defendant. However, the primary reason that courts refuse to allow such evidence is because no matter how well a suspect may fit into the child molester profile, it can never prove whether the actual event took place (Peters & Murphy, 1992).

Future research involving the use of psychological/psychiatric testimony in relation to criminal profiles must continue. This especially includes studies examining its efficacy in the court system. Relevant policy implications depend on these results.

Suggestions for Future Research

More empirical research is needed to support the validity of crime scene and offender profiling. The D.C. sniper case highlighted the weaknesses of offender profiles and the importance of remaining mindful of their limitations. Profiling is typically used in cold cases or investigations where the physical evidence (or leads) are limited. Research could help to refine the effectiveness of this investigative tool. There is clearly a need for careful, systematic evaluation of criminal profiles (Alison, Smith, Eastman, & Rainbow, 2003). More victimological research could also further inform accurate offender profiles (Graney & Arrigo, 2002).

One could say that the future of criminological profiling has already arrived. In years past, investigators relied only on personal knowledge involving experience and wisdom. Inferences were drawn based on corroboration with peers and personal hunches. In the modern computer era, comprehensive and extensive computerized databases exist which allow thousands of variables to be cross-examined between criminals, crime scenes, and case details. Computerized searches look for specific patterns, consistencies, and inconsistencies, in order to determine the most likely course of action for law enforcement agents to act upon (Turvey, 2002).

At the FBI's National Center for the Analysis of Violent Crime (NCAVC), experts in criminal personality profiling developed a computerized system of crime pattern analysis. The Violent Criminal Apprehension Program, a computerized system, termed VICAP, uses a collection of crime pattern recognition programs to detect and predict the behavior of violent criminals. Future research is needed to examine the accuracy and reliability of such computer programs and to develop a method in which all law enforcement agencies could utilize a system on a cost-efficient and practical level. Further, the development of a national database may bring large statistical power to such evaluations. Research examining these possibilities is certainly required.

Research is also needed in evaluating the possible detrimental effects of criminal profiling. As mentioned, many jurisdictions do not allow for the inclusion of psychological profiles as evidence in their courts. Will profiling a person negatively persuade a jury to convict a potential felon if the profile is too broad or if it encompasses too many personality characteristics? Research is needed to determine, scientifically, if profiling is indeed efficacious.

USE OF FORCE

Introduction

The question of force used by police first received attention in 1974, in Memphis, Tennessee, when a 15-year-old boy named Edward Garner broke into a home and stole $10 and a purse. At the arrival of the police, Garner, who was unarmed, fled from the home and ran across the backyard. As the police began pursuit of the suspect, Garner reached a six-foot fence surrounding the yard. In an attempt to avoid police custody, he continued to flee and began to climb over the fence. The police officer, fearing that the suspect would get away if he made it over the fence, fired at the back of Garner's head and killed him.

The decision to use force in the apprehension of a citizen, whether it be excessive or deadly, ultimately lies in the hands of the police officer at the moment of conflict. Although the goal of the officer is always to resolve a conflict in the most peaceful manner possible, it is understood that there are situations in which a peaceful resolution is not possible. Guidelines are established to assist the officer, who at times must make a "split-second" decision as to the type of force necessary. In order to appreciate these use of force guidelines, it is first necessary to understand how dangerous situations in need of force unfold, as well as how the decisions that follow are made.

Literature Review

The history behind the police officer's right to use force dates back to common law under English rule. Known as the "fleeing felon" law, common law states that a police officer could use deadly force in situations that would protect the life of the officer or an innocent third party, to overcome resistance to arrest, or to prevent the escape of any felony suspect (Inciardi, 1993; Pursley, 1994). The loose generalization of the fleeing felon law leaves a series of questionable circumstances and issues that remain unaddressed due to the changing criminal activities of our present day. Our current legal system now classifies more crimes as felonies, which in turn allows for more felony-related crimes that are neither necessarily dangerous nor life-threatening. Furthermore, technology provides more effective means of communication and organization within police forces that can aid in the apprehension of criminals (Pursley, 1994; Walker & Kreisel, 2001).

Such unspecified circumstances established by the fleeing felon law were left to the discretion of the police jurisdiction. Many jurisdictions continued to use the common law guidelines until the landmark decision in *Tennessee v. Garner* (1985), which sought to outline the qualifications of the use of force in a constitutional frame. It was argued that the level of force the officer used against Edward Garner was extreme and unnecessary given the circumstances of the crime. Following *Tennessee v. Garner*, the use of force was restricted to circumstances where it was necessary to prevent the escape of a suspect believed to be a significant threat to the officer or others (Inciardi, 1993).

Within the creation of more defined standards for the use of force are the motives, behaviors, and decision-making processes that underlie such an action. Many social scientists have researched these aspects and have offered some insights that can serve as aids in organizing such standards of police practice. In the past, the problems associated with the use of force were seen as the result of "a few bad apples" within the law enforcement community (Kappeler, Sluder, & Alpert, 1998). Such an explanation is weighted in the view that many police officers possess a stereotypical aggressive and authoritative nature (Claussen-Rogers & Arrigo, 2004). This concept has received a great deal of attention within the public due to the highly controversial Rodney King incident (see the following case illustration). Although the officers involved maintained that they acted according to police standards and that such force was necessary in the apprehension of King, the beating of Rodney King has been cited as a clear representation of the use of excessive force and stands to support the idea of the authoritative and aggressive police officer (Kappeler, Sluder, & Alpert, 1998).

In the early morning hours of March 3, 1991, in a suburb of Los Angeles, police began a high-speed chase in pursuit of a suspect who was driving recklessly and believed to be dangerously intoxicated. The driver, Rodney King, led police on a chase that reached approximately 100 m.p.h. and ended when he reached an entrance to a park which had been closed off with a cable. After King, who was unarmed, stepped out of his car, police attempted to restrain him by striking him with a Taser gun and then followed by beating him repeatedly with their batons. King suffered multiple fractures, broken bones, and internal injuries. As this was occurring, a citizen who lived across from the park grabbed his video camera and proceeded to record the event. The tape was then sold to television stations which broadcasted the tape nationwide. Initially the officers were acquitted in court, although upon appeal two of the four officers were convicted of excessive use of force. The King incident produced widespread public outrage that spawned numerous questions and concerns about police power and brutality.

Following the Rodney King incident, many police departments looked to establish a clearly defined set of guidelines for the use of excessive and deadly force. However, more recent explanations of force suggest it is impossible for such specified standards to be established and maintain that the act of force is based on a split-second decision that involves an immediate analysis of the situation by the police officer (Fyfe, 1985; Kappeler, Sluder, & Alpert, 1998). Intense stress and the possibility of a life-threatening situation accompany such an analysis. Some experts believe that to expect an officer to make an appropriate decision under these circumstances is unrealistic.

In contrast, there have been several studies that attempt to understand the process by which an officer makes his or her decision and the circumstances behind it. For example, Binder and Scharf (1980) researched the circumstances that evolve during a conflict and developed a four-phase model description the stages resulting in the decision to use deadly force. As they noted, "the violent police–citizen encounter is considered a developmental process in which successive decisions and behaviors by either police officer or citizen, or both, make the violent outcome more or less likely" (Binder & Scharf, 1980, p. 111). The model consists of the Anticipation Phase, Entry and Initial Contact Phase, Information Exchange, and Final Phase. Each phase describes the emotional as well as the environmental details as they unravel in a potentially violent situation.

The Anticipation Phase is composed of the immediate involvement of the officer when he or she is first called to intervene and the information that is relayed as a result. Entry and Initial Contact include what the officer is confronted with when arriving at the scene and the development of the crisis. The Information Exchange Phase consists of any verbal or nonverbal exchange of information between the suspect and the officer which also contributes to the officer's assessment of the dangerousness of the situation. In the Final Phase, the officer makes the decision of whether to use force by incorporating the information received in the previous phases, as well as any final action by the suspect or any other immediate threat.

As described, this model reflects the application of a series of decisions actively made by the police officer. Appropriate decisions are made when the police officer consciously evaluates the situation based on the development of the event. Many police departments have used a similar philosophy to develop a series of guidelines which establish a more definitive circumstance for the use of force. Such policies can aid the officer in making a rational choice in a time of great pressure.

An examination of the role of neighborhood context on police use of force by Terrill and Reisig (2003) revealed that officers are significantly more likely to use higher levels of force when they confront suspects in disadvantaged neighborhoods and in those areas with higher homicide rates. Jacobs and Carmichael (2002) contend that police officer homicides in particular were most likely in cities with the largest discrepancies in black-white resources. This would clearly weigh heavily on an officer's mind when performing duties in these areas. Using the 1994 General Social Survey to examine effects of race, gender, and geographical region on support of various criminal justice policies, Halim and Stiles (2001) found that African Americans were less likely to support police use of force than their racial counterparts. This phenomenon is most certainly a major factor in strained relations between police officers and their minority constituents in disadvantaged communities.

Forensic Psychology and Policy Implications

One way to combat the chances of using force unnecessarily is by incorporating effective training programs that prepare an officer in the event that such a quick decision must be made (Ross & Jones, 1996). Developing extensive policies that outline the criteria which might necessitate the use of force can act as means of training police officers to recognize the key elements involved. These key elements include specific response levels on the part of the officer that must be evaluated during the course of the confrontation. Providing officers with applicable response levels, such as appropriate dialogue and verbal direction with the citizen, appropriate means of restraint, and the use of weapons and incapacitation, can alleviate some of the intense pressure in that split-second decision. In addition, such policies can address the various subject factors such as age, size, seriousness of crime, and weapon usage as compared to the officer's factors of size, number of officers present, an officer's defensive tactics, and legal requirements. As explored in the Edward Garner case, his youth, the fact that he was unarmed, and the fact that he had not committed a dangerous crime all indicate that under such a policy deadly force was not appropriate given the context of the situation. Similarly, in the Rodney King case, policy questions remain about the amount of force necessary to subdue a suspect. Such guidelines could prove to be highly effective in the fast-paced discretionary decision making realm of office use of force (Walker & Kreisel, 2001).

Another effective means of preventing unnecessary use of force would be in the screening and counseling of those officers who harbor a greater propensity toward violence (Scrivner, 1994). Sugimoto and Oltjenbruns (2001) note that law enforcement personnel who continue to work, despite experiencing symptoms of posttraumatic stress disorder (PTSD) resulting from a critical incident, may incur risks of reduced self-control, escalated use of force, and inappropriate behavior. This inappropriate behavior may manifest due to anger outbursts or irritability associated with their PTSD. Screening and counseling provisions would allow the police departments to gain greater control over the likelihood of an incident occuring, rather than relying solely on the circumstances of the crime or on the suspect (Claussen-Rogers & Arrigo, 2004).

In addition, monitoring officers' behaviors can also serve as a defense against the unnecessary use of force (Scrivner, 1994). By alerting supervisors to those patrol personnel who demonstrate actions that represent a risk for violence, intervention techniques can be performed early. In addition, monitoring officers in the field can create much needed a role models, as well as aid in the enforcement of the policies established within the department.

Suggestions for Future Research

There is a great need for further research in the evaluation of the environmental aspects that lead to the use of force. As discussed, the environment in which the situation arises can determine the appropriativeness of force and its potential outcome. With a more complete understanding of how the environment develops, what role the environment plays, and how the critical incident can be manipulated for safety, the use of force as a means to uphold justice with minimal conflict can be assured. Furthermore, it is important to understand the psychological as well as the sociological aspects of using force. Comprehending the emotional and cognitive functions of both the suspect and the police officer involved in such a crisis is pivotal. Moreover, it is essential to investigate how gender and ethnicity relate to the use force by officers. Addressing these environmental, sociological, and psychological concerns can be beneficial when training police officers to recognize the scenarios that develop and can facilitate an informed choice of whether or not to use force.

COERCED CONFESSIONS

Introduction

No other piece of evidence is more damaging to a criminal than a stated confession. Throughout history, confessions have been obtained in a variety of ways. Due process specifically states that interrogators may use certain tactics to obtain confessions from an accused, provided that the confession is voluntary and a product of an essentially free and unhindered person. However, many tactics employed by an interrogator do not fall within these guidelines and are therefore considered "coerced."

This section outlines and discusses the legal definition of a coerced confession, its psychological and sociological bases and implications, and discusses some of the specific tactics used by investigators and interrogators in obtaining confessions. The following fictional case provides an example in which a variety of interrogation issues, legal or otherwise, are brought into play.

> Ned and Jake, desperate for cash and needing to obtain drugs to support their addictions, decide that robbing a downtown convenience store would be a quick and convenient way to obtain money. The two arrive in Ned's car, and it is decided that Jake will run into the store, hold up the convenience clerk, and make a quick escape. Upon entering the store, Jake becomes worried and apprehensive when he realizes that the store has approximately five other people inside. Nervously, Jake approaches the clerk, pulls a gun, and demands all the money in the cash register. The clerk, unwilling to be a victim of this type of crime any longer, pulls his own firearm out from under the counter and points it at Jake. In a panic, Jake fires, killing the store clerk. Hearing a shot fired, Ned also panics and quickly drives away, leaving Jake behind. Jake, seen by numerous eyewitnesses, flees into the night on foot, only to be apprehended later by the police who take him in to be questioned.
>
> In the interrogation room, two officers enter and introduce themselves to Jake, who has been waiting for the officers for approximately 45 minutes in the isolated room. The officers, after offering Jake some water and/or use of the bathroom, quickly review Jake's Miranda rights. Jake listens and does not respond in any notable fashion. The officers then begin questioning Jake about the attempted robbery that took place earlier that evening. Jake, unwilling to give any information, states that he is innocent and wishes to speak with a lawyer. The officers tell Jake that the process can take place in one of two ways: cooperate and answer all questions immediately or cease questioning now and wait for legal counsel, thereby not cooperating with investigative procedures. Feeling somewhat intimidated, Jake concedes to answering more questions. Later, the officers come to another roadblock in Jake's testimony. He refuses to answer a question dealing with his accomplice. The officers state that if he implicates his friend in the murder of the clerk, the courts may reward his cooperation with leniency. Afraid and hopeful of a more lenient sentence, Jake admits full guilt and gives the name and description of his accomplice.

Would you consider the above confession to be coerced? If so, what specific techniques did you feel were inappropriate? The following section examines specific issues related to appropriate and inappropriate interrogation strategies. It also reviews the psychological power these techniques excercise over many arrested subjects, as well as other topics related to coerced confessions.

Literature Review

According to police procedure and the Fifth Amendment, prosecutors cannot use statements obtained by a subject as evidence in court unless the arresting party has ensured that the subject's Miranda rights have been offered and explained. The courts believe that subjects pulled from their familiar environment and surrounded by potentially intimidating authority figures may reveal information that they otherwise would not disclose. The right to remain silent until counsel is made available protects one against such an abuse (*Davis v. United States*, 1994).

When a suspect is read his or her Miranda warnings, it is sometimes questionable whether or not the person understands them and is able to make rational, independent decisions based on that information. The more vulnerable members of our society — the mentally ill, mentally retarded, and the young — are particularly at risk for manipulation and exploitation. In a study examining pre-adjudicative and adjudicative competency in juveniles and young adults, results indicated that Mirada competence and adjudicative competence were strongly related (Redlich, Silverman, & Steiner, 2003). Age and suggestibility were also related to Miranda competence. Viljoen, Roesch, and Zapf (2002) found that defendants with primary psychotic disorders had more impairment than defendants with affective disorders, substance abuse disorders, and no diagnosed major mental illness, in their understanding of interrogation rights, the nature of criminal proceedings, the possible consequences of those proceedings, and their ability to have a meaningful interchange with their attorneys.

As with many laws, ambiguity exists when determining exactly when a subject requests counsel. For example, during an interrogation the subject states, "Maybe I should talk to a lawyer." Does the officer interpret this as a clear request to receive counsel? If so, the interrogator must immediately stop questioning and hold the subject until a lawyer is available. If not, has the officer breached the subject's Miranda rights, creating the possibility of coercing a confession?

Three basic rules aid law enforcement agents in understanding whether a subject is requesting counsel. The first is termed The Threshold of Clarity

Rule and states that the subject's request for counsel must meet a "threshold of clarity." Under this rule, a person must clearly demonstrate a request for counsel. As one may guess, this rule is itself somewhat vague and offers no specific guidelines identifying what is "clear."

The second rule related to the right not to self-incriminate is termed the Per Se Rule. According to this rule, any reference to counsel during an interrogation session must result in the immediate cessation of questioning and the appointment of counsel to the subject. This rule has more clarity and leaves little question as to whether the person is indeed requesting counsel.

Last, The Clarification Rule states that if a subject makes an ambiguous request for counsel, the officers may ask for further clarification. However, if the officers, in their request for clarification, continue to discuss the arrest, the law may be breached (*Davis v. United States*, 1994).

Once a subject's Miranda rights are read and the subject waives those rights or agrees to continue questioning until counsel arrives, the interrogator may then begin questioning the subject on matters related to the crime. Officers utilize a variety of techniques in interrogation to provide them with the most important, relevant information related to the crime. As discussed in other portions of this book, the significant amount of stress felt by police often leads to an attitude of indifference or frustration. This results in tactics that ensure quick, albeit often inappropriate, justice.

Given the variety of stressors and their severity, it is understandable why an officer may use underhanded tactics to obtain a confession. For example, in the case study provided earlier, the suspect was clearly guilty of homicide and was identified by a variety of witnesses. The arresting officer, convinced that the subject was guilty, tried to expedite justice by bringing this criminal the punishment he deserved. Other cases may be encumbered with confusion and inconsistencies, and officers may then feel the need to use strategies to coerce a confession.

According to Dripps (1988), there is a conflict in every criminal case between personal autonomy and the need for evidence. Dripps stated that the majority of confessions do not take place freely and with rational intellect. Rather, confessions are procured only through manipulation, irrationality of the subject, and mistakes made by the suspect during interrogation. Obviously, the courts need clear evidence of guilt if a subject is to be convicted of a crime. As stated previously, the most impressive and conclusive evidence one can obtain is a confession by the accused. This evidence must not come at the expense of the individual's personal autonomy; if personal autonomy were to be sacrificed, then unlawful tactics might as well be utilized to obtain the same end.

While one may be tempted to believe that police interrogations take place in prime-time television fashion, complete with 200-watt light bulbs, 8-hour grueling question-and-answer sessions, yelling in the face of the accused, and fist pounding, the reality is that the majority of interrogations normally do not take place in such a style. R. A. Leo (1996) described, using observations from 122 interrogations involving 45 different detectives, the processes and tactics utilized during a variety of interrogation sessions incorporating everything from homicide to property crimes. His results indicated that overall, coerced confessions occur less often than one may believe. However, he stated that he "... occasionally observed behavior inside the interrogation room — such as yelling, table pounding, or highly aggressive questioning — that straddled the margins of legality" (p. 270).

When R. A. Leo's results are reviewed more closely, we find that about 78% of the interrogated subjects ultimately waived their Miranda rights. In seven (4%) of the cases observed, the detective continued questioning the subject even after Miranda rights were invoked. The types of tactics used were appealing to the suspect's self-interest (88%), confronting suspect with existing evidence of guilt (85%), undermining suspect's confidence in denial of guilt (43%), identifying contradictions in suspect's story (42%), behavioral analysis interview questions (40%), appealing to the importance of cooperation (37%), moral justifications/psychological excuses (34%), confronting suspect with false evidence of guilt (30%), using praise or flattery (30%), appealing to detective's expertise/authority (29%), appealing to the suspect's conscience (23%), and minimizing the moral seriousness of the offense (22%).

Less frequently used tactics were also implemented, possibly suggesting coercion: invoking metaphors of guilt (10%), exaggerating the facts/nature of the offense (4%), yelling at suspect (3%), accusing suspect of other crimes (1%), and attempting to confuse the subject (1%). In all, detectives used an average of 5.62 interrogation tactics.

R. A. Leo (1996), after analyzing this data, stated that according to his necessary conditions for coercion, police questioning involving coercive methods took place in only four (2%) of the cases. Further analysis of these four cases revealed that only psychologically coercive methods were used as opposed to physically coercive methods. In one case, detectives intentionally questioned a heroin addict suffering from acute withdrawal symptoms during the second day of his incarceration, knowing his symptoms were at their worst. In another case, the "good cop/bad cop" routine was utilized on a young gang member. One detective promised the youth's release if he cooperated, while the other stated that he would provide the prosecutor with incriminating information. The suspect provided the desired information and was subsequently released. All officers using coercive methods stated that they felt nothing could be lost by employing such tactics with these subjects, since they were treated essentially as informants or witnesses.

DiPietro (1993) described a number of factors related to interrogation of subjects. He stated that officers should assess the suspect's background and personal characteristics such as age, race, intelligence, and educational level before beginning interrogation. Certain subjects may be more conducive to coercive techniques, thus rendering a subsequent confession inadmissible if such strategies were employed. Further, DiPietro noted that some types of deceptive techniques are appropriate, given that they are not openly coercive, but that officers must not trick a subject into waiving his or her Miranda rights. He then offered a two-part definition of deception: (1) lies that relate to a suspect's connection to the crime and (2) trickery that introduces extrinsic considerations. Perske (2000) explained that individuals with mental retardation or other development disabilities are very susceptible to coerced or false confessions. He strongly recommended that mental health professionals or other types of human service workers be present, as soon as possible, during the interview process.

DiPietro (1993) also described a number of interrogation techniques, which may, by some definitions, be considered coercive. The first of these are lies that connect the suspect to the crime. These include telling the subject that fingerprints were found at the crime scene when in fact they were not. Also, trickery that falsely introduces extrinsic evidence might be considered coercive. This could include telling a subject that they would lose their welfare benefits if they were found guilty, but that leniency would be granted in exchange for cooperation. Another potentially coercive method is the effect of promises on voluntariness. This is a technique used in which an officer promises some sort of benefit to the subject in return for cooperation. Promises of leniency are also used in the facilitation of confessions, as are promises to tell higher authorities (such as the courts), that cooperation was given. Conceivably, a cooperative subject may be told that he or she will be treated less harshly if cooperation is given.

Promises of collateral benefits, such as the release of a family member or treatment for the subject's substance abuse problem, are also given.

More specifically, the courts have found that promises to protect the accused, promises to protect the accused's family, and promises not to arrest the defendant are considered to be coercive. Finally, threats may be viewed as inherently coercive and are therefore not allowed in the interrogation process.

While the discussion thus far has focused mainly on coercive interviewing techniques, good interviewing techniques do exist and are encouraged in virtually all interrogation situations. Hess and Gladis (1987) described a variety of good interrogation techniques, which they liken to successful advertising in marketing. These techniques include such principles as the establishment of credibility, a feeling of reciprocity, the giving of compliments, conveying a sense of urgency, and casting doubts on current beliefs. These techniques, according to the authors, helped the interrogator to establish a facile rapport with the subject and to obtain information in an efficient fashion rather than resorting to coercive methods.

Forensic Psychology and Policy Implications

A variety of policy implications exist for ensuring that confessions are not obtained primarily through coercive methods. M. B. Johnson and Hunt (2000, p. 17) recommended that entire police interrogations be electronically recorded, not only the resulting confession in order "to facilitate the court's task of determining the suspect's competence to waive constitutional rights and questions regarding the reliability of incriminating statements." More and more police departments have utilized video recorders in the interrogation room to provide the courts with real evidence related to the interrogation process. For example, a survey conducted in 1990 revealed that approximately one-third of law enforcement agencies were videotaping the interrogation process (Geller, 1994). That number is expected to rise, giving more concrete evidence of the value of such a technique. The future will no doubt see the implications of video recording debated and discussed in the court system.

Dripps (1988) discussed the constitutional right guaranteeing the privilege against self-incrimination. He stated that constructing the Constitution as an inflexible set of mores or rules results in faulty thinking about and interpretation of what is being protected. For example, some commentators claim that the privilege against self-incrimination binds the courts by denying as admissible the most impressive and appropriate evidence regarding a defendant's admission of guilt or innocence. Policies dealing with the privilege to not incriminate oneself in a court of law have surprisingly been absent. Further explanation of this privilege, coupled with its possible ramifications, could help elucidate convictions when necessary.

Other policies might include a restructuring of the Fifth Amendment. In particular, making the currently ambiguous wording more clear would be useful. Clarification of this amendment would conceivably make coercion illegal and reduce appeals dealing with the interpretation of a detective's interrogation techniques.

Suggestions for Future Research

Research studying the dynamics surrounding coerced confessions is deficient. Virtually every aspect of coercive practices involved in obtaining confessions are unexamined and in need of exploration. The videotaping procedure, previously described, lacks supporting studies that evaluate this procedure's psychological effects on the subject as well as on detectives' possible inhibition regarding being recorded.

Personality characteristics associated with interrogators who routinely use coercive methods also are lacking. What types of personality traits make up a detective who uses coercive methods? Is it one who is "burned out" or has grown overly cynical toward the criminal justice system? Research investigating the level of experience required to become a routine interrogator should be examined.

What makes a particularly good interrogator? While the techniques used by certain detectives have been explored and examined, the actual characteristics associated with personality types have not. It may be that certain personality types will never, under normal conditions, develop good, efficient interviewing techniques.

What are the psychological aftereffects of the subject who has been coerced into giving a confession? Are there long-lasting psychological consequences of being deceived or tricked? What is the public's perception of coerced confessions? The public may feel that any means necessary to obtain justice are within reasonable limits. Others may feel that only the strictest of procedures should be followed, which leaves little room for deviation. In addition, more research needs to be conducted to assess what the acceptable methods are by which to interrogate individuals with mental retardation, especially including the subjects with high degrees of suggestibility coupled with subaverage intelligence. These topics and many more are available avenues for the continued study of coerced confessions. Interrogation must always take place; therefore, psychology's contribution to this phenomenon must be explored.

THE POLICE PERSONALITY AND PRE-EMPLOYMENT SCREENINGS

Introduction

Police officers hold a position that is replete with stress and responsibility. These officers face dangerous situations, aggressive suspects, and agitated citizens. Line officers must comply with their supervisors and uphold the law. These individuals are entrusted with a tremendous amount of power and with a great deal of discretion in how they use that power. As a result, various methods have been employed to assess the personality and any psychopathology exhibited by the officer candidates (Claussen-Rogers & Arrigo, 2004). Most frequently, psychological tests and civil service interviews are used to ascertain this information. Some researchers argue that this information is only detected through on-the-spot observation of on-the-street interactions (Toch, 1992). With increasing media attention linked to cases of police brutality, there is a growing concern about the mental health screening of police officers. Are these cases examples of a few violence-prone men or are they more indicative of a "police personality" that pervades law enforcement? Some investigators question whether the screening of officer candidates is sufficiently sound when identifying personnel who subsequently will be unable to cope with the responsibilities of the job (Claussen-Rogers & Arrigo, 2004). Consider the following case illustration.

Cameron's father had been a police officer and Cameron admired the "tough-guy" image and excitement that he perceived to be embodied in police work. He had always been outgoing and seemingly fearless. All of his friends and family knew that he would be an excellent candidate for law enforcement. Cameron applied for a job with the local police department. After what seemed like hours of psychological tests and panel interviews, Cameron was relieved to hear that he qualified to be on the police force. Being a new officer on his probationary period, he was eager to belong and to perform his duties to the utmost of his abilities. He had heard countless stories by the "veterans" about the difficulty of gaining compliance from a particular category of civilians. In addition, Cameron was warned that it was best to take a firm, consistent approach in dealing with this group as suspects.

In his second month of duty, Cameron tried to obtain identification from a suspect who fit the description of "difficult" civilian. The suspect met his expectations by being belligerent and threatening. Cameron responded by being increasingly demanding and forceful. The conflict escalated into an altercation between the suspect and Cameron.

Literature Review

Conflicting conceptualizations of "police personality" are found in the literature (Claussen-Rogers & Arrigo, 2004). Some researchers contend that individuals with certain personality traits are drawn to police work (Cortina, Doherty, Schmitt, Kaufman, & Smith, 1992). Cameron's fearless attitude would seem to have led him to a law enforcement career. These researchers note that personality traits or any psychopathology present are detected during one's initial screening for the police academy. Other investigators maintain that although would-be officers have similar occupational interests, the police subculture of violence and cynicism that leads to particular actions such as excessive force or police brutality (Graves, 1996). In Cameron's case it is difficult to determine if it was his personality characteristics alone or the influence of other officers that led to the violent interaction with a civilian. Still other commentators assert that years of working with hostile civilians, occupational stagnation, and the loss of faith in our criminal justice system lead to personality and attitude changes in police officers (Kappeler, Sluder, & Alpert, 1998). While some believe that one of these scenarios is most dominant, others contend that these influences can be interdependent. Clearly, there is controversy surrounding how to establish whether an individual is suitable for police work (Claussen-Rogers & Arrigo, 2004).

Researchers maintain that the considerable demands routinely placed on police officers requires that persons hired not only be free from psychopathology, but be very well adjusted, with good coping skills (Beutler, Nussbaum, & Meredith, 1988). Police officers encounter life-threatening situations, aggressive offenders, and have to answer to the community as well as to their supervisors. Officers face the worst elements of society and then have to handle the most delicate of human crises with sensitivity. The unique stressors that officers confront make emotional strengths and weaknesses the focus of screening procedures for officer candidates.

Research indicates that psychological assessment tools have been increasingly utilized in the past 2 decades as a means to screen and select police officer candidates (Arrigo & Claussen, 2003; Beutler et al., 1988). MMPI and MMPI-2 are the psychological tests that are most commonly used as a screening device in police officer selection (Beutler et al., 1988; Cortina et al., 1992; Kornfeld, 1995; J. J. Murphy, 1972). The MMPI is primarily a test of psychopathology and is used most successfully when testing for this purpose (Graham, 1993). The literature suggests that these instruments are employed to determine which candidates are the most likely to fail during training or probationary periods (Cortina et al., 1992; Detrick, Chibnall, & Rosso, 2001; Inwald, 1988; J. J. Murphy, 1972). In addition, they are used to indicate which candidates are most likely to use excessive force or misuse weapons while on duty. Other researchers maintain that efforts to correlate MMPI scores to job performance have not been effective (Cortina et al., 1992). By identifying personality styles and any psychopathology, police departments hope to save time and money, as well as avoid any negative publicity or litigation that would ensue following an excessive force claim.

Cortina et al. (1992) noted that police officer candidates exhibit a distinguishable pattern on the MMPI. For example, the validity scales for these candidates, which measure the accuracy of the test, usually show defensiveness or an unwillingness to acknowledge distress. The Psycho-pathic Deviate (Pd) scale is frequently elevated. Interestingly, the elevation of the Pd scale is typically seen in individuals who engage in criminal behavior. Interpretive possibilities for an elevated Pd score include aggressive or assaultive behavior, substance abuse, or poor tolerance of boredom. A study by Kornfeld (1995), in which the MMPI-2 was administered to 84 police officer candidates, indicated low scores on scales 0 and 2. Male candidates had a low scale 5, while female candidates had an elevated scale 5. For a nonclinical sample, low scale 2 scores suggest that these individuals are less likely to worry, to have problems reaching decisions, and to worry about being rejected (Graham, 1993; Kornfeld, 1995). They are also more likely to be self-confident. A low scale 0 on the MMPI denotes an individual who is sociable, extroverted, and friendly (Graham, 1993; Kornfeld, 1995). A low scale 5 for a male indicates an extremely masculine presentation, with stereotypical masculine interests, and someone who is action oriented (Butcher, 1990; Graham, 1993;

Kornfeld, 1995). A female with an elevated scale 5 could be a woman who has rejected the traditional feminine role, embracing more commonly masculine interests. Overall, Kornfeld (1995) found that these police officer candidates were psychologically well adjusted, comfortable with people, free of worry, and self-confident.

The MMPI was not designed particularly for the selection of police officers, and some researchers have expressed concern over its use in this context (Arrigo & Claussen, 2003; Cortina et al., 1992). In response to this concern, the Inwald Personality Inventory (IPI) was developed (Cortina et al., 1992; Detrick & Chibnall, 2002). The IPI is a 310-item questionnaire that "...attempts to assess the psychological and emotional fitness of recruits as well as some of their job-relevant behavioral characteristics" (Detrick & Chibnall, 2002, p. 20). In a validity study conducted by Inwald, Knatz, and Shusman (1983), the IPI was found to be superior to the MMPI in predicting job-relevant criteria such as absences, lateness, and derelictions (disciplinary interviews). However, according to Cortina et al. (1992), neither the MMPI nor the IPI could add much more than the Civil Service Exam, a multiple-choice exam testing cognitive ability, in predicting performance ratings and officer turnover rates.

In a recent study, the IPI was administered to police officer candidates during a pre-employment screening and these scores were utilized in predicting applicant performance, as rated by supervisors after one year of active duty (Detrick & Chibnall, 2002). The results of the study indicated that IPI scales, including Family Conflicts, Guardedness, and Driving Violations significantly predicted performance. Another study by Detrick, Chibnall, and Rosso (2001) examined the relationship between the IPI and the MMPI-2 as police officer screening tools. The MMPI-2 and the IPI were administered to 467 police officer candidates and moderate correlations were found with the clinical scales. However, substantial correlations were found with two validity scales. A defensive profile was noted on the MMPI-2 with elevations on the validity scales L and K. Additionally, scales 2 (Depression) and 0 (Introversion) were low, while scale 5 (Masculine/Feminine) was extreme (Detrick et al., 2001).

Eber (as cited in Lorr & Strack, 1994) obtained objective psychometric data on 15,000 candidates for positions in law enforcement agencies around the country. Using the Clinical Analysis Questionnaire, one of Eber's objectives was to determine a distinct police personality style that might explain the sporadic occurrence of excessive force or assaultive behavior in typically rational, stable, and professional officers. The Clinical Analysis Questionnaire consists of personality measure scales and 12 measures of psychopathology. Overall, the candidates were found to have very little psychopathology. They were less depressed, less confused, and less likely to engage in self-harm than the general population. However, they were more thrill seeking and had a disregard for social conventions based on these measures. Regarding their personality styles, Eber found that these candidates were self-disciplined, very tough-minded, and slightly independent.

Expanding on Eber's work, Lorr and Strack (1994) divided the police personality profile into three robust profile groups. The largest cluster was identified as the typical "good" cop or those who were self-disciplined, were low in anxiety, extroverted, and emotionally tough. One in four candidates fell into a cluster that had relatively high levels of paranoia, schizophrenia, and psychasthenia, as well as high anxiety and lower self-control. Despite their relatively high occurrence compared to "good" cops, these instances of psychopathology were relatively low compared with the general population.

Arrigo and Claussen (2003) suggested that pre-employment screening should be utilized in the prediction, control, and prevention of police officer corruption. These authors examined the effectiveness of the IPI and the Revised-NEO Personality Inventory in evaluating antisocial behavioral proclivities and conscientious personality traits. They concluded that their joint use, in combination with their appropriate administration, offered a reliable and valid predictor of good job performance (Arrigo & Claussen, 2003).

Other researchers maintain that adverse psychological changes occur in officers after some time has elapsed on the job. A study conducted by Beutler et al. (1988), using the MMPI, looked at 25 officers directly after recruitment, 2 years later, and, finally, 4 years later. These researchers found that the officers presented personality styles suggestive of substance abuse risk and stress-related physical complaints. In addition, they concluded that this risk increased with time in service. Beutler et al. (1998) and Beutler, Storm, Kirkish, Scogin, & Gaines (1985) maintained that, overall, this group was guarded and was hesitant to seek mental health treatment. Russell and Beigel (1982) reported that the alcoholism and suicide rates among police officers, by far, surpassed those of the general population, suggesting the harsh impact of law enforcement work on these individuals.

In a study undertaken by Saathoff and Buckman (1990), the most common primary diagnosis among 26 state police officers who requested, or were referred to, psychiatric services by their department was adjustment disorder, followed by substance abuse and then personality disorder. The majority of officers believed that there was a stigma attached to receiving mental health services. Despite infrequent occurrences, Saathoff and Buckman (1990) stressed that the extremes of violence, homicide, and suicide must be taken into consideration with police agents, as they carry guns in the course of their duties.

Some researchers contend that the negative behavior displayed by a select number of officers is related to a personality style that officers embody when they join the force. However, other researchers maintain that incidents like police brutality stem from a belief system that forms as members begin to feel betrayed by the system and, thus, lose respect for the law (Graves, 1996). These researchers explained that officers see the worst of society on a daily basis and begin to lose faith in others, trust only fellow officers, and suffer "social estrangement." Some investigators note that the police develop a survival personality defined by rigidity, increased personal restriction, and cynicism (Kroes, 1976; Saathoff & Buckman, 1990).

Most of the research on police cynicism occurred in the late 1960s and mid-1970s (Graves, 1996). Cynicism is defined as a distrust in humans and their intentions. According to Graves, "... cynicism is the antithesis of idealism, truth, and justice — the very virtues that law enforcement officers swear to uphold" (p. 16). He notes that cynicism was the precursor to emotional problems that led to misconduct, brutality, and possibly corruption. In addition, he stressed the negative impact on officer productivity, morale, community relations, and even the relationship that the officer had with his own family.

Researchers have found that cynicism is more prevalent in large urban police departments, particularly with college-educated, lower ranking officers, during their first 10 years of service (Graves, 1996). Graves suggested that the heavy demands of law enforcement lead to these incidents of burnout, stress, and cynicism. He argued that these factors foster unhealthy emotional responses such as a withdrawal from society and an antipathy to idealism, or a loss of respect for law and society.

Toch (1992) explained that there are "violent men" among the ranks of police officers. He further added that while these men have certain fears, insecurities, and self-centered perspectives with which they enter the force, their brutality is often protected by a code of mutual support among them. According to Toch:

> In theory, aggressive police officers could be dealt with as dangerous deviants by their peers and by the administrator of their departments. Instead, they are seen as overly-forceful practitioners of a philosophy that comprises themes such as "lots of

suspects are scumbags," "one cannot tolerate disrespect," "situations must be (physically) controlled," and "the real measure of police productivity is number of arrests." (pp. 242–243)

Toch suggested that it is a fallacy to believe that the "police problem" is a function of personality disturbances among a small group of officers that can be detected during initial psychological screenings or a function of racial beliefs that can be eradicated by cultural sensitivity lectures. He argued that some officers have a proclivity to escalate interpersonal interactions into explosive situations. In addition, he maintained that this propensity for violence could only be identified through on-the-spot observations of their street patrol interactions. Clearly in Cameron's case, early detection of this type of behavior could help prevent future citizen abuse. In addition, his department would have benefited from additional staff training in resolving hostile situations without resorting to violence.

Forensic Psychology and Policy Implications

Overall, it is clear that mental health professionals need to have a role in police training as well as to provide psychological services and evaluations after the occurrence of a critical incident or trauma. Many forensic psychologists specialize in the unique psychological dynamics of police work, the emotional needs of police officers, and the complexities of law enforcement organizations. In order for a mental health professional to be effective within an organization, they must understand the special needs or issues of their constituency, which in this case are police officers.

Within the police department, Beutler et al. (1988) suggested that departments should enhance coping strategies for officers by including intradepartmental programs for stress management, psychological interventions, and educational programs on the abuses of alcohol. Saathoff and Buckman (1990) recommended that when psychiatrists or psychologists conduct a psychological evaluation of officers, they should not be cajoled by the officer or the department into limiting the scope of their evaluation. Continuing mental health counseling/education for officers has endless implications for their own safety and the safety of the community. These researchers also suggested including officers' families in the mental health process in order to elicit critical information and to increase the level of support for that officer.

It is imperative for police departments to take all possible steps to reduce the stigma attached to psychological services for officers. Police supervisors should receive training to help them identify those patrol personell in need of psychological referrals. These interventions should be encouraged and rewarded by supervisors and even made mandatory after critical events.

Regarding cynicism, Graves (1996) suggested that competent, principle-centered, people-oriented leadership could help to inspire and motivate employees and prevent negativity. In addition, these administrators should actively recognize the positive actions by police officers within the department as well as within the community. He also maintained that by offering continuous training about the intent regarding rules of evidence, officers could be empowered within the criminal justice system rather than manipulated by it. Graves noted that a participatory management style that allows officers to have a voice would increase their satisfaction with their jobs and reduce cynicism that flowed out toward the community. Finally, he suggested that a realistic job preview should be offered to police officer candidates during recruitment.

Toch (1992) suggested that rather than focus only on the individual recruit's personality style, his or her pattern of social interaction should be examined in order to assess the violence potential. He pointed out that young officers should strongly be advised to communicate to civilians the reasons for their actions. For example, Toch cited multiple incidents where police officers demanded a certain response from a suspicious civilian, and that their increasingly authoritative and demanding demeanor contributes to the escalation of violence. Toch recognized that the ambiguity in the power delegated to police officers frequently resulted in the abuse of those powers. He suggested that more guidance should be offered in handling discretion. Officers are bombarded with phrases like "reasonable force" without a clear understanding of their meanings or applicability in street encounters. In the above case illustration, Cameron was faced with a noncompliant suspect and had no plan to diffuse the situation.

In order to confront these situations, Toch (1992) suggested that officers should be provided with criteria of conduct with a realistic preparation for their use on the street. Specifically, he recommended directive, in-service training experiences rather than passive learning experiences. In addition, he recommended that while on their probationary periods, officers should be shadowed. During this observation period, when violence-producing situations materialized, a resolution *should be* worked out and errors *should be* open to analysis and correction.

Suggestions for Future Research

The literature in this area calls for more objective or qualitative data on the mental disorders experienced by police officers. The categorization of the personality traits identified in the current research does little to elucidate the experience of police officers. Traditionally a guarded group, it is difficult to obtain an accurate indication of their psychological functioning. Longitudinal studies of personality and mood changes could help identify the effect of continued police service on the mental health of officers.

Regarding the psychological assessment instruments used to screen officer candidates, Kornfeld (1995) reported the need for new normative data on the MMPI-2, especially for female and minority police officer candidates, to help promote fairness in the selection process. Additional research is needed to better understand the relevance of personality constructs for specific jobs and the impact of changing federal guidelines on employment testing (Camara & Merenda, 2000). Overall, more validation research needs to be done on the effectiveness of these various instruments or personality clusters in the prediction of job suitability (Claussen-Rogers & Arrigo, 2004).

More inquiries need to be conducted on the notion that principle-centered, person-oriented leadership reduces cynicism among police officers. Program evaluations can be carried out in departments that implement leadership styles and policies reflecting participatory management. Finally, agencies that utilize the "shadowing" concept provided by Toch (1992) should be evaluated. This assessment would explore whether incidents of excessive force or police brutality would be reduced by more direct evaluations of, and preparations for, violence-producing situations and training for violence-prone individuals.

POLICING MINORITY POPULATIONS

Introduction

Research indicates that police officers are given discretion in enforcing victimless crimes such as traffic violations (Hecker, 1997; Schifferle, 1997). As a result, a police officer's personal biases may have an effect on whom he or she chooses to stop. Studies from the 1970s found that in predominantly African American precincts in Boston, Chicago, and Washington, over three-quarters of the Caucasian policemen expressed highly prejudiced attitudes (Wintersmith, 1974). More recent occurrences do not indicate that police attitudes toward minorities, particularly African Americans, have changed. For example, despite ex–Los Angeles Police Department (LAPD) officer Mark Fuhrman's outward expression of racism, making statements such as "Anything out of a nigger's mouth for the first five or six sentences is a f::: lie:::" (Texeira, 1995, p. 235), he was not fired from the police department. Instead, Mark Fuhrman was promoted and given the best assignments (Texeira, 1995).

Although not all police officers share the same racist attitudes, many officers say that there is a code of silence to which they must conform, or at least pretend to conform, based on the beliefs of other officers (Texeira, 1995). Police recruits do not necessarily bring a racist attitude to the job with them; they learn it from older, more experienced officers who expect the new officers to conform (Wintersmith, 1974). Because many police organizations foster racist attitudes, it is not surprising that minorities tend to be targeted for traffic stops and for suspicion of criminal activity (Hecker, 1997; Schifferle, 1997; Texeira, 1995). In fact, African Americans are targeted so much more than Caucasians, that there is a violation many African Americans refer to as DWB, that is, "driving while black" (Hecker, 1997). The following scenario is an example of a traffic stop based on race, which clearly outlines how discrimination occurs in policing and helps to explain why African American citizens would coin a term such as DWB.

Ben, a 30-year-old African American man living in Maryland, recently graduated from law school and started working at a law firm. He went and purchased a new red Lexus to celebrate his new job and graduation from law school. One weekend, Ben was driving his Lexus when he noticed a Caucasian police officer following him. He was not wearing his usual suit, as it was the weekend, but was wearing jeans, a T-shirt, and a hat instead. Ben continued to drive and was extra cautious because the police officer continued to follow him. Ben finally came to his exit and turned on his signal to exit right. After he exited, the police officer pulled him over, indicating he violated a traffic law; Maryland law requires a signal be activated at least 100 feet before turning right.

When the officer pulled Ben over, he asked if he could search the vehicle. At this point Ben realized he was the victim of discrimination. Ben told the officer he could not search the vehicle and that the Constitution prohibited the police from searching the vehicle without reasonable suspicion of crime. The officer ordered Ben out of his car and called a unit with a narcotics dog in to search the vehicle. The officer found nothing illegal, left Ben with a warning about the signal law, and drove away (Hecker, 1997).

This section utilizes the case of Ben to explain how current law allows police to use complete discretion in enforcing the law, discusses how this discretion may affect minority populations socially, reviews arguments that suggest police racism does not occur, and examines the policy implications for this controversy. Because most research on this topic has been conducted specifically on the African American community, racial bias toward African Americans is primarily discussed. This focus does not imply that other minority populations are not discriminated against or are unworthy of discussing; in fact, there is certainly a need for additional research in this field.

Literature Review

Research clearly indicates that police discrimination toward minorities exists. However, the issue is more complex than racism among officers. There are laws that actually allow such racism to occur. Oliver (2001) maintained that cultural racism that dominates our society contributes to structural violence against African Americans. There are psychological issues for both police officers and minorities affected by discrimination, and there are policies that can be adopted to reduce the likelihood of its occurence. Although the case of Ben is fictional, it is an accurate description of what has happened to many upstanding African Americans. In 1996, a journalist who interviewed delegates to the Black Caucus convention reported that nearly every delegate he spoke with, including doctors, lawyers, and professors, had been stopped by police on several occasions without being cited a traffic violation (Hecker, 1997).

The Law and Discretion

Selective law enforcement has always been used to oppress minorities (Schifferle, 1997). For example, in 19th century Oregon, the "[C]hinese were more than sixty percent of all persons arrested for violations of city ordinances during the years of 1871–1885" (Schifferle, 1997, p. 4). Although police may or may not use selective enforcement to oppress minorities as they did years ago, they do excercise its use. One researcher described how the jail at the police station in which she worked was filled with Mexican and African Americans, and how, surprisingly, the watch sergeant never questioned it (Texeira, 1995). Unfortunately, the law allows for selective over-enforcement because there are no guidelines or limitations helping police determine when they should or should not enforce a law. Although there is no specific law that authorizes this practice, police have nearly unlimited discretion in deciding whether to enforce a particular violation (Hecker, 1997; Schifferle, 1997). Schellenberg (2000) noted that an officer's discretionary behavior could be impacted by raising the visibility of police front line work through the use of mobile audiovisual systems. The traffic code is where many police exercise selective enforcement (Schifferle, 1997). Police are given discretion in determining who to stop for traffic violations or when they suspect criminal activity (Hecker, 1997; Schifferle, 1997). Traffic stops have been used by police officers who suspect criminal activity such as drug trafficking (Schifferle, 1997).

In the above case illustration Ben was a victim of such selective enforcement. Police officers saw an African American man dressed in casual clothing driving an expensive vehicle and automatically suspected criminal activity. Much of the justification for such stops is based on gang and drug-dealer profiles. Police departments have compiled information on what the "typical" drug dealer or gang member looks like (Hecker, 1997; Schifferle, 1997). Such profiles result in stereotyping in which police equate race with criminal activity (Schifferle, 1997). Most likely, the officer suspected Ben of being a drug dealer and police profiles of drug dealers probably supported their belief.

A police officer can pull over any automobile, and if he or she needs justification for such a stop, the officer is allowed to follow a vehicle until a traffic violation occurs (Hecker, 1997). If a police officer has reasonable cause to believe that the individual is breaking another law, such as drug trafficking, he or she may conduct a plain-view search of the vehicle and seek consent for a complete search. If the individual does not consent to the search, a narcotics dog can be brought in to search the vehicle for drugs; this is exactly what happened in Ben's case.

Traffic stops have been challenged in court cases, providing some limits to such stops. For example, in *Terry v. Ohio* (1968), the Supreme Court indicated that searches and seizures without probable cause could only be conducted if the officer had a reasonable suspicion of criminal activity (Hecker, 1997; E. Long, J. Long, Leon, & Weston, 1975). This ruling also indicates that reasonable suspicion requires "specific and articulable facts which, taken together with rational inferences from those facts, reasonably warrant" a search (Hecker, 1997, p. 7). Although this ruling attempted to protect minorities from unreasonable searches, it most likely does little. Police profiles of drug traffickers and gang members provide law enforcement with the factual information they need to justify stopping and searching vehicles.

Another more recent case that challenged traffic stops was the situation of Michael Whren (*United States of America v. Whren*, 1997). Whren and another occupant in his car were driving a Nissan Pathfinder with temporary plates in Washington, D.C. Officers in an unmarked car indicated that the driver was not paying full attention to his or her driving so they followed the vehicle to investigate. When the officers pulled alongside the Pathfinder, they saw plastic bags that appeared to be drugs. The police then arrested the driver and passenger, searched the vehicle, and found more drugs. Michael Whren was convicted on four counts, all of which were possession of or intent to distribute drugs.

Whren took his case to the U.S. Supreme Court, claiming the stop was unreasonable under the Fourth Amendment and, as a result, the evidence was not obtained legally. However, the court ruled that, although the Constitution does not allow selective enforcement of the law, "the constitutional basis for objecting to intentionally discriminatory application of the laws is the Equal Protection Clause, not the Fourth Amendment" (Whren, as cited in Schifferle, 1997, p. 8). The ruling on Whren only provides that discretion not be based on race. Clearly, it would be difficult to prove whether a stop was based solely on race. In Ben's case, the officer could have claimed that Ben met the description of a drug trafficker, thus warranting a stop. Despite constitutional protection against discrimination, it appears as though vague laws and stereotypical police profiles prevent true protection for minorities when selective enforcement of the law is considered. Indeed, minorities report taking precautions such as wearing conservative clothing, driving conservative cars, and carefully obeying traffic laws to prevent being harassed by police officers (Hecker, 1997; Oliver, 2001).

How Discretion Affects Minorities

Based on research that suggests police tend to target minority groups for traffic stops and drug investigations, it is not surprising that African Americans are disproportionately arrested in relation to their representation in the general population (Schifferle, 1997). In addition, although research does not specifically indicate the impact the high arrest rate has on African Americans, one could reasonably speculate that the arrest rate perpetuates further stereotyping toward this population (Cooper, 2001).

Police discretion affects minorities many ways, both socially and psychologically. Because police tend to single out minorities for traffic stops, minorities, especially African Americans, tend to fear police harassment (Hecker, 1997). One might question how minorities could possibly perceive the police as protectors and helpers in their communities when they are harassed by those who "protect and serve."

In a British study in which 641 black, white, and Asian men were polled, researchers found that blacks had worse perceptions of law enforcement officers than whites and Asians (Jefferson & Walker, 1993). Although it is difficult to determine why blacks had worse perceptions, the researchers indicate that blacks perceived police discrimination. The previously noted case of Ben is an excellent example of how a successful, upstanding citizen who values the laws on which America is based (he was an attorney) could develop a negative perception of police similar to those of blacks in the British study (Cooper, 2001). When Ben was stopped by the officer and forced to allow the canine to search his vehicle, most likely his respect for law enforcement officers deteriorated. As one author stated, "The belief among a substantial segment of the population that law enforcement officers act with bias or prejudice undermines the authority and effectiveness of law enforcement and threatens law" (Hecker, 1997, p. 3).

Questioning Police Racism

Despite evidence that suggests police discriminate against minorities and despite the fact that this wrongful practice has a negative impact on them, some maintain that police discrimination is not responsible for such high arrest rates. Indeed, there are other factors which account for the high arrest rates of African Americans.

Meanwhile, some argue against the notion that most police officers are racist. Although some rationales more supportive of the police do not deny that police target minority populations, they justify the targeting by suggesting that the offense rate among African Americans is higher. The arguments defending police that more minorities are arrested because the areas in which they live tend to be patrolled more, that more minorities are of low SES and therefore commit more crime, and that minorities, African Americans especially, engage in more criminal activity than the general population, thus resulting in higher arrest rates (Schifferle, 1997; Texeira, 1995).

Wilbanks (as cited in Schifferle, 1997) provided several reasons why minorities are more likely to be arrested. He indicated that minority neighborhoods are subject to more police surveillance, which would lead to higher arrest rates. This argument is supported by other researchers as well (Texeira, 1995). However, Texeira (1995) noted that such surveillance resulted from police racism toward minorities. Still, researchers could assert that minority neighborhoods are watched more closely by police because minorities commit more crime. This appears to be the belief of Wilbanks who claimed that differential offending by African Americans could explain the differences in arrest rates.

Other studies indicate that minorities are more likely to be of low SES, which leads them to commit more crime (Jefferson & Walker, 1993). Researchers noted that once SES is controlled for in further police bias investigations, it will be possible to determine if police bias or low SES results in disproportionately high arrest rates for minorities (Cooper, 2001). While the notion of low SES may adequately explain the disproportionately high arrest rate for minorities, it does not explain the significant number of minority traffic stops in which no traffic violation occurred (Schifferle, 1997).

There is no absolute way to determine if the position, that African Americans commit more crime and are therefore arrested more than Caucasians, is true. Not all offenders are known to police, and an officer's decision not to arrest an offender may not be documented (Schifferle, 1997). Some researchers indicate that racial bias plays a role in police decisions to arrest (Cooper, 2001). Others note that police may be more suspicious of African Americans because they commit more crime. As a result, police stop African Americans more often, which allows police to uncover criminal activity (Wilbanks, as cited in Schifferle, 1997).

Although it is difficult to determine the actual cause of high arrest rates for minorities, research supports the notion that high arrest rates, for African Americans in particular, are at least partially due to racial bias of police officers. Although racial bias is apparent, it is difficult to determine if police bias toward minorities is a function of institutionalized racism within the police organization, or if police target racial minorities because minorities commit more crime. Nevertheless, action should be taken to ensure that the police are not discriminating against minorities.

Forensic Psychology and Policy Implications

Researchers and legal scholars have made suggestions that could prevent discriminatory traffic stops. Hecker (1997) suggested that civilian review boards should insist that police agencies accused of repeated discriminatory law enforcement practices to report statistics on every police stop made. The act of recording the data alone may reduce police discrimination. Civilian review boards should question whether drug profiles are suggestive enough of criminal activity to warrant their use.

Another tactic utilized to prevent racism in the police force is to hire more minorities. In the 1980s the Detroit police force shed its reputation as being racist by employing a police force that was 50% African American (Jackson, 1989). However, with the decreasing popularity of affirmative action, it is not likely that this hiring practice will continue.

Legal scholars have proposed other methods to limit police discretion. Although many investigators recognize that police discretion is necessary, some argue that it needs to be limited. Some recommend judicially mandated internal police rulemaking to govern selective enforcement (Hecker, 1997). Other research suggests that departments develop guidelines for controlling police discretion (Weber-Brooks, 2001). Although these guidelines would ideally help reduce the problem, it is questionable that they would be effective in reality, especially because racism is so ingrained in many police organizations (Cooper, 2001).

Governmental policies need to be enacted that specifically constrain police discretion. In addition, police organizations accused of selective law enforcement should be required to report statistics on every individual stopped. Until policies are enacted to limit the amount of discretion police are given, and to monitor the amount of race-based traffic stops, minorities will be unable to view police as their protectors.

Suggestions for Future Research

Most of the research on racism in policing focuses on African Americans; however, Latin Americans are also overrepresented in jail and prison populations. In addition, there are reports of discrimination against Asian Americans. There is a clear need for research on selective law enforcement for all minority groups. There is also a need for studies that deal with how selective enforcement impacts minority citizens. Although the impact of selective enforcement was addressed in this section, much of the information was based on speculation given the lack of extensive, reliable, and valid in inquiries.

Practice Update Section: Adult Issues in Policing

Psychology is inextricably linked to in the interrogation process. For instance, interrogation strategies for a psychopathic murderers pertaining to the whereabouts of a victim's body would need to take into account their narcissism, callousness, and lack of empathy and remorse. Attempting to appeal to their sense of sympathy for the family, or the right of the victim to a decent burial, would be a futile effort. Appealing to their narcissism or implying that their crimes were unimpressive might yield better results in encouraging the accused to divulge details of the crime. A forensic or police psychologist could provide training or serve as a consultant to law enforcement, regarding the most effective strategies for interrogating different personality types or psychopathology. While in this type of case, the interrogation process could help lead to justice or closure for a family, improper interrogation strategies with the mentally retarded can result in injustice for all parties.

Individuals with mental retardation are, perhaps, the most grossly under researched group with regard to their interaction with the police and legal system. The potential for rights infringement has been realized over and over again. The recent Supreme Court ruling that prohibits the execution of the mentally retarded (*Atkins v. Virginia*, 2002) can be closely connected to the many injustices these individuals typically confront throughout the criminal justice system. The American Association of Mental Retardation (2002, p. 13) provided a new definition describing this condition: "Mental retardation is a disability characterized by significant limitations both in intellectual functioning and in adaptive behavior as expressed in conceptual, social, and practical adaptive skills. This disability originates before age 18."

Although everyone is an individual and ability levels differ, research demonstrates that there are certain characteristics and cognitive limitations that are very common among the mentally retarded. For example, these individuals are very susceptible to coerced confessions and are at a higher risk of being unable to understand their Miranda warnings. Moreover, mentally retarded citizens are plagued by impulsive behaviors, poor planning and coping skills, and have a tendency to acquiesce in order to please those seen as authority figures (Everington & Keyes, 1999).

Leading questions by law enforcement can result in exploitation. Those evaluating or interrogating individuals with mental retardation should avoid leading questions and "yes or no" queries. For example, the same question could be asked in two different ways, requiring a no answer in one instance but a yes response in another. This line of questioning could then be used to detect a pattern of acquiescence (Appelbaum, 1994).

The mentally retarded are particularly motivated to seek approval, especially from those in authority, even if it means giving incorrect or untruthful answers. They are very responsive to disapproval and will feel disempowered or unable to refuse the persistent demands of the officer pressing for a confession. Unable to truly conceptualize the long-term consequences of a confession, true or false, the mentally retarded individual might accept blame from an accuser for immediate approval, or for removal from uncomfortable surroundings.

Further complicating the issue, is the tendency for persons with mental retardation to minimize or deny the severity of their deficits in an attempt to appear normal. An officer who has little knowledge of these issues might dramatically overestimate the intellectual capacities of a suspect. Compared to individuals with average IQs, the mentally retarded have a limited capacity to reason, to consider consequences, and to make effective choices (Baroff, 1996). They have many expressive and receptive language deficits and have difficulty understanding directions or procedures (certainly complex legal rights), rapid speech, complex sentences, and more abstract concepts. The interrogation or interview should be conducted at a level commensurate to the suspect's cognitive level, with simple and concrete vocabulary. Information should be presented slowly, and repetition will likely be necessary. Rather than simply asking a mentally retarded suspect if he or she understands what was just read or spoken, the person should be asked to explain it back in one's own words. Hypothetical situations are likely to be too abstract for these citizens to effectively process. In order to facilitate the constitutional protections of the mentally retarded, and to not encourage false/coerced confessions, law enforcement should use mental health consultants who are trained in working with this population. Police departments should expose their officers to the dangers and pitfalls of using standard interrogation techniques with the mentally retarded.

CHAPTER 8

Juvenile Issues in Policing/Psychology

OVERVIEW

Police involvement in the lives of juveniles has varied considerably throughout the history of the United States. What is unmistakable, however, is that wayward youths can and do find themselves subject to law enforcement intervention. At the core of these interventions is a struggle over how to address the "best interests" of the child while, at the same time, maintain the public's concern for safety, order, security, and control. It is at this juncture that psychology assumes a pivotal role in the (successful) outcome of law enforcement interventions with juveniles.

This chapter examines a number of critical areas where the intersection of policing and adolescent behavior generates forensic psychological controversies. Topics explored in this chapter include (1) dealing with troubled youths in school and in the community, (2) policing juvenile gangs, (3) juvenile attitudes toward the police, and (4) adolescent female prostitution. The issues investigated in this chapter barely scratch the surface of where and how the interface of policing, psychology, and juvenile justice affects the lives of police officers, youthful offenders, and the public at large. As with all chapters throughout this textbook, the intent here is to describe a number of the more compelling crime and justice controversies identified in the field.

Police officers confront all sorts of troubled youths; for example, some adolescents engage in underage drinking, join gangs, are truant, or become suicidal. How do police officers in their crime control interventions promote the rehabilitation of the adolescent? How do officers promote the aims of punishment? Does the mental health of juveniles impact their legal status and if so, are appropriate treatment and placement options being applied?

Law enforcement personnel deal directly with youth gang members. What kinds of antigang police tactics are used to inhibit membership? What sorts of antigang control strategies are adopted to curb juvenile violence? What perceptions do non-gang-affiliated adolescents have about these police interventions?

Juveniles in general harbor attitudes and beliefs about law enforcement and social control practices. Where do these adolescent perceptions come from? Can these beliefs and attitudes be changed in any meaningful way? Police officers also find themselves responding to youths who engage in some very physically and emotionally debilitating behavior. Addressing child sexual exploitation (e.g., adolescent female prostitution) is perhaps one of the most difficult forms of police interventions imaginable. How do officers cope with the sexual victimization of children? How do the principles of rehabilitation or retribution operate within this forensic problem? Are these youths hard-core criminals or unsuspecting victims?

The field of policing deviant, risky, and/or illicit juvenile conduct is by far more complex than is described in the pages that follow. In addition, the perceptions adolescents engender regarding law enforcement behavior and practices are also more intricate and subtle than the space limits this chapter allows. However, what is clear is the important role of psychology and the psychological sciences at the crossroads of policing and juvenile justice. As the individual sections of this chapter repeatedly point out, improving relations between officers and (wayward) youths is certainly needed. The impact of such efforts potentially could improve juvenile recidivism rates and foster better, more meaningful police–community ties. One facet to this more civic-minded agenda entails additional research. The manner in which troubled youths, adolescent gangs, juvenile attitudes and beliefs, and child sexual exploitation relate to policing is not well developed in the overlapping criminological and psychological literature. Thus, as the material developed in this chapter recommends, the future success of juvenile justice and law enforcement necessitates more cross-disciplinary efforts along these, and similar, lines of scholarly inquiry.

DEALING WITH TROUBLED YOUTHS AT SCHOOL AND IN THE COMMUNITY

Introduction

The youth of today are faced with a variety of problems that put them at risk. These problems include underage drinking and driving, drug abuse, pregnancy, suicide, truancy, gang activity, and prostitution. It is not uncommon to pick up a newspaper on any given day and find an article describing such behaviors. What follows is an illustration of how serious these problems can be.

> Jill is a 14-year-old high school student who is currently facing criminal charges for being an accomplice to murder. Jill has a history of running with the wrong crowd. Many of the crowd's activities include drinking, doing drugs, and skipping school. She has a long history of truant behavior.
>
> During the time Jill was away from school, she was burglarizing local neighborhood homes to support her drug habit. On one particular occasion, she was with her boyfriend, Mike, burglarizing a nearby residence. They were in the midst of robbing the house when the resident surprised them. Startled and scared, Mike pulled out his gun and shot the victim to death. Jill exemplifies how a life of drugs, truancy, and crime can lead to a tragic ending.

Historically, the tradition has been that the police assume ultimate responsibility for fighting crime and maintaining order. When dealing with wayward youths, the aim has been to rehabilitate, rather than to punish. Despite common public misperception, juvenile crime is actually on the decline (Comes, Bertrand, Paetseh, & Hornick, 2003; Doob & Sprott, 1998; Stevenson, Tufts, Hendrick, & Kowalski, 1999). According to data reported by the Federal Bureau of Investigation (FBI) in the *Uniform Crime Reports* (Rand, 1998) and the National Center of Education Statistics (U.S. Department of Education, 1999), adolescent violent acts have declined over the past 20 years and are continuing to do so. The public's overestimation of the frequency and severity of juvenile crime is perpetuated by the media's nonstop coverage of extreme instances of school violence or other sensational cases of teen violence like the school shootings at Columbine, Colorado, and Paducah, Kentucky (Austin, 2003; Comes et al., 2003; Sullivan & Miller, 1999). However, despite an overall decline in juvenile crime, particularly in the late nineties, a growing number of juveniles are being jailed or are engaged in the criminal justice system in some way, as the focus in our juvenile justice system shifts further from the rehabilitative model to a more punitive one (Granello & Hanna, 2003; B. Smith, 1998). The perspective regarding rehabilitation versus retribution for these offenders is sometimes challenged by those who feel that the criminal justice system needs to resort to punishing offenders for their crimes.

Police organizations nationwide are currently questioning the effectiveness of the early strategies of crime control, which date back to the turn of the century. At present these agencies are exploring ways to combat the problem of dealing with troubled youths, either through retributive or rehabilitative measures. Police strategies to address this issue vary with each jurisdiction. Some agencies are implementing programs that target specific at-risk behaviors such as drinking and driving and drug abuse. In this section, the focus is on truant youths and juvenile delinquency. Several examples, explaining how various law enforcement agencies nationwide confront these issues, are presented. Additionally, the prevalence of mental disorders in juvenile offenders is discussed, as well as the impact this prevalence has on youthful offending and overall treatment.

Literature Review

As early as the 1800s, social reformers recognized the link between truancy and delinquency (Gavin, 1997). Truant behavior has been correlated with crimes such as burglary, vandalism, motor vehicle theft, and robbery. As a result of this relationship, law enforcement officials, community agencies, and school administrators have worked on developing various programs to address truant behavior as well as the resulting delinquent acts. The majority of these programs attempt to keep youngsters in school and to control daytime crimes. With a focus on rehabilitation, many of these programs strive to offer alternative choices for youths. The aim is to keep them out of the juvenile justice system. Depending on the policies and procedures of law enforcement and school agencies, combating truant behavior varies. The truant youths can be returned to school, taken home, or taken to local police departments where the parent or guardian is contacted.

When addressing the problems of truancy and delinquency, the responsibility lies with parents; school officials; law enforcement personnel; and local, state, and federal organizations. This makes truancy and adolescent crime a multifaceted problem. Thus, it is essential to have the cooperation and support from all participants in order to successfully combat the problem. In a study examining the principal factors of school violence, two of the five factors identified were (1) a decline in family structure and (2) family violence and drug use (Speaker & Peterson, 2000). Research has demonstrated a correlation between violence perpetrated by youth in the community and violence committed in the schools (Leone, Mayer, Malmgren, & Meisel, 2000). Thus, as Austin (2003, p. 21) observed, "Partnerships involving local law enforcement, business, social service agencies, teachers, administrators, and families create a sense of shared purpose and collaboration in reducing both school and community violence."

In 1983, the Phoenix Arizona Police Department created a School Resource Officer (SRO) program in an attempt to reduce the number of truant children and juvenile delinquents. The program was funded through a 3-year federal grant. By the end of the grant period, the truancy rate at two pilot schools decreased by 73% and crimes committed on campus and in surrounding neighborhoods significantly decreased (Soto & Miller, 1992). As a result of the success, the school district agreed to continue to fund the project by paying 75% of each SRO's salary. The SRO program was expanded to include the servicing of 36 schools throughout the Phoenix area.

The officers involved with the SRO program volunteer their time. In order to participate in the program, they must complete an extensive application process and pass a review procedure. Upon their acceptance, they receive intense training and education regarding juvenile issues. The SRO officers deal with problems both on and off school grounds. Their responsibilities include educating faculty and students on safety strategies to reduce crime, and to recognize signs of child abuse and neglect. The officers spend a great deal of time and energy attempting to establish a good working relationship with parents living in housing projects in nearby areas. This is done in an effort to educate the parents on the importance of monitoring their child's school habits and to encourage their children to stay in school. The SRO unit is also responsible for detecting, reporting, and investigating suspected cases of child abuse and neglect.

The SRO team initiated 23,015 contacts with students, parents, school administrators, and faculty members during the 1990–1991 academic year. Officers made 476 arrests on school grounds, referred 596 cases to other social service agencies, recovered $14,000 in stolen property, and filed 578 truancy reports for students in kindergarten through 8th grade (Soto & Miller, 1992). The goal and objective of the SRO program is to enforce truancy laws educate school officials, and to build a trusting, working relationship with parents and children. These objectives are intended to serve as an effective crime prevention strategy in the hopes of combating criminal activity before it begins.

Researchers have concluded that for the purpose of predicting future criminality, the most likely juvenile recidivists are those whose first referral involves truancy, burglary, motor vehicle theft, or robbery (Snider, as cited in Gavin, 1997). Various law enforcement agencies across the country have developed truancy interdiction programs to counter both short- and long-term effects of truancy. Nationwide, the vast majority of truancy interdiction efforts produce significant reduction in crimes traditionally associated with juvenile offenders (Gavin, 1997). The St. Petersburg Police Department in Florida decided to implement a truancy interdiction program in hopes of minimizing the relationship that exists between truancy and delinquency. The ultimate goal of this initiative was to reduce the opportunities for youths to get into trouble by informing parents to encourage their children to stay in school.

One of the first obstacles the St. Petersburg Police Department faced was what to do with these truant youths once officers apprehended them. Because St. Petersburg was a large jurisdiction, the time it took officers to personally return the child to his or her school consumed too much time and took away from other police duties needing attention. The St. Petersburg police officials recognized the potential problem this would pose and realized that having officers return the truant youths directly to school would not actively involve the parents. They decided to establish a centralized truancy center where the truant youths waited for their parents to pick them up, ensuring that the parents took an active role in the situation.

Once the truant youths arrive at the center via the patrol officer, a receiving officer or a juvenile detective contacts both the school and the parents and proceeds to tend to the youngster until the parents or guardians arrive. If the youngster is on probation, the juvenile officer notifies the youth's case worker immediately. The initial process was intended by program developers to be very brief in nature so that the patrol officers could get back to patrolling.

It is the responsibility of the parent or guardian to return their child to school. When they arrive at the center to pick up their child, the juvenile detective presents the parent or guardian with an accurate record of their child's attendance in an effort to make them realize the seriousness of the truant behavior. The parents are also presented with a letter signed by the chief of police and the school superintendent stressing the importance of ensuring that children go to school as well as a copy of the state statute mandating school attendance. The parents are advised that the law requires them to have their child in school and that failure to do so is a criminal act (Gavin, 1997). Before the child can be readmitted to school, the parent or guardian must bring a referral slip with the child to school. This, then, notifies school officials that the child was in custody. Many times, guidance counselors and school officials use this as an opportunity to meet with the child and parent or guardian.

Another element of the interdiction program is geared toward counseling truant youths. The juvenile detective interviews the children and asks them about their truant behavior, their home life, and other variables that may be influencing their truant conduct. They also stress to the child the importance of staying in school and getting a good education. However, a number of the juveniles in question could benefit from actual therapy or counseling from a mental health professional. Many times, the juvenile officers recognize financial problems, or other issues, and refer the family to the appropriate social service agency. When these situations arise, the officers give the parents lists and names of various community agencies that specialize in assisting with family problems.

When evaluating successful truancy interdiction programs, the Inglewood, California Police Department serves as an outstanding and effective model. The current literature on effective interdiction programs mentions the results as well as the ways in which the program was designed and implemented. The City of Inglewood's program was initiated to prevent and reduce the relationship between juvenile delinquency and truancy. The project is called Helping Others Pursue Education (HOPE). The city of Inglewood, California, worked in conjunction with five public agencies to plan the program. The five agencies involved with the project included the school district, the Los Angeles County Probation Department, the Los Angeles County Department of Social Services, the Inglewood Superior Court, juvenile judges, and the Inglewood Police Department (Rouzan & Knowles, 1985).

Police officers, assisted by school security personnel, are responsible for picking up and transporting truants to the project HOPE center. The project center is staffed full-time by a director, counselor, teacher, secretary, security guard, and a county probation officer. The atmosphere of the project center resembles that of an academic setting. The juveniles are forced to adhere to rules and are disciplined and remanded when noncompliant. Once the juveniles are apprehended by officers and taken to the center, the staff interview and counsel the youths. They are also forced to participate in a rigorous academic schedule intended to get them "back on track" with other children their age. Similar to the earlier programs mentioned, the counselors of the HOPE initiative emphasize parental interaction and aspire to assist the family if an emergency arises. This is usually accomplished through providing the parents with updated lists of various community service contacts. The main intent of the HOPE initiative is to rehabilitate the youngster and assist the family by understanding the underlying behaviors that influence the truancy. If these efforts fail, the staff probation officers direct the youth to a hearing in juvenile court.

The HOPE program was extremely successful. Comparison of the school year without the HOPE program (1982–1983) to the year with the HOPE program (1983–1984), for the entire city of Inglewood, revealed that daytime residential burglaries decreased by 32%, auto burglaries decreased by 64%, strong-arm robberies decreased 45%, and grand theft auto dropped 36% (Rouzan & Knowles, 1985).

In order for truancy interdiction programs to effectively address the issues of truancy and delinquency, it is imperative to have parental, community, school, and police support. Studies and analyses of crime and truancy rates in communities around the country confirm that today's truants commit a significant proportion of daytime crime (Gavin, 1997). Successful truancy interdiction programs serve both long- and short-term objectives: keeping kids in school and preventing future criminal activity. By keeping youths off the streets, the police can reduce crime today, and by encouraging youths to stay in school, the police can help reduce dropout rates and prevent more serious criminal activity tomorrow (Gavin, 1997).

Psychologists, social workers, and teachers are also on the front lines of confronting truancy, delinquency, and violence in school settings. Austin (2003) examined effective interventions that help prevent school violence. The danger of zero tolerance policies created to rid schools of allegedly dangerous youth, or to send a strong message to first-time offenders, has had some extremely detrimental effects on students, particularly those with mental illness. The 1997 amendments to the Individuals with Disabilities Education Act (IDEA) have actually enabled schools to unilaterally remove students for weapons or drug offenses, whether or not they are a manifestation of a student's disability (Austin, 2003). There is a public panic that schools have become extraordinarily violent in recent years, when in fact they are safer than a child's home or neighborhood (H. N. Snyder & Sickmund, 1999). The probability that a student will be killed in school is less than 1 in 1 million (U.S. Department of Education, 1999).

While zero tolerance policies are designed to protect students and staff from youths who pose a threat to others, these policies are discriminating against students of color and those with behavioral disorders. Twenty percent of students suspended in 1999 were those with disabilities or those classified with a learning disorder or as emotionally disturbed, despite the fact that nationwide only 11% of students ages 6 to 21 are receiving special education (Austin, 2003). Research indicates that removing students with emotional disabilities from school is the standard practice, rather than more preventative or proactive measures (Austin, 2003; Leone et al., 2000).

Students from ethnic minority groups are disproportionately represented in suspension rates. For example, African American students only represent 17% of the national school enrollment, yet, they make up 32% of all out-of-school suspensions (Austin, 2003). Studies also show that African American and Latino students are more likely to receive harsher punishments that are considered excessive when compared to their behavior (Austin, 2003; Bireda, 2000; Harvard Civil Rights Project, 2000).

While the zero tolerance policies give the appearance of getting tough on crime and making schools more safe, the youth that is expelled or suspended is likely at greater risk for an escalation in deviant behaviors (Austin, 2003; Maeroff, 2000). Programs that focus on retribution and control are not effective in preventing school violence and can actually exacerbate criminal behaviors (Leone et al., 2000). Examples of the damaging effects of extreme, nondiscriminative, unilateral policies are presented in the following case examples.

> ...a middle school student was observed using the file of a miniature Swiss Army knife to pare his fingernails. He was arbitrarily expelled from school for 1 year, in accordance with the school district's zero tolerance policy for possessing a "weapon"...a 7-year-old was suspended for bringing nail clippers to school in Illinois, and a 15-year-old was suspended for dying his hair blue (Zirkel, 1999; Essex, 2000, as cited in Austin, 2003).

Forensic Psychology and Policy Implications

Police interactions with delinquent juveniles can be very demanding. With the rise of juvenile crime, it is inevitable that police are going to have a relationship with these juveniles, which often becomes quite critical in nature. The encounters they have with one another can have a profound effect on the juvenile's future. Police are often challenged by the role they play within the juvenile justice system. They vacillate between the need to help steer the youths away from a life of crime versus traditional police duties entailing crime prevention and maintaining order. When addressing issues of truancy and delinquency as well as the relationship that exists between the two, many police departments have focused on rehabilitative efforts to curtail the problem. In collaboration with other agencies, many of these programs have been effective.

When looking at juvenile delinquency from a psychological perspective, the notion of pre-delinquent intervention has been explored. The idea is to identify and treat youths who are inclined to have encountered with the law. Experts in the fields of psychology, sociology, and criminology who support this approach feel that youth crime is an individual problem requiring an individually oriented solution (R. Lundman, 1993).

This approach to delinquency focuses on personality problems that youths have. Various biological, psychological, and social conditions can work together to influence the thought and behavior patterns of these individuals. According to this perspective, one's personality may predispose juveniles to engage in delinquent activities. When looking at the example of Jill and the delinquent activities she participated in, early intervention efforts through her school should have addressed her truant behavior once it started. Treatment efforts to work with her on an individual basis, or on a family system level, should have also been attempted to identify the underlying problems.

Research does not support the effectiveness of zero tolerance policies in schools, but it does support programs that reflect an understanding of the precipitating factors to school violence, including preventing their development in the very early stages (Austin, 2003; Braddock, 1999; Knoster & Kincaid; Stein & Davis, 2000). Austin (2003, p. 19) recommended that schools incorporate as many of the following components as possible in the development of schoolwide violence-prevention initiatives: (1) using functional behavior assessment and behavior intervention plan effectively, (2) screening for risk factors, (3) teaching acceptance of diversity, (4) building self-esteem and teaching social skills, (5) resolving conflict through peer mediation, (6) involving the family and the community, and (7) focusing on the classroom as a community. Psychologists can play a critical role in training others and/or implementing these components in a violence-prevention program. The risk-assessment training of a forensic psychologist would prove invaluable.

To support pre-delinquent intervention, it is essential to identify youths inclined toward a life of delinquency and then to intervene. This can be accomplished by intervening early in the youth's development. Prevention efforts should focus on the environment of the child and the parental relationship. Studies indicate that the child's home life is a key factor in delinquent behavior (Feld, 1999; Siegel & Senna, 1994). Without proper discipline and a nurturing and structured environment, the child's chances for healthy development are hindered, therefore making the child more predisposed to engage in delinquent activities.

When efforts to reach the child early in development fail, it is imperative to implement treatment efforts in an attempt to reach the child before he or she engage in more serious offender behaviors (Grisso & Schwartz, 2003). Mental health agencies and child welfare agencies as well as the juvenile justice system can either mandate treatment for the entire family or specifically work to assess the youth's behavioral problems.

Treatment options to address the needs of the family and the individual include alcohol and drug programs, child abuse and sexual abuse programs, or community-based programs where the focus is on a community-oriented approach (Feld, 1999). The community-oriented approach to the prevention of juvenile delinquency believes that youth crime is a community problem (R. Lundman, 1993). Whether the programs developed are targeted for the family or the individual, it is essential to have the help of local, community, state, and federal entities as well as experts in the field working together to identify and address juvenile intervention and crime prevention (Grisson & Schwartz, 2003).

In the efforts to address the issue of juvenile delinquency and early crime prevention, the literature has identified the issue of restrictive state statutes as a hindrance in the process. Frequently, those in charge of such programs have a difficult time trying to implement programs due to restrictive or narrowly defined state legislative guidelines. In these instances, law enforcement agencies, psychologists, and social scientists should work with state legislatures to amend those statutes which are considered too restrictive.

The wording of some individual state statutes regarding compulsory school attendance does have significant impact on attempts to interdict truants (Gavin, 1997). To adapt to restrictive or unhelpful statutes, there are a number of steps program developers can take. Police administrators can work with local legislative delegations to address the issues at hand. Once they are discussed, the parties involved can negotiate and devise a mutual compromise that will ultimately help the youths. Statutes regarding compulsory school attendance will have a considerable affect on attempts to interdict truants (Gavin, 1997). As such, it is important to have a good working relationship with state legislatures so that they will help support and validate various truancy interdiction programs and proactive, mental-health-based, violence-prevention initiative in the future (Grisso & Schwartz, 2003).

Suggestions for Future Research

When addressing the issue of truant and delinquent youth, it is obvious that the problem is multifaceted. These issues have been a concern since the

1800s, yet with the increasingly violent nature of some current juvenile crime, the seriousness of the offenses, and public panic, new efforts are being examined to combat juvenile crime (Feld, 1999). Additional studies need to be undertaken comparing the effectiveness of zero tolerance policies on preventing or controlling school violence. Moreover, longitudinal studies could be conducted examining their respective impact on future antisocial behaviors. Other strategies targeting more effective school violence prevention should be implemented and their effectiveness should be examined.

A major area of interest for future research includes how various agencies throughout the United States deal with truancy and delinquency. One must keep in mind, however, that research addressing truancy in large cities incorporates more variables when compared to smaller communities. One of the most important areas for future development is to accurately assess the repercussions these programs have on the community, the citizens, and the offenders. It cannot be emphasized enough how important it is to seek out help and support from various agencies in order to successfully combat the problems that youths face today. Programs and relationships need to be cultivated with social service organizations in order to provide effective services to juveniles.

Police have the ultimate front-line responsibility of enforcing the laws that govern juvenile offenders. The help of social service organizations, such as youth service bureaus, mental health services, the school system, recreational facilities, and welfare agencies, coupled with parental involvement, truancy interdiction programs and violence-prevention strategies, can help keep kids in school as well as prevent future serious crimes. Jill's case above represents a very tragic and real example of how truant behavior and juvenile delinquency led one person to confront the criminal justice system.

POLICING JUVENILE GANGS

Introduction

As juvenile gangs grow in size and become increasingly violent, the community and media pressure for law enforcement officers to suppress their activity and curtail their membership has become intense. The threat of gangs is no longer just an inner-city problem. Juvenile gangs are found in every type of community, even branching out into rural areas (W. P. Evans,

Fitzgerald, Weigel, & Chvilicek, 1999; Owens & Wells, 1993). A study that examined factors associated with gang involvement among rural and urban juveniles found that there was no significant difference in gang membership or pressure to join gangs between the rural and urban samples (W. P. Evans et al., 1999). However, there were differences in other gang violence indicators. Communities large and small are demanding action from law enforcement, and the police have had to take a more aggressive stance in their fight against gang activity. Antigang policing tactics such as gang-tracking databases and civil gang injunctions have been created and employed around the country in an attempt to suppress gang activity. If granted by the court, a civil gang injunction is a lawsuit that limits conduct by members of a gang that would otherwise be considered lawful. However, enforcement strategies alone fail to address the root causes of the juvenile gang epidemic. According to Brantley and DiRosa (1994), understanding the factors that drive youths to join gangs is the first step in addressing the problem.

Supporters of such strategies maintain that they are effective forms of gang control, while opponents hold that these tactics infringe upon civil liberties, particularly those of ethnic minorities (N. Siegal, 1997). It is argued that aggressive tactics broadly applied to law–abiding youths encourage negative attitudes toward officers to flourish in areas where a fragile police–community relationship already exists. Police officers have the challenge of implementing these strategies without targeting juveniles who are not affiliated with gangs. Consider the following case illustration.

> Sixteen-year-old Claudio Ceja of Anaheim, California, is an 11th grader at Loara High School. From 8:00 a.m. until 2:35 p.m. he attends class. From 4 to 6 p.m. he hands out fliers for a local business. From 6 to 9:30 p.m. he completes his homework before he goes to his second job at an Anaheim convention center. But the Anaheim police do not see Ceja as a hard-working young student. In the past few years, they have stopped, detained, and photographed Ceja five times and put his photograph in the city's gang-tracking computer database. Each time, Ceja told them he was not involved with a gang. But each time they ignored his claims, he says. Despite the police attention, Ceja has never been arrested or charged with any crime. "They seem to be doing it for the fun of it," says Ceja. "They take my picture, and they put it in a gang file. But I'm not a gangster. I don't want to be identified as one." (N. Siegal, 1997, p. 28)

Literature Review

Aggressive policing tactics and legal interventions into the lives of gang members, particularly those that criminalize activities that are typically lawful, are becoming more widespread. However, many argue that such tactics often lead to the harassment of law-abiding youths who may fit stereotypes of a gang member as in Claudio Ceja's case, creating a negative impact on community–police relations (Hoffman & Silverstein, 1995). Ceja's case illustrates the fine line between cracking down on gang members and further alienating at-risk youths.

As the literature demonstrates, antigang policing tactics serve as an imperfect attempt to treat the symptoms and not the causes of our juvenile gang epidemic. Two of the most common antigang policing tactics are gang-tracking databases and civil gang injunctions. These policing tactics attempt gang suppression or deterrence by their speed of enforcement, certainty of punishment, and severity of sanctions, while the targeting of these sanctions is extended through an increase in gang intelligence tracking (Klein, 1995).

Gang-tracking databases are employed as an intelligence-gathering strategy as gangs become increasingly mobile and organized. Territorial graffiti, tattoos, symbols, and specialized clothing (for example, those indicating gang colors) are all visual symbols that can indicate gang affiliation and are frequently combined with a database to provide patrol officers with identification information (Owens & Wells, 1993). Gang intelligence information gathered or received by law enforcement or juvenile-related personnel are included in the database. Police departments that utilize these gang-tracking databases detain and photograph youths who are charged with gang activity as well as those who are only suspected of it, as in Ceja's case. Youths often deny gang membership, leaving officers to distinguish between delinquent conduct and gang behavior.

Critics of these gang databases claim that minorities are disproportionately represented. Ed Chen, staff attorney with the American Civil Liberties Union (ACLU) of Northern California stated:

> There's a racially discriminating aspect to all these programs. In every case that we've seen, the targets are Latino or African American youth. They can concentrate on young black, brown, and sometimes yellow men. It's rarely used against non-minorities (N. Siegal, 1997, p. 31).

Despite claims of harassment by youths who are not affiliated with gangs, Torok and Trump (1994) stated that crimes are often solved quickly or prevented altogether by stripping gang members of their anonymity. The U.S. Treasury Department's Bureau of Alcohol, Tobacco, and Firearms (ATF) contends that not only do gang-tracking databases give accurate pictures of gang activities and membership, but that a national intelligence network is necessary if law enforcement is to effectively confront violent gangs (Higgins, 1993). An example of an elaborate gang-tracking system was developed and implemented by the National Major Gang Task Force (NMGTF), an organization devoted to networking, training, and creating information–sharing about gangs and security threat group management in correctional settings (American Correctional Association, 2001). This system connects all 50 state correctional systems, the Federal Bureau of Prisons, major jails, law enforcement, and probation and parole officers across the nation (American Correctional Association, 2001). Juvenile gang membership often persists into adult gang member-ship. Subsequently, when their criminal behavior lands them in prison, a burgeoning, dangerous prison gang subculture also exists.

Civil gang injunctions are also being used as a preemptive strike against gang-related crime. Using civil gang injunctions, prosecutors can prohibit members of a particular street gang from participating in criminal activities such as graffiti or weapons possession as well as from engaging in conduct which facilitates criminal activity that is typically deemed legal. According to the Los Angeles City Attorney Gang Prosecution Section (1995), "... aggressive enforcement of an injunction enables law enforcement to effectively prevent imminent criminal activity by arresting persons for prohibited patterns of conduct which are known to precede and facilitate these crimes" (p. 325). For example, those members of the gang named in the injunction could be enjoined (prohibited) by a court from activities like wearing pagers, dressing in gang attire, flashing "handsigns," approaching and soliciting business from pedestrians and passing vehicles, or gathering at specified locations such as a city park. This is a proactive technique that is designed to enable uniformed officers to arrest gang members before a drug deal is consummated or any other gang-related crime is committed.

Heinkel & Reichel (2002) explored the use of the driver's license as a new strategy that does not lead to harassment or violate constitutional rights, while effectively reducing gang activity in both smaller and larger cities. Examination of the driver's license status of 383 gang members (ages 16 to 34) found that 77% did not have a valid license. Gang members were significantly more likely to be driving without a valid license, more so males than females. The strategy would require police officers to reduce potential gang activity by engaging in rolling driver's license checks on known gang members and by stopping those individuals identified in the license check as driving without a license and taking them into custody when allowed by statute or department policy (Heinkel & Reichel, 2002).

Critics question whether the desire for safe streets overrides constitutionally protected rights such as free assembly. This includes the concern for where gang members will congregate as a result of being pushed from one park or neighborhood to another (Pyle, 1995). Research suggests that the underlying causes for juvenile gang participation are largely ignored by enforcement strategies alone.

Traditional law enforcement agencies tend to have only a reactive plan to managing street gangs (Etter, 2003). Individuals who consider themselves to be members of an organized gang are more likely to participate in all kinds of delinquent behaviors (Bjerregaard, 2002). Juvenile street gangs are a serious problem that cannot be understood, managed, or prevented by reactive law enforcement tactics on their own.

A study that focused on young Mexican American girls (aged 14–18 years) who were not formal gang members but participated in street-based activities of male gangs and risky behaviors such as sexual relations, partying, substance use, and crime found that these behaviors resulted in a number of negative outcomes (Cepeda & Valdez, 2003). The study indicated that the females' problems went beyond individual characteristics and were impacted by the social, cultural, and economic conditions of their environment. A study that examined the differences between female and male juvenile gang members, using a sample of 5,935 8th graders in a multisite evaluation, found that girls report greater isolation from family and friends than do boys (Esbensen, Deschenes, & Winfree, 1999). Research has also indicated that when youths are physically and sexually abused, the likelihood of gang involvement is four times greater than for those who do not suffer abuse (Thompson & Braaten-Antrim, 1998).

In order to effectively address the problems at the root of gang membership, mental health professionals and law enforcement must first understand that within their own subculture, gang involvement can actually be adaptive from the perspective of at-risk youths. In a study of 395 adjudicated juveniles, over half ($n = 194$) of the male youths and almost half of the females ($n = 29$) reported being affiliated with a gang (W. Evans, Albers, Macari, & Mason, 1996; Granello & Hanna, 2003). The study further indicated that male juveniles involved in a gang had lower rates of suicidal ideation and suicide attempts as those males who were not involved in a gang. This is an example of how gang membership can have some adaptive functions no matter how misguided (E. J. Hanna, C. A. Hanna, & S. G. Keys, 1999).

Forensic Psychology and Policy Implications

The current trend in gang policy involves gang suppression and deterrence, while some argue that prevention and rehabilitation possibilities are neglected. Law enforcement is certainly under significant pressure to address the problem, as gang members disproportionately contribute to serious crimes, particularly homicide (Decker & Curry, 2002). According to the Los Angeles City Attorney Gang Prosecution Section (1995), little effort has been made to change the social conditions that make juvenile gangs a viable option for a growing number of youths. Civil gang injunctions and gang-tracking databases are representative of this thrust in gang policy. Opponents question their effectiveness and maintain that the civil rights of gang members are being abridged.

According to Klein (1995), the gang subculture discourages the acceptance or assignment of legitimacy to police, prosecution, and court definitions of acceptable behaviors. Additionally, he stated that deterrence strategies may not only inhibit the expression of fear of sanctions, but encourage the bravado that accompanies antisocial or criminal activities while increasing group cohesiveness. Recognizing the limitations of enforcement strategies alone, gang policies need to encompass more comprehensive programs that address the root causes of juvenile gangs conformity.

Research indicates that aggressive policing strategies might curb the incidence of gang activity in a particular area for a period of time; however, factors influencing juveniles to join gangs have tremendous psychological and sociological origins. Various factors such as a sense of belonging; the need for recognition and power; a sense of self-worth and status; the desire for a place of acceptance; a search for love, structure, and discipline; the need for physical safety and protection; and, in some instances, a family tradition motivate juveniles to join gangs (M. Walker, Schmidt, & Lunghofer, 1993). Juveniles who are drawn to gangs generally live in a subculture where attachments to families, friends, and teachers are lacking and involvement in pro-social activities are minimal or nonexistent. As a result, the stringent enforcement of gang laws or policing tactics may only decrease gang activity in one neighborhood while displacing it into another.

Forensic psychologists have a critical role to play in a more comprehensive strategy of gang suppression. With specialized training in the psychological aspects of a gang, as well as the criminological theories and sociocultural factors that influence one's membership and activity in it, forensic psychologists can work in conjunction with various law enforcement agencies and school districts to identify and counsel those youths at risk for or already involved in a gang.

Conflict resolution and conflict mediation strategies are utilized by forensic psychologists working with juvenile gang members (Noll, 2003). These strategies are used to provide youths with the skills and insight to nonaggressively manage conflict. A structured network of aggressive policing, as well as the prosecution of illegal gang activity, serves as a deterrent to active membership. Providing educational programs, conflict resolution strategies, and professional psychological services to both juvenile gang members and those juveniles at risk for joining such a group could help address the problem of juvenile gangs. Moreover, programs that provide educational and occupational opportunities to at-risk youth could help curb the economic and environmental correlates of gang participation.

As juvenile gang membership continues to grow, an examination of the issues that make gangs so attractive to our youth could have a more lasting and significant impact on this societal problem. Research demonstrates that gangs satisfy important needs for many youths denied access to power, privileges, and resources. These same youths find it difficult to meet many psychological and physical needs, and feel alienated and neglected at home (Bjerregaard, 2002; Glick, 1992). In the face of such strong motivating influences, arrest or incarceration is infrequently a deterrent.

Aggressive enforcement of antigang tactics is only one component of an overall comprehensive gang strategy that includes intelligence gathering, school intervention, graffiti abatement, vertical prosecution, community support, conflict resolution strategies, and professional psychological services. Wraparound programs should exist that not only address the problems of the individual, but that also involve the family and the community. Juvenile gangs are a complex problem requiring a thoughtful solution. According to Brantley and DiRosa (1994), the need for a coordinated response is imperative after first understanding the reasons that compel youths to join gangs.

Suggestions for Future Research

Very little research exists regarding the role of forensic psychologists working with at-risk youths or juvenile gang members. As more comprehensive programs are implemented, including prevention and rehabilitation components, comparative studies need to be undertaken to test their effectiveness. For example, which conflict resolution or mediation strategies best enable these youths to nonaggressively manage conflict?

What types and durations of psychological services are the most effective? Research examining the effects of various psychoeducational and recreational programs are needed. In addition, the effects of involving families and siblings in the psychological interventions of at-risk youths should be investigated. Once programs are in place, arrest records, school dropout rates, and other forms of acting out can be monitored to determine the effectiveness of the various services that are offered.

Research regarding the attitudes and perceptions that the police hold about juvenile gangs is almost nonexistent. As gangs become greater in number and increasingly violent, the effect that working with this volatile population has on police officers is a vital concern. Their perceived threat of danger and the demeanor of gang members can greatly impact officers' interactions with these youths as well as the direction of antigang tactics. Additionally, the levels of stress and their effects on officers who work in gang units is an area in need of examination. Finally, as Claudio Ceja's case demonstrates, more effective means to identify juvenile gang members should be continually explored.

JUVENILES' ATTITUDES TOWARD THE POLICE

Introduction

The attitudes of juveniles toward the police develop as a result of numerous influences in their lives. Although police officers are frequently the primary contact that adolescents have with the legal system, these experiences are only a small part of what forms their views of police officers. They learn about law enforcement from their parents, their peers, their community, the educational system, the media, and from personal contacts with the police. These attitudes are likely to have a large impact on the choices they make throughout their lives, especially as young people.

Devon is a 15-year-old African American male who is currently living in permanent foster care, awaiting the arrival of his 18th birthday so that he may have the freedom to live on his own and make his own decisions. He states that the police are "out to get him" and that all they want to do is "ruin people's lives." Devon cannot remember a positive interaction with the police and

(continued)

(Continued)
reports that his first memory of police involvement was before the age of 3. He remembers being frightened and hiding under his bed while his parents screamed and broke things in the house. After what seemed like hours of loud noises, pushing, and hitting, he recalls two police officers dragging his father from his home, leaving his mother in a state of panic. Devon remembers watching his mother's pain and hating the men who took away the man they loved. They had stripped her of a husband and Devon of a father.

Two years later Devon learned of the police's desire to take anything that he valued from him by placing him in foster care. He will never forget the afternoon he was taken from his own home and forced to live with strangers in a house filled with other children he did not know. Devon was told that he had to live with these people because his mother did drugs and was not taking good care of him. Devon knew that things were crazy at home, but that was where his family lived. What would he do without his brothers? Where were they? He hated this new place and the new people. They would not let him see his family, the only people he knew. He blamed the police for ruining his life by taking his family from him. Now he understood why his mother always spoke so negatively of these people who were supposed to make things better.

Literature Review

Although attitudes toward law enforcement and social control have been studied quite extensively over the past few decades, researchers have focused primarily on the perceptions of adults. The fact that juveniles might have an entirely different set of attitudes and opinions, which also might include their own etiology, has been only minimally examined. However, the interaction between juveniles and the police is certainly not a recent phenomenon and it does not seem to be disappearing. In fact, the perceptions of the police by young people have become so important that interventions such as Police–School Liaisons, where a police officer becomes an integral part of the children's lives in a particular school, are being introduced to change children's attitudes toward law enforcement. Interventions such as these indicate that young people tend to have a negative view of police, and in order to effectively alter their perception, the etiology of these attitudes must be understood.

Unfortunately, many studies regarding the attitudes of juveniles toward the police conducted in years past have been limited by the assumption that these attitudes are primarily a result of personal interaction with law enforcement (Leiber, Nalla, & Farnworth, 1998). However, as investigators become more interested in examining numerous possible influences, it is apparent that there are many factors which contribute to these beliefs. Low and Durkin (2001) examined whether or not misrepresentations of police work in television police dramas were reflected in children's ($n = 96$, Grades 1, 3, 5, and 7) perceptions of law enforcement activities in real life. The results indicated that activities overrepresented on television were perceived by children as fairly frequent in reality. Activities under-represented (paperwork, routine activities) were perceived by children as occurring relatively infrequently. The more a child watched police shows and perceived them as adding to their knowledge of law enforcement, particularly for the younger children, the more inaccurate their interpretation of real-life police work became (Low & Durkin, 2001).

Leiber et al. (1998) conducted a study proposing that attitudes toward the police developed as a result of the sociocultural context of which children were a part. They specifically hypothesized that the attitudes of young people "develop as a function of socialization in their communities' social environment, of their deviant subcultural 'preferences,' and of the prior effect of these sociocultural factors on juveniles' contacts with the police" (p. 151). Leiber et al. found that the attitudes of juveniles toward the police were not a direct result of police–juvenile contacts. In fact, many sociocultural factors were directly related to young people's perceptions of the police. Commitment to delinquent norms was found to be a significant predictor of negative attitudes toward the police. Race and ethnicity most strongly predicted juveniles' perceptions of police discrimination and police fairness, and minority youths tended to have more negative perceptions of the police than Caucasians. These results indicated that young people's image of the police was a direct result of their sociocultural upbringing and that in many communities the negative view of law enforcement was so much a way of life that youths developed resistance toward the police without ever having had contact with them. This finding is also supported by a 1995 study conducted in Britain, which found that a relationship existed between the attitudes of children and adults living in the same household toward the police (Maung, 1995). Inquiries like these demonstrate the difficulty inherent in attempting to change negative views of police, social control, and the law. Many youths are taught to have disrespect for the law itself, and police are the most visible representatives of the legal system.

A study examined the perceptions of community members in a poor, urban neighborhood in Boston regarding the police and their actions directed at reducing youth violence (Stoutland, 2001). In examining the mistrust of the police, trust was broken down into four questions related to priorities, competence, dependability, and respectfulness. More than 50 qualitative interviews with community members were conducted. The findings suggested that many residents felt that the police's level of competence and dependability met their expectations but not so with priorities or respect. In particular, respect was highlighted as the most important component of trust that was often missing (Stoutland, 2001).

A study by Waddington and Braddock (1991) found that in Britain adolescent boys either saw the police as officers of order or bullies, and when divided into the racial groups of Asian, black, or white, their attitudes differed. Individuals in the white and Asian groups saw police in both ways, whereas the vast majority of the black sample regarded police as bullies. Changing juveniles' negative perceptions of the police requires making contact with those youth who harbor resentment toward the law.

A program at the Stoughton, Massachusetts, police department emphasizes crime prevention by having police officers hang out with kids (Atkin, 1999). The basic premise of the Cops and Kids program is that local police officers foster relationships with youth and reduce juvenile crime by changing attitudes and relationships, rather than by relying on intimidation. In this locale, the National Recreation and Park Association (NRPA) plays larger role in community policing and crime prevention efforts. To make a program like this work, the police department must be willing to give up some control and be willing to work with the NRPA. The shift in approach from arrest to mentoring is notable. The types of programs include running team sports leagues, going on a group mountain bike ride on Saturdays, a badminton club, and judo and karate. An after-school program is also provided that offers snacks, tutoring, and activities. The parks and recreation specialists typically implement the programs, while the police help sell the public on funding them (Atkin, 1999). Opening the channels of communication between youth and law enforcement is an important goal. Teachers in their community have noted an improvement in grades, attendance, and classroom behavior for those involved with the initiative. This program is 1 of 17 in the state of Massachusetts that uses grant money to fund supervised youth programs, during nonschool hours.

In addition, intervening at the school level gives police an opportunity to have a positive impact on the lives of those children who might not otherwise have positive interactions with the legal system. This idea has led to the development of Police–School Liaison programs. These programs were developed to create a positive view of the police and to decrease the adherence to criminal and delinquent lifestyles. In schools with such a program, a police officer becomes a full-time School–Liaison Officer (SLO). The role of this individual is to improve the police image and to offer young people positive interactions with law enforcement. School––Liaison Officers provide many functions in the school including interacting with school officials and teachers about particular students, disciplining and warning pupils, investigating illegal activity such as theft or vandalism, offering supervision, or participating in school assemblies. These varied activities offer a wide array of opportunities for students to have contact with their SLO; however, most students see this individual while the officer patrols school grounds or eats in the cafeteria (Hopkins, Hewstone, & Hantzi, 1992).

Policymakers hope that Police–School Liaison programs will change the negative attitudes of juveniles toward both law enforcement and criminal offending. In a 1992 study by Hopkins et al., the impact of these programs was investigated. They targeted six schools with SLOs and seven control schools without SLOs. They used a detailed questionnaire to assess a number of factors from the student's point of view including police stereotypes, amount of contact with police, attitudes toward the police, and perceptions of crime. These psychologists found that there was a very low level of direct contact between students and their SLO in the target schools. Upon interviewing others in the school it was learned that although the direct contact might have been minimal, there was a great deal of police input into the school. In regard to attitude change, there was no significant difference in the attitude development of the students in the target and control schools over the time studied. This finding could be related to the age of the students (14–16), as this is when adolescents establish negative views of law enforcement. The most important outcome of this study relates to the students' perception of *their* SLO and to the police in general. Students in the target schools viewed their SLO more positively than police in general. It seems that students did not perceive their SLO as a typical representative of the police and therefore did not generalize their positive feelings about their SLO to the entire police force.

This finding is demonstrated by the case of Devon, a student who attended a high school with a Police–School Liaison Program. He had a number of interactions with his school's SLO, Officer Riley, who was present throughout much of Devon's secondary education. Not only did he attend many school functions during which Officer Riley spoke, but Devon also developed an individual relationship with him. He had a habit of missing and of being late for class, and Officer Riley took it upon himself to discuss Devon's behavior with him. He became aware of Devon's dislike and fear of police, and he therefore attempted to instill a positive impression of law enforcement upon Devon. Even though many of their interactions revolved around Devon's delinquent behavior, such as being suspected of destroying school property and the possession of illegal drugs, Officer Riley and Devon developed a relationship marked by mutual respect and understanding. Officer Riley worked hard to educate Devon about the consequences of his conduct and encouraged him to attend and succeed in school. Devon believed his SLO was not "out to get him" and that he was honest and trustworthy. Unfortunately, this perception did not generalize to other police officers. When Devon came into contact with police in the community, he was defensive, angry, and scared. He thought that he must have done something wrong and that they were looking for him. He viewed his SLO as an exception to the rule, and that Officer Riley was the only police officer with whom he could talk to and who might actually listen and believe him.

Forensic Psychology and Policy Implications

Community policing and problem-solving policing are law enforcement strategies designed to promote the positive role of policing in the community. These tactics may be successful for instilling a positive attitude in juveniles toward the police. Community policing involves the development of a working partnership between a given locale and the police to better citizens' lives by addressing issues of crime and disorder. Community members work with officers to identify problems and find workable solutions (Cordner, 2001; Schmalleger, 1997). These solutions often have a significant effect on children and their view of the police.

For instance, the efforts of community policing have involved making the law enforcement system visible through school activities, antidrug and alcohol programs, and sporting events. By encouraging parents to support these prosocial initiatives, children become educated about the positive role of police. It is important for juveniles to know their SLO. In addition, their view of other members of the police force and their ability to develop a positive view of police in general should be encouraged. This may be enhanced by ensuring that minority police are highly involved in portraying a positive image reflective of the entire department. Minority youth may be inclined to perceive the police negatively because they represent an approach to crime control and order maintenance different from many school-age children. Dispelling this point of view may engender benefits for both the juveniles and the community.

Problem-solving policing is a style of law enforcement that addresses the underlying social conditions or problems that relate to crime (Cordner, 2001). It assumes that many crimes are a result of specific circumstances in a given community. Through this type of policing, community members are educated about issues related to crime prevention, and the police make use of community resources such as counseling centers or job-training facilities in their efforts to control crime (Schmalleger, 1997). By insisting on this type of policing, officers could then target the conditions that cause juveniles to adopt delinquent attitudes and pursue criminal activities. Understanding the root of these behaviors could also help prevent the development of these views into adulthood. Psychologists can play an important role in training police officers how to more effectively interface with these juveniles, and can help educate law enforcement about appropriate mental health referrals in the community. Moreover, psychologists should actively conduct program evaluations in order to access the effectiveness of the community policing strategies and the crime prevention initiatives.

Suggestions for Future Research

It would be helpful to know whether juveniles living in urban areas are more prone to have negative views of the police as compared to their rural counterparts. In addition, whether there is a difference in attitude toward authorities along racial lines in urban and rural areas warrants investigation. This information would help target those populations that harbor the most negative views toward the police, subsequently addressed through community policing or educational programs. Moreover, the effectiveness of Police–School Liaison initiatives should be further examined. The results of one study do not necessarily generalize to all programs, and future inquiries could explore the differences regarding how various programs are implemented. Some initiatives may require more direct contact with the police than others, which may certainly effect program efficacy. However, this type of program evaluation and comparison would allow for ineffective initiatives to adapt their model, hopefully increasing their respective levels of effectiveness.

ADOLESCENT FEMALE PROSTITUTES: CRIMINALS OR VICTIMS?

Introduction

The criminal justice response to juvenile prostitution is composed of distinct departments with conflicting philosophies. Varying aspects of child exploitation are handled by different divisions of law enforcement. Typically, the juvenile division works closely with child protective service agencies and handles child abuse and neglect cases or those cases that involve intrafamilial abuse (Weisberg, 1985). Sexual exploitation cases such as adolescent prostitution are usually assigned to the vice division. While juvenile divisions generally embrace a rehabilitative model, viewing these prostitutes as victims, vice division police officers tend to favor a punitive approach, perceiving these juveniles as criminals.

Flowers (1995) defined teen prostitution as the "use of or participation of persons under the age of 18 in sexual acts with adults or other minors where no force is present, including intercourse, oral sex, anal sex, and sadomasochistic activities where payment is involved" (p. 82). Jesson (1993) explained that payment is not only defined by money but with anything of exchangeable value such as drugs, food, shelter, or clothing. Although adult female prostitution is explored as a form of work in feminist theory, the adolescent prostitute is still excluded from this perspective. She is viewed as a victim of deviant adult behavior and frequently of her own past.

Often, these individuals have suffered physical, emotional, and sexual abuse within their family unit. The ranks of juvenile prostitutes abound with runaways or "throwaways." A study on the later effects of child sexual abuse in females in pre- or early adolescence, found that victims of abuse were described as struggling with feelings of depression, death, and suicidal ideation, experiencing lower self-esteem, running away from home, having multiple sexual partners, having an increased risk of becoming pregnant, and/or an increased risk of contracting sexually transmitted diseases, including HIV and AIDS (P. Johnson, 2001). According to Weisberg (1985), intervention by officers usually occurs in the form of an arrest or harassment with little regard for treatment or rehabilitation. Although these individuals engage in a variety of other criminal or delinquent behaviors, they have very complex mental health needs that are not adequately addressed through the juvenile justice system. Consider the following case illustration.

Kara is a 15-year-old Caucasian female living in a large metropolitan area. Kara comes from a single-parent household, her father having left before she was born. She has never met or spoken with him. From as far back as she can remember, her mother has had various "boyfriends" living with them in the two-bedroom apartment that also houses Kara's two younger brothers. As Kara's mother has been employed infrequently, and her various "boyfriends" have contributed little financially to the family, they have often been confined to modest, if not altogether poor, living circumstances. At times, they have nearly been evicted as rent money has not always been available.

Beginning in early childhood, at age 5 or 6, Kara was subjected to hurtful and psychologically devastating verbal abuse. While her mother rarely struck her physically, her violent outbursts were often directed at Kara. Starting at age 7, she was sexually molested by her mother's live-in "boyfriend." Perhaps the most damaging element of his attacks was her mother's refusal to believe the sexual abuse was occurring.

At the age of 13, Kara took to the streets to "get away" from her troubles at home. Having no money, shelter, or food, Kara was quick to accept the help offered to her by other young girls living on the streets. These girls gave Kara the sort of friendship and "care-structure" that was not available to her at home. As Kara would come to find out, however, these girls were prostitutes, utilizing the only resource they believed they had to survive. At the age of 14, Kara began prostituting herself.

Now Kara has been discovered by the local police. While she has had no prior contact with the police and is otherwise a "good citizen," she has nonetheless engaged in activities that are illegal. Kara assures the police that she has chosen this way of life both knowingly and in a rational manner. She insists that she will continue to prostitute herself, as it allows her to "get the things she wants" and "not have to go back home." What are the police to do in Kara's situation?

Literature Review

Cases like Kara's illustrate the dilemma law enforcement confronts when dealing with adolescent prostitutes. They are faced with an individual breaking the law; however, what options are available to this child? Despite the abundance of research and various perspectives on adult female prostitution, adolescent female prostitution is an entirely different phenomenon. For example, with regard to adult prostitution, feminist theories look at issues such as power relationships between men and women and the lack of opportunities in the labor market for these women (Jesson, 1993). Sereny (1984) explained that juvenile prostitution addresses the power differential between adults and children who have not yet entered the work force.

Although the available literature on policing adolescent prostitution in the United States is sparse, it is clear that this behavior cannot be appropriately considered using theories of adult female prostitution.

The scope of juvenile prostitution in the United States is alarming. Police figures estimate between 100,000 and 300,000 active prostitutes exist under the age of 18 (Flowers, 1998). Nonofficial sources claim that for children under the age of 16, the numbers are around half a million "with the numbers doubling or tripling when including 16- and 17-year-old prostitutes." Approximately two-thirds of these prostitutes are female.

The research indicates that a variety of contributing factors and motivations lead to adolescent prostitution. The literature overwhelmingly suggests that prior to entering prostitution, the vast majority of these girls suffer physical, emotional, or, most frequently, sexual abuse (Flowers, 1998; Jesson, 1993; Schaffer & DeBlassie, 1984; Weisberg, 1985; Widom & Kuhns, 1996). The story of Kara illustrates how many teenagers flee from a dangerous household to a dangerous lifestyle on the streets as a prostitute. The Huckleberry House Project concluded that 90% of the adolescent female prostitutes studied were sexually molested (Harlan, Rodgers, & Slattery, 1981). Research examining adolescent prostitution in Canada and the Philippines found that runaways from abusive homes were particularly susceptible to pimps and drug dealers on the streets (Bagley, 1999). Widom and Kuhns (1996) found that childhood neglect was also a risk factor for entry into juvenile prostitution. These researchers indicated that the children on the streets alone were more vulnerable to the lures offered by pimps or other juveniles. "Early childhood abuse and neglect appear to place children at increased risk of becoming prostitutes, which reinforces the importance of viewing prostitution in a victimization context" (p. 1611).

Investigators have repeatedly found that sexual abuse leads to running away and the combination of the two is critical in the juvenile's risk for entering prostitution (Farley, 2003; Jesson, 1993). Researchers agree that there is a strong correlation between running away and juvenile prostitution. Many of these girls who leave home to escape abuse or to seek independence and excitement quickly become prostitutes to pay for drugs, food, shelter, and the like (Farley, 2003; Flowers, 1998). Some are lured by the sweet-talking pimp offering love, protection, and companionship. Benson and Matthews (1995) suggested that the majority of women enter street prostitution when they are "vulnerable and impressionable." Other studies noted that the primary reason these adolescents become involved in prostitution is to support a drug habit (Bagley & Young, 1987).

According to the U.S. Department of Justice, Federal Bureau of Investigation's *Uniform Crime Reports* for 1995 (1996), 504 females under 18 years old were arrested for prostitution and commercialized vice, and approximately 108,840 females under the age of 18 were arrested as runaways. Far more female adolescents were arrested for loitering (34,011), vagrancy (313), and suspicion (322) than for prostitution and vice. Research shows that officers will arrest these adolescent girls under various other status offenses in order to prevent stigmatizing them as "prostitutes." In addition to prostitution, these girls frequently engage in diverse criminal and delinquent activities. Flowers (1995) found that the crimes most typically committed by these juvenile prostitutes include theft, robbery, drug dealing, and the use of drugs. Greater than 80% of the arrests of both females and males were between 15–17 years of age.

Overall, officers exercise a great deal of discretion in their decisions to arrest or not arrest and on what charge (Flowers, 1998). The literature is consistent in that the overwhelming majority of juvenile females arrested for prostitution are Caucasian (Flowers, 1998; Weisberg, 1985). African Americans compose a distant second-largest category of juvenile prostitutes (Weisberg, 1985). However, a study was conducted that explored the association between severity of childhood trauma and adult prostitution behaviors with a sample of 676 heterosexual drug addicts in San Antonio, Texas. The findings indicated that black women reporting severe degrees of emotional abuse, emotional neglect, or physical neglect were more likely to engage in prostitution behavior than Hispanic or white women with similar levels of trauma (Medrano, Hatch, Zule, & Desmond, 2003). Juvenile prostitutes can come from all socioeconomic backgrounds. Flowers (1998) maintained that studies with smaller samples have found that they are overrepresented in lower socioeconomic classes. However, research with larger samples indicates that the majority of juvenile prostitutes come from middle- and upper-class backgrounds.

A number of federal legislative provisions have been enacted since the 1970s to curtail the sexual exploitation of children. According to Weisberg, states are creating "criminal statutes that fail to punish adolescent prostitutes either by omitting any mention of sanctions or specifically excluding adolescents involved in prostitution from any liability" (as cited in Flowers, 1998, p. 152). Weisberg (1985) further explained that in civil legislation, many states look at adolescent prostitution as a form of child abuse/sexual exploitation, rather than as a result of delinquent behavior. In both cases, the adolescent prostitute is viewed as a victim, not as an offender.

As previously mentioned, most cases of juvenile prostitution are handled by either a police department's vice squad or juvenile division. According to Weisberg (1985), the various units and police officers involved in a juvenile prostitution case create the lack of a coordinated response. He maintained that vice squad officers perceive these juveniles as troublemakers as a result of their involvement with various types of crime and their "streetwise" demeanor. In addition, he explains that frequently officers are unaware of the resources available in the community to help these adolescents. Their typical response is to arrest. In contrast, Weisberg suggested that the juvenile division officers are much more in tune with a rehabilitative approach and have the capability to make the appropriate referrals to community organizations and treatment programs. He noted officers who simply arrest are failing to provide any long-lasting solution to the problems posed by juveniles.

Some researchers suggest that an officer's lack of knowledge about community resources for adolescent female prostitutes is not problem. The problem is that some officers believe that these programs are not effective in making either short- or long-term changes in the lives of juveniles (Weisberg, 1985). Frequently, the same youths are rearrested on charges related to prostitution time and time again. Weisberg suggested that officers are left with a lack of faith in the courts and the treatment programs in place to help these individuals. The literature indicates that officers are also frustrated by the quick release of adolescents from juvenile hall, arrested for status offenses such as running away. In Kara's case, she is blatantly telling officers that she will return to prostitution as soon as she is released. Officers are regularly left with the discretion to treat the adolescent female prostitute as either a criminal or a victim. In both instances police officers are habitually dissatisfied with the outcome, as the same juveniles are cycled through the system.

Forensic Psychology and Policy Implications

Adolescent female prostitution is in many cases an unfortunate result of abuse or neglect. Young women with various emotional scars are left feeling worthless, degraded, and depressed. Research shows that 10–20% of these teenagers have been in psychiatric hospitals, many on multiple occasions (J. Johnson, 1992). Additional studies indicate that almost half of these girls have attempted suicide. Many of these juveniles enter prostitution with a variety of emotional problems and few have sought professional help (Flowers, 1998).

This is clearly a population that would benefit from mental health services. Unfortunately, the link between officers and mental health professionals is not established in many cases. Some officers are not aware of the available resources or do not recognize the juvenile prostitute as having been victimized. The literature suggests that adolescent females selling sex are often the most alienated from social services, despite their obvious need for help (Community Care, 2003). Forensic psychologists are particularly well suited to recognizing the psychological correlates to the criminality of these juveniles. The plethora of emotional and psychological problems often experienced by adolescent female prostitutes are not being addressed and the cycle of crime and arrest is perpetuated. Moreover, having additional protections against child sexual abuse would best prevent the manifestation of female adolescent prostitution. When the instance of abuse is not immediately known, the victim should be placed in a safe environment and provided with counseling in order to cope with the effects of the abuse.

Schaffer and DeBlassie (1984) noted that when in contact with the criminal justice system, these juveniles are exposed to practices that suggest they are mainly being punished for sexual promiscuity. They argued that treatment is at best secondary. According to Schaffer and DeBlassie, those in law enforcement authority are "security-oriented" and the police personnel who are interested in rehabilitation are no more than tolerated, having very little impact on policy. Programs to address these needs could be implemented, with the critical factor being adequate education for line officers trained to recognize adolescent girls who could benefit from these services. The training offered to both juvenile division officers also and vice officers also could be more uniform. Although vice squad officers are extensively schooled in the different components of prostitution, the special needs of the troubled adolescent often go unrecognized. Officers who see these juveniles on the street committing various crimes could easily miss the child victim that many of these teenagers used to be.

Future Research

There is a paucity of research regarding policing female adolescent prostitution. While the literature on adult female prostitution is abundant, more research must consider the unique aspects of juvenile prostitution. The literature overwhelmingly suggests that there are special emotional and psychological issues that must be considered with this population. However, there are no investigations documenting what differences occur between those adolescent prostitutes who receive psychological services from their contact with the criminal justice system and those who do not. Program evaluations comparing police departments that take a more rehabilitative approach with juvenile prostitutes as opposed to those that take a more retributive approach are needed. Recidivism rates and suicide rates also should be compared. Additional studies on how officers view juvenile prostitutes, as criminals or victims, would be of great value. Research is needed on those juvenile prostitutes who come from middle- and upper-class backgrounds. This is a growing phenomenon with seemingly different precipitating factors. Overall, female adolescent prostitution is an area in need of further examination.

Practice Update Section: Issues in Juvenile Policing

Bilchik (1997) reported that there are over one million cases of confirmed child abuse and neglect in the United States each year compared to approximately 150,000 cases of violent offenses committed by juveniles, a nearly 7 to 1 ratio. Regarding the reduction of juvenile crime and violence, Bilchik (1997) stated:

...the lack of positive adult supervision and role models in too many of our children's lives, the transience within our communities, the lack of full attention to children with special education needs, poor parenting, the absence of clear and appropriate standards, the seemingly ever-increasing size of the public school classroom and the shortage in the number, staffing and resources of after-school and recreational programs in the community...None of these things are controlled by children, yet these are precisely the conditions we should focus on if we want to reduce the levels of juvenile, and ultimately, adult crime (p. 42).

There is a cycle of violence that is perpetuated, when the family, community, and mental health and criminal justice systems fail children who have been abused. More often than not juveniles who engage in school violence, gangs, or prostitution have suffered emotional, physical, and/or sexual abuse or neglect. Despite these serious issues, the mental health services available are grossly inadequate. Policing strategies to address these problems are also insufficient. The mental health needs of juvenile offenders should be routinely assessed. Mental health professionals need to play a critical role in the detection and treatment of mentally ill juveniles, particularly those with a high risk for violence. Gurian-Sherman (2001) contends that many children incarcerated with mild to serious mental health disorders are in trouble for committing a delinquent act; however, the schools, as well as mental health and criminal justice systems, neglected their needs. In addition, many probation officers, police officers, and residential staff working with juveniles are not required to have any behavioral or mental health training, and many do not know how to appropriately incorporate treatment and counseling into their case management plans or placements (Gurian-Sherman, 2001).

Far too many violent, adult offenders are beyond reach because opportunity after opportunity for intervention or prevention during their youth was neglected. Research indicates that those youths who are most likely to survive abusive and neglectful homes are those who are more resilient by way of gaining meaningful relationships outside of the home (Keating, Tomishima, Foster, & Alessandri, 2002;Rutter, 1995; Stein, Fonagy, Ferguson, & Wiseman, 2000). Psychologists, psychiatrists, teachers, mentors, clergy, and pro-social peer relationships are just some examples of positive therapeutic relationships or positive attachments from which these more resilient children could benefit. A strong law enforcement or school policy approach will only significantly reduce juvenile crime if paired with a strong prevention element as well.

Psychologists have an ethical and often legal duty to report suspected cases of child abuse they encounter, when acting in their professional capacity. The undeniably detrimental effects on children who experience such treatment highlight the importance of that ethical and legal responsibility. Far too often forensic psychologists are hired by defense counsel in adult and adolescent criminal cases to discuss the trauma of abuse and how these circumstances might provide mitigating circumstances for sentencing, particularly in capital murder cases. At this point in the life of a violent offender, the examination of many tragic life circumstances might mean the difference between life and death or result in fewer years in prison. Arguably, more social service and mental health resources in childhood (the younger the better), could help prevent the crime in the first place, as well as save many more lives.

CHAPTER 9

Family/Community Issues
in Policing

OVERVIEW

At the crossroads of policing and psychology are controversies that affect adult and juvenile offenders as well as society in general. Chapters 7 and 8 examined a number of crime and justice issues linked to these particular domains. However, other related areas of inquiry in the field are law enforcement and family or community issues. As developed in this chapter, family/community issues in policing refer to how the psychological sciences are or can be used to understand the manner in which police officers address domestic dilemmas in their own lives or in the lives of citizen suspects. The overlapping fields of policing and psychology are not limited to crime and justice controversies afflicting adult and juvenile offenders. There are also many issues that impact society in general. The domain of community issues in forensic psychology and law enforcement encompasses those topics in which the relationship between the police and the public is called into question and more closely examined. There are many facets to this relationship. Psychology is one medium that allows us to understand where and how police, families, and the public interface.

In this chapter, six controversial matters are investigated. These topics include (1) officers as mediators in domestic disputes, (2) police stress, (3) police work and family stress, (4) police and the mentally ill, (5) community-oriented policing, and (6) police training in communication skills and conflict resolution. While certainly not exhaustive, the six issues investigated in this section represent some of the more controversial concerns at the forefront of the family and community area of policing and psychology.

Law enforcement personnel are called upon to resolve domestic disputes. To this extent, the police function as mediators attempting to peacefully settle family strife. What police methods are used to mediate family squabbles? What are the prevention strategies officers employ to quell protracted domestic violence?

Police work is stressful. This stress assumes many forms and impacts the family of which the officer is a member. How does substance abuse, the use of firearms, work-related violence, and stigma contribute to an officer's experience of stress? How, if at all, do law enforcement personnel express their concerns about these experiences in their home life?

The stress of police work also directly impacts an officer's family members. This is not surprising since crime, suffering, and death are routine components of law enforcement. How do occupational stressors (e.g., shootings) create family trauma and turmoil? What is the impact of an officer's authoritarianism, cynicism, and violence on his or her family members? What support, if any (e.g., grief therapy), is provided to surviving spouses of officers killed in the line of duty? How do family members cope in the aftermath of an officer's suicide?

The police increasingly find themselves responding to citizen encounters with the mentally ill. What preconceived notions, if any, do officers harbor regarding the psychiatrically disordered? How do officers deal with the mentally ill? Does police academy training sufficiently prepare cadets to interface with the psychiatrically ill?

Recent strategies designed to improve the law enforcement presence in various urban, rural, and suburban neighborhoods have relied upon community-oriented policing techniques. What are these techniques? Is this strategy a viable solution to fighting crime? Is it a law enforcement trend with limited effectiveness? How does the public perceive community-oriented policing?

Police departments find that communication skills and conflict resolution training are integral dimensions to effective police–citizen encounters. What kind and degree of training do officers receive? How do these skills affect victims and offenders?

The controversies considered in this section suggest that law enforcement and psychology are undeniably linked in matters that affect the domestic life of officers, their families, and the public. As the specific topics collectively disclose, it is also clear that little attention has thus far been given to this important, though underexamined, area of forensic and police psychology. In an era where much is made about violence, crime, and how our law enforcement agencies respond to it, it is essential that we not forget or overlook how matters of peace and justice also operate at the intersection of policing and psychology.

In addition, more research at the crossroads of psychology and policing would help educate future generations of forensic experts with interests in these and related issues. Indeed, if forensic psychology is to affect the organization, culture, and practice of policing in society, then responding to crime and justice controversies such as those canvassed in this chapter is not only necessary but essential.

POLICE AS MEDIATORS IN DOMESTIC DISPUTES

Introduction

Domestic violence has occurred, and has even been condoned, within certain cultures throughout history. In fact, the often-heard phrase "rule of thumb" actually refers to the old practice that a man could not beat his spouse with an object greater than the width of his thumb. Clearly, domestic violence is a pervasive societal problem that affects not only victims and their offenders, but also the police who frequently must deal with this delicate, emotionally laden, and often controversial subject.

The following case illustration is a typical, yet compelling, scenario of a domestic violence situation.

An officer is patrolling in his squad car when he receives a call from dispatch to respond to a complaint of domestic violence. The officer recognizes the address and mumbles to himself in an irritating manner, "Why, should I even bother to respond?"

This address with this same complaint has occurred numerous times since he joined the police force some 13 years ago. This scenario happens about once a month. Typically, a complaint is received from Mrs. Jones that her husband is being verbally and often physically abusive and that she requires assistance immediately. However, each time an officer confronts this situation, Mrs. Jones refuses to cooperate with the arresting or prosecuting procedures, stating that her call to the police was premature, a mistake, and that she does not wish to prosecute despite her blackened eyes and bruised cheeks. Often, Mr. Jones is not present in the home, making it a waste of valuable time to try and find him.

Instances such as this are commonplace for the police officer who responds to domestic violence calls. Depending on the policy and procedures of the police department's jurisdiction, officers are instructed to deal with these situations differently. Some law enforcement departments have a mandatory arrest policy for the perpetrator as well as the victim. In a time of increased public concern and increased police involvement, officers are faced with the task of having to handle domestic disputes via mandatory arrest or through mediation. Far too often, domestic violence calls can be the most physically dangerous for the responding officers as compared to other types of calls.

A significant amount of literature exists on the dynamics, causes, prevention strategies, and policing methods related to this subject. Mediators are most often trained officers who deal with these types of situations on a daily basis. The focus of this section is on the role of police officers as mediators in domestic disputes. A variety of aspects related to mediation in domestic disputes are examined including police practices and tactics, existing policies regarding offenders, recommendations, and prevention strategies.

Literature Review

Research indicates that about one-third of all police calls result from domestic disturbances in which intimate partners have engaged in loud or abusive arguments, or even physical violence (Bell & Bell, 1991). As a result, police officers are forced to attend to such disputes in an effort to maintain order as well as to protect potential victims from imminent physical injury. Depending on the particular officer, the person may not feel comfortable assisting in domestic violence calls, given one's training or knowledge in the area of domestic violence and dispute resolution. Indeed, studies show that police have historically been reluctant to intervene in domestic disputes (Bayley & Garafalo, 1989; Danis, 2003). In large measure, many officers maintain that social workers are better suited to deal with the problem of domestic violence than are law enforcement personnel. Despite the idealism of this philosophy, it is the inherent duty of law enforcement to maintain order, as well as to enforce the law. For the past three decades, a variety of legal challenges, an increase in public awareness, and an outcry about domestic violence, have led to changes in law enforcement policies to include: required training in domestic violence, misdemeanor arrests without warrants; enforcement in some jurisdictions of civil restraining orders (otherwise known as protective orders) as well as requirements for officers to provide information and referrals for victim services (Danis, 2003; Zorza, 1992).

The police response to domestic violence is regarded as a controversial and ever-changing social problem. Traditional responses to such disputes have several distinct characteristics. They include case screening, avoidance of intervention by police, and bias against arrest. Research indicates that historically less than 10% of domestic violence incidents were reported to the police (E. S. Buzawa & C. G. Buzawa, 2001). This suggests that due to socioeconomic and racial factors, only a small percentage of incidents were ever reported. Studies also show that domestic violence assaults resulting in emergency room treatment were four times higher than estimates of domestic violence incidents reported to law enforcement agencies (Danis, 2003; Rand, 1997). Violence in middle to higher socioeconomic groups was often communicated to medical or religious personnel. Additionally, the research indicates that victims of domestic violence were often advised to contact social service entities instead of expecting the assistance of police officers (Danis, 2003). One study found that in a sample of cases, over two-thirds of domestic violence incidents were "solved" without the dispatch of officers (E. S. Buzawa & C. G. Buzawa, 2001). Because of the pervasive lack of social concern, these practices were unofficially accepted. According to Danis (2003), many unintended consequences can occur as a result of police intervention to include additional violence by the perpetrators, mutual arrests, and the possible lack of cultural sensitivity to victims and perpetrators.

Investigations examining police attitudes and perceptions of domestic violence, consistently reveals that most police officers, regardless of individual or departmental characteristics, strongly dislike responding to domestic violence calls (E. S. Buzawa & C. G. Buzawa, 2001). There are several reasons for this. These include organizational impediments, lack of training, police attitudes, and fear of injury.

Prior to the 1970s and 1980s almost all 50 states limited police in arresting for misdemeanor and domestic violence assaults. Police could only intervene with an arrest if they directly witnessed the assault. This policy affected police officers' perceptions regarding their role in domestic disputes. Many felt that their role was merely peripheral. Without being able to make arrests, they were limited in their abilities. In addition to organizational constraints, many officers have experienced a lack of training in the areas of domestic violence and conflict mediation. This further impedes their efforts to effectively combat the issue. A recent study examining 485 victim surveys from a domestic violence victim advocacy center, over a period of 12 months, found that reasons for a woman returning to an abusive relationship included lack of money (45.9%), lack of a place to go (28.5%), and lack of police help (13.5%) (Anderson et al., 2003).

Traditionally, police departments denied the importance of their role in domestic violence because of society's view, organizational and legislative constraints, and a general lack of training and knowledge in the area. However, modern policies have changed dramatically. The catalyst to such change involved pioneering legislation in the state of Pennsylvania, enacted in 1977. As a result, all 50 states, including the District of Columbia, passed domestic violence reforms. Depending on the jurisdiction, arrests were encouraged or even mandated by legislation. New statutory-specific domestic violence offenses have been incorporated into the criminal code. In contrast to traditional policing, punitive solutions are emphasized as well.

Today some jurisdictions have mandatory arrest laws in which both the victim and the offender are taken into custody. Mandatory arrest laws have been studied by Mignon and Holmes (1995). Their research indicated that police officers were much more likely to arrest offenders when mandatory arrest laws were in place, particularly in cases of violation of restraining orders. In addition, it was discovered that two-thirds of offenders were not arrested, and that physical assaults provided the strongest evidence for arrest. The greater the injury to the victim, the more likely the offender was to be arrested. Hutchinson (2003) found that women are significantly more likely to call the police when their male partners abuse both alcohol and drugs, and when they are frequently intoxicated.

The police officer who responds to a domestic violence call must, in some way, play the role of a psychologist. Upon arriving at the scene of a domestic dispute, the officer must discriminate between conflicting stories, examine the psychological status of the victim, evaluate the potential dangerousness of the alleged offender, and provide support and comfort to the victim. Police officers may face civil liability for inappropriate responses if they are apathetic, respond untimely to 911 calls, failure to enforce a state statute, or if they are motivated by animus against women (Blackwell & Vaughn, 2003).

Quantitatively speaking, a variety of factors contribute directly to an officer's decision to make an arrest. In order of importance they are (1) use of violence against police officers, (2) commission of a felony, (3) use of a weapon, (4) serious injury to the victim, (5) likelihood of future violence, (6) frequent calls for police assistance from the household, (7) alcohol-/drug-intoxicated assailant, (8) disrespect for police officers, (9) previous injury to victim or damage to property, (10) previous legal action (restraining order), and (11) victim insisting on arrest (Dolon, Hendricks,

& Meagher, 1986). It is clear that the police must consider a large array of factors, either consciously or unconsciously, when faced with a domestic dispute. In addition to these influences, other variables, such as personal attributes and officers' perceptions regarding their role in domestic violence, contribute to their decision to make an arrest.

Forensic Psychology and Policy Implications

The establishment of policies related to domestic violence took center stage in the feminist movement of the 1970s. During this time, advocates demanded that policies and laws be reformed so as to further protect a woman from her abusive partner (Stalans & Lurigio, 1995a; 1995b). Today, research exists that calls for further public policy reform relating to domestic disputes.

Studies indicate that mandatory arrest laws, overall, significantly contribute to increased arrest rates for domestic violence offenders. Although about 40 states currently have mandatory arrest laws, this policy should be extended to all states, with strict enforcement. This policy would help ensure complete protection for women regardless of geographical location.

Danis (2003) discussed the importance of developing counseling intervention programs for batterers that reduce dropout and no-show rates, address cultural differences, develop outcome measures, and apply specific interventions for different batterer subtypes. Required court appearances have been found to reduce these dropout and no-show rates (Gondolf, 2000).

Prevention should be the ultimate goal of any potentially violent situation. In 1991, the Massachusetts Criminal Justice Training Council and the Framingham Police Department combined with local educators and victim advocacy groups to establish a program that attempted to lower domestic violence rates. This program targeted students in the 7th and 8th grades and educated them in the skills necessary to help them avoid destructive behaviors. The program was incorporated into local schools as part of a health class. Ideally, a female officer and a male teacher informed the students, based on their own extensive training from experts in domestic violence, of the dangers, consequences, and avoidance methods of violent home situations. The initiation of this program, while too new to objectively evaluate, showed remarkable positive results as measured by students' attitudes toward violence in current or future relationships and other related measures of partner relations and abuse (W. D. Baker, 1995).

As previously mentioned, the establishment of more informed and rigorous training programs for police officers is seen as the most important step when controlling or mediating domestic dispute situations. These initiatives should include mental health expertise conducted by police psychologists to aid officers in more effectively interfacing with victims of domestic violence. Training, coupled with the implementation of available legal and social resources, is the method of choice for the Albuquerque Police Department. Legal and social resource availability such as domestic violence shelters, medical care, counseling, and even escorted transportation and assistance in the removal of items from the victim's residence, are all powerful strategies that help ensure police immunity from civil liability, as well as provide much needed comfort force to victims of partner abuse (Baca, 1987).

Suggestions for Future Research

There are a number of areas ripe for research in the field of domestic violence mediation. Research is needed that examines public support for different interventions in the criminal justice system. Victim counseling efficacy and financial/legal service usefulness has yet to be examined. Public perception and support for plea bargaining of offenders is under-investigated, as are victims' views of the criminal justice system as related to domestic violence (Stalans, 1996).

Other research could examine the effects of chronic spousal abuse on victims' psychological symptom development and their refusal to prosecute offenders. Also, more studies are needed that examine the psychological profiles of officers who deal with domestic violence situations.

Police attitudes toward domestic violence have been evaluated, albeit rarely, in the professional literature. However, comprehensive studies examining the relationship between certain police personality characteristics such as cynicism and other possible causal or relational links to domestic violence responses, are not found in the literature. Because domestic violence calls constitute such a large percentage of police responses, the dynamics of domestic abuse can also affect the police officer and not just the offender or victim.

Due to the process of change surrounding and controversy in domestic violence, the particular style of policing used by different officers within a department, as well as between departments, varies to a greater extent than before (E. S. Buzawa & C. G. Buzawa, 2001). Traditionally, police have avoided responding to domestic disputes, but due to societal pressure, they have been forced to deal with domestic disputes at increased frequencies. Because of the debate associated with police responses to domestic violence, it is imperative that they receive adequate training.

Simpson (2003, p. 631) stated, "Continued empirical examination is vital to the understanding of how police may influence the reporting behavior of domestic violence victims." When looking at the case illustration of Mrs. Jones, the repeated nature of her domestic disputes and the lack of follow-up probably became very frustrating for the officer who responded. Depending on the departmental policy, the officer must have had certain limitations, leading to additional frustration. Training by psychologists could help officers learn effective mediation methods, thereby reducing the frequency of incidents, as well as increasing options for persons like Mrs. Jones. By utilizing other agencies within the community, the officer could act as a liaison for victims of repeated violence.

POLICE STRESS

Introduction

Many different definitions from various disciplines have attempted to define the term "stress." However, with such inherent issues as constant danger, severe intensity of job responsibilities, threat of personal injury, grueling shift changes, and a myriad of rules and regulations, police work may in some ways typify the very meaning of it. Not surprisingly, then, police officers experience a tremendous amount of stress, often leading to tragic circumstances such as substance abuse, termination from the police force, or even suicide.

> Imagine for a moment that you are a police officer. You have been assigned to work the graveyard shift this particular night, a shift you have not worked for about 2 weeks. Your assignment for the night is to patrol a particularly dangerous area of town. You have had only a few hours of sleep due to the abrupt shift change, and you are certainly not feeling very alert. As luck would have it, you receive a call over the radio stating that you are to investigate a complaint of gang activity in the area you are patrolling. Without hesitation, you arrive at the scene, and are greeted by a number of men holding a variety of weapons. As you step out of the car, you cannot help but think that this confrontation may very well cost you life or limb.

Literature Review

Incidents such as that just described may cause feelings of fear, resistance, and acute stress. Researchers have examined the topic of police stress to some extent. These inquiries help us understand the dynamic processes involved with a law enforcement officer's job requirements and their association to the amount of stress experienced.

A survey conducted by J. M. Violanti and Aron (1995) demonstrated that police officers experience two basic types of stressors: organizational practices and the inherent nature of police work. Organizational stressors refer to events stemming from police administration, which are found to be bothersome or intolerable to members of the police force. They include such issues as authoritarian structure, lack of participation in decision-making processes, and unfair discipline. Inherent nature stressors refer to those occurrences that may threaten to harm the police officer either physiologically or psychologically. Included in this category are such items as high-speed chases, dealing with crises, and personal physical attacks (J. M. Violanti & Aron, 1993). According to the results of this study, killing someone in the line of duty was found to be the most stressful event one could experience as a police officer. Experiencing a fellow officer being killed was found to be the second most stressful experience. Both of these stressors could be considered inherent in ongoing police work. A more recent examination of police stress literature found that there are several different types of stressors which include four main categories: (1) intra-interpersonal (i.e., personality-related stressors), (2) occupational (i.e., job-related stressors), (3) organizational, and (4) health consequences of police stress (Abdollahi, 2002).

In the study by J. M. Violanti and Aron (1993), the highest ranked organizational stressor was found to be shift work, followed by inadequate support, incompatible patrol partner, insufficient personnel, excessive discipline, and inadequate support by supervisors. Interestingly, 7 of the top 20 stressors were found by the authors to be organizational/administrative. The authors further broke down stressors by job ranking and experience. Those with 6 to 10 years of police experience were found to have the highest levels of overall stress (organizational and inherent combined). The ranking of desk sergeant was found to be most associated with overall stress, as were those officers between the ages of 31–35, Caucasian, and female.

Substance Abuse

Remembering the incident described above, one can only imagine the cumulative effects that years of police work can have on one's psychological functioning. Given the varied sources of police stress, it is of little surprise that officers often turn to unhealthy coping strategies. One of the most common, yet under-reported, ways police officers cope with stress is through the use/abuse of drugs and alcohol.

Of particular interest is the number of officers who abuse alcohol as a means of dealing with their stressful lives. J. M. Violanti, Marshall, and Howe (1985) claimed that reported alcohol abuse is underrated due to fear of retribution or demotion within the police department. Further, the authors stated that known alcohol abusers are "hidden" in positions where they cannot detrimentally influence the department or the public's interaction with the department. Davey, Obst, and Sheehan (2001), in a study of Australian state police officers, found that 30% were at risk of harm from excessive alcohol consumption. Furthermore, they noted that officers would frequently attribute their drinking patterns to celebration and socialization with peers, thereby justifying it to themselves as more acceptable. However, factors relating to stress emerged as the most predictive of scores indicating possible alcohol use disorders on the Alcohol Use Disorders Identification Test (AUDIT) (Davey et al., 2001).

J. M. Violanti et al. (1985) described a model of how a police officer might be led to drink as a result of job-related stress. Job demands could lead to a number of possibilities for the police officer. These demands might be dealt with by using various coping techniques, some of which might include feelings of stress followed by alcohol/drug use. Probably most common, rather than a direct route, is a combination of pathways eventually leading to alcohol/drug use (Abdollahi, 2002). Kohan and O'Connor (2002) found that among police officers, job stress was mainly associated with negative affect and alcohol consumption.

With proper psychological coping mechanisms, the abuse of alcohol and other substances can be avoided. Indeed, it is the destruction or breakdown of the coping mechanisms available to the officer that most often lead to chemical dependence. Consequently, alcohol/drug abuse may foster unsatisfactory job performance, resulting in reprimand, which may then lead to increased alcohol/drug use, thus forming a maladaptive cycle of dysfunctional behavior (Abdollahi, 2002).

The Impact of Using a Firearm

As mentioned earlier, there are numerous factors, which contribute to police stress. These factors can be broken down into finite categories of stressors. Not surprisingly, research reveals that the use of a firearm by a police officer resulting in another death, is often the single most stressful event experienced by that officer (Arrigo & Garsky, 2001; J. M. Violanti & Aron, 1995).

The use of a firearm by a police officer often leads to a number of detrimental psychological states. Much like a soldier using a firearm to defend oneself or others, the police officer may experience flashbacks, perceptual distortions, isolation, emotional numbing, sleep difficulties, depression, or a heightened sense of danger following the event. Sleep disturbance is another common symptom. A study that examined critical incident exposure and sleep quality in police officers found that duty-related critical incident exposure to on-line policing and work environment stress associated with routine administrative and organizational elements were the main predictive variables to subjective sleep disturbances (Neylan et al., 2002). Cumulative critical incident exposure was related to nightmares, whereas, general work environment stress was strongly associated with poor global sleep quality. Exposure to the threat of death or to death events is required in the manifestation of posttraumatic stress disorder (PTSD) (Sugimoto & Oltjenbruns, 2001). Researchers acknowledge that death-related stressors are inherent in law enforcement. Sugimoto and Oltjenbruns (2001) contended that police personnel who continue to work while actively experiencing symptoms of PTSD may be at risk for experiencing reduced self-control, escalated use of force, and other behaviors related to irritability or outbursts of anger linked to PTSD.

In fact, it is often after the use of a firearm that many officers decide to leave their profession, due to the traumatic psychological nature of the event (R. Solomon & Horn, 1986). The experience of acute stress in police work can lead to chronic stress, burnout, professional resignation, and other somatic or physical health concerns (Anshel, 2000). When these factors are combined with the hours of paperwork justifying the use of the firearm, the entire impact of the event becomes incredibly stressful for the officer.

Police as Targets of Violence

Perhaps no other single event is more stressful than the threat of personal bodily harm. Immersing yourself in the imagined scenario described at the beginning of this section may have induced feelings of stress. Considering this, one can certainly understand the level of stress an officer faces when the nature of the profession threatens violence against him or her every day.

A study conducted by McMurray (1990) revealed that of the 161 police officers surveyed from Washington, D.C. and/or Newark, New Jersey, police departments, 90% indicated that they felt assaults against the police had increased over the past year. These same officers also felt that support services within their departments were inadequate.

An interesting and distinct pattern emerged when the officers were asked to rank events that most disturbed them following an assault. Seventy-four percent explained that not knowing that the assault was coming was most disturbing to them. This was followed by feelings of powerlessness (53%) and nonsupport from onlookers (48%), from the courts (47%), from police officials (35%), from fellow officers (26%), from friends (23%), and lack of support from family (8%). It is clear that the absence of a support structure on both professional and personal levels is a substantial source of distress for the police officer who has been assaulted (McMurray, 1990).

The law enforcement category indicated that 90% of officers claimed they were as aggressive in law enforcement after the assault than prior to it. Half of the officers surveyed indicated that they would be more likely to use force if a situation called for it prior to their being assaulted. McMurray (1990) further stated that while an aggressive officer might cause fewer officer injuries, this could also have implications for placing the community and police department at undue risk, especially if unwarranted or excessive force was implemented against the citizens.

Concluding the discussion on police as targets of violence necessitates a summary of the detrimental effects of being assaulted while on active duty. One need not be a psychologist or a criminologist to understand that being assaulted, especially unexpectedly, can result in a tremendous amount of stress and emotional turmoil. Everything from recurring nightmares to a "quick-trigger syndrome" may develop as a result of being a victim of assault (Fyte, 2001). Considering that the police officer is placed in a potentially hostile environment every day, it is no wonder that some officers harbor feelings of violation and psychological disarray.

Suicide

There is no doubt that the ultimate and most tragic result of an inability to cope with police stress is suicide. An occupation riddled with constant death, deceit, antisocial behaviors and personalities, defiance, ridicule, criticism, boredom, rigid hierarchical structures, and lack of social support may result in suicide in some cases. T. E. Baker and J. P. Baker (1996) reported that in 1994, 11 New York City police officers committed suicide. However, only two officers were actually killed by criminals in New York City that same year. It is clearly an unacceptable and distressing ratio when police are killing themselves at a rate more than five times greater than that performed by criminals. A more recent study examined the suicide rates of New York City police officers from 1977 to 1996 and compared them to the suicide rates of New York's general population (Marzuk, Nock, Leon, Portera, & Tardiff, 2002). The police suicide rate was 14.9% per 100,000 residents, compared with the general population's 18.3% per 100,000. Overall, it was found that the rate of suicide among New York City's police officers was equal to or even less than that of the city's resident population (Marzuk et al., 2002).

An article by Arrigo and Garsky (2001) investigated a police officer's decision to commit suicide. The authors stated that a combination of occupational stress, nonsupportive family structure, and alcoholism might contribute to suicidal ideation in the police officer. The inherent and chronically stressful nature of police work accumulates in the form of such feelings as helplessness and hopelessness. Also, organizational stressors such as those described earlier lead to feelings of suppressed hostility, frustration, and a sense of having little influence in one's work. A number of important and often undesirable responsibilities such as shift work and disabling injuries occur with police work. These and other factors have a tremendous impact on the officer's family, who must deal with these issues daily. A police officer's job requires a large amount of time and energy in order ensure that he or she is performing properly and "by the book." As a result, the spouses of police officers are often neglected in the process. Also, police officers training typically instills such psychological coping techniques as detachment from emotional situations. All too often this detachment is reflected in the personal lives of the officers. This results in a breakdown of family communication and a lack of emotional intrigue, attachment.

The final component described by Arrigo and Garsky (2001) is the officer's use of alcohol and its effects on the decision to commit suicide. Many people use alcohol as a means to escape a reality that they would rather not experience; at the very least, they seek to distance themselves from it. As described in the section on the use of alcohol by police officers, the typical officer's use is higher than that of the general population. When one examines the nature of police work, it is not difficult to understand this phenomenon.

Alcohol is often used by police officers as a sleep-inducing agent to help them deal with biological rhythm disruptions associated with shift work. It is also used to help control deep-seated cynicism, another coping strategy employed by police officers who have become disenchanted with the operation of the department in which they work (Kappler, Sluder, & Alpert, 1998).

T. E. Baker and J. P. Baker (1996) described the warning signs associated with the police officer who might commit suicide. According to these authors, supervisors should look for clusters of symptoms such as a recent loss, sadness, frustration, disappointment, grief, alienation, depression, loneliness, physical pain, mental anguish, and mental illness. Other signs should also be examined. The most obvious include previous suicide attempts or other type of self-mutilation. When an officer does commit suicide, police departments often have difficulty dealing with the loss (Loo, 2001). Police psychologists can play an invaluable role in the healing process.

Stigma in Asking for Help

As with many other occupations, law enforcement includes its own unwritten code of conduct and its own subculture. A traditionally masculine occupation, many male police officers feel the need to keep psychological distress signs to themselves for fear of being viewed as "soft." Likewise, female police officers often do not wish to display their more negative psychological states for fear that they will be perceived as weak in character. Many police officers also refuse to reveal their emotional needs or concerning, believing that they will not obtain one of the very few promotional positions available within the department (Arrigo & Garsky, 2001; Shearer, 1993). Consequently, officers maintain that asking for help might result in such things as forced leave, demotion, or ridicule and lack of respect by colleagues. As a result, emotions, feelings, and sometimes faulty or unhealthy thinking patterns remain bottled up inside for indefinite amounts of time, causing such dysfunctional states as depression.

Depression is characterized as a mood disorder that may encompass a person's entire range of functioning: increased or decreased appetite or sleep, bouts of crying, feelings of worthlessness, guilt, difficulty concentrating, difficulty making decisions, and thoughts of suicide and death. Clearly, this psychological state can detrimentally affect the police officer's ability to competently and objectively perform his or her duties. Realizing this, the police officer often chooses silence as a means of avoiding these work-related problems.

Mindful of stigma, supervisors must take a more active role in identifying concerns that officers might have. It is not enough for administrators to simply tell officers that they are available if anyone has an issue to discuss. Supervisors must actively question their officers. They must provide periodic check-ups that will enable them to assess whether an officer is dealing with a resolvable issue or experiencing a large amount of stress warranting psychological counseling.

Forensic Psychology and Policy Implications

A variety of topics were discussed in this section, and a multitude of policy implications exist for each topic. Police stress is a problem that has existed since the inception of law enforcement and will certainly not disappear any time in the near future. Despite this, surprisingly few policies have been implemented that protect the police officer from the detrimental effects of exposure to stressors, and prevent and treat stress-related syndromes.

As discussed earlier, abuse of substances such as drugs and alcohol is used as a means for police officers to avoid the discomfort associated with their occupation and to escape its harsh realities. Therefore, policy implications surrounding the use/abuse of alcohol and/or drugs within the police force must deal with the very root of the problem in addition to the abusive substances themselves. In other words, helping the officer to utilize more effective coping mechanisms and encouraging a more open discussion of one's concerns will, in effect, reduce likely reliance on alcohol or drugs.

Police departments incorporate virtually no policies to help the officer effectively cope with the potential psychological trauma associated with the most stressful event one could experience on the job; namely, using a firearm. Aside from the hours of paperwork, the officer mostly copes with the posttraumatic stress associated with this event on his or her own. Fortunately, many police agencies are now incorporating mental health care, including critical incidents debriefings, in their efforts to assist the officer with the psychological consequences of his or her actions. Having said this, more formal policies need to be enacted as standard procedure after police officers use a firearm to ensure their psychological well-being.

Many policy implications follow when police officers have been victims of assault. McMurray (1990) described a number of them. For instance, he noted that supervisors need to be trained to deal with the posttraumatic stress associated with assault, need crisis intervention, assistance, and need to know "how to listen." In addition, assaulted police officers should be allowed time off with pay until they are deemed fit to return to work. Finally, the paperwork associated with the event should be performed by another officer familiar with the case.

Many officers interviewed in McMurray's (1990) study claimed that the police department only concerned itself with physical, not psychological, injuries. Psychological screening should become mandatory following an event involving an assault. Moreover, many officers reported that they were not even sure what resources, if any, were available to them following a traumatic event. As a policy matter, officers should know at all times what psychological resources are available, as well as be encouraged to use them whenever necessary.

Policies linked to police suicide are lacking and in need of development. Because troubled officers often resist seeking help, supervisors should instill the notion that no officer will suffer economic or promotional consequences. Further, all information given to supervisors must remain confidential, and this policy must be relayed to the officers. In addition, any information given to a supervisor by an officer should ultimately lead to a professional referral source, such as a psychologist or other counselor (T. E. Baker & J. P. Baker, 1996). Also, psychological interventions should be made available at any time an officer deems it necessary. Crisis counseling, specifically for police officers, is often nonexistent, causing the officer to rely on the same resources available to the public. This may leave officers with a feeling of hesitancy, especially if they believe the treatment will be lengthy or costly. Therefore, the intervention supplied to officers by the police agency should be free of charge.

Arrigo and Garsky (2001) advocated three main policies that might help deter the officer from engaging in self-mutilation or suicide. The first of these includes stress management and stress-reduction techniques. The authors recommended that a special class explaining how to cope with anxiety and stressors, in addition to reducing them, needs to be incorporated into all training programs. The aspects of the course could focus on such themes as nutrition and dieting, physical health, fitness, humor, play and amusement strategies, and others.

In addition to stress management and stress-reduction techniques, group "rap" or process sessions should be made available to all police officers. This would incorporate group sessions emphasizing peer support for issues such as the death of a partner or the use of deadly force. This training, according to Arrigo and Garsky (2001), should occur early in the candidate's training and regularly while in the police force. The intention of this policy is to help demystify the concept of counseling for the police officers, hopefully leading to more voluntary use of these services.

Finally, Arrigo and Garsky (2001) advocated police mentoring. While some mentoring programs already exist within the police force, the instruction might not be governed by a standard of quality. This could lead to negative influences regarding policing, stress build-up, and possibly even suicidal ideation. Skilled mentoring could allow more disciplined officers to incorporate a higher degree of respect for colleagues into their work, benefitting those whom they train.

Police officers should not be reluctant to ask for help. With the promise of confidentiality, absence of ridicule, and no advancement or employment threats, officers should not feel hesitant to ask for assistance. Inclusion of even a few of these policies would no doubt make for a less dangerous, more psychologically (and physically) healthy lifestyle for police officers. With the opportunity for officers to vent frustrations and use appropriate emotional outlets, better decision making will no doubt take place, resulting in more efficient policing techniques and procedures and fewer inappropriate and dangerously hostile outbursts by officers will likely occur as well.

Suggestions for Future Research

The subject of police stress encompasses a wide array of issues. As a result, many opportunities for future research in this area are available. The use of alcohol by police officers, for example, has been blamed on the rigid structure associated with the police department as well as with faulty coping mechanisms (e.g., cynicism) employed by line staff. These issues warrant further scrutiny.

As previously discussed, the use of a firearm is judged by many officers to be an extremely stressful event. However, a small percentage of officers actually have engaged in such behavior. This not withstanding, future research is needed in order to determine the psychological ramifications associated with this traumatic occurrence.

Additionally, investigations in the area of assaulted police officers are essential. Relatively few studies exist examining issues such as attitudes toward the perpetrator, self-esteem reductions associated with being physically injured, attitudes toward counseling and psychological treatment, and the psychology of anticipating physical confrontations. If officers were trained to anticipate the intentions of a would-be attacker, less injury might result.

Research in the area of police suicide also is in dire need of attention. Studies examining the impact of suicide on family members, friends, the community, criminals, and other law enforcement personnel are clearly lacking. More importantly, research dealing with teaching police officers effective psychological coping mechanisms must be undertaken. Also, research regarding the inherent elements of police work and how to reduce the detrimental psychological impact of this work must be considered. Inquiries of this sort could help reduce the rate of police suicides.

Police work is by no means a stress-free job. A myriad of potential stressors plague the officer daily. This section identified some of these sources and reviewed some of their consequences. Police officers are not immune to the effects of psychological and physical manifestations of dis-ease (Abdollahi, 2002). A clear understanding of this must follow if law enforcement agencies and their officers are to function to the best of their respective abilities.

POLICE WORK AND FAMILY STRESS

Introduction

The precarious nature of police work not only affects officers, but their families as well. There is ample research suggesting that the job demands of police officers can have an adverse effect on their psychological, as well as physical, well-being. This is evident when looking at issues such as stress, suicide, alcoholism, and cynicism. Based on research regarding the police profession and the extreme stress officers endure on a daily basis, it is inevitable that this dis-ease will manifest itself within the family structure.

This entry, identifies several stressors, examines the various effects of police work on family members, and presents ways in which members can learn to cope with the demands that are placed upon them. Specific issues reviewed include various occupational stressors and PTSD as a result of critical incidents such as officer-involved shootings and police suicide. Research is discussed which addresses these issues. Observations on coping strategies designed to ultimately help police families understand and process stress from law enforcement work are also presented.

Imagine that you have just received a phone call from the Los Angeles Police Department informing you that your spouse, a seasoned police officer, has been shot and killed in the line of duty. Once the shock wears off, you fade back to reality. An event such as this is one that you have always thought about, yet never expected would happen to you. You begin to think about how you will recover from this traumatic occurrence and how you will continue to raise two small children, while at the same time try to cope with the loss of a loved one.

This tragic example is an extreme illustration of how policing can have an adverse effect on the lives of an officer's family. Studies indicate that police officers experience one of the highest levels of stress among all occupations (J. Violanti, 1995). Based on what is known about the heightened stress of police work, it is imperative to recognize how its various forms directly impact family members.

Literature Review

There are several occupational stressors that can potentially have an adverse effect on the police officer (Abdollahi, 2002). Many of the stressors identified by peace officers as particularly problematic have a direct and immediate impact on spouses and family members (White & Honig, 1995).

A shooting incident is one of the most severe occupational stressors that an officer is likely to experience during his or her career (Blak, 1995). Police officers are trained to use authorized weapons in the event that they might encounter a life-threatening situation, yet every officer hopes that he or she will not have to resort to such an extreme. Shooting incidents will inevitably impact the life of the officer as well as the lives of his or her family (Blak, 1995).

The clinical research regarding officer-involved shootings focuses on both physical and psychological reactions to the incident. PTSD is defined as an expected, but functional reaction to an abnormal and trauma-producing situation (Blak & Sanders, 1997). Officers often feel estranged, isolated, depressed, anxious, and emotionally unprepared. They also experience increased irritability (Blak, 1995). Oftentimes these reactions are projected into the home environment of the officer involved, resulting in interpersonal problems.

The spouses and children of officers involved in these incidents naturally undergo psychological and physical trauma as well. The stress that they endure is considered "secondary stress reaction," or secondary trauma, which is a common reaction experienced by family members (Blak, 1995; White & Honing, 1995). It is not uncommon for there to be a strain on the marital relationship as a result of the emotional upheaval that each spouse encounters.

According to research on the effects of PTSD on family members, the family system is affected in numerous ways. The family may exhibit their own symptoms such as a lack of self-worth and helplessness. They naturally want to help, but may feel frustrated in the attempt, resulting in some helplessness. Typically, the officer experiences depression as a result of the lack of support from his or her family. Because the officer is often isolated and detached from others, family members sense that their loved one is emotionally dead, or uncaring, and they experience defeat and failure. The family may even express bewilderment (Blak & Sanders, 1997).

Suicide is a route some officers choose to take as a response to the stress encountered on a daily basis (Arrigo & Garsky, 2001). In the case of officers who commit suicide, it is the survivors left behind who must try to understand and cope with the tragedy.

Families of the deceased officer oftentimes experience emotional anguish as well as feelings of guilt. In the midst of this grieving and mourning process, the families are frequently left to take care of funeral expenses. Because suicide is perceived as dishonorable, families may not be afforded the full honors of a police, military-style burial (J. Violanti, 1995).

Moreover, police departments often abandon surviving family members after 1 or 2 weeks of condolences, leaving them to mostly grieve on their own (J. Violanti, 1995). This is a harsh reality for many families who experience the aftermath of police suicide.

Stressors are hardships that affect the family unit because of the choice to pursue a policing career by one or both of the spouses (Canada, 1993). As stated earlier, there are specific occupational stressors that are well documented in the research (Abdollahi, 2002). Several authors have described the extreme discomfort associated with police work and the repetitive exposure to crime, suffering, and death (Dietrich, 1989).

Depersonalization is a process where officers learn to become desensitized to the unpleasant conditions to which they are exposed on a daily basis. Through this process, they become emotionally detached. As some authors have stated, peace officers see not only the worst aspects of life, but see everyone at their worst (Dietrich, 1989).

Emotional hardening is a personality characteristic commonly found among many police officers. It is a protective maneuver that may be successful at work, but disastrous in terms of maintaining the intimacy necessary within a family (Kannady, 1993). Numerous authors have documented the tendency of peace officers to demonstrate emotional detachment, emotional blunting, or emotional repression in response to the environment in which they work (Roberts & Levenson, 2001; White & Honig, 1995). As a result of this personality characteristic, there is an incongruence between job-related activities and real human emotions. This leads to interpersonal problems within the family environment, such as a lack of intimacy between the spouse and the officer. The officer may appear to be distant, withdrawn, noncommunicative, and nonempathetic to the needs of family members.

The occupation of police work fosters a particular culture as well as a particular outlook on the world. This world view not only develops within the officer, but is also brought home, where it influences the family's perception of reality (Kannady, 1993). The family's understanding of reality, based on the officer's account, is somewhat distorted. They begin to perceive the world as threatening, dangerous, and view others as untrustworthy. The officer and spouse may become overly protective of each other as well as of their children (Arrigo & Garsky, 2001).

Authoritarianism is a fundamental aspect of the police occupation. The officer must function according to a preset list of legal and organizational guidelines (Dietrich, 1989). It is common for the officer to experience stress related to this work aspect because the individual lacks control over many decisions that affect routine patrol activities. This experience can have a negative effect on family members. Some officers overcompensate at home, given this perceived lack of control at work (Arrigo & Garsky, 2001).

Many times the officer can be rigid or overly demanding of his or her spouse and children. In a study conducted in 1990, rigid, authoritarian peace officer parents were regarded as unapproachable and "nonhuggable" (Southworth, 1990). As a result of this perception, children of peace officers were more likely to become rebellious adolescents, as well as to have more emotional problems.

Danger preparation is the realization that an officer is risking his or her life when on duty. This realization invariably affects the family members, resulting in anxiety and psychological stress. Threats to an officer's safety can create emotional fatigue for a spouse (Arrigo & Garsky, 2001).

A majority of the research regarding the relationship between police stress and its impact on the family is dated. Despite this fact, much of the research focuses on issues such as domestic violence and divorce within law enforcement families, as well as the a lack of unity and trust between child–parent relationships. Displacement of anger, decreased communication and conflict-management skills, alienation and withdrawal, and decreased trust all serve to create an environment that can place a law enforcement relationship at greater risk for domestic violence (White & Honig, 1995).

A recent study examined the impact of job stress and physical exhaustion on marital interaction in police couples. Roberts and Levenson (2001) found that the police officers studied carried their job stress home with them and it adversely affected their interactions with their spouses. It was noted that the physiologically aroused states that were measured on high stress days made it quite difficult for police officers to think clearly and to solve problems effectively. This led to more defensive and self-protective behaviors. This more defensive and vigilant posture was carried home from work and was inserted into the marital interaction. This pattern of behavior could increase marital strife and could result in eventual dissolution (Robert & Levenson, 2001). Days with high levels of work-related stress were also correlated with more negative affect. Overall, these researchers found that job stress was more detrimental for a police couple than physical exhaustion. The husband's job stress created heightened arousal, increased negative emotions, and greater emotional distance (Robert & Levenson, 2001).

The various stressors presented in this entry are inherent to the police profession. An officer may be regarded as a success on the job, yet not very successful within the family structure. "The traits and dispositions that make exceptional police officers unfortunately make very poor spouses, parents, and friends" (Southworth, 1990, p. 20).

Forensic Psychology and Policy Implications

Stress is common and inevitable among police families. How they cope with the stress will determine the quality of their marriage (Canada, 1993). This determination is contingent upon the coping mechanisms that they choose to employ. Coping mechanisms must be utilized to successfully combat the stressors of police work as well as to learn how to become resistant to them. Roberts and Levenson (2001) recommended that police couples utilize stress management techniques, attempting to include more positive emotions into marital discourse, and employ strategies to talk about job stress in adaptive ways instead of avoiding it.

It is the responsibility of the law enforcement agency to provide the families of peace officers with the resources necessary to successfully cope with ongoing stressors. The first and most important intervention must be at the management and organizational levels (White & Honig, 1995). Education must start within the organizational structure to address occupational stressors and their adverse effects on the family unit.

Spouse orientations, trainings, and workshops to address issues related to occupational demands and stressors must be developed. Orientations provide spouses the opportunity to acclimate themselves to their spouses' job requirements. Ongoing workshops and seminars function as support groups for spouses as new problems surface during peace officers' career development.

Moreover, when an officer is involved in a critical incident, the family members need to be educated. They need to know the range of normal responses to such an abnormal and extreme event. If family members are fully informed of the responses they can expect to encounter as a result of such trauma, the disabling impact of the event may be ameliorated significantly (Blak, 1995).

In the tragic event of an officer fatality, law enforcement agencies must go beyond departmental boundaries to assist the families of all deceased officers, including those who take their own lives (J. Violanti, 1995). The department can facilitate the grieving process by offering assistance to the families. This can include financial matters, pension rights, counseling, and maintaining contact with the survivors. In addition, employers are now slowly beginning to recognize the need for more in-depth assistance to the families of law enforcement personnel (White & Honig, 1995). It is imperative for law enforcement organizations to take an active role in recognizing the effect of policing on families and in providing viable interventions and support services for the family members.

As stated earlier, families of police officers must manage many difficult stressors. Without appropriate resources such as good communication and problem-solving techniques, psychological services, and organizational training and support systems, many families find it difficult to adapt to the demands of the police profession.

Suggestions for Future Research

It is evident that stress associated with police work can and does manifest itself within the family arena, resulting in poor interpersonal relationships with spouses and children, divorce, domestic violence, and other emotionaly devastating consequences. There is an abundance of research which examines the adverse reactions police officers endure because of their jobs; however, yet there is a paucity of information specifically targeting the relationship between police work and family stress.

As with the case illustration presented at the beginning of this section, it exemplifies the most severe form of stress a law enforcement family can experience. In order to have a conceptual understanding of the effects of occupational stress upon the family, future research needs to further examine the aforementioned stressors including the direct physical and psychological effects of police work. Law enforcement agencies need to be responsible for program implementation as well as evaluation, in order to gauge the effectiveness of specific programs which address this issue.

POLICE AND THE MENTALLY ILL

Introduction

A police officer's job is one riddled with a variety of pitfalls and potential dangers. As if maintaining control over "normal" populations is not difficult enough, law enforcement agents often find themselves having to deal with populations that are incapable of rational and reasonable thought. More specifically, mentally ill people often find themselves interacting with law enforcement after having made some specific threat or engaged in some inappropriate or illegal action. Consider the following example of how a mentally ill individual came face-to-face with the law.

A police officer receives a call and is told that there is an involuntary commitment request at a large psychiatric institution downtown. The officer calls for an ambulance to arrive at the scene before he arrives. By the time he has reached the institution, he is greeted by a medley of interested pedestrians, disarrayed staff members, and a hostile-looking man holding a butter knife he apparently stole from the kitchen. The man in question is pacing and mumbling something to himself, apparently severely agitated. It looks to the police officer like any movement toward the patient might result in a violent outburst. Due to the fact that the patient is in possession of a potentially dangerous weapon, the situation must be handled with extreme caution, diligence, and cunning in order to prevent the patient from hurting himself or anyone else.

The manner in which the police officer handles the above situation is critical for a variety of reasons. For example, would a wrong or inappropriate statement made by the officer invoke some sort of rage response? Would other patients observing the ordeal become agitated as well after seeing such an encounter, thus resulting in other psychotic outbreaks? If the patient refused to submit, how will physical restraints be applied? Will anyone get hurt in the process? These questions and others are faced by officers every day. However, a surprising paucity of literature exists on exactly how an officer should deal with the mentally ill in the line of duty (Patch & Arrigo, 1999). This section attempts to answer these questions. It also reviews related concerns: the public's perception of the mentally ill and law enforcement, how police should handle disordered patients; the psychological makeup of the mentally ill lawbreaker, the co-occurring or comorbid diagnosis often given to jailed mentally ill inmates, and public policy implications dealing with the appropriate and effective response to the mentally ill and policing.

Literature Review

As a result of deinstitutionalization and a dramatic increase of individuals with severe mental illness in the community, police officers are often the first line responders to the psychiatrically disordered in crisis and potential gatekeepers for mental health services (Lamb, Weinberger, DeCuir, & Walter, 2002). Traditionally, attitudes of police officers toward the mentally ill have included ignorance and misunderstanding. In particular, officers historically have been somewhat cynical toward this population (Nunnally, 1961). This is not surprising, considering the tremendous amount of stress experienced by police officers every day. Arguably, the failure of police academies and training programs to adequately address issues related to mental health have fostered the misconceptions about those with psychiatric disorders.

By examining 84 medium and large law enforcement agencies, Hails and Borum (2003) found that departments varied greatly in the amount of police training on mental health topics, with a median of 6.5 hours for basic recruits and one hour of in-service training. Around one-third of the departments had some degree of specialized responding for handling calls involving individuals with mental illness. Twenty-one percent had a special unit within the department to aid in these types of calls and 8% had the availability of a mobile mental health crisis team (Hails & Borum, 2003).

Research conducted by Stuart and Arboleda-Florez (2001) demonstrated that people with mental illness and substance abuse disorders were not major contributors to police-identified criminal violence. They further stated that public perceptions of the mentally ill as criminally dangerous were exaggerated. However, this is not to say that the mentally ill, particularly those who are fearful or paranoid as a result of psychosis, do not commit violent acts. The Secret Service are forced to arrest approximately 100 people per year for causing or attempting to cause disruptions at the White House. Gottesman and Bertelson (1989) found that of 328 people attempting to cause problems at the White House, 91% met the criteria for schizophrenia. It is clear from these statistics that the mentally ill do engage in certain behaviors that are likely to bring police action. While officers are called upon for transportation services to escort disordered citizens to acute psychiatric units or emergency rooms, other situations arise necessitating more finite and definitive policing skills.

Lamb et al. (2002) cautioned that the unnecessary criminalization of the mentally ill can occur if police officers do not appropriately perform and balance their respective roles as protectors of those with disabilities as well as guardians of the community's welfare. These authors strongly emphasized the importance of criminal justice and mental health collaboration through mental health training for officers, mobile crisis units, knowledge of appropriate community mental health resources, and identification of the psychiatrically disordered.

Research has shown that there are differences between police departments in big cities and smaller communities when training officers to avoid shootings involving emotionally disturbed persons (Fyfe, 2000). While larger cities have seen a decline in these tragedies, more mid-sized cities have not. Fyfe (2000) contends that big cities are more sophisticated in handling situations with emotionally disturbed persons because of increased exposure to and knowledge about the mentally ill.

Steadman et al. (2001) explained that some communities have developed pre-booking diversion programs that depend on specialized crisis response sites where the police officers can drop off individuals in psychiatric crisis and return to duty. These programs are designed to facilitate collaboration between law enforcement and mental health professionals. They also help individuals receive appropriate treatment and reduce referrals to overburdened jails.

An experiment conducted by Finn and Stalans (1997) showed that police officers harbor certain preconceived notions regarding male versus female victims and assailants. Mentally ill assailants in particular were viewed in a somewhat different light than their non-mentally ill counterparts. The study examined the influence of assailant or victim role, gender, and mental status on police officers' attitudes regarding the naïveté of both assailants and victims, passiveness, dangerousness, future criminality, psychological sickness, responsibility, credibility, blameworthiness, and control over actions. The researchers hypothesized that if mental state was a large contributing factor in officers' inferences, then both male and female assailants who displayed signs of mental illness would be less capable of understanding the wrongfulness of violence, would be less passive, more dangerous, more likely to engage in future crime, more psychologically sick, less responsible, less credible, less blameworthy, and less in control of their actions than assailants who were not mentally ill.

The investigators found (based on reactions to fictional vignettes) that stereotypes of the mentally ill appeared to shape officers' beliefs and inferences regarding assailants when signs of mental illness were recognized. More specifically, mentally ill assailants were believed to be more dangerous and less in control regardless of their gender. Further, findings suggested that when no mental illness was evident in the vignettes, gender stereotyping did take place (Finn & Stalans, 1997).

In evaluating the effectiveness of a mental health training intervention with the police force in England, a total of 109 police officers attended training workshops and completed pre- and post-surveys including knowledge, attitudes, and behavioral interventions (Pinfold et al., 2003). It was noted that positive impact on police work, particularly improvements in communication between officers and persons with mental illness, was reported in one-third of the cases. Stereotypes linking the mentally ill and violent behavior overall were not successfully challenged. However, short educational interventions produced change in the officer's attitudes toward the mentally disordered and left officers feeling more informed and confident to interact with such persons (Pinfold et al., 2003).

Forensic Psychology and Policy Implications

Given the current state of police attitude, inference, and beliefs regarding the mentally ill, what can be done to improve the knowledge base surrounding this issue? Clearly, literature and programs designed to change police officers' understanding of the handling and treatment of the mentally ill are lacking (Patch & Arrigo, 1999). What information does exist, tends to be limited in scope. However, certain programs have been implemented, with varying degrees of success, in an attempt to help bridge the gap between the mentally ill and law enforcement procedures and policies.

Mentally disordered persons very often find themselves in jail for committing illegal acts. Typically, they are incarcerated in a jail setting, not because they are criminals, per se, but because there are no other available resources to utilize at the time of the offense (V. B. Brown, Ridgely, Petter, Levine, & Ryglewicz, 1989).

Abram and Teplin (1991) found that the vast majority of 728 severely ill jail inmates met criteria for alcohol disorders, drug disorders, or antisocial personality disorder. Further, these inmates were found to have other comorbid psychiatric disorders. The researchers concluded that co-disordered arrestees require mental health policy development in three key areas: improving the treatment of the co-disordered citizen when in crisis, improving the jails' identification of and response to the co-disordered mentally ill, and developing community treatment facilities to address the needs of the co-disordered mentally ill. These same researchers concluded that there was little choice but to reform the current health care delivery system in order to adequately accommodate and properly treat the mentally disordered in jail.

Alleviating problems such as those just described could start at a more basic level by invoking mandatory mentally ill training sessions for police officers. These training sessions could be designed to keep the mentally ill from initially ending up in jail, making it more difficult to remove them from those conditions after the fact. Educational sessions would appear to be a useful concept in this regard as well.

Godschalx (1984) described a program developed to educate police officers on the various aspects of mental illness. The problem endeavored to have officers deal more effectively and efficiently with this population. In addition it helped officers more accurately understand the psychological processes involved with the emotionally disturbed. A brief questionnaire was given to a sample of officers before undergoing a training session on the mentally ill. After the educational program was completed, the questionnaire was administered again. Officers not attending the program made no change in their understanding of mental illness. Conversely, those who completed the program understood a statistically significant greater amount about the mentally ill. However, these same officers did not change their inherent attitudes toward this population despite the training.

These results beg one question. Should police officers be mandated to learn more in-depth information regarding the mentally ill so as not to make faulty decisions related to their treatment. Policy implications linked to these findings would be good evidence that programs of this nature should be implemented.

Suggestions for Future Research

Areas related to future research are, not surprisingly, wide open. The few articles described here are valuable contributions to the study of the police and the mentally ill. However, there is a need for additional scientific information which could help police officers understand the mentally ill.

More specifically, additional pre- and post-test evaluations of police officers' training in, and understanding of, the mentally disordered would be of value in detecting how much police officers have learned about the mentally ill in the United States and in other countries. Further, data obtained from psychiatrically disordered persons would permit a converse view of their treatment by police officers or law enforcement in general. This would allow for further understanding of effective and ineffective interactions between the police and the mentally ill.

Finally, research on the effectiveness of various educational programs is sorely needed. These inquiries could help promote officer comprehension regarding the mentally ill. Conceivably, once greater understanding is achieved, better decisions regarding crisis intervention and police–citizen encounters can occur. Ultimately, these educational activities could lead to the de-escalation of potentially dangerous situations, thus making the police force's ability to respond to the mentally ill that much more effective.

COMMUNITY POLICING: TRENDY OR EFFECTIVE?

Introduction

The past several decades have produced a tolerance for crime and a growing distrust of police officers. This phenomenon is particularly evident in low socioeconomic communities and among ethnic minorities. According to T. M. Joseph (1994), while citizens fear becoming victims of crime, they have an increasing tolerance toward criminal activity and its impact on their communities. In order to combat crime rates and the deteriorating relationships between police officers and members of the community, many departments are implementing community-oriented policing (Adams, Rohe, Willren, & Arcury, 2002; Thurman , Giacomazzi, & Bogen, 1993).

Community-oriented policing is an attempt to move the focus of law enforcement from reaction to criminal activity to prevention of crime. While no single definition of "community-oriented policing" exists, a broad definition includes a combination of strategies designed to prevent crime through the establishment of a strong community–police relationship. Skogan (1994) identified various strategies that are utilized with this approach:

> opening small neighborhood substations, conducting surveys to identify local problems, organizing meetings and crime prevention seminars, publishing newsletters, helping form Neighborhood Watch groups, establishing advisory panels to inform police commanders, organizing youth activities, conducting drug education projects and media campaigns, patrolling on horses and bicycles, and working with municipal agencies to enforce health and safety regulations (pp. 167–168).

Despite the advantages associated with the cooperation and collaboration between citizens and police officers, the implementation of these strategies presents many challenges for administrators and officers. The ambiguity in defining community policing has raised concerns. Issues, such as the community's willingness to participate, and officers' attitudes regarding community policing, have caused many to question if this strategy is a viable solution to crime prevention or just another ineffective trend in law enforcement. Consider the following case illustration.

Dear Lakeshore Police Department,

This letter is in regard to the recent change in policing procedures in my neighborhood. While I am appreciative that your department has taken notice of the rampant crime in this community, as a resident I have many concerns. Not a day goes by that I do not hear gunshots or see some adolescent on the street selling drugs. Gangs and drugs seem to have taken over our community and many residents do not feel safe in their own homes. Although this neighborhood is full of crime, most people living here are not criminals. I am a single mother struggling to raise two school-age children.

I have heard on the news and read in the paper that your department is implementing "community policing" in our neighborhood. I have heard of Neighborhood Watch programs and the like but usually in upscale neighborhoods. Having more officers on foot patrol and a substation on our block will make me feel safer and will hopefully reduce crime. However, I would not feel comfortable providing tips about neighborhood crime or testifying in court

(continued)

(Continued)
about any crimes I have witnessed. I have no doubt that some form of
retaliation against my children, home, or myself would be inevitable.

Unfortunately, many residents keep to themselves and frequently distrust
the police. I fear that my neighbors would label me a "snitch" if I were to join a
police-run organization. While I hope this new approach will make the
neighborhood safer, community participation would surprise me. Once again, I
appreciate that your department has taken steps toward reducing crime in this
neighborhood.

Sincerely,

Sandra

Literature Review

For the past 20 years, the trend in anticrime policy has been to implement
community policing. During the 1970s and 1980s, the citizen's role in
solving crime was the focus in police research (Rosenbaum & Lurigio,
1994). The fact that private citizens were often major partners in solving
crimes or obtaining arrests became the foundation for community policing.
Research found that low clearance rates in most police departments could
be attributed to the lack of useful tips offered to officers (Eck, 1982;
Rosenbaum & Lurigio, 1994). Residents of a neighborhood are usually the
best sources when identifying community problems (Pate, Wycoff, Skogan,
& Sherman, 1986). However, police departments must consider if citizens
like Sandra would be willing to participate. This issue is particularly relevant
in areas with high crime rates.

The first attempt to make law enforcement more community
oriented occurred with team policing. In 1967, the police task force
of the President's Commission on Law Enforcement and the Administration of Justice suggested team policing as a way to improve the relationship
between line officers and the community. Team policing consisted of long-
term beat assignments and "walk-and-talk" foot patrols. Problems with
implementation led to the failure of team policing. The problems associated
with decentralized decision making were credited with the downfall of this
approach. It was discredited by the majority of police departments by the
end of the 1970s (Rosenbaum & Lurigio, 1994).

However, the 1980s saw the rise of community policing. Despite
the ambiguity of this concept, common themes are mentioned by
Rosenbaum (1988): "an emphasis on improving the number and quality
of police–citizen contacts, a broader definition of 'legitimate' police work,

decentralization of the police bureaucracy, and a greater emphasis on proactive problem-solving strategies" (p. 334). Typically, this approach has been utilized in specialized units and within specific police districts. It has yet to be implemented departmentwide throughout a large police organization (Rosenbaum & Lurigio, 1994). Thatcher (2001), stated, "...community policing has fundamental (and probably desirable) implications for police practice because it forces police to attend to many neglected dimensions of their mandate" (p. 765).

According to Cordner (2001), community policing became the dominant strategy of policing in the 1990s. In fact, the 1994 Crime Bill mandated that 100,000 newly funded police officers must be involved in community policing. However, Cordner pointed out the difficulty of producing reliable knowledge regarding the effectiveness of community policing. He maintained that most community policing studies have considerable research design limitations which include lack of control groups, nonrandom treatments, and the tendency to only measure short-term effects. While very few investigations have used experimental designs and victimization surveys to evaluate the effect of community policing on crime, many studies have utilized before-and-after comparisons and single-item victimization questions taken from community surveys (Cordner, 2001). Given these methodological limitations, researchers argue that credible evaluations of this approach do not exist, leaving police officers, citizens, and forensic psychologists to debate whether community policing works.

A current study examined the effectiveness of community policing in reducing urban crime by using the Law Enforcement Management and Administrative Statistics survey, the FBI's Uniform Crime Reports, and city-level census data. At issue here were the factors effecting robbery and homicide rates in 164 cities in the United States (MacDonald, 2002). The results indicated that community policing had little effect on the control or reduction of violent crime. However, proactive policing strategies related to arrest were associated with decreases in violent crime over time (MacDonald, 2002).

Although the results are mixed, the fear of crime and calls for service have been reduced due to the police–citizen contact with community policing (Cordner, 2001). In addition, an overwhelming number of studies suggest that community relations have been improved. Residents in Sandra's neighborhood need to obtain a better perception of the police in order to create a productive alliance. According to Skogan (1994), 9 of 14 areas in six cities using community policing demonstrated improvement in the community's perception of the police. In addition, seven areas had a decrease in the fear of crime, six areas reduced their perceptions of neighborhood disorder, and in three areas victimization rates were lower. Again, critics maintain that results like these should be viewed with caution as they only represent short-term outcomes and contain questionable methodologies (Cordner, 2001).

Studies investigating police officer job satisfaction have generally shown positive results. However, these results do not represent long-term effects or all officers, just those in specialized units (Cordner, 2001). Conflict between officers in these specialized units and those in the rest of the department has been cited in some studies. This suggests that many officers not working in a substation or a beat utilizing community policing view these assignments as social work rather than as real police work (Rosenbaum & Lurigio, 1994). T. M. Joseph (1994) maintained that the collapse of social institutions such as the deterioration of the traditional family structure, the lack of affordable housing and health care, and the paucity of residential care for the mentally ill have created the need for a more humanistic, collaborative approach to policing. The perception that community service officers do less work under more favorable conditions adds to the resentment felt by other officers (J. Patterson, 1995). Resentment can also be felt by neighborhoods that are not targeted by community policing.

Adams et al. (2002) examined the impact of community-oriented policing on officer attitudes toward their jobs in six small to mid-size law enforcement agencies. Results indicated community police officers were more supportive of community-oriented policing methods and goals, and more satisfied with their jobs when compared to traditional officers. In addition, the majority of traditional officers also supported community-oriented policing goals and the transition to community-oriented policing in their departments (Adams et al., 2002). A study that investigated the extent to which awareness of community policing had permeated immigrant communities in central Queens, New York City, revealed that respondents from the long-established ethnic communities were far more aware than those from recently established communities, and were also more likely to have participated in community policing activities (R. C. Davis & Miller, 2002). Increasing foot patrols and holding more meetings with the community were found to be the most effective means of improving police–community relations (R. C. Davis & Miller, 2002).

Another criticism of community policing is that community membership in neighborhood or block organizations usually includes only a small portion of residents and even fewer are active members (Buerger, 1994).

In addition, membership is typically "...dominated by homeowners and by white residents in racially mixed areas" (p. 412). Research suggests that citizens in neighborhoods that need community policing are frequently the most distrustful of the police. This phenomenon was illustrated by Sandra's letter. The fear of retaliation from drug dealers or gang members as a result of cooperating with the police can also hinder community involvement (T. M. Joseph, 1994).

Forensic Psychology and Policy Implications

Research clearly demonstrates the need for more systematic evaluations of community policing programs. Anticrime policy needs to be supported by social science research reflecting long-term effects and rigorous methodologies. Forensic psychologists can undertake the task of program evaluation and the testing of new policing strategies in order to help identify which are most effective. Kennedy and Moore (1997) stated that:

> [b]y implication, since social science does not now play this role in policing on any large scale, social science, practiced by outsiders, should gradually come to be a considerably more central and influential part of policing than is currently the case (p. 474).

The forensic psychologist has the benefit of training in research methodologies, criminological theories, and criminal justice administration.

Community policing is an attempt to foster stronger relationships between officers and the community in order to facilitate crime prevention. For this approach to work, police departments must shift the focus of training from paramilitaristic techniques to those that promote cooperation with citizens. Walters (1993) indicated that the highest standards of discipline and professionalism must be exhibited by officers in order to maintain credibility as well as to maintain community involvement. Careful personnel selection and training is critical, particularly with regard to police discretion. Forensic psychologists can assist this process by utilizing psychological tests and employment interviews or screenings (Claussen-Rogers & Arrigo, 2004).

In addition, criminal justice administrators must be sensitive to the needs of both the citizens in the community and those officers in the department. Large-scale implementation of this approach is needed. Department-wide training and implementation of community policing strategies will provide more useful information about its effectiveness and reduce animosity between officers. However, cost-effectiveness remains a critical issue.

The cooperation between citizens and officers could lead to more arrests and crime prevention. The more traditional role of officers does not encourage community participation in decision making and strategy in law enforcement. Currently, there is a push to include victim organizations as collaborative partners in community policing in order to encourage more victim-oriented criminal justice responses (Laszlo & Rinehart, 2002). Forensic psychologists can assist police departments and communities in adopting a more social problem-oriented approach to crime prevention; however, whether community policing is an effective means of crime prevention remains to be seen.

Suggestions for Future Research

More research is needed to determine if community policing works. In addition to finding ways by which to evaluate the approach, new methods for determining officer performance must be created. The traditional means, such as number of arrests and the number of tickets issued, are not appropriate performance measures for community-oriented police officers (T. M. Joseph, 1994). The utilization of proactive techniques for crime prevention and greater adherence to community demands has fostered the need for more creative strategies in response to increasing calls for police service (Walters, 1993).

Another important aspect of this approach is community participation. Research exploring what encourages this participation and what individual expectations include is sorely needed (Buerger, 1994). What would convince a resident like Sandra to participate in community policing? The concerns of those residents least likely to trust officers need to be examined in order for this approach to be effective in the communities that would benefit the most. Additionally, the role of victims in enhancing community policing is an important area ripe for analysis (Ready, Weisburd, & Farrell, 2002). Specific problems within the target areas identified must be carefully examined in order to implement the most effective strategies. Rosenbaum and Lurigio (1994) suggested that the continued use of case study methodology would provide more accurate and complete data on the effectiveness and long-term effects of community policing. In addition, these authors maintained, "[t]he process of working together and the barriers to cooperative relationships are essential for future research" (p. 304).

POLICE TRAINING: COMMUNICATION SKILLS AND CONFLICT RESOLUTION

Introduction

The nature of a police officer's job requires routine interaction with members of the public. Often, these encounters entail the resolution of some existing, or potentially existing, conflict. Interactions with vicitms and offenders, interviewing witnesses, answering citizen questions, making arrests, and giving citations can result in police-citizen conflict. Consequently, the police officer must possess effective communication and conflict resolution skills. Indeed, training and education in these areas assume fundamental roles in police interactions. This section discusses some of the issues regarding police officers and conflict resolution skills. Commonly used tactics, as well as strategies that would arguably be more effective in some situations, are also addressed.

> Two officers were dispatched to [a] halfway house where resident Henry had been causing a disturbance. The staff wanted him expelled. The first officer to arrive gave him an intense lecture. Henry, feeling unjustly chastised, walked off and went outside. The officer grabbed him by the back of the shirt and told him he was not finished talking to him. Henry pushed the officer and the officer pushed back. A backup officer arrived at the scene and stepped in between the two men just before the situation got out of control. Through the use of verbal skills he calmed Henry and helped his fellow officer regain composure. He then persuaded the staff members into allowing Henry to remain at the center. Henry agreed to modify his behavior. The result? Because of good communication skills on the second officer's part, everyone was appeased (Woodhull, 1993).

Literature Review

Police officers estimate that 75–90% of their time is spent in some form of communication (Woodhull, 1993). Training in communication skills, however, has failed to reflect this fact. An estimation of training time allocated to learning communication skills is less than 10%. One officer noted, in addressing the significance of communication in his work, that communication was the basis for all police work and was necessary for the effective enforcement of laws (Woodhull, 1993). Thus, police officers are aware of the large portion of time that they spend communicating with the public. Further, they recognize the importance of adequate training in this area. Administrators and educators also agree that police officers need to be trained in interpersonal communication (Woodhull, 1993).

The necessity of these abilities, and the failure of existing training to acknowledge the importance of communication and conflict skills, is illustrated in current programs. Woodhull (1993) noted that police officers "undergo more intense training than perhaps any other professionals" (p. 4). Officers are extensively trained in the use of firearms and subsequently required to demonstrate proficiency in firearm use. Most officers, however, will rarely, if ever, use their weapons in the line of duty. In contrast, officers will inevitably spend most of their time communicating, but are not as extensively trained in such skills (Manning, 1998). This contradiction was alluded to over 2000 years ago by Aristotle, who claimed that people should not train themselves in fist-and-weapon tactics while neglecting to train themselves in verbal tactics (Woodhull, 1993). As communication characterizes the human being, effective communication can develop understanding, while ineffective communication can result in violence (Woodhull, 1993). Thus, even before the day of the modern police officer, the importance of communication versus physical tactics in human encounters was well understood. Given the extent of communication in a police officer's job, and the significance of effective skills, some of the reasons why conflict occurs between police and citizens warrants attention.

The police are asked to maintain public order, including defusing volatile or potentially volatile situations. As noted earlier, these situations may involve criminal, disorderly, intoxicated, and/or mentally ill citizens; individuals who are angry about more general police practices or motivated by political views; and a host of other situations. The instability of citizens in these encounters creates significant risk to the officers, the citizen, and the bystanders (L. Wrightsman, Nietzel, & Fortune, 1994). Often, these disputes between police officers and the public exist because of differing opinions about the duties of police officers. The *role* of police officers is an area where there has been much disagreement among scholars, the public, and the police (Manning, 1998). There is general agreement that the police officer's job consists of multiple duties, including situations where no crime has occurred. In addition to law enforcement practices (crime detection, making arrests, questioning individuals about criminal activity, etc.), the police must concern themselves with keeping peace, maintaining order, and servicing the public in general. While the disagreement often revolves around exactly for what duties the police are responsible, there is little debate that the job includes dealing with many different types of problems (L. Brooks, 1997).

Public encounters may result in conflict when the officer's perception of his or her duties or role differs from the citizen's perception (Bennett & Hess, 1996). A prime example is the otherwise upstanding citizen who is cited or ticketed for a traffic violation and replies, "Why are you bothering me when there are real criminals running around on the streets? Don't you have anything better to do with your time?" Such complaints are common in police work and often open the door for conflict. Once one understands the motivating factors behind conflict situations, the next step is to understand the other side. In other words, what are some basic tactics of conflict resolution and how are they employed by police officers?

A growing number of communities, including New York City, are beginning to use mediation programs to facilitate the potential resolution of complaints made by citizens against the police (Berger, 2000). Berger (2000) indicated that the lack of understanding regarding police duties and poor communication by both the police and the public are at the root of most police-community conflicts. Berger (2000, p. 211) believed that "the mediation process itself can work in a transformative way, improving strained relations between the police and the general population."

Tactics of conflict resolution include a large group of behaviors that are intended to either gain compliance in an interaction or resolve the interaction in a way which is satisfactory to both parties (C. Wilson & Gross, 1994). Such tactics are necessary when two parties have goals or desires in an encounter which are incompatible, yet the interaction must end in some sort of compromise. This scenario describes the great majority of interactions involving the police and the public. The question becomes, "What tactics do police officers generally employ in public situations, and what other (better) options are available to them?"

C. Wilson and Gross (1994) noted that the tactics officers use are dependent upon the citizen's socioeconomic status, gender, ethnicity, and age. Chosen tactics have also been related to the degree of citizen compliance and perception of intoxication (R. Worden, 1989), as well as to the neighborhood in which the encounter occurs and the specific police department's attitude toward tactics for gaining compliance (D. Smith & Klein, 1984). Toch (1985) and others have implied that the attitude of specific officers upon entering an interaction can increase the likelihood of a conflict occurring or even escalating. Some officers, whose chosen goal is to obtain compliance from the citizen, may behave in a way that increases the probability of a negative (confrontational or escalated) interaction. These officers may perceive coercive tactics as the most effective available strategy for dealing with the situation. On the other hand, officers who prefer problem-solving tactics would be less likely to increase the existing tension in interactions with citizens (C. Wilson & Gross, 1994). Problem solving is one method of *nonconventional* conflict resolution.

Common, or conventional, methods of conflict resolution for police officers include legitimate use of physical force, arrest, coercion and/or threats to arrest, and avoidance (Cooper, 1997). These tactics are commonly employed in conflict situations and, admittedly, are necessary on occasion. The issue is whether more appropriate tactics are available that would allow an officer to address a volatile (or potentially volatile) situation in a more productive and less injurious way. Cooper (1997) referred to methods that do not involve force, coercion, or arrest as *nonconventional* conflict-resolution methods. These methods include mediation, arbitration, third-party negotiation, facilitation, reconciliation, counseling, problem solving, and problem management. He contends that these methods are suitable for addressing situations such as "disputes or conflicts characterized as public, barricade situations, community-based, and interpersonal" conflict (p. 88). Further, the effectiveness of such techniques on a global scale requires not only increased usage, but also perfecting the *manner* in which they are used. A more in-depth discussion of the various methods previously outlined is not necessary here. The point worth noting is that there are a number of conflict-resolution tactics available to police officers which might not be typically employed, but are useful in appropriate situations.

Forensic Psychology and Policy Implications

Given the extent and nature of conflict between police and citizens, as well as the large amount of time officers spend in communicative encounters, the need for training is undeniable. It is apparent that existing policy for training officers in communication skills, as well as extended training throughout their careers, is currently inadequate in many departments. In the case of Henry, the first officer to arrive on the scene was clearly not effective in communicative abilities. His communication, in fact, escalated the conflict rather than brought it to a peaceful resolution. Based on the above case illustration, we can assume that initially the first officer's attempt to communicate with Henry was ineffective for a number of reasons; namely, his "intense lecture" immediately left Henry feeling like the officer was against him, instead of with him or for him. Naturally, Henry's perception was that the officer was there to lecture him and punish him rather than peacefully resolve the conflict between Henry and the staff. Later, when Henry felt "chastised" and walked away, the officer responded with an even more authoritarian attitude, bringing threats and physical force into the interaction. At this point, the encounter could have easily become unnecessarily inflated to the point of violence and the arrest of Henry. Luckily, the second officer arrived on the scene in time to calm the situation. The communication and conflict-resolution skills of the second officer became vitally important, and a potentially explosive conflict was controlled.

Approaching a situation like the first officer in Henry's case will regrettably create unnecessary consequences for citizens and police. The more aware the public becomes of such behaviors, and the more communicative conflicts that citizens themselves have with officers, the more likely society is to doubt and disrespect the police. For police to enjoy the kind of relationship it aspires to maintain with citizens, communicating effectively becomes as important as other duties. Whenever possible, resolving volatile or conflict situations without the use of unnecessary force, threat, or arrest should be the goal of every police officer. Consequently, natural communicative ability and effective training become a necessity.

Recently, psychology has made important contributions to police–citizen conflict situations. Generally, psychologists are called upon to educate the police about matters such as dealing with the mentally ill, hostage situations, domestic violence situations, and other crises (Manning, 1998). Psychology has proven an effective tool for developing approaches to such situations but has more to offer than just training. The knowledge of human relations and general communication skills establishes a place for psychology in the education and training of police officers. Further, psychology avails itself well to the establishment and ongoing evaluation of training programs. Forensic psychology, in its mutual regard for psychological and criminal justice matters, has established a place for itself in police administration and consultation. Recently, more departments are realizing the value that psychology can bring, and are beginning to employ psychologists in roles outside of the traditional clinical and crisis situations. Police departments are beginning to realize the importance of officers having the necessary communicative skills (like the second officer in the scenario with Henry) and thus are looking to increase training in such areas in the future.

Suggestions for Future Research

Given increasing public awareness and citizen complaints regarding police use of force, brutality, and "attitude," such nonconventional tactics are worthy of additional research the policy level. Certainly, additional research needs to be done on the effectiveness of nonconventional tactics and their applicability to various situations. The lack of officer training in nonconventional techniques and communication skills in general makes them difficult to employ and even more difficult to measure in terms of their effectiveness. Henry's situation provides convincing evidence of the positive benefits of communication and nonthreatening and nonforceful measures by the police. The fact that, as of yet, appropriate education and training is often not supplied renders only speculative accounts of the effectiveness and usefulness of these methods.

Practice Update Section: Issues in Family/Community Policing

In 1996, Amber Hagerman, a 9-year-old girl from Arlington, Texas, was abducted and murdered. Congress and President Bush recently passed the National Amber Alert Plan as an extension of the Amber Alert emergency response system. The Amber Plan is likely the most far-reaching and impactful extension of community policing. According to the Federal Communications Commission (2003), its purpose is to galvanize communities across the country aiding law enforcement in the safe return of the child and the apprehension of the suspect. Once police have confirmed a missing child report, an alert is sent to radio stations, television stations, and cable companies. These sources interrupt programming and repeat news bulletins about abducted children typically with descriptions of the children, suspect vehicles, and the like. The Amber Alerts are used only in the most serious child abduction cases when the police believe the child is in danger of serious bodily harm. The Amber Alert program is credited with the resolution of at least eight abductions since its inception in 1997. Under revised guidelines, the new Amber Plan is only activated if the missing child is under age 15, disabled, or believed to be in danger (Burns, 2001). As of October, 2003, 46 states have adopted the Amber Plan. The Amber Plan is likely one of the most aggressive and wide-reaching policing strategies to be implemented in the fight against child abduction and murder. Now law enforcement is incorporating more community resources into the fight against child victimization.

   Police officers face a number of job-related stressors that are very traumatic and unique to law enforcement, for example, child abduction and murder. Some police officers are attacked or wounded by an assailant, fear for their lives, view horrific crime scenes, and interact with living victims and with the families of those who are deceased. Certainly, no one could imagine the horrors faced by law enforcement officers who responded to the 9/11 attacks on the

World Trade Center and the Pentagon. Both the physical and psychological demands placed on some law enforcement officers can have a profound impact on their mental and physical health. Psychological services addressing both pro- and reactive measures should be firmly in place in police departments around the country. Critical incident debriefing is one such reactive measure. Tobin (2001) contends that it is only useful when a major incident has happened, typically when there has been significant loss of life. He recommended that CISD be used sparingly, with highly trained personnel, who also act as peer supporters of the at-risk population. This is a very important service that a police psychologist properly trained in issues relating to policing, psychology, and trauma can provide. Tobin (2001) indicated that CISD helps to reduce the anger that is often felt toward those in authority and promotes unit cohesiveness when effective. He further warned of the legal liability if done improperly.

Buchanan, Stephens, and Long (2001) conducted a study that examined the number of traumatic events experienced by police recruits and other officers. These authors suggested that the number and type of traumatic event young adults experience, including assaults, disasters, and motor vehicle accidents, are important variables in determining vulnerability to developing psychological symptoms if exposed to future trauma. These are potentially important factors for police psychologists to take into consideration when considering the psychological impact of a job related critical incident.

Van Patten and Burke (2001) found that the child homicide investigator experienced significantly higher levels of stress when compared with ordinary adults. Additionally, the traumatic scene of a child homicide was the most significant predictor of stress. Police departments and police psychologists should be particularly mindful of the extreme stress experienced by homicide investigators, particularly child homicide investigators. In addition to critical incident debriefing as a reactive measure, individual counseling and other proactive measures such as stress reduction education and programs should also be implemented.

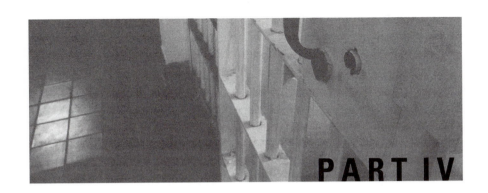

PART IV

Corrections and Prison Practices

CHAPTER 10

Adult Issues in Corrections/ Correctional Psychology

OVERVIEW

The adult prison population presents society with a complex set of issues and controversies requiring thoughtful, manageable, and effective responses. The assorted tools of the psychological sciences and the law are increasingly called upon to make sense out of difficult correctional questions affecting the lives of prisoners and the community of which they are a part. Thus, not only are the skills of the forensic/correctional professional utilized for purposes of evaluating, diagnosing, and treating inmates, they are also employed for purposes of understanding the correctional milieu itself.

This chapter describes a limited number of topics that are of considerable concern for psychologists working in prison settings or responding to matters of confinement for offenders. While other subjects could have been investigated in this chapter, the issues explored represent some of the more controversial matters affecting correctional psychology today. These topics include (1) an offender's right to refuse medical treatment; (2) incarcerating and executing the mentally ill; (3) suicide, inmate screening, and crisis intervention; (4) sex offender treatment; (5) prison violence; and (6) inmate sexuality.

The legal system has acknowledged that persons civilly committed for psychiatric treatment have, under specified conditions, the right to refuse medical intervention (see Chapter 4). Is the right to refuse treatment for persons criminally confined any different? What types of involuntary treatments do inmates typically refuse? What constitutional protections exist for offenders exercising their right to refuse treatment? Persons experiencing mental illness can be incarcerated and sentenced to death. What are the constitutional limits to executing the mentally ill? What role does a psychological competency evaluation play in a decision to carry out an execution? What moral and ethical dilemmas do psychologists confront when finding that a person is competent to be put to death? Suicides in jails and prisons occur at a higher rate than in the general population. Are correctional institutions doing enough to prevent potential suicides? Is the lack of institutional policies addressing comprehensive suicide prevention contributing to the suicide attempts and completions of detainees? Could inmate mental health screenings upon admission, treatment, and crisis intervention programs assist the mentally ill inmate and prevent suicides? Some incarcerated individuals are convicted of various sex crimes, including molesting or otherwise violating children. Psychologists with specialized training are relied upon to treat sex offenders. Do sex offender interventions work? Is the treatment beneficial? What impact, if any, does sex offender treatment have on recidivism (i.e., the prisoner's potential for future victimization)?

In addition to the important role forensic psychologists assume regarding mentally ill prisoners, they also help determine how best to address related correctional dilemmas. Violence is a part of prison life. How do substandard correctional conditions impact prison violence? How is institutional life psychologically stressful for inmates? What is the relationship between prison violence and overcrowding? Inmate sexuality is not necessarily the same outside the confines of the penal institution. What are the definitions of inmate homosexuality? Are all prison homosexuals gay/lesbian outside the facility as well? What are the roles and functions of nonheterosexuality in prison?

The domain of adult forensics and corrections moves the psychologist into a more social arena in which to investigate noncriminal behavior, attitudes, beliefs, and so on pertaining to prisoners, correctional personnel, institutional practices, and the public's responses to them. Future investigators would do well to engage in research along these and similar lines of inquiry as it would substantially advance our knowledge of prisoners, correctional workers, and society's understanding of offender behavior. The adult correctional/forensic field is replete with an assortment of controversial issues or topical themes affecting prisoners and the institutions that house them. Psychologists help provide solutions to a number of these more vexing matters. Not only are forensic experts called upon to assess how best to deal with offenders who are mentally ill and in need of some form of therapeutic intervention, they help correctional facilities interpret the overall climate in which institutional problems surface, are resolved, and can be altogether avoided. As the individual sections of this chapter demonstrate, by its very nature there is a profound psychological dimension to any criminal confinement. Thus, well-trained correctional psychologists are sorely needed if the challenges that confront the adult prison population are to be thoughtfully, effectively, and efficiently addressed.

AN OFFENDER'S RIGHT TO REFUSE TREATMENT

Introduction

The basic rights provided to citizens under most of the constitutional amendments have been extended to the inmates in our prisons. The source of the right to refuse treatment can be traced to case law beginning in the mid-1970s (Winick, 1997). During this time period, U.S. civil rights advocates, after successfully arguing for the rights of minorities, turned their attention to psychiatric patients. They argued for a greater recognition of the general rights of involuntary patients and for the specific right of these patients to refuse treatment. Because a voluntary patient cannot be treated against his or her will unless found incompetent to make treatment decisions, they reasoned that an involuntary patient should have a similar right. Since the late 1970s, an increasing number of state courts have recognized this common law principle as the doctrine of "informed consent." The state courts have not been receptive to countering arguments, namely, economic considerations about lowering treatment costs and the need of mentally ill patients to be treated. Involuntarily committed though competent patients are allowed the right to refuse treatment because state courts are creating laws that provide them with a review board or court to make treatment decisions in their best interest.

An offender's right to refuse treatment raises significant questions in terms of constitutional law (Arrigo & Tasca, 1999; Arrigo & Williams, 1999). When treatment is focused on changing the mind of the offender, the right to refuse treatment is based on the First Amendment right to free speech. The cruel and unusual punishment associated with experimental drugs and unstable treatment programs used on inmates has generated the controversial issue of the Right to Refuse Treatment doctrine (Bullock, 2002). Inmates may suffer from severe psychological problems when involuntarily given experimental drugs. However, mandating experimental drugs for medical treatment addresses some different issues than court-ordered antipsychotic medications. The *Washington v. Harper* (1990) case exemplified the controversy of mandating antipsychotic medication.

In the case *Washington v. Harper* (1990), a prisoner's right to refuse treatment was in question. The Supreme Court decision considered the right of inmate Harper to refuse antipsychotic medication. The Department of Corrections for the state of Washington maintained a Special Offender Center to diagnose and treat convicted felons who were state prisoners and had serious mental disorders. Under the Washington Special Offender Center's policy, if a prisoner does not agree to treatment with antipsychotic drugs ordered by a psychiatrist, the prisoner is entitled to a hearing before a committee consisting of a psychiatrist, a psychologist, and another prison official, none of whom can be, at the time of the hearing, involved in the prisoner's treatment. Also, the prisoner can be subjected to involuntary treatment with the drugs only if the committee determines that the prisoner suffers from a mental disorder and is gravely disabled or poses serious harm to him- or herself, others, or their property.

Walter Harper had consistently taken antipsychotic medication for 6 years to curb his aggression and to silence voices he was hearing. In 1982, he refused his medication because of its side effects. In 1988, the Washington Supreme Court agreed with inmate Harper ruling that antipsychotic drugs could only be given to an involuntary inmate following a court hearing at which time the state was required to show that the medication was both necessary and effective. The Washington Supreme Court held that under the Fourteenth Amendment a state prisoner's interest in avoiding the groundless administration of antipsychotic drugs is not insignificant, since the forcible injection of medication into an unwilling person's body represents an indisputable interference with that person's freedom. Antipsychotic drugs can have serious, even fatal, side effects, such as a severe involuntary spasm of the upper body, tongue, throat, or eyes; motor restlessness, a condition which can lead to death from cardiac dysfunction; and a neurological disorder characterized by involuntary, uncontrollable movements of various muscles.

The Washington Supreme Court's ruling was reversed and remanded in 1990 when the U.S. Supreme Court decided that the Constitution does not require a court hearing prior to a prisoner being involuntarily medicated. The Court held that the Fourteenth Amendment Due Process Clause permits the state to treat a prison inmate who has a serious mental illness with antipsychotic drugs against his will, if he is dangerous to him- or herself, or others, and the treatment is in his medical interest. The Center's policy agreed with due process requirements because it protected others from potentially dangerous mentally ill inmates. The U.S. Supreme Court held that the Center's policy was acceptable because it applied exclusively to potentially dangerous mentally ill inmates who were gravely disabled or posed a threat to others. The Court held that the drugs could be given only for treatment and under the direction of a licensed psychiatrist. Therefore, the Due Process Clause did not require a judicial hearing before the state could treat a mentally ill prisoner with antipsychotic drugs against his or her will.

In the case of *Knecht v. Gillman* (1973), the court questioned the extent to which injections of the drug apormorphine could be used as an unwilling stimulus. The injections were oftentimes administered by a nurse without the presence of a doctor or specific authorization from a doctor. The United States District Court for the Southern District of Iowa, Central Division, dismissed the complaint and Knecht appealed. The Court of Appeals held that administering a drug which induces vomiting to nonconsenting mental institution inmates on the basis of alleged violations of behavioral rules constituted cruel and unusual punishment.

Written consent from the inmate, however, may obviate this situation's unconstitutionality. This applies if the written consent specifies the nature of treatment, purpose, risk, and effects as well as advises the inmate of his or her right to terminate consent at any time. The inmate must also be given the opportunity to cancel consent at any time, and the injection must be authorized by a physician and administered by a physician or nurse. Also, the fact that civil rights statutes do not specify the scope of judicial relief available in actions successfully sustained under them does not preclude federal courts from fashioning an effective equitable remedy.

Literature Review

One way to consider the issue of the right to refuse treatment is to examine the problems occurring with experimental drugs and involuntary treatment on inmates. For example, behavior modification is one such program that centers on the modification of an offender's actions (Allen & Simonsen, 1989; Freeman, 1994). One type of behavior modification is aversive conditioning for deviant sexual behavior. Freeman (1994) indicated that aversive conditioning is the reduction or elimination of behavior patterns by associating them with unpleasant stimuli. Nausea-inducing drugs were used extensively in early experiments in aversive conditioning. The drugs were primarily given by injection to induce vomiting during an undesirable behavior. This procedure is very unpleasant and traumatic to the offender. Siegel et al. also explained that in later experiments electric shock replaced drugs as an aversive stimulus. Behavior modification is a highly criticized program. It can make excessive claims about results, use inmates as guinea pigs, and increase the use of behavior modification programs that are actually thinly disguised initiatives for furthering institutional objectives at the expense of prisoners. As a result, proponents of behavior modification are now using more sophisticated and humane treatment techniques with inmates. Nevertheless, as a protection, numerous institutional authorities have dropped the term "behavior modification" from the names of their treatment programs, knowing that the term carries negative connotations.

A program that applies learning theory with the aim of altering criminal behavior is the contingency management program. A contingency is something that may or may not happen and management involves increasing the chances that it will happen. Lillyquist (1985) found that with contingency management in a correctional setting, the aim is to increase the likelihood of occurrence of certain kinds of desired behaviors by reinforcing the behaviors when they occur. For example, participation in educational or vocational training programs, conforming behavior, and prosperous interviewing for jobs are some of the behaviors that have been dealt with in contingency management programs. Siegal et al. (2001) suggested that tangible reinforcements such as candy, soft drinks, cigarettes, and snacks can be increased with access to desired activities such as watching television, making phone calls, exercising, and receiving extra visits from family members.

Another area of great contention is the state's right to involuntary medicate a criminal defendant for the purpose of restoration of trial competency or to plead guilty (Morse, 2003). "When a defendant who has been adjudicated incompetent to stand trial invokes the right to refuse psychiatric treatment, the defendant's interest in being free from unwanted bodily intrusions is in conflict with the government's interest in obtaining an adjudication of the defendant's guilt or innocence in a criminal matter" (Bullock, 2002, p. 1). While the individual's rights are compelling, Morse (2003) maintained that the state does have a right to restore trial competence through medicating the defendant charged with most crimes and that this and other remedies are available to ensure a fair trial.

Forensic Psychology and Policy Implications

When an inmate's right to refuse treatment is legally quashed to the point that the prisoner becomes involuntarily medicated, as in the *Washington v. Harper* (1990) case, cruel and unusual punishment may occur. If an inmate is involuntarily medicated and a problem occurs with the medication, then the prisoner would have favorable grounds to initiate a lawsuit against the correctional facility. In other cases, class action litigation has been initiated for inadequate psychiatric or mental health treatment in correctional institutions (Welch & Gunther, 1997). In some cases, careful medication management and monitoring of the severely psychotic inmate can help prevent harm to the inmate or his or her peers, as well as dramatically improve the quality of life for the individual (e.g., reduction of auditory hallucinations, confusion, disorganized speech and thought process).

However, many inmates in correctional settings are quite creative in their requests for medication or will feign symptoms of mental illness in an effort to obtain psychiatric medications for their mood-altering characteristics. Inmates with a history of substance abuse who are experiencing detoxification are particularly demanding in their pursuit of medication (Carr, Hinkle, & Ingram, 1991). Other inmates will feign symptoms of mental illness to avoid placement in the general population (Freeman & Alaimo, 2001). If an inmate's symptoms, diagnosis, or course of treatment is in question, correctional psychiatrists will frequently refer these inmates for an evaluation by correctional psychologists (e.g., assess for malingering, differential diagnosis).

Public policymakers must create stringent requirements and assurances that it is in the inmate's best health interest before an inmate is medicated. As mentioned earlier, the *Knecht v. Gillman* (1973) case is one example of involuntary treatment leading to cruel and unusual punishment. Legal standards involving mental health care provisions are among the most composite regulations affecting jails, jail policy, and public policy. Court decisions regarding the provision of medical care to jail detainees, criminal responsibility for an illegal act, and treatment of the mentally ill in jail play a vital role in legal standards related to the administration of mental health treatment and medication of prisoners. Because of this, these matters also need to be considered.

Suggestions For Future Research

More research needs to be directed toward implementing safe regulations and procedures regarding inmate treatment administration. For example, a therapist has the ability to exert a high level of control over a prisoner. Experimental methods such as drug therapy and electric shock can change the behavior of an inmate in dramatic and often harmful ways. Unnecessary adverse side effects may occur when these procedures are administered. One example of an unstable and unpredictable treatment procedure is when the prison's needs are placed in priority over the needs of the inmate, and treatment programs are temporarily withheld because of prison activity or disciplinary behaviors. For instance, offenders who violate institutional rules may be placed in solitary confinement for a period of time without intervention. Treatment can be terminated when the needs of the institution are more important, causing the treatment to lose its effect and assist the offender. As a result, inmates lose confidence in the prison's therapeutic programming. In these instances, prisoners do not have faith in the correctional facility's promise to provide effective treatment because it can be discontinued based on the needs and financial status of the institution.

The lack of prison industry and the presence of enforced inactivity have led to the development of treatment programs that fill time. The long-term value of such programs is questionable at best, and they are a topic of heated discussion, which requires further research. Unless some highly effective treatment programs are installed and supported by solid evaluation, intervention initiatives will be seriously jeopardized. As a result of failing to improve intervention programs for offenders, future appeals by the offender will not be aimed at the specific actions that brought the person to prison but, rather, will be targeted at the treatment programs themselves. Clearly, more research and testing need to be conducted in order to ensure that prisoners receive safe and effective treatment programs today, and in the future.

INCARCERATING AND EXECUTING THE MENTALLY ILL

Introduction

On any given day, over 100,000 mentally ill individuals are incarcerated in prisons and jails throughout the United States (Penner & Oss, 1996). The deinstitutionalization of state hospitals has led to an influx of mentally ill persons in the jail and prison systems, which means that as many individuals who were once hospitalized are now incarcerated for their behavior (Belcher, 1988; Lurigio, Fallon, & Dincin, 2000; Perez, Leifman, & Estrada, 2003). According to the U.S. Department of Justice, Bureau of Justice Statistics (1999), about 10% of prison and jail inmates reported a mental or emotional condition and approximately 16% or an estimated 283,800 inmates reported either a mental condition or an overnight stay in a psychiatric hospital, and were classified as mentally ill. Despite the prevalence of mental illness in the criminal justice system, it is not uncommon for the mentally ill to receive little or no treatment during their incarceration. Perhaps even more disturbing is the staggering number of mentally ill individuals on death row. Although it is unconstitutional in the United States to execute a mentally ill person who is unaware of the nature or reason for his or her punishment, such individuals continue to be executed (Arrigo & Tasca, 1999; Jacobs, 1998). In addition to the legal issues that are raised by the unconstitutionality of such a practice, a number of psychological issues are raised as well (Broadsky, Zapf, & Boccaccini, 2001). In order for the court to determine whether a particular mentally ill inmate is fit for execution, a mental health professional must conduct a competency-for-execution evaluation and provide an expert opinion as to the inmate's understanding of the nature and reason for his or her punishment. Psychologists who conduct such evaluations are often faced with numerous ethical and moral dilemmas due to the literal life-and-death nature of their decision. The following illustration of Horace Kelly depicts a recent case involving the execution of a mentally ill person.

There is evidence that Horace Kelly suffered brain damage at birth. He was born over 2 months premature, weighing less than 2 pounds. By the time he was 18 months old he had endured chronic physical and sexual abuse at the hands of his father. By the age of 4 his mother reported that he frequently was observed shivering in a trance-like state. His childhood was further characterized by horrific headaches, terrible nightmares, and seeing and drawing demons.

When Mr. Kelly was 24 years old he murdered three people over a 6-day period, crimes for which he is currently awaiting execution. During the course of his trial, Mr. Kelly reportedly spent weeks in the corner of his cell curled into a fetal position, sleeping under the sink, and crying frequently. Horace Kelly appeared for court looking extremely disheveled with an odor of urine and visible lice in his hair.

Mr. Kelly had virtually stopped talking by the time he reached death row. There are many documented accounts of his bizarre behavior, delusional thoughts, confused state, severe distortions of reality, enuresis, nightmares, and suicide attempts. During his time on death row he has been prescribed numerous different psychotropic medications; however, his psychological decline has persisted. When asked about the meaning of execution, Mr. Kelly stated that it was the day that the payrolls would be processed.

Although several psychologists have diagnosed Mr. Kelly with schizophrenia and mental retardation and a number of neurologists have reported severe brain damage, he was rendered competent to be executed. Once the decision of competency was delivered, numerous attempts were made to spare

(continued)

(Continued)

Mr. Kelly from the death penalty. However, despite appeals, letters to the governor, and public outcry, the state of California denied clemency for Mr. Kelly. He was eventually executed.

Literature Review

The case of Horace Kelly is not an anomaly. It has been estimated that approximately 10% of the incarcerated population are mentally ill (Penner & Oss, 1996; H. J. Steadman, McCarty, & Morrissey, 1989). Moreover, according to the National Coalition for the Mentally Ill in the Criminal Justice System, an estimated 40,000 prisoners suffer from schizophrenia (Penner & Oss, 1996). In a study that examined the self-reported lifetime histories of psychiatric hospitalizations of male jail detainees with mental disorders, approximately 52% reported at least one psychiatric hospitalization (Fisher et al., 2002). Brinded, Simpson, Laidlaw, Fairley, and Malcolm (2001) found that there were markedly elevated prevalence rates for major mental disorders in New Zealand prisons with a very high comorbidity with substance use disorders. These researchers found that while approximately 81% of inmates with bipolar disorder were receiving psychiatric treatment, only 46% of depressed inmates, and 37% of psychotic inmates were receiving treatment. They contended that a dramatic increase in the availability of mental health services is necessary to accommodate the large number of mentally ill inmates (Brinded et al., 2001).

As depicted in the case illustration, schizophrenia is a psychotic disorder which is characterized by a detachment from reality, perceptual distortions, disorganized thoughts, odd or eccentric behavior, and delusional thinking that is often accompanied by paranoia (American Psychiatric Association, 1994). While schizophrenia is a chronic mental illness, it can often be less debilitating and kept somewhat under control when properly treated. However, in Los Angeles County jails, an investigation by the Department of Justice revealed that inmates who suffer from mental disorders such as schizophrenia oftentimes have to wait dangerously long periods of time before medication will be prescribed and frequently the medication will be improperly administered (Sherer, 1998). While it is common for inmates with mental illness not to receive proper treatment in jail or prison, it is also far too common for mental illness to remain undetected in this population.

H. J. Steadman et al. (1989) reported that the method by which jails evaluate for mental illness is insufficient. These researchers stated that typically a brief questionnaire that is administered at the time an inmate is booked is used for the purposes of detecting mental illness. In addition to the fact that a simple questionnaire is an inadequate means for assessing mental illness, many inmates become mentally disordered as a result of the stressful environment of their incarcerated setting (H. J. Steadman et al., 1989). This suggests that ongoing evaluations are necessary in order to adequately assess for mental illness throughout a detainee's period of incarceration.

Cohen and Dvoskin (1992) recommended that the provision of mental health services in prisons should include adequate screening and triage, follow-up evaluations by mental health professionals, crisis intervention services, crisis beds, longer term residential treatment units, outpatient clinic services, inpatient services, and consultation services. While incarceration of the mentally ill is controversial in and of itself, the issue is further complicated when mentally ill individuals commit capital offenses and face the death penalty (Brodsky et al., 2001). Every state that has a death penalty acknowledges that it is inhumane to execute an individual who is mentally incompetent and has adopted a law prohibiting such executions from occurring (K. S. Miller & Radelet, 1993). In the landmark case of *Ford v. Wainwright* (1986), the United States Supreme Court ruled that it was unconstitutional to execute a mentally ill death-row inmate who did not understand the nature and reason for his execution. Despite such prohibitions, executions of the mentally ill continue to occur (Arrigo & Williams, 1999).

In addition to the unconstitutionality of executing mentally ill inmates, there are a number of psychological issues that are raised as well. If the sanity of a death-row prisoner is questioned prior to his or her execution, a psychologist is called upon to conduct a competency-for-execution evaluation. Such an evaluation is requested in order to assist the court in determining whether inmates have a mental illness which prevents them from understanding that they are going to be executed and the reason why (Brodsky et al., 2001).

There is oftentimes a great deal of skepticism associated with the reliability of psychologists' clinical diagnoses of mental illness. For example, in *Ford v. Wainwright* (1986), although three separate evaluators found Ford to be competent for execution, they all found him to be suffering from some sort of mental illness; yet, they could not agree on his diagnosis (B. J. Winick, 1992). This illustrates the fact that it is necessary but not sufficient for a death-row inmate to have a mental disorder to be found incompetent. Examination of case law shows that neither mental illness

(*Ford v. Wainwright*, 1986; *Garrett v. Collins*, 1992) nor mental retardation (*Penry v. Lynaugh*, 1989) in and of itself renders a person incompetent for execution. Conducting competency-for-execution evaluations frequently poses a number of moral and ethical issues for psychologists. Melton Petrila, Poythress, & Slobogin (1997) cautioned psychologists to examine whether their own belief systems would interfere with their objective assessment of an individual's competency for execution. Often, psychologists conducting such evaluations find themselves in a difficult position, given that their expert opinion can lead directly to an individual's execution (Brodsky et al., 2001). Moreover, if a psychologist finds a death-row inmate incompetent for execution, the individual's life is not automatically spared. In fact, there have only been two cases in this country where a death-row inmate has been found incompetent for execution (Radelet & Miller, 1992). In one such case, *Singleton v. State* (1991), the Court ruled of Singleton's incompetence.

On February 10, 2003, with a majority of six to four and one abstention, the federal appeals court in Saint Louis, Missouri, ruled that Charles Laverner Singleton, on death row since 1979 for the murder of a grocery store clerk, could be involuntarily administered antipsychotic medication to restore his competence for execution (Lancet, 2003). Mr. Singleton's mental health deteriorated in 1987, when he began manifesting delusions that his cell was inhabited by demons. He was diagnosed with schizophrenia and initially took medications voluntarily but was later compelled to take them based on the notion that he posed a danger to self and/or others. A *habeas corpus* petition was filed in 1999–2000, after his execution date had been set, challenging the constitutionality of competency restoration through involuntary medication for the purpose of execution (Hensl, 2004). His petition was denied but he was granted a stay of execution on appeal. During this decision, the court found that the antipsychotic medication was administered for the protection of Mr. Singleton and other inmates, rather than for restoration of competency (Heath, 2000). Lancet (2003, p. 621) identified the Singleton case decision in 2003, as the first at the federal level to examine the question of treatment restoration and competency for purposes of execution, and notes that in a dissenting opinion a Justice commented that "the medical community was being forced to practice in a manner contrary to its ethical standards."

In the second case of its kind, Gary Alvord was found incompetent for execution and remains on death row today (K. S. Miller & Radelet, 1993). This case illustrates a second issue that is difficult for many psychologists who encounter death-row prisoners while working in the forensic arena. As in the case of Gary Alvord, if an inmate is found incompetent, he or she is sent to a state mental hospital to be restored to competency. Thus, the primary responsibility of a psychologist rendering treatment to a death-row inmate is to restore the inmate to competency so that the state can execute him or her (Brodsky et al., 2001). As might be expected, the psychologist often has ambiguous feelings about providing treatment under such circumstances. Similarly, individuals within the field of psychology have mixed feelings about the appropriateness of a psychologist's involvement in capital cases (Hensl, 2004).

One such argument among those who believe that psychologists and psychiatrists should not treat those found incompetent to be executed pertains to weighing the costs and benefits of treatment. Opponents of such intervention believe that it is more detrimental to restore a death-row inmate to competency, since the result will be execution, than it is to withhold treatment from that individual (Heilbrun, Radelet, & Dvoskin, 1992). Second, those opposed to treating individuals found incompetent for execution acknowledge the potential adverse effects that such treatment could have on the clinician when he or she knows that rendering their services may result in the death of another human being (Heilbrun et al., 1992).

Slobogin (2000, p. 667) identified three reasons why death sentences should never or rarely be imposed on individuals with mental illness: (1) execution of the mentally ill "violates equal protection of the law in those states that prohibit the execution of children (all states), or people with mental retardation" (now all states); (2) the majority of death sentences forced on the mentally ill are deprivations of life without due process of law, as a result of capital sentencing juries typically treating mental illness as an aggravating rather than a mitigating factor; and finally (3) even if the death sentence is valid, the Eighth Amendment will usually prevent the sentence from being carried out because the sentenced mentally ill are incompetent under the *Ford* standard, or are made competent solely because of the unconstitutional administration of forced medication. The official text (passed October 23–24, 2000) of the American Psychiatric Association Board of Trustees' (cited in Fava, 2001, p. 168) stated, "The American Psychiatric Association endorsed the moratorium on capital punishment in the United States until jurisdiction seeking to reform the death penalty implement policies and procedures to assure that capital punishment, if used at all is administered fairly and impartially in accord with the basic requirements of due process."

On the other hand, those who support treating incompetent death-row inmates believe that everyone has the right to receive psychiatric and psychological treatment if they so desire. However, this begs the question: Are incompetent individuals capable of providing informed consent? For example, suspected or documented mental retardation is commonly used as a reason for examining a death-row inmate's competency for execution. In this country to date, 33 individuals with mental retardation have been executed, including those with the cognitive functioning of a 7-year-old child (Keyes, Edwards, & Perske, 1998). The recent *Atkins v. Virginia* decision rendered executing the mentally retarded unconstitutional. Lancet (2003) maintained that if the *Singleton* case goes to the Supreme Court, the Court has an opportunity to build on the *Atkins* decision in protection of the mentally ill. Those in support of treating the incompetent argue that refusing to provide such treatment is nothing more than a protest against the death penalty, and although the principle of doing no harm applies in nonforensic settings, it is not as applicable to forensic treatment settings (Heilbrun et al., 1992).

One final issue that is raised in the controversy over treating mentally incompetent death-row inmates pertains to medication. As in the case of Horace Kelly, a psychotic disorder such as schizophrenia is a common mental illness for which a competency-for-execution evaluation may be requested. Psychotic disorders are most commonly treated by some form of psychotropic medication. Therefore, death-row inmates found incompetent for execution may be sent to a state mental hospital to be restored to competency through the administration of antipsychotic medication or may be treated by a correctional/forensic psychiatrist at the correctional institution. A problem that arises in cases such as these is the fact that individuals have the right to refuse treatment, including medication (*Washington v. Harper*, 1990). However, the United States Supreme Court in *Perry v. Louisiana* (1990) failed to resolve whether a death-row inmate possesses the right to refuse treatment (B. J. Winick, 1992).

Forensic Psychology and Policy Implications

There are a number of policy implications for the fields of criminal justice and mental health pertaining to the incarceration and execution of the mentally ill. There was a time in this country when mentally ill individuals were primarily housed in state mental hospitals. However, the deinstitutionalization of the mentally ill has in reality reinstitutionalized such individuals in the local jails and state prisons. As noted by Belcher (1988), mentally ill persons who are homeless or who have been previously hospitalized are particularly vulnerable to subsequent incarceration. Perhaps it is society's lack of appropriate strategies for caring for the mentally ill that leads to the incarceration of such individuals. Policy reform would do well to introduce alternative services to the mentally ill that would ensure that they received the proper treatment needed in order for them to adequately function in society.

Execution of the mentally ill holds significant implications for both the criminal justice and mental health systems (Hensl, 2004). From a legal standpoint, the ruling of *Ford v. Wainwright* (1986) perhaps raised more questions than it answered. There is a lack of specificity in defining several issues which cross the divide between psychology and the law. For example, although an individual must have a mental illness in order to be rendered incompetent, the Court has yet to specify which mental illnesses or conditions (with the exception of mental retardation) can be used to exempt an individual from execution. As illustrated by several cases, this results in psychologists diagnosing death-row inmates as mentally ill, while still rendering them competent for execution. Similarly, the Court has not yet ruled on the appropriate protocol to follow when psychologists disagree in their expert opinions. Finally, with so few cases in which death-row prisoners were found incompetent for execution, clear guidelines have not yet been established in terms of what to do with those deemed incompetent.

Suggestions for Future Research

There are a number of areas that need further exploration regarding the incarceration and execution of the mentally ill (Brodsky et al., 2001). Research is needed that compares mentally ill offenders who have been hospitalized with those who have been incarcerated in terms of their psychological symptomatology, as well as their risk to the community upon release. Such research would assist in understanding which environment provides the most benefit to the individual as well as to society.

Studies that assess the reliability of psychologists' expert opinions on death penalty cases would provide valuable information to the courts in determining the weight that should be given to such testimony. Moreover, it would be helpful to both the criminal justice and the mental health fields to have research available that identifies those factors, which account for the discrepancies among psychologists' opinions in capital cases. Finally, research could contribute significantly to operationalizing some of the legal terminology involved so that the legal standards could be appropriately applied to the practice of conducting competency-for-execution evaluations.

SUICIDE RISK, SCREENING, AND CRISIS INTERVENTION FOR INMATES

Introduction

Jail and prison suicides continue despite the fact that many are both foreseeable and preventable (Welch & Gunther, 1997). As prisons and jails keep filling up with the mentally ill, many correctional institutions still fail to implement proactive policies or programs for suicide prevention (Vaughan & Stevenson, 2002). Growing litigation is compelling correctional institutions to provide adequate mental health screenings, crisis intervention, and treatment for the prevention of suicide. Welch and Gunther (1997, p. 229) maintained that "insufficient staff, maintaining inadequate training and supervision, deficient jail conditions, lack of written rules and procedures to screen and monitor potentially suicidal detainees, and overcrowding" are all factors involved in many jail suicides and subsequent litigation.

Jails and prisons are filled with high-risk individuals to include those who abuse substances, the mentally ill, the indigent, young adults, and those facing a major life stressor. In order to prevent suicide in our correctional systems, prevention and intervention programs are necessary. Once identified, special housing needs, mental health treatment, and increased supervision can be implemented for those inmates at risk for harming themselves. However, without proper identification, no preventative measures can be put into practice.

Sometimes, even if properly screened, an inmate will deny a history of mental illness or current symptoms, or perhaps symptoms of mental illness were not present at that time. The need for crisis intervention services in corrections is undeniable and is a major responsibility for forensic/correctional psychologists. The case of Mr. M illustrates the importance of screening incoming inmates for mental health services and potential for suicide (Freeman & Alaimo, 2001, pp. 449–450).

Mr. M, a 26-year-old African American man charged with first-degree murder, had been jailed three times previously on drug charges. During intake, he was interviewed by a mental health specialist with a bachelor's degree who administered a primary mental health screening instrument. This questionnaire addresses various aspects of psychiatric history, drug and alcohol use, suicide history, and current risk of suicidal behavior, homicidal behavior, or both.

Mr. M reported no history of psychiatric treatment, but admitted to smoking upward of $150 of crack cocaine per day for the past 2 years. He also denied any history of suicide attempts and suicidal or homicidal ideation at intake. On closer questioning, the mental health specialist elicited that Mr. M was charged with murdering his mother. He spoke softly, appeared disheveled, and tears welled up in his eyes several times during the brief interview. Later he became mute and refused to answer further questions.

The mental health specialist conducted a secondary interview immediately. The secondary interview determined whether Mr. M should be referred for admission to the acute care psychiatric unit. A more in-depth assessment, the secondary interview included questions about mental status and background information designed to both elicit risk factors for suicide and detect mental instability. Although Mr. M was unresponsive to secondary interview questions, he was referred for admission to the acute care psychiatric unit based on his despondent behavior and the fact that he was charged with murdering his mother. He also was considered high risk because of possible depression related to cocaine withdrawal. His disheveled appearance suggested possible underlying mental illness, an unstable living situation, and possible cognitive impairments related to substance withdrawal. These factors increase concerns about suicidal behavior.

Literature Review

According to the U. S. Department of Justice, Bureau of Justice Statistics (1995), from 1993 to 1994 more than 400 inmates took their life annually. Hayes (1989) found that there were 107 suicides per 100,000 inmates, with a rate greater than nine times that of the general population. This national study of jail suicides also found that most jails did not screen for suicide risk or mental illness and many individuals who completed suicide had been placed in isolation and killed themselves within 24 hours of their incarceration. The most common method of suicide was hanging (Hayes, 1989). While death by suicide is approximately the tenth leading cause of death in the overall population, it is a leading cause of death in correctional institutions (Cox & Morschauser, 1997). The suicide rates in Texas county jails from 1986 through 1995 averaged 58 suicides per 100,000 inmates (Texas Commission on Jail Standards, 1996). The highest rates were found in 1984 with 151 suicides per 100,000 inmates.

Most correctional institutions are ill equipped to identify and treat the numerous mentally ill offenders that are admitted daily. Some individuals with no prior history of mental illness also commit suicide soon after incarceration. Often the suicide attempt or completion was precipitated by other factors such as intoxication and the shame or humiliation of being arrested for a crime. Durand, Curtiss, Burtka, Federman, Haycox, & Smith (1995) indicated that factors such as intoxication, a history of depression or suicide attempts, and having been charged with murder or manslaughter are associated with high risk of suicide. As previously mentioned, the commission of suicide in a jail most often occurs during the first 24 hours, but suicide can be related to a variety of other factors. Freeman and Alaimo (2001) contend that the literature on jail suicides suggests that a number of combinations of situational factors, inmate adjustment and coping factors, and environmental forces or conditions of confinement are responsible for suicidal behavior. While there are often a number of precipitating factors, many researchers agree that incarceration itself is often traumatic and related to suicide (Bonner, 1992; Freeman & Alaimo, 2001; L. M. Hayes, 1989, 1998).

Two of the most salient factors for inmate suicide are the jail conditions and a personal crisis situation the detainee faces (L. M. Hayes, 1989). The factors related to conditions inherent in the jail include shame of incarceration, separation or isolation from family and friends, fear and distrust of their surroundings, a lack of control of the future, and the degrading features of the confinement. Furthermore, L. M. Hayes (1989) identified the crisis situation factors that predispose the inmate to suicide as excessive drinking and/or using drugs, severe shame over the conduct resulting in arrest, a recent loss, active mental illness, a history of past suicidal ideation or attempts, and an upcoming court date. The individuals may have already been facing a crisis or may be experiencing a mental illness that contributed to the commission of the crime prior to incarceration.

Inmate suicide can also be explored by examining a detainee's vulnerability to stress (Bonner, 1992). A detainee may have lacked the capacity to cope with the stresses of incarceration or may have lost the capacity once confined. Once the prisoner encounters more than he can bear, the result might be suicidal ideation, behavior, or completion. In addition to having difficulty coping with the immediate shock of incarceration, over time the stress may be exacerbated by victimization or conflicts within the institution, loss of relationships, continuing legal difficulties, and increasingly unstable emotions.

Welch and Gunther (1997) conducted a study to determine the areas of institutional policy and customs that were the most problematic in relation to jail suicide. Out of 77 cases examined, 52% cited inadequate training and supervision as the institutional problem most significantly related to suicide; 22% cited lack of policies and procedures for screening and monitoring potentially suicidal inmates; 21% specifically cited deficient jail conditions; 5% cited insufficient staff; and none of the cases cited overcrowding. Deficient jail conditions not only refer to placing suicidal inmates in isolation cells but also refer to physical characteristics of the institution's architecture and design, particularly in the cells, that facilitate suicide, for example "an exposed light fixture (*Silva v. State; Thomas v. Benton County, Ark.*), a ceiling grate (*Natriello v. Flynn*), and a shower curtain rod (*Vega v. Parsley*)" (Welch & Gunther, 1997, p. 235). *Cabrales v. County of Los Angeles* specifically cited insufficient staff in the suit; whereas, *Buffington v. Baltimore County* highlighted the importance of not ignoring behavioral and psychological indicators (e.g., substance intoxication, severe depression, self-destructive behavior, delusional ideation) of suicide risk. Consider the following two cases as described by Welch & Gunther (1997, p. 236).

> In *Cabrales v. County of Los Angeles* (1989), for example, the decedent was examined by the institution's psychiatrists following a suicide attempt. The psychiatrist, however, concluded that the suicide attempt was merely a "gesture" to manipulate the staff. The decedent was no longer ruled a suicide risk and returned to the general population, where he committed suicide several days later. The plaintiff alleged that the institution deprived the decedent of adequate mental health services and supervision. The jury found the jail commander and county liable because medical understaffing prevented psychiatrists from providing adequate assessments.
>
> ...As mentioned in *Buffington v. Baltimore County* (1990), the decedent, with a long history of depression and substance abuse, was arrested and placed in protective custody after leaving a suicide note and departing his home with several rifles and handguns. During the booking, the decedent admitted to the officer that he was planning to commit suicide. The decedent was placed in an isolation cell where he hanged himself by his trousers. Two officers were found liable for suicide.

Although suicides while in confinement should never happen, in reality they are a fairly rare event. Staff inaction to prevent suicide could result from a lack of training or in other cases, the perception that some inmates are manipulative and are only "gesturing" without real intent to harm themselves (Welch & Gunther, 1997, p. 240). They may view parasuicidal behaviors such as cutting and head banging as attempts to get sympathy or attention. However, researchers stress the importance that these incidents should also be taken seriously because these actions can lead to death. "Current research on suicidal gestures and attempts within the correctional setting is replete with evidence to view *all* threats of self-injury as potentially suicidal behavior" (NCIA, 1992, cited in Welch & Gunther, 1997, p. 240). In more recent research, Dear, Thomson, and Hills (2000, p. 160) found that "Prison staff cannot assume that prisoners who appear manipulative or report manipulative motives were not suicidal at the time of self-harming."

Having a central intake and screening program can help correctional staff classify detainees for housing and appropriate mental health services (Snow & Briar, 1990). These investigators indicated that despite considerable research on risk factors associated with suicide, particularly for detainees, many jails do not have detoxification and mental health units. This can only serve to increase the risk for substance abusers suffering through withdrawal and suicidal ideation. Those with mental illness are misunderstood and their treatment needs often go unmet. "Environmental and service deficits accelerate the disorientation and decompensation of such inmates and result in unmeasurable human costs for the victim and severe management problems for the jail.... In short, the mentally ill are not prepared to cope with jail life and jails are not prepared to cope with the mentally ill. Punishing their bizarre behavior with segregation or suspended privileges only increases their fear and suspicion. Suicide is one result" (Snow & Briar, 1990, p. 154).

Cohen and Dvoskin (1992) recommended that the delivery of mental health services in prisons should include screening and triage, follow-up evaluations, crisis intervention services, crisis beds, longer term residential treatment units, and outpatient clinic services (general population but with psychotropic medications, individual and group therapy, and case management). Prisons must be able to screen incoming inmates to identify those who might need mental health treatment, suicide precautions, and/or special housing. Non-mental-health staff, to include nurses and correctional officers, often conduct first level screenings. However, there should be a very low threshold for referral to a trained mental health professional (masters or doctoral level) for a follow-up evaluation. Additionally, crisis intervention services should be available for all inmates, not only those classified as mentally ill. Crisis intervention should be timely and adequate to prevent escalation of violence to self or others, as well to prevent further decompensation into more serious mental illness (Cohen & Dvoskin, 1992).

Forensic Psychology and Policy Implications

The lack of appropriate community mental health or other social service programs for persons with disabilities often contributes to the criminalization of the mentally ill, leaving jails and prisons to fill the gap in custodial care and services (Snow & Briar, 1990; Vaughan & Stevenson, 2002). According to Welch and Gunther (1997), lessons learned from class action litigation have obvious implications for correctional institution reform and proactive measures to prevent and reduce the risk of jail suicide. These researchers contend that important changes must be made in institutional policies affecting inadequate training and supervision, deficient jail conditions, the lack of adequate mental health screenings, treatment, and crisis intervention, as well as insufficient staff, particularly mental health professionals.

Consent decrees are another form of litigation where the court can order correctional institutions to be reformed in a particular area, for example, by implementing a comprehensive suicide prevention program. These changes can be very detailed and are judicially enforced and penalties are compulsory for noncompliance. Due to budgetary concerns and ideological differences, this path of institutional reform for the treatment of the mentally ill and/or suicide prevention is necessary in many instances. A consent decree in *Garcia v. Board of County Commissioners of the County of El Paso* (1985) resulted in the jail being compelled to create a comprehensive suicide prevention program to include intensive supervision to all admitted inmates during the first 24 hours of confinement. All inmates were required to undergo screening, including the completion of an in-depth questionnaire. Those inmates identified as "at-risk" were required to remain under active visual observation on either irregular intervals (no more than 15-minute checks) or constant supervision without interruption (Welch & Gunther, 1997). Mental health/medical staff will typically recommend this level of supervision for a high-risk inmate to help prevent suicide.

Other consent decrees have resulted in written policies and procedures for institutions to provide "special needs" cells with a clear, unobstructed view of the inmate, which pass inspection by a suicide-prevention expert. In addition, inmate screening and specialized training of correctional and mental health staff in suicide prevention have been mandated. The training of staff and having them available is essential. Correctional psychologists should play a central role in training staff in the identification of high-risk individuals and situations, as well as suicide intervention techniques. The reality of the inmate to mental health professional ratio and the very limited contact line staff, particularly correctional officers, have with these offenders necessitates that staff are adequately trained in identifying those in need for a more in-depth screening or crisis intervention by mental health professionals. Many inmates are either missed during the initial mental health screening or their mental state deteriorates over the course of confinement. It is essential that correctional staff be equipped to refer those individuals needing more evaluation or immediate crisis intervention to the appropriate medical and psychology staff. Correctional psychologists often are on call for crisis intervention to further evaluate a detainee who is threatening suicide or who is exhibiting or experiencing bizarre or agitated behavior. Correctional/forensic psychologists must take a leadership role in implementing and monitoring the screening/intake procedures for the correctional institution, as well as mental health treatment and crisis intervention.

Most likely, given their inability or reluctance to seek out mental health treatment during the early stages of their illness, the only contact many psychiatrically disordered offenders have with mental health professionals in the community and in the criminal justice system is compelled by crisis (Vaughan & Stevenson, 2002). In both settings, a failure to provide continuity of care after the crisis is common. Mental health follow-up during their confinement is essential. Furthermore, after a period of incarceration and having had time to think about their situation and potentially recover from the effects of drug and alcohol abuse, some individuals are able to realize their need for mental health treatment and social support. Prison or jail-based mental health treatment teams need to link the detainee to appropriate community resources before their release (Vaughan & Stevenson, 2002). Including a system of aftercare in the community to avoid a break in mental health care should be another dimension of mental health services for detainees. "Finally, when all else fails, it is the police who are left to pick up the pieces, particularly in a crisis" (Vaughan & Stevenson, 2002, p. 19). In this instance, the cycle begins all over again.

Suggestions for Future Research

Additional research is needed to further identify risk factors specifically related to detainees. Data collection regarding the effectiveness of suicide prevention programs in correctional settings is also needed. Continued research on the provision of mental health services in jails and prisons and the preferred treatment modalities, based on effectiveness, could be very beneficial in improving the quality of treatment and the reduction of detainee suicides. Studies examining the impact of class action litigation and consent decrees on jail and prison administrators' attitudes toward mental health services are needed. Additionally, studies exploring the numbers and types of mental health policies and procedures that have been implemented in jails and prisons as a result of litigation could be very enlightening. A forensic/correctional psychologist, particularly one serving an administrative capacity or consulting role, could use this data to educate wardens and other correctional officials about the costs/benefits to both the inmate and the institution for the delivery of inadequate mental health services.

SEX-OFFENDER TREATMENT

Introduction

The most appropriate way of addressing sex offenders continues to be an issue debated among psychologists, criminologists, private citizens, and the legislature. The disposition options for convicted sex offenders are wide-ranging and include life imprisonment, civil commitment, chemical castration, and psychological treatment. Perhaps the area that has received the most attention from the fields of psychology and criminology is whether it is beneficial to provide treatment to sex offenders. This matter continues to be controversial even among the foremost experts in the field of sex offender research. On the one hand, some believe that sex-offender treatment is beneficial (Alexander, 1997; D. T. Lee, 2003; Marques, 1999; L. E. Marshall, 2001; W. L. Marshall, 1996), while there are some who do not (Furby, Weinrott, & Blackshaw, 1989; Quinsey, 1998).

The method most often used in determining whether a particular treatment modality has been successful is the measure of recidivism. Recidivism is considered the best measure of treatment efficacy since the primary goal of sex-offender treatment is the reduction of future victimization (R. Prentky & Burgess, 1990). Therefore, in exploring whether the treatment of sex offenders is beneficial, it is essential to examine recidivism rates between those offenders who receive treatment and those who do not. Below, the case of Jesse depicts a convicted sex offender incarcerated without treatment for a number of years for child molestation. Jesse knows that he will re-offend if released from prison because he is no better equipped to deal with his deviant behavior now than he was 10 years ago.

> Jesse is a 36-year-old child molester who has been incarcerated for the past 10 years for molesting a 9-year-old boy. As his parole date approached, Jesse acknowledged that he did not know why he committed his offense in the first place and he was afraid that he would commit another offense if he was released. Jesse pleaded with the parole board not to release him.
>
> The parole board recognized Jesse's plea as a sign of remorse and released him into the community. For 1 year, Jesse remained offense-free. Then one day a neighborhood boy visited Jesse for a piano lesson and Jesse re-offended.
>
> When Jesse returned to prison, he learned about sex-offender treatment. He wrote letters and spoke with prison officials requesting that he receive this treatment. The only response to Jesse's efforts was a prison chaplain who visited him weekly.

Literature Review

Jesse is perhaps a rare case in that he outwardly acknowledged that he would re-offend if released, and he believed that the only way to prevent a re-offense was to remain incarcerated. Some experts would disagree with Jesse's position that remaining incarcerated was the only way in which to prevent a re-offense. In the 10 years that he was in prison, Jesse did not receive any treatment. It is possible that Jesse would not have re-offended if he had received the proper treatment to address his inappropriate sexual fantasies and behaviors.

Despite the fact that numerous experts have shown that treatment does indeed reduce recidivism among sex offenders (Blanchette, 1996; Heilbrun, Nezu, Keeney, Chung, & Wasserman, 1998; R. J. McGrath, Cumming, Livingston, & Hoke, 2003), there has been a decrease in funding for sex-offender treatment programs since the late 1980s (Alexander, 1997). R. J. McGrath et al. (2003) examined the recidivism rates of 195 adult male sex offenders who were referred to a prison-based cognitive-behavioral treatment program. Out of this sample, 56 of the offenders completed treatment, 49 entered treatment but did not complete, and 90 refused treatment services. After approximately six years, the sexual re-offense rate for the completed treatment sample was 5.4% as compared to 30.6% for the partial treatment, and 30% for the no-treatment groups. Those participants who had aftercare treatment and correctional supervision services in the community had even lower recidivism rates (McGrath et al., 2003). The lack of funding and available treatment for sex offenders is, in part, due to public opinion that sex offenders cannot be successfully treated. The accuracy of such an opinion needs to be explored and is best accomplished through an examination of recidivism rates among sex offenders.

In a comprehensive study on the effectiveness of sex-offender treatment, Alexander (1997) conducted a meta-analysis of 81 sex-offender treatment studies involving 11,350 subjects. The results overwhelmingly showed that sex offenders who received treatment while in prison had a lower rate of recidivism than those offenders who did not receive treatment. Among the sex offenders who received treatment in prison, 9.4% re-offended, whereas those offenders who did not receive treatment had a re-offense rate of 17.6%.

A retrospective study that examined recidivism rates with sex offenders treated at a secure facility with a cognitive behavioral program, as compared to an untreated correctional sample, found that successfully treated offenders were significantly less likely to re-offend (Scalora & Garbin, 2003). These researchers found that those who recidivated were significantly younger, single, had engaged in more victim grooming or less violent offending behavior, and had significantly more property crimes.

In order to accurately assess the issue of treatment efficacy among sex offenders, it is imperative to differentiate disaggregate the offenders and not address the entire sex-offender population as a homogenous group. In this regard, numerous studies show that incest offenders have a very low rate of recidivism (Alexander, 1997; Hanson & Bussiere, 1996; Hanson, Steffy, & Gauthier, 1993). Referring again to Alexander's (1997) meta-analysis, the recidivism rate of treated incest offenders was 4.0%, whereas untreated incest perpetrators had a recidivism rate of 12.5%. For the incest-perpetrator population, it is apparent that treatment is quite effective in reducing future victimization. The comparison between treated and untreated rapists, however, does not provide encouraging results. Rapists who received treatment had a recidivism rate of 20.1%, while untreated rapists had a re-offense rate of 23.7%. These findings clearly illustrated the point that treating sex offenders as a homogenous group will lead to erroneous conclusions regarding the effectiveness of treatment.

McGuire (2000) found that not all sex offenders lapse in similar manners, and those with adult victims show more impulsive-criminal trends in lapse behavior when compared to those with child victims. He found that the different categories of sex offenders relapse in different rates and manners.

The empirical research shows that treatment is quite successful for incest perpetrators; however, it is less effective for rapists. Therefore, perhaps the question that needs to be addressed is not whether to treat sex offenders, but rather, what model of sex-offender treatment is most effective for which type of sex offender?

Another area that has received a considerable amount of research attention pertains to the type of treatment that is most beneficial for sex offenders. Until very recently, the consensus among those who treat this population was that a cognitive-behavioral program focused on relapse prevention was the most effective (Laws, 1989; Marshall & Barbaree, 1990; R. A. Prentky, Knight, & Lee, 1997). Such treatment programs have been referred to as "state-of-the-art" in terms of sex-offender treatment (Freeman-Longo & Knopp, 1992). As mentioned previously, rapists tend to have a lower success rate in terms of reducing recidivism after treatment. However, based on the meta-analysis conducted by Alexander (1997), all sex offenders, including rapists, had a recidivism rate under 11% after receiving treatment that utilized relapse prevention techniques. Thus, instead of asking whether to treat sex offenders, perhaps the focus needs to be placed on which type of treatment program is most effective for this population. There is a considerable amount of current research, which lends support to the idea that cognitive-behavioral treatment, particularly when coupled with a relapse prevention component, is quite effective in reducing recidivism among sex offenders.

Heilbrun et al. (1998) pointed out that relapse prevention as a treatment strategy was not initially developed as a stand-alone treatment, but rather as one component combined with other interventions. Recent research (Laws, 2003; Polaschek, 2003) has discovered that the relapse-prevention model incorporated in cognitive behavioral sex-offender treatment is not well suited to some types of sex offenders. This mode of sex-offender treatment operated under the assumption that there was only a single model of relapse; a relapse was always triggered by negative emotions or events, all offenders were attempting to avoid offending, and that offending was the result of skills deficits (Ward & Hudson, 1998, 2000). While the relapse prevention offense process model was once thought to be a one size fits all model, an alternative approach focusing on the individual characteristics of the offender and offense patterns is gaining wider acceptance. Ward and Hudson (1998, p. 701) concluded that research has "provided evidence for the existence of diverse offense pathways containing a number of distinct phases ... offenders vary in their goals, their capacity to plan offenses, and in the kinds of emotions they experience throughout the offense process."

Ward and Hudson (1998; 2000) presented a self-regulation model for relapse prevention in sex offenders that took into account the individual differences in offenders; for example, some offenders are not triggered by a negative event, but rather plan and seek out offensive sex. Some offenders are not affected or influenced by a lack of social skills and this would not be an appropriate focus of their sex-offender treatment program. A cognitive behavioral approach to address cognitive distortions, victim empathy, and deviant sexual arousal are still critical components of sex-offender treatment. However, researchers and practitioners recognize that certain components of treatment will be different for an offender who is underregulated and lacks cognitive planning and social skills, in addition to experiencing deviant arousal patterns, problems with intimacy, and cognitive distortions. This is especially so when compared to an offender who experiences cognitive distortions, dysfunctional schemas, deviant arousal, psychopathy, and loneliness (Ward & Hudson, 1998; 2000).

Despite the amount of psychological literature which illustrates the effectiveness of certain treatment modalities for particular types of sex offenders, the legislature continues to decrease funding for these treatment programs and exerts a great deal of energy supporting the chemical castration of child molesters (Alexander, 1997). There are a number of reasons why law enforcement, legislators, and the public disregard the scientific research that demonstrates rehabilitation of sex offenders is indeed possible. One criticism identified by individuals who believe that "nothing works" is the notion that a large number of sex offenses go undetected and therefore skew recidivism results. However, when addressing the issue of sexual offending, it unfortunately goes without saying that many sex offenders are not brought to the attention of the authorities. This is a commonly held assumption, even among those who believe in the efficacy of sex-offender treatment (Hanson & Bussiere, 1996). Thus, the reported recidivism rates reflecting an underreporting of sex offenses remains a valid consideration. It is important to keep in mind, however, that while the statistics underestimate actual victimization rates, this does not discount the vast discrepancy in the recidivism rates between those offenders who receive treatment and those who do not.

Forensic Psychology and Policy Implications

The issue of whether to treat sex offenders remains controversial. Perhaps one reason why this topic continues to be debated is that there are few subjects that raise as much consternation as the issue of child sexual abuse. It is understandable that many of the foremost leaders in the struggle to obtain stricter punishments for sex offenders are the parents of victims of child molestation. However, from a policy standpoint, it is important to bear in mind that even with the emotional disgust and rage exercised against sex offenders, they too are eventually released from prison. Given the research, which supports the effectiveness of treatment for this population, consideration needs to be given to increasing rather than decreasing the funding for sex-offender treatment programs. Withholding treatment from such individuals does not address the issue at the core of this controversy. Both those who treat sex offenders and those who seek to punish them have the common goal of reducing future victimization. Within the current criminal justice system, the vast majority of sex offenders are released from prison and returned to communities where potential victims reside. Recognizing this fact, it is important to question whether the public prefers to have sex offenders in their neighborhood who have received treatment or those who have not received any treatment whatsoever and, therefore, have not learned how to control their deviant sexual behavior.

Another issue to consider regarding policy reform is the cost of incarceration versus the cost of treatment for sex offenders. Blanchette (1996) presented data which illustrated that treating the average sex offender on an outpatient basis costs approximately $7,000 per year less than incarceration. As noted by Williams (1996), even if treatment was successful only for a small number of individuals, the cost-effectiveness of treatment is clear. Further, it cannot be overlooked that reducing recidivism by even a small amount spares numerous potential victims from suffering the devastating effects of sexual abuse.

Suggestions for Future Research

In recent years, an abundance of psychological literature has addressed the issue of treatment efficacy for sex offenders. However, the fields of law and criminology have scarcely produced any research on this topic. Perhaps this is because professionals in the mental health arena are those who most often provide the treatment. However, it is essential for individuals working within the mental health and the criminal justice systems to find common ground on the issue if the goal of reducing victimization is to be actively pursued. As noted by Alexander (1997), when agencies become convinced that a cause is worthwhile and urgent, the money will be appropriately allotted. Therefore, it is necessary that research be conducted addressing the reluctance by legislatures to implement treatment programs for sex offenders. Perhaps there is a lack of communication between the respective disciplines, and, thus, research would do well to target educating the public, the legislature, and the prison system on the efficacy of sex-offender treatment.

Heilbrun et al. (1998) suggested that one way to assist lawmakers was to provide more outcome data on base rates of re-offending by released sex offenders, factors associated with different levels of risk, and impact of treatment on recidivism. The current literature on the topic of sex-offender treatment is lacking in certain areas as well. The ineffectiveness of treatment with particular groups of sex offenders clouds public perception of the overall effectiveness of treatment. For this reason, research is sorely needed that addresses those sex offenders who do not respond well to existing treatment modalities. Specifically, limited studies assess how best to treat rapists, exhibitionists, and homosexual pedophiles. As suggested by Alexander (1997), research needs to focus on the heterogeneity of sex offenders in order to present a more accurate picture of what type of treatment works best for whom. Laws (2003) encouraged more research into the self-regulation model and encouraged investigators to not so readily accept this approach but to continue to explore and broaden the overall treatment strategy, thereby increasing the efficacy for all types of sex offenders.

PRISON VIOLENCE

Introduction

Christopher Scarver attacked Jeffrey Dahmer while he was cleaning a prison gymnasium bathroom, smashing his head with a metal bar borrowed from an exercise machine. Violence has become a central component of prison life. Dee Farmer, as another example, was convicted merely of credit card fraud, yet he suffered a savage attack at the hands of a fellow inmate. When Farmer refused an inmate's demand for sexual intercourse, the inmate punched and kicked Farmer. After threatening Farmer with a homemade knife, the attacker tore off Farmer's clothes and raped him. The attacker threatened to kill Farmer if he reported the incident.

The Dahmer and Farmer tragedies represent the controversial issue of poor prison conditions which cause institutional violence. Numerous research studies indicate that inmate violence is the product of the psychologically stressful and oppressive conditions within the prison itself (McCorkle, Miethe, & Drass, 1995). Measures of poor conditions, such as inadequate prison management and lack of prison programs due to overcrowding, are associated with high levels of prison violence.

Literature Review

Situations like those previously described are very common in prison life. The Farmer incident raises the question: If poor prison conditions are improved, does that indicate that psychological stress will decrease among inmates, causing a decrease in violence? In response to this question, there is growing consensus among investigators that prisons with exceptional conditions, such as efficient prison management, numerous prison programs, and comfortable prison capacity, experience a decrease in prison violence compared to facilities with poor prison conditions (McCorkle et al., 1995). Prison overcrowding and lack of satisfactory correctional management were conditions that contributed to the Dee Farmer attack. In Farmer's case, the assailant reacted to the psychologically stressful prison environment by attacking him. Effective prison management, suitable prison capacity, and programs designed to keep inmates busy contribute to relieving psychological tension in the prison.

Research indicates that the social and environmental factors that primarily produce prison violence include inmates' personal histories of violence, the youthfulness of the prison population, the lower socio-economic class of most inmates, racial conflict between prisoners, inmate norms promoting violent behavior, and the psychological effects of prison conditions suffered by inmates. Additionally, reduced security from criminal victimization, the loss of autonomy, and the scarcity of goods and services add to this stress. To lessen the physical and psychological effects of these deprivations, inmates sometimes undertake different illicit activities such as drug trafficking, murder, gambling, and selling protection from victimization. These illegal behaviors, in turn, require means for resolving disputes and thus invite the use of prison violence. The following case illustration best exemplifies this process.

J. T. owes C. L. several bottles of scotch. C. L. reports that this debt covers gambling losses; J. T. insists he has been paying for protection. C. L. gives J. T.

1 month to settle, but J. T. is unable to do so. The best J. T. can do is supply several packs of cigarettes, which only covers a small portion of the amount owed. At the end of the 1-month period, J. T. is violently assaulted and killed by V.P., who is often used by C. L. to "collect debts."

A psychological research prison study by McCorkle et al. (1995) found that poor prison management increased prison violence. Data were collected from 371 state prisons and included measures of both individual and collective violence. In this study, only adult male state correctional facilities were examined; federal prisons, institutions for youths and women, medical facilities, drug and alcohol centers, boot camps, work camps, and community correction facilities were excluded. Of the 371 state prisons, 99 were maximum security, 140 medium security, and 132 minimum security. Institutions were asked to report major incidents for the period of July 1, 1989 to June 30, 1990. Three types of prison violence were examined: inmate assaults against inmates, inmate assaults against staff, and riots. Riots were defined as assaults with five or more inmates involved, which required the intervention of outside assistance resulting in serious injury and/or property damage. McCorkle et al. (1995) found that the average rate of inmate-on-inmate assaults reported by prisons for the year was approximately 2 per 100 prisoners. Staff assaults occurred at a rate of less than 1 per 100 inmates, and 8% of prisons had experienced a riot during the year.

Prison management variables included the guard-to-inmate ratio, the guard turnover rate, the ratio of white to black correctional staff, program involvement, and institutional size as reported in 1990. McCorkle et al. (1995) found that several management variables were significant causes of individual-level violence. For example, higher white to black guard ratios were identified with higher rates of both inmate and staff assaults. Prisons in which a major percentage of the correctional population involved itself in educational, vocational, and prison industry programs had a lower incidence of violence against staff and inmates. This suggests that prisons depriving inmates of program involvement have a higher incidence of violence than prisons that encourage program involvement. Both individual and collective violence were more common in medium- and maximum-security institutions than in minimum-security facilities. Large prisons reported slightly lower rates of inmate-on-inmate assaults. This study (McCorkle et al., 1995) found that external conditions play a role in influencing prison violence. For example, prisons in states with high unemployment experienced lower rates of inmate assaults than prisons in states with lower unemployment. One explanation is that when there is high unemployment, parole boards may be more restrained and less likely to grant early release. Under such conditions, there is less turnover in prison populations, a factor proposed by some to be a major cause of prison violence.

Huebner (2003) surveyed 4,168 male inmates and found that those who were involved in work programs were significantly less likely to assault staff. Additionally, African American respondents who were gang members with a long-standing history of criminal behavior were the most likely to assault staff and inmates. Finally, subjects who were older and educated were less likely to commit assaults (Huebner, 2003). Hollin and Palmer (2003) suggested that screening for drug and alcohol problems is an important prerequisite for working with violent offenders. These researchers recommended screening for intensity of service delivery and identifying target or goals for change upon the commencement of a prison term.

P. Johnson (2001) examined structural causes of violence among African American inmates in U.S. prisons. He indicated that media images of violent black men in the news, the utilization of underpaid prison labor, and the rise of prisoner militancy since the 1960s and 1970s were all structural causes of violence. P. Johnson (2001) contended that there had been a 510% increase in the number of incarcerated drug offenders from 1983 until 1993, many of whom were African American.

In a study by Mills and Kroner (2003), alienation, impulse expression, and age were antisocial constructs that were related to institutional disruptions and infractions by violent offenders. Another study examined the relationship between Axis II (personality) disorders and community and institutional violence among a sample of 261 incarcerated women (Warren et al., 2002). Results revealed that a significant relationship occurred between antisocial personality disorder and institutional violence, as well as narcissistic personality disorder and incarceration for a violent crime. Harer and Langan (2001) examined data for 24,765 women and 177,767 men admitted to federal prison from 1991 through 1998. These researchers found that while in prison, women committed less violence overall and less serious violence than men. However, they also found that the same classification instrument predicted violent behavior equally well for both genders.

Trulson and Marquart (2002) conducted a study whereby 10 years of inmate-on-inmate assault data were used to compare the rates of violence among inmates racially integrated in a double cell versus inmates racially segregated in a double cell. The results indicated that the violence between integrated inmates was actually lower than between segregated inmates.

DiIulio (1987) suggested that prison violence, both individual and collective, is the result of failed prison management, including security lapses, high staff turnover, a lack of discipline among guards, unsearched inmates, and lack of prison programs. Useem and Kimball (1989) found that organizational and management factors were the most important determinants of prison violence. Toch (2001) asserted that supermax confinement or high-tech segregation settings create additional mental health problems in already violent offenders that result in the enhancement, not the reduction, of inmate violence potential. The increase in the prisoner population, which now numbers more than 2 million, has been relentless since the 1980s and shows no signs of diminishing. Indeed, the steady increase in the prison population since the late 1980s has been staggering. For example, the number of prisoners in America increased by 115% (from 329,000 to 710,000) between 1980 and 1989 (Marquart et al., 1994). Prison statistics such as these raise the psychological issue: How can prison programs be effective to inmates in an overcrowded facility? In response to this question, some researchers engaged in a study focusing on the effects of prison overcrowding on correctional educational programs.

Marquart and colleagues (1994) found that prison overcrowding decreased the opportunity for inmates to participate and complete prison education programs. This study examined the Windham School System in Texas. Windham's mission is to raise inmate literacy levels as well as to provide prisoners with vocational skills in order to enable them to join the workforce on release from prison. Windham's academic programs are geared toward raising the functional level of prisoners. The Windham School System regards a one-grade-level increase for an inmate to be a significant personal and organizational accomplishment. The Windham School System measures the performance and effectiveness of the vocational courses by the total number of certificates earned. Information was collected from two separate state databases: the Texas Department of Criminal Justice Institutional Division and the Windham School System.

The types of data collected from the prison system included prison number, average sentence length, and average time served in prison on 73,990 new inmates admitted and on 66,160 prisoners who were paroled or discharged in Texas prisons between 1990 and 1992. The second database consisted of prisoner education files maintained by the Windham

School System. As a result of an implemented population cap and redistribution of funds in the prison system, a significant amount of problems occurred with the Windham academic program and vocational courses. Due to prison overcrowding, there was a limited number of vocational courses; thus, inmates were forced to wait a period of time before participating in a particular course. There was a 6-month wait before the first vocational class commenced.

The data indicated that 974 out of 6,919 prisoners were released from prison while participating in vocational courses. Therefore, 1 of 7 inmates enrolled in a vocational course started the course, and then left prison before certification. The results of this study strongly suggest that prison administrative personnel enrolled inmates in Windham's School System programs with the expectation that they would complete them, but those expectations were thwarted by early release practices and prison over-crowding policies. The combined effects of population–control policies and early release severely attenuated the Windham School System's perfor-mance measures. Consequently, prison overcrowding caused inmates to wait on a space-available basis for educational programs and vocational courses. Arguably, delays for admittance to these educational programs and courses could have a psychologically profound and stressful impact on an inmate's life. For example, delays frustrated prisoners and created more idle time for them to get into trouble and perpetrate violence. When inmates are enrolled in educational programs, they are less likely to experience violence (McCorkle et al., 1995).

Forensic Psychology and Policy Implications

Life in prison entails facing a chronically stressful environment with its demanding regimentation, loss of control, and daily potential for violence. Prison educational programs offer inmates an escape from these stressors and a lower risk for violence. However, current criminal justice policies aimed at regulating prison populations have negative consequences for correc-tional education programs and the public. For example, an implemented population ceiling allows thousands of inmates early release and results in a rapid decrease in time served. Therefore, the opportunity to benefit and rehabilitate from educational programming eludes many prisoners. As a policy matter, returning unprepared and untrained prisoners to the community poses a threat to public safety. Prison educational programs are the most powerful methods to help advance prison governance, institutional stability, and control over inmate violence. For example, inmates who attend several hours of class each day are occupied rather than idle. Inmates who are busy are not security problems and, as supported by the aforementioned McCorkle et al. (1995) study, present a low risk for violence. However, when prison overcrowding forces policymakers to implement criminal justice initiatives, such as a population cap and a redistribution of funds to other prison necessities (additional cells, clothes, and food), the results can have a disastrous impact on educational programming.

For example, depriving prisoners of such assistance creates a psychologically stressful environment. Inmates are not rehabilitated through programs nor kept busy with educational work. Abolition of educational initiatives would mean that other programs to keep the inmates active would need to be created, funded, and staffed. Therefore, prison stability and control over prison violence is hampered when educational programs are cut: Inmates have increased idle time, which can produce violence and chaos. Research on correctional educational programs demonstrates that they help prison organizations run efficiently and keep inmates at a low risk for violence.

Correctional/forensic psychologists can play an important role in screening inmates for their potential for institutional violence. The HCR-20 and the Psychopathy Checklist: Screening Version (PCL:SV) were used to assess the prediction of institutional violence in 41 long-term sentenced offenders in two maximum-security correctional institutions (Belfrage, Fransson, & Strand, 2000). Results demonstrated a high predictive validity for the clinical and risk-management items of the HCR-20 but almost none for its historical items. Overall, the findings suggested that correctional institutional violence could be predicted adequately by the use of the HCR-20 and the PCL:SV.

Suggestions for Future Research

One method for minimizing incidents of violence is to use comprehensive environmental scanning systems to regularly monitor behaviors in prisons and identify potential "hot spots" for violence. The use of advanced scanning systems, such as management support systems, is a relatively recent phenomenon in corrections. The ultimate goal of these systems is to enhance the ability of correctional administrators and managers to better monitor the prison environment on a continuing basis. The environment is monitored by collecting and analyzing a variety of factors that provide information on the morale, behaviors, and perceptions of prison staff, administrators, and inmates.

Environmental scanning consists of four steps. First, a process is developed to identify emerging behaviors, such as increases or decreases in typical accepted prison tension indicators including assaults and fights. Second, the findings of the scanning process are organized in an information package and distributed to administrators. Third, upon reviewing the information, the administrators must decide whether the behaviors represent a threat to the prison (threats can emerge from factors such as increases in assaults, drug finds, and inmate misbehavior or decreases in such factors as inmate program participation, counseling contracts, or health care services). Fourth, they must determine if there is a need for intervention policies and/ or procedures to address these behaviors.

Scanning systems have a critical role in prison violence prevention. First, potential prison problem areas can be detected before serious concerns emerge. Second, scanning systems force prison administrators to consider which factors best measure the well-being of their institution, the employees, and the inmate population. Third, scanning systems create a database for prison information and help correctional administrators better detect normal versus abnormal data entries. Finally, scanning systems force administrators to ask questions such as: Why did the trends emerge? Why are they shifting? Did any policy and/or personnel actions influence the trends? Should action be taken? These questions help corrections administrators make informed management decisions (Labecki, 1994). The comprehensive scanning systems enable administrators to better understand, predict, and design for the needs of offenders and programs, staffing, and security demands. Most important, a scanning system can help administrators distinguish between a psychologically acceptable and a psychologically oppressive and tension-filled environment.

Program involvement helps inmates stay out of trouble and reduces the violence in prisons. Conflict-resolution training teaches inmates the skills and resources to handle their own and other inmates' anger. It also teaches correctional officers the communication skills needed for positive interaction with inmates. Conflict-resolution training usually requires 15 hours of instruction. The course curriculum is designed to provide special skills in handling conflict with an emphasis on developing and improving skills in listening, problem solving, encouraging positive values, and mediation. Additionally, the course emphasizes anger control, forgiveness, and nonviolence. The conflict-resolution training objective is to improve communication, promote self-esteem, build relationships, and encourage respect for cultural differences and people's emotions. It also teaches techniques to resolve disputes without emphasizing winning or losing.

Love (1994) found that conflict-resolution training was effective in prisons with highly aggressive and violence-prone inmates. For example, conflict-resolution training was developed at the State Correctional Institution at Huntington, Pennsylvania, which houses some of the state's most aggressive inmates and where staff must deal with violence daily. Of the 2200 inmates, nearly one-third are serving life sentences and many have extensive histories of assaultive behavior. In 1988, Community First Step, an inmate organization at SCI-Huntington, decided to bring the conflict-resolution program to that facility. The course was well received, and after 3 years, Community First Step invited prison officers to participate in a training session with inmates. They believed, correctly, that this would improve relationships between inmates and officers.

One Huntington inmate who was serving 10 to 20 years for a violent assaultive crime participated in the training with corrections officers. He noted that one of the officers who took part was a strict disciplinarian from a military background who believed that inmates were "nobodies." According to the inmate, after completing the conflict-resolution course, the officer was more humane and professional in his relationships with prisoners (Love, 1994). The most powerful example of the effectiveness of conflict-resolution training occurred during the 1989 riots at the State Correctional Institution at Camp Hill. Inmates in the New Values drug-and-alcohol program, who had recently completed a course in conflict resolution, were the only inmates who did not participate in the disturbance. Also, these inmates were credited with helping officers so they would not be violently attacked. More research on the effectiveness of comprehensive scanning systems and conflict-resolution training in corrections is needed.

INMATE SEXUALITY

Introduction

For many people, it seems that the topic of sex and sexuality is one that causes discomfort and maybe even embarrassment. When viewing such an awkward topic in the context of inmates who are incarcerated in unisex prisons, people's discomfort levels seem to increase even further. This subject calls to mind the idea of gang rape, forced sexual interactions, and especially homosexuality. Inmate sexual assault is undoubtedly a pervasive problem in correctional systems (Hensley, R. W. Dumond, Tewksbury, & D. A. Dumond, 2002). In a recent review of empirical studies, Hensley and Tewksbury (2002) explored the dynamics of institutional sex and delineated male and female inmate consensual behavior and male and female inmate coerced sexual activity. As mentioned, in addition to sexual assaults in prisons, there are instances of consensual homosexual relationships. Hensley, Tewksbury, and Wright (2001) surveyed 142 inmates at a maximum-security institution and found that race and religion had a significant impact on same-sex relationships in prison. White subjects were more likely to be involved in consensual homosexual behavior than non-white subjects. Additionally, non-Protestant inmates were also more likely than Protestant offenders to engage in homosexual behavior while in prison.

Despite the societal progress made in being able to openly discuss and understand homosexuality, it is still a subject that causes a great deal of concern and emotional reaction. Inmate homosexuality is not immune from this controversy. In fact, there are considerably more dilemmas found with same-sex partnerships in prison. One controversy is the definition of homosexuality within a prison. This is an issue because many inmates who engage in homosexual behaviors while incarcerated are not homosexuals outside of prison (G. T. Long, 1993). This section discusses various aspects of inmate sexuality and sexual assaults in order to provide a better understanding of this phenomenon.

Sam was a 21-year-old first-time offender sentenced to a state prison where he knew no one. He was very lonely and depressed and was quickly befriended by Bud, who had been in the prison for several years and knew how the system worked. Bud took Sam under his wing and introduced him to prison life, including the inmate marriages between the "jockers" and the "punks." Bud stressed how normal an activity this was in prisons because he hoped to turn Sam into his punk. Once Bud had courted Sam for several weeks, he finalized the relationship by having Sam transferred to his cell where he could sodomize him away from the guards' view (Huffman, as cited in G. T. Long, 1993).

Charles was in his cell one morning when a large man entered asking to borrow something that belonged to his cellmate. The inmate asked Charles if he engaged in homosexual acts, and Charles emphatically stated no.

The inmate threatened physical injury if Charles would not have sex with him. When Charles attempted to defend himself, three other inmates entered the cell and hit and kicked Charles until he fell down. They then ripped off his pants and each one sodomized Charles while the others restrained him (Davis, as cited in G. T. Long, 1993).

Literature Review

The above case illustrations are very different, yet both situations exist in prisons as ways to engage in sexual behaviors and exert resistance to prison rules and regulations (Donaldson, 1990). In response to allegations of homosexuality, the perpetrators in these case illustrations would most likely deny that they were gay and might attack a fellow inmate who "accused" them of such. Donaldson states that the inmate subculture allows prisoners to be in the penetrating role without raising questions about their heterosexuality. Yet, one who submits to penetration is perceived as giving up his masculinity. Donaldson reports that the majority of prisoners engage in the former role and are called jockers or "men." The jockers engage in heterosexual behaviors both before and after their period of incarceration. A jocker's penetration of another prisoner only serves to validate his masculinity. It also serves to give the jocker some power by having control over other prisoners and thus diminishing the power the institution has over him. Donaldson (1990) describes another class of inmates called "queens." These are men who exhibit homosexual patterns outside of the prison and thus exhibit similar behaviors while incarcerated. They are typically effeminate and are always in the role of a receiver. The queens are usually pressured by the jockers to maintain the feminine role. They typically consist of a small percentage of the inmate population. The queens often are separated from the other prisoners by guards in order to provide protection for them and attempt to diminish homosexual behaviors within the prison. The protection is necessary because homosexuals may be abused by the other inmates and correctional staff tend to believe that homosexuals are troublemakers (G. T. Long, 1993).

Alarid (2000b) examined the experience of gay and bisexual men who were housed in protective custody. Her findings revealed that although all inmates surveyed felt safer in protective custody than in the general population, gay men were more likely to pressure bisexual and heterosexual men in protective custody for sex. Additionally, bisexual offenders who preferred women to men were more likely to seek protection from another inmate, felt less safe than gay or bisexual men who preferred men, and reported more pressure from other offenders to have sex (Alarid, 2000b).

Donaldson (1990) reported that a third category of inmates is referred to as punks. This category is typically larger than the queens, and the punks are considered to be the lowest class of inmates by other prisoners because they are forced into playing the receiver role. They are usually heterosexual, yet they are often "turned out" by other prisoners. This turning-out process typically involves rape, often gang rape. Charles is an example of a punk who was turned out by gang rape. These inmates are usually somewhat smaller and less experienced in the prison system. They usually have been charged with nonviolent offenses and may even have come from a middle-class upbringing. The punks will usually return to their heterosexual patterns once released from prison, but may experience distress in the form of rape trauma syndrome. However, G. T. Long (1993) reported that as a result of being turned out, those who were heterosexual might prefer homosexual behaviors once released from prison. In fact, all turnouts in one study reported to engage in exclusively homosexual behavior after being released from prison, although they were heterosexual before incarceration (Sagarin, as cited in G. T. Long, 1993).

As mentioned above, forcible rape exists in the prison subculture. It typically exists in a much higher percentage in maximum-security prisons because the inmates are usually incarcerated for more violent crimes and less worried about the risks involved with such prohibited behavior (Donaldson, 1990). C. Struckman-Johnson, D. Struckman-Johnson, Rucker, Bumby, and Donaldson (1996) found that in a state prison system, 22% of male inmates were pressured or forced to have sexual contact of some type. Those who were victims of forced sex stated that threat of harm and physical intimidation were the methods most often used by the perpetrators. Inmates' accounts of their turnouts reported that they were raped or "so completely terrified by physical threats that they were unable to resist" (Sagarin, as cited in G. T. Long, p. 155).

Hensley, Tewksbury, and Castle (2003) interviewed 174 male inmates incarcerated in three correctional facilities in Oklahoma and found that approximately 14% of their participants had been sexually targeted by other inmates. Those who engaged in forcible rape did not need to worry about an inmate reporting them because there were serious consequences for informers in the prisoner subculture (Donaldson, 1990). The C. Struckman-Johnson et al. (1996) study found that of those males who had been pressured or forced into having sexual contact, only 29% reported the incident(s) to staff. In fact, often the sexual activities were engaged in as a group with prisoners watching out for guards and deterring other prisoners from the area being used (Donaldson, 1990). The C. Struckman-Johnson et al. (1996) study also reported that of the male inmates who were victims, 25% were forced to complete the entire act of intercourse by two or more inmates.

In addition to the aftereffects of the rape trauma syndrome mentioned above, those forced into sexual behaviors might experience immediate distress. C. Struckman-Johnson et al. (1996) discovered that 75% of those who were forced to engage in sex experienced at least one negative consequence. Feelings of distrust, anxiety around others, and depression were the most common negative consequences. Sixteen percent of those forced into sexual behaviors received physical injuries. Sagarin (as cited in G. T. Long, 1993) stated that inmates reported feelings of shame, disgust, and humiliation after their first homosexual experience in prison. These feelings continued during their period of incarceration.

The above descriptions relate solely to sexual behaviors in all-male prisons, but female prisons share some of the same characteristics with respect to inmate sexuality. Donaldson (1990) reported that some women engage in lesbian relationships because they do not have access to members of the opposite sex. These women are labeled "penitentiary turnouts" and are similar to the jockers in male prisons. Those who engage in homosexual relationships outside of prison are labeled "lesbians" and are similar to the queens. The inmate who assumes the traditional female role in the relationship is called "femme" or "mommy," and the inmate who assumes the traditional male role is called "stud" or "daddy."

It is more common for female prisoners as compared to male prisoners, to engage in sexual behaviors that do not involve physical force or pressure. However, Bell et al. (1999) referred to the sexual coercion of women in prison as one of America's most "open" secrets. C. Struckman-Johnson et al. (1996) reported a 7% rate of forced or pressured sexual contact among women prisoners. Instead of basing the relationships upon fear and intimidation, they base them on consent between the inmates involved.

Mahon (1996) found that female inmates reported widespread consensual sex which included mutual masturbation, sharing of sex toys, and oral and anal sex. The sexual behaviors occurred in places such as the showers, bathrooms, and cell areas. The relationships developed in prison take on a significant role for women because they provide a source of meaningful personal and social interconnections with other people. These relationships may develop due to what G. T. Long (1993) describes as "a need for intimacy and closeness with another person" (p. 158).

However, more recent research found that out of 150 women in one women's prison, 27% had been coerced into sexual activity in the state system and 19% in their present facility (C. Struckman-Johnson & D. Struckman-Johnson, 2002). One-third of these targets reported that one perpetrator had assaulted them, while greater than 40% had been confronted by a group of two to three individuals. Out of the reported incidents, one-half of the perpetrators were women and one-half were men. Approximately one-half of the incidents were perpetrated by female inmates and 45% of the incidents involved one or more prison staff (C. Struckman-Johnson & D. Struckman-Johnson, 2002). Most incidents involved genital touching and about one-fifth of sexual coercion that occurred in three Midwestern women's prisons could be classified as rape (C. Struckman-Johnson & D. Struckman-Johnson, 2002). Women are also sexually assaulted in prisons by other inmates and staff members. Alarid (2000a) conducted a qualitative analysis of one female inmate's experiences and observations of sexual assault during a 5-year sentence. The female subject indicated that coercive sexual behavior was very common, although acts classifiable as rape were the least common. Multiple women often perpetrated these acts with anger being the primary motivator. Greer (2000) found that economic manipulation could also play a significant role in female sexual conduct.

With the prevalence of sexual activity that occurs within prisons, it would seem that the administrative and correctional staff would be aware of its existence. Hensley et al. (2002) examined what wardens ($N = 226$) believed regarding the effectiveness of institutional policies and procedures, staff training, and increased supervision by staff on reducing sexual assaults perpetrated by inmates. Most wardens believed that these practices could reduce the amount of sexual coercion among inmates.

There are an increasing number of cases where female inmates are suing correctional institutions for sexual exploitation (Bell et al., 1999; Springfield, 2000; C. Struckman-Johnson & D. Struckman-Johnson, 2002). Although administrators may often deny that such sexual behavior occurs, Donaldson (1990) reported that they know that a prisoner who becomes difficult, or is disliked by staff, can be placed in a position where he will become a victim of forced sexual behaviors by other inmates. In fact, prison staff may even sexually victimize inmates. C. Struckman-Johnson et al. (1996) reported that 18% of their victimized sample were forced to engage in sexual behaviors with prison staff. Mahon's (1996) inmate participants informed her that nonconsensual and even consensual sexual activity occurred between prisoners and the male correctional staff.

The reasons given were for protection, wanted items, privileges, and access to services.

There is a final category of inmates, which is often overlooked and not taken seriously within the prison system. This category consists of both pre- and postoperative transsexuals. Transsexuals are those who identify themselves as the opposite gender from their biological genitalia and may attempt surgery to change their genitalia (R. Smith, 1995). Petersen, Stephens, Dickey, and Lewis (1996) indicated that these prisoners pose a significant difficulty to prison management, yet results from their survey reflect that only 20% of 64 corrections departments indicated the existence of any formal policy regarding housing or treating transsexuals. Their study noted that nearly every department lacked specialized therapy for these inmates. For postoperative transsexuals, only 32% of the departments stated that they would definitely house the prisoners according to their new gender (i.e., male-to-female transsexuals would be sent to a female prison).

When viewing these inmates from a sexual behavior perspective, it would seem that they would be at greater risk for sexual assault and abuse. However, the Petersen et al. (1996) study found that 85% of the departments reported that this was not felt to be an important issue. In fact, less than 15% considered transsexual inmates to be at greater risk for sexual or physical assault. However, one particular Supreme Court case suggested that transsexuals are at risk for harm. *Farmer v. Brennan* (1994) involved a preoperative transsexual who exhibited feminine characteristics. He was transferred to a higher security penitentiary and claimed to have been beaten and raped by another inmate after being placed in the general population. The inmate brought suit against the prison officials who housed him in the general population upon transfer. In his previous location he was segregated. The Supreme Court ruled that "prison officials may be held liable under Eighth Amendment for denying humane conditions of confinement only if they know that inmates face a substantial risk of serious harm and disregard that risk by failing to take reasonable measures to abate it" (p. 1270).

Based on this ruling, prison officials may need to be more aware of how they handle transsexuals and take more seriously their risks for being harmed. From this review, it appears that sexual behaviors do exist among inmates and that the sexual behaviors in prisons are not restricted solely to offenders. Mahon (1996) provided an appropriate summary in which she quotes a female jail inmate, "Male COs [correctional officers] are having sex with females. Female COs are having sex with female inmates, and the male inmates are having sex with male inmates. Male inmates are having sex with female inmates. There's all kinds, it's a smorgasbord up there" (p. 1212).

Forensic Psychology and Policy Implications

After examining the data on inmate sexual behaviors, one alarming concern is the extent of AIDS and the spread of HIV. Mahon (1996) reported that at the end of 1994, the rate of AIDS cases in state and federal prisons was seven times higher than that in the total population of the United States. If prisoners are engaging in a prohibited activity, then it is highly unlikely that they are participating in it safely. Some type of policy must be developed to provide inmates with the means to engage in safe sex. It would be next to impossible to ensure that inmates abandoned their sexual behaviors, so instead of pretending that it does not exist, policies need to be developed to ensure that it occurs safely. May and Williams (2002) reported that less than 1% of the jails and prisons in the United States allow inmates access to condoms. A Washington, D.C. Central Detention facility initiated a program to make condoms accessible to inmates. Data was collected from 307 male inmates and 100 correctional officers who were present at the facility during its first year and results indicated that the program was generally supported and considered important by inmates and correctional staff (May & Williams, 2002).

Another consideration that should be examined is the provision of counseling for inmates raped and sexually assaulted. These prisoners most likely do not want to come forth and discuss their experiences, so measures should be taken to ensure confidentiality. The trauma that one experiences after being raped is considerable, and ignoring the consequences could lead to future acting-out behaviors by those victimized. The inmate code regarding informants is probably too strong to ignore, especially for those who have been raped. Policies need to be developed, which allow these inmates to be in protective housing without needing to inform the staff who sexually assaulted them.

With respect to transsexual inmates, formal policies must be enacted in each prison for handling these cases. R. Smith (1995) suggested that it is important to house the prisoner based on what the inmate's genitalia currently is. She noted that other considerations included how long the inmate had been receiving hormone therapy, what type of surgical procedures had been conducted, what the psychosocial needs of the inmate were, and how long the person was to be incarcerated.

Suggestions for Future Research

An area of research requiring attention includes effective methods for the prevention of HIV in the prisons and jails. Effective mental health intervention and treatment for inmates who have been victims of sexual assaults should also be undertaken (C. Struckman-Johnson et al., 1996). It is important to understand what types of treatments work for these offenders so that the impact of any trauma can be reduced. Another important area for future research concerns sexual relations between prison staff and inmates. Attempting to identify what types of staff characteristics are associated with such behavior could help in screening out these candidates at the beginning of the hiring process. Thus, future psychological harm to prisoners could be averted. Also, more in-depth studies of administrators' awareness of inmate sexual behaviors and their responses to it would provide a better understanding of exactly where officials stand on this issue and what needs to be done to educate them on the effects of sexual assaults. C. Struckman-Johnson and D. Struckman-Johnson (2002) suggested that certain characteristics in female inmates such as attractiveness, passivity, toughness, or sexual orientation could be studied to examine their correlation with being targeted as a victim of sexual assault. Additionally, they encouraged future research into the long-term impact of sexual assault on the ability to form new social-sexual relationships outside of prison.

Practice Update Section: Counseling/Treating Offender Populations in Corrections

Psychologists who work in correctional settings face a myriad of ethical and treatment-related challenges in working with difficult offender populations. The very environment itself can be a source of considerable stress for the inmates and sometimes the treatment provider. The policies and procedures of the institution are typically not conducive to a therapeutic environment. Clearly, the focus of incarceration remains on retribution not rehabilitation.

One example is the inmate that is seen for individual counseling and discloses suicidal ideation with a plan. The inmate describes the method he intends to use to harm himself and indicates that he is currently in possession of that means (e.g., a razor tucked inside his mattress). While it is necessary to immediately initiate suicide precautions and to prevent access to the weapon or razor described in the plan, a series of institutional policies must now be followed that will have quite punitive repercussions for the inmate. Some prison systems require that the inmate who poses an imminent risk for suicide be stripped naked to search for other potential weapons and to prevent any

(*continued*)

(*Continued*)

clothing from being used as a self-harming weapon. He might then be placed naked into a protective cell, where he must be observed by correctional staff. The razor the inmate possessed is considered contraband and he has now committed an infraction by having it in his possession. Committing an institutional infraction can have implications for parole hearings, inmate worker positions, and other privileges. It is likely the inmate will feel punished for expressing his suicidal ideation and plan to the psychologist and he might be reluctant or unwilling to report any future plans or wishes to harm himself. Additionally, feeling degraded and punished will do little to alleviate depression, hopelessness, or suicidal thoughts. When the environmental restraints to prevent suicide are lifted, the inmate might be less inclined to reach out for mental health services. Yet, the need for policies to protect a dense prison population, as well as ensure the security of the institution, is undeniable.

Correctional psychologists are typically understaffed and are required to perform a number of roles such as assessment and treatment, acting as research consultants for administrators, and training for correctional and medical staff. Specific assessment and treatment-related duties often include: psychological testing (e.g., differential diagnosis, malingering, cognitive deficits, etc.), inmate screenings, homicidal and suicidal risk assessments, crisis assessment and intervention, mental status examinations, competency to execute evaluations for death-row inmates, reviewing infractions committed by mentally ill inmates, individual therapy, group therapy, sex-offender treatment, substance abuse treatment, risk assessment for parole boards, and the like. Although general clinical skills relating to assessment and treatment are essential, an understanding of institutional dynamics, policies and procedures, and characteristics and research specifically relating to offender populations is also critical to competently providing mental health services in a prison or jail.

Due to a history of violence and institutional security policies, group rooms or rooms for counseling and assessment must be clearly visible by correctional and/or nursing staff to ensure the safety of clinicians. Some institutions provide body alarms for mental health professionals to wear. Although the clinician wants to create a therapeutic alliance for individual or group therapy, safety must be paramount.

The level of confidentiality in a correctional institution can be quite different from the community, especially since inmates have much less privacy. Prisoners must be clear on the limits of confidentiality inherent in a correctional or forensic setting, where often the protection of society or other individuals supersedes the individual. In cases where a psychologist is called in to assess an inmate who is engaging in bizarre or self-injurious behavior, a member of the correctional staff is typically present. Some psychologists conduct a psychological evaluation in the Administrative Segregation (AdSeg) or the Security Housing Unit (SHU) with prisoners who have been aggressive toward staff or other inmates. Typically, the psychologist is required to wear a protective vest and if the inmate must be taken out of the individual cell, the prisoner is in ankle and wrist shackles with the correctional officer present throughout the evaluation for the safety of the psychologist.

Mental health professionals working in jails or prisons also regularly encounter antisocial personalities or very manipulative and potentially dangerous clients. They quickly learn that what is reported to them frequently cannot be accepted at face value. It is very common for correctional staff to become "cynical, sarcastic, or negative," and these attitudes are very "detrimental to staff morale and therapeutic relationships" (Carr et al., 1991, p. 84). These researchers suggested the following tips for interacting with manipulative patients or inmates (pp. 84–85):

1. Be firm, but not abusive.
2. Set limits.
3. Do not make promises you cannot keep.
4. Be clear about what you will and will not do.
5. For security reasons you cannot and therefore do not tell inmates everything or answer all their questions.
6. Distinguish between genuine and manipulative complaints using past history, evident gains, and personal experience.
7. Do not get into making deals. This puts patients in control.
8. Put the responsibility back on the patient.
9. Determine what is immediate and what can wait. Many patients will try to convince you that every concern they have is urgent and immediate.
10. Do not bend the rules unless it is a safety issue.
11. Get consultation. It is easy to be manipulated until you have some distance.
12. Try to determine the motive of the patient's behaviors and statements. Do not make assumptions.
13. Recognize that some patients are manipulative because it is the only way they know how to get their needs met. Try to educate them regarding more adaptive coping mechanisms.

Overall, Carr et al. (1991, p. 89) suggested to "set limits and maintain a firm, but compassionate approach to the patients." Correctional psychologists are charged with providing mental health services to a high-risk population with complicated treatment needs in a setting that is not conducive to rehabilitation. Appropriately trained correctional psychologists working with offender populations in jails and prisons are balancing ethical issues such as confidentiality, treatment, institutional security, and patient welfare.

CHAPTER 11

Juvenile Issues in Corrections

OVERVIEW

Juveniles break the law and find themselves punished because of it. On occasion, this punishment includes some form of incarceration. Psychologists, however, typically raise doubts about the efficacy of correctional punishment for adolescents and argue that juveniles who act delinquently are not criminals but, rather, are troubled youths. The field of juvenile corrections, then, examines whether criminal justice or mental health responses are best suited to the needs and interests of juveniles who engage in illicit conduct. In addition, the domain of juvenile corrections explores the impact of correctional remedies for children who break the law.

This chapter investigates five controversies in the juvenile correctional arena. The issues examined in the following pages represent some of the more hotly contested matters at the crossroads of juvenile justice, psychology, and corrections. While the reader is presented with a limited selection of topics to review and digest, the variety of issues considered demonstrates the breadth of the field and the need for experts trained in this subspecialty area. The five controversies explored include (1) juveniles in adult jails, (2) juveniles on death row, (3) juveniles in boot camps, (4) suicide among incarcerated youth, and (5) the incarceration of status offenders. Finally, the Practice Update section addresses issues psychologists face who work in corrections or other juvenile facilities.

Delinquent adolescents can and do find themselves in adult jails. What type of crimes do juveniles commit and how are they different from their adult counterparts? What psychological problems do children experience when placed in the adult jail system? What forms of (physical and sexual) violence do youths confront while in the adult system? Juveniles can be sentenced to death and a representative minority of convicted youths are awaiting execution. Does the age and/or mental state of the juvenile offender matter for purposes of sentencing determinations? What psychological difficulties do adolescents confront while awaiting execution? In response to the problems caused by adolescent delinquency, correctional experts have recently advocated juvenile boot camps that prepare youths to engage in productive, pro-social behavior. How do these facilities function? Do juvenile boot camps promote the aims of rehabilitation and treatment or the aims of retribution and punishment? What impact, if any, do juvenile boot camps have on recidivism? Some incarcerated boys and girls commit suicide. What are the links between juvenile delinquency and suicide? What are the links between juvenile incarceration and suicide? What psychological prevention and intervention strategies exist to address the phenomenon of suicide among incarcerated youths? Adolescents can be placed in correctional facilities for violating "status offenses." These offenses include such behaviors as running away from home, truancy from school, incorrigibility, and curfew infractions. Why do these behaviors subject youths to incarceration? What role, if any, does the mental health system play in responding to delinquent children? What mental health services, if any, are available for troubled youths?

The juvenile forensic arena of corrections shows us how the mental health and the criminal justice systems differentially respond to the problems posed by adolescent misconduct. Where the correctional community generally promotes retributive measures of justice (i.e., punishment), the psychological establishment typically advances rehabili- tative measures of justice (i.e., treatment). As the sections of this chapter reveal, there are a number of pressing issues affecting the lives of youths caught in the crossfire of "intervention politics." Thus, it is not surprising that forensic psychologists, cross-trained in the areas of corrections, adolescent delinquency, and psychology, are most especially competent to understand how the criminal justice and mental health systems *can* work in concert to meet the best interests of delinquent youths and society. Clearly, as the chapter implies, without such careful and thoughtful interventions developed and implemented by forensic psychological experts, we risk losing too many children to the devastation of crime and violence. This is a loss that our society cannot afford to absorb or sustain.

JUVENILES IN ADULT JAILS

Introduction

Thousands of children are placed in adult jails each year. The conditions in which these children are held, and the circumstances they encounter, pose serious threats to their physical and mental well-being. Children's advocates have long been aware of the dangers that children face in this environment, and their concerns have prompted litigation to end the incarceration of juveniles in adult jails. Despite many years of litigation to abolish the holding of children in adult facilities, approximately 40 states continue to do so, placing thousands of children in dangerous situations a year. Oftentimes, when juveniles are imprisoned with adults in an attempt to reform their behavior, they leave the jail even less equipped to deal with the outside world than before incarceration (Tomasevski, 1986).

There are numerous cases depicting specific problems of incarcerating juveniles in adult jails. Children are particularly vulnerable to suicide when confronted with the adult jail environment. The following example illustrates the problem of keeping children in isolation.

Kathy Robbins was a 15-year-old girl who was arrested for running away from home in 1984. She was taken to Glenn County Jail in California, where she was strip-searched and placed in a small dark cell with a solid steel door. She was held in virtual isolation for 4 days until her hearing date. At her hearing, she begged the judge to send her home.

The court ordered that her case be continued and that Kathy remain incarcerated in the jail until such time. That afternoon, Kathy committed suicide by hanging herself with a sheet from the guardrail of the top bunk. Disturbing information concerning Kathy Robbins was disclosed during the case of *Robbins v. Glenn County* (1986). Kathy had physical evidence of previous suicide attempts, yet no measures were taken in jail to supervise Kathy or ensure her safety. She was only allowed one brief visit with her mother and was not given any reading material that her mother had provided. Further, the jail staff had refused to take her phone messages from her mother. Most troubling in this case is the fact that space was available at a local group home while Kathy was incarcerated in the jail.

It should be noted that girls who are so traumatized by the experience of being held in an adult jails are not the only ones who resort to suicide. Every year there are cases of young boys who commit suicide while subjected to the conditions in adult jails. Oftentimes for boys, suicide follows their victimization in a rape assault by adult inmates. Whereas boys are subjected to rape victimization by adult prisoners, girls are often victims of rape by the jail staff, as can be seen from the following examples.

In *Doe v. Burwell*, a 15-year-old girl from Ohio had left home for 1 day without her parents' permission. In order to "teach her a lesson," the juvenile court judge ordered her to be incarcerated in the county jail for 5 days. During her 4th night in jail, she was raped by a deputy jailer.

A 14-year-old runaway girl was held in a county jail in Pennsylvania when she was raped by the deputy sheriff as well as by two male inmates. One of the inmates was a convicted murderer who was awaiting sentencing. The sheriff released the inmates in order for them to participate in the rape of the young girl (Chesney-Lind, 1988).

Violence in correctional settings is a common occurrence. When children are intermixed with adults, they become prime targets for such assaults as a result of their vulnerability. The following case illustration demonstrates this disturbing fact.

In *Yellen v. Ada County* (1985), a 15-year-old boy was incarcerated in an adult jail for failing to pay $73 in traffic fines. He was held for a 14-hour period during which time he was brutally tortured by other inmates and eventually beaten to death.

Literature Review

Examining the psychological and criminological literature provides us with a better understanding of the pervasive and severe problems encountered when incarcerating juveniles in adult jails. Soler (2002) noted the increased prosecution of juveniles as adults and the incarceration of juveniles in adult jails, despite a serious lack of mental health resources and services in the correctional system. In addition, state legislatures have increasingly reduced judges' discretion in sending particularly heinous juvenile offenders to adult court, mandating that all adolescents of a certain age accused of a certain crime be sentenced as adults and sent to adult jails (Beinart, 1999). The Coalition for Juvenile Justice advocated for increased access to mental health services designed specifically for the problems of incarcerated youth in their 2000 annual report (Thomas & Penn, 2002). The specific recommendations included the need for wraparound services, improved planning and coordination between agencies, and further research (Thomas & Penn, 2002).

Ziedenberg and Schiraldi (1998) reported that there is a scarcity of data on the rape, suicide, and assault rates of the 4,000 juveniles who are sent to adult prisons and the 65,000 adolescents who pass through adult jails each year. According to the Annual Survey of Jails in 1989, there were approximately 53,994 juveniles held in adult jails and the numbers are growing. Of particular concern was the fact that many of them were status offenders (runaways, truants, and children out of parental control). Only a small percentage of the children held in jails were charged with violent crimes (Soler, 1988). Murray (1983) reported that of the nearly half a million children in adult jails, only 14% of them had been charged with a serious offense such as homicide, rape, or burglary.

A lawsuit was filed against the City of Long Beach and the County of Los Angeles in *Baumgartner v. City of Long Beach* (1987) when a taxpayer was outraged that the cities incarcerated more than 4,000 juveniles each year in the Long Beach City Jail. Nearly 1,000 of the children had not been charged with an offense. Instead, these children were victims of abandonment, neglect, and abuse by their parents and, thus, were removed from their homes. While proper placements in foster or group homes were pending for these children, they remained locked up in jail with adult inmates. This environment further placed these abused children in the face of danger. Additionally, a nursery equipped with cribs and toys was located in the jail where infants were placed until such time as proper placements could be arranged for them (Soler, 1988; Steinhart, 1988). Another 1,000 of the youths were status offenders, while less than 10% were charged with violent offenses. All of the children were kept in dark cells behind bars.

The adult jail environment is not conducive to the detainment of juveniles (Godwin & Helms, 2002). Tomasevski (1986) presented the results from a comprehensive study conducted by the Defense for Children International in 1983, in an attempt to create awareness about the problem of detaining children in adult facilities. Children held in the adult facilities are subjected to circumstances, which are direct threats to their emotional and physical health. In order to "protect" children in such an environment, they are often separated from the adult inmate population. The result of this action is isolation, often resembling solitary confinement. Tomasevski's (1986) international study of children in adult prisons revealed that the United States displayed the most evidence of virtual solitary confinement.

When children are required to remain separate from adult prisoners by "sight and sound," they are oftentimes completely isolated from human contact. Adolescents are particularly vulnerable to depression and suicide when they are isolated and fearful. Further, the correctional officers are not trained to identify the signs of depression in adolescents, and, therefore, intervention frequently does not occur in time.

In the above case of Kathy Robbins, the depression that children suffer and the desperate measures they take when held in isolation are apparent. When children in jail are not isolated, they encounter severe problems of a different nature. Juveniles are particularly vulnerable to sexual and physical abuse by staff and adult inmates. Adolescents are abused more frequently and driven to desperation more quickly in correctional facilities (Ziedenberg & Schiraldi, 1998).

Females in jail are held under more restrictive conditions than males (Chesney-Lind & Shelden, 1992). Often, they are housed in a subsection of a male facility. For this reason, they are rarely granted equal opportunity for recreation, education, or work-release programs as their male counterparts (Mann, 1984). Women will often spend most, if not all, of their time inside their cell. This is difficult for adult women, but it is particularly trying for young girls. It is particularly dangerous for girls who have backgrounds involving sexual and physical abuse. The repeated trauma makes them especially susceptible to depression and even suicide (A. Browne & Finkelhor, 1986). A pilot study revealed that psychoeducational group intervention for incarcerated girls (aged 13–17 years old) may be effective in alleviating depression and trauma symptoms (Pomeroy, Green, & Kiam, 2001). Chesney-Lind and Shelden (1992) reported that girls in jail tend to be younger, commit less serious offenses (primarily status offenses), and, despite their less severe offenses, remain in custody for approximately the same length of time as their male counterparts.

Forensic Psychology and Policy Implications

The incarceration of children in adult jails is a social, political, and human rights problem (Atkinson & Young, 2002). Despite the litigation efforts to end the incarceration of children with adults, an estimated 27,000–50,000 juveniles are still held in adult facilities each year (L. S. Wrightsman, 1991). As efforts increase to curb the rate of juvenile crime, the special needs and rights of children must not be ignored. Adolescent detention facilities are especially equipped to address the special needs of youthful offenders. Specialized treatment programs are designed to offer juveniles an opportunity for rehabilitation. To hold youths in adult facilities is to deny them this opportunity, as well as to subject them to severe psychological distress, physical and sexual abuse, and an environment where they are influenced by career and violent offenders. Nevertheless, society apparently supports the stricter, more punitive approach to dealing with juvenile offenders. Tomasevski (1986) described the Canadian Adult Prisoners' association response regarding adult facilities as places that should not house children. Those youths who do not succumb to molestation or get hurt tend to become tougher than when they entered the facility; their young age and their exposure to adult facilities only ensures that they will return.

Suggestions for Future Research

There has not been a great deal of recent research conducted on juveniles incarcerated in adult jails. The long-term effects of such an environment on children need to be examined from a psychological as well as a criminological perspective. Specifically, follow-up studies on adolescents who have been held in adult facilities would provide useful information regarding their psychological functioning, as well as their subsequent criminal behavior. Further, such analyses could then be compared to youthful offenders who were held in juvenile facilities. This would provide a clear illustration of the ramifications of incarcerating juveniles with adults as opposed to other adolescents. Additionally, the exploration into alternative placements for juveniles needs to continue. Future research on the prevalence of mental illness among juvenile offenders is needed. Finally, future inquiries might entail an analysis surrounding the reasons why previous litigation has failed to effectively end the incarceration of juveniles in adults jails, despite cases as tragic as Kathy Robbins.

JUVENILES ON DEATH ROW

Introduction

Capital punishment has remained an unabated controversy for decades. The constitutionality of the death penalty, the cost of capital cases and executions, and the impact the death penalty has on deterring crime in our society have all been repeatedly questioned. This controversy is further complicated by the issue of sentencing juveniles to death. The United States is only one of a few nations to allow the execution of juvenile offenders. The other nations include Iran, Nigeria, Pakistan, Saudi Arabia, and Yemen (Blum, 2002). The United States is not only one of the six countries permitting adolescent capital punishment, it is the leading country. Fifty-eight juveniles in the United States were serving their sentences on death row as of March 1997 (Streib, 1998). Moreover, juveniles on death row typically exhibit neurological damage, psychoses, and have suffered severe physical and/or sexual abuse as younger children (Lewis et al., 1988). The following case illustrates the complexities involved when a juvenile faces capital punishment.

> James Terry Roach was executed on January 10, 1986, in South Carolina, the same state in which he was born. Terry was raised by an ill mother and a father who was absent most of the time. Terry suffered from mental retardation with an IQ near 70. He dropped out of school early, became involved with drugs, and was diagnosed with a personality disorder. When Terry was 16 years old, he lived in a home with unemployed antisocial people who were involved in extensive drug use. Due to Terry's limited mental capacities, he was easily influenced by others. When Terry was 17 years old, he was convinced by an older housemate to spend the day riding around in a car while drinking beer and using marijuana and PCP. The boys came upon a 17-year-old male with his 14-year-old girlfriend, both from prominent families in the community. On a signal from his friend, Terry fatally shot the male three times. The boys then took the girl to a secluded area where they repeatedly raped her. Terry's friend then shot and killed the girl and he later returned to mutilate her body.
>
> The community was outraged by the crimes, especially given the prominent status of the victims' families. The death penalty was sought and received for both Terry and his friend. It should be noted that Terry's court-appointed attorney was disbarred 2 years after his representation of the case for irregularities in his practice. However, his handling of Terry's case was deemed constitutionally adequate. Despite letters to the governor pleading for clemency from Mother Theresa and former President Carter, Terry's execution was carried out. Although Terry had reached the chronological age of 25 at the time of his execution, his mental age remained fixed at 12 (*Roach v. Aiken*, 1986).

Literature Review

The case of Terry Roach depicts both the gravity of crimes that are committed by the tragedy of executing an individual who only has the mental capacity of a 12-year-old boy. This case demonstrates the need to explore the sociological, criminological, and psychological dynamics of capital punishment for juvenile offenders. In March 1997, juveniles on death row constituted approximately 2% of that total population (Streib, 1998). All of these offenders were males who received death sentences for murder. Of these 58 juveniles, 49% were African American, 17% Latino, and 34% Caucasian. This is consistent with the high percentage of minority executions that are found in adult capital punishment cases as well. Moreover, 59% of the executed juvenile offenders were convicted of murdering a Caucasian adult. Since the 1970s, 221 juvenile offenders have received death sentences in the United States and 21 have been executed (Blum, 2002). Blum (2002) stated that greater than 80% of the juvenile death sentences since that time have either been reversed or commuted as compared to 40% of adult death sentences.

From a criminological stance, punishment for crime serves one of three primary purposes: deterrence, retribution, or rehabilitation. For obvious reasons, the death penalty cannot serve a rehabilitative function. However, rehabilitation is the premise of the juvenile justice system in the United States. Therefore, the basic assertion of the juvenile justice system (i.e., rehabilitation of juvenile offenders) is inherently incompatible with the death penalty.

In two separate decisions in the 1980s, the U.S. Supreme Court upheld the death penalty for crimes committed at the age of 16 or 17, but ruled that it was unconstitutional to impose the death penalty for crimes that were committed at age 15 or below (Blum, 2002). A study examining public opinion on the death penalty for juvenile and adult offenders found that 14% of the 535 individuals surveyed were willing to execute juveniles who were 15 years or younger at the time they committed the crime (B. L. Vogel & R. E. Vogel, 2003). There was less support for executing juveniles than adults and 28.2% of those surveyed strongly opposed the execution of juveniles, while 42.5% of the subjects that supported the use of the death penalty for juveniles would support life without parole as an alternative (B. L. Vogel & R. E. Vogel, 2003).

Capital punishment has been further examined in its relationship to deterrence of criminal activity. The Federal Bureau of Investigation Uniform Crime Reports indicated that since the death penalty was reinstated in 1976, the number of death-row inmates and executions has increased substantially. There has, however, been virtually no change in the commission rate of murders (FBI, 1997). Furthermore, comparisons between those states which utilize the death penalty and those that do not, reveal that the majority of death-penalty states have higher rates of murder. This finding supports those who oppose the death penalty because it shows how capital punishment fails to deter crime (FBI, 1997).

Particularly in the case of Terry Roach, it is highly unlikely that his execution will deter others like him. His attorney addressed the improbability of a deterrence effect, stating that Terry (and those with similar problems) did not have the ability to think more than a few hours in advance and could likely not even conceive of possibilities for his actions such as arrest or execution (Streib, 1987). This is consistent with developmental theory, which acknowledges that adolescents have a deficient understanding of mortality. This furthers the previous discussion on rehabilitation in the juvenile justice system. According to his attorney, Terry lacked the ability to think about the consequences of his actions. This is common among adolescents and certainly something to be expected from a mentally retarded adolescent.

The public outrage at Terry's sentence illustrates the general perception that the punishment did not fit the offender. Constitutional law focuses primarily on the fact that the death penalty for juvenile offenders is in violation of the Eighth Amendment. In 1976, the landmark Supreme Court case of *Gregg v. Georgia* held that the death penalty does not violate the Eighth Amendment to the Constitution. Although the essence of this case does not involve the age of the offender, the concern over an offender's age did emerge. In this ruling, the Court maintained that the jury needed to consider characteristics of the offender that might mitigate against a capital punishment ruling. Among such characteristics mentioned was the age of the offender.

Special consideration of the constitutionality of the death penalty for juveniles was addressed in *Eddings v. Oklahoma* (1982). This case involved a 16-year-old defendant who was potentially facing capital punishment. Regarding the age of the offender, the Court found that a person's youthfulness is worthy of consideration as a mitigating factor. In *Eddings,* the Supreme Court avoided making a determination on the constitutionality issue and sent the case back for re-sentencing; however, Justices Burger, Blackmun, Rehnquist, and White stated that there was no constitutional basis to bar the death penalty for the 16-year-old defendant. The Supreme Court continues to avoid ruling on the federal constitutionality of sentencing juveniles to death; rather, the legality of the death penalty for juveniles remains a determination for individual jurisdictions.

The June 6, 1989, decision in *Perry v. Lynaugh* explicitly allowed the continued execution of mentally retarded offenders. However, it was overturned 13 years later on June 20, 2002, with the *Atkins v. Virginia* decision (Weeks, 2003). The majority opinion held that the Eighth Amendment prohibited the continued execution of the mentally retarded because it constituted "cruel and unusual" punishment. This decision represented a significant shift in ideology from previous majority opinions.

Some speculate that such reversals could soon lead to the exclusion of all juveniles from capital punishment (Weeks, 2003).

It is interesting to note that these same juveniles sentenced to death are not legally old enough to vote, enter into a contract, marry, or sit on the juries like those who convict them (Streib, 1987). Perhaps for this reason, the age for sentencing juveniles to death in many states is 18. However, not all states hold age 18 as the threshold, and some states do not abide by a minimum age for capital punishment at all. In 1962, the death penalty existed in 41 states, in which the minimum age was 7 in 16 states, age 8 in 3 states, age 10 in 3 states, and ages 12–18 in 19 states (Streib, 1987). This has changed considerably over the past 3 decades. Currently, only 22 states allow capital punishment for crimes committed before the age of 18 (Blum, 2002). Four states have death penalty eligibility for those 17 and above, 11 states for 16 and above, and 7 states have no minimum age specified (Weeks, 2003). Virginia laws allowing capital punishment for minors might have been the precipitating factor in sending D.C. sniper suspects John Allen Muhammad, 41, and John Lee Malvo, 17, first to Virginia to face trial, despite the fact that the majority of their victims were shot in Maryland (Blum, 2002). In both the federal system and in Maryland, individuals must be at least 18 to face capital punishment, while Washington, D.C., has no death penalty (Blum, 2002).

From a psychological standpoint, it is important to assess the juveniles' perceptions and attitudes toward capital punishment and their death sentence. Streib (1987) reported that younger juveniles on death row experience greater fear as well as a strong sense of abandonment. Streib (1987) described such juveniles as exhibiting uncontrollable crying, severe depression, and "childlike pleas for rescue to a parent or authoritative adult" (p. 158). The previous case illustration of Terry Roach, the 17-year-old mentally retarded boy, demonstrates how the public viewed him as evil for his heinous crimes. A study conducted by Lewis et al. (1988) examined 14 juveniles on death row concerning their psychological characteristics and disorders. The researchers reported that the typical juvenile offender on death row had serious injuries to the central nervous system, exhibited psychotic symptoms, and had been physically and sexually abused.

A study evaluating the precursors to lethal violence found that when examining the social and family histories of 16 men sentenced to death in California, institutional failure had occurred in 15 cases, including 13 cases of severe physical or sexual abuse while in foster care or under state youth authority jurisdiction (Freedman & Hemenway, 2000). Schaefer and Hennessy (2001) reported that neuropathy, psychiatric illness, substance abuse, and child abuse might be found in greater proportions in executed capital offenders versus among other violent incarcerated offenders. Finally, recent studies question the developmental maturity of juveniles. Magnetic resonance imaging (MRI) studies have allowed scientists to postulate that the human brain may not be fully mature until a person reaches his or her mid-twenties (Tamber, 2003). The frontal lobe, which controls executive functioning tasks such as planning, inhibition, and abstraction is the last part to develop (Tamber, 2003).

Forensic Psychology and Policy Implications

The appropriateness of imposing the death penalty on juveniles was explored from a criminological, sociological, and psychological perspective. When combining views from experts representing the American Society of Criminology, the Academy of Criminal Justice Sciences, and the Law and Society Association, the death penalty has not proven itself to be a general deterrent to crime (Radelet & Akers, 1995). Therefore, the death penalty has not served its primary function in society. For this reason, policy analysts must question why children are executed, despite the research showing that the intended effects of the death penalty have failed. Moreover, if the juvenile justice system continues to maintain that rehabilitation is the most appropriate goal for youthful offenders, then the death penalty is obviously incompatible with such a goal. The Terry Roach case illustrates the need for special considerations in sentencing juveniles, particularly when capital punishment is involved. Terry's attorney stated that his client lacked the ability to think about the consequences of his actions. By killing such children, society abdicates its responsibility to teach appropriate ways to control behavior as well as the skills needed to think and understand consequences for one's conduct. Since the juvenile justice system prides itself on rehabilitation, it needs to consider, and explain to the public, why killing a child becomes the appropriate remedy when rehabilitation has not even been attempted.

Suggestions for Future Research

Few studies address the psychological impact of death row on juveniles. This knowledge is crucial in order to provide appropriate services to these children. Research also needs to explore what factors influence the jurors who decide to impose the death penalty upon youthful offenders. The law states that age could be considered as a possible mitigating factor in capital cases. The literature has not established when jurors accept age as a mitigating factor and when they do not. The majority of experts in the disciplines of criminology, sociology, and psychology oppose the death penalty for juveniles. However, research is sparse concerning the reasons for their opinion. In addition, we know little about the effects of sentencing a child to death for society. Investigators need to explore why the majority of the population favors the death penalty especially when new laws regulating its use in the case of juvenile offenders are not well developed.

JUVENILE BOOT CAMP

Introduction

Juvenile boot camp facilities have become an increasingly popular response to adolescent crime in the United States. Often referred to as shock incarceration, boot camps are based on the premise that instilling regimen and discipline in young offenders will decrease subsequent criminal behavior. Controversy exists as to whether recidivism reduction has actually been achieved with the implementation of boot camps throughout the United States. Some experts argue that the implementation of boot camp programs does nothing to change the environment from which the juvenile emerges, and, therefore, once the program has ended, the juvenile's return to the same environment perpetuates their engagement in criminal behavior. For this reason, it has been argued that boot-camp facilities do not curb long-term recidivism rates among juvenile offenders. The hypothetical case of Johnny illustrates a common trend among boot camp participants.

Johnny is a 16-year-old boy who was recently arrested for the first time. He was caught breaking into a house while under the influence of a controlled substance. Because this was Johnny's first offense, he was sentenced to the local juvenile boot camp which had recently been built in his small town. While at the boot camp, Johnny's day began at 5:00 a.m. and ended at 9:00 p.m. His 16-hour day consisted of rigorous calisthenics, strict discipline, difficult work, job training, and educational programs. Johnny became very comfortable with the routine and was a role-model to new recruits. After 90 days in the boot

(continued)

(*Continued*)

camp, Johnny was released to his parents. He would remain on probation for the next month, during which time he was not to leave his house except to go to school and meet with his probation officer.

Johnny's first night at home reminded him of what his life was like prior to boot camp. His parents were both intoxicated and began yelling at one another within the first hour Johnny was home. Johnny decided to tell his parents about his experience at boot camp and the changes he intended to make in his life. Johnny's father, irate at his son for interrupting, began to beat Johnny and tell him how worthless he was. The physical and verbal abuse lasted for one hour at which time the neighbors called the police for the disturbance. Johnny, afraid of the police seeing his bloody and bruised body, ran away. The next day Johnny was arrested for violating his probation.

Literature Review

A rapid growth of boot camps for adult offenders evolved in the United States in the 1980s. At the time, there were questions as to whether such programs would be appropriate for youthful offenders. The growing number of cases of troubled youth who die while participating in rigorous boot camp programs brings this question into sharp focus (Janofsky, 2001). The Office of Juvenile Justice and Delinquency Prevention (OJJDP) sought to explore whether adult boot camps could in fact be adapted to suit the needs of juveniles. The OJJDP funded a study in 1992 to examine three existing boot camp programs in order to determine the possible adaptations that would be required to make them suitable for juvenile offenders (Bourque et al., 1996). Throughout the 1990s, numerous juvenile boot camps have been developed as an alternative to traditional incarceration.

Boot camp facilities provide a militaristic regimen of strenuous physical conditioning and strict discipline. Specifically, boot camps are intended to provide a cost-effective means of dealing with delinquent youths, instill morality and ethics, strengthen academic achievement, and hold adolescents accountable for their actions while providing them with the tools necessary to prevent re-offense. It is questionable whether boot camps are in fact providing juveniles with the necessary tools to curb recidivism. As illustrated above in the case of Johnny, it might not be enough to simply provide these youths with the skills and then expect them to leave the boot camp and function appropriately in their natural environment.

Peterson (1996) reported that the pilot programs evaluated by the OJJDP revealed that there was no significant difference in recidivism between those in the boot camp programs and those in control programs. Similarly, in a study conducted by MacKenzie and Souryal (1994), an evaluation of boot camp programs in eight states revealed that such programs did not reduce recidivism rates for juvenile offenders in five of the eight states investigated. In the three states that did show lower recidivism rates for program participants, juveniles were provided intensive follow-up supervision (Reid-MacNevin, 1997).

A study examining the re-offense patterns of 162 youth transferred and sentenced to, adult court during 1999 through June of 2001 revealed that the youths receiving adult probation or boot camp services were 1.74 to 2.29 times more likely to re-offend than were youth receiving juvenile sanctions (Mason, Chapman, Chang, & Simons, 2003). A juvenile boot camp that was implemented in a public school setting was named Specialized Treatment and Rehabilitation (STAR). Although operated jointly by the school, the juvenile court, and the juvenile probation department, this program also demonstrated very little impact on recidivism (Trulson, Triplett, & Snell, 2001). The Acting Assistant Attorney General for Civil Rights in the state of Georgia noted that boot camps were not only ineffective, but can be harmful to some adolescents (Tyler, Darville, & Stalnaker, 2001).

After examining their meta-analysis, Lundman (1993) and Morash and Rucker (1990) reported that boot camp participants might actually have higher rates of recidivism than those who participate in traditional incarceration. It is difficult to properly determine whether this is due to the increased monitoring that boot camp graduates receive following their release, thereby increasing their chance for subsequent apprehension. However, supporters of boot camp facilities suggest that recidivism rates are not appropriate measures of a successful program (Osler, 1991). The literature suggests that boot camps are more costly than most other traditional options and they are much less effective than what the public perceives (Tyler et al., 2001). The OJJDP has reported that most boot camps run an average of 10 times the cost of a juvenile on probation (Tyler et al., 2001).

Several explanations have been offered describing why boot camps do not have a general effect on recidivism. From a criminological perspective, boot camps are theoretically based on deterrence theory. As noted by Reid-MacNevin (1997), "correctional research has shown time and again that deterrence-based criminal justice interventions do not work" (p. 156). This philosophy of deterrence has been repeatedly tested within the criminal justice system through such programs as Scared Straight. These programs assume that juvenile delinquents can be scared and intimidated into engaging in pro-social behavior leading to a respect for authority (Welch, 1997). Unfortunately, such programs have consistently reported unsuccessful deterrence effects. In 1992, Lipsey conducted a meta-analysis of 443 studies between 1950 and 1992. The study revealed that deterrence programs such as boot camps had negative effects on juvenile delinquents. Therefore, research has not only shown that boot camps do not lower the rate of re-offending by juveniles, but more importantly, that youths may be negatively affected by such initiatives.

From a psychological perspective, research has examined the image of masculinity, which is portrayed in boot camp programs. Morash and Rucker (1990) suggested that the confrontation and demanding nature of boot camps illustrated aggression and thus produce aggressive behavior among participants. This can be explained through social learning theory, which maintains that behavior is acquired through modeling the behavior of others. Such learning is particularly found among adolescents. Therefore, according to Morash and Rucker, the goal of teaching juveniles pro-social behavior is not being achieved in correctional boot camps. Trulson et al. (2001) postulated that boot camps were popular with the public and political leaders because they presented a strong appearance of being tough on juvenile crime. However, they note that boot camps are not reaching the goal of reducing juvenile crime.

As noted by Correia (1997), boot camps are implemented in an artificial environment and, therefore, any behavioral changes that are made by an offender will most likely not be reinforced when the juvenile returns to his or her natural environment in society. Learning theory maintains that it is essential for a behavior to be performed in one's natural environment for a permanent change in conduct to occur. Furthermore, Correia (1997) explained that criminal behavior was strongly influenced by environmental factors. Thus, if changes were not made to an individual's natural environment, any progress made while at boot camp was unlikely to continue post release. In the case of Johnny, it is unlikely that any of his progress made at boot camp will present and sustain itself in his home environment; within the first 2 hours of being released, Johnny's life returned to what it was prior to his participation in the boot camp program. The California Department of Corrections closed its boot camp in 1997, due to its expense and failure to reduce recidivism (Parenti, 2000).

According to Peterson (1996), differences between boot camp and control group participants did emerge in various arenas. Substantial improvement in academic achievement occurred among participants in the boot camp program. On average, youths increased their achievement scores in reading, language, spelling, and math by at least one academic grade level. Moreover, a significantly higher number of graduates from the boot camp program became employed while in aftercare. Aftercare is a dimension of the program that follows one's participation in the residential component of the boot camp and entails stringent monitoring for 6 to 9 months in the community.

In order to ensure maximum effectiveness of boot camp programs, target populations are selected for participation. The criteria initially established included juvenile males who did not have violent criminal histories. Most juveniles who were selected for such programs had been convicted of property or drug offenses. Therefore, the applicability of boot camps was purposefully limited. The OJJDP maintains that the boot camp focus remains within the rehabilitation model of the juvenile justice system. The lack of positive results emerging from recidivism studies begs the question: Are boot camps truly serving their rehabilitative function?

Forensic Psychology and Policy Implications

Millions of dollars are used in funding the development of new boot camp programs for juvenile offenders each year. With such an investment, it is imperative that programs provide the rehabilitation services they propose. Psychologists have acquired a great deal of knowledge in terms of the family environment and the psychological characteristics of the offender that lead to subsequent delinquency. Given this knowledge, it is apparent that boot camp programs do not fully address the complexity of the issues involved in juvenile criminality. The environment to which the adolescent will return post release from the boot camp is lacking in attention. Developmental theory shows us that children do not adapt well to drastic changes in their environment. This is exactly what occurs when a child does not receive any means of discipline in the home, aside from perhaps physical abuse (as in the case of Johnny), and then is placed in a militaristic, rigid environment for 90 days. When 3 months have elapsed, the child is once again placed in an unstructured environment and expected to maintain the regimen that he or she has "learned." According to behavioral theory, the behavior will not generalize to the natural environment because the ecological cues are completely different and the person's conduct is neither required nor reinforced. For these reasons, it appears that psychologists can provide a great deal of insight into the methods for improving existing boot camp programs; this would allow for the comprehensive impact of environmental influences on human behavior and child development. Furthermore, criminal justice research has illustrated for years that programs based on deterrence are not effective in reducing recidivism. With the vast amount of literature supporting this notion, policymakers should question why millions of dollars continue to be spent to build new boot camp facilities. Such programs have yet to prove they decrease juvenile recidivism. Indeed, at times, they have deleterious effects on adolescents.

Suggestions for Future Research

Outcome studies would provide a more thorough understanding of the lasting effects of boot camp placement on subsequent offending. Future research would do well to focus on which aspects of existing boot camp programs are working and which are not. In some instances, academic achievement increases among those who participate in boot camps. However, there are no studies examining the psychological well-being of the children when they enter as opposed to when they leave the program. Moreover, no studies exist assessing whether strict militaristic discipline has any negative psychological effects on children's self-esteem or self-worth. Finally, future research needs to explore potential program development including a family and community reunification component so that situations such as Johnny's can be better addressed.

SUICIDE AMONG INCARCERATED JUVENILES

Introduction

Suicide claims the lives of thousands of adolescents each year. Currently, suicide is the third leading cause of death among youths. Moreover, it is important to note that for every adolescent who completes suicide, hundreds of others attempt it. Among the youths at high risk for suicide are those who are incarcerated. The isolation, despair, guilt, and hopelessness felt by many incarcerated juveniles is portrayed through suicidal ideation, nonfatal self-injurious (parasuicidal) behavior, and, ultimately, the desperate act of taking one's own life. The research and clinical intervention concerning life-threatening behavior among incarcerated juveniles is relatively sparse. The link between delinquency and suicide, as well as between incarceration and suicide, has been clearly documented in the literature. However, currently there are no concentrated efforts to address this issue in terms of prevention or intervention measures. The following cases illustrate the gravity of the situation, depicting both a male and female juvenile who resorted to suicide while incarcerated.

> Within 1 year at Westchester County Jail in New York City, two juveniles committed suicide while incarcerated. Nancy Blumenthal was 17 years old when she hanged herself in her cell from her own bedsheet. She was being held in jail while she awaited trial for robbery charges. Her bail had been revoked. Nancy was placed on a suicide watch while she participated in a court-ordered psychiatric evaluation. Following the evaluation, she was placed in the psychiatric ward where she could be observed every 30 minutes. During the investigation of her suicide, it was discovered that Nancy had been taking the antidepressant Zoloft for 2 years prior to her incarceration. During her month in jail, however, she was taken off of the drug.
>
> Ivan Figueroa was another 17 year old who committed suicide in the same jail within 3 months of Nancy's death. Similar to Nancy, Ivan hanged himself in his jail cell. He had been in jail for 4 days and was awaiting trial for rape and assault charges. When he was first arrested, he too was placed on suicide watch. He was subsequently returned to the general inmate population and soon committed suicide (Anonymous, 1997).

Literature Review

Cases like Nancy's and Ivan's remind us that suicide among incarcerated juveniles exists, needs to be examined and, ultimately, prevented. Adolescent suicide in general has been a focal point of research over the past 2 decades. As a result of such close scrutiny, the mental health field is far better equipped to assess, treat, and prevent suicidal behavior than ever before. It appears, however, that examination of suicidal behavior occurring among incarcerated juveniles is a particular concern that has not received a great deal of research attention (Giraldi & Greenberg, 2002). Incarcerated adolescents have unique environmental, social, and interpersonal factors that render them especially susceptible to suicidal ideation and behavior. Yet, as the literature illustrates, this population has not been studied nor has it received the amount of clinical intervention for suicide as has the general adolescent population.

The alarming suicide rate among adolescents has resulted in considerable research regarding the incidence, prevalence, and causes of life-threatening behavior. According to the National Center for Health Statistics (1997), adolescent suicide has more than tripled in the past 3 decades. Some studies incorporate individuals ages 15–24 in their investigations of adolescent suicide. Padgitt (1997) stated that within this age group, there are approximately 10,000 reported teen suicides a year and estimates that there are between 100,000 and 200,000 adolescent suicide attempts annually. Further, others note that every 78 seconds an adolescent attempts suicide and every 90 seconds one succeeds (National Center for Health Statistics, 1996). Moreover, research repeatedly has shown that boys are far more likely than girls to complete suicide; however, there is little gender difference in terms of suicidal ideation.

Although there is an extensive literature regarding adolescent suicide, there is relatively little research conducted on suicide among adjudicated adolescents (Evans, Albers, Macari, & Mason, 1996). Within the existing literature, there are conflicting results regarding the prevalence of suicide among incarcerated juveniles. Some suggest that one reason for this might be due to the underreporting of such occurrences by detention facility officials (Flaherty, 1983). Flaherty noted that it is a sensitive and embarrassing issue for officials to discuss, particularly when suicides occur within their facilities. Therefore, many results are skewed in the direction of underestimating the incidence rate. A 1997 report on prison suicides by the British Prison Reform Trust found that while individuals aged 15 to 21 composed only 13% of the prison population, they represented 22% of all the suicide deaths (Ziedenberg & Schiraldi, 1998).

A distinction needs to be made between completed suicide and parasuicide. Completed suicide refers to the suicidal act resulting in an individual's death, whereas parasuicide refers to nonfatal intentional self-harm. Research has shown that younger inmates are more vulnerable to parasuicide (Ivanoff, Jang, & Smyth, 1996). Others suggest that an increase in the incidence of parasuicide among younger inmates may be attributed to impulsivity (G. L. Brown, Linnoila, & Goodwin, 1992). One study reported that in a sample of 11,000 juveniles in detention facilities, 18,000 acts of attempted suicide, suicidal gestures, or self-mutilation occurred within the institution.

Research that examined 81 adolescents (aged 13–16) in a short-term juvenile facility and a matched group of 81 adolescent psychiatric inpatients compared the correlates of suicide risk between these two high-risk groups (Sanislow, Grilo, Fehon, Dwain, Axelrod, & McGlashan, 2003). The adolescents in both groups reported similar levels of distress on measures of suicide risk, depression, impulsivity, and drug abuse. After controlling for depression, impulsivity and drug abuse remained significantly associated with suicide risk for the juvenile detention group only (Sanislow et al., 2003).

Previous research has linked delinquency to physical and sexual abuse (Albers & Evans, 1994; De Wilde, Kienhorst, Diekstra, & Wolters, 1992). More specifically, studies have reported that incarcerated juveniles are at an increased risk for suicide due to their high incidence of substance abuse as well as physical and sexual abuse (A. O. Battle, M. V. Battle, & Tolley, 1993). In a study conducted by Evans et al. (1996), no difference was found between gang and nongang members in terms of reported physical abuse; however, nongang members reported higher levels of suicidal ideation. In this same study, gang members who had a history of sexual abuse had higher levels of suicidal ideation than their nongang counterparts.

Contrary to the previously mentioned research, results have emerged which conclude that incarcerated juveniles are at less risk for suicide. Flaherty (1983) reported that youths in juvenile detention facilities committed suicide at a lower rate than adolescents in the general population. However, this study also reported that juveniles detained in adult jails were at a far greater risk for completing suicide. Flaherty found that 17 of the 21 suicides were committed by youths who were held in adult jails in complete isolation. This was clearly the situation in the previous case illustration of Kathy Robbins. As demonstrated by this section's case examples, the most common means of committing suicide among incarcerated juveniles is hanging.

A recent study examined the lifetime history of suicide attempts in incarcerated youths ($N = 289$ adolescents) and psychological factors related to suicidal and self-mutilative behaviors during incarceration (Penn, Esposito, Schaeffer, Fritz, & Spirito, 2003). Of the 289 adolescents, 12.4% reported a prior suicide attempt and 60% of the attempts were made using violent methods. The results of the study suggested that incarcerated juveniles have higher rates of suicide attempts with more violent methods than juveniles in the general population (Penn et al., 2003).

Several characteristics distinguish young offender suicides from the general population of inmate suicides. A study by Liebling (1993) revealed that youthful inmates were more likely to commit suicide after their conviction, but prior to their sentencing. Most suicides among the young inmates occurred during the first month of custody. Additionally, Liebling concluded that young inmates who committed suicide were less likely to have ever received psychiatric treatment.

Previous research found that Caucasian delinquents made more serious and lethal suicide attempts than African American delinquents or delinquents of mixed ethnicity (Alessi, McManus, Brickman, & Grapentine, 1984). Alessi et al. further reported that offenders diagnosed with major affective disorders or borderline personality disorders attempted suicide at a much greater rate. These results are consistent with suicidal behavior among individuals suffering from these disorders in the general population. Wool and Dooley (1987) reported the explanations given by younger inmates who attempted suicide while in custody. The most frequent explanations included the following: a close relationship was threatened, a visit did not take place, and, the prison environment was intolerable. When adolescent needs are not fulfilled, many youths enter a state of emotional crisis. Sometimes this manifests itself as a cry for help or self-injury, other times the child literally escapes from the crisis through the desperate act of suicide.

Forensic Psychology and Policy Implications

Juvenile suicide is a tragic end to a young life. Psychologists have studied the predictors and the reasons for suicide for many years. Specific studies have been conducted on adolescent suicide and how it differs from its adult counterpart, as well as on subgroups of adolescents who are at a greater risk for suicide. The research clearly draws a link between delinquency and suicide as well as incarceration and suicide. It should be of no surprise that a combination of delinquency and incarceration places a youth at high risk for suicidal ideation and behavior. In the cases of Nancy and Ivan, two suicides committed within 3 months of one another should alert correctional facilities, mental health agencies, and the public to the severity of suicidal behavior among incarcerated juveniles.

Within the field of psychology there is an increased awareness of suicide prevention strategies and an ability to implement crisis intervention with suicidal individuals (Giraid et al., 2002). If incarcerated youths are at such a high risk for suicide, why is so little being done to prevent such occurrences? Relying on the results of empirical studies, we find that specific youths can be identified who are particularly vulnerable. We also know that adolescents who commit suicide while incarcerated often do so within the first month of custody. Thus, in order to provide the necessary preventative measures, these individuals need to be identified and given counseling and crisis intervention as soon as they arrive in custody. When dealing with a human life and, in particular, a young vulnerable life, the focus must be on addressing the problem of suicidality before it occurs. Society places a strong emphasis on research and intervention with suicidal individuals, yet virtually ignores the issue of suicide among incarcerated adolescents. This suggests that some believe that the lost life of an incarcerated youth does not equal that of a nonincarcerated youth. As long as this bias exists, so too will the problem of suicide among incarcerated adolescents.

Suggestions for Future Research

Over the past 3 decades, research on adolescent suicide in the general population has expanded; however, relatively scant research exists which examines suicidal ideation and behavior among incarcerated adolescents. Suicide prevention programs need to be designed and implemented in juvenile detention facilities. Moreover, these programs need to be empirically studied in order to determine the proper method of identifying those individuals in need, as well as the location and time for the prevention program to be most beneficial. Incarcerated settings for juveniles that have crisis intervention and regular psychological services need to be compared with those that do not offer such assistance. Furthermore, studying the similarities and differences among adolescents who attempt or commit suicide within an incarceration facility, with those who engage in suicidal behavior in the community would help provide a more thorough understanding of what treatment needs best serve this vulnerable population.

INCARCERATION OF STATUS OFFENDERS

Introduction

According to the FBI's 1994 Uniform Crime Report, approximately 237,000 juveniles under the age of 18 were arrested for status offenses (Godwin & Helms, 2002). A status offense is any offense that is committed by a juvenile that would not constitute an offense if committed by an adult. Examples of such offenses include running away from home, curfew violation, truancy from school, and out of parental control. In 1994, approximately 152,000 children were arrested for running away from home. With such a large number of juveniles engaging in this behavior, the question arises: Are these children better dealt with through the juvenile justice system or by mental health professionals? Historically, the criminal justice system has dealt with status offenders in the same manner in which other juvenile offenders have been handled. For this reason, juveniles who run away from home are oftentimes incarcerated in the same secure detention facilities as juveniles who commit more serious and violent crimes. However, by definition, status offenders have no victims, and in fact their crimes would not even be illegal except by a function of the individual's age. Many in the mental health profession believe that a more appropriate method of dealing with status offenders is to provide psychological services to the juvenile, and to his or her family, as opposed to incarceration. Congress has enacted laws which require the deinstitutionalization of status offenders; however, despite such movements, thousands of juveniles continue to be incarcerated for status offenses.

Johnny is 13 years old and currently lives with a foster family. He was 8 years old when his parents were divorced, at which time he decided to reside with his mother. When Johnny was 10, his mother remarried, and he suddenly had a stepfather, Derek. Within the first 2 months of living in the same house, Derek began entering Johnny's room in the middle of the night. Derek sodomized and forced Johnny to orally copulate him an average of three times a week for the next 3 years. After years of enduring such abuse, Johnny ran away from home. Johnny was arrested not even 1 mile away from his home, where he was sitting behind a vacant store. Johnny spent 2 weeks in juvenile hall. Like most children who are sexually abused, Johnny was too frightened to tell anyone about the molestation. Upon release from juvenile hall, Johnny was returned home to his mother and stepfather. One week after Johnny returned home, Derek began the molestations again. Johnny ran away from home two more times before he disclosed the abuse. On each occasion, he was arrested and incarcerated in juvenile hall. Following his report of the molestation, a medical exam was conducted which confirmed Johnny's story. Johnny was removed from his home and placed in foster care, where he remains today.

Literature Review

Johnny's case illustrates the complex psychological dynamics that are involved in the lives of many status offenders. The critical issue for forensic psychologists to address is whether juveniles like Johnny are more appropriately dealt with as delinquents or victims of child abuse. With juvenile crime occurring at an alarming rate in the United States, the legislature and the public are increasingly more inclined to deliver stiffer sentences to juvenile offenders. However, perhaps it is wholly inappropriate to apply a blanket approach to the punishment of adolescent offenders.

The literature regarding the incarceration of status offenders is extremely scant. The research in this area was conducted primarily in the 1980s. Gary Melton spoke on behalf of the American Psychological Association in 1991, during which time he stated "a search of the PsychLit database failed to uncover a single article on status offenses or status offenders published after 1988" (Melton, Petrila, Poythress, & Slobogin, 1997, p. 438). Melton suggested that the real issue at hand is a lack of services available to families and troubled youths. He concluded his testimony by suggesting that petitions to incarcerate status offenders "are clear exemplars of blaming the victim — subjecting a child who already may have a traumatic history to a quasi-punitive process because of a lack of adequate services" (Melton et al., 1997, p. 439).

Thus, given the dearth of recent research, this review of the literature relies on somewhat dated material. An historical analysis of status offenders reveals that around 1960, New York and California amended their statutes concerning juvenile delinquents in order to differentiate between delinquents and status offenders (Zatz, 1982). At that time it was acknowledged that status offenders were more in need of community-based programs designed to address psychological issues; however, such programs were not established. In 1974, the Juvenile Justice and Delinquency Prevention (JJDP) Act further addressed the issue of dealing with status offenders in the juvenile justice system. According to the JJDP Act, states were not allowed to incarcerate status offenders in secure juvenile detention facilities. Yet, the Illinois courts strongly supported the incarceration of status offenders as evidenced by the decision in *People v. Presley* (1974). In this decision the court concluded that due to *parens patriae*, the state has the authority to incarcerate children who run away from home. It was not until 1992, with the amendments to the JJDP Act, that status offenders were removed from juvenile court jurisdiction altogether. It should be noted that now, 30 years after the JJDP Act was passed, approximately 27% of status offenders continue to be held in secure detention facilities (Godwin & Helms, 2002; Krisberg & DeComo, 1993).

Chesney-Lind (1988) stated in a paper presented at the Annual Meeting of the American Society of Criminology, that the existence of status offenses poses a distinct threat to young women. She reported that girls charged with status offenses are usually treated more harshly than male status offenders or other types of female offenders. Research suggests that urban African American adolescent girls who engage in early sexual activity and those who become pregnant are more likely to be using substances and engaging in status offenses (Lanct & Smith, 2001). Another study found that adolescent males (aged 13–15), who live in single-parent homes, reported greater incidents of status offenses, property crime, and person crime (Anderson, 2002).

In addition to the psychological and criminological debate regarding the treatment of status offenders, is the economic controversy. McIntyre (1996) studied the number of status-offender petitions that were filed over the past 20 years. She reported that there was a 54% decline in status petitions from 1979 to 1995, and that such a reduction saved the American taxpayers approximately 6 million dollars. However, although the decrease in status-offender petitions is cost-effective, it remains questionable as to whether the needs of these juveniles are being addressed. Among those who fought for a distinction between status offenders and delinquents, it was hoped that specific treatment programs would be developed in order to better meet the psychological needs of status offenders (Zatz, 1982). Linney (1982) examined the alternatives to incarceration that had been offered for status offenders. In terms of counseling services availed to these offenders, Linney found that all the programs reported that counseling was available to the juveniles. Upon closer examination, however, the definition and frequency of counseling varied across programs. For instance, in certain programs, any time a social worker spoke with a juvenile, "counseling" took place. Furthermore, when individual counseling was provided, Linney determined that it centered around helping the juvenile adjust to the residential placement, and once this was accomplished, the counseling ceased. It is clear from Linney's study that although community-based programs do exist for status offenders as alternatives to incarceration, they are extremely lacking in terms of the treatment they provide.

Eighty-four percent of the facilities examined in Linney's (1982) study reported the juveniles' families as being the primary causal factor in the commission of status offenses. Similarly, as noted by Melton et al. (1997), the behaviors of status offenders are oftentimes attributable to psychological dysfunction within their families. A study on the later effects of child sexual abuse indicated that in addition to a number of other emotional difficulties, these individuals experienced more verbal altercations with their parent(s), running away from home, multiple sexual partners, and sexual activity at an earlier age (P. Johnson, 2001). With this in mind, it is necessary to treat juveniles as troubled youths in need of psychological services.

As seen in the above case illustration of Johnny, his running away was clearly a function of the abuse that he suffered at home as opposed to the development of a criminal lifestyle. However, if individuals such as Johnny continue to be placed among violent juvenile offenders in detention facilities, it is likely that they will be influenced by the delinquent behavior of their peers. Adolescence is a time when individuals are highly impressionable, and the influences of those with whom juveniles come into contact play a critical role in the shaping of their future behavior (Chance, 1988). Therefore, in addition to the specific psychological needs of status offenders, the removal of these delinquents from juvenile detention facilities is offered as a means to curb their recidivism. The current trend, however, is either to incarcerate the individual, despite laws which prohibit such action, or to place the juvenile in a residential program in which treatment supposedly exists, although the nature and extent of the treatment is extremely deficient.

Forensic Psychology and Policy Implications

There are a number of policy implications regarding the incarceration and handling of status offenders. It is clear that the Juvenile Justice and Delinquency Prevention Act established in 1974 sought to end the incarceration of status offenders in detention facilities. Moreover, the JJDP Act encouraged viewing status offenders and delinquents separately, in that status offenders were troubled youths in need of special services, while delinquents were those in need of punishment for committing criminal behaviors. It is particularly telling that, although a law exists which mandates the deinstitutionalization of status offenders from secure detention facilities, approximately one in four status offenders remains incarcerated. The fact that the federal government's legislation is not being carried out illustrates that significant policy reforms are needed. The purpose of deinstitutionalizing status offenders was to provide the special psychological services these individual youths needed. Research has shown that even when deinstitutionalization is successfully implemented, the treatment services are severely lacking. Thus, it appears that the JJDP Act has not been successful in accomplishing its desired goals for status offenders.

Suggestions for Future Research

Recent psychological and criminological literature in the area of status offenders, and specifically regarding the incarceration of status offenders, is relatively sparse. Studies need to be conducted comparing status offenders who receive treatment with those who do not. A shared goal among those who oppose and those who support the incarceration of status offenders is the reduction of future offenses. With this in mind, comparative studies are essential to making a determination about what action best curbs recidivism. In a similar fashion, those status offenders who have been incarcerated need to be evaluated against those who have not, particularly in terms of subsequent commission of offenses. Recidivism among status offenders needs to be explored in a twofold manner. Those who re-offend with subsequent status offenses need to be compared to those who subsequently commit more serious, or violent, offenses.

An additional area of research pertains to the families of status offenders. Most individuals within the mental health and criminal justice fields who come into contact with status offenders agree that dysfunctional families play a central role in juveniles' behaviors. It therefore becomes crucial to develop and implement comprehensive programs designed to address the specific needs of a particular dysfunctional family. Once these programs are in place, it will then be possible to compare the recidivism rates of those juveniles who participate in such programs with those who receive other sentences.

Practice Update Section: Issues in Juvenile Corrections

Early intervention and prevention is clearly the best approach for reducing juvenile crime from status offenses to capital murder. However, forensic/correctional psychologists are being asked to evaluate and treat increasingly violent and mentally ill juveniles. More often than not, these children have slipped through the cracks or the services indicated were just not available. In general, children in the juvenile court system do not have an enforceable right to treatment and are only entitled to whatever services are available in their jurisdiction (Haller, 2000). Frequently, psychologists are asked to evaluate a juvenile and make recommendations regarding their disposition to their caseworker, probation officer, and/or other participants in the juvenile court system. Clinicians are encouraged by referring agencies to be realistic in their recommendations based on what services can be obtained in the community. With little money or resources being provided for intervention or mental health programs for delinquent or troubled youth, the options are often limited. Unfortunately, what is offered often falls short of what is recommended. There is a growing need for mental health services that involve not only the children, but their families and community resources as well. The Department of Justice, Office of Juvenile Justice and Delinquency Prevention has identified additional research on the prevalence of mental disorders in juvenile offenders, the development of mental health screening assessment protocols, and improved mental health services as the three main factors in addressing the mental health needs of delinquent youth (Thomas & Penn, 2002).

The mentally ill and often dually diagnosed juvenile offenders present unique issues for follow-up. More often than not, symptoms of mental illness in children and adolescents will manifest behaviorally, as compared to their adult counterparts. For example, depression in children and adolescents is frequently exhibited through irritability and anger, rather than the depressed mood more typically associated with depression in adults (American Psychiatric Association, 1994). Additionally, there are a number of behavioral disorders associated with childhood and adolescence. As previously discussed, juveniles who act out as a result of emotional disturbance may be charged with status offenses for running away, truancy, or more serious charges, based on their actions. Psychologists may be asked to evaluate juveniles whose crimes are a cry for help, as a result of emotional and family problems.

Suicide and parasuicidal behaviors are a serious concern in jail and prison settings, particularly with juveniles. Psychologists are typically involved in the screening, prevention, and assessment of risk for these behaviors. When juvenile offenders are incarcerated in adult jails or prisons, the screening and follow-up on these issues are even more critical. In addition to other factors, juvenile offenders are at a far greater risk for being sexually assaulted or other types of violent victimization. The Juvenile Suicide Assessment (JSA) is an instrument for the assessment and management of suicide risk with incarcerated juveniles. This instrument can help mental health professionals identify both factors that increase and decrease an incarcerated juvenile's risk for suicide (Gallousis & Francek, 2002).

There are a growing number violent crimes perpetrated by juveniles, where a complete lack of empathy for victims, remorse, or responsibility for ones own actions is apparent. This is a disturbing trend that will create an ever-increasing demand for adolescent violence risk assessments. A number of highly publicized school shootings and the D. C. sniper case have demonstrated the devastation that an extremely violent youth can create. Unfortunately, most juvenile offenders suffer the gravest of consequences for their exceedingly rare, more psychopathic behavior, not unlike their adult counterparts who also engage in this type of extreme and lethal violence.

CHAPTER 12

Family/Community Issues in Corrections/Correctional Psychology

OVERVIEW

Psychologists are called upon to address a myriad of problems that directly affect the adult prison populations. In addition, psychologists are relied upon to assess other correctional dilemmas regarding the intellectual, personality, and behavioral characteristics of offenders and those who work in the institutions, as well as to interpret society's responses to particular offender groups and general correctional practices. This is the domain of family and community-oriented corrections. Unlike its adult and juvenile counterparts, the family/community corrections field explores many of the social variables that inform noncriminal inmate behavior, ongoing prison practices, and the public's responses to both.

This chapter includes six topical themes, which represent the breadth of the field affecting correctional/forensic psychology. It is not possible to present a complete and thorough cataloging of issues and/or controversies contained in this subspecialty area. However, those subjects examined in the pages that follow include some of the more interesting and pressing concerns at the interface of corrections, psychology, and civil justice. Topics investigated include (1) psychological stress and correctional work, (2) intellectually disabled prisoners, (3) society's response to sex offenders, (4) women working in male prisons, (5) "make-believe" families, and (6) women in prison and mother–child separation.

The conditions under which correctional work occurs are emotionally and physically demanding. Symptoms of chronic fatigue, depression, cynicism, burnout, and the like are not uncommon for many correctional officers. What is the psychological impact of work-related stress for correctional personnel? How do employees cope with it, and what prevention and intervention programs exist to curb the excesses of stress? A representative minority of prisoners are mentally retarded. How are the rehabilitative and retributive philosophies of corrections managed for prisoners with intellectual disabilities? What special services and/or programs exist for mentally retarded inmates? How are prisoners screened and assessed for mental retardation, and what role exists for correctional psychologists to assist in the evaluation process? A number of societal responses have been proposed to address the problems posed by convicted sex offenders. Some of these include chemical castration, community notification, civil commitment, and formalized registration. How, if at all, do these interventions prevent future victimization? What is the relationship between these societal responses and recidivism? Do proposals such as these violate the constitutional rights of sex offenders who have already paid their debt to society? Increasingly, women correctional officers work in male prisons. How are such officers perceived by their male correctional officer counterparts? How do women correctional officers (COs) cope with the hostility, sexual harassment, and discrimination they experience on the job? How do female COs and correctional psychologists cope with the stress of working in male prisons?

People have a fundamental need to express intimacy and affection. The same is true for persons in prison, especially women. One response to this need is to create make-believe families. What emotional needs do surrogate or "play" families fill for women in prison? What specific roles do prisoners assume in these kinship systems? How do pseudofamilies operate in the correctional milieu? Women in prisons represent a special group of offender. Who are they demographically? Many female prisoners are mothers. To what extent do mothers in prison feel shame, guilt, and grief as a result of their (criminal) life choices? How do they cope with the grief that comes from the loss of parental bonding and parenting? What are the emotional and health-care consequences to both mothers and their children when the parent is incarcerated? How do children (and mothers) deal with the anxiety of separation? How can correctional/forensic psychologists help ease the pain of separation caused by criminal confinement? What services exist (i.e., support groups) to address these psychological problems? What advocacy work is being done to improve the standards for prison visitation by family members?

At the intersection of corrections, psychology, and family studies are an array of issues and controversies affecting the lives of persons incarcerated and their loved ones. Correctional/forensic psychologists are uniquely trained to explore these dynamic issues and assist prison systems in meeting the challenges posed by such constituencies. The domain of community/ family corrections moves the psychologist into a more social arena in which to investigate noncriminal behavior, attitudes, beliefs, and so on pertaining to prisoners, correctional personnel, institutional practices, and the public's responses to them. As seen in this chapter, little is known about the family/ community domain of correctional/forensic psychology. Future investigators would do well to engage in research along these and similar lines of inquiry as it would substantially advance our knowledge of prisoners, children of inmates, correctional workers, and society's understanding of offender behavior.

PSYCHOLOGICAL STRESS AND CORRECTIONAL WORK

Introduction

The *American Heritage Dictionary* defines stress as "a mentally or emotionally disruptive or disquieting influence" (Berube, 1982, p. 1205). This definition does not fully describe the types of stress that COs experience on a day-to-day basis, as they are under a continual threat of physical danger. They experience hostility from the inmates and often the public. They respond to political changes in attitudes toward the role of institutional corrections. They work daily in a tedious and unrewarding environment. Finally, they completely depend on their coworkers to provide for their safety (Finn, 1998; Grossi & Berg, 1991). Working in such an atmosphere every day can lead to some very debilitating consequences, including depression, chronic fatigue, physical illness, and even posttraumatic stress disorder (PTSD). The following illustration describes a stressful situation that officers often must face.

> The day began like any other at the prison. The day staff came in and were briefed on any problems or incidents of which they needed to be aware, and then they began their duties of moving the prisoners through their daily routines. After a few hours, when the work was becoming tedious and the guards began to relax, three inmates attacked a guard walking by and managed to get his gun away from him. They used him as a hostage and demanded that
>
> *(continued)*

(Continued)
the other guards give up their guns. The officers had to comply to avoid having their coworker killed. The inmates were able to gain control of the prison unit by holding approximately 30 employees hostage. The guards that were able to avoid becoming hostages locked themselves in the administrative offices but could not escape from the prison. This highly intense and stressful situation lasted for over 2 hours with the officers under constant fear for their lives. The incident ended without any serious injuries but with a great deal of property damage (Bergmann & Queen, 1987). The officers who had to endure this hostage situation were exposed to a type of stress that most people will never experience in their lifetime. Even the officers that were not held hostage felt the effects of the stress because they had to return to work in this environment wondering if such an incident might happen again.

Literature Review

Although the above illustration is a severe example, it represents the type of stressful situation that COs are potentially faced with and must learn to accept as part of their job. Research shows that most COs do feel this stress. In a study that asked officers to rate their levels of day-to-day job-related stress, only 26.2% reported feeling low levels of stress. Most of the officers experienced medium to high levels of stress every day, with 10.0% reporting very high levels of work stress (Robinson, 1992). Generally, the type of stress that officers experience is related to the work that they do, that is, guarding the inmates. With overcrowded prisons, officers have a more difficult time controlling inmates, especially when the inmates know that they will be there for a long time and do not fear punishment (Finn, 1998; Martinez, 1997). The above case illustration shows how it is possible for prisoners to become uncontrollable just by outnumbering the guards. Robinson (1992) reported that the most frequently cited source of stress by COs is related to security. Twenty-seven percent of the officers reported a fear of offenders and a lack of security procedures. Their second and third most reported sources of stress were a lack of communication in the prison and a heavy workload. In addition, Robinson determined that officers' job commitment was affected by stress. He found that officers who reported higher levels of work-related stress had lower levels of commitment to their jobs.

Lambert, Hogan, and Barton (2002) stated that correctional staff job stress has grown dramatically due to increasing prison populations and differing ideologies. These researchers found that role ambiguity and work creating family conflict decreased overall job satisfaction. Another study examined CO stress and burnout by surveying 250 COs from a southwestern state (Morgan, Van Haveren, & Pearson, 2002). Results indicated that older and more educated COs experienced a greater sense of personal accomplishment, whereas younger and less experienced officers experienced greater depersonalization and emotional exhaustion, as well as decreased levels of personal accomplishment.

A recent literature review examined job stress and burnout of COs (Schaufeli & Peeters, 2000). The empirical literature identified the most notable stressors to include role problems, work overload, demanding social contacts (with inmates, coworkers, and supervisors), and poor social status. Finn (1998) described several factors that have contributed to increased CO stress to include inmate overcrowding, increased inmate assaults against staff, longer inmate sentences resulting in less fear of punishment, and more prison gangs. Furthermore, Finn (1998) identified organizational and work-related categories of stressors, as well as stressors from outside of the system. The four most common organizational conditions that most frequently cause stress are understaffing, overtime, shift work, and supervisor demands. Role conflict and role ambiguity were less consistent organizational stressors. Research indicates that the most common work–related stressors include threat of inmate violence, actual inmate violence, inmate demands and attempts at manipulation, and problems with coworkers (Finn, 1998). Finally, stress from outside the criminal justice system most commonly included a poor public image or negative societal stereotypes of COs and low pay. Finn (1998) found that the effects of CO stress can include impaired physical health from heart disease to eating disorders, excessive use of sick time, burnout, high staff turnover, reduced safety (e.g., sloppy searches, increased use of force), early retirement, and impaired family life (e.g., displacing aggression, isolating).

Martinez (1997) identified two different types of stress that COs experience in the course of their duties. The first was described in the previous case illustration. This was an episodic stressor where a traumatic incident happened to, or was witnessed by, a guard. The other type of discomfort is referred to as chronic stress. This is stress that officers encounter every day. It is the routine of doing the same thing over and over. This can be very damaging psychologically if the officers do not have the appropriate abilities to deal with it. It may even lead to a psychological disability. For example, in the case of *Fasanaro v. County of Rockland* (1995), the petitioner was a CO who began to suffer from a stress–related disability. The doctor who evaluated him indicated that the pressures from his job had become too much for him and recommended that the officer take a leave of absence. This case arose because the CO was denied disability benefits. The court ruled in favor of the CO and stated that if stress exists at work, then any stress–related anxiety disorders and disabilities can be causally related to the job and the employee should be allowed to collect worker's compensation.

A stress–related anxiety disorder is just one possible consequence for COs. A more serious consequence may be suicide. Kamerman (1995) found that speaking about CO suicide is taboo. After examining New York City statistics for a 5-year period, he reported that CO suicides were at least as great a problem as police suicides, and that the number of suicides were most likely greater than what was actually reported. In little over a year, a correctional facility in New York had three guards commit suicide. Kamerman (1995) proposed that the overcrowded prisons and the building of new facilities without the necessary funding for additional COs increased the pressures faced by these personnel. Kamerman (1995) further indicated that the lack of research on officer suicides reflects the public's diminished concern for the stress that correctional guards confront. However, clearly, the effects will continue to manifest themselves in extreme ways such as mental disability and suicide.

The traumatic events occasionally experienced by COs, as in the above case illustration, can also have debilitating outcomes. Bergmann and Queen (1987) reported that there are three characteristics which must be present for an event to be traumatic. There must be an extremely high level of stress, a denial of the importance of the event or a shock-like response, and a normal set of feelings or consequences following the event. They labeled this normal set of feelings an acute stress response where individuals withdraw from important people and activities, reexperience the event through flashbacks, feel depressed, have sleep difficulties and nightmares, feel anxious and hypervigilant, feel guilty, and have difficulty returning to work.

M. Davis (1995) also examined stress related to traumatic incidents. He described a traumatic incident as being a routine day where suddenly a fight breaks out among the inmates, and one inmate cuts the other in the neck and creates a gaping wound with blood spraying everywhere. According to the author, possible consequences for the guards are confusion, sweating, depression, anger, grief, and changes in eating and sleeping behaviors. Both Bergmann and Queen (1987) and M. Davis (1995) identified long-term side effects from stress, including alcoholism, divorce, unemployment, violent relationships, and suicide if the COs did not receive appropriate mental health services.

These traumatic incidents can also cause PTSD in certain employees. In the case of *Wertz v. Workmen's Compensation Appeal Board* (1996), the plaintiff worked at a prison during a prison riot. He suffered PTSD and was awarded total disability benefits. When he returned to a modified duty position at the prison, his PTSD symptoms began to increase again, forcing him to leave his job permanently. Despite the fact that there were no riots when he returned to work, he was still awarded disability payments because his psychological stress was related to the workplace.

Although many studies have examined the nature and extent of stress experienced by COs, few have researched ways to reduce it. As can be seen from the worker's compensation lawsuits, stress can have some serious consequences and lead to additional expenses for institutions. A study that did examine methods for reducing stress researched the benefits of exercise programs for COs (Kiely & Hodgson, 1990). The authors found that the exercise programs were a success, although they relied on self-reports for their data. The staff was able to see how they benefited from the exercise programs and therefore were in favor of them. They reported higher staff morale, improved attitudes, increased confidence, and greater physical fitness which improved resistance to stress. The authors did find that COs had a difficult time recognizing stress in themselves or others, and therefore concluded that heightening CO awareness of potential stressors along with preventative actions such as exercise would be the best way to minimize the negative consequences of stress. Their overall findings revealed the benefits of physical fitness as a way to reduce stress and assist guards in overcoming the effects of stress–related illnesses.

Another variable that intuitively would seem to reduce stress is peer support. However, Grossi and Berg (1991) found that peer support actually increased work stress. They hypothesized that in a prison setting, COs might have to compromise their personal values and integrity in order to obtain peer support, particularly when overlooking infractions made by other officers. This could produce more feelings of stress instead of less. However, it might be that other forms of support could be stress–reducing, such as the role of administration or family support. Regrettably, these variables were not examined in this study.

Finn (1998) reported that there are programs or services to help prevent and treat CO stress. He identified four categories of programs: academy training, in-service training, critical incidents stress management, and individual counseling. However, he pointed out that the criticism most often levied at these programs is their lack of specificity to correctional environments and their related stressors. In other words, those correctional systems that offer these types of programs often examine stress in general and provide generic coping strategies without real-life utility to the unique circumstances faced by COs.

Forensic Psychology and Policy Implications

After examining the effects that stress has on COs, it is clear that programs need to be developed to help them handle work tension before they burn out. One type of program that has received a considerable amount of attention is critical incident stress debriefing. This is a stage method whereby individuals are taken back through the incident to explore their thoughts and feelings with one another regarding the incident. The group processing of such a fact-finding-thinking-feeling model, combined with relaxation training, as well as individual counseling aimed at reducing flashbacks of the incident, can help prevent the development of PTSD or assist in reducing the intensity of the experience (Finn, 1998; McWhirter & Linzer, 1994). According to the 1997 article "Battle Staff Burnout," critical incident stress debriefing with correctional staff should be done within 1 or 2 days after the event and should include all personnel. The article also recommended creating a policy for debriefing that includes the following points: clear definitions of debriefing, an outline of what critical incidents would require debriefing, rules of confidentiality, and an outline of responsibilities.

Other recommendations for preventing long-term consequences of traumatic stress were outlined by Bergmann and Queen (1987). Departments should organize their response before a traumatic incident occurs. Psychological responses of survivors should be included in the policies and procedures for handling prison disturbances. Departments should make sure that posttraumatic services are only provided by qualified and trained staff. Finally, creative ways must be found to finance posttraumatic services.

Another important policy matter that needs to be addressed is CO suicide. Training programs need to be implemented to handle all officers' confrontations with death. There should be institutional training for suicide prevention focused on guards and inmates. The gains from such training initiatives could extend beyond suicide prevention (Kamerman, 1995). Correctional psychologists should also be available for individual counseling regarding stress, depression, and the like. Finn (1998) reported that most COs only have their Employee Assistance Programs (EAPs) to turn to and that many officers feel that these initiatives do not protect their confidentiality and that EAP staff are unfamiliar with CO stress. Correctional and forensic psychologists who are trained to understand both the systemic or organizational problems within the prison system and general clinical psychology would be the best equipped to effectively work with correctional personnel on these issues.

A final policy consideration for CO stress is funding. As mentioned previously, with overcrowded prisons and the building of new facilities, correctional staff have not been able to keep up with the growth. Instead of funneling more funds into building prisons, attention needs to be placed on providing services for COs, including adequate numbers of staff. The problem of crime is not going to disappear with the addition of new prisons, but the problem of stress-related disease and disability could be greatly reduced if COs were to receive the appropriate mental health services.

Suggestions for Future Research

The major area in which research is lacking concerns the benefits of stress-reduction programs for COs. Although exercise was found to decrease stress and provide additional advantages, a more rigorous empirical study needs to be conducted. This could take a holistic approach examining ways to create healthy workplaces in terms of overall organizational structure, as well as expanding personal coping mechanisms such as the exercise programs (Kiely & Hodgson, 1990). Also, a more systematic study of critical-incident stress-debriefing programs, including follow-up investigations (Finn, 1998; McWhirter & Linzer) and their direct applications in a correctional setting, provides further evidence that such programs are beneficial. Other creative ways for reducing the job-related stress of institutional work need to be examined. Finally, more research must be conducted on CO suicide (Kamerman, 1995). This could foster a better understanding of the causes of suicide, and the effects suicide has on those who are left to deal with it.

INTELLECTUALLY DISABLED INMATES

Introduction

According to Conley, Luckasson, and Bouthilet (1992), the prevalence of prisoners with mental retardation is relatively small, consisting of approximately 2% of inmates in state and federal prisons. However, this small population of inmates provides a great challenge to the correctional system given their need for specialized services. The dilemma that exists concerns the handling of prisoners with mental retardation. There is a concern for public safety due to their criminal behavior and there is a concern for providing appropriate services (Exum, Turnbull, Martin, & Finn, 1992). As a result, there is a constant struggle to maintain a balance between habilitation and punishment that does not occur with the typical offender.

> Richard, a 28 year old with mental retardation, was sentenced to prison for 3.5 to 7 years for criminal mischief. This was his fifth arrest over a period of 3 years, and the judge did not know what else to do but place Richard in prison. Richard was living in a community home but had to be released because he resisted the services provided by staff, who also were at a loss as to what would be best for him. During a period of 6 months in prison, Richard committed four infractions. The disciplinary review board lost patience with him and decided to take away 6 months of good time for his last infraction of fighting with other inmates. The guards are aware that Richard is not like other prisoners, but they do not know how to help him stay out of trouble. Richard also does not know how to stay out of trouble and feels that he must continue fighting in order to keep harassment from other inmates to a minimum. He worries that he will not be safe if he lets his guard down (Exum et al., 1992).

Literature Review

With the rise in correctional populations all over the country, there also has been an increase in inmates like Richard who have functional disabilities and low IQs, falling in the mentally retarded range (J. N. Hall, 1992). Individuals with intellectual disabilities are overrepresented in the criminal justice system, as compared to their prevalence in the general population (S. C. Hayes, 2002; S. C. Hayes & Farnill, 2003). Because of this, prisons have had to develop appropriate services and programs to assist these individuals. Before an inmate can be given these special services, he or she must first be diagnosed as mentally retarded. Accurate diagnosis of mental retardation has important implications for correctional administrators, probation and parole, and community services (S. C. Hayes & Farnill, 2003). The American Association of Mental Retardation (2002, p. 13) has provided a new definition: "Mental retardation is a disability characterized by significant limitations both in intellectual functioning and in adaptive behavior as expressed in conceptual, social, and practical adaptive skills. This disability originates before age 18." Screening and evaluating an inmate prior to placing the person in a housing unit is perhaps the most important aspect in developing appropriate services for a prisoner with mental retardation (Exum et al., 1992; S. C. Hayes, 2002). This is the stage where intellectual disability characteristics can be determined for prisoners. S. C. Hayes (2002) stressed the importance of early detection in order to provide these individuals with appropriate services, protection, diversion, and rehabilitation.

Bowker and Schweid (1992) reported a profile of the mentally retarded offender: 91% were male, 57% were African American, 48% were between the ages of 20 and 24, 73% were single, 13% completed high school, 67% were repeat offenders, and the mean full-scale IQ was 68. A program in Florida reported that a majority of the mentally retarded inmates were male, African American, and under age 30. Due to the higher number of African American mentally retarded inmates, Ho (1996) conducted a study which examined race as a factor in predicting those inmates who would be diagnosed as mentally retarded. The researcher found that the effect of race did not make any significant addition to the prediction. "Regardless of race, the offender who had a low IQ or a severe deficit in adaptive behavior was most likely to be diagnosed as having severe retardation" (Ho, 1996, p. 343). Ho reported that IQ was the strongest determinant for predicting mental retardation among offenders.

The type of instrument used to measure intelligence is an important factor to consider because the way in which inmates are screened can affect the prevalence of retardation. Often a group test is administered to incoming offenders because it saves time. Yet, Spruill and May (1988) found that group testing overestimates the prevalence of mental retardation. They found that if inmates were administered an individual intelligence test, such as the Wechsler Adult Intelligence Scale, then there was a lower prevalence of retardation. Upon questioning inmates who had been tested, they learned that many were very anxious upon entering prison, and the group testing did not allay their anxieties. The inmates also reported that they did not understand why they were being tested and, therefore, some did not try to do their best on the tests. S. C. Hayes and Farnill (2003) also used the Kaufman Brief Intelligence Test (K-BIT) to assess intelligence and the Vineland Adaptive Behavior Scales to assess for deficits in adaptive behavior.

Despite the findings reported by Spruill & May (1988) prisons still administer group screening tests because of the sheer volume of inmates that must be processed. Georgia State Prison has a mental retardation program, which uses a group screening test to identify individuals who score less than 80 (J. N. Hall, 1992). The Texas Department of Corrections also screens all incoming inmates for mental retardation. If a prisoner scores less than 73 on a standard intelligence test, then he or she is sent to the mental retardation unit for a 30-day evaluation (Santamour, 1990).

Once an inmate has been identified with mental disabilities, what types of services are available? J. N. Hall (1992) described how South Carolina and Georgia treated this population. The South Carolina Department of Corrections has a Habilitation Unit. This is a minimum-security unit reserved for those with developmental disabilities. Services such as special education, life-skills training, vocational preparation, recreation, counseling, and pre-release preparation are offered. These programs are run by a team of professionals which includes psychologists, special education teachers, and vocational specialists. The primary goal is to provide appropriate training which will improve the inmate's socialization skills. Therefore, the inmate will be prepared to live on the outside and hopefully not return.

The other program described by J. N. Hall (1992) is the Georgia State Prison Mental Retardation Unit. Unlike South Carolina's program, this is run through a maximum-security facility. The prisoners typically are repeat offenders who have committed violent crimes. Similar to South Carolina, this program teaches socialization and life-skills development. However, the goal is not to prepare the inmate for the outside world but to emphasize institutional adaptation. An effort is made to train the inmate on how to live inside the prison without committing further crimes. Barron, Hassiotis, and Barnes (2002) identified those offenders with intellectual disabilities as a group with complex needs who have the potential to create a continuing risk to their communities. These researchers suggested that despite the number of offenders with intellectual disabilities, little is known about treatment effectiveness or outcomes. Finally, they noted that these offenders often receive inadequate services due to not being identified in the criminal justice system, and that there is a tremendous lack of research into treatment effectiveness for this population in general (Barron et al., 2002).

Santamour (1990) described a special program for prisoners with mental retardation implemented in the Texas Department of Corrections. Once an inmate is identified as possibly disabled, the prisoner is sent to a special unit for evaluation. Multidisciplinary teams made up of doctors, social workers, educators, psychologists, vocational trainers, and security conduct the evaluations and work with inmates in the program. If the decision is made to admit the person into the program, then housing is available in one of five units designed to fit particular needs. One unit consists of dual-diagnosis inmates who have mental retardation and another psychological disorder. The prisoners housed in this unit also tend to act aggressively. A second unit houses inmates identified as being particularly vulnerable to abuse and therefore in need of extra protection. A third unit houses those inmates who are aggressive or disruptive and have histories of belligerent behavior. A fourth unit consists of those who have only mental retardation and no other identified problems. A fifth unit is reserved for model prisoners with mental retardation who are allowed the highest level of privileges. Once an inmate has been identified and housed, then an individualized habilitation and education plan is developed by the treatment team. This plan emphasizes four areas: (1) habilitation, which includes academic, vocational, and social skills; (2) social support, which includes counseling by psychologists and trained COs who work as case managers; (3) institutional security; and (4) continuity of treatment, which prepares the inmate for the outside world when his or her release date approaches.

When an inmate is released from prison, he or she may still require special services. Therefore, an Ohio county has developed a Mentally Retarded Offender (MRO) Unit in their probation department (Bowker & Schweid, 1992). To be assigned to this unit, an inmate must score a 75 or lower on the Wechsler Adult Intelligence Scale, which must be administered by a licensed psychologist. This unit is run on a case management model where the probationer receives individualized services determined by the probation officer, the clinical director of the MRO unit, and others as deemed necessary. The supervision levels for these probationers range from "super-high," which means contact with the probation officer once a week, to "extended," which means only monthly contacts via mail with the probation officer. A probation officer working in this unit generally carries a caseload of approximately 55–65 individuals compared to the regular officers' caseloads of approximately 200. Due to the case management model, the MRO Unit officers take a much more active role in their probationers' post release services. If Richard, from the previous case illustration, had been assigned to such a unit, then more appropriate services might have been found for him, and he might have remained in the community instead of being sent to prison.

The programs that have been described all focus on aspects such as habilitation and vocational and social skills. Yet, are these skills important or even necessary for an inmate with mental retardation? A study conducted by Munson (1994) suggested that there are three important processes that take place once an offender is released into a community. These include beginning an appropriate occupation, selecting a home, and developing appropriate and positive leisure skills. He hypothesized that offenders who were provided career development training would score significantly higher than a control group on self-esteem and participation and commitment in the worker, homemaker, and leisure roles. His participants were youthful offenders who had mental retardation and/or learning disabilities as well as behavioral problems. He found that the offenders in the group who received career development training increased their self-esteem, while it decreased for those in the control group. Also, participation and commitment in the homemaker role increased more for the group receiving training than the control group. Although commitment to the worker and leisure roles did not show a significant difference between groups, the training did increase the offenders' commitment to finding and maintaining a home, and it did increase their self-esteem. These two benefits could provide enough incentive for released offenders to remain in the community and avoid criminal activities, which is the ultimate goal of most training programs.

Bowker and Schweid (1992) provided another reason for implementing specialized programs within prisons. Offenders with mental retardation, such as Richard in the case illustration, often become victims of physical attacks and psychological abuse. Beail (2002) stated that people with intellectual disabilities are also victims of violent crimes. They can be manipulated for goods or blamed for infractions by more intelligent inmates. This type of behavior only becomes worse with overcrowding, and many prisons are overcrowded. If separate units are not created for those with mental retardation, then they must be housed with the mentally or physically ill, where they will not receive the types of services they need.

Placing inmates with mental retardation in the general population of a prison can create many conflicts. If the inmate breaks the rules, as Richard continuously did, then COs may place him or her in disciplinary isolation because COs are not concerned with why the prisoner broke the rules, only that they were broken. The stress of the punishment may only frustrate the mentally retarded inmate further, and he or she may verbally or physically act out this frustration because of a lack of understanding about what is happening. The aspects of prison life may actually place the mentally retarded prisoner at risk, despite attempts to help the person (J. N. Hall, 1992). This is why it is so important to develop separate units and programs for this population.

Forensic Psychology and Policy Implications

Although programs for mentally retarded inmates do exist, not all prisons have them, and not all of the programs are adequate. Policymakers need to develop programs focused on the special needs of these inmates, especially their slower learning capabilities and limited ability to understand the rules of the prison. Policies should be developed that decrease mainstreaming them into the general population and increase the creation of special facilities (Spruill & May, 1988). Policies also need to be developed to create interagency communications, which would smooth the way for a continuum of care from prison into the community (J. N. Hall, 1992). Psychologists, social workers, probation officers, and correctional staff should begin working together to assist prisoners in habilitating and transitioning back into the community so that they refrain from future criminal activities. Without this type of teamwork, offenders like Richard will keep cycling back through the system because they do not know how to live in their communities. Mental health professionals and other correctional staff who work with the mentally retarded should have training regarding their special needs. Communication with these individuals should be commensurate with their intellectual abilities. Correctional staff should also be acutely aware of the potential for manipulation of these individuals by higher functioning inmates. In addition, they should be informed that in some instances behavior interpreted as oppositional may actually be a result of failing to understand of instructions.

Suggestions for Future Research

Further research needs to be conducted on what types of programs are appropriate for inmates with mental retardation and those with additional problems or disabilities (J. N. Hall, 1992). Because of the difficulties inherent in group testing, more effective methods of screening for mental retardation should be studied further. The tests currently used for identifying mental retardation among inmates should be examined for validity with different ethnic groups (Ho, 1996). If these tests are culturally biased, then the reported higher prevalence of African American inmates with mental retardation may not be accurate. Inmates who really are not retarded, but have been raised with different cultural values and ideals, may be receiving services that are not suitable for them. Research also should be conducted on community-based programs that have had success in housing and habilitating prior offenders so that more effective initiatives can be developed to help this population stay out of prison. Additional research is needed on what are the most effective treatment strategies for individuals with mental retardation.

SOCIETY'S REACTION TO SEX OFFENDERS

Introduction

There are currently more than 200,000 convicted sex offenders in the United States (U.S. Department of Justice, Federal Bureau of Investigation, 1996). These offenders are perhaps the most detested individuals in today's society. Since the late 1980s, there have been numerous movements calling for tougher penalties for sex offenders by law enforcement, legislatures, and communities. These movements support chemical castration, community notification, formalized registration, and civil commitment. At first glance, such actions may appear as proper precautions to ensure the safety of society against further victimization by convicted sex offenders. However, these actions also need to be examined in terms of whether they serve their intended function of curbing recidivism. Further, one needs to question whether the constitutional rights of the offender are violated. The next case illustrates the repercussions that recent implementation of community notification laws have had on both sex offenders and their families.

Jose is a 19-year-old Latino male who has been participating in sex-offender-specific treatment for the past 6 months. Jose attends high school and works 30 hours a week in order to pay for his treatment. One Monday night during a group therapy session, Jose disclosed the devastation that he and his family have encountered as a result of his sexual offense, and, specifically, the mandated registration and community notification laws. Jose revealed how he was recently confronted by five men whom he considered friends. They located Jose's name on the CD-ROM which contains information about all registered sex offenders. Accessible information included Jose's name, picture, zip code, and a description of his offense. Jose tearfully described how his friends did not stop after confronting just him. They also confronted Jose's sister, who, they learned, was his victim.

They then took it upon themselves to notify Jose's girlfriend (who subsequently left him), Jose's place of employment (which subsequently fired him), and students at his school. Feeling extremely scared and alone, Jose disclosed his feelings of worthlessness and hopelessness. He stated, "I will never overcome my status as a sex offender, and no matter how much treatment I receive, I will continue to be hated by everyone. My family is being hurt because of me, and life is not worth it anymore." Jose then disclosed that he was intending to commit suicide.

Literature Review

The above case is an example of a young man who completed a jail sentence for his offense and received outpatient sex-offender treatment while on probation. Despite these punishment and rehabilitation efforts, society imposes additional requirements for the protection of the community against individuals such as Jose. These additional requirements are explored in terms of their respective advantages and disadvantages within the literature. The three issues examined are the registration and community notification laws, the statute for Sexually Violent Predators, and chemical castration.

Sex-Offender Registration and Community Notification

The death of 7-year-old Megan Kanka sparked a nationwide movement to release information about the location and identity of sex offenders in the community. New Jersey was the first state to pass "Megan's Law" after the young girl was raped and murdered by a convicted child molester who had moved into her neighborhood. Megan's Law is upheld in every state under federal legislation. The purpose of the law is to equip the community with information necessary for the protection of children against child molesters (Cody, 1997). According to this law, the identification of the victim is not to be released. However, as illustrated in the case of Jose, the victim's name does not need to be present in order for identification to occur. A description of the sexual offense is provided, which can, at times, be sufficient for victim identification. As in the case of Jose, victim identification occurred after it was stated that the sexual offense was committed against his sister. Regardless of the public's opinion on the rights (or lack thereof) of sex offenders, most would agree that the rights of victims, and particularly their identities, need to be protected.

In terms of the practical application of this law, it is important to examine whether it serves its intended purpose of protecting children from sexual abuse as well as reducing recidivism among sexual offenders. The law is too recent for studies to have been conducted, which examine the rate of sexual offenses before and after its passage. Molett, Arnold, and Meyer (2001) contend that there is not enough scientific evidence that community notification and registration laws are effective in protecting society from sexual re-offenders. A study at a 240-bed state inpatient psychiatric hospital in Nebraska indicated the sex offenders in this sample showed little familiarity with community notification laws and perceived some aspects of these laws as unfair (Elbogen, Patry, & Scalora, 2003).

The literature provides a great deal of information concerning sexual offenses and offenders, which can help to address whether the law will meet its goals. Perhaps the most important issue is that most sexual offenses are not committed by strangers in the community; rather, most sexual offenses are perpetrated by members of the family. This illustrates one misperception by society that sexual offenders are crazed predators who are waiting to pounce on the first child they see. This misconception is easier for the public to understand than the fact that, by far, most offenses are incestuous in nature. As noted by Williams (1996), it is the stereotypic image of a sex offender that creates fear and misunderstanding within society. However, it is precisely such fear and misunderstanding that provide the basis for an emotional response by legislatures, as witnessed by the sex-offender registration and community notification laws.

A group of 138 professionals who work with sex offenders were surveyed regarding their opinions of public sex offender registry Web sites (Malesky & Keim, 2001). Results indicated that greater than 80% of the participants did not believe that sex offender registry Web sites would affect the number of children who were sexually abused each year and 70% of respondents believed that a listing of sex offenders would actually create a false sense of security for parents. Over 60% of the mental health professionals surveyed believed that sex offenders listed on the Web sites would become targets of vigilantism in their communities (Malesky & Keim, 2001). Edwards and Hensley (2001) stated that the stigma and backlash from the community might discourage offenders from reporting their behaviors and seeking counseling. Some researchers argue that the gains in public awareness come at a high cost for corrections by way of personnel, time, and budgetary resources (Zevitz & Farkas, 2000a).

A study was conducted to explore the experience of residents who attended community notification meetings regarding the notification of convicted sex offenders (Zevitz & Farkas, 2000b). Results indicated that these meetings could perform an important role in managing behavior of known sex offenders in the community, but would come at the cost of increased community anxiety. Zevitz and Farkas (2000b) reported that the anxiety was related to how those in attendance were notified of the meeting, how clearly the purpose was conveyed, and how organized the presentation approved during the meeting. Younglove and Vitello (2003, p. 25) pointed out the paradox of discretionary community notification by stating "perception of public safety is increased only by decreasing perception of public safety."

Sexually Violent Predator Act

Another way in which society chooses to deal with sexual offenders is by following their incarceration with civil commitment. The definition of a sexually violent predator varies slightly across states; however, the basic premise is the same. California has defined the statute in the following way:

> A person who has been convicted of one or more sexually violent offenses against two or more victims for which he or she received a determinate sentence and who has a diagnosed mental disorder that makes the person a danger to the health and safety of others in that it is likely that he or she will engage in sexually violent criminal behavior. (D. A. Cohen, 1997)

The purpose of the law is to identify, locate, apprehend, and prosecute habitual sexual offenders (D. A. Cohen, 1997). Wood, Grossman, and Fichtner (2000) reported that the intent of sexually violent predator laws is to reduce sexually violent crimes through treatment and involuntary confinement. Since 1999, civil commitment for sexually violent predators has been implemented in 15 states, with the newest approach occurring in Texas where civil commitment is utilized on an outpatient basis (Bailey, 2002; Molett et al., 2001). When examined more closely, there are numerous issues inherent in this statute that call into question its constitutionality. There has long been a debate as to whether sex offenders need treatment or imprisonment. The Sexually Violent Predator Act, which became effective in California on January 1, 1996, allows the state to subject the offender to both treatment and imprisonment. In essence, it permits an indefinite civil commitment to be imposed on an offender after a full prison sentence has been served and prior to his release from prison. The *ex post facto* clause of the United States Constitution prohibits retroactive application of penal statutes. Given that the Sexually Violent Predator Act is a civil law, analysis of *United States v. Ward* (1980) extends the *ex post facto* clause to civil cases. In this case, it was found that civil laws violate the *ex post facto* law if the statute is "so punitive either in purpose or effect as to negate its intention." This applies to the Sexually Violent Predator Act in that the said intent was to provide mental health treatment to the offender; however, the underlying goal was to extend the confinement of the individual.

In a similar fashion, the Sexually Violent Predator Act is in conflict with prohibitions against double jeopardy. Double jeopardy is said to have occurred if one of three situations is present: (1) a second prosecution for the same offense after acquittal, (2) a second prosecution for the same offense after conviction, and (3) multiple punishments for the same offense. In terms of the Sexually Violent Predator Act, violations of the latter two occur. The major defense that has been used in court to claim that the Sexually Violent Predator Act does *not* constitute double jeopardy is that a civil commitment is not punitive in character (*Department of Revenue of Montana v. Kurth Ranch*, 1994). One must determine whether the motivation for the commitment is truly for the offender to receive treatment or whether the purpose is to keep the offender confined in a secure facility apart from the rest of society. Further, if treatment is needed for the individual, such treatment needs to be provided immediately upon this determination, rather than after a prison sentence has been completed. *Young v. Weston* (9th Circuit, 1999), which was an appeal of a writ of *habeas corpus* on indefinite commitment under Washington State's Sexually Violent Predator Statute, was reversed and remanded (Walcott, 2000). The appeals court held that the conditions of confinement and the quality of treatment at a special center violated the *ex post facto* and double jeopardy clauses of the U.S. Constitution. However, in the case of *Hubbart v. Superior Court of Santa Clara County*, the court upheld California's Sexually Violent Predator Act (Scott & Yarvis, 2000).

Supporters of the Texas outpatient civil commitment statute contend that it is an effective and low cost, less restrictive means to protect the community and treat the sexual offender, with the cost of outpatient civil commitment at $20,000 per person/year as compared to more than $100,000 for inpatient commitment in other states (Meyer, Molett, Richards, Arnold, & Latham, 2003). Outpatient civilly committed sex offenders in Texas are managed by a team made up of a case manager (supervision), mental health professionals, public safety officer (global positioning satellite monitoring), and other professionals (Meyer et al., 2003). These researchers found that out of 21 committed individuals, 7 were in treatment, 1 passed away, 10 were in custody after violating the conditions of commitment that constitute a felony, and 3 awaited release from prison.

Chemical Castration

Perhaps the most drastic measure that has been implemented as a means of protecting society against sex offenders is the chemical castration law. In addition to psychotherapy, some researchers contend that pharmacotherapy is another important tool or treatment option for sex offenders, particularly for paraphilias (Briken, Hill, & Berner, 2003). According to Maletzky and Field (2003, p. 391), there are three classes of medications currently used to reduce sex drive: "(1) hormonal agents acting peripherally, predominantly medroxyprogesterone acetate (MPA; Depo-Provera); (2) hormonal agents acting centrally, predominantly leuprolide (Lupron); and (3) serotonin-active antidepressants, such as fluoxetine (Prozac) and paroxetine (Paxil)." Again, the chemical castration law varies slightly from state to state; however, the fundamentals of the law remain the same. In California, two-time sex offenders can be required to take Depo-Provera upon parole. Depo-Provera is a hormone-suppressing drug which lowers testosterone levels, thereby decreasing a man's sex drive. The court has also allowed for discretion in using this procedure for first-time sex offenders. In support of the chemical castration law, European studies have been cited in which offenders who underwent chemical castration had a recidivism rate under 15.0%. Review of the California Department of Corrections' statistics, however, reveals that sexual offenders who serve a prison sentence and do not receive treatment during incarceration have a recidivism rate of approximately 18.5%, whereas the recidivism rates for drug and violent offenders are approximately 25.0 and 30.0%, respectively (Lotke, 1996).

The American Civil Liberties Union of Florida has argued that the use of chemical castration is unconstitutional for several reasons (Spralding, 1997). First, chemical castration interferes with an individual's rights to procreate and to refuse treatment. Second, Depo-Provera is not approved by the Food and Drug Administration for chemical castration. Third, judges, not physicians, will be making the ultimate decision as to whether an offender should be given the drug and when the drug can be discontinued. Fourth, there are serious side effects from Depo-Provera which include diabetes, gallstones, hypertension, fatigue, weight gain, nightmares, and muscle weakness. For these reasons, the chemical castration law can be viewed as judges practicing medicine without a license.

Perhaps one of the most important opposing arguments to the chemical castration law is that it will not curb recidivism in many offenders. The treatment strategy that has the best effect on curbing recidivism among sexual offenders is cognitive-behavioral therapy that incorporates a relapse prevention plan or a self-regulation model depending on the specific type of sex offender in question (Gibbons, 2003; Laws, 1989; Polaschek, 2003). Some basic empirical animal research also does not support the use of chemical castration to deter deviant sexual aggression in humans (Moore, 2001). Chemical castration does nothing to treat the psychological roots of sexually aberrant behavior. Numerous sexual offenders do not offend as a result of an overactive sex drive. Many offenders commit sexual offenses for reasons that have nothing to do with sex such as power, control, and anger. In fact, when comparing untreated sexual offenders to those who received sex-offender treatment, the recidivism rate dropped from 18.5% to approximately 10.9% (Alexander, 1997). This clearly demonstrates that treatment can effectively reduce recidivism among sexual offenders.

Forensic Psychology and Policy Implications

There is a great need for forensic psychologists to provide information to the public and legislature regarding sexual offenders and their recidivism and treatment. It appears that several of the recent actions taken against sexual offenders will be ineffective in accomplishing the goal of protecting society. Cordoba and Chapel (1983) acknowledged that society is more willing to allow sex offenders back into the community if they have undergone anti-androgen therapy (chemical castration). It is important, however, to examine whether such measures are based simply on emotion and community misperceptions or whether thorough research was conducted to support their implementation. It appears that there is a direct conflict between society's outcry for severe punishment of sex offenders and mental health experts who maintain that there is effective treatment for such individuals. Given this conflict, the legislature has attempted to satisfy both sides through legally sanctioned penal and civil commitments.

Chemical castration, community notification, registration, and the Sexually Violent Predator Act are all aimed at protecting society from sex offenders who are likely to recidivate upon release from prison. In lobbying the chemical castration bill in California, proponents stated that recidivism would drop from almost 100 to 2% (E. Moses, 1996). In reviewing the literature on recidivism among sexual offenders, no study documented that recidivism occurs in almost 100% of the cases (Proulx et al., 1997). This illustrates the public's misperceptions about sexual offenders and specifically about their likelihood for re-offense. Furthermore, policymakers should be educated on the fact that public awareness needs to be focused primarily on the family, where most sexual offenses occur. Numerous studies have shown the effectiveness of cognitive behavioral treatment for sexual offenders in reducing recidivism. With this in mind, attention needs to be focused on funding prison and parole treatment programs, which are designed specifically for this population.

Suggestions for Future Research

Sexually violent predator laws are all relatively new in the United States. Longitudinal analyses need to be conducted, examining recidivism rates before and after the laws. This will provide a more accurate measure of whether the laws are meeting their goal of curbing recidivism. In order to illustrate the discrepancy between society's perceptions of sex offenders and the empirical literature, studies should be conducted which directly compare the statistical data gathered in the department of corrections with society's perceptions of recidivism among sex offenders. These data should then be assessed in relation to the effectiveness of treatment for this population. It is likely that the results will show that the legislature supports the misperceptions within society, notwithstanding the empirical findings available from corrections and mental health professionals.

WOMEN WORKING IN MALE PRISONS

Introduction

Today when you walk into a male prison it is not uncommon to see women there, not as inmates but as COs guarding the male prisoners. Prior to the passage of Title VII of the Civil Rights Act of 1964, this would have been a rare sight. Women were delegated to work in all-female institutions and juvenile corrections (Etheridge, Hale, & Hambrick, 1984). Fortunately, Title VII prohibited sex discrimination by state and local governments, so female COs began to move into the male prison system. Unfortunately, they have not had a warm welcome, especially by their male coworkers. The toughest task female COs have to face is not guarding the prisoners, but trying to find a way to coexist with the male COs in an atmosphere of hostility, harassment, and nonsupportiveness.

The following example illustrates the process that many female COs face when trying to fit into the male prison system.

When Jane first began her career as a CO, she chose to work in a female prison because there were more job openings and she felt more comfortable working with this population. After several years, she decided to move to an all-male prison because she had two kids to help support and needed the pay raise this job would bring. Although she was very familiar with the job requirements of a CO and had never worked in a male prison, she was aware that every prison had its own rules.

On her first day, she went in with a friendly, open attitude. She smiled and introduced herself to her new coworkers. She noticed that she was the only female CO in her unit. She got a couple of nods and one person even grunted hello. Nobody returned her friendly attitude, though. She knew the name of the CO who was to train her, but it took her half an hour to find him because he started his rounds without waiting for her. Upon finding him, he immediately ordered her to be quiet and watch everything he did. Several times that day she asked him questions about the job, and he often did not give her a sufficient answer or ignored her altogether. After one question, he accused her of being stupid and of not knowing anything about being a CO.

During her lunch break, none of the male COs would sit with her. She overheard them talking and laughing about her, and one even cornered her and asked her to go out for a drink after work. After telling him she was married, he just laughed and said he was sure her husband expected such things since she worked with "real men." When Jane left work after that first day, she felt very discouraged and was afraid to return.

After thinking it over, she vowed to go back with a different attitude. She began to act more assertively and to not let her male coworkers demean her. She began to use more offensive language and joked around with the men so that she would fit in better. Gradually, the men began to accept her, but only after she showed she could be tough like them and not act feminine. She had to change her personality to fit their beliefs about how a CO should act. Her problem then became one of trying to leave her work personality at work. Her comments were that "it's a macho environment and I have to act aggressively to succeed. I work here all day, talk loud, act tough. I go home at night and find myself talking in a deep, loud voice to my kids" (Jurik, as cited in S. E. Martin and Jurik, 1996, p. 197). So, Jane found that she could fit into the male prison system, but at the cost of giving up her own identity to conform to her male counterparts.

Literature Review

Jane's situation is not an uncommon one among female COs working in all-male prisons. Although Jane was able to fit in, she had to conform to the male officers' behaviors. When women do not conform, their experience can be very stressful, because some male COs will harass and discriminate against them.

The first signs of discrimination began after Title VII was passed. All-male prisons tried to prohibit women from even being hired by using the BFOQ clause, which states that sex discrimination can occur if it is a Bona Fide Occupational Qualification (Pollock-Byrne, 1990). *Dothard v. Rawlinson* (1977) is an example of this. The state of Alabama prohibited a woman from working in an all-male prison because it claimed the violence of the state prisons would be dangerous for women. The state used the BFOQ clause as their justification. The U.S. Supreme Court upheld the state's case, although it did overturn the use of height and weight restrictions in hiring unless it could be shown how it related to the job. Although this seems like a negative outcome for women, it was really a narrow ruling applying only to Alabama. Other states have had a difficult time proving that height, weight, or gender influence what is necessary to be a CO (Pollock-Byrne, 1990).

Although prisons have not been able to prevent women from being hired, some male COs have not welcomed them into their subculture. Fry and Glaser (1987) conducted a study on female COs and found that they were not viewed positively by the male guards. In fact, they found that the male officers' resistance was the greatest problem the female COs faced in male prisons. S. E. Martin and Jurik (1996) found, more specifically, that it is in the area of actual security work in men's prisons where women are least likely to be included. Women consist of 43% of the total correctional work force, yet they only make up 13% of CO security in men's prisons. Because their numbers are so low, it is not surprising that the biggest problem faced by female COs is being recognized and treated as equals (Szockyj, 1989). Jane's situation captures this problem.

Recent research suggests that maybe the perceptions of female correctional staff are not as negative as they once were. Hemmens, Stohr, Schoeler, and Miller (2002) conducted a survey of 467 prison workers employed by a variety of institutions and found that the perceptions of female correctional staff were generally positive. The majority of subjects viewed several sexually harassing behaviors as inappropriate, such as jokes, insults, personal comments, or sexual relations between staff and inmates. Individuals who worked at maximum-security facilities had the lowest perceptions of female correctional staff's abilities, while those who worked at women's facilities had the highest view of their capabilities. Subjects over the age of 50 had the lowest perceptions of female correctional staff and females had better impressions of the work of other female staff. Finally, previous military service also negatively impacted positive impressions of female correctional workers (Hemmens et al., 2002).

The unequal position of female COs can often begin before they even start their job. Many do not receive any type of training before their first day of work (S. E. Martin & Jurik, 1996). They are supposed to receive on-the-job training, yet their trainers generally are male COs who do not want them there (Zimmer, 1987). Sometimes, they actively undermine the woman's ability to succeed by withholding information about how to deal with the inmates (Zimmer, 1987). In Jane's case, the training officer often refused to answer her questions about the job. S. E. Martin and Jurik (1996) also found that male coworkers excluded women COs from training exercises and even sabotaged them to the point of threatening the women's physical safety. They also reported that, due to this hostility by the coworkers, the inmates actually provided the needed information and training.

From their first day, women COs are confronted with the problem of fitting in with their coworkers. This problem does not always go away with time. Female COs face steady opposition and sometimes sexual harassment from the male guards (Zimmer, 1987). The opposition can take many different forms. Although male coworkers at times show overt hostility, they also engage in more subtle ways of undermining female COs. They can put pressure on women by constantly questioning or scrutinizing their performance (S. E. Martin & Jurik, 1996). They sometimes reverse decisions made by women, thereby undermining women's authority over prisoners (Zimmer, 1987). For women in supervisory positions, their male subordinates engage in subtle and blatant forms of resistance such as rolling their eyes, inattentiveness, and feigning an inability to hear orders. They can also undermine a woman's authority by "going over her head," thus causing her to lose the respect of her superiors due to ineffective management (S. E. Martin & Jurik, 1996).

Sexual harassment is another technique male COs use to keep women in an unequal status. Women become victims of rumors and allegations of sexual misconduct. There are overt propositions made by male COs and even more subtle behaviors such as joking, teasing, and name calling (S. E. Martin & Jurik, 1996). In the previous case illustration, Jane was propositioned by her coworker and then ridiculed when she refused his advances. Women COs even report that male officers proposition them in front of male inmates (Pollock-Byrne, 1990). It seems as if this might encourage the inmates to behave in a similar manner, yet Horne (1985) reported that obscenities more often came from the male coworkers than from the inmates. In a study of San Quentin Prison, it was found that women COs were sexually harassed at work and by phone at home. The overtly sexist language and conduct was openly tolerated (Owen, as cited in S. E. Martin & Jurik, 1996). This sexual harassment makes relationships with male COs "difficult in that a balance always has to be struck between being friendly and being thought of as sexually available — being 'one of the boys' or designated as the fraternity whore" (Pollock-Byrne, 1990, p. 118). S. E. Martin and Jurik (1996) stated that further problems arise when female COs refuse their counterparts' protection and sexual advances and attempt to show their competence. The male COs will label them as "too mannish, 'man-haters,' bitches, or lesbians" (S. E. Martin & Jurik, 1996, p. 174).

Women have had some success in trying to stop sexual harassment. For example, in *Bundy v. Jackson* (1981), a woman prison counselor was harassed by her male supervisors. When she rejected their advances, they prevented her from advancing in her job. When she charged them with sexual harassment, the court ruled in her favor, saying that her employer had allowed a hostile and discriminating work environment that violated Title VII (S. E. Martin & Jurik, 1996). Boothby and Clements (2000) conducted a national survey of correctional psychologists ($N = 830$) and found that the majority were Caucasian males. Despite the holding in Bundy, S. E. Martin and Jurik (1996) said that sexual harassment in all-male prisons has not decreased. The correctional field has been slow to prevent this type of behavior. Women fear that if they complain it may cause a negative evaluation of their job performance or even job loss.

Another aspect of opposition that female COs must face is that male COs evaluate women's job performances more negatively than they do their own (S. E. Martin & Jurik, 1996). A study by Fry and Glaser (1987), which gave questionnaires to staff, reported that the men found women COs to be less capable than themselves in duties that related to security and safety. Szockyj (1989) noted a similar finding in that male COs viewed themselves as more effective in handling situations that involved physical strength and preferred male back-up over female back-up. Male COs viewed women as too physically and emotionally weak to work in all-male prisons, and, therefore, as usable to do their jobs adequately in violent situations resulting in likely injury (S. E. Martin & Jurik, 1996). There is also a fear that women will get too friendly with the inmates, so female officers' intentions with the prisoners are scrutinized, although male officers' intentions are rarely monitored (S. E. Martin & Jurik,

1996). Crouch (1985) found that the problem was not an inability by female COs to handle the job demands, but rather one of male guards' perceived standards of appropriate behavior for both genders. Therefore, it is often necessary for female COs to prove that they can perform their job well before being accepted, whereas this is not necessary for male COs. This negative perception of women and their ability to do their job creates a disadvantage for promotions because they are often evaluated by male supervisors (Crouch, 1985). Thus, it is more difficult for women to get into positions of power where they could attempt to change the atmosphere of hostility female COs endure.

Because most of the resistance faced by female COs comes from male coworkers, some ideas have been offered that explain this occurrence. First, female COs are viewed as intruders in an all-male world (Horne, 1985). Female officers threaten an established subcultural code; they threaten a self-image held by male officers that guard work is dangerous and therefore only suitable for men. In other words, women are a status threat to men. One reason why men treat women in a sexually harassing way is to deny women acceptance on the job. Therefore, their status as men will not be diminished (Crouch, 1985). If women can perform the guard job as well as men, the job can no longer be used as a way of defining their masculinity (S. E. Martin & Jurik, 1996).

Another explanation is that women COs conduct their job in a different way than men. They are more likely to have a social worker's attitude about the job. They spend more time actually listening to the inmates' problems, having conversations about families, and assisting them in their plans for release. They do this as a way of creating alliances with the prisoners so that the inmates will voluntarily comply with orders and the women will not have to use force or intimidation (Zimmer, 1987). Male COs may perceive this behavior as sympathy toward inmates and feel that female guards are incapable of handling the job properly. Research exploring CO burnout indicated that female COs were less likely than their male colleagues to interact with inmates in a detached, impersonal way (Morgan et al., 2002). Moreover, Grekul (1999) noted that those COs who held views sympathetic to inmates often felt that they were an isolated minority and were extremely different from their coworkers.

Although no one agrees on the reason why male COs treat female officers with such opposition, what can be agreed upon is that women in "male" fields such as corrections face many hindrances, including expressed and subtle hostilities, exclusion from the male CO subculture, and sexual harassment (S. E. Martin & Jurik, 1996).

Forensic Psychology and Policy Implications

The hostility endured by female COs in all-male prisons is a significant social problem. The harassment women face "is a source of mistrust, resentment and job-related stress" (S. E. Martin & Jurik, 1996, p. 178). In fact, female COs experience more work-related stress than male COs. This reinforces the concept of women as outsiders and subordinates. Research suggests that role conflict or the challenge of balancing custodial responsibilities (e.g., maintaining security) and treatment roles (e.g., helping inmates to rehabilitate, or modeling pro-social interactions) is a significant source of stress for COs (Finn, 1998). In the absence of any support, they must adapt to the masculine culture (S. E. Martin & Jurik, 1996). This forces them to ignore and stifle their femininity, which is a part of who they are. Jane found that in order to fit in with her male coworkers she had to develop a macho persona. This behavior and attitude can lead to a negative self-image and low self-esteem, which can have adverse effects on health and family interactions. It could even influence a female guard's ability to do her job effectively, perpetuating the negative stereotypes placed on women by men and preventing job advancement. Thus, it is a self-fulfilling prophecy: female COs are treated as subordinates, causing them to do their job in a way they are uncomfortable with, thereby forcing them to be seen as incompetent, which leaves them in subordinate positions. Etheridge et al. (1984) emphasized that a major barrier to advancement by women is the expectancies held by the women themselves.

Because the numbers of female COs in all-male prisons are so small, they are often considered token employees. Therefore, their performance is highly visible, leading to further stress and pressure on the job (Crouch, 1985). They must represent the ability of all female COs, proving that they can do the job as well as their male counterparts. This can cause female COs to be wary of making mistakes, so they imitate the male officers, which may not be the most effective way to perform their job.

The fact that sexual harassment is still occurring in all-male prisons underscores an important political dynamic for women working as COs. This type of behavior interferes with basic civil rights and therefore should be assessed by policymakers in an attempt to prevent women from having to endure such degrading experiences in their place of business. Sexual harassment further reinforces the notion that women are subordinate and not worthy of being treated as equals in the job environment. Policy analysts must address this false sentiment.

Female correctional/forensic psychologists who work in prison systems often encounter similar attitudes and misconceptions. Not only are female psychologists employed in a masculinized system, but they are in a profession that is misunderstood and regarded with suspicion. Too often, women who hold this position are viewed as a "bleeding heart" or a "pushover" or as babying the inmates. Correctional officers frequently misunderstand the role of the correctional psychologist and underestimate her training in working with very manipulative and dangerous clients. Psychologists in prison systems may encounter passive aggressive antics by COs such as "forgetting" to process requests for group therapy or may harass prisoners who are trying to pass through security with approved group materials (e.g., notebooks, homework assignments). Correctional/forensic psychologists can play an active role in providing in-service training to COs by educating them about mental illness and about the psychologist's role as a mental health professional in a penal environment.

Suggestions for Future Research

Although work-related sexual harassment was dealt with to a certain extent during the first few decades after Title VII was passed, this trend has not continued. The effects of stricter, more defined sexual harassment laws in regard to women working in all-male prisons is a major area of needed research. Are women COs more willing to bring these situations out into the open now that sexual harassment is in the public eye? Do women now garner better results in getting this behavior to stop without having to sacrifice their jobs or level of respect by their coworkers?

Another area of inquiry warranting attention is the effects this profession has on the female's family members. Developing a tougher, more aggressive personality could have a major impact on a female CO's loved ones. For example, it could change the dynamics of the marital relationship or have an impact on the way the mother raises her children. In Jane's situation, she had a difficult time leaving her work personality at work. She spoke to her children the way she spoke to the inmates and guards. Consequently, does being a CO cause women to redefine their entire identity in order to succeed in the correctional setting? Research is needed in this area.

Zimmer (1987) proposed that perhaps women should not be evaluated the same way as men, given these traditionally held male jobs. Specifically, an assessment could be undertaken, exploring the requirements for a CO's job, followed by an evaluation as to whether the officer met them without looking at the manner in which they were met. A precedent needs to be set for acknowledging that women can perform their duties differently from men and be just as effective.

Finally, how are female correctional and/or forensic psychologists perceived by security staff? Are incidents of stress and burnout higher for the female psychologist in a correctional setting? Is she afforded less credibility or respect than her male counterparts? Do these women have personality styles that make this line of work more attractive than general practice? Are female psychologists more or less at risk for inmate assault? These areas are virtually unresearched and could provide valuable information to aid with recruitment, job satisfaction, and job retention.

MAKE–BELIEVE FAMILIES

Introduction

When men and women who commit crimes are sent to prison, it is easy for many people to say that they are being punished and that offenders should not be entitled to the same liberties or rights made available to ordinary citizens. However, some criminals spend many years confined in the prison environment, and they still experience the same emotions and feelings as when they were not imprisoned. It is unrealistic to assume that these inmates can shut themselves off from wanting intimacy and affection, especially in such a lonely environment where the need for affection is quite intense (Watterson, 1996). Male and female prisoners recreate their desires and needs inside of the correctional facility, yet they do so in different ways. In female prisons, women create caring relationships (MacKenzie, Robinson, & Campbell, 1989), referred to as kinship systems (Giallombardo, 1966), play families (MacKenzie et al., 1989), surrogate families (Church, 1990), and pseudofamilies (Pollock-Byrne, 1990).

Kelly was 28 years old when she was convicted of selling drugs on the streets. She was sentenced to 5 years in a state correctional facility. Kelly had spent a few weeks in the local jail before, but she had never been to prison. She had

(continued)

(Continued)

heard all sorts of stories about prison and was not sure what to expect when she arrived. She was scared and felt very alone. She had no family to speak of, and her so-called friends were other drug dealers and addicts who she could not rely on to be supportive during her time of need. On Kelly's first day in prison, she was placed in a cell with a 23-year-old inmate named Sabrina. Although Sabrina was 5 years younger than Kelly, she seemed much older and wiser. Sabrina instantly began sharing her feelings with Kelly in an attempt to have Kelly talk about her fears. Sabrina stated that it would make things easier if Kelly would talk about them. Kelly immediately felt a connection to Sabrina, which she had never experienced with anyone before. In a very short amount of time, Kelly began to view Sabrina as a mother figure and even began calling her "mom." She also was surprised to learn that Sabrina was married to another female inmate who was housed in a different unit. This inmate's name was Christina, but everyone called her Chris. Kelly soon began to call her "dad" because Chris behaved like a father and treated Kelly like her own daughter. The three of them were just like a regular family and Kelly was able to adjust to prison life with their help and support.

Literature Review

As exemplified in Kelly's case, women who are sentenced to serve time in prison find ways to cope with their environment. One way many of these women accomplish this is by modeling real families (Watterson, 1996). They use these play mothers, fathers, daughters, and lovers to make up for losing their real parents, children, and lovers (C. Burke, 1992; D. Morgan, 1997). The inmates do not necessarily enter prison to consciously create these families, but when they are scared and lonely, they either retreat into their own misery or create new relationships which develop into substitute families (Watterson, 1996).

Giallombardo (1966) defined a prison family as "a group of related kin linked by ties of allegiance and alliance who sometimes occupy a common household and are characterized by varying degrees of solidarity" (p. 163). She noted that many of these women come together in homosexual relationships to create a marriage unit. Some of the prisoners take on the role of a man and adopt masculine traits such as wearing their hair short, wearing pants, and expressing typical societal male characteristics of strength and authority. Other inmates take on the feminine role of wife or mother and wear makeup and more feminine clothing (Giallombardo, 1966; Watterson, 1996).

Pollock-Byrne (1990) described the male and female roles as being stereotypical where the males are domineering and leading and the females are nurturing and pleasing. Because the inmates play these roles in such a stereotypical fashion, those playing the male role may seem so masculine that they are referred to as "he" and "him." These "men" also can get carried away with their roles and treat their wives as slaves, ordering them around. The women who go along with this behavior probably have been involved in similar relationships while outside of prison. Therefore, it is a habit for them to do anything in order to keep their man (Watterson, 1996). Despite the sometimes negative consequences of developing prison marriages, these relationships actually serve to meet the inmates' needs for affection, and they provide closeness and a sense of belonging (Giallombardo, 1966). The women turn to each other for comfort and create these homosexual relationships and surrogate families (Church, 1990; Morgan, 1997). The marriages may not even have anything to do with sex. In fact, some women may never consummate their marriage in a sexual manner (Watterson, 1996). Instead, possibly for the first time ever, the women base their relationships on kinship and intimacy as opposed to sex (Pollock-Byrne, 1990).

Relationships among female prisoners may not be restricted to homosexual unions. Entire families organize themselves by choice and give each other titles (MacKenzie et al., 1989). Women of varying ages assume roles of mothers, daughters, aunts, and fathers (Church, 1990; MacKenzie et al., 1989). As in Kelly and Sabrina's situation, age does not necessarily dictate what role the women play. These families are not bound by ethnic categories either. Many families will include members of several ethnicities (Church, 1990). Pollock-Byrne (1990) reported that the mother–daughter dyad is the most common familial relationship. A prison mother may have several daughters, and if she has a prison husband, then he may become their father, as Chris did for Kelly. Pollock-Byrne also indicated that when playing the role of mother in prison, the inmate may be a better parent to her role-playing daughter than she ever was to her real children on the outside. For the inmates playing the role of the child, their prison mother serves as a type of role model and may become like a real mother, who helps instead of neglects them (Watterson, 1996). In Kelly's situation, Sabrina became a real mother for her.

Whether this is true in all situations, prison families, especially the roles of parent and child, are viewed as very special. The relationships consist of consideration and warmth (Giallombardo, 1966). The families are similar to regular friendships where the inmates support each other in order to decrease the stress of life in prison. Coming together as a family allows them to feel a sense of security, ease, and connection with others (Watterson, 1996). The family also serves as a form of protection for each member. If a member of the family is in physical danger from some other inmate, then the "father" or "brother" can protect that person (Giallombardo, 1966; Watterson, 1996).

Some researchers suggest that these prison families may not be as common as they used to be and may serve a purpose for only some women. MacKenzie et al. (1989) conducted a study and found that many women newly admitted to prison were involved in play families. However, those who had been in prison for a great deal of time did not partake in this phenomenon. The researchers suggested that these play families assist inmates in adjusting to prison life, but then once acclimated, the need for safety and security disappears. Pollock-Byrne (1990) discussed something similar. She stated that when an inmate approaches her release date or when she maintains close ties to her real family, then the need for a pseudofamily is not as strong as for those inmates who are alone and have no outside connections. Kelly is an example of this latter type of inmate. Without those outside relationships, the prison families become real families. Pollock-Byrne (1990) also suggested that with increased efforts at family programming and community support, female inmates are able to preserve their outside connections, which therefore decreases the need for a prison family.

In a study conducted by Ansay (as cited in Silverman & Vega, 1996), it was found that the most common group in prison was more like a gang than a family. Approximately 6 to 12 inmates who were serving long sentences comprised these gang groups and had labels such as "associates" and "cousins," thus providing more support for the notion that prison families may not be as common as they once were.

Genders and Player (1990) questioned prison staff about these inmate families, and their responses appeared to concur with what inmates reported. They suggested that relationships were more about finding affection and emotional support than they were about engaging in sexual behaviors. The staff reported that many women engaged in lesbian behaviors at some time during their imprisonment. In fact, the staff indicated that this was an eventual phase for women serving long terms in prison; however, these women were not thought to be lesbians when not imprisoned. Morgan (1997) noted that the lesbian relationships fostered in prison are often not the angry, violent ones portrayed on TV but a relationship based on a need for support and companionship. Prison administrators have indicated that they believe that fewer than 5% of female inmates have engaged in lesbian relationships outside of prison (Watterson, 1996).

Prison staff also reported that problems with these families can occur when a couple breaks up because jealous feelings and even suicidal thoughts erupt (Genders & Player, 1990). Watterson (1996, p. 294) indicated that problems occur when a female inmate "drops her belt." This is when the woman reverts back to her female role after playing a male role. It creates problems because there are not enough female inmates who want to play the male role. The woman is then seen as a phony and this is threatening to other inmates.

Despite the difficulties prison families can create, it appears as though they are necessary to help inmates adjust. As one inmate stated, ". . . inside this place, when I do something with a girl, usually I feel like someone's comforting me and just making me feel good. It's not really a sex thing, even when it's sex, because in here you feel so damn little and alone . . ." (Watterson, 1996, p. 285).

Forensic Psychology and Policy Implications

An important consideration in these make-believe families is understanding why the inmates find them necessary. As the previous literature suggested, female inmates find that they are an important source of support and a requisite when adjusting to the prison environment. Psychologists and mental health workers should play a significant role in helping inmates and correctional staff identify this need. Policies should be implemented to assist these women in their initial adjustment to prison. Psychologists must make correctional staff aware of the types of issues these women confront upon entering the prison system so that staff can assist them during the transition. This could prevent some acting-out behaviors that the women might otherwise exhibit, given their feelings of fear and insecurity.

Policies also should be developed to prevent women from being labeled as lesbians and placed in separate housing units if they do not view themselves in such a manner. If female inmates assume a role in a homosexual relationship only while in prison, then when nearing release, they should be assisted in coming to terms with this. They also will need assistance in transitioning back into heterosexual relationships and into their real families.

Another dimension to consider when dealing with female inmates is their natural families on the outside. Policies should be developed to help women maintain connections with their friends and families so that the need to create make-believe ones will not be necessary. If a woman enters prison and does not have connections to anyone outside of prison, then correctional staff and psychologists should assist her in developing ties to the community in the form of education, vocation, and community service. In this way, the inmate may have something to look forward to upon release and not feel so alone upon having to leave her prison family.

Suggestions for Future Research

Minimal research has been conducted on female inmates' make-believe families. Much of the research was conducted in the late 1960s and 1970s, with a few scattered studies in the early 1990s. If this is a phenomenon which is no longer prevalent in prisons, then studies should be conducted to determine why this is so and what may have taken its place. If women no longer feel the need for these families, then what are they doing to adjust to prison life? More current investigations need to be undertaken. Additionally, inquiries into the prevalence of more traditional prison gangs in female institutions should be conducted.

An area of research that has been neglected is how men adjust to and cope with prison life. If they do not create surrogate families in prison, then it is important to learn what they do instead. Are their mechanisms for coping effective, and, if not, what can be done to assist them? If men are able to maintain ties with their real families, then it would be helpful to know how they manage to do so. In this way, maybe female prisons can implement the policies and programs that assist men in continuing their relationships with their families.

WOMEN IN PRISON AND MOTHER–CHILD SEPARATION

Introduction

While it is widely recognized that the United States has the highest incarceration rate in the world, women prisoners have not received as much attention from the media, the legislature, and the fields of psychology and criminology as compared with their male counterparts. Yet the recent trend toward retributive justice dramatically effects the incarceration rates of women. This is primarily because most women in prison are incarcerated as a result of nonviolent offenses (Luke, 2002; Watterson, 1996). The vast majority of female offenders commit drug-related crimes. While the increase in prison populations may create a sense of security in the community, there are numerous detrimental effects which result from incarcerating less serious offenders. Among the most important issues regarding incarcerated women is their status as mothers. Therefore, confinement serves to emotionally and physically separate mothers from children, which in turn creates a host of debilitating effects on both the women and their children. Additionally, the majority of women prisoners have a substance abuse problem for which they do not receive treatment while imprisoned (Boudin, 1998; Luke, 2002). The lack of services provided to women prisoners contributes greatly to their perpetual criminal behavior, and this is connected to their drug addiction.

Furthermore, children of inmates are often overlooked victims, and this group is not small. One report noted that in 1999 an estimated 721,5000 State and Federal prisoners were parents to 1,498,800 children under the age of 18. Additionally, 22% of all minor children with a parent in prison were under the age of 5 (U.S. Department of Justice, Bureau of Justice Statistics, 2003a). According to the U.S. Department of Justice, Bureau of Justice Statistics (1999), in 1998 approximately 950,000 women were involved with either federal, state, or local corrections, including those incarcerated in jails and prisons and out on parole. Brownell (1997) reported that at least 75% of female inmates have children, with the average of two children per prisoner. The U.S. Department of Justice, Bureau of Justice Statistics (2000) indicated that from 1991 to 1999, there was a 98% increase in the number of children with a mother in prison. Children of color are far more likely to have a parent incarcerated (Luke, 2002). According to the U.S. Department of Justice, Bureau of Justice Statistics (2000), in 1999, African American children were nine times as likely as their Caucasian counterparts to have a parent incarcerated, while Latino children were three times more likely. Having an incarcerated parent can be very traumatic and can lead to severe consequences for most children, including "anxiety, hyperarousal, depression, bedwetting, eating and sleeping disorders, behavior and conduct disorders, attention disorders, and prolonged developmental regression" (Center for Children of Incarcerated Parents, as cited in Adalist-Estrin, 1994, p. 165). As examined in this section, the mother–child separation can have negative consequences for the mother as well.

When Annie was sent to prison for 1 to 3 years, she was 8 months pregnant. Upon giving birth in prison, her baby was taken away from her and sent to live with Annie's mother, who was interested in becoming a foster parent. Annie became depressed after being separated from her baby and after realizing that she might lose custody. She is worried about the baby living with her mother because Annie reported being physically abused by this woman while growing up. Despite this, she feels there are no other alternatives: She cannot rely on the baby's father to help her because he beat and threatened her both before and during her pregnancy. Annie's depression has escalated to the point of her mentioning ways to commit suicide (Brownell, 1997).

Leslie is a first-time offender who is incarcerated. She has a 9-year-old son who was living with her prior to her incarceration. Her son now lives with his father from whom Leslie is separated. The father does not want their son to go to the jail but agreed to allow visitation. The son wants to visit his mother, yet he is afraid of the jail. Leslie is worried that her son will no longer respect her and that she may be causing psychological damage to him. Although she wants to see her son, she does not want him to see her in jail because she fears this will create more damage than has already been done (Hairston, 1991b).

Literature Review

Women comprise one of the fastest growing prison populations in the United States (Haywood, Kravitz, Goldman, & Freeman, 2000; D. F. Reed & E. L. Reed, 1998). Between 1986 and 1995, the number of incarcerated women in the United States increased by more than 250% (A. J. Beck & Gilliard, 1995). In 2001, women were 6.6% of the State prison inmates, up from 6% in 1995 (U.S. Department of Justice, Bureau of Justice Statistics, 2003). The criminal justice system is much more likely to sentence a woman to prison now than ever before (Watterson, 1996). According to the U.S. Department of Justice, Bureau of Justice Statistics (2003), the prevalence of imprisonment in 2001 was higher for black females (1.7%) and Hispanic females (0.7%) than for white females (0.3%). Further, women are receiving much longer prison sentences at both the state and the federal levels (Watterson, 1996). However, this is not to suggest that women are becoming more violent or committing more crimes; rather, the criminal justice system has broadened the scope of criminal behavior for which it deems incarceration a necessary remedy. Due largely to the "war on drugs," California prisons actually showed a decrease in their percentage of violent offenders from 1985 to 1991, while their percentage of substance abuse offenders doubled (California Department of Corrections, 1991). The majority of women prisoners are incarcerated as a result of drug-related crimes. Women of color are disproportionately represented within groups of women incarcerated for both possession and trafficking drugs (Loper, 2002). A. Y. Davis (2000, p. 151) maintained that "women in prison are among the most wronged victims in the war on drugs." Thus, it is clear why this population has been particularly affected by the new laws, which require stiffer sentences for drug offenses.

Given the recent influx of women prisoners nationwide, it is important to look at the overall impact that such a movement has on society. First, there are numerous psychological considerations that pertain to incarcerated women that do not pertain to incarcerated men. Boudin (1998) identified central issues that women prisoners encounter during their period of confinement. Because the vast majority of women inmates are mothers, the issue of parenting permeates throughout all of these core concerns. Boudin claimed that a woman's personal traumatic experiences prior to incarceration have dramatic effects on her life choices before, during, and after confinement. The U.S. Department of Justice (1994) reported that over 40% of incarcerated women report a history of physical or sexual abuse. The U.S. Department of Justice, Bureau of Justice Statistics (2003) reported that 48% of jailed women indicated that they had been physically or sexually abused prior to admission with 27% having been raped. Fletcher, Rolison, and Moon (1993) reported that the typical female prisoner was sexually abused in childhood by a male member of her immediate family. While Boudin (1998) agreed that there is a high prevalence of physical, sexual, and emotional abuse in the lives of women prisoners, she reported that there are very few opportunities for women to receive help in resolving such matters during the time they are incarcerated. Greene, Haney, and Hurtado (2000) described how mothers who are frequently incarcerated for nonviolent, drug-related offenses experience poverty, physical and sexual abuse, and drug addiction, and how the cycle is often repeated by their children.

Many incarcerated mothers report that the worst part of being incarcerated is having to be separated from their children (Church, 1990; Hairston, 1991b; Luke, 2002). As the previous case illustrations show, there are many issues involved when dealing with children of incarcerated parents. Indeed, children are not the only ones who can experience the negative consequences of being separated. In Leslie's instance, she felt embarrassed and guilty about being in jail and having to subject her children to such an environment. Because of this, imprisoned mothers like Leslie might not even want their children to visit them in jail or prison (Hairston, 1991b). Even if they want to see their children, other factors may prevent them from attending visiting days. Often women's prisons are in places far away from children's homes and in areas difficult to reach by public transportation, which makes it difficult for traveling (Church, 1990; Kiser, 1991). Many incarcerated mothers experience intense guilt, loss, and sadness and fear for the loss of custody of their children (Luke, 2002).

Luke (2002) discussed the shift in focus of the U.S. child welfare policy with the implementation of the Adoption and Safe Families Act of 1997, which allows for shorter time periods before the termination of parental rights is sought. She indicated that while the intent of this new law is to better protect children from abusive or neglectful homes, it does not take into consideration the circumstances of the many mothers who are incarcerated for crimes unrelated to their parenting, including harsh penalties for low-level drug offenses. A recent study found that many women engaged in economic crimes such as drug dealing as a solution to hunger or homelessness (Ferraro & Moe, 2003).

Similar to Annie's case above, sometimes children are placed with foster families during the mother's incarceration, and the foster parents may not want the child to visit the mother because of their own desires to adopt the child (Osborne, 1995). Sometimes even the mother's own relatives do not want the children to visit her in prison (Kiser, 1991). A survey conducted by Hairston (1991b) found that 71% of incarcerated mothers did not have any visitation with their children during their period of confinement.

Watterson (1996) reported that 75% of the jails in 1994 did not allow contact visits between prisoners and their children. When such visits are allowed, it is often a traumatic experience for everyone involved. Children have a difficult time with the intimidating environment of a prison. They often do not understand why they have limited or no contact with their mothers, and they have difficulty saying goodbye to their mothers once the visit is over. For the mother, once a contact visit is granted, she knows that in order to be with her child she might be subject to the humiliation of a strip-search immediately after the visit.

> [T]he reality is that she knows before she begins that after seeing her children and family and perhaps feeling very good about herself, she will have to take off all her clothing and stand naked in front of the guards, who will check under her arms and breasts for contraband. She'll have to open her mouth and let them look under her tongue and in her cheeks. Then she has to squat, pull apart her buttocks and cough, so the guard in charge can check her vagina and anus for any hidden objects (Watterson, 1996, p. 214).

For this reason, contact visits can simultaneously be a rewarding and positive experience as well as a humiliating and punishing one. Acknowledging the importance of interaction between mothers and children, programs were developed in the 1980s to support such contact. However, in the 1990s such programs were largely discontinued due to a loss of state and federal funding (Watterson, 1996).

When children lose their mothers to incarceration, there are many negative consequences. Luke (2002, p. 933) indicated "Behavioral and emotional problems, school problems, fear, anxiety, anger, sadness, and guilt are within the normal range of experiences for children of incarcerated parents, as are abuse of chemicals at a young age, early sexual activity, teen pregnancy, truancy, and juvenile delinquency." Kiser (1991) found that children felt they were to blame for their mother's offense and became very depressed. They continued to experience these negative emotions years after their mother's incarceration and some even attempted suicide. Falk (1995) noted that children feel powerless when they have to sit by and watch their mother go to jail. While the separation is now unavoidable, the attachment between the mother and child is critical as a protective factor for the child's future development. The author stated that these children experience grief emotions such as anger, denial, and depression. They may withdraw from others, or they may begin to act out and become aggressive. Feinman (1994) suggested that children experience emotions such as insecurity, lack of trust, confusion, and loneliness. These emotions can show themselves in mental and physical illnesses and a drop in school grades. Additionally, children with parents who are incarcerated are up to six times more likely to be incarcerated during their lifetime, as compared to peers without a family history of incarceration (Luke, 2002; Myers, Smarsh, Amlund-Hagen, & Kennon, 1999).

If a child loses his or her mother to incarceration, then who takes care of the child? Hairston's (1991b) survey found that in 34% of the cases, the maternal grandmother became the caretaker. These children often live with relatives or friends of the mother. If these are not possibilities, then state-financed foster families care for them (Falk, 1995; Osborne, 1995). Occasionally, siblings have to be separated and live in different homes (Falk, 1995), thus increasing the loss they experience. Feinman (1994) reported that some states have laws which allow the state to determine whether an incarcerated mother is unfit and to take away her children via a foster home or adoption. Once again, this creates additional loss for the child.

According to a fact sheet provided by the Chicago Legal Aid to Incarcerated Mothers (1997), nearly 90% of male prisoners report that while they are incarcerated their children are being cared for by the children's mothers, whereas only 25% of similarly confined women report that their children are being cared for by their fathers. The result is that thousands of children end up in "the system." At times, relatives will care for the children of incarcerated mothers; however, all too often the children are placed in foster homes, separated from their siblings, and denied visitation with their mothers. In a study conducted by Bloom and Steinhart (1993), 54% of the mothers reported that their children had never visited them while they were in prison. Participants in this study attributed the distance between their place of residence and their mother's place of incarceration as a primary reason for the lack of visitations. Thus it becomes obvious how the incarceration of mothers greatly impacts society overall, not solely on the lives of the women in prison.

There are several solutions that could be implemented so that the child did not have to go through the trauma of enduring the incarceration of one's mother. The implementation and funding of programs is an important preventative measure to reduce the number of emotionally damaged children with an increased risk of future substance abuse, criminality, and incarceration. Perhaps the most comprehensive solution is one that permits children to live with their mothers while in prison for a certain length of time (Feinman, 1994; Jaffe, Pons, & Wicky, 1997). Jaffe et al. (1997) reported that the negative impact of this solution is that a child will have to experience the prison environment. Others opposed to this solution believe that prison is not a place for raising children and that these youths would learn to become criminals by associating with their offending mothers (Feinman, 1994). Jaffe et al. (1997) suggested the positive impact of this solution is that it emphasizes the mother–child bond and the important part it plays in a developing child. Being with one's mother is critical for a developing child and having her taken away during the early years could create some very negative consequences.

Some correctional institutions have implemented programs to allow children to remain with their incarcerated mothers. In the city of New York, the Legal Aid Society brought a lawsuit against the Department of Corrections based on the notion that separating a mother and newborn child is an action of cruel and unusual punishment under the Eighth Amendment. Apparently, there was a New York State law which allowed infants to remain in state prisons until the age of 1 year, so the Legal Aid Society wanted that law applied to the city jail. The court agreed with this argument, and, since 1985, incarcerated mothers have been allowed to have their newborn children remain with them in a special area of the jail designed for such a purpose (Feinman, 1994). The Bedford Hills Correctional Facility in New York has been a model prison for such programs as it was the first women's prison to implement a nursery for mothers and their infants (Brownell, 1997). Positive results have been reported in relation to these nursery programs. They decrease tensions and increase obedience and morale among female inmates. They also affect the staff in a positive way (Feinman, 1994).

A similar program in Nebraska was implemented in order to decrease the effects of separation between a mother and her child due to incarceration. Children younger than 18 months old can remain at the correctional facility with their mothers in a nursery equipped for six infants. The mothers must take prenatal courses, and other inmates can become involved by babysitting or providing support for the mothers (Hromadka, 1995).

California also offers incarcerated mothers a chance to remain with their children. The program is called Mother-Infant Care, and it is available to minimum-security female prisoners. These women are allowed to live with their young children throughout the length of their sentence. However, they must participate in parental education courses and community service, and they are given opportunities for job training and continuing education (Gifford, 1992).

Most programs which allow children to live with their mothers in prison have been developed for only very young children. There have been attempts to create other options for older children through visitation programs. Having children visit their mothers is viewed as an important ingredient to maintaining attachment bonds (Adalist-Estrin, 1994). Despite this, there are still few initiatives, which provide visitation for children on a consistent basis (M. C. Moses, 1995). However, some alternatives that have been developed include expanded visitations, longer visitation hours, and overnight to week-long visits (Adalist-Estrin, 1994).

The Minnesota Correctional Facility at Shakopee is credited with having the most extensive and well-developed parenting programs of this kind in the country (Alley, 1998; Luke, 2002). Incarcerated mothers are offered a number of specialized parenting classes and two extended visitation programs (Luke, 2002). The two extended visitation programs include the Children's Program, for children up to 11, and the Parenting Teens Program, for inmates with children ages 12 through 17 years old (Luke, 2002). These programs are designed to increase cohesiveness between parent and child, enhance parenting skills in a safe environment, and to provide the inmate an opportunity to assess her capabilities and desire to parent her children. Once again, these types of programs also compel good behavior by inmates who desire to see their children. The Children's Program consists of extended, well-structured, overnight weekend visits with one and sometimes two of the mother's children, depending on space. The Parenting Teens Program consists of monthly "teen days" or visits from teenage children contingent upon the inmate participating in weekly support group meetings for parents of teens. In addition to parenting skills, these groups also serve to provide a support network for mothers who are suffering, as a result of being separated from their children. The teens and their mothers often play in the gym, work on crafts, watch a movie, or just spend time talking alone during the scheduled teen day visits (Luke, 2002).

Forensic Psychology and Policy Implications

The number of women incarcerated in the United States is increasing with every new law that requires stiffer sentences for minor offenses. Although the vast majority of women prisoners are incarcerated as a result of drug-related crimes, few programs exist inside the prisons to provide the treatment that such women need in order to recover from their addictions. Research has repeatedly shown that incarceration alone does not alter the subsequent criminal behavior of drug-abusing offenders (Moon, Thompson, & Bennett, 1993; National Institute of Corrections, 1991). Policy reforms are drastically needed, given that most women prisoners are substance abusers, most prisons do not offer substance abuse treatment, and incarceration without a treatment component does not curb recidivism for offenders who abuse drugs or alcohol. Programs or psychotherapy groups designed to address their histories of abuse are also scarce or nonexistent.

Although efforts have been made to improve programs for children and their incarcerated mothers, there are still many issues that remain unresolved. For instance, as Falk (1995) pointed out, because of their restrictions, many of these projects exclude one or more children of the same family from visiting their mother. This could create a new set of problems for the family. It may be unreasonable for all of a woman's children to live with her in the prison, but programs should be developed where all the children in one family can visit their mother for extended periods of time.

Because incarcerated women have suggested that being separated from their children is the most difficult aspect of their confinement, support services designed specifically to assist them in adjusting to this separation should be developed further (Hairston, 1991b; Luke, 2002). As evidenced from the previous case illustration, Annie would have benefited greatly from assistance on how to cope with being separated from her child.

Correctional/forensic psychologists can also be instrumental in developing programs that support contact between imprisoned mothers and their children. Given that such programs did exist for a short period of time, it can be assumed that the legislature once saw promise in such initiatives, but subsequently found that they were not beneficial or cost-effective. With the expertise and insight of both criminology and psychology, programmatic solutions need to be explored.

Psychologists can also work with correctional staff and facilities on how best to implement and run programs where children would live within the prison or come for overnight visitation. Not all staff will be knowledgeable about how to provide a positive environment for children, so child development specialists should be involved in the programming. Also, the correctional facilities need to develop visitation areas which promote family bonding (Hairston, 1991b) and help children overcome their fears of going to the prison for visitation. As Leslie's case shows, children are afraid of jails and prisons and may not want to see their mothers for this reason. Psychologists could also facilitate psychotherapy groups for women in need of support, as a result of their separation from their children.

Once programs and services have been developed within the correctional institution, then policies should be developed to assist these same women when released from prison. Currently, there is no set standard for continuing services outside of the prison (Adalist-Estrin, 1994). As in Annie's case, these mothers may be struggling with someone seeking to terminate their parental rights. Mothers released from prison need assistance with this process. Correctional facilities could have social workers on staff to help these women transition back into their families. Luke (2002) strongly recommended that changes in current child welfare policy be made in order to reflect the unique needs of children of incarcerated parents.

One area that has been neglected is the development of more comprehensive programs for fathers who become incarcerated. In some situations, the father is the sole caretaker. As such, his children likely experience the same sense of grief over the loss of the male parent. Even if the children have a mother at home, they still have a connection with their father and they should be able to visit him in order to maintain that connection. Male correctional facilities could assist with this by improving their visitation areas and by allowing for extended child visits. If the father is the sole caretaker of a young child, then policies for developing live-in programs at male prisons also should be developed.

Suggestions for Future Research

Compared to the literature on male prisoners, the research on imprisoned women is relatively scarce. Female prisoners have only recently received concentrated attention as a separate cohort from their male counterparts. While the existing research strongly supports contact between women prisoners and their children, studies are needed that compare those women who do receive such visits with those who do not especially in terms of their psychological well-being, their behavioral conduct within the prison, and their future criminal behavior. One of the primary goals of the criminal justice system is the reduction of future criminal behavior. Therefore, recidivism studies need to be conducted that compare women who receive substance abuse treatment while incarcerated with those who do not. For many reasons, alternative sentencing programs need to be examined for women who have committed nonviolent offenses. If such programs are found to be as effective at reducing recidivism among women offenders as are correctional placements, then their implementation would be sensible economically, psychologically, and criminologically.

An important area of research is to determine which situations are beneficial and which are detrimental for children who maintain contact with their incarcerated parents (Hairston, 1991a). In some instances, seeking termination of parental rights may be in the best interest of the child, but a better understanding of what those instances are should be explored. Similarly, the effects on children from visiting or not visiting their incarcerated parent must be studied further (Hairston, 1991a).

Additional research should be conducted regarding the possible effects on young children who live with their mothers in correctional institutions. More information is needed, particularly regarding whether this is beneficial or detrimental to youths. If benefits are assured, then examining whether they would extend to older children should be the next step.

Finally, investigators need to examine what the effects are on children whose fathers are incarcerated, even if that father is not the sole provider. Do these children experience the same sense of loss as losing a mother? Are the bonds as strong with a father as they are with a mother? The father plays an important role in his children's lives, and more information needs to be learned about what kind of an effect his absence creates.

Practice Update Section: Issues in Corrections/ Correctional Psychology

Boothby and Clements (2002) indicated that while the number of psychologists choosing to work in correctional settings is increasing, little research is done to evaluate their job experiences or job satisfaction. The number of correctional psychologists has doubled in the last 20 years with the majority being Caucasian males (Boothby & Clements, 2000). These researchers surveyed 800 correctional psychologists and discovered that, overall, they had a moderate level of job satisfaction (Boothby & Clements, 2002). Safety, job security, and relationships with clients were ranked as the job characteristics that were the most satisfying, while opportunities for advancement and professional growth were ranked as the least satisfying. Finally, psychologists who worked for federal prisons or less crowded institutions were comparatively more satisfied with their jobs (Boothby & Clements, 2002). Although working with violent offenders, psychologists working in a forensic hospital or correctional institution may have increased feelings of security due to the presence of security staff, cameras, and other safety precautions taken in these settings. Psychologists working in community mental health centers are typically not afforded many of these same protections or security measures, while some-times working with potentially dangerous clients.

A study examining the priorities of psychological services in a correctional environment identified assessment, harm prevention, and other clinical services, as well as being a role model and evaluating and training other staff, as important duties to be developed (S. Byrne, M. K. Byrne, & Howells, 2001). Boothby and Clements (2000) found that administrative duties have grown and now consume about one-third of a psychologist's professional time in correctional settings. This can be a source of frustration for some psychologists who feel that there is already a shortage of psychologists to offer clinical services such as group therapy or psychological testing. Some prisons require that staff psychologists review infractions committed by inmates with a documented mental illness to determine the impact of the disorder on their actions. In essence, these reviews are similar to a miniature mental state at the time of the offense evaluation for institutional infractions. Procedures such as these in some correctional environments are a result of previous litigation regarding the treatment of mentally ill inmates.

In the past, psychologists who worked in a correctional environment were regarded with suspicion by individuals who questioned their ability to function in a private practice arena. While the security and benefits of a prison-based job are alluring to some, the specialized practice of correctional/forensic psychol-ogy has attracted many highly qualified clinicians trained in working with

(continued)

(*Continued*)

offender populations. Psychologists who are trained with a specialty in forensic psychology are often skilled and knowledgeable about treatment interventions designed for criminal populations. They are trained in subject matter and skill areas focused on psycholegal issues and in the dynamics of correctional or courtroom settings, enabling them to function more effectively in these contexts. The correctional client and the organizational dynamics (e.g., chain of command, security issues) are different from those in the community. In addition each correctional setting is quite different. Private practitioners routinely interface with insurance companies and typically deal with pro-social clientele rather than violent offenders, CCOs, and wardens. There are differing implications as set forth by the Standards for Psychology Services in Jail and Prisons regarding informed consent, confidentiality, and "duty to warn" (American Association for Correctional Psychology, 2000). The American Association for Correctional Psychology (2000) revised its 1980 Standards in order to promote the highest quality of mental health services to those in custody and to increase the scope of the correctional psychologists' role to include policy making, psychological screening of security staff, and consultation. Understanding the differences in roles between the correctional/forensic psychologist, the community, or the general clinical psychologist can have important implications for the recruitment and retention of mental health staff in correctional settings.

Abadinsky, H., & Winfree, L. (1992). *Crime and justice: An introduction* (2nd ed.). Chicago: Nelson-Hall.

Abdollahi, M. K. (2002). Understanding police stress research. *Journal of Forensic Psychology Practice, 2*(2), 1–24.

Abram, K. M., & Teplin, L. A. (1991). Co-occurring disorders among mentally ill jail detainees: Implications for public policy. *American Psychologist, 46*(10), 1036–1045.

Ackerman, M. J., & Ackerman, M. C. (1996). Child custody evaluation practices: A 1996 survey of psychologists. *Family Law Quarterly, 30*, 565–586.

Ackerman, M. J., & Ackerman, M. C. (1997). Custody evaluation practices: A survey of experienced professionals revisited. *Professional Psychology: Research and Practice, 28*, 137–145.

Acklin, M. W. (2002). Forensic psychodiagnostic testing. *Journal of Forensic Psychology Practice, 2*(3), 107–112.

Adalist-Estrin, A. (1994). Family support and criminal justice. In S. L. Kagan & B. Weissbourd (Eds.), *Putting families first America's family support movement and the challenge of change* (pp. 161–185). San Francisco: Jossey-Bass.

Adams, R., Rohe, W., Willren, C., & Arcury, T. (2002, July). Implementing community-oriented policing: Organizational change and street officer attitudes. *Crime & Delinquency, 48*(3), 399–430.

Adoption and Safe Families Act. No. 105–89, 101–501, 111 Statute 2115 (1997).

Alarid, L. F. (2000a). Sexual assault and coercion among incarcerated women prisoners: Excerpts from prison letters. *The Prison Journal, 80*(4), 391–406.

Alarid, L. F. (2000b, March). Sexual orientation perspectives of incarcerated bisexual and gay men: The county jail protective custody experience. *The Prison Journal, 80*(1), 80–95.

Albers, E., & Evans, W. (1994). Suicide ideation among a stratified sample of rural and urban adolescents. *Child and Adolescent Social Work Journal, 11*(5), 379–389.

Alessi, N. E., McManus, M., Brickman, A., & Grapentine, L. (1984). Suicidal behavior among serious juvenile offenders. *American Journal of Psychiatry, 141*, 286–287.

Alexander, M. A. (1997). *Sex offender treatment probed anew.* Unpublished manuscript.

Alison, L., Bennell, C., Mokros, A, & Ormerod, D. (2002, March). The personality paradox in offender profiling: A theoretical review of the processes involved in deriving background characteristics from crime scene actions. *Psychology, Public Policy, & Law, 8*(1), 115–135.

Alison, L., Smith, M. D., Eastman, O., & Rainbow, L. (2003, June). Toulmin's philosophy of argument and its relevance to offender profiling. *Psychology, Crime & Law, 9*(2), 173–183.

Allard, P., & Young, M. C. (2002). Prosecuting juveniles in adult court: The practitioner's perspectives. *Journal of Forensic Psychology Practice, 2*(2), 65–77.

Allen, H., & Simonsen, C. E. (1989). *Corrections in America.* New York: Macmillan.

Alley, M. (1998). The mother offspring life development program. In C. Blinn (Ed.), *Maternal ties: A selection of programs for female offenders* (pp. 151–165). Lanham, MD: American Correctional Association.

Amato, P. R., & Sobolewski, J. M. (2001). The effects of divorce and marital discord on adult children's psychological well-being. *American Sociological Review, 66*(6), 900–921.

American Association for Correctional Psychology. (2000, August). Standards for psychology services in jails, prisons, correctional facilities, and agencies. *Criminal Justice & Behavior, 27*(4), 433–494.

American Association of Mental Retardation (2002). *Mental retardation: Definition, classification, and systems of supports* (10th ed.). Washington, DC: American Association on Mental Retardation.

American Bar Association. (1980). *Juvenile justice standards on dispositions.* Cambridge, MA: Ballinger Press.

American Civil Liberties Union Lesbian & Gay Rights Project (2002). *Too high a price: The case against restricting gay parenting.* Available from: 125 Broad Street, 18th Floor, New York, NY 10004.

American Correctional Association. (2001). ACA welcomes its newest affiliate. *Corrections Today, 63*(3), 18.

American Psychiatric Association. (1987). *Diagnostic and statistical manual of mental disorders* (3rd ed. revised). Washington, DC: Author.

American Psychiatric Association. (1994). *Diagnostic and statistical manual of mental disorders* (4th ed.). Washington, DC: Author.

American Psychiatric Association Insanity Defense Work Group. (1983). American Psychiatric Association Statement on insanity defense. *American Journal of Psychiatry, 140,* 681–688.

American Psychological Association. (1992). Ethical principles of psychologists and code of conduct. *American Psychologist, 47*(12), 1597–1611.

American Red Cross (2001). Available: http://www.trauma-pages.com

Anastasi, A., & Urbina, S. (1997). *Psychological testing* (7th ed.). Upper Saddle River, NJ: Prentice Hall.

Anderson, M., Gillig, P., Sitaker, M., McCloskey, K., Malloy, K., & Grigsby, N. (2003, June). "Why doesn't she just leave?" A descriptive study of victim reported impediments to her safety. *Journal of Family Violence, 18*(3), 151–156.

Anonymous. (1984, April). Forensic guidelines: Collection and preservation of arson evidence. *The Police Chief,* pp. 56–58.

Anonymous. (1997). Hell on Block 1G. *Westchester County Weekly*. Retrieved February 15, 1998, from http://www.westchesterweekly.com/articles/suicied2.html

Appelbaum, P. L. (1994). Assessment of criminal justice related competencies in defendants with mental retardation. *Journal of Psychiatry & Law, 22*, 311–327.

Anshel, M. H. (2000, September). A conceptual model and implications for coping with stressful events in police work. *Criminal Justice & Behavior, 27*(3), 375–400.

Arcaya, J. M. (1989). The police and the emotionally disturbed: A psychoanalytic theory of intervention. *International Journal of Offender Therapy and Comparative Criminology, 33*(1), 37–48.

Arens, D. A. (1993). What do the neighbors think now? Community residences on Long Island, New York. *Community Mental Health Journal, 29*, 235–245.

Arrigo, B. (1993). Paternalism, civil commitment, and illness politics: Assessing the current debate and outlining a future direction. *Journal of Law and Health, 7*(3/4), 131–168.

Arrigo, B. (1996). *The contours of psychiatric justice: A postmodern critique of mental illness, criminal insanity, and the law.* New York: Garland.

Arrigo, B. (1999). A review of graduate training models in forensic psychology: Implications for practice. *Journal of Forensic Psychology Practice, 1*(1), 1–20.

Arrigo, B., & Claussen, N. (2003, June). Police corruption and psychological testing: A strategy for preemployment screening. *International Journal of Offender Therapy & Comparative Criminology, 47*(3), 272–290.

Arrigo, B. A., & Garsky, K. (2001). Police suicide: a glimpse behind the badge. In R. G. Dunham & G. P. Alpert (Eds.), *Critical issues in policing: Contemporary readings (5th ed.)*, (pp. 664–680), Prospect Heights, IL: Waveland.

Arrigo, B. A., & Purcell, C. E. (2001). Examining paraphilias and lust murder: Towards an integrated model. *International Journal of Offender Therapy and Comparative Criminology, 45*, 6–31.

Arrigo, B., & Shipley, S. (2001). The confusion over psychopathy (I): Historical considerations. *International Journal of Offender Therapy and Comparative Criminology, 45*(3), 325–344.

Arrigo, B., & Tasca, J. (1999). Right to refuse treatment, competency to be executed, and therapeutic jurisprudence: Toward a systemic analysis. *Law and Psychology Review, 23*(1), 1–47.

Arrigo, B. A., & Williams, C. R. (1999). Law, ideology and critical inquiry: The case of treatment refusal for incompetent prisoners awaiting execution. *New England Journal on Criminal and Civil Confinement, 25*, 367–412.

Ashworth, A. (1999). *Principles of Criminal Law* (3rd ed.). Oxford: Clarendon Press.

Atkin, R. (1999, June 16). Hey mom — I'm going for a ride with the cops. *Christian Science Monitor, 91*(140), 11.

Atkinson, J. M., & Garner, H. C. (2002, July). Least restrictive alternative — Advance statements and the new mental health legislation. *Psychiatric Bulletin, 26*(7), 246–247.

Atkinson, J., & Young, T. L. (2002). Keeping high-risk youth from becoming incarcerated adults. In N. G. Ribner (Ed.), *The handbook of juvenile forensic psychology*, (pp. 608–624), San Francisco, CA: Jossey-Bass.

Austin, V. L. (2003). Fear and loathing in the classroom: A candid look at school violence and the policies and practices that address it. *Journal of Disability Policy Studies, 14*(1), 17–22.

Austin, W. G. (2001, October). Partner violence and risk assessment in child custody evaluation. *Family Court Review, 39*(4), 483–496.

Azar, S., & Cote, L. (2002, May/June). Sociocultural issues in the evaluation of the needs of children in custody decision making: What do our current frameworks for evaluating parenting practices have to offer? *International Journal of Law & Psychiatry, 25*(3), 193–217.

Baca, S. V. (1987, August). Domestic violence: One police department's solution. *The Police Chief*, pp. 40–41.

Bachrach, L. (1980). Is the least restrictive environment always the best? Sociological and semantic implications. *Hospital and Community Psychiatry, 31*, 97–103.

Bagley, C. (1999). Adolescent prostitution in Canada and the Philippines. *International Social Work, 42*(4), 445–455.

Bagley, C., & Young, L. (1987). Juvenile prostitution and child sexual abuse: A controlled study. *Canadian Journal of Community Mental Health, 6*, 55–126.

Bailey, R. K. (2002). The civil commitment of sexually violent predators: A unique Texas approach. *Journal of the American Academy of Psychiatry & the Law, 30*(4), 525–532.

Baker, T. E., & Baker, J. P. (1996, October). Preventing police suicide. *FBI Law Enforcement Bulletin*, pp. 25–27.

Baker, W. D. (1995, September). Prevention: A new approach to domestic violence. *FBI Law Enforcement Bulletin*, pp. 18–20.

Banach, M. (1998). The best interests of the child: Decision-making factors. *Families in Society, 79*, 331–340.

Bandura, A. (1998). Mechanisms of moral disengagement. In W. Reich (Ed.), *Origins of terrorism: Psychologies, ideologies, theologies, states of mind* (pp. 161–191). Washington, DC: Woodrow Wilson Center Press.

Barnes, J. E. (2000, March 23, 2000). Insanity defense fails for man who threw woman onto track (cover story). *New York Times, 149*(51336), pA1.

Bardwell, M. C., & Arrigo, B. A. (2002). Competency to stand trial: A law, psychology, and policy assessment. *Journal of Psychiatry & Law, 30*(2), 147–269.

Baroff, G. S. (1996). The mentally retarded offender. In J. W. Jacobson, & J. A. Mulick (Eds.), *Manual of diagnosis and professional practice in mental retardation*, (pp. 311–321), Washington, DC.: APA Books.

Barr, W. P. (1992). Violent youths should be punished as adults. In M. D. Biskup & C. P. Cozic (Eds.), *Youth violence*. San Diego, CA: Greenhaven Press.

Barrett, S. E. (1997). Children of lesbian parents: The what, when, and how of talking about donor identity. *Children's Rights, Therapists' Responsibilities, 20*, 43–55.

Barron, P., Hassiotis, A., & Barnes, J. (2002). Offenders with intellectual disability: The size of the problem and therapeutic outcomes. *Journal of Intellectual Disability Research, 46*(6), 454–463.

Batterman-Faunce, J. M., & Goodman, G. S. (1993). Effects of context on the accuracy and reliability of child witnesses. In G. S. Goodman & B. L. Bottoms (Eds.), *Child victims, child witnesses: Understanding and improving testimony* (pp. 301–330). New York: Guilford Press.

Battle, A. O., Battle, M. V., & Tolley, E. A. (1993). Potential for suicide and aggression in delinquents at juvenile court in a southern city. *Suicide and Life Threatening Behavior, 23*(3), 230–244.

Battle staff burnout with critical incident stress debriefing. (1997, November 7). *Corrections Professional, 21*, p. 3.

Bauserman, R. (2002). Child adjustment in joint-custody versus sole-custody arrangements: A metanalytic review. *Journal of Family Psychology, 16*(1), 91–102.

Baxter, H., Duggan, C., Larkin, E., Cordess, C., & Page, K. (2001, September). Mentally disordered parricide and stranger killers admitted to high-security care: A descriptive comparison. *Journal of Forensic Psychiatry, 12*(2), 287–299.

Bayley, D. H., & Garafalo, J. (1989). The management of violence by police patrol officers. *Criminology, 27,* 1–25.

Beail, N. (2002). Constructive approaches to the assessment, treatment and management of offenders with intellectual disabilities. *Journal of Applied Research in Intellectual Disabilities, 15*(2), 179–182.

Beck, A. J., & Gilliard, D. K. (1995). *Prisoners in 1994.* Washington, DC: Bureau of Justice Statistics Bulletin.

Beck, J. (1990). Home confinement and the use of electronic monitoring with federal parolees. *Federal Probation, 54,* 22–31.

Beinart, P. (June 14, 1999). Bill of goods. *New Republic, 220*(24), 6.

Belcher, J. R. (1988). Are jails replacing the mental health system for the homeless mentally ill? *Community Mental Health Journal, 24*(3), 185–195.

Belfrage, H., Fransson, G., & Strand, S. (2000). Prediction of violence using the HCR-20: A prospective study in two maximum-security correctional institutions. *Journal of Forensic Psychiatry, 11*(1), 167–175.

Bell, C., Coven, M., Cronan, J., Garza, C., Guggemos, P. & Storto, L. (1999). Rape and sexual misconduct in the prison system: Analyzing America's most "open" secret. *Yale Law & Policy Review, 18,* 195–223.

Bell, D. J., & Bell, S. L. (1991). The victim offender relationship as a determinate factor in police dispositions of family violence incidence: A replication study. *Policing and Society, 1,* 225–237.

Bennett, W., & Hess, K. (1996). *Management and supervision in law enforcement* (2nd ed.). St. Paul, MN: West Publishing.

Benson, C., & Matthews, R. (1995). Street prostitution: Ten facts in search of a policy. *International Journal of the Sociology of Law, 23,* 395–415.

Berger, V. (2000, July). Civilians versus police: Mediation can help to bridge the divide. *Negotiation Journal, 16*(3), 211–235.

Bergmann, L. H., & Queen, T. R. (1987). The aftermath: Treating traumatic stress is crucial. *Corrections Today, 49,* 100–104.

Bernet, W. (2002, October). Child custody evaluations. *Child & Adolescent Psychiatric Clinics of North America, 11*(4), 781–804.

Berube, M. S. (Ed.). (1982). *The American Heritage dictionary* (2nd ed.). Boston: Houghton Mifflin.

Beutler, L. E., Nussbaum, P. D., & Meredith, K. E. (1988). Changing personality patterns of police officers. *Professional Psychology: Research and Practice, 19*(5), 503–507.

Beutler, L. E., Storm, A., Kirkish, P., Scogin, F., & Gaines, J. A. (1985). Parameters in the prediction of police officer performance. *Professional Psychology: Research and Practice, 16,* 324–335.

Bhui, K., Outhwaite, J., Adzinku, P., Dixon, P., et al. (2001). Implementing clinical practice guidelines on the management of imminent violence on two acute psychiatric in-patient units. *Journal of Mental Health, 10*(5), 559–569.

Bidrose, S., & Goodman, G. S. (2000, May/June). Testimony and evidence: A scientific case study of memory for child sexual abuse. *Applied Cognitive Psychology, 14*(3), 197–213.

Bilchik, S. (1997, April). Prevention and teamwork key to fighting juvenile crime. *Corrections Today, 59*(2), 42–45.

Binder, R. L. (2002). Liability for the psychiatrist expert witness. *American Journal of Psychiatry, 159*(11), 1819–1825.

Binder, A., & Scharf, P. (1980). The violent police-citizen encounter. *Annals of the American Academy of Political and Social Science, 452,* 111–121.

Bindman, J. (2002, Fall). "Safe, sound, and supportive": Mental health care policy in England. *International Journal of Mental Health, 31*(3), 3–13.

Bindman, S. (1991, October 14). Top court revisits abuse defense. Murder conviction appeal to focus on instructions to jury about "battered-woman syndrome." *The Ottawa Citizen,* p. A1.

Bireda, M. R. (2000). Education for all. *Principal Leadership, 1*(4), 8–13.

Birgden, A., & Vincent, F. (2000). Maximizing therapeutic effects in treating sexual offenders in an Australian correctional system. *Behavioral Sciences & the Law, 18*(4), 479–488.

Bjerregaard, B. (2002, September). Self-definitions of gang membership and involvement in delinquent activities. *Youth & Society, 9*(4), 45–56.

Black, B. (1988). *Work and mental illness.* Baltimore: Johns Hopkins University.

Blackwell, B. S., & Vaughn, M. S. (2003, Mar/April). Police civil liability for inappropriate response to domestic assault victims. *Journal of Criminal Justice, 31*(2), 129–146.

Blak, R. (1995). *Use of deadly force. The psychological impact of officer involved shootings.* Available at the Institute for Psychology, Law, and Public Policy, Fresno, CA.

Blak, R., & Sanders, S. (1997). *Post traumatic stress (PTSD) in law enforcement.* Available at the Institute for Psychology, Law, and Public Policy, Fresno, CA.

Blanchette, K. (1996). *Sex offender assessment, treatment and recidivism: A literature review.* Unpublished manuscript.

Blau, T. H. (1998). *The psychologist as expert witness* (2nd ed.). New York: John Wiley & Sons, Inc.

Bleich, A., Gelkopf, M., & Solomon, Z. (2003, August). Exposure to terrorism, stress-related mental health symptoms, and coping behaviors among a nationally representative sample in Israel. *Journal of the American Medical Association, 290*(5), 612–620.

Bloom, B. (1995). Public policy and the children of incarcerated parents. In K. Gabel & D. Johnston (Eds.), *Children of incarcerated parents* (pp. 271–284). New York: Lexington Books.

Bloom, B., & Steinhart, D. (1993). *Why punish the children? A reappraisal of the children of incarcerated mothers in America.* San Francisco: National Council on Crime and Delinquency.

Blum, V. (2002). Allowing execution of juveniles gives Virginia its edge in case. *The Legal Intelligencer, 227*(97), 1–3.

Blumberg, M. (1989). The AIDS epidemic and the police. In R. Dunham and & G. Alpert (Eds.), *Critical issues in policing: Contemporary readings* (pp. 208–219). Prospect Heights, IL: Waveland Press.

Blumenthal, S. (2000). Developmental aspects of violence and the institutional response. *Criminal Behaviour & Mental Health, 10*(3), 185–198.

Bonner, R. L. (1992). Isolation, seclusion, and psychological vulnerability as risk factors for suicide behind bars. In A. L. Berman, R. W. Maris, J. T. Maltsberger, & R. I. Yufit (Eds.), *Assessment and prediction of suicide* (pp. 389–419). New York: Guilford.

Boothby, J. L., & Clements, C. B. (2000, December). A national survey of correctional psychologists. *Criminal Justice & Behavior, 27*(6), 716–732.

Boothby, J. L., & Clements, C. B. (2002, June). Job satisfaction of correctional psychologists: Implications for recruitment and retention. *Professional Psychology: Research & Practice, 33*(3), 310–315.

Borgman, R. (1981). Antecedents and consequences of parental rights termination for abused and neglected children. *Child Welfare, 60,* 391–403.

Borum, R., & Grisso, T. (1995). Psychological test use in criminal forensic evaluations. *Professional Psychology: Research and Practice, 26*(5), 465–473.

Borum, R., & Reddy, M. (2001). Assessing violence risk in Tarasoff situations: A fact-based model of inquiry. *Behavioral Sciences & the Law, 19*(3), 375–385.

Bottoms, B. L. (1993). Individual differences in perceptions of child sexual assault victims. In G. S. Goodman & B. L. Bottoms (Eds.), *Child victims, child witnesses: Understanding and improving testimony* (pp. 229–261). New York: Guilford Press.

Boudin, K. (1998). Lessons from a mother's program in prison: A psychosocial approach supports women and their children. *Women & Therapy, 21*(1), 103–125.

Bourque, B. B., Cronin, R. C., Felker, D. B., Pearson, F. R., Han, M., & Hill, S. M. (1996). Boot camps for juvenile offenders: An implementation evaluation of three demonstration programs [On-line].

Bow, J. N., & Quinnell, F. A. (2001, June). Psychologists' current practices and procedures in child custody evaluations: Five years after American Psychological Association. *Professional Psychology: Research & the Law, 32*(3), 261–268.

Bowker, A. L., & Schweid, R. E. (1992). Habilitation of the retarded offender in Cuyahoga County. *Federal Probation, 56,* 48–52.

Bracco, K. (1997). Patriarchy and the law of adoption: Beneath the best interests of the child. *The Alberta Law Review, 35,* 1035–1055.

Braddock, D. (Ed.). (1999). *Positive behavior support for people with developmental disabilities: A research synthesis.* Washington, DC: American Association on Mental Retardation.

Brantley, A. C., & DiRosa, A. (1994). Gangs: A national perspective. *FBI Law Enforcement Bulletin, 63*(5), 1–6.

Braver, S. L., Fabricius, W. V., & Ellman, I. M. (2003, June). Relocation of children after divorce and children's best interests: New evidence and legal consideration. *Journal of Family Psychology, 17*(2), 206–219.

Breci, M. G., & Simons, R. (1987). An examination of organizational and individual factors that influence police response to domestic disturbances. *Journal of Police Science and Administration, 15*(2), 93–104.

Breuner, C. C., & Farrow, J. A. (1995). Pregnant teens in prison: Prevalence, management, and consequences. *Western Journal of Medicine, 162,* 328–330.

Briken, P., Hill, A., & Berner, W. (2003, August). Pharmacotherapy of paraphilias with long-acting agonists of luteinizing hormone-releasing hormone: A systemic review. *Journal of Clinical Psychiatry, 64*(8), 890–897.

Brinded, P. M. J., Simpson, A. I. F., Laidlaw, T. M., Fairley, N., & Malcolm, F. (2001). Prevalence of psychiatric disorders in New Zealand prisons: A national study. *Australian and New Zealand Journal of Psychiatry, 35,* 166–173.

Briscoe, J. (1997). Breaking the cycle of violence: A rational approach to at-risk youth. *Federal Report, 61,* 3–13.

Brodsky, S. L., Caputo, A. A., & Domino, M. L. (2002). The mental health professional in court: Legal issues, research foundations, and effective testimony. In B. Van Dorsten (Ed.), *Forensic psychology: From classroom to courtroom* (pp. 17–33). New York: Kluwer Academic/Plenum Publishers.

Bronitt, S., & McSherry, B. (2001). *Principles of criminal law.* Sydney: LBC.

Brooks, L. (1997). Police discretionary behavior: A study of style. In R. Dunham & G. Alpert (Eds.),*Critical issues in policing* (3rd ed.). Prospect Heights, IL: Waveland Press.

Brooks, S. L. (2002). Kinship and adoption. *Adoption Quarterly, 5*(3), 55–66.

Brown, G. L., Linnoila, M. I., & Goodwin, F. K. (1992). *Impulsivity, aggression, and associated affects: Relationship to self-destructive behavior and suicide.* New York: Guilford Press.

Brown, J. D. (2003, Spring). Is involuntary outpatient commitment a remedy for community mental health service failure? *Ethical Human Sciences & Services, 5*(1), 7–20.

Brown, J. G. (1994). The use of mediation to resolve criminal cases: A procedural critique. *Emory Law Journal, 43,* 1–45.

Brown, S. (1999, September). The mental health tribunal of Queensland: A use model for UK forensic psychiatry? *Journal of Psychiatry, 10*(2), 325–332.

Brown, V. B., Ridgely, M. S., Pepper, B., Levine, I. S., & Ryglewicz, H. (1989). The dual crisis: Mental illness and substance abuse. *American Psychologist, 44,* 565–569.

Browne, A., & Finkelhor, D. (1986). Impact of child sexual abuse: A review of the research. *Psychological Bulletin, 99*(1), 66–77.

Browne, K., & Herbert, M. (1997). *Preventing family violence.* New York: Wiley.

Brownell, P. (1997). Female offenders in the criminal justice system: Policy and program development. In A. R. Roberts (Ed.), *Social work in juvenile and criminal justice settings* (2nd ed., pp. 325–349). Springfield, IL: Charles C Thomas.

Buchanan, A., & Leese, M. (2001). Detention of people with dangerous severe personality disorders: A systematic review. *Lancet, 358,* 1955.

Buchanan, G., Stephens, C., & Long, N. (2001). Traumatic events of new recruits and serving police. *Australasian Journal of Disaster and Trauma Studies, 5*(2), NP.

Buerger, M. E. (1994). A tale of two targets: Limitations of community anticrime action. *Crime & Delinquency, 40*(3), 411–436.

Buhrke, R. A. (1996). *A matter of justice: Lesbians and gay men in law enforcement.* New York: Routledge.

Bullock, J. L. (2002). Involuntary treatment of defendants found incompetent to stand trial. *Journal of Forensic Psychology Practice, 2*(4), 1–33.

Burford, G., Pennell, J., MacLeod, S., Campbell, S., & Lyall, G. (1996). Reunification as an extended family matter. *Community Alternatives: International Journal of Family Care, 8*(3), 33–55.

Burke, C. (1992). *Vision narratives of women in prison.* Knoxville: University of Tennessee Press.

Burke, M. (1993). *Coming out of the blue: British police officers talk about their lives in "the job" as lesbians, gays, and bisexuals.* New York: Cassell.

Burke, M. (1994). Homosexuality as deviance: The case of the gay police officer. *British Journal of Criminology, 34*(2), 192–203.

Burns, R. (2001, September). Amber Plan: Hue and cry. Retrieved November 5, 2003 from http://www.communitypolicing.org/publications/comlinks/cll6/cll6_burns.htm

Bussey, K., Lee, K., & Grimbeck, E. J. (1993). Lies and secrets: Implications for children's reporting of sexual abuse. In G. S. Goodman & B. L. Bottoms (Eds.), *Child victims, child witnesses: Understanding and improving testimony* (pp. 147–168). New York: Guilford Press.

Bussey, M. (1996). Impact of kids first seminar for divorcing parents: A three-year follow-up. *Journal of Divorce and Remarriage, 26,* 129–149.

Butcher, J. N. (1990). *MMPI-2 in psychological treatment.* New York: Oxford University Press.

Butcher, J. N. (2002). Assessment in forensic practice: An objective approach. In B. Van Dorsten (Ed.), *Forensic psychology: From classroom to courtroom* (pp. 65–81). New York: Kluwer Academic/Plenum Publishers.

Butler, B. M., & Moran, G. (2002, April). The role of death qualification in venire persons' evaluations of aggravating and mitigating circumstances in capital trials. *Law & Human Behavior, 26*(2), 175–184.

Buzawa, E. S., & Buzawa, C. G. (2001). Traditional and innovative police responses to domestic violence. In R. G. Dunham & G. P. Alpert (Eds.), *Critical issues in policing: Contemporary readings (5th ed.),* (pp. 216–237), Prospect Heights, IL: Waveland.

Byrne, S., Byrne, M. K., & Howells, K. (2001). Defining the needs in a contemporary correctional environment: The contribution of psychology. *Psychiatry, Psychology, & Law, 8*(1), 97–104.

California Department of Corrections. (1991). *California prisoners and parolees 1990.* Sacramento: State of California.

Camara, W. J., & Merenda, P. F. (2000, December). Using personality tests in preemployment screening: Issues raised in Soroka v. Dayton Hudson Corporation. *Psychology, Public Policy, & Law, 6*(4), 1164–1186.

Campbell, J., Sharps, P., Laughon, K., Webster, D., et al. (2003, July). Risk factors for femicide in abusive relationships: Results from a multisite case control study. *American Journal of Public Health, 93*(7), 1089–1098.

Canada, G. (1993, August). Developing stress-resistant police families. *The Police Chief,* pp. 92–95.

Carlson, B. E., & Cervera, N. (1992). *Inmates and their wives: Incarceration and family life.* Westport, CT: Greenwood Press.

Carlson, K. A. (1992). Doing good and looking bad: A case study of prison/community relations. *Crime and Delinquency, 38,* 56–69.

Carpenter, M. (1978). Residential placement for the chronic psychiatric patient: A review and evaluation of the literature. *Schizophrenia Bulletin, 4,* 384–398.

Carr, K., Hinkle, B., & Ingram, B. (1991). Establishing mental health and substance abuse services in jails. *Journal of Prison & Jail Health, 10*(2), 77–89.

Ceci, S. J., & Bruck, M. (1993). Suggestibility of the child witness: A historical review and synthesis. *Psychological Bulletin, 113,* 403–439.

Ceci, S. J., & Bruck, M. (1995). *Jeopardy in the courtroom: A scientific analysis of children's testimony.* Washington, DC: American Psychological Association.

Cepeda, A., & Valdez, A. (2003, January). Risk behaviors among young Mexican American gang-associated females: Sexual relations, partying, substance use, and crime. *Journal of Adolescent Research, 18*(1), 90–106.

Chamelin, N. (1975). *Introduction to criminal justice.* Englewood Cliffs, NJ: Prentice Hall.

Chan, R. W., Raboy, B., & Patterson, C. J. (1998). Psychosocial adjustment among children conceived via donor insemination by lesbian and heterosexual mothers. *Journal of Child Development, 69,* 443–451.

Chance, P. (1988). *Learning and behavior* (2nd ed.). Belmont, CA: Wadsworth.

Chandler, R., & Plano, J. (1988). *The public administration dictionary.* Santa Barbara, CA: ABC-Clio.

Chappelle, W., & Rosengren, K. (2001). Maintaining composure and credibility as an expert witness during cross-examination. *Journal of Forensic Psychology Practice, 1*(3), 51–68.

Chesney-Lind, M. (1988). Girls in jail. *Crime and Delinquency, 34,* 150–168.

Chesney-Lind, M., & Shelden, R. G. (1992). *Girls, delinquency, and juvenile justice.* New York: Brooks/Cole.

Chicago Legal Aid to Incarcerated Mothers. (1997). *Women in prison: Fact sheet.* Retrieved April 21, 1998 from http://www.c-l-a-i-m.org/factsheet.htm

Chopra, M. P., Weiss, D., Stinnett, J. L., & Oslin, D. W. (2003, March/April). Treatment-related decisional capacity. *American Journal of Geriatric Psychiatry, 11*(2), 257–258.

Church, G. J. (1990). The view from behind bars. *Time, 135,* 20–22.

Claussen-Rogers, N. L., & Arrigo, B. A. (2004). *Police corruption and psychological testing,* Durham, NC: Carolina Academic Press.

Cleckley, H. (1941). *The mask of sanity: An attempt to clarify some issues about the so-called psychopathic personality.* St. Louis, MO: C. V. Mosby.

Cody, B. (1997). San Mateo county sheriff's office: Megan's law in the state of California. Retrieved October 5, 1998 from http://www.5mcsheriff.com/n-f/is-m.htm#top

Cohen, D. A. (1997). Sexual psychopaths. Retrieved August 16, 2003 from http://members.tripod.com/≫dazc/sexopat.htm#watiz

Cohen, F., & Dvoskin, J. (1992, July/August). Inmates with mental disorders: A guide to law and practice. *Mental & Physical Disability Law Reporter, 16*(4), 462–470.

Cohen, H. S., & Feldberg, M. (1991). *Power and restraint: The moral dimension of police work.* New York: Praeger.

Cohn, A. W. (2003, June). Juvenile focus. *Federal Probation, 67*(1). Retrieved August 16, 2003 from http://web22.epnet.com/citation.asp?tb

Coles, E. M., & Veiel, H. O. F. (2001). Expert testimony and pseudoscience: How mental health professionals are taking over the courtroom. *International Journal of Law & Psychiatry, 24*(6), 607–625.

Comes, J. T., Bertrand, L. D., Paetseh, J. J., & Hornick, J. P. (2003, Spring). Self-reported delinquency among Alberta's youth: Findings from a survey of 2,001 junior and senior high school students. *Adolescence, 38*(149), 75–92.

Community Care. (2003, May 1). Prostitution study points to alienation. *Community Care, 1470,* 11–18.

Conley, R. W., Luckasson, R., & Bouthilet, G. N. (Eds.). (1992). *The criminal justice system and mental retardation.* Baltimore, MD: Paul H. Brookes.

Conner, K., Duberstein, P., & Conwell, Y. (2000, Winter). Domestic violence, separation and suicide in young men with early onset alcoholism: Reanalyses of Murphy's data. *Suicide & Life-Threatening Behavior, 30*(4), 354–359.

Connolly, A. (2003, September). Psychoanalytic theory in times of terror. *Journal of Analytical Psychology, 48*(4), 407–431.

Cook, J. R. (1997). Neighbors' perceptions of group homes. *Community Mental Health Journal, 33,* 287–299.

Coons, J., Mnookin, R., & Sugarman, S. (1993). Deciding what's best for children. *Notre Dame Journal of Law and Public Policy, 7,* 465–490.

Cooper, C. (1997). Patrol police officer conflict resolution processes. *Journal of Criminal Justice, 25*(2), 87–101.

Cooper, C. (2001). An afrocentric perspective on policing. In R. G. Dunham, & G. P. Alpert (Eds.), *Critical issues in policing: Contemporary readings (4th ed.),* (pp. 376–400), Prospect Heights, IL: Waveland.

Cooprider, K. W. (1992). Pretrial bond supervision: An empirical analysis with policy implications. *Federal Probation, 56,* 41–49.

Corbett, C., & Simon, F. (1991). Police and public perceptions of the seriousness of traffic offences. *British Journal of Criminology, 31*(2), 153–164.

Cordner, G. W. (2001). Community policing: elements and effects. In R. G. Dunham & G. P. Alpert (Eds.), *Critical issues in policing: Contemporary readings (5th ed.),* (pp. 493–510), Prospect Heights, IL: Waveland.

Cordoba, O. A., & Chapel, J. L. (1983). Medroxyprogesterone acetate antiandrogen treatment of hypersexuality in a pedophiliac sex offender. *American Journal of Psychiatry, 140,* 1036–1039.

Cornwell, J. K. & Deeney, R. (2003, Mar/June). Exposing the myths surrounding preventive outpatient commitment for individuals with chronic mental illness. *Psychology, Public Policy, & Law, 9*(1–2), 209–232.

Correia, M. E. (1997). Boot camps, exercise, and delinquency. An analytical critique of the use of physical exercise to facilitate decreases in delinquent behavior. *13,* 94–113.

Cortina, J. M., Doherty, M. L., Schmitt, N., Kaufman, G., & Smith, R. G. (1992). The "Big Five" personality factors in the IPI and MMPI: Predictors of police performance. *Personnel Psychology, 45,* 119–140.

Costin, L. B., Karger, H. J., & Stoesz, D. (1996). *The politics of child abuse in America.* New York: Oxford University Press.

Cowley, G., Springen, K., Miller, S., Lewis, S., & Titunik, V. (1993, August 16). Who's looking after the interests of the children? *Newsweek,* pp. 54–55.

Cox, J. F., & Morschauser, P. C. (1997). A solution to the problem of jail suicide. *Crisis, 18*(4), 178–184.

Crank, J. P. (1992). Police style and legally serious crime: A contextual analysis of municipal police departments. *Journal of Criminal Justice, 20,* 401–412.

Crank, J. P., Payn, B., & Jackson, S. (1993). The relationship between police belief systems and attitudes toward police practices. *Criminal Justice and Behavior, 20*(2), 199–221.

Crenshaw, M. (1998). The logic of terrorism: Terrorist behavior as a product of strategic choice. In W. Reich (Ed.), *Origins of terrorism: Psychologies, ideologies, theologies, states of mind* (pp. 7–24). Washington, DC: Woodrow Wilson Center Press.

Crisanti, A. S., & Love, E. J. (2001, July/October). Characteristics of psychiatric inpatients detained under civil commitment legislation: A Canadian study. *International Journal of Law & Psychiatry, 24*(4–5), 399–410.

Crisanti, A. S., & Love, E. J. (2002, November/December). From one legal system to another? An examination of the relationship between involuntary hospitalization and arrest. *International Journal of Law & Psychiatry, 25*(6), 581–597.

Crockenberg, S., & Forgays, D. (1996). The role of emotion in children's understanding and emotional reactions to marital conflict. *Merrill-Palmer Quarterly, 42,* 22–47.

Crocker, A. G., Favreau, O. E., & Caulet, M. (2002). Gender and fitness to stand trial: A 5-year review of remands in Quebec. *International Journal of Law and Psychiatry, 25,* 67–84.

Crosby-Currie, C. (1996). Children's involvement in contested custody cases: Practices and experiences of legal and mental health professionals. *Law and Human Behavior, 20,* 289–310.

Crouch, B. M. (1985). Pandora's box: Women guards in men's prisons. *Journal of Criminal Justice, 13,* 535–548.

Cupric, S., Fuller, K., & Schneider, R. (2003, July). Divergent ethical perspectives on the duty-to-warn principle with HIV patients. *Ethics & Behavior, 13*(3), 263–278.

Danis, F. S. (2003, April). The criminalization of domestic violence: What social workers need to know. *Social Work, 48*(2), 1–12.

Davey, J., Obst, P., & Sheehan, M. (2001, May). It goes with the job: Officers' insights into the impact of stress and culture on alcohol consumption within the policing occupation. *Drugs: Education, Prevention & Policy, 8*(2), 141–149.

Davis, A. Y. (2000, September). Women in prison. *Essence, 31*(5), 150–152.

Davis, C. G., & McKearney, J. M. (2003, October). How do people grow from their experience with trauma or loss? *Journal of Social & Clinical Psychology, 22*(5), 477–492.

Davis, D., & Follette, W. C. (2002). Rethinking the probative value of evidence: Base rates, intuitive profiling, and the "postdiction" of behavior. *Law & Human Behavior, 26*(2), 133–158.

Davis, J. M. (2002). Countering international terrorism: Perspectives from international psychology. In C. E. Stout (Ed.), *The psychology of terrorism, Volume Four: Programs and practices in response and prevention.* Westport, CT: Praeger.

Davis, M. (1995). Critical incident stress debriefing: The case for corrections. *The Keeper's Voice, 16.* Retrieved September 20, 1997 from http://www.acsp.uic.edu/iaco/kv160145.htm

Davis, R. C., & Miller, J. (2002). Immigration and integration: Perceptions of community policing among members of six ethnic communities in central Queens, New York City. *International Review of Victimology, 9*(2), 93–111.

Dawson, J. M., & Langan, P. A. (1994). *Murder in families.* Washington, DC: Bureau of Justice Statistics.

Dear, G. E., Thomson, D. M., & Hills, A. M. (2000, April). Self-harm in prison: Manipulators can also be suicide attempters. *Criminal Justice & Behavior, 27*(2), 160–175.

Decker, S., & Curry, D. G. (2002). Gangs, gang homicides, and gang loyalty: Organized crimes or disorganized criminals. *Journal of Criminal Justice, 30*(4), 343–352.

Defina, M., & Wetherbee, L. (1997, October). Advocacy and law enforcement: Partners against domestic violence. *FBI Law Enforcement Bulletin,* pp. 22–26.

D'Emilio, J. (1983). *Sexual politics, sexual communities: The making of a homosexual minority in the United States 1940–1970.* Chicago: University of Chicago Press.

De La Fuente, L., De La Fuente, E. I., & Garcia, J. (2003, June). Effects of pretrial juror bias, strength of evidence and deliberation process on juror decisions: New validity evidence of the Juror Bias Scale scores. *Psychology, Crime & Law, 9*(2), 197–209.

Department of Health. (1998). *Modernising mental health services: Safe, sound and supportive.* Retrieved February 8, 1998 from http://www.doh.gov.uk/nsf/mentalh.htm

Dernevik, M., Grann, M., & Johansson, S. (2002). Violent behaviour in forensic psychiatric patients: Risk assessment and different risk-management levels using the HCR-20. *Psychology, Crime & Law, 8,* 93–111.

Detrick, P., & Chibnall, J. T. (2002). Prediction of police officer performance with the Inwald Personality Inventory. *Journal of Police & Criminal Psychology, 17*(2), 9–17.

Detrick, P., Chibnall, J. T., & Rosso, M. (2001, October). Minnesota Multiphasic Personality Inventory-2 in police officer selection: Normative data and relation to the Inwald Personality Inventory. *Professional Psychology: Research & Practice, 32*(5), 484–490.

Dewa, C., & Lin, E. (2000, July). Chronic physical illness, psychiatric disorder and disability in the workplace. *Social Science & Medicine, 51*(1), 41–50.

De Wilde, E. J., Kienhorst, I. C., Diekstra, R. F., & Wolters, W. H. (1992). The relationship between adolescent suicidal behavior and life events in childhood and adolescence. *American Journal of Psychiatry, 149*(1), 45–51.

Dexter, H., Cutler, B., & Moran, G. (1992). A test of voir dire as a remedy for the prejudicial effects of pretrial publicity. *Journal of Applied Social Psychology, 22*(10), 819–832.

Diamond, S. (1990). Scientific jury selection: What social scientists know and do not know. *Judicature, 73,* 178–183.

Dietrich, J. (1989, November). Helping subordinates face stress. *The Police Chief,* pp. 44–47.

DiIulio, J. (1987). *Governing prisons.* New York: Free Press.

Dillen, A. (2003, October). Queer family values: Debunking the myth of the nuclear family. *Archives of Sexual Behavior, 32*(5), 489–490.

DiPietro, A. L. (1993, July). Lies, promises, or threats: The voluntariness of confessions. *FBI Law Enforcement Bulletin,* pp. 27–31.

Dobson, V., & Sales, B. (2000). The science of infanticide and mental illness. *Psychology, Public Policy, & Law, 6,* 1098–1109.

Dodge, K. S. (1993). "Bashing back": Gay and lesbian street patrols and the criminal justice system. *Law & Equality: A Journal of Theory and Practice, 11,* 295–368.

Dolgin, J. L. (1996). Why has the best interest standard survived? The historic and social context. *Children's Legal Rights Journal, 16,* 2–10.

Dolon, R., Hendricks, J., & Meagher, M. (1986). Police practices and attitudes toward domestic violence. *Journal of Police Science and Administration, 14*(3), 187–192.

Donaldson, S. (1990). Prisons, jails, and reformatories. In W. R. Dynes (Ed.), *Encyclopedia of homosexuality.* New York: Garland.

Doob, A. N., & Sprott, J. B. (1998, April). Is the "quality" of youth violence becoming more serious? *Canadian Journal of Criminology,* pp. 185–194.

Douglas, J. E., & Burgess, A. E. (1986, December). Criminal profiling: A viable investigative tool against violent crime. *FBI Law Enforcement Bulletin,* pp. 9–13.

Doyle, J. (1996). Homosexuals in law enforcement: A contemporary study. *Journal of California Law Enforcement, 30*(4), 77–81.

Doyle, M., Dolan, M., & McGovern, J. (2002). The validity of North American risk assessment tools in predicting in-patient violent behaviour in England. *Legal and Criminological Psychology, 7,* 141–154.

Dripps, D. A. (1988). Supreme court review. Foreward: Against police interrogation—and the privilege against self incrimination. *Journal of Criminal Law and Criminology, 78*(4), 699–734.

Druss, B. G., Marcus, S. C., Rosenheck, R. A., Olfson, M., Tanielian, T., & Princus, H. A. (2001). Understanding disability in mental and general medical conditions. *American Journal of Psychiatry, 157*, 1485–1491.

D'Silva, K., & Ferriter, M. (2003). Substance use by the mentally disordered committing serious offences—A high-security hospital study. *Journal of Forensic Psychiatry & Psychology, 14*(1), 178–193.

Dunphy, F. R., & Garner, G. (1992, April). A guide to effective interaction with the news media. *The Police Chief*, pp. 45–48.

DuRand, C. J., Burtka, G., Federman, E., Haycox, J., & Smith, J. (1995). A quarter century of suicide in a major urban jail: Implications for community psychiatry. *American Journal of Psychiatry, 152*(7), 1077–1080.

DuRant, R. H., Barkin, S., & Krowchuk, D. P. (2001). Evaluation of a peaceful conflict resolution and violence prevention curriculum for sixth-grade students. *Journal of Adolescent Health, 28*(5), 386–393.

Durbin, J., Cochrane, J., Goering, P., & Macfarlane, D. (2001, February). Needs-based planning: Evaluation of a level-of-care planning model. *Journal of Behavioral Health Services & Research, 28*(1), 67–80.

Easteal, P. (2001, March). Women in Australian prisons: The cycle of abuse and dysfunctional environments. *Prison Journal, 81*(1), 87–112.

Eaves, D. (2002). The International Association of Forensic Mental Health Services: Working toward interdisciplinary and international collaboration. *International Journal of Forensic Mental Health, 1*(1), 3–5.

Eck, J. E. (1982). *Solving crimes: The investigation of burglary and robbery*. Washington, DC: Police Executive Research Forum.

Edelstein, S. B., Burge, D., & Waterman, J. (2002, March/April). Older children in preadoptive homes: Issues before termination of parental rights. *Child Welfare, 81*(2), 101–121.

Edwards, W., & Hensley, C. (2001). Contextualizing sex offender management legislation and policy: Evaluating the problem of latent consequences in community notification laws. *International Journal of Offender Therapy and Comparative Criminology, 45*(1), 83–101.

Elbogen, E. B., Patry, M., & Scalora, M. J. (2003). The impact of community notification laws on sex offender treatment attitudes. *International Journal of Law & Psychiatry, 26*(2), 207–219.

Elias, R. (1986). *The politics of victimization*. New York: Oxford University Press.

Elrod, P., & Brown, M. P. (1996). Predicting public support for electronic house arrest. Results from a New York county survey. *American Behavioral Scientist, 39*, 461–473.

Enelow, A. J., & Leo, R. J. (2002). Evaluation of the vocational factors impacting on psychiatric disability. *Psychiatric Annals, 32*(5), 293–297.

Erickson, P. E. (2000, Spring). Federal child abuse and child neglect policy in the United States since 1974: A review and critique. *Criminal Justice Review, 25*(1), 77–92.

Ericson, R. V. (1991). Mass media, crime, law, and justice: An institutional approach. *British Journal of Criminology, 31*(3), 219–249.

Esbensen, F. A., Deschenes, E. P., & Winfree, T. L. (1999). Differences between gang girls and gang boys: Results from a multisite survey. *Youth & Society, 31*(1), 27–53.

Etheridge, R., Hale, C., & Hambrick, M. (1984). Female employees in all-male correctional facilities. *Federal Probation, 48,* 54–65.

Etter, G. W. (2003, Spring). Strategic planning for law enforcement agencies: Management as a gang fighting strategy. *Journal of Gang Research, 10*(3), 13–23.

Evans, W., Albers, E., Macari, D., & Mason, A. (1996). Suicide ideation, attempts and abuse among incarcerated gang and nongang delinquents. *Child and Adolescent Social Work Journal, 13,* 115–126.

Evans, W. P., Fitzgerald, C., Weigel, D., & Chvilicek, S. (1999). Are rural gang members similar to their urban peers? Implications for rural communities. *Youth & Society, 30*(3), 267–282.

Everington, C. & Keyes, D. W. (1999, July/August). Mental retardation: Diagnosing mental retardation in criminal proceedings: The critical importance of documenting adaptive behavior. *Forensic Examiner, 8*(7–8), 31–34.

Everly, G. S. (2003). Psychological counterterrorism. *International Journal of Emergency Mental Health, 5*(2), 57–59.

Evers, T. (1998). A healing approach to crime: Victim-offender mediation. *The Progressive Inc., 9*(62), 30–36.

Ewing, C. P. (1997). *Fatal families: The dynamics of intrafamilial homicide.* Thousand Oaks, CA: Sage.

Exum, J. G., Turnbull, H. R., Martin, R., & Finn, J. W. (1992). Points of view: Perspectives on the judicial, mental retardation services, law enforcement, and corrections systems. In R. W. Conley, R. Luckasson, & G. N. Bouthilet (Eds.), *The criminal justice system and mental retardation* (pp. 1–16). Baltimore: Paul H. Brookes.

Exworthy, T., Mohan, D., Hindley, N., & Basson, J. (2001). Seclusion: Punitive or protective? *Journal of Forensic Psychiatry, 12*(2), 423–433.

Fagan, A. A. (2001, Aug). The gender cycle of violence: Comparing the effects of child abuse and neglect on criminal offending for males and females. *Violence & Victims, 16*(4), 457–474.

Falk, J. A. (1995). Project exodus: The corrections correction. In L. Combrinck-Graham (Ed.), *Children in families at risk: Maintaining the connections* (pp. 375–392). New York: Guilford Press.

Farley, M. (2003). Prostitution and the invisibility of harm. *Women & Therapy, 26*(3–4), 247–280.

Farr, K. A. (2002, June). Battered women who were "being killed and survived it": Straight talk from survivors. *Violence & Victims, 17*(3), 267–281.

Fava, G. A. (2001, May/June). Physicians, medical associations and death penalty. *Psychotherapy & Psychosomatics, 70*(3), 168.

Feeman, V. L. (1994). Reassessing forced medication of criminal defendants in light of Riggins v. Nevada, *Boston College Law Review, 35,* 681–721.

Federal Bureau of Investigation (FBI). (1985a, August). The men who murdered. *FBI Law Enforcement Bulletin,* pp. 2–11.

Federal Bureau of Investigation (FBI). (1985b, August). Crime scene and profile characteristics of organized and disorganized murderers. *FBI Law Enforcement Bulletin,* pp. 18–25.

Federal Bureau of Investigation (FBI). (1994) *Uniform Crime Report 1993.* Washington, DC: U.S. Government Printing Office.

Federal Bureau of Investigation (FBI). (1997). Facts about deterrence and the death penalty. Retrieved March 12, 1998 from http://www.essential.org/dpic/dete...f

Federal Communications Commission (2003). *Consumer advisory: The Amber Plan.* Retrieved September 8, 2004 from http://www.fcc.gov/cgb/consumerfacts/AMBER-Plan.html

Federal Probation (2000, June). It has come to our attention. *Federal Probation, 64*(1). Retrieved September 15, 2003 from http://www.web22.epnet.com/citation.Asp

Feinman, C. (1994). *Women in the criminal justice system* (3rd ed.). Westport, CT: Praeger.

Feld, B. C. (1999). *Bad kids: Race and the transformation of the juvenile court*, New York, NY: Oxford University Press.

Feld, B. C. (1997, Fall). Abolish the juvenile court: Youthfulness, criminal responsibility, and sentencing. *Journal of Criminal Law & Criminology*, i(1), 68–69.

Felthous, A., & Kachigian, C. (2001). To warn and to control: Two distinct legal obligations or variations of a single duty to protect. *Behavioral Sciences & the Law, 19*(3), 355–373.

Ferraro, K. J., & Moe, A. M. (2003, February). Mothering, crime, and incarceration. *Journal of Contemporary Ethnography, 32*(1), 9–40.

Festinger, T., & Pratt, R. (2002). Speeding adoptions: An evaluation of the effects of judicial continuity. *Social Work Research, 26*(4), 217–224.

Finch, J. R., & Wheaton, J. E. (1999). Patterns of services to vocational rehabilitation consumers with serious mental illness. *Rehabilitation Counseling Bulletin, 42*(3), 214–227.

Finn, M. A., & Stalans, L. J. (1997). The influence of gender and mental state on police decisions in domestic assault cases. *Criminal Justice and Behavior, 24*(2), 157–176.

Finn, P. (1998, December). Correctional officer stress: A cause for concern and additional help[a]. *Federal Probation, 62*(2), 65–75.

Firush, R., & Shukat, J. R. (1995). Content, consistency, and coherence of early autobiographical recall. In M. S. Zaragoza, J. R. Graham, G. C. N. Hall, R. Hirschman, & Y. S. Ben-Porath (Eds.), *Memory and testimony in the child witness* (pp. 5–23). Thousand Oaks, CA: Sage.

Fischoff, S. (2003, September). Stack and sway: The new science of jury consulting. *Political Psychology, 24*(3), 628–631.

Fishbein, P., Davis, J. M., & Hamparin, D. (1984). *Restitution programming for juvenile offenders.* Columbus: Ohio Serious Juvenile Offender Program, Department of Corrections.

Fisher, W. H., Packer, I. K., Banks, S. M., Smith, D., Simon, L. J., & Roy-Bujnowski, K. (2002, November). Self-reported lifetime psychiatric hospitalization histories of jail detainees with mental disorders: Comparison with a nonincarcerated national sample. *Journal of Behavioral Health Services & Research, 29*(4), 458–465.

Fishman, L. T. (1990). *Women at the wall: A study of prisoners' wives doing time on the outside.* Albany: State University of New York Press.

Flaherty, M. G. (1983). The national incidence of juvenile suicide in adult jails and juvenile detention centers. *Suicide and Life Threatening Behavior, 13*, 85–93.

Flaks, D. K., Ficher, I., Masterpasqua, F., & Joseph, G. (1995). Lesbians choosing motherhood: A comparative study of lesbian and heterosexual parents and their children. *Developmental Psychology, 31*, 105–114.

Flanagan, L. W. (1995). Meeting the special needs of females in custody: Maryland's unique approach. *Federal Probation, 59*, 49–53.

Fletcher, B. R., Rolison, G. L., & Moon, D. G. (1993). The woman prisoner. In B. R. Fletcher, L. D. Shaver, & D. G. Moon (Eds.), *Women prisoners: A forgotten population* (pp. 15–26). Westport, CT: Praeger.

Flowers, R. B. (1995). *Female crime, criminals and cellmates: An exploration of female criminality and delinquency*. Jefferson, NC: McFarland.

Flowers, R. B. (1998). *The prostitution of women and girls*. Jefferson, NC: McFarland.

Franklin, K. (2003). Practice opportunities with an emerging family form: The planned lesbian and gay family. *Journal of Forensic Psychology Practice, 3*(3), 47–64.

Freedman, D., & Hemenway, D. (2000, June). Precursors of lethal violence: A death row sample. *Social Science & Medicine, 50*(12), 1757–1770.

Freeman, A., & Alaimo, C. (2001). Prevention of suicide in a large urban jail. *Psychiatric Annals, 31*(7), 447–452.

Freeman-Longo, R. E., & Knopp, H. F. (1992). State-of-the-art sex offender treatment: Outcome and issues. *Annals of Sex Research, 5*(3), 141–160.

Fried, C. S., & Reppucci, N. D. (2001, February). Criminal decision making: The development of adolescent judgment, criminal responsibility, and culpability. *Law & Human Behavior, 25*(1), 45–61.

Fritsch, E., & Hemmens, J. D. (1995). Juvenile waiver in the United States 1979–1995: A comparison and analysis of state waiver statutes. *Juvenile and Family Court Journal, 46*(3), 17–35.

Fry, L. J., & Glaser, D. (1987). Gender differences in work adjustment of prison employees. *Journal of Offender Counseling, Services, and Rehabilitation, 12*, 39–52.

Furby, L., Weinrott, M. R., & Blackshaw, L. (1989). Sex offender recidivism: A review. *Psychological Bulletin, 105*, 3–30.

Fyfe, J. J. (1985). The split-second syndrome and other determinants of police violence. In A. Campbell & J. Gibbs (Eds.), *Violent transactions: The limits of personality* (pp. 207–223). New York: Basil Blackwell.

Fyfe, J. J. (1996). Methodology, substance, and demeanor in police observational research: A response to Lundman and others. *Journal of Research in Crime and Delinquency, 33*(3), 337–348.

Fyfe, J. J. (2000). Policing the emotionally disturbed. *Journal of the American Academy of Psychiatry & the Law, 28*(3), 345–347.

Fyfe, J. J. (2001). The Split-second syndrome and other determinants of police violence. In R. G. Dunham, & G. P. Alpert (Eds.), *Critical issues in policing: Contemporary readings* (5th ed.), (pp. 583–598), Prospect Heights, IL: Waveland.

Fyfe, J. J., Klinger, D. A., & Flavin, J. M. (1997). Differential police treatment of male-on-female spousal violence. *Criminology, 35*(3), 455–473.

Gaarder, E., & Belknap, J. (2002). Tenuous borders: Girls transferred to adult court. *Criminology, 40*(3), 1–33.

Gabel, K., & Johnston, D. (1995). *Children of incarcerated parents*. New York: Lexington Books.

Gacono, C. B. (2002). Forensic psychodiagnostic testing. *Journal of Forensic Psychology Practice, 2*(3), 1–10.

Galea, S., Ahern, J., Resnick, H., et al. (2002). Psychological sequelae of the September 11 terrorist attacks in New York City. *New England Journal of Medicine, 346*, 982–987.

Gallousis, M., & Francek, H. (2002, Summer). The juvenile suicide assessment: An instrument for the assessment and management of suicide risk with incarcerated juveniles. *International Journal of Emergency Mental Health, 4*(3), 181–200.

Garner, B. A. (Ed.). (1996). *Black's law dictionary*. St. Paul, MN: West Publishing.

Garrison, M. (1996). Parent's rights versus children's rights: The case of the foster child. *New York University Review of Law and Social Change, 22*(2), 371–396.

Gavin, T. (1997, March). Truancy: Not just kids' stuff anymore. *FBI Law Enforcement Bulletin, 8*(3), 9–15.

Geller, W. A. (1994, January). Research forum: Videotaping interrogations and confessions. *FBI Law Enforcement Bulletin*, pp. 24–27.

Gelles, R. J. (1996). *The book of David: How preserving families can cost children's lives*. New York: Basic Books.

Genders, E., & Player, E. (1990). Women lifers: Assessing the experience. *The Prison Journal, 80*, 46–57.

Genova, J. (1989, April). Automating crime labs and evidence control. *The Police Chief*, pp. 34–40.

Gerlock, A. A. (2001, June). A profile of who completes and who drops out of domestic violence rehabilitation. *Issues in Mental Health Nursing, 22*(4), 379–400.

Gesalman, A. B. (2002, January 21). Signs of a family feud: The trial of Andrea Yates tests the insanity defense as relatives try to cope. An "unspeakable" crime. *Newsweek*, 22–23.

Giallombardo, R. (1966). *Society of women: A study of a women's prison*. New York: Wiley.

Gibbons, P. (Ed.) (2003, March). Managing sex offenders: Is there a role for psychiatry? *Irish Journal of Psychological Medicine, 20*(1), 4–5.

Gifford, E. A. (1992). California's mother-infant care program: An alternative model for prison mothers. *UCLA Women's Law Journal, 2*, 279–281.

Gioia, D., & Brekke, J. S. (2003). Use of the American with Disabilities Act by young adults with schizophrenia. *Psychiatric Services, 54*(3), 302–304.

Giraldi, E., & Greenberg, M. (2002). The role of the psychiatrist with incarcerated yourth: Psychiatric medication management. In N.G. Ribner (Ed.), *The handbook of juvenile forensic psychology*, (pp. 389–412), San Francisco, CA: Jossey-Bass.

Glick, B. (1992). In New York: Governor's task force tackles growing juvenile gang problem. *Corrections Today, 54*, 92–97.

Glover, A. J. J., Nicholson, D. E., Hemmati, T., et al. (2002, June). A comparison of predictors of general and violent recidivism among high-risk federal offenders. *Criminal Justice and Behavior, 29*(3), 235–249.

Godschalx, S. M. (1984). Effect of a mental health educational program upon police officers. *Research in Nursing and Health, 7*, 111–117.

Godwin, C. D., & Helms, J. L. (2002). Statistics and trends in juvenile justice and forensic psychology. In N. G. Ribner (Ed.), *The handbook of juvenile forensic psychology*, (pp. 3–28), San Francisco, CA: Jossey-Bass.

Goldfried, M. R. (2001, November). Integrating gay, lesbian, and bisexual issues into mainstream psychology. *American Psychologist, 56*(11), 977–988.

Goldstein, J., Solnit, A. J., Goldstein, S., & Freud, A. (1996). *The best interests of the child: The least detrimental alternative*. New York: Free Press.

Goldstein, R. L. (1999). Commentary on "Attorneys' pressures on expert witness." *Journal of the American Academy of Psychiatry & the Law, 27*(4), 554–558.

Gondolf, E. W. (2000). A 30-month follow-up of court-referred batterers in four cities. *International Journal of Offender Therapy and Comparative Criminology, 44*(1), 111–128.

Goodman, G. S., Tobey, A. E., Batterman-Faunce, J. M., Orcutt, H., Thomas, S., Shapiro, C., & Sachsenmaier, T. (1998). Face-to-face confrontation: Effects of closed circuit technology on children's eyewitness testimony and jurors' decisions. *Law and Human Behavior, 22,* 165–203.

Gothard, S., Viglone, D., Meloy, J., & Sherman, M. (1995). Detection of malingering in competency to stand trial evaluations. *Law and Human Behavior, 19,* 493.

Gottesman, I. I., & Bertelsen, A. (1989). Confirming unexpressed genotypes of schizophrenia. Risk in the offspring of Fischer's Danish identical and fraternal discordant twins. *Archives of General Psychiatry, 46,* 867–872.

Gottman, J. S. (1990). Children of gay and lesbian parents. In F. W. Bozett & M. B. Sussman (Eds.), *Homosexuality and family relations* (pp. 177–196). New York: Harrington Park Press.

Gourley, E. V., & Stolberg, A. L. (2000). An empirical investigation of psychologists' custody evaluation procedures. *Journal of Divorce & Remarriage, 33*(1–2), 1–29.

Graham, J. R. (1993). *MMPI-2 assessing personality and psychopathology.* New York: Oxford University Press.

Granello, P. F., & Hanna, F. J. (2003, Winter). Incarcerated and court-involved adolescents: Counseling an at-risk population. *Journal of Counseling & Development, 81*(1), 11–19.

Graney, D. G., & Arrigo, B. A. (2002). *The power serial rapist: A criminology–victimology typology of female victim selection.* Springfield, IL: Charles C Thomas.

Graves, W. (1996). Police cynicism: Causes and cures. *FBI Law Enforcement Bulletin, 65,* 16–20.

Gray, K. (2001, September). Juvenile justice. *Essence, 32*(5), 147–153.

Gray, L., & Harding, A. (1988). Confidentiality limits with clients who have the AIDS virus. *Journal of Counseling and Development, 66,* 219–223.

Greene, A. F., Coles, C. J., & Johnson, E. H. (1994). Psychopathology and anger in interpersonal violence offenders. *Journal of Clinical Psychology, 50,* 906–912.

Greene, S., Haney, C., & Hurtado, A. (2000). Cycles of pain: Risk factors in the lives of incarcerated mothers and their children. *Prison Journal, 80*(1), 3–23.

Greer, D. (1994). A transatlantic perspective on the compensation of crime victims in the United States. *Journal of Criminal Law and Criminology, 85*(2), 333.

Greer, K. R. (2000). The changing nature of interpersonal relationships in a women's prison. *The Prison Journal, 80,* 442–468.

Grekul, J. (1999, October). Pluralistic ignorance in a prison community. *Canadian Journal of Criminology, 41*(4), 513–535.

Griffin, J. L. (1993, August 25). Primary label for gay police officers is cop. *Chicago Tribune,* p. 5.

Grisso, T. (1986). *Evaluating competencies: Forensic assessments & instruments.* New York: Plenum.

Grisso, T. (1996a). Pretrial clinical evaluations in criminal cases: Past trends and future directions. *Criminal Justice and Behavior, 23*(1), 90–106.

Grisso, T. (1996b). Society's retributive response to juvenile violence: A developmental perspective. *Law and Human Behavior, 20*(3), 229–247.

Grisso, T. (2000, April). The changing face of juvenile justice. *Psychiatric Services, 51*(4), 425–426, 438.

Grisso, T. (2003). *Evaluating competencies: Forensic assessments & instruments: Second Edition.* New York: Kluwer Academic/Plenum.

Grisso, T., & Schwartz, R. G. (2003). *Youth on trial: A developmental perspective on juvenile justice,* Chicago, IL: University of Chicago Press.

Groscup, J. L., Penrod, S. D., Studebaker, C. A., Huss, M. T., & O'Neil, K. M. (2002). The effects of *Daubert* on the admissibility of expert testimony in state and federal criminal cases. *Psychology, Public Policy, & Law, 8*(4), 339–372.

Grossi, E. L., & Berg, B. L. (1991). Stress and job dissatisfaction among correctional officers: An unexpected finding. *International Journal of Offender Therapy and Comparative Criminology, 35,* 73–81.

Groves, B., Zuckerman, B., Marans, S., & Cohen, D. (1993). Silent victims: Children who witness violence. *Journal of the American Medical Association, 269,* 262–264.

Guadalupe, J. L., & Bein, A. (2001). Violence and youth: What can we learn? *International Journal of Adolescence & Youth, 10*(1–2), 157–176.

Gunroe, M. L., & Braver, S. L. (2001). The effects of joint legal custody on mothers, fathers, and children controlling for factors that predispose a sole maternal versus joint legal award. *Law & Human Behavior, 25*(1), 25–43.

Gurian-Sherman, S. (2001). The challenge of juvenile justice: Advocating for troubled children in trouble. *Issues in Mental Health Nursing, 22,* 207–224.

Hagan, J. (1982). Victims before the law: A study of victim involvement in the criminal justice process. *Journal of Criminal Justice, 73,* 317–330.

Hails, J., & Borum, R. (2003, January). Police training and specialized approaches to respond to people with mental illnesses. *Crime & Delinquency, 49*(1), 30–51.

Hairston, C. F. (1989). Men in prison: Family characteristics and family views. *Journal of Offender Counseling, Services, and Rehabilitation, 14*(1), 23–30.

Hairston, C. F. (1991a). Family ties during imprisonment. Important to whom and for what? *Journal of Sociology and Social Welfare, 18,* 87–104.

Hairston, C. F. (1991b). Mothers in jail: Parent-child separation and jail visitation. *Affilia, 6,* 9–27.

Halim, S., & Stiles, B. L. (2001, February). Differential support for police use of force, the death penalty, and perceived harshness of the courts: Effects of race, gender, and region. *Criminal Justice & Behavior, 28*(1), 3–23.

Hall, A. S., Pulver, C. A., & Cooley, M. J. (1996). Psychology of best interest standard: Fifty state statutes and their theoretical antecedents. *American Journal of Family Therapy, 24,* 171–180.

Hall, G. C. N. (1990). Prediction of sexual aggression. *Clinical Psychology Review, 10,* 229–245.

Hall, J. N. (1992). Correctional services for inmates with mental retardation: Challenge or catastrophe? In R. W. Conley, R. Luckasson, & G. N. Bouthilet (Eds.), *The criminal justice system and mental retardation* (pp. 167–190). Baltimore, MD: Paul H. Brookes.

Haller, L. H. (2000, October). Forensic aspects of juvenile violence. *Child and Adolescent Psychiatric Clinics of North America, 9*(4), 859–881.

Hanna, E. J., Hanna, C. A., & Keys, S. G. (1999). Fifty strategies for counseling defiant, aggressive, adolescents: Reaching, accepting, and relating. *Journal of Counseling & Development, 77,* 395–404.

Hansen, M. (1994a, March). Troopers' wrongdoing taints cases. *American Bar Association Journal,* p. 22.

Hansen, M. (1994b, November). Fears of the heart. *American Bar Association Journal,* pp. 58–63.

Hansen, M. (1997). Repairing the damage: Citizen boards tailor sentences to fit the crimes in Vermont. *American Bar Association Journal, 83*(20), 1–2.

Hanson, R. K., & Bussiere, M. T. (1996). Sex offender risk predictors: A summary of research results. Retrieved December 3, 1998 from http://www.csc-scc.gc.ca/crd/forum/e082/e082c.htm

Hanson, R. K., Steffy, R. A., & Gauthier, R. (1993). Long-term recidivism of child molesters. *Journal of Consulting and Clinical Psychology, 61*(4), 646–652.

Hare, R. D. (1991). *The Hare Psychopathy Checklist-Revised.* Toronto, Canada: Multi-Health Systems.

Hare, R. D. (1993). *Without conscience: The disturbing world of the psychopaths among us.* New York: Guilford.

Hare, R. D. (2000, January). *Assessing psychopathy with the PCL-R.* Paper presented at Sinclair Seminars, San Diego, CA.

Hare, R. D., & Hart, S. (1993). Psychopathy, mental disorder, and crime. In S. Hodgins (Ed.), *Mental disorder and crime* (pp. 104–115). Newbury Park, CA: Sage.

Harer, M. D., & Langan, N. P. (2001, October). Gender differences in predictors of prison violence: Assessing the predictive validity of a risk classification system. *Crime & Delinquency, 47*(4), 513–536.

Harlan, S., Rodgers, L. L., & Slattery, B. (1981). *Male and female adolescent prostitution: Huckleberry Sexual Minority Youth Services Project.* Washington, DC: U.S. Department of Health and Human Services.

Harland, P., Reijneveld, S. A., Brugman, E., Verloove-Vanhorick, S. P., & Verhulst, F. C. (2002, December). Family factors and life events as risk factors for behavioral and emotional problems in children. *European Child & Adolescent Psychiatry, 11*(4), 176–184.

Harris, G., Rice, M., & Cormier, C. (2002, August). *Law and Human Behavior, 26*(4), 377–394.

Harris, G., Rice, M., & Quinsey, V. (1993). Violent recidivism of mentally disordered offenders: The development of a statistical prediction instrument. *Criminal Justice and Behavior, 20,* 315–335.

Harris, G., Rice, M., Quinsey, V., Lalumiere, M., Boer, D., & Lang, C. (2003, September). A multisite comparison of actuarial risk instruments for sex offenders. *Psychological Assessment, 15*(3), 413–425.

Harris, P., & Smith, S. (1996). Developing community corrections: An implementation perspective. In A. T. Harland (Ed.), *Choosing correctional options that work: Defining the demand and evaluating the supply* (pp. 183–222). Thousand Oaks, CA: Sage.

Hart, S. D. (1998). The role of psychopathy in assessing risk for violence: Conceptual and methodological issues. *Legal and Criminological Psychology, 3,* 121–137.

Hart, S. D., Cox, D., & Hare, R. (1995). *The Hare PCL:SV Psychopathy Checklist: Screening Version.* New York: Multi-Health Systems.

Hart, S. D., & Hare, R. D. (1997). Psychopathy: Assessment and association with criminal conduct. In D. M. Stoff, J. Breiling, & J. D. Maser (Eds.), *Handbook of antisocial behavior* (pp. 22–35). New York: John Wiley.

Harvard Civil Rights Project. (2000). *Opportunities suspended: The devastating consequences of zero tolerance and school discipline policies: Report from a national summit on zero tolerance.* Washington, DC: Author. (ERIC Document Reproduction Service No. ED454314).

Hastings, J. E., & Hamberger, L. K. (1988). Personality characteristics of spouse abusers: A controlled comparison. *Violence and Victims, 3,* 31–48.

Hayes, L. M. (1989). National study of jail suicides: Seven years later. *Psychiatric Annals, 31*(7), 447–452.

Hayes, L. M. (1998). Suicide prevention in correctional facilities: An overview (pp. 245–256). In M. Puisis (Ed.), *Clinical practice in correctional medicine,* St. Louis, MO: Mosby.

Hayes, S. C. (2002). Early intervention or early incarceration? Using a screening test for intellectual disability in the criminal justice system. *Journal of Applied Research in Intellectual Disabilities, 15*(2), 120–128.

Hayes, S. C., & Farnill, D. (2003, April). Correlations for the Vineland adaptive behavior scales with Kaufman brief intelligence test in a forensic sample. *Psychological Reports, 92*(2), 573–580.

Haywood, T. W., Kravitz,, H. M., Goldman, L. B., & Freeman, A. (2000, July). Characteristics of women in jail and treatment orientations: A review. *Behavior Modification, 24*(3), 307–324.

Hazelwood, R. R. (1983, September). The behavior-oriented interview of rape victims: The key to profiling. *FBI Law Enforcement Bulletin,* pp. 8–15.

Heath, I. (2000). May state treat, over his objection, a capital murder inmate who, as a result of mental illness, is found to be a danger to self and others, when a concurrent effect of the treatment is the restoration of competency to be executed, *Journal of the American Academy of Psychiatry & the Law, 28*(2), 247–248.

Hecker, S. (1997). Race and pretextual traffic stops: An expanded role for civilian review board. *Columbian Human Rights Law Review, 28,* 1–37.

Hecker, T., & Steinberg, L. (2002, June). Psychological evaluation at juvenile court disposition. *Professional Psychology: Research and Practice, 33*(3), 300–306.

Heide, K. M. (1992). *Why kids kill parents: Child abuse and adolescent homicide.* Columbus: Ohio State Press.

Heilbrun, K. (1992). The role of psychological testing in forensic assessment. *Law and Human Behavior, 16*(3), 257–272.

Heilbrun, K. (2001). *Principles of forensic mental health assessment.* New York: Kluwer Academic/Plenum Publishers.

Heilbrun, K., Hart, S. D., Hare, R. D., Gustafson, D., Nunez, C., & White, A. J. (1998). Inpatient and post-discharge aggression in mentally disordered offenders. *Journal of Interpersonal Violence, 13,* 514–527.

Heilbrun, K., Nezu, C., Keeney, M., Chung, S., & Wasserman, A. L. (1998). Sexual offending: Linking assessment, intervention, and decision making. *Psychology, Public Policy, and Law, 4*(1/2), 138–174.

Heilbrun, K., Radelet, M. L., & Dvoskin, J. (1992). The debate on treating individuals incompetent for execution. *American Journal of Psychiatry, 149*(5), 596–605.

Heinkel, J. O., & Reichel, P. L. (2002). The driver's license: A suggested gang suppression strategy. *Journal of Gang Research, 9*(4), 45–56.

Heinze, M. C., & Purisch, A. D. (2001). Beneath the mask: Use of psychological tests to detect and subtype malingering in criminal defendants. *Journal of Forensic Psychology Practice, 1*(4), 23–52.

Helfer, R. E., & Kempe, C. H. (Eds.). (1986). *Child abuse and neglect: The family and the community.* Cambridge, MA: Ballinger.

Hemmens, C., Miller, M., Burton, V. S., & Milner, S. (2002, April). The consequences of official labels: An examination of the rights lost by the mentally ill and mentally incompetent ten years later. *Community Mental Health Journal, 38*(2), 129–140.

Hemmens, C., Stohr, M. K., Schoeler, M., & Miller, B. (2002, November/December). One-step up, two steps back: The progression of perceptions of women's work in prisons and jails. *Journal of Criminal Justice, 30*(6), 473–489.

Henning, K., Jones, A., & Holdford, R. (2003, August). Treatment needs of women arrested for domestic violence: A comparison with male offenders. *Journal of Interpersonal Violence, 18*(8), 839–856.

Henry J. Kaiser Family Foundation. (2001). *Inside-Out: A report on the experiences of lesbians, gays and bisexuals in America and the public's views on issues and policies related to sexual orientation.* Retrieved October 18, 2002 from http://www.kff.org

Hensl, K. (2004). Restored to health to be put to death: Reconciling the legal and medical dilemmas of medicating to execute in *Singleton v. Norris. Villanova Law Review 49,* 291–328.

Hensley, C., Dumond, R. W., Tewksbury, R., & Dumond, D. A. (2002, Fall). Possible solutions for preventing inmate sexual assault: Examining wardens' beliefs. *American Journal of Criminal Justice, 27*(1), 19–33.

Hensley, C., & Tewksbury, R. (2002, July). Inmate-to-inmate prison sexuality: A review of empirical studies. *Trauma, Violence, & Abuse, 3*(3), 226–243.

Hensley, C., Tewksbury, R., & Castle, T. (2003, June). Characteristics of prison sexual assault targets in male Oklahoma correctional facilities. *Journal of Interpersonal Violence, 18*(6), 595–606.

Hensley, C., Tewksbury, R., & Wright, J. (2001, Fall). Exploring the dynamics of masturbation and consensual same-sex activity within a male maximum security prison. *Journal of Men's Studies, 10*(1), 59–71.

Herbert, P. (2002). The duty to warn: A reconsideration and critique. *Journal of the American Academy of Psychiatry & the Law, 30*(3), 417–424.

Hess, J. E., & Gladis, S. D. (1987, July). Benevolent interrogation. *FBI Law Enforcement Bulletin,* pp. 20–23.

Heyman, R., & Slep, A. M. S. (2002, November). Do child abuse and interparental violence lead to adulthood family violence? *Journal of Marriage & Family, 64*(4), 864–870.

Hickman, L. J., & Simpson (2003). Fair treatment or preferred outcome? The impact of police behavior on victim reports of domestic violence incidents. *Law & Society Review, 37*(3), 607–633.

Higgins, S. E. (1993). Interjurisdictional coordination of major gang interventions. *The Police Chief, 60*(6), 46–47.

Higson-Smith, C. (2002). A community psychology perspective on terrorism: Lessons from South Africa. In C. E. Stout (Ed.), *The psychology of terrorism, Volume Four: Programs and practices in response and prevention.* Westport, CT: Praeger.

Hill, C. D., Rogers, R., & Bickford, M. E. (1996). Predicting aggressive and socially disruptive behaviour in a maximum-security forensic hospital. *Journal of Forensic Sciences, 41,* 56–59.

Ho, T. (1996). Assessment of retardation among mentally retarded criminal offenders: An examination of racial disparity. *Journal of Criminal Justice, 24,* 337–350.

Hodgins, S. (2002). Research priorities in forensic mental health. *International Journal of Forensic Mental Health, 1*(1), 7–23.

Hoffman, P., & Faust, L. (1977). Least restrictive treatment of the mentally ill: A doctrine in search of its senses. *San Diego Law Review, 14,* 1100–1154.

Hoffman, P., & Silverstein, M. (1995). Safe streets don't require lifting rights. In M. W. Klein, C. L. Maxon, & J. Miller (Eds.), *The modern gang reader.* Los Angeles: Roxbury.

Hollin, C. R., & Palmer, E. J. (2003, September). Level of service inventory–revised profiles of violent and nonviolent prisoners. *Journal of Interpersonal Violence, 18*(9), 1075–1086.

Holub, R. J. (1992). *Forensic psychological testing: A survey of practices and beliefs.* Unpublished manuscript, Minnesota School of Professional Psychology, Bloomington.

Hong, G. K. (2002). Psychiatric disabilities. In M. G. Brodwin, F. A. Tellez, & S. K. Brodwin (2nd eds.), *Medical, psychosocial, and vocational aspects of disability* (pp. 107–118). Athens, GA: Elliott and Fitzpatrick.

Hopkins, N., Hewstone, M., & Hantzi, A. (1992). Police-schools liaison and young people's image of the police: An intervention evaluation. *British Journal of Psychology, 83,* 203–220.

Hopper, S., & McSherry, B. (2001). The insanity defence and international human rights obligations. *Psychiatry, Psychology and Law, 8*(2), 161–173.

Horne, P. (1985). Female correction officers: A status report. *Federal Probation, 49,* 46–54.

Horvath, L. S., Logan, T. K., & Walker, R. (2002, December). Child custody cases: A content analysis of evaluations in practice. *Professional Psychology: Research & Practice, 33*(6), 557–565.

Hostetter, E. C., & Jinnah, D. T. (1993). Families of adult prisoners. Retrieved July 12, 1998 from http://www.ifs.univie.ac.at/uncjin/mosaic/famcorr/fmcorrpt.html

House Ways & Means Committee. (1998). *Green book.* Washington, DC: Committee Print.

Howells, K., Hall, G., & Day, A. (1999, November). The management of suicide and self-harm in prisons: Recommendations for good practice. *Australian Psychologist, 34*(3), 157–165.

Hromadka, P. (1995). Innovative York program allows babies to stay with inmate moms. *Nebraska Nurse, 28,* 14.

Hubbard, K. L., Zapf, P. A., & Ronan, K. A. (2003, April). Competency restoration: An examination of the differences between defendants predicted restorable and not restorable to competency. *Law & Human Behavior, 27*(2), 127–139.

Huber, M., Balon, R., Labbate, L., Brandt-Youtz, S., Hammer, J., & Mufti, R. (2000, June). A survey of police officers' experience with Tarasoff warnings in two states. *Psychiatric Services, 51*(6), 807–809.

Huebner, B. M. (2003, March/April). Administrative determinants of inmate violence: A multilevel analysis. *Journal of Criminal Justice, 31*(2), 107–117.

Hufft, A. G. (1992). Psychosocial adaptation to pregnancy in prison. *Journal of Psychosocial Nursing, 30,* 19–23.

Hunt, G., Riegel, S., Morales, T., & Waldorf, D. (1993). Changes in prison culture: Prison gangs and the case of the Pepsi generation. *Social Problems, 40*(3), 398–409.

Huprich, S. K., Fuller, K. M., & Schneider, R. B. (2003, July). Divergent ethical perspectives on the duty-to-warn principle with HIV patients. *Ethics & Behavior, 13*(3), 263–278.

Hutchinson, I. W. (2003, April). Substance use and abused women's utilization of the police. *Journal of Family Violence, 18*(2), 93–113.

Icove, D. J. (1994). Police use of discretion: A comparison of community, system, and officer expectations. Retrieved from http://www.totse.com/files/FA019/res rev.htm

Inciardi, J. A. (1993). *Criminal justice.* Orlando, FL: Harcourt Brace Jovanovich.

Ingrassia, M., & Springen, K. (1993, May 3). Standing up for fathers. *Newsweek,* pp. 52–53.

Ingrassia, M., & Springen, K. (1994, March 21). She's not baby Jessica anymore. *Newsweek*, pp. 60–65.

Inwald, R. (1988). Five-year follow-up study of departmental terminations as predicted by 16 preemployment psychological indicators. *Journal of Applied Psychology, 73,* 703–710.

Inwald, R., Knatz, H., & Shusman, E. (1983). *Inwald Personality Inventory manual.* New York: Hilson Research.

Ivanoff, A., Jang, S. J., & Smyth, N. (1996). Clinical risk factors associated with parasuicide in prison. *International Journal of Offender Therapy and Comparative Criminology, 400,* 135–146.

Jackson, P. I. (1989). *Minority group threat, crime, and policing: Social context and social control.* New York: Praeger.

Jacobs, C. (1998). California to execute man with schizophrenia. Retrieved February 9, 1999 from http://w1.480.telia.com/≫u48003561/kellyhorace.htm

Jacobs, D. (2002, June). Police use of force against drug suspects: Understanding the legal need for policy development. *Social Forces, 80*(4), 1223–1251.

Jacobs, D., & Carmichael, J. T. (2002, June). Subordination and violence against state control agents: Testing political explanation for lethal assaults against the police. *Social Forces, 80*(4), 1223–1251.

Jacobs, P. (1966). *Prelude to riot.* New York: Vintage Press.

Jaffe, P. D., Pons, F., & Wicky, H. R. (1997). Children imprisoned with their mothers: Psychological implications. In S. Redmonds, V. Garrido, J. Perez, & R. Barberet (Eds.), *Advances in psychology and law: International contributions* (pp. 399–407). Berlin: de Gruyter.

Jager, A. D. (2001). Forensic psychiatry services in Australia. *International Journal of Law and Psychiatry, 24,* 387–398.

James, S. E. (2002, July). Clinical themes in gay- and lesbian-parented adoptive families. *Clinical Child Psychology & Psychiatry, 7*(3), 475–486.

Janko, S. (1994). *Vulnerable children, vulnerable families: The social construction of child abuse.* New York: Teachers College Press.

Janofsky, J. S. (2001). Reply to Schafer: Exploitation of criminal suspects by mental health professionals is unethical. *Journal of the American Academy of Psychiatry & the Law, 29*(4), 449–451.

Jaskiewicz-Obydzinska, T., & Czerederecka, A. (1995). Psychological evaluation of changes in testimony given by sexually abused juveniles. In G. Davies & S. Lloyd-Bostock (Eds.), *Psychology, law, and criminal justice: International developments in research and practice* (pp. 160–169). Berlin: de Gruyter.

Jefferson, T., & Walker, M. (1993). Attitudes to the police of ethnic minorities in a provincial city. *British Journal of Criminology, 33,* 251–266.

Jesson, J. (1993). Understanding adolescent female prostitution: A literature review. *British Journal of Social Work, 23,* 517–530.

Johnson, H., & Hotton, T. (2003, February). Losing control: Homicide risk in estranged and intact relationships. *Homicide Studies: An Interdisciplinary & International Journal, 7*(1), 58–84.

Johnson, J. (1992). *Teen prostitution.* Danbury, CT: Franklin Watts.

Johnson, J. G. (2001). Violence in prison systems: An African American tragedy. *Journal of Human Behavior in the Social Environment, 4*(2–3), 105–128.

Johnson, M. B. (1996). Examining risks to children in the context of parental rights termination proceedings. *New York University Review of Law and Social Change, 22*(2), 397–424.

Johnson, M. B. (1999). Psychological parent theory reconsidered: The New Jersey "JC" case, part II. *American Journal of Forensic Psychology, 17*(2), 41–56.

Johnson, M. B., Baker, C., & Maceira, A. (2001). The 1997 Adoption and Safe Families Act and parental rights termination consultation. *American Journal of Forensic Psychology, 19*(3), 15–28.

Johnson, M. B., & Hunt, R. C. (2000). The psychological interface in juvenile Miranda assessment. *American Journal of Forensic Psychology, 18*(3), 17–35.

Johnson, P. (2001). In their own voices: Report of a study on the later effects of child sexual abuse. *Journal of Sexual Aggression, 7*(2), 41–56.

Johnson, S., & O'Connor, E. (2001). *The gay baby boom: A psychological perspective.* New York: New York University Press.

Johnston, D. (1995a). Effects of parental incarceration. In K. Gabel & D. Johnston (Eds.), *Children of incarcerated parents* (pp. 59–88). New York: Lexington Books.

Johnston, D. (1995b). Intervention. In K. Gabel & D. Johnston (Eds.), *Children of incarcerated parents* (pp. 199–236). New York: Lexington Books.

Johnston, D., & Gabel, K. (1995). Incarcerated parents. In K. Gabel & D. Johnston (Eds.), *Children of incarcerated parents* (pp. 3–20). New York: Lexington Books.

Jordan, K. (2003, April). What we learned from the 9/11 first anniversary. *Family Journal of Counseling & Therapy for Couples & Families, 11*(2), 110–116.

Joseph, K. L. (1996). Victim-offender mediation: What social and political factors will affect its development? *Ohio State Journal of Dispute Resolution, 11*(207), 1–14.

Joseph, T. M. (1994, September). Walking the minefields of community-oriented policing. *FBI Law Enforcement Bulletin,* pp. 8–12.

Kagle, J., & Kopels, S. (1994). Confidentiality after Tarasoff. *Health and Social Work, 19*(3), 217–222.

Kain, C. (1988). To breach or not to breach: Is that the question? A response to Gray and Harding. *Journal of Counseling and Development, 66,* 224–225.

Kaltenborn, K. (2001, February). Children's and young people's experience in various residential arrangements: A longitudinal study to evaluate criteria for custody and residence decision making. *British Journal of Social Work, 31*(1), 81–117.

Kamerman, J. (1995). Correctional officer suicide. *The Keeper's Voice 16.* Retrieved October 29, 1998 from http://www.acsp.uic.edu/iaco/kv160307.htm

Kandel, R. F. (1994). Just ask the kid! Towards a rule of children's choice in custody determinations. *University of Miami Law Review, 49,* 299–376.

Kannady, B. (1993, August). Developing stress-resistant police families. *The Police Chief,* pp. 92–95.

Kappeler, V. E., Sluder, R. D., & Alpert, G. P. (1998). *Forces of deviance: Understanding the dark side of policing,* Prospect Heights, IL: Waveland.

Katz, L. F., & Gottman, J. M. (1997). Buffering children from marital conflict and dissolution. *Journal of Clinical Child Psychology, 26,* 157–171.

Keating, L. M. (2002, Winter). The effects of a mentoring program on at-risk youth. *Adolescence, 37*(148), 717–735.

Keating, L. M., Tomishima, M. A., Foster, S., & Alessandri, M. (2002, Winter). The effects of a mentoring program on at-risk youth. *Adolescence, 37*(148), 717–734.

Keilin, W. G., & Bloom, L. J. (1986). Child custody evaluation practices: A survey of experienced professionals. *Professional Psychology: Research and Practice, 17,* 338–346.

Keilitz, S. (1994). Legal report: Civil protection orders: A viable justice system tool for deterring domestic violence. *Violence and Victims, 9,* 79–84.

Kelley, J. B. (1997). The best interests of the child: A concept in search of meaning. *Family and Conciliation Courts Review, 35,* 377–387.

Kelley, J. B. (2003, April). Parents with enduring child disputes: Focused interventions with parents in enduring disputes. *Journal of Family Studies, 9*(1), 51–62.

Kennedy, D. M., & Moore, M. H. (1997). Underwriting the risky investment in community policing: What social science should be doing to evaluate community policing. In R. G. Dunham & G. P. Alpert (Eds.), *Critical issues in policing: Contemporary readings* (pp. 469–488). Prospect Heights, IL: Waveland Press.

Keyes, D., Edwards, W., & Perske, R. (1998). Mental retardation and the death penalty. Retrieved October 24, 1998 from http://www.essential.org/dpic/dpicmr.html

Kiely, J., & Hodgson, G. (1990). Stress in the prison service: The benefits of exercise programs. *Human Relations, 43,* 551–572.

Kilchling, M., & Loeschnig-Gspandl, M. (2000). Legal and practical perspectives on victim/offender mediation in Austria and Germany. *International Review of Victimology, 7*(4), 305–332.

Kinder, K., Veneziano, C., Fichter, M., & Azuma, H. (1995). A comparison of the dispositions of juvenile offenders certified as adults with juvenile offenders not certified. *Juvenile and Family Court Journal, 46*(3), 37–42.

Kirkland, K., & Kirkland, K. L. (2001). Frequency of child custody evaluation complaints and related disciplinary action: A survey of the Association of State and Provincial Psychology Boards. *Professional Psychology: Research & Practice, 32*(2), 171–174.

Kirschner, S. M., & Galperin, G. J. (2001). Psychiatric defenses in New York County: Pleas and results. *Journal of the American Academy of Psychiatry & the Law, 29*(2), 194–201.

Kiser, G. C. (1991). Female inmates and their families. *Federal Probation, 55,* 55–63.

Klein, M. W. (1995). Attempting gang control by suppression: The misuse of deterrence principles. In M. W. Klein, C. L. Maxon, & J. Miller (Eds.), *The modern gang reader.* Los Angeles: Roxbury.

Klinger, D. A. (1994). Demeanor or crime? Why "hostile" citizens are more likely to be arrested. *Criminology, 32*(3), 475–493.

Klinger, D. A. (1996). Bringing crime back in: Toward a better understanding of police arrest decisions. *Journal of Research in Crime and Delinquency, 33*(3), 333–336.

Klockars, C. B. (1984). Blue lies and police placebos. *American Behavioral Scientist, 27*(4), 529–544.

Knapp, S., & VandeCreek, L. (2001). Ethical issues in personality assessment in forensic psychology. *Journal of Personality Assessment, 77*(2), 242–254.

Knoster, T., & Kincaid, D. (1999). Effective school practice in educating students with challenging behaviors. *TASH Newsletter, 11*(25), 8–11.

Knox, G., & Tromanhauser, E. (1991). Gangs and their control in adult correctional institutions. *The Prison Journal, 71*(2), 15–21.

Kocsis, R. N. (2003a, February). An empirical assessment of content in criminal psychological profiles. *International Journal of Offender Therapy & Comparative Criminology, 47*(1), 37–46.

Kocsis, R. N. (2003b, April). Criminal psychological profiling: Validities and abilities. *International Journal of Offender Therapy and Comparative Criminology, 47*(2), 126–144.

Kocsis, R. N., Cooksey, R. W., & Irwin, H. J. (2002, October). Psychological profiling of sexual murders: An empirical model. *International Journal of Offender Therapy & Comparative Criminology, 46*(5), 532–554.

Kocsis, R. N., Irwin, H. J., Hayes, A. F., & Nunn, R. (2000, March). Expertise in psychological profiling. *Journal of Interpersonal Violence, 15*(3), 311–331.

Koehler, S. P., & Willis, F. N. (1994). Traffic citations in relation to gender. *Journal of Applied Social Psychology, 24*(21), 1919–1926.

Koenen, K. C., Moffitt, T. E., Caspi, A., Taylor, A., & Purcell, S. (2003, June). Domestic violence is associated with environmental suppression of IQ in young children. *Development & Psychopathology, 15*(2), 297–311.

Koetting, M. G., Grabarek, J., Van Hasselt, V. B., & Hazelwood, R. R. (2003). Criminally committed inpatients in a residential forensic pre-release treatment program: An exploratory study. *Journal of Offender Rehabilitation, 37*(2), 107–122.

Kohan, A., & O'Connor, B. P. (2002a, May). Police officer job satisfaction in relation to mood, well-being, and alcohol consumption. *Journal of Psychology, 136*(3), 1–12.

Kohan, A., & O'Connor, B. (2002b, May). Police officer job satisfaction in relation to mood, well-being, and alcohol consumption. *Journal of Psychology, 136*(3), 307–318.

Kornfeld, A. D. (1995). Police officer candidate MMPI-2 performance: Gender, ethnic, and normative factors. *Journal of Clinical Psychology, 51*(4), 536–540.

Kovera, M. B., Dickinson, J. J., & Cutler, B. L. (2003). Voir dire and jury selection. In A. M. Goldstein (Ed.), *Handbook of psychology: Forensic psychology, Vol. 11* (pp. 161–175). New York: John Wiley & Sons.

Krauss, D. A., & Sales, B. D. (2000). Legal standards, expertise, and experts in the resolution of contested custody cases. *Psychology, Public Policy, & Law, 6*(4), 843–879.

Krisberg, B., & DeComo, R. (1993). *Juveniles taken into custody: Fiscal year 1991 report.* Washington, DC: United States Department of Justice, Office of Juvenile Justice and Delinquency Prevention.

Kroes, W. H. (1976). *Society's victim: The policeman.* Springfield, IL: Charles C Thomas.

Kurtz, L. (1997). Comment: Protecting New York's children: An argument for the creation of a rebuttable presumption against awarding a spouse abuser custody of a child. *Albany Law Review, 60,* 1345–1376.

Labecki, L. A. (1994). Monitoring hostility: Avoiding prison disturbances through environmental screening. *Corrections Today, 56*(5), 104–111.

Lamb, D., Clark, C., Drumheller, P., Frizzell, K., & Surrey, L. (1989). Applying Tarasoff to AIDS-related psychotherapy issues. *Professional Psychology: Research and Practice, 20,* 37–43.

Lamb, H., Weinberg, L., DeCuir, W., & Walter, W. (2002, Oct). The police and mental health. *Psychiatric Services, 53*(10), 1266–1271.

Lambert, E. G., Hogan, N. L., & Barton, S. M. (2002, Fall). The impact of work-family conflict on correctional staff job satisfaction: An exploratory study. *American Journal of Criminal Justice, 27*(1), 35–52.

Lancet (February 22, 2003). Execution: an unwanted side-effect. *Lancet, 361*(9358), 621.

Lanctôt, N., & Smith, C. A. (2001). Sexual activity, pregnancy, and deviance in a representative urban sample of African American girls. *Journal of Youth and Adolescence, 30,* 349–372.

Lanyon, R. I. (1986). Psychological assessment procedures in court-related settings. *Professional Psychology: Research and Practice, 17*(3), 260–268.

Lasher, L. (2003, April). Munchausen by proxy (MBP) maltreatment: An international educational challenge. *Child Abuse & Neglect, 27*(4), 409–411.

Laszlo, A. T., & Rinehart, T. A. (2002). Collaborative problem-solving partnerships: Advancing community policing philosophy to domestic violence victim services. *International Review of Victimology, 9*(2), 197–209.

Lawal, O. A. (2002). Social-psychological considerations in the emergence and growth of terrorism. In C. E. Stout, ed., *The psychology of terrorism, Volume Four: Programs and practices in response and prevention.* Westport, CT: Praeger.

Laws, R. D. (Ed.). (1989). *Relapse prevention with sex offenders.* New York: Guilford Press.

Laws, R. D. (2003, March). The rise and fall of relapse prevention. *Australian Psychologist, 38*(1), 22–30.

Lee, D. T. (2003). Community-treated and discharged forensic patients: An 11-year follow-up. *International Journal of Law & Psychiatry, 26*(3), 289–300.

Lee, M. (1997). Post-divorce interparental conflict, children's contact with both parents, children's emotional processes, and children's behavioral adjustment. *Journal of Divorce and Remarriage, 27,* 61–82.

Lee, R. W., & Gillam, S. L. (2000). *Clinical Supervisor, 19*(1), 123–136.

Leiber, M., Nalla, M., & Farnworth, M. (1998). Explaining juvenile's attitudes toward the police. *Justice Quarterly, 15*(1), 151–173.

Leinen, S. (1993). *Gay cops.* New Brunswick, NJ: Rutgers University.

Leo, R. A. (1996). Criminal law: Inside the interrogation room. *Journal of Criminal Law and Criminology, 86*(2), 266–303.

Leo, R. J. (2002). Social Security Disability and the mentally ill: Changes in the adjudication process and treating source information requirements. *Psychiatric Annals, 32*(5), 284–292.

Leon, K. (2003, July). Risk and protective factors in young children's adjustment in parental divorce: A review of the research. *Family Relations: Interdisciplinary Journal of Applied Family Studies, 52*(3), 258–270.

Leonard, E. D. (2000, January/July). Battered women prisoners as agents of social change: Cross-cultural implications. *Caribbean Journal of Criminology & Social Psychology, 5*(1–2), 154–164.

Leone, P. E., Mayer, M. J., Malmgren, K., & Meisel, S. M. (2000). School violence and disruption: Rhetoric, reality, and reasonable balance. *Focus on Exceptional Children, 33*(1), 1–20.

Levin, A., & Mills, L. G. (2003, October). Fighting for child custody when domestic violence is at issue: Survey of state laws. *Social Work, 48*(4), 463–470.

Levinson, A., & Fonagy, P. (1999). *Adult attainment patterns in forensic nonpsychiatric patients.* Manuscript submitted for publication.

Levinson, D. (1988). Family violence in cross-cultural perspective. In V. Van Hasselt, R. L. Morrison, A. S. Bellack, & M. Herson (Eds.), *Handbook of family violence* (pp. 435–456). New York: Plenum.

Levy, R., & Rubenstein, L. (1996). *The rights of people with mental disabilities.* Carbondale: Southern Illinois University Press.

Lewis, D. O., Pincus, J. H., Bard, B., Richardson, E., Prichep, L. S., Feldman, M., & Yeager, C. (1988). Neuropsychiatric, psychoeducational, and family characteristics of 14 juveniles condemned to death in the United States. *American Journal of Psychiatry, 145,* 584–589.

Lewis, J. L., Simcox, A. M., & Berry, D. T. R. (2002). Screening for feigned psychiatric symptoms in a forensic sample by using the MMPI-2 and the Structured Interview of Malingered Symptomatology. *Psychological Assessment, 14*(2), 170–176.

Lidz, C., Mulvey, E., & Gardner, W. (1993). The accuracy of predictions of violence to others. *Journal of The American Medical Association, 269,* 1007–1111.

Liebling, A. (1993). Suicides in young prisoners: A summary. *Death Studies, 17*(5), 381–409.

Lilly, R. J. (1992). The Pride Inc. program: An evaluation of 5 years of electronic monitoring. *Federal Probation, 54,* 42–47.

Lillyquist, M. J. (1985). *Understanding the changing criminal behavior.* Englewood Cliffs, NJ: Prentice Hall.

Lin, C. (2003, June). Ethical exploration of the Least Restrictive Alternative. *Psychiatric Services, 54*(6), 866–870.

Linney, J. A. (1982). Alternative facilities for youth in trouble: Descriptive analysis of a strategically selected sample. In J. F. Handler & J. Zatz (Eds.), *Neither angels nor thieves: Studies in deinstitutionalization of status offenders.* Washington, DC: National Academy Press.

Lipsey, M. (1992). *Juvenile delinquency treatment: A meta-analytic inquiry into the variability of effects in meta-analysis for explanation: A casebook* (T. Cook et al., Eds.). New York: Russell Sage Foundation.

Logan, T. K., Walker, R., Horvath, L. S., & Leukefeld, C. (2003). Divorce, custody, and spousal violence: A random sample of circuit court docket records. *Journal of Family Violence, 18*(5), 269–279.

Logan, T. K., Walker, R., Jordan, C. E., & Horvath, L. S. (2002, December). Child custody evaluations and domestic violence: Case comparisons. *Violence & Victims, 17*(6), 719–742.

Long, E., Long, J., Leon, W., & Weston, P. B. (1975). *American minorities.* Englewood Cliffs, NJ: Prentice Hall.

Long, G. T. (1993). Homosexual relationships in a unique setting: The male prison. In L. Diamond (Ed.), *Homosexual issues in the workplace.* Washington, DC: Taylor & Francis.

Loo, R. (2001). Effective postvention for police suicide. *Australasian Journal of Disaster and Trauma Studies, 5*(2), NP.

Loper, A. B. (2002, Fall). Adjustment to prison of women convicted of possession, trafficking, and nondrug offenses. *Journal of Drug Issues, 32*(4), 1033–1050.

Lord, D. D. (2001, March/April). Jury selection: Part one. *Forensic Examiner, 10*(3–4), 27–30.

Lorr, M., & Strake, S. (1994). Personality profiles of police candidates. *Journal of Clinical Psychology, 50*(2), 200–207.

Los Angeles City Attorney Gang Prosecution Section. (1995). Civil gang abatement: A community based policing tool of the office of the Los Angeles City Attorney. In M. W. Klein, C. L. Maxon, & J. Miller (Eds.), *The modern gang reader.* Los Angeles: Roxbury.

Lotke, E. (1996). Sex offenders: Does treatment work? *Corrections Compendium, 21*(5), 1–8.

Love, B. (1994). Program curbs prison violence through conflict resolution. *Corrections Today, 56*(5), 144–156.

Low, J., & Durkin, K. (2001). Children's conceptualization of law enforcement on television and in real life. *Legal and Criminological Psychology, 6*, 197–214.

Lowenstein, L. F. (2002a). Joint custody and shared parenting: Are courts listening? *Family Therapy, 29*(2), 101–108.

Lowenstein, L. F. (2002b). The value of mediation in child custody disputes (recent research 1996–2001). *Justice of the Peace, 166*(38), 739–744.

Luke, K. P. (2002, November/December). Mitigating the ill effects of maternal incarceration on women in prison and their children. *Child Welfare League, LXXX1*(6), 929–948.

Lundman, R. (1993). *Prevention and control of juvenile delinquency* (2nd ed.). New York: Oxford University Press.

Lundman, R. J. (1996a). Demeanor and arrest: Additional evidence from previously unpublished data. *Journal of Research in Crime and Delinquency, 33*(3), 306–323.

Lundman, R. J. (1996b). Extralegal variables and arrest. *Journal of Research in Crime and Delinquency, 33*(3), 349–353.

Lurigio, A. J., Fallon, J. R., & Dincin, J. (2000). Helping the mentally ill in jails adjust to community life: A description of a postrelease ACT program and its clients. *International Journal of Offender Therapy & Comparative Criminology, 44*(5), 532–548.

Lyon, T. D., Saywitz, K. J., Kaplan, D. L., Dorado, J. S. (2001, February). Reducing maltreated children's reluctance to answer hypothetical oath-taking. *Law & Human Behavior, 25*(1), 81–92.

MacDonald, J. M. (2002, October). The effectiveness of community policing in reducing urban violence. *Crime & Delinquency, 48*(4), 592–618.

MacDonald-Wilson, K., Rogers, E. S., & Anthony, W. A. (2001). Unique issues in assessing work function among individuals with psychiatric disabilities. *Journal of Occupational Rehabilitation, 11*(3), 217–232.

MacKenzie, D. L., Robinson, J. W., & Campbell, C. S. (1989). Long-term incarceration of female offenders: Prison adjustment and coping. *Criminal Justice and Behavior, 16*, 223–228.

MacKenzie, D. L., & Souryal, R. (1994). Results of a multisite study of boot camp prisons. *Federal Probation, 58*, 60–66.

Maeroff, G. I. (2000). *A symbiosis of sorts: School violence and the media* (Choices Briefs No. 7). New York: Columbia University. (ERIC Document Reproduction Service No. ED445138).

Maghan, J. (1997). Prison violence. *Crime and Justice International, 13*(9), 18–21.

Mahon, N. (1996). New York inmates' HIV risk behaviors: The implications for prevention policy and programs. *American Journal of Public Health, 86*, 1211–1215.

Malesky, A., & Keim, J. (2001). Mental health professionals' perspectives on sex offender registry web sites. *Sexual Abuse: Journal of Research & Treatment, 13*(1), 53–63.

Maletzky, B. M., & Field, G. (2003, July/August). The biological treatment of dangerous sexual offenders, A review and preliminary report of the Oregon pilot Depo-Provera program. *Aggression & Violent Behavior, 8*(4), 391–412.

Manchester, J. (2003). Beyond accommodation: Reconstructing the insanity defense to provide an adequate remedy for postpartum psychotic women. *The Journal of Criminal Law & Criminology, 93*(2–3), 713–752.

Mandela, N. (1994). *Long walk to freedom: The autobiography of Nelson Mandela*. London: Abacus.

Manning, P. K. (1998). *Police work: the social organization of policing* (2nd ed.), Prospect Heights, IL: Waveland.

Mann, C. (1984). *Female crime and delinquency*. Birmingham: University of Alabama Press.

Marini, I. (2003). What rehabilitation counselors should know to assist Social Security beneficiaries in becoming employed. *Work: Journal of Prevention, Assessment & Rehabilitation, 21*(1), 37–43.

Marion, N. (1995). The federal response to crime victims. *Journal of Interpersonal Violence, 10*(4), 419–436.

Marquart, J. W., Cuvelier, S. J., Burton, V. S., Adams, K., Gerber, J., Longmire, D., Flanagan, T. J., Bennett, K, & Fritsch, E. (1994). A limited capacity to treat: Examining the effects of prison population control strategies on prison education programs. *Crime and Delinquency, 40*(4), 516–531.

Marques, J. K. (1999, April). How to answer the question "Does sexual offender treatment work?" *Journal of Interpersonal Violence, 14*(4), 437–451.

Marshall, L. E. (2001, July). Excessive sexual desire disorder among sexual offenders: The development of a research project. *Sexual Addiction & Compulsivity, 8*(3–4), 301–307.

Marshall, W. L. (1996). The sexual offender: Monster, victim, or everyman? *Sexual Abuse: A Journal of Research and Treatment, 8,* 317–336.

Marshall, W. L., & Barbaree, H. E. (1990). An integrated theory of the etiology of sexual offending. In W. L. Marshall, D. R. Laws, & H. E. Barbaree (Eds.), *Handbook of sexual assault: Issues, theories, and treatment of the offender* (pp. 257–275). New York: Plenum Press.

Martin, D. (1989). Human immunodeficiency virus infection and the gay community: Counseling and clinical issues. *Journal of Counseling and Development, 68,* 67–71.

Martin, M. A., Allan, A., & Allan, M. M. (2001). The use of psychological tests by Australian psychologists who do assessments for the courts. *Australian Journal of Psychology, 53*(2), 77–82.

Martin, S. E., & Jurik, N. C. (1996). *Doing justice, doing gender: Women in law and criminal justice occupations*. Thousand Oaks, CA: Sage.

Martin, S. L., Kim, H., Kupper, L. L., Meyer, R. E., & Hays, M. (1997). Is incarceration during pregnancy associated with infant birth weight? *American Journal of Public Health, 87,* 1526–1531.

Martin, S. L., Rieger, R. H., Kupper, L. L., Meyer, R. E., & Qaqish, B. F. (1997). The effect of incarceration during pregnancy on birth outcomes. *Public Health Reports, 112,* 340–346.

Martindale, D. A. (2001). Cross-examining mental health experts in child custody litigation. *Journal of Psychiatry & Law, 29*(4), 483–511.

Martinez, A. R. (1997). Corrections officer: The other prisoner. *The Keeper's Voice 18.* Retrieved December 3, 1998 from http://www.acsp.uic.edu/iaco/kv1801/180108.shtml

Marzuk, P., Nock, M., Leon, A., Portera, L., & Tardiff, K. (2002, December). Suicide among New York City police officers, 1977–1996. *American Journal of Psychiatry, 159*(12), 2069–2071.

Mason, C. A., Chapman, D. A., Chang, S., & Simons, J. (2003). Impacting re-arrest rates among youth sentenced in adult court: An epidemic examination of the juvenile sentencing project. *Journal of Clinical Child and Adolescent Psychology, 32,* 205–214.

Mastrofski, S. D., Ritti, R. R., & Snipes, J. B. (1994). Expectancy theory and police productivity in DUI enforcement. *Law and Society Review, 28*(1), 113–146.

Maung, N. (1995). *Young people, victimization and the police: British crime survey findings on experiences and attitudes of 12 to 15 year olds.* London: H. M. Stationery Office.

May, J. P., & Williams, E. L. (2002, October). Acceptability of condom availability in a U.S. jail. *AIDS Education & Prevention,* 14(SupplB), 85–91.

McCord, J. (1991). The cycle of crime and socialization process. *Journal of Criminal Law and Criminology, 82,* 211–228.

McCorkle, R. C., Miethe, T. D., & Drass, K. A. (1995). The roots of prison violence: A test of the deprivation, management, and "not-so-total" institution models. *Crime and Delinquency, 41*(3), 317–331.

McCormack, R. (1991). Compensating victims of violent crime. *Justice Quarterly, 8*(3), 329–343.

McCormack, R. (1994). United States crime victim assistance: History, organization and evaluation. *International Journal of Comparative and Applied Criminal Justice, 18*(2), 209–220.

McGrath, R. (1991). Sex-offender risk assessment and disposition planning: A review of empirical and clinical findings. *International Journal of Offender Therapy and Comparative Criminology, 35*(4), 328–350.

McGrath, R. J., Cumming, G., Livingston, J. A., & Hoke, S. E. (2003). Outcome of a treatment program for adult sex offenders: From prison to community. *Journal of Interpersonal Violence, 18*(1), 3–17.

McGuire, T. J. (2000). Correctional institution based sex offender treatment: A lapse behavior study. *Behavioral Sciences & the Law, 18*(1), 57–71.

McIntyre, N. (1996). Project SODA FY95 progress report. Retrieved from November 10, 1998 http://www.dccn.org/communit/projsoda/soda.htm

McMurray, H. L. (1990). Attitudes of assaulted police officers and their policy implications. *Journal of Police Science and Administration, 17*(1), 44–48.

McSherry, B. (1993). Defining what is a "disease of the mind": The untenability of current legal interpretations. *Journal of Law and Medicine, 1,* 76–90.

McSherry, B. (2001). Expert testimony and the effects of mental impairment: Reviving the ultimate issue rule. *International Journal of Law & Psychiatry, 24*(1), 13–21.

McWhirter, E. H., & Linzer, M. (1994). The provision of critical incident stress debriefing services by EAPs: A case study. *Journal of Mental Health Counseling, 16,* 403–414.

Medrano, M. A., Hatch, J. P., Zule, W. A., & Desmond, D. P. (2003). Childhood trauma and adult prostitution behavior in a multiethnic heterosexual drug-using population. *American Journal of Drug & Alcohol Abuse, 29*(2), 463–486.

Melancon, R. (1998). Arizona's insane response to insanity. *Arizona Law Review, 40,* 287.

Meloy, J. R. (2000). Violence risk and threat assessment: A practical guide for mental health and criminal justice professionals. San Diego, CA: Specialized Training Services.

Melton, G., Petrila, J., Poythress, N., & Slobogin, C. (1987). *Psychological evaluations for the courts: A handbook for mental health professionals and lawyers.* New York: Guilford Press.

Melton, G., Petrila, J., Poythress, N., & Slobogin, C. (1997). *Psychological evaluations for the courts: A handbook for mental health professionals and lawyers* (2nd ed.). New York: Guilford Press.

Melville, J. D., & Naimark, D. (2002). Punishing the insane: The verdict of guilty but mentally ill. *Journal of the American Academy of Psychiatry & the Law, 30*(4), 553–555.

Menzies, R. (2002). Historical profiles of criminal insanity. *International Journal of Law and Psychiatry, 25*, 379–404.

Meyer, W. J., Molett, M., Richards, C. D., Arnold, L., & Latham, J. (2003, August). Outpatient civil commitment in Texas for management and treatment of sexually violent predators: A preliminary report. *International Journal of Offender Therapy and Comparative Criminology, 47*(4), 396–406.

Mignon, S., & Holmes, W. (1995). Police response to mandatory arrest laws. *Crime and Delinquency, 41*(4), 430–442.

Miller, G. (1993). The psychological best interests of the child. *Journal of Divorce and Remarriage, 19*, 21–36.

Miller, K. S., & Radelet, M. L. (1993). *Executing the mentally ill: The criminal justice system and the case of Alvin Ford.* Newbury Park, CA: Sage.

Miller, M., & Morris, N. (1988). Predictions of dangerousness: An argument for limited use. *Violence and Victims, 3*(4), 263–283.

Miller, R. (1990). Involuntary civil commitment. In R. Simon (Ed.), *Annual review of psychiatry and the law.* Washington, DC: American Psychiatric Press.

Miller, R. (1992). An update on involuntary civil commitment to outpatient treatment. *Hospital and Community Psychiatry, 43*(1), 79–81.

Miller, R. D. (2003). Testimony by proxy: The use of expert testimony to provide defendant testimony without cross-examination. *Journal of Psychiatry & Law, 31*(1), 21–41.

Mills, J., & Kroner, D. G. (2003, June). Antisocial constructs in predicting institutional violence among violent offenders and child molesters. *International Journal of Offender Therapy & Comparative Criminology, 47*(3), 324–334.

Mills, L. (1996). Empowering battered women transnationally: The case for postmodern interventions. *Social Work, 41*, 261–267.

Milner, J. S., & Campbell, J. C. (1995). Prediction issues for practitioners. In J. C. Campbell (Ed.), *Assessing dangerousness: Violence by sexual offenders, batterers, and child abusers.* Thousand Oaks, CA: Sage.

Mokros, A., & Alison, L. J. (2002, February). Is offender profiling possible? Testing the predicted homology of crime scene actions and background characteristics in a sample of rapists. *Legal & Criminological Psychology, 7*(1), 25–43.

Molbert, B., & Beck, J. C. (2003, January). Assessing violence in patients: Legal implications. *Psychiatric Times, XX*(1). Retrieved April 9, 2003 from http://www.psychiatrictimes.com/p030122.html

Molett, M. T., Arnold, L., & Meyer, W. J. (2001, November). Commitment as an adjunct to sex offender treatment. *Current Opinion in Psychiatry, 14*(6), 549–553.

Monahan, J. (1981). *The clinical prediction of violent behavior.* Beverly Hills, CA: Sage.

Monahan, J. (1996). Violence prediction: The past twenty and the next twenty years. *Criminal Justice and Behavior, 23*(1), 107–120.

Monahan, J. (2002). The MacArthur studies of violence risk. *Criminal Behaviour & Mental Health, 12*(4), S67–S72.

Monahan, J., Steadman, H., Silver, E., Appelbaum, P., Robbins, P., Mulvey, E., Roth, L., et al. (2000). Developing a clinically useful actuarial tool for assessing violence risk. *British Journal of Psychiatry, 176,* 312–319.

Monahan, J., Steadman, H., Silver, E., Appelbaum, P., Robbins, P., Mulvey, E., Roth, L., et al. (2001). *Rethinking risk assessment: The MacArthur study of mental disorder and violence.* New York: Oxford University Press.

Monson, C. M., Gunnin, D. D., Fogel, M. H., & Kyle, L. L. (2001). Stopping (or slowing) the revolving door: Factors related to NGRI acquittees' maintenance of a conditional release. *Law & Human Behavior, 25*(3), 257–267.

Montoya, J. (1999). Child hearsay statutes: At once over-inclusive and under-inclusive. *Psychology, Public Policy, and Law, 5*(2), 304–322.

Moon, D. G., Thompson, R. J., & Bennett, R. (1993). Patterns of substance use among women in prison. In B. R. Fletcher, L. D. Shaver, & D. G. Moon (Eds.), *Women prisoners: A forgotten population* (pp. 45–54). Westport, CT: Praeger.

Moore, T. O. (2001). Testosterone and male behavior: Empirical research with hamsters does not support the use of castration to deter human sexual aggression. *North American Journal of Psychology, 3*(3), 503–520.

Moran, G. (2001). Trial consultation: Why licensure is not necessary. *Journal of Forensic Psychology Practice, 1*(4), 77–85.

Moran, M. J., Sweda, M. G., Fragala, M. R., & Sasscer-Burgos, J. (2001). The clinical application of risk assessment in treatment-planning process. *International Journal of Offender Therapy and Comparative Criminology, 45*(4), 421–435.

Moran, R. (1981). Knowing right from wrong. *Corrections Today, 57,* 124–126, 142.

Morash, M., & Rucker, L. (1990). A critical look at the idea of boot camp as a correctional reform. *Crime and Delinquency, 36,* 204–222.

Morgan, D. (1997). Restricted love. *Women & Therapy, 20*(4), 75–84.

Morgan, R. D., Van Haveren, R., & Pearson, C. A. (2002, April). Correctional officer burnout: Further analyses. *Criminal Justice & Behavior, 29*(2), 144–160.

Morris, G. H. (2002). Commentary: Punishing the unpunishable — the abuse of psychiatry to confine those we love to hate. *The Journal of the American Academy of Psychiatry and the Law, 30,* 556–562.

Morrison, E., Morman, G., Bonner, G., Taylor, C., Abraham, I., & Lathan, L. (2002). Reducing staff injuries and violence in a forensic psychiatric setting. *Archives of Psychiatric Nursing, 16*(3), 108–117.

Morse, S. J. (2003). Involuntary competence. *Behavioral Sciences & the Law, 21*(3), 311–328.

Moses, E. (1996). Ogles proposes castration law. Retrieved Septeber 12, 1998 from http://www.bhip.com/news/9ogles.htm

Moses, M. C. (1995). Girl scouts behind bars: A synergistic solution for children of incarcerated parents. *Corrections Today, 57,* 124–126.

Mossman, D. (2003). Daubert, cognitive malingering, and test accuracy. *Law & Human Behavior, 27*(3), 229–249.

Mullen, P. E. (2002). Commentary: Competence assessment practice in England and Australia versus the United States. *The Journal of the American Academy of Psychiatry and the Law, 30,* 486–487.

Mullen, P. E., Briggs, S., Dalton, T., & Burt, M. (2000, September/December). Forensic mental health services in Australia. *International Journal of Law & Psychiatry, 23*(5–6), 433–452.

Munetz, M., & Geller, J. (1993). The least restrictive alternative in the postinstitutional era. *Hospital and Community Psychiatry, 44*(10), 967–973.

Munson, W. M. (1994). Description and field test of a career development course for male youth offenders with disabilities. *Journal of Career Development, 20*, 205–218.

Murphy, C. M., Meyer, S. L., & O'Leary, K. D. (1993). Family of origin violence and MCMI-II psychopathology among partner assaultive men. *Violence and Victims, 8*, 165–175.

Murphy, J. J. (1972). Current practices in the use of the psychological testing by police agencies. *Journal of Criminal Law, Criminology, and Police Science, 63*, 570–576.

Murray, J. P. (1983). Status offenders: roles, rules, and reactions. In J. P. Murray (Ed.), *Status offenders: A sourcebook*, (pp. 5–45), Boystown, NE: The Boys Town Center.

Myers, B., Smarsh, T., Amlund-Hagen, K., & Kennon, S. (1999). Children of incarcerated mothers. *Journal of Child and Family Studies, 8*(1), 11–25.

Myers, J. E. (1983–1984). Involuntary civil commitment of the mentally ill: A system in need of change. *Villanova Law Review, 29*, 367–433.

Myers, J. E. B. (1993a). A call for forensically relevant research. *Child Abuse and Neglect, 17*, 573–579.

Myers, J. E. B. (1993b). The competency of young children to testify in legal proceedings. *Behavioral Sciences and the Law, 11*, 121–133.

National Broadcasting Corporation (NBC) Research. (1998). Retrieved from http://www.msnbc.com/news/wld/iframes/schoolshootings.Asp

National Center for Health Statistics. (1996). A generation at risk. Retrieved from http://www.rainbows.org/Rain5a.htm

National Center for Health Statistics. (1997). Teen suicide rate. Retrieved January 12, 1998 from http://home. ptd.net/≫buzz/fam-cide.htm

National Center for Posttraumatic Stress Disorder (PTSD). (2001). *The range, magnitude, and duration of effects of natural and human-caused disasters: A review of the empirical literature.* Retrieved August 16, 2003 from http://www.ncptsd.org/facts/disasters/fs_range.html

National Center on Child Abuse and Neglect. (1994). *Child maltreatment 1992: Reports from the states to the National Center on Child Abuse and Neglect.* Washington, DC: U.S. Department of Health and Human Services.

National Institute of Corrections. (1991). *Intervening with substance-abusing offenders: A framework of action* (Report No. 296–934/40539). Washington, DC: U.S. Government Printing Office.

Neil, E., Beek, M., & Schofield, G. (2003). Thinking about and managing contact in permanent placements: The differences and similarities between adoptive parents and foster carers. *Clinical Child Psychology & Psychiatry, 8*(3), 401–418.

Nemitz, T., & Bean, P. (2001). Protecting the rights of the mentally disordered in police stations: The use of the appropriate adult in England and Wales. *International Journal of Law and Psychiatry, 24*, 595–605.

New York State Investigation Commission. (1981). *Corruption and abuses in the correctional system: The Green Haven correctional facility.* New York: New York State Investigation Commission.

Newman, G. R. (1990). Popular culture and criminal justice: A preliminary analysis. *Journal of Criminal Justice, 18*(3), 261–272.

Neylan, T., Metzler, T., Best, S., Weiss, D., Fagan, J., et al. (2002, March/April). Critical incident exposure and sleep quality in police officers. *Psychosomatic Medicine, 64*(2), 345–352.

Nicholson, R., & Kugler, K. (1991). Competent and incompetent criminal defendants: A quantitative review of comparative research. *Psychological Bulletin, 109*(3), 355–370.

Nicholson, R. A., & Norwood, S. (2000, February). The quality of forensic psychological assessments, reports, and testimony: Acknowledging the gap between promise and practice. *Law & Human Behavior, 24*(1), 9–44.

Niederhoffer, A. (1967). *Behind the shield.* New York: Doubleday.

Noffsinger, S. G. (2001). Restoration to competency: Practice guidelines. *International Journal of Offender Therapy and Comparative Criminology, 45*(3), 356–362.

Noll, D. E. (2003). Restorative justice: Outlining a new direction for forensic psychology. *Journal of Forensic Psychology Practice, 3,* 5–24.

Norman, J. A. (1995). Children of prisoners in foster care. In K. Gabel & D. Johnston (Eds.), *Children of incarcerated parents.* New York: Lexington.

Nugent, W., Umbreit, M. S., Wiinamaki, L., & Paddock, J. (2001, January). Participation in victim-offender mediation and reoffense: Successful replications? *Research on Social Work Practice, 11*(1), 5–23.

Nunnally, J. C. (1961). *Popular conceptions of mental health.* New York: Holt, Rinehart, & Winston.

Ogloff, J. R. P., Roesch, R., & Eaves, D. (2000). International perspectives on forensic mental health systems. *International Journal of Law and Psychiatry, 23,* 429–431.

Oliver, W. (2001). Cultural racism and structural violence: Implications for African Americans. *Journal of Human Behavior in the Social Environment, 4*(2–3), 1–26.

Oppenheim, E., & Bussiere, A. (1996). Adoption: Where do relatives stand? *Child Welfare League of America, 5*(47), 1–488.

Oppenheimer, K., & Swanson, G. (1990). Duty to warn: When should confidentiality be breached? *Journal of Family Practice, 30*(2), 179–184.

Orcutt, H., Goodman, G., Tobey, A., Batterman-Faunce, J., & Thomas, S. (2001, August). Detecting deception in children's testimony: Factfinder's abilities to reach the truth in open court and closed-circuit trials. *Law & Human Behavior, 25*(4), 339–372.

Osborne, O. H. (1995). Jailed mothers: Further explorations in public sector nursing. *Journal of Psychosocial Nursing, 33,* 23–28.

O'Shea, B. (2003, March). Factitious disorders: The Baron's legacy. *International Journal of Psychiatry in Clinical Practice, 7*(1), 33–39.

Osinowo, T. O., & Pinals, D. A. (2003). Competence to stand trial. *Journal of the American Academy of Psychiatry & the Law, 31*(2), 261–264.

Osler, M. W. (1991). Shock incarceration: Hard realities and real possibilities. *Federal Probation, 55,* 34–42.

Otto, R. K., Edens, J. F., & Barcus, E. H. (2000, July). The use of psychological testing in child custody evaluations. *Family & Conciliation Courts Review, 38*(3), 312–340.

Otto, R. K., Heilbrun, K., & Grisso, T. (1990). Training and credentialing in forensic psychology. *Behavioral Sciences and the Law, 8,* 217–231.

Owens, R. P., & Wells, D. K. (1993). One city's response to gangs. *The Police Chief, 60*(2), 25–27.

Padgitt, S. T. (1997). Suicide by teens. Working with today's youth for a better future tomorrow, http://www.tott.org/text/teen.html.

Palermo, G. B. (2002, August). Criminal profiling: The uniqueness of the killer. *International Journal of Offender Therapy & Comparative Criminology, 46*(4), 383–385.

Palmer, B., Nayak, G., Dunn, L., Appelbaum, P., & Jeste, D. (2002, March/April). Treatment-related decision-making capacity in middle-aged and older patients with psychosis: A preliminary study using the MacCAT-T and HCAT. *American Journal of Geriatric Psychiatry, 10*(2), 207–211.

Parenti, C. (2000, October). When 'tough love' kills. *Progressive, 64*(10), 31–34.

Parrish, P. (1993, September). Police and the media. *FBI Law Enforcement Bulletin,* pp. 24–25.

Patch, P., & Arrigo, B. A. (1999). Police officer attitudes and use of discretion in situations involving the mentally ill: The need to narrow the focus. *International Journal of Law and Psychiatry, 22*(1), 23–25.

Pate, A. M., Wycoff, M. A., Skogan, W. G., & Sherman, L. W. (1986). *Reducing fear of crime in Houston and Newark: A summary report.* Washington, DC: Police Foundation.

Patterson, C. (1994). Children of the lesbian baby boom: Behavioral adjustment, self-concepts, and sex-role identity. In B. Greene & G. Herek (Eds.), *Contemporary perspectives on gay and lesbian psychology: Theory, research, and applications* (pp. 156–175). Beverly Hills, CA: Sage.

Patterson, C. J., & Chan, R. W. (1999). Families headed by lesbian and gay parents. In M. E. Lamb (Ed.), *Parenting and child development in "nontraditional" families* (pp. 191–219). Mahway, NJ: Lawrence Erlbaum Associates, Inc.

Patterson, C. J., & Redding, R. E. (1996). Lesbian and gay families with children: Implications of social science research for policy. *Journal of Social Issues, 52,* 29–50.

Patterson, J. (1995, November). Community policing: Learning the lessons of history. *FBI Law Enforcement Bulletin,* pp. 5–10.

Pawlukewicz, J. (2003). World Trade Center trauma interventions: A clinical model for affected workers. *Psychoanalytic Social Work, 10*(1), 79–88.

Pedro-Carroll, J., Nakhnikian, E., & Montes, G. (2001, October). Assisting children through transition: Helping parents protect their children from the toxic effects of ongoing conflict in the aftermath of divorce. *Family Court Review, 39*(4), 377–392.

Penn, J. V., Esposito, C. L., Schaeffer, L. E., Fritz, G. K., & Spirito, A. (2003, July). Suicide attempts and self-mutilative behavior in a juvenile correctional facility. *Journal of the American Academy of Child & Adolescent Psychiatry, 42*(7), 762–769.

Penner, N., & Oss, M. E. (1996, November). Barred on the inside: Mental illness in prisons. *Open Minds Quarterly, 3,* 14–16.

Perez, A., Leifman, S., & Estrada, A. (2003, January). Reversing the criminalization of mental illness. *Crime & Delinquency, 49*(1), 62–78.

Perlin, M., Gould, K., & Dorfman, D. (1995). Therapeutic jurisprudence and the civil rights of institutionalized mentally disabled persons: Hopeless oxymoron or path to redemption. *Psychology, Public Policy, and the Law, 1*(1), 80–119.

Perske, R. (2000, December). Deception in the interrogation room: Sometimes tragic for persons with mental retardation and other developmental disabilities. *Mental Retardation, 38*(6), 532–537.

Peters, J. M., & Murphy, W. D. (1992). Profiling child sexual abusers: Legal considerations. *Criminal Justice and Behavior, 19*(1), 38–53.

Petersen, M., Stephens, J., Dickey, R., & Lewis, W. (1996). Transsexuals within the prison system: An international survey of correctional services policies. *Behavioral Sciences and the Law, 14,* 219–229.

Peterson, E. (1996). Juvenile boot camps: Lessons learned. Retrieved October 4, 1997 from http://www.ncjrs.org/txtfiles/fs-9636.txt

Peterson-Badali, M., & Abramovitch, R. (1993). Grade related changes in young people's reasoning about plea decisions. *Law and Human Behavior, 17,* 537–552.

Pinfold, V., Huxley, P., Thornicroft, G., Farmer, P., Toulmin, H., & Graham, T. (2003, June). Reducing psychiatric stigma and discrimination: Evaluating an educational intervention with the police force in England. *Social Psychiatry & Psychiatric Epidemiology, 38*(6), 337–344.

Pipe, M. E., & Goodman, G. S. (1991). Elements of secrecy: Implications for children's testimony. *Behavioral Sciences and the Law, 9,* 33–41.

Pitt, S., & Bale, E. (1995). Neonaticide, infanticide, and filicide: A review of the literature. *Bulletin of the American Academy of Psychiatry and Law, 23,* 375–386.

Podboy, J. W., & Kastl, A. J. (1993). The intentional misuse of standardized psychological tests in complex trials. *American Journal of Forensic Psychology, 11,* 47–54.

Polaschek, D. L. L. (2003, August). Relapse prevention, offense process models, and the treatment of sexual offenders. *Professional Psychology: Research & Practice, 34*(4), 361–367.

Poletiek, F. H. (2002). How psychiatrists and judges assess the dangerousness of persons with mental illness: An "expertise bias." *Behavioral Sciences & the Law, 20*(1–2), 19–29.

Pollock-Byrne, J. M. (1990). *Women, prison, & crime.* Belmont, CA: Wadsworth.

Pomeroy, E. C., Green, D. L., & Kiam, R. (2001, April). Female juvenile offenders incarcerated as adults: A psychoeducational group intervention. *Journal of Social Work, 1*(1), 101–115.

Poythress, N. G., & Feld, D. B. (2002). "Competency restored"—what forensic hospital reports should (and should not) say when returning defendants to court. *Journal of Forensic Psychology Practice, 2*(4), 51–57.

Prentky, R., & Burgess, A. (1990). Rehabilitation of child molesters: A cost benefit analysis. *American Journal of Orthopsychiatry, 60,* 108–117.

Prentky, R. A., Knight, R. A., & Lee, A. F. (1997). Child sexual molestation: Research issues. Retrieved September 12, 1997 from http://www.ncjrs.org/txtfiles/163390.txt

President's Commission on Mental Health. (1978). *Report to the President.* Washington, DC: U.S. Government Printing Office.

Pritchett, G. L. (1993, July). Interpersonal communication: Improving law enforcement's image. *FBI Law Enforcement Bulletin,* pp. 22–26.

Proulx, J., Pellerin, B., Paradis, Y., McKibben, A, Aubut, J., & Ouimet, M. (1997). Static and dynamic predictors of recidivism in sexual aggressors. *Sexual Abuse: A Journal of Research and Treatment, 9*(1), 7–27.

Pursley, R. D. (1994). *Introduction to criminal justice.* New York: Macmillan.

Puzzanchera, C. M. (2000). Delinquency cases waived to criminal court, 1988–1997. *OJJDP Fact Sheet,* U.S. Department of Justice.

Pyle, A. (1995). County takes first step to prohibiting gangs from parks. In M. W. Klein, C. L. Maxon, & J. Miller (Eds.), *The modern gang reader.* Los Angeles: Roxbury.

Quinn, K. M. (2002). Juveniles on trial. *Child & Adolescent Psychiatric Clinics of North America, 11*(4), 719–730.

Quinnell, F. A., & Bow, J. N. (2001). Psychological tests used in child custody evaluations. *Behavioral Sciences & the Law, 19*(4), 491–501.

Quinsey, V. L. (1998). Comment on Marshall's "A Monster, victim, or everyman." *Sexual Abuse: A Journal of Research and Treatment, 10,* 65–69.

Quinsey, V. L., Lalumiere, M. L., Rice, M. E., & Harris, G. T. (1995). Predicting sexual offenses. In J. C. Campbell (Ed.), *Assessing dangerousness: Violence by sexual offenders, batterers, and child abusers* (pp. 114–137). Thousand Oaks, CA: Sage.

Radelet, M. L., & Akers, R. L. (1995). Deterrence and the death penalty: The views of the experts. Retrieved October 18, 1997 from http://sun.soci.niu.edu/≫critcrim/dppa-pers/mike.deterrence

Radelet, M. L., & Borg, M. J. (2000, February). Comment on Umbreit and Vos: Retributive versus restorative justice. *Homicide Studies: An Interdisciplinary & International Journal, 4*(1), 88–92.

Radelet, M. L., & Miller, K. S. (1992). The aftermath of *Ford v. Wainwright. Behavioral Sciences and the Law, 10,* 339–351.

Rand, M. (1997). Violence-related injuries treated in hospital emergency departments. Washington, DC: U.S. Department of Justice.

Rand, M. (1998). Criminal victimizations 1997: Changes 1996–7 with trends 1993–97. Washington, DC: U.S. Department of Justice, Bureau of Justice Statistics.

Ready, J., Weisburd, D., & Farrell, G. (2002). The role of crime victims in American policing: Findings from a national survey of police and victim organizations. *International Review of Victimology, 9*(2), 175–195.

Redding, R. E., Floyd, M. Y., & Hawk, G. L. (2001). What judges and lawyers think about the testimony of mental health experts: A survey of the courts and bar. *Behavioral Sciences & the Law, 19*(4), 583–594.

Redding, R. E., & Reppucci, N. D. (1999, February). Effects of lawyers' socio-political attitudes on their judgments of social science in legal decision making. *Law & Human Behavior, 23*(1), 31–54.

Redlich, A. D., Silverman, M., & Steiner, H. (2003). Pre-adjudicative and adjudicative competence in juveniles and young adults. *Behavioral Sciences & the Law, 21*(3), 393–410.

Reed, D. F., & Reed, E. L. (1998). Children of incarcerated parents. *Social Justice, 24*(3), 152–169.

Reed, J. (1999). Current status of the admissibility of expert testimony after Daubert and Joiner. *Journal of Forensic Neuropsychology, 1*(1), 49–69.

Reich, W. (1998). Understanding terrorist behavior: The limits and opportunities of psychological inquiry. In W. Reich (Ed.), *Origins of terrorism: Psychologies, ideologies, theologies, states of mind* (pp. 261–279). Washington, DC: Woodrow Wilson Center Press.

Reid-MacNevin, S. A. (1997). Boot camps for young offenders. *Journal of Contemporary Criminal Justice, 13,* 155–171.

Reisner, R., & Slobogin, C. (1990). Law and the mental health system: Civil and criminal aspects. St. Paul, MN: West Publishing.

Reming, G. C. (1988). Personality characteristics of supercops and habitual criminals. *Journal of Police Science and Administration, 16*(3), 136–167.

Renzema, M., & Skelton, D. T. (1990). *The use of electronic monitors by criminal justice agencies.* Kutztown, PA: Kutztown University Foundation.

Reppucci, N. D., & Crosby, C. A. (1993). Law, psychology, and children: Overarching issues. *Law and Human Behavior, 17,* 1–10.

Reske, H. J. (1995). Victim–offender mediation catching on: Advocates say programs, typically for nonviolent offenses, benefit both parties. *American Bar Association Journal, 81*(14), 1–4.

Rice, M. E. (1997). Violent offender research and implications for the criminal justice system. *American Psychologist, 52*(4), 414–423.

Rigby, K., & Black, D. (1993). Attitudes toward institutional authorities among aboriginal school children in Australia. *Journal of Social Psychology, 133*(6), 845–852.

Riggs, S. A. (2003). Response to *Troxel v. Granville*: Implications of attachment theory for judicial decisions regarding custody and third-party visitation. *Family Court Review, 41*(1), 39–53.

Roach, K. (2000, July). Changing punishment at the turn of the century: Restorative justice on the rise. *Canadian Journal of Criminology, 42*(3), 249–280.

Roberts, N. A., & Levenson, R. W. (2001, November). The remains of the workday: Impact of job stress and exhaustion on marital interaction in police couples. *Journal of Marriage & the Family, 63*(4), 1052–1067.

Robinson, D. (1992). Commitment, attitudes, career aspirations and work stress: The experiences of correctional staff. *Focus on Staff 4.* Retrieved November 5, 1998 from http//198.103.98.138/crd/forum/e04/e04li.htm

Rogers, F., Bagby, R., & Dickens, S. (1992). *Structured interview of reported symptoms: Professional manual.* Odessa, FL: Psychological Assessment Resources.

Rogers, R., & Ewing, C. P. (2003). The prohibition of ultimate opinions: A misguided enterprise. *Journal of Forensic Psychology Practice, 3*(3), 65–75.

Rogers, R., Grandjean, N., Tillbrook, C. E., Vitacco, M. J., & Sewell, K. W. (2001). Recent interview-based measures of competency to stand trial: A critical review augmented with research data. *Behavioral Sciences & the Law, 19*(4), 503–518.

Rosenbaum, D. P. (1988). Community crime prevention: A review and synthesis of the literature. *Justice Quarterly, 5,* 328–395.

Rosenbaum, D. P., & Lurigio, A. J. (1994). An inside look at community policing reform: Definitions, organizational changes, and evaluation findings. *Crime and Delinquency, 40*(3), 299–314.

Ross, D. L., & Jones, M. (1996). Frequency of training in less-than lethal force tactics and weapons: Results of a two-state survey. *Journal of Contemporary Criminal Justice, 12*(3), 250–263.

Rouzan, J. T., & Knowles, L. (1985, January). A streamlined truancy sweep program that really works. *The Police Chief,* pp. 44–45.

Roy, S. (1993). Two types of juvenile restitution programs in two midwestern counties: A comparative study. *Federal Probation, 57,* 48–53.

Russell, H. E., & Beigel, A. (1982). *Understanding human behavior for effective police work.* New York: Basic Books.

Rutter, M. (1995). Psychosocial adversity: Risk, resilience and recovery. *Southern African Journal of Child & Adolescent Psychiatry, 7*(2), 75–88.

Ryan, T. A., & Grassano, J. B. (1992). Taking a progressive approach to treating pregnant offenders. *Corrections Today, 57,* 184–186.

Saathoff, G. B., & Buckman, J. B. (1990). Diagnostic results of psychiatric evaluations of state police officers. *Hospital and Community Psychiatry, 41*(4), 429–432.

Sachs, N. P. (2000, Fall). Is there a tilt toward abusers in child custody decisions? *The Journal of Psychohistory, 28*(2), 203–228.

Safyer, S. M., & Richmond, L. (1995). Pregnancy behind bars. *Seminars in Perinatology, 19*, 314–322.

Sakuta, T. (2003, September). Constitutional and organizational elements of forensic psychiatry in Japan. *Current Opinion in Psychiatry, 16*(5), 553–557.

Sanislow, C. A., Grilo, C. M., Fehon, D. C., Axelrod, S. R., & McGlashan, T. H. (2003, February). Correlates of suicide risk in juvenile detainees and adolescent inpatients. *Journal of the American Academy of Child & Adolescent Psychiatry, 42*(2), 234–240.

Santamour, M. B. (1990). Mentally retarded offenders: Texas program targets basic needs. *Corrections Today, 52*, 92, 106.

Saunders, N. (2003, February). Domestic-violence protection act. *Essence, 33*(10), 26.

Say, R. E., & Thomson, R. (2003, September). The importance of patient preferences in treatment decisions—challenges for doctors. *British Medical Journal, 327*(7414), 542–545.

Saywitz, K. J. (1995). Improving children's testimony: The question, the answer, and the environment. In M. S. Zaragoza, J. R. Graham, G. C. N. Hall, R. Hirschman, & Y. S. Ben-Porath (Eds.), *Memory and testimony in the child witness* (pp. 113–140). Thousand Oaks, CA: Sage.

Scalora, M. J., & Garbin, C. (2003). A multivariate analysis of sex offender recidivism. *International Journal of Offender Therapy & Comparative Criminology, 47*(3), 309–323.

Scarpa, A. (2003, July). Community violence exposure in young adults. *Trauma Violence & Abuse, 4*(3), 210–227.

Schaefer, K. D., & Hennessy, J. J. (2001). Intrinsic and environmental vulnerabilities among executed capital offenders, revisiting the Bio-Psycho-Social Model of criminal aggression. *Journal of Offender Rehabilitation, 34*(2), 1–20.

Schaffer, B., & DeBlassie, R. R. (1984). Adolescent prostitution. *Adolescence, 19*(75), 689–696.

Schaufeli, W. B., & Peeters, M. C. W. (2000, January). Job stress and burnout among correctional officers: A literature review. *International Journal of Stress Management, 7*(1), 19–48.

Schellenberg, K. (2000, December). Policing the police: Surveillance and the predilection for leniency. *Criminal Justice & Behavior, 27*(6), 667–687.

Schifferle, C. J. (1997). After *Whren v. United States*: Applying the equal protection clause to racially discriminatory enforcement of the law. *Michigan Law and Policy Review, 2*, 1–25.

Schmallenger, F. (1997). *Criminal justice: A brief introduction* (2nd ed.). Upper Saddle River, NJ: Prentice Hall.

Schmidt, A., & Curtis, C. (1987). Electronic monitors. In B. R. McCarthy (Ed.), *Intermediate punishments* (pp. 137–152). Monsey, NY: Willow Tree Press.

Schuster, M. A., Stein, B. D., Jaycox, L., Collins, R. L., Marshall, G. N., Elliott, M. N., Zhou, A. J., et al. (2001). A national survey of stress reactions after the September 11, 2001, terrorist attacks. *New England Journal of Medicine, 345*, 1507–1512.

Schwartz, I. M. (1992). Juvenile crime-fighting policies: What the public really wants. In I. M. Schwartz (Ed.), *Juvenile justice and public policy: Toward a national agenda*. Lanham, MD: Lexington Books.

Scott, C. L., & Yarvis, R. M. (2000). *Hubbart v. Superior Court of Santa Clara County. Journal of the American Academy of Psychiatry & the Law, 28*(1), 82–85.

Scrivner, E. M. (1994). Controlling police use of excessive force. *Series: National Institute of Justice Research in Brief.* Retrieved July 10, 1998 from http://www.ncjrs.org/txtfiles/ppsyc.txt

Seifert, D., Jahn, K., Bolten, S., & Wirtz, M. (2002). Prediction of dangerousness in mentally disordered offenders in Germany. *International Journal of Law and Psychiatry, 25,* 51–66.

Sereny, G. (1984). *The invisible children.* London: Pan Books.

Severson, M. M., & Bankston, T. V. (1995). Social work and the pursuit of justice through mediation. *Social Work, 40,* 683–690.

Shader, R. I., Jackson, A. H., Harmatz, J. S., & Applebaum, P. S. (1977). Patterns of violent behavior among schizophrenic patients. *Diseases of the Nervous System, 38*(1), 13–16.

Shalala, D. E. (1994). Domestic terrorism. *Vital Speeches of the Day, 15,* 450–453.

Shalif, Y., & Leibler, M. (2002). Working with people experiencing terrorist attacks in Israel: A narrative perspective. *Journal of Systemic Therapies, 21*(3), 60–70.

Shamir, J., & Shikaki, K. (2002, September). Self-serving perceptions of terrorism among Israelis and Palestinians. *Political Psychology, 23*(3), 537–557.

Shapiro, J. (1993, August 9). Bonds that blood and birth cannot assure. *US News and World Report,* p. 13.

Shaw, P., Hotopf, M., & Davies, A. (2003). In relative danger? The outcome of patients discharged by their nearest relative from sections 2 and 3 of the Mental Health Act. *Psychiatric Bulletin, 27*(2), 50–54.

Shearer, R. W. (1993, August). Police officer stress: New approaches for handling tension. *The Police Chief,* pp. 96–99.

Shelley-Sireci, L., & Ciano-Boyce, C. (2002). Becoming lesbian adoptive parents: An exploratory study of lesbian adoptive, lesbian birth, and heterosexual adoptive parents. *Adoption Quarterly, 6*(1), 33–43.

Sherer, R. A. (1998). Allegations of poor psychiatric care in county jails prompt increased funding[On-line]. Available: webmaster@mhsource.com

Sheridan, M. (2003, April). The deceit continues: An updated literature review of Munchausen syndrome by proxy. *Child Abuse & Neglect, 27*(4), 431–451.

Sherman, L. G., & Morschauser, P. C. (1989). Screening for suicide risk in inmates. *Psychiatric Quarterly, 60*(2), 119–138.

Shilts, R. (1982). *The mayor of Castro Street: The life and times of Harvey Milk.* New York: St. Martin's.

Shipley, S., & Arrigo, B. (2001). The confusion of psychopathy (II): Implications for forensic (correctional) practice. *International Journal of Offender Therapy and Comparative Criminology, 45*(4), 407–420.

Shipley, S. L., & Arrigo, B. A. (2004). *The female homicide offender: Serial murder and the case of Aileen Wuornos.* Upper Saddle River, NJ: Pearson Education/Prentice Hall.

Short, J. L. (1998). Evaluation of a substance abuse prevention and mental health promotion program for children of divorce. *Journal of Divorce and Remarriage, 28,* 139–155.

Short, J. L. (2002). The effects of parental divorce during childhood on college students. *Journal of Divorce & Remarriage, 38*(1–2), 143–156.

Shuman, D. W., & Sales, B. D. (2001). Daubert's wager. *Journal of Forensic Psychology Practice, 1*(3), 69–78.

Siegel, D. M., Grudzinskas, A. J., & Pinals, D. A. (2001). Old law meets new medicine: Revisiting involuntary psychotropic medication of the criminal defendant, *Wisconsin Law Review, 24,* 307–371.

Siegal, N. (1997). Ganging up on civil liberties: Anti-gang policing and civil rights. *The Progressive, 61*(10), 28–31.

Siegel, L. J., & Senna, J. J. (1994). *Juvenile delinquency, theory, practice, and law* (5th ed.). St. Paul, MN: West Publishing.

Sigler, R. T., & Lamb, D. (1995). Community-based alternatives to prison: How the public and court personnel view them. *Federal Probation, 59,* 3–9.

Silverman, I. J., & Vega, M. (1996). *Corrections: A comprehensive view.* St. Paul, MN: West Publishing.

Simonelli, C., Mullis, T., Elliot, A., & Pierce, T. (2002, February). Abuse by siblings and subsequent experiences of violence within the dating relationship. *Journal of Interpersonal Violence, 17*(2), 103–121.

Simpson, A. I. F., Allnutt, S., & Chaplow, D. (2001). Inquiries into homicides and serious violence perpetrated by psychiatric patients in New Zealand: Need for consistency of method and result analysis. *Australian and New Zealand Journal of Psychiatry, 35,* 364–369.

Skeem, J. L., Golding, S. L., Cohn, N. B., & Berg, G. (1998). The logic and reliability of evaluations of competence to stand trial. *Law and Human Behavior, 22,* 519–547.

Sklarew, B., Krupnick, J., Ward-Wimmer, D., & Napoli, C. (2002, July). The school-based mourning project: A preventive intervention in the cycle of inner-city violence. *Journal of Applied Psychoanalytic Studies, 4*(3), 317–330.

Skogan, W. G. (1994). *The challenge of community policing: Testing the promises.* Thousand Oaks, CA: Sage.

Skolnick, A. (1998). Solomon's children: The new biologism, psychological parenthood, attachment theory, and the best interests standard. In M. A. Mason & A. Skolnick (Eds.), *All our families: New policies for a new century* (pp. 236–255). New York: Oxford University Press.

Slobogin, C. (1994). Involuntary community treatment of people who are violent and mentally ill: A legal analysis. *Hospital and Community Psychiatry, 45*(7), 685–689.

Slobogin, C. (2000, July/August). Mental illness and the death penalty. *Mental & Physical Disability Law Reporter, 24*(4), 667–677.

Slobogin, C. (2003). Pragmatic forensic psychology: A means of "scientizing" expert testimony from mental health professionals? *Psychology, Public Policy, & Law, 9*(3–4), 275–300.

Slobogin, C., & Fondacaro, M. (2000). Rethinking deprivations of liberty: Possible contributions from therapeutic and ecological jurisprudence. *Behavioral Sciences & the Law, 18*(4), 499–516.

Slovenko, R. (2002). The role of psychiatric diagnosis in the law. *Journal of Psychiatry and Law, 30*(3), 421–444.

Smith, A. B., & Gollop, M. M. (2001, June). What children think separating parents should know. *New Zealand Journal of Psychology, 30*(1), 23–31.

Smith, B. (1998). Children in custody: 20-year trends in juvenile detention, correctional, and shelter facilities. *Crime & Delinquency, 44,* 526–543.

Smith, B., Sloan, J., & Ward, R. (1990). Public support for the victim's rights movement: Results of a statewide survey. *Crime and Delinquency, 36*(4), 488–502.

Smith, D., & Klein, J. (1984). Police control of interpersonal disputes. *Social Problems, 31*(4), 468–481.

Smith, R. (1995). Transgendered....and taken to jail. *Journal of Psychosocial Nursing, 33,* 44–46.

Snow, C. R. (1997). *Family violence: Tough solutions to stop the violence.* New York: Plenum Press.

Snow, J., & Weed, R. (1998). Mental health forensic issues in Georgia: The role of the expert witness. *Georgia Journal of Professional Counseling, 6*(1), 53–65.

Snow, W. H., & Briar, K. H. (1990). The convergence of the mentally disordered and the jail population. *In Clinical Treatment of the Criminal Offender,* (pp. 147–162). Binghamton, NY: The Haworth Press, Inc.

Snyder, H. N., & Sickmund, M. (1999). *Juvenile offenders and victims: 1999 national report.* Washington, DC: Office of Juvenile Justice and Delinquency Prevention.

Snyder, R. T. (2001). *The protestant ethic and the spirit of punishment.* Grand Rapids, MI: William B. Erdmans Publishing Company.

Social Security Administration. (2001). *Disability evaluation under Social Security* (SSA Publication No. 64–039). Washington, DC: U.S. Government Printing Office.

Social Security Advisory Board. (2001, January). *Charting the future of Social Security's disability programs: The need for fundamental change.* Retrieved February 8, 2003 from http://www.ssab.gov

Soler, M. (1988). Litigation on behalf of children in adult jails. *Crime and Delinquency, 34,* 190–208.

Soler, M. (2002). Health issues for adolescents in the justice system. *Journal of Adolescent Health: Official Publication of the Society for Adolescent Medicine, 31*(6 Suppl), 321–333.

Solomon, P. (1983). Analyzing opposition to community residential facilities for troubled adolescents. *Child Welfare, 62,* 361–366.

Solomon, R., & Horn, J. (1986). Post-shooting traumatic reactions: A pilot study. In J. Reese & H. Goldstein (Eds.), *Psychological services for law enforcement.* Washington, DC: U.S. Government Printing Office.

Soto, G., & Miller, M. (1992, August). Keeping kids in school. *Police Practices.*

Southworth, R. (1990, November). Taking the job home. *FBI Law Enforcement Bulletin,* pp. 8–11.

Speaker, K. M., & Peterson, G. J. (2000). School violence and adolescent suicide: Strategies for effective intervention. *Educational Review, 52*(1), 65–73.

Spencer, D. J. (2002). The suicide bomber—is it a psychiatric phenomenon? *Psychiatric Bulletin, 26,* 436.

Spissel, H., Krischker, S., & Cording, C. (1998). Aggression in the psychiatric hospital. A psychiatric basic documentation based 6-year study of 17,943 inpatient admissions. *Psychiariche Praxis, 25,* 227–230.

Spralding, L. H. (1997). Chemical castration: A return to the dark ages. *American Civil Liberties Union.* Retrieved March 18, 1998 from http://www.shadow.net/aclu/t-chem.htm

Springfield, D. (2000). Sisters in misery: Utilizing international law to protect United States female prisoners from sexual abuse. *Indiana International & Comparative Law Review, 10,* 457–486.

Sprott, J. B., & Doob, A. N. (2000, April). Bad, sad, and rejected: The lives of aggressive children (N1). *Canadian Journal of Criminology, 42*(2), 1–8.

Spruill, J., & May, J. (1988). The mentally retarded offender: Prevalence rates based on individual versus group intelligence tests. *Criminal Justice and Behavior, 15,* 484–491.

Stahl, P. M. (1994). *Conducting child custody evaluations.* Thousand Oaks. CA: Sage.

Stalans, L. J. (1996). Family harmony or individual protection? *American Behavioral Scientist, 4,* 433–448.

Stalans, L. J., & Lurigio, A. (1995a). Responding to domestic violence against women. *Crime and Delinquency, 41*(4), 387–398.

Stalans, L. J., & Lurigio, A. J. (1995b). Public preferences for the court's handling of domestic violence situations. *Crime and Delinquency, 41,* 399–413.

Stamps, L. E. (2002). Maternal preference in child custody decisions. *Journal of Divorce & Remarriage, 37*(1–2), 1–11.

Stanard, R., & Hazler, R. (1995). Legal and ethical implications of HIV and duty to warn for counselors: Does Tarasoff apply? *Journal of Counseling and Development, 73,* 397–400.

Steadman, H., McGreevy, M., Morrissey, J., Callahan, L., Robbins, P., & Cirincione, C. (1993). *Before and after Hinckley: Evaluating insanity defense reform.* New York: Guilford Press.

Steadman, H., Monahan, J., Hartstone, E., Davis, S., & Robbins, P. (1982). Mentally disordered offenders: A national survey of patients and facilities. *Law and Human Behavior, 6,* 31–38.

Steadman, H. J., McCarty, D. W., & Morrissey, J. P. (1989). *The mentally ill in jail: Planning for essential services.* New York: Guilford Press.

Steadman, H. J., Stainbrook, K., Griffin, P., Draine, J., Dupont, R., & Horey, C. (2001, February). A specialized crisis response site as a core element of police-based diversion programs. *Psychiatric Services, 52*(2), 219–222.

Stein, H., Fonagy, P., Ferguson, K. S., & Wisman, M. (2000). Lives through time: An ideographic approach to the study of resilience. *Bulletin of the Menninger Clinic, 64,* 281–305.

Stein, M., & Davis, C. A. (2000). Direct instruction as a positive behavioral support. *Beyond Behavior, 10*(1), 7–12.

Steinhart, D. (1988). California legislature ends the jailing of children: The story of a police reversal. *Crime and Delinquency, 34,* 169–189.

Stevenson, K., Tufts, J., Hendrick, D., & Kowalski, M. (1999, Summer). Youth and crime. *Canadian Social Trends,* 17–21.

Stone, A. (1975). *Mental health and law: A system in transition.* Rockville, MD: National Institute of Mental Health.

Stout, C. E. (Ed.). (2002). The psychology of terrorism, Volume Four: Programs and practices in response and prevention. Westport, CT: Praeger.

Stoutland, S. E. (2001, August). The multiple dimensions of trust in resident/police relations in Boston. *Journal of Research in Crime & Delinquency, 38*(3), 226–257.

Straus, M. B. (1994). *Violence in the lives of adolescents.* New York: W. W. Norton.

Streib, V. (1987). *The death penalty for juveniles.* Bloomington: Indiana University Press.

Streib, V. (1996). Current death row inmates under juvenile death sentences. Retrieved from http://www.essential.org/dpic/juvchar.html

Streib, V. (1998). Juveniles and the death penalty: Brief facts and figures. Retrived June 12, 1998 and July 18, 1998 from http://www.prince.essential.org/dpic/juvchar.html

Strier, F. (2001). Why trial consultants should be licensed. *Journal of Forensic Psychology Practice, 1*(4), 69–76.

Strous, R. D., Stryjer, R., Keret, N., Bergin, M., & Kotler, M. (2003, February). Reactions of psychiatric and medical inpatients to terror and security instability in Israel. *Journal of Nervous & Mental Disease, 191*(2), 126–129.

Struckman-Johnson, & C., Struckman-Johnson, D. (2002, August). Sexual coercion reported by women in three Midwestern prisons. *Journal of Sex Research, 39*(3), 217–227.

Struckman-Johnson, C., Struckman-Johnson, D., Rucker, L., Bumby, K., & Donaldson, S. (1996). Sexual coercion reported by men and women in prison. *Journal of Sex Research, 33,* 67–76.

Stuart, H., & Arboleda-Florez, J. (2001, May). A public health perspective on violent offenses among persons with mental illness. *Psychiatric Services, 52*(5), 654–659.

Stuart, H., Arboleda-Florez, J., & Crisanti, A. S. (2001). Impact of legal reforms on length of forensic assessments in Alberta, Canada. *International Journal of Law and Psychiatry, 24,* 527–538.

Sugimoto, J. D., & Oltjenbruns, K. A. (2001). The environment of death and its influence on police officers in the United States. *Omega: Journal of Death & Dying, 43*(2), 145–155.

Sullivan, M. L., & Miller, B. (1999). Adolescent violence, state processes, and the local context of moral panic. In J. M. Heyman (Ed.), *States and illegal practices* (pp. 261–283). New York: Berg.

Sun, Y., & Li, Y. (2002, May). Children's well-being during parents' marital disruption process: A pooled time series analysis. *Journal of Marriage & Family, 64*(2), 472–488.

Swerling, J. B. (1978). *A study of police officers' values and their attitudes toward homosexual officers.* Unpublished dissertation, California School of Professional Psychology, Los Angeles.

Sykes, G. M. (1967). *Crime and society.* New York: Random House.

Szockyj, E. (1989). Working in a man's world: Women correctional officers in an institution for men. *Canadian Journal of Criminology, 31,* 319–328.

Taborda, J. G. V. (2001). Criminal justice system in Brazil: Functions of a forensic psychiatrist. *International Journal of Law and Psychiatry, 24,* 371–386.

Tamber, C. (2003, April 29). Minors on death row may have new hope. *The Legal Intelligencer, 228*(82), 32–38.

Tasker, F., & Golombok, S. (1995). Adults raised as children in lesbian families. *American Journal of Orthopsychiatry, 65,* 203–215.

Taylor, A. J. W. (2002, December). Coping with catastrophe: Organising psychological first-aiders. *New Zealand Journal of Psychology, 31*(2), 104–109.

Teaster, P. B., & Roberto, K. A. (2002, June). Living the life of another: The need for public guardians of last resort. *Journal of Applied Gerontology, 21*(2), 176–187.

Terrill, W., & Reisig, M. D. (2003, August). Neighborhood context and police use of force. *Journal of Research in Crime & Delinquency, 40*(3), 291–321.

Texas Commission on Jail Standards. (1996). State standards and suicide prevention: Lone Star. *Jail/Suicide/Mental Health Update, 6,* 9–11.

Texeira, M. T. (1995). Policing the internally colonized: Slavery, Rodney King, Mark Fuhrman and beyond. *Western Journal of Black Studies, 19,* 235–243.

Thatcher, D. (2001, June). Conflicting values in community policing. *Law & Society Review, 35*(4), 765–798.

Thomas, C. R., & Penn, J. V. (2002, October). Juvenile justice mental health services. *Child and Adolescent Psychiatric Clinics of North America, 11*(4), 731–748.

Thompson, K. M., & Braaten-Antrim, R. (1998). Youth maltreatment and gang involvement. *Journal of Interpersonal Violence, 13*(3), 328–345.

Thurman, Q. C., Giacomazzi, A., & Bogen, P. (1993). Research note: Cops and community policing: An assessment of a community policing demonstration project. *Crime and Delinquency, 39*(4), 554–564.

Tillbrook, C. (2003). Avoiding expert opinions on the ultimate legal question: The case for integrity. *Journal of Forensic Psychology Practice, 3*(3), 77–87.

Tillbrook, C., Mumley, D., & Grisso, T. (2003). Avoiding expert opinions on the ultimate legal question: The case for integrity. *Journal of Forensic Psychology Practice, 3*(3), 77–87.

Tobey, A. E., Goodman, G. S., Batterman-Faunce, J. M., Orcutt, H. K., & Sachsenmaier, T. (1995). In M. S. Zaragoza, J. R. Graham, G. C. N. Hall, R. Hirschman, & Y. S. Ben-Porath (Eds.), *Memory and testimony in the child witness* (pp. 214–239). Thousand Oaks, CA: Sage.

Tobin, J. (2001). The limitations of critical incident stress debriefing. *Irish Journal of Psychological Medicine, 18*(4), 142.

Toch, H. (1985). The catalytic situation in the violence equation. *Journal of Applied Social Psychology, 15*(2), 468–481.

Toch, H. (1992). *Violent men: An inquiry into the psychology of violence.* Washington, DC: American Psychological Association.

Toch, H. (2001, September). The future of supermax confinement. *Prison Journal, 81*(3), 376–388.

Toller, W., & Tsagaris, B. (1996). Managing institutional gangs. *Corrections Today, 58*(6), 110–112.

Tolman, A. O. (2001). Clinical training and the duty to protect. *Behavioral Sciences & the Law, 19*(3), 387–404.

Tolman, A. O., & Mullendore, K. B. (2003, June). Risk evaluations for the courts: Is service quality a function of specialization? *Professional Psychology-Research & Practice, 34*(3), 225–232.

Tomasevski, K. (1986). *Children in adult prisons: An international perspective.* London: Printer.

Torok, W. C., & Trump, K. S. (1994). Gang intervention: Police and school collaboration. *FBI Law Enforcement Bulletin, 63*(5), 13–17.

Towl, G. (1999, September). What do forensic psychologists in prison do? *British Journal of Forensic Practice, 1*(3), 9–11.

Trowbridge, B. (2003). Psychologists' roles in evaluating child witnesses. *American Journal of Forensic Psychology, 21*(3), 27–70.

Trulson, C., & Marquat, J. W. (2002, June). The caged melting pot: Toward an understanding of the consequences of desegregation in prisons. *Law & Society Review, 36*(4), 743–781.

Trulson, C., Triplett, R., & Snell, C. (2001, October). Social control in a school setting: Evaluating a school-based boot camp. *Crime & Delinquency, 47*(4), 573–610.

Turco, R. N. (1990, September). Psychological profiling. *International Journal of Offender Therapy and Comparative Criminology,* pp. 147–154.

Turvey, B. E. (2002). *Criminal profiling: An introduction to behavioral evidence analysis,* San Diego, CA: Academic Press.

Tye, M. C. (2003, January). Lesbian, gay, bisexual, and transgender parents: Special considerations for the custody and adoption evaluator. *Family Court Review, 41*(1), 92–103.

Tyler, J., Darville, R., & Stalnaker, K. (2001). Juvenile boot camps: A descriptive analysis of program diversity and effectiveness. *Social Science Journal, 38*(3), 445–461.

Umbreit, M. S. (1993). Crime victims and offenders in mediation: An emerging area of social work practice. *Social Work, 38,* 69–73.

Umbreit, M. S. (1994). *Victim meets offender: The impact of restorative justice and mediation.* Monsey, NY: Criminal Justice Press.

Umbreit, M. S. (1995). Holding juvenile offenders accountable: A restorative justice perspective. *Juvenile and Family Court Journal, 46*(2), 31–42.

Umbreit, M. S., & Bradshaw, W. (1997). Victim experience of meeting adult vs. juvenile offenders: A cross-national study. *Federal Probation, 61,* 33–39.

Umbreit, M. S., Coates, R. B., & Roberts, A. W. (2000, Spring). The impact of victim-offender mediation: A cross-national perspective. *Mediation Quarterly, 17*(3), 215–229.

Umbreit, M. S., Coates, R. B., & Vos, B. (2001, December). The impact of victim-offender mediation: Two decades of research. *Federal Probation, 65*(3), 29–35.

Umbreit, M. S., & Vos, B. (2000, February). Homicide survivors meet the offender prior to execution. *Homicide Studies: An Interdisciplinary & International Journal, 4*(1), 63–87.

U.S. Department of Education. (1999). *The condition of education 1999.* Washington, DC: National Center for Educational Statistics. (ERIC Document Reproduction Service No. ED430324)

U.S. Department of Justice. (1994). *Special report: Women in prison* (Report No. NCJ-145321). Washington, DC: Bureau of Justice Statistics.

U.S. Department of Justice, Bureau of Justice Statistics. (1995). *Jails and jail inmates 1993–1994* (Publication NCJ-151651). Washington, DC: U.S. Department of Justice, Bureau of Statistics.

U.S. Department of Justice, Bureau of Justice Statistics. (1997). Criminal offender statistics. Retrieved October 6, 1998 from http://www.ojp.usdoj.gov/bjs/crimoff

U.S. Department of Justice, Bureau of Justice Statistics. (1999a). Mental health and treatment of inmates and probationers. Retrieved March 1, 1998 from http://www.ojp.usdoj.gov/bjs/abstract/mhtip.htm

U.S. Department of Justice, Bureau of Justice Statistics. (1999b). *Women offenders* (Publication No. NCJ-175688). Washington, DC: Snell. Retrieved January 20, 1998 from http://www.ojp.usdoj.gov/bjs/pub/press/wo.pr

U.S. Department of Justice, Bureau of Justice Statistics. (2000). *Incarcerated parents and their children* (Publication No. NCJ-182335). Washington, DC: Mumola.

U.S. Department of Justice, Bureau of Justice Statistics. (2002). Homicide trends in the U.S.: Intimate homicide. Retrieved June 8, 2003 from http://www.ojp.usdoj.gov/bjs/homicide/intimates.htm

U.S. Department of Justice, Bureau of Justice Statistics. (2003a). Incarcerated parents and their children.Retrieved August 18, 2003 from http://www.ojp.usdoj.gov/bjs/abstract/iptc.htm

U.S. Department of Justice, Bureau of Justice Statistics. (2003b). Characteristics of state prison inmates. Retrieved February 12, 2002 from http://www.ojp.usdoj.gov/bjs/crimoff.htm

U.S. Department of Justice, Federal Bureau of Investigation. (1996). *Crime in the United States: Uniform Crime Reports 1995.* Washington, DC: U.S. Government Printing Office.

U.S. Department of Justice, Federal Bureau of Investigation. (1999a). *Terrorism in the United States 1999.* Retrieved February 24, 1999 from http://www.fbi.gov/publications/terror/terror99.pdf.

U.S. Department of State. (2000). *Patterns of global terrorism 1999* (Department of State Publication 10687). Washington, DC: Office of the Secretary of State, Office of the Coordinator for Counterterrorism.

Useem, B., & Kimball, P. A. (1989). *States of siege: U.S. prison riots 1971–1986.* New York: Oxford University Press.

Van Biema, D. (1995, December 11). A shameful death. *Time, 146,* pp. 33–36.

Van Patten, I., & Burke, T. (2001, May). Critical incident stress and the child homicide investigator. *Homicide Studies: An Interdisciplinary & International Journal, 5*(2), 131–152.

Van Zelst, W., De Beurs, E, & Smit, J. (2003, February). Effects of the September 11th attacks on symptoms. *International Journal of Geriatric Psychiatry, 18*(2), 190.

Vaughan, P. J., & Stevenson, S. (2002). An opinion survey of mentally disordered offender service users. *The British Journal of Forensic Practice, 4*(3), 11–20.

Veiel, H. O. F., & Coles, E. M. (1999, May). Measuring fitness to stand trial: Psychological analysis of a legal issue. *Canadian Journal of Psychiatry, 44*(4), 356–362.

Viljoen, J. L., Roesch, R., & Zapf, P. A. (2002, October). An examination of the relationship between competency to stand trial, competency to waive interrogation rights, and psychopathology. *Law & Human Behavior, 26*(5), 481–506.

Viljoen, J. L., Roesch, R., & Zapf, P. A. (2002, December). Interrater reliability of the Fitness Interview Test across 4 professional groups. *Canadian Journal of Psychiatry, 47*(10), 945–953.

Violanti, J. (1995). The mystery within: Understanding police suicide. *FBI Law Enforcement Bulletin, 64,* 19–23.

Violanti, J. M., & Aron, F. (1993). Sources of police stressors, job attitudes, and psychological distress. *Psychological Reports, 72,* 899–904.

Violanti, J. M., & Aron, F. (1995). Police stressors: Variations in perception among police personnel. *Journal of Criminal Justice, 23*(3), 287–294.

Violanti, J. M., Marshall, J. R., & Howe, B. (1985). Stress, coping, and alcohol use: The police connection. *Journal of Police Science and Administration, 13*(2), 106–110.

Vitacco, M. J., & Packer, I. K. (2003). Civil commitment. *Journal of the American Academy of Psychiatry & the Law, 31*(2), 264–266.

Vogel, B. L., & Vogel, R. E. (2003, March/April). The age of death: Appraising public opinion of juvenile capital punishment. *Journal of Criminal Justice, 31*(2), 169–183.

Waddington, P., & Braddock, Q. (1991). Guardians or bullies? Perceptions of the police amongst adolescent black, white and Asian boys. *Policing and Society, 2*(1), 31–45.

Wadman, R. C., & Ziman, S. M. (1993, February). Courtesy and police authority. *FBI Law Enforcement Bulletin,* pp. 23–26.

Wahl, O. F. (1993). Community impact of group homes for mentally ill adults. *Community Mental Health Journal, 29,* 247–259.

Wakefield, H., & Underwager, R. (1993). Misuse of psychological tests in forensic settings: Some horrible examples. *American Journal of Forensic Psychology, 11,* 55–75.

Walcott, D. M. (2000). Sexually violent predator commitment successfully challenged on basis of conditions of confinement and treatment. *Journal of the American Academy of Psychiatry & the Law, 28*(2), 244–245.

Walcott, D. M., Cerundolo, P., & Beck, J. C. (2001). Current analysis of the Tarasoff duty: An evolution towards the limitation of the duty to protect. *Behavioral Sciences & the Law, 19*(3), 325–343.

Walker, A. G. (1993). Questioning young children in court: A linguistic case study. *Law and Human Behavior, 17,* 59–81.

Walker, M., Schmidt, L., & Lunghofer, L. (1993). Youth gangs. In M. I. Singer, L. T. Singer, & T. M. Anglin (Eds.), *Handbook for screening adolescents at psychosocial risk* (pp. 504–552). New York: Lexington Books.

Walker, S., & Katz, C. (2001). *The police in America: An introduction (4th ed.)*, New York, NY: McGraw-Hill.

Wall, J. C., & Amadio, C. (1994). An integrated approach to child custody evaluation: Utilizing the best interest of the child and family systems frameworks. *Journal of Divorce and Remarriage, 21,* 39–57.

Walters, P. M. (1993). Community-oriented policing: A blend of strategies. *FBI Law Enforcement Bulletin, 62,* 20–23.

Ward, T., & Hudson, S. M. (1998). A model of the relapse process in sexual offenders. *Journal of Interpersonal Violence, 13*(6), 700–725.

Ward, T., & Hudson, S. M. (2000). A self regulation model of relapse prevention. In: D. R. Laws, S. M. Hudson, & T. Ward (Eds.), *Remaking relapse prevention with sex offenders: A sourcebook.* London: Sage Publications.

Warren, J. I., Burnette, M., South, S. C., Chauhan, P., Bale, R., & Friend, R. (2002). Personality disorders and violence among female prison inmates. *Journal of the American Academy of Psychiatry & the Law, 30*(4), 502–509.

Warshak, R. A. (1996). Gender bias in child custody decisions. *Family and Conciliation Courts Review, 34,* 396–409.

Wattenberg, E., Kelley, M., & Kim, H. (2001, July/August). When the rehabilitation ideal fails: A study of parental rights termination. *Child Welfare, 80*(4), 405–431.

Watterson, K. (1996). *Women in prison: Inside the concrete womb* (Rev. ed.). Boston: Northeastern University Press.

Watts, D., Leese, M., Thomas, S., Atakan, Z., & Wykes, T. (2003). The prediction of violence in acute psychiatric units. *International Journal of Forensic Mental Health, 2*(2), 173–180.

Weaver, R. S. (1992). Violent youth need rehabilitation, not harsh punishment. In M. D. Biskup & C. P. Cozic (Eds.), *Youth violence.* San Diego, CA: Greenhaven Press.

Weber-Brooks, L. (2001). Police discretionary behaviour: A study of style. In R. G. Dunham & G. P. Alpert (Eds.), *Critical issues in policing: Contemporary readings (4th ed.),* (pp. 117–131), Prospect Heights, IL: Waveland.

Webster, C. D., Douglas, K. S., Eaves, D., & Hart, S. D. (1997). *HCR-20: Assessing risk for violence—version 2,* British Columbia, Canada: Mental Health, Law, and Policy Institute, Simon Fraser University.

Weeks, R. M. A. (2003). Comparing children to the mentally retarded: How the decision in *Atkins v. Virginia* will affect the execution of juvenile offenders. *B. Y. U. Journal of Public Law, XVII,* 441–486.

Weinberg, M. S., & Williams, C. J. (1974). *Male homosexuals: Their problems and adaptations.* New York: Penguin.

Weiner, I. B. (2003). Prediction and postdiction in clinical decision making. *Clinical Psychology: Science & Practice, 10*(3), 335–338.

Weiner, J. R. (2003). Tarasoff warnings resulting in criminal charges: Two case reports. *Journal of the American Academy of Psychiatry & the Law, 31*(2), 239–241.

Weinstein, H. C. (2002). Ethics issues in security hospitals. *Behavioral Sciences & the Law, 20*(5), 443–461.

Weinstein, L., & Geiger, J. F. (2003). Insanity and its various interpretations. *Psychology & Education, 40*(3–4), 19–24.

Weisberg, D. K. (1985). *Children of the night: A study of adolescent prostitution.* Lexington, MA: Lexington Books.

Weiss, M. (1997). A legal evaluation of criminal competency standards. *Journal of Contemporary Criminal Justice, 1*(3), 213–223.

Welch, M. (1997). A critical interpretation of correctional boot camps as normalizing institutions: Discipline, punishment and the military model. *Journal of Contemporary Criminal Justice, 13*(2), 184–205.

Welch, M., & Gunther, D. (1997). Jail suicide and prevention: Lessons from litigation. *Crisis Intervention, 3*, 229–244.

Wenocur, S., & Belcher, J. R. (1990). Strategies for overcoming barriers to community-based housing for the chronically mentally ill. *Community Mental Health Journal, 26*, 319–333.

Werth, J. L. (2001, Fall). U.S. involuntary mental health commitment statutes: Requirements for persons perceived to be a potential harm to self. *Suicide & Life-Threatening Behavior, 31*(3), 348–357.

Wertlieb, D. (1997). Children whose parents divorce: Life trajectories and turning points. In I. H. Gotlib & B. Wheaton (Eds.), *Stress and adversity over the life course* (pp. 179–195). New York: Cambridge University Press.

West, D. J. (1988). Psychological contributions to criminology. *British Journal of Criminology, 28*(2), 77–89.

Westcott, H. L., & Page, M. (2002, May/June). Cross-examination, sexual abuse and child witness identity. *Child Abuse Review, 11*(3), 137–152.

Weyer, M., & Sandler, I. (1998). Stress and coping as predictors of children's divorce-related ruminations. *Journal of Clinical Psychology, 27*, 78–86.

Whitcomb, D. (2003, April). Legal interventions for child victims. *Journal of Traumatic Stress, 16*(2), 149–157.

White, E. K., & Honig, A. L. (1995). Law enforcement families. In M. Kurke & E. Scrivener (Eds.), *Police psychology into the 21st century* (pp. 189–205). Hillside, NJ: Lawrence Erlbaum.

Whitfield, C., Anda, R., Dube, S., Felitti, V. (2003, February). Violent childhood experiences and the risk of intimate partner violence in adults: Assessment in a large health maintenance organization. *Journal of Interpersonal Violence, 18*(2), 166–185.

Widom, C., and Kuhns, J. (1996). Childhood victimization and subsequent risks for promiscuity, prostitution, and teenage pregnancy: A prospective study. *American Journal of Public Health 86*(11), 1607–1612.

Widom, C. S. (1992). The cycle of violence. *Journal of Marriage and the Family, 43*, 331–337.

Williams, S. M. (1996). A national strategy for managing sex offenders. *Forum on Corrections Research, 8*(2), 33–35.

Wilson, C., & Gross, P. (1994). Police-public interactions: The impact of conflict resolution tactics. *Journal of Applied Social Psychology, 24*(2), 159–175.

Wilson, J. S., & Leasure, R. (1991). Cruel and unusual punishment: The health care of women in prison. *Nurse Practitioner, 16,* 32–39.

Winick, B. (1995). Ambiguities in the meaning of mental illness. *Psychology, Law, and Public Policy, 1*(3), 534–611.

Winick, B. J. (1992). Competency to be executed: A therapeutic jurisprudence perspective. *Behavioral Sciences and the Law, 10,* 317–337.

Wintersmith, R. F. (1974). *Police and the black community.* Lexington, MA: Lexington Books.

Wood, R., Grossman, L., & Fichtner, C. (2000). Psychological assessment, treatment, and outcome with sex offenders. *Behavioral Sciences & the Law, 18*(1), 23–41.

Woods, P., Reed, V., & Collins, M. (2003). The relationship between risk and insight in a high-security forensic setting. *Journal of Psychiatric and Mental Health Nursing, 10,* 510–517.

Woodhull, A. (1993). *Police communication in traffic stops.* Rochester, NY: Schenkman Books.

Woodworth, M., & Porter, S. (2000). Historical foundations and current applications of criminal profiling in violent crime investigations. *Expert Evidence, 7*(4), 241–264.

Wool, R. J., & Dooley, E. (1987). A study of attempted suicides in prisons. *Medicine Science Law, 27*(4), 297–301.

Woolard, J. L., Reppucci, N. D., & Redding, R. E. (1996). Theoretical and methodological issues in studying children's capacities in legal contexts. *Law and Human Behavior, 20,* 219–228.

Wooldredge, J. D., & Masters, K. (1993). Confronting problems faced by pregnant inmates in state prisons. *Crime and Delinquency, 39,* 195–203.

Worden, R. (1989). Situational and attitudinal explanations of police behavior: A theoretical reappraisal and empirical assessment. *Law and Society Review, 23*(4), 667–711.

Worden, R. E., Shepard, R. L., & Mastrofski, S. D. (1996). On the meaning and measurement of suspects' demeanor toward the police: A comment on "demeanor and arrest." *Journal of Research in Crime and Delinquency, 33*(3), 324–332.

Wrightsman, L., Nietzel, M., & Fortune, W. (1994). *Psychology and the legal system* (3rd ed.). Pacific Grove, CA: Brooks/Cole.

Wrightsman, L. S. (Ed.). (1991). *Psychology and the legal system* (2nd ed.). Belmont, CA: Wadsworth.

Wynne, E. E. (1997). Children's rights and the biological bias in biological parent versus third-party custody disputes. *Child Psychiatry and Human Development, 27,* 179–191.

Younglove, J. A., & Vitello, C. J. (2003). Community notification of "Megan's Law" from a therapeutic jurisprudence perspective: A case study. *American Journal of Forensic Psychology, 21*(1), 25–38.

Zatz, J. (1982). Problems and issues in deinstitutionalization: Historical overview and current attitudes. In J. F. Handler & J. Zatz (Eds.), *Neither angels nor thieves: Studies in deinstitutionalization of status offenders.* Washington, DC: National Academy Press.

Zeiss, R., Tanke, E., Fenn, H., & Yesavage, J. (1996). Dangerousness commitments: Indices of future violence potential. *Bulletin of the American Academy of Psychiatry and Law, 24,* 247–253.

Zevitz, R. G., & Farkas, M. A. (2000a). The impact of sex-offender community notification on probation/parole in Wisconsin. *International Journal of Offender Therapy and Comparative Criminology, 44*(1), 8–21.

Zevitz, R. G., & Farkas, M. A. (2000b). Sex offender community notification: Examining the importance of neighborhood meetings. *Behavioral Sciences & the Law, 18*(2–3), 393–408.

Ziedenberg, J., & Schiraldi, V. (1998, August). The risks juveniles face. *Corrections Today, 60*(5), 22–25.

Zimmer, L. (1987). How women reshape the prison guard role. *Gender and Society, 1,* 415–431.

Zinger, I., & Forth, A. E. (1998). Psychopathy and Canadian criminal proceedings: The potential for human rights. *Canadian Journal of Criminology, 40,* 237–276.

Zorza, J. (1992). The criminal law of misdemeanor domestic violence, 1970–1990. *Journal of Criminal Law & Criminology, 83*(1), 46–72.

Zuberbuhler, J. (2001, April). Early intervention mediation: The use of court-ordered mediation in the initial stages of divorce litigation to resolve parenting issues. *Family Court Review, 39*(2), 203–206.

CASES

Alaska Statute Title 11, Chapter 56, Article 4, Section 610-As 11.56.610 (1997).
Atkins, v. Virginia, 536 U.S. 304 (2002).
Barefoot v. Estelle, 103 S. Ct. 3383, 463 U.S. 880 (1983)
Bartley v. Kremens, 402 F. Supp. 1039 (1975)
Baston v. Kentucky, 476 U.S. 79 (1986)
Baumgartner v. City of Long Beach, Civil No. C-54782 (L.A. Super. 1987)
Bundy v. Jackson, 641 F. 2d 934 (D.C. Cir. 1981)
Chambers v. Mississippi, 410 U.S. 284 (1973)
Coleman v. Wilson, 912 F. Supp. 1282 (1995)
Coy v. Iowa, 108 S. Ct. 2798 (1988)
Daubert v. Merrell, 509 U.S. 579, 591 (1993)
Davis v. United States, 512 U.S. 452-464 (1994)
Department of Revenue of Montana v. Kurth Ranch, 511 U.S. 128 L.Ed. 2d 767, 777 (1994)
Dodd v. Hughes, 81 Nev. 43, 398 P.2d 540 (1965)
Dothard v. Rawlinson, 433 U.S. 321 (1977)
Durham v. United States, 214 F.2d 862 (D.C. Cir. 1954)
Dusky v. United States, 362 U.S. 402 (1960)
Eddings v. Oklahoma, 455 U.S. 104 (1982)
Estelle v. Gamble, 429 U.S. 97 (1976)
Farmer v. Brennan, 114 S. Ct. 1970 (1994)
Fasanaro v. County of Rockland, 166 Misc. 2d 152, 632 N.Y.S. 2d 453 (NY 1995)
Finlay v. Finlay, 240 N.Y. 429, 148 N.E. 624 (1925)
Ford v. Wainwright, 477 U.S. 399 (1986)
Foucha v. Louisiana, 504 U.S. 71 (1992)
Frye v. United States, 293 F. 1013 (DC Cir 1923)
Garcia, v. Board of County Commissioners, El Paso County, NO. 83-Z-222 U.S. Dist. Ct. Co, 1985.

Garrett v. Collins, 951 F. 2d 57, 58 (5th Cir. 1992)

General Electric Co. v. Joiner (1997)

Gregg v. Georgia, 428 U.S. 1301 (1976)

Guardianship of Richard Roe III, 421 N.E. 2d 40 (1981)

In re Gault, 387 U.S. 1 (1967)

In re Winship, 397 U.S. 358 (1970)

Jackson v. Indiana, 406 U.S. 715 (1972)

Jennings v. New York State Office of Mental Health, 90 N.Y.2d 227 (1997)

Juvenile Justice and Delinquency Prevention Act, 42 U.S.C. 5603(23) (1974)

Katz v. United States, 389 U.S. 347 (1967)

Kent v. United States, 383 U.S. 541 (1966)

Knecht v. Gillman, 488 F. 2d 1136 (1973)

Lake v. Cameron, 364 F. 2d 657 DC Cir (1966)

Maryland v. Craig, 110 S. Ct. 3157 (1990)

McKeiver v. Pennsylvania, 403 U.S. 528 (1971)

North Carolina v. Alford, 400 U.S. 25 (1970)

Olmstead v. United States, 277 U.S. 438, 48 S. Ct. 564 (1928)

Parham v. J. R., 442 U.S. 584 (1978)

Penry v. Lynaugh, 109 S. Ct. 2934 (1989)

People v. Aris, N.E. 005418 Cal. App. Lexis 1187 (1989)

People v. Presley, 47 Ill. 2, 50 (1974)

Perry v. Louisiana, 111 S. Ct. 449 (1990)

R. v. Frith, 22 St. Tr. 307 at 318 (1790)

R. v. Presser, V. R. 45 (1958)

R. v. Pritchard, Carrington & Payne, 303 (1836)

Rex v. Brasier (1770)

Roach v. Aiken, Warden et al., 474 U.S. 1039 (1986)

Robbins v. Glenn County, No. CIVS-85-0675 RAR (U.S.D.C., E.D. Ca. 1986)

Rock v. Arkansas, 107 S. Ct. 2704 (1987)

Santobello v. New York, 404 U.S. 257 (1971)

Schall v. Martin, 104 S. Ct. 2403 (1984)

Singleton v. State, 90-CP-36-66 (Newberry County) (1991)

Stanford v. Kentucky, 492 U.S. 361 (1989)

Swain v. Alabama, 380 U.S. 202 (1965)

Tarasoff v. Regents of the University of California, 551 P.2d 334 (1976)

Tennessee v. Garner, 471 U.S. 1 (1985)

Terry v. Ohio, 392 U.S. 1 (1968)

Thompson v. Oklahoma, 487 U.S. 815 (1988)

Todaro v. Ward, 431 F. Supp. 1129 (1977)

Town of Gates v. Commissioner of New York State Office of Mental Retardation and
    Developmental Disabilities and Finger Lakes Developmental Disabilities Services Office,
    667 N.Y.S. 2d 568 (1997)

United States of America v. Michael A. Whren, 324 U.S. App. D.C. 197 (1997)

United States v. Salerno, 481 U.S. 739 (1987)

United States v. Sanusi, 813 F. Supp. 149 (1992)

United States v. Timmins, 9th Circuit (2002)

United States v. Ward, 448 U.S. 242, 248 (1980)

Washington v. Harper, 494 U.S. 210, 110 S. Ct. 1028 (1990)

Wertz v. Workmen's Compensation Appeal Board, 683 A.2d 1287 (Penn. 1996)

Wheeler v. United States, 159 U.S. 523 (1895)

Wilkins v. Missouri, see Stanford v. Kentucky, 492 U.S. 361 (1989)

Winterwerp v. The Netherlands (1979)

Yellen v. Ada County, Civil No. 83-1026 (U.S.D.C. Idaho 1985)

Index

A

AACWA, *see* Adoption Assistance and
    Child Welfare Act
AAFP, *see* American Academy of Forensic
    Psychology
ABFP, *see* American Board of Forensic
    Psychology
Abuse
battered mother, 77
    batterer treatment, 90
    mentally retarded offenders, 460
    physical abuse, 77, 436–437, 485
    sexual abuse, 77, 316, 436–437, 485
    substance abuse, 47–48, 50, 333,
        349, 437
Abusive father, custody decisions, 194–195
Abusive husband, murder by wife, 83
ACLU, *see* American Civil Liberties Union
Acquired immunodeficiency syndrome
    adolescent female prostitutes, 314
    informing *vs.* confidentiality, 170
    inmate sexual behavior, 412
ADA, *see* Americans with Disabilities Act
Adolescent female prostitutes
    arrests, 318
    factors and motivations, 316
    federal legislation, 317
    future research, 319–320
    law enforcement considerations, 315–316
    officer discretion, 317
    overview, 314
    policy issues, 318–319
    scope of problem, 316
    sexual abuse role, 316
    statistics, 317

Adoption Assistance and Child Welfare Act,
    227, 229–230
Adoption and Safe Families Act, 230–231,
    486
Adoptive parents, gay/lesbian *vs.*
    heterosexual, 239–240
Adult corrections
    counseling and treatment, 413
    inmate sexuality, 405–416
    juveniles in
        case example, 419–420
        future research, 423
        isolation and depression, 421–422
        overview, 419–420
        policy issues, 422–423
        problems, 420–421
    mentally ill incarceration and execution,
        376–384
    offender's treatment refusal, 371–376
    overview, 369–371
    prison inmate suicide risk, 384–391
    prison violence, 397–405
    sex offender treatment, 391–397
Adult court, juvenile transfer to, 57–58
Adult criminal profiling
    biological theories, 251
    case example, 249
    categories, 250–251
    FBI definition, 250
    FBI research, 251
    future research, 256–257
    habitual criminal personality, 253
    overview, 248–249
    policy issues, 256
    profiler definition, 249–250